D0174280

2 A 1999

J

Revealing Antiquity

· 11 ·

G. W. Bowersock, General Editor

POMPEII

Public and Private Life

PAUL ZANKER

Translated by Deborah Lucas Schneider

Harvard University Press
Cambridge, Massachusetts
London, England
1998

Publication of this volume was assisted by a grant from Inter Nationes.

Originally published in German as *Pompeji: Stadtbild und Wohngeschmack* (1995).

Library of Congress Cataloging-in-Publication Data
Zanker, Paul.
[Pompeji. English]
Pompeii : public and private life / Paul Zanker ; translated by
Deborah Lucas Schneider.
p. cm. – (Revealing antiquity ; 11)
Includes bibliographical references and index.
ISBN 0-674-68966-6 (cloth : alk. paper)
ISBN 0-674-68967-4 (pbk. : alk. paper)
1. Pompeii (Extinct city).
2. Cities and towns, Ancient—Rome.
3. City planning—Rome.
4. Politics and culture—Rome.
5. Pompeii (Extinct city)—Social life and customs.
I. Title. II. Series.
DG70.P7Z3613 1998
937′.7—dc21
98-24720

Contents

Preface

Every author is pleased to be read, and so I hope readers will understand why I agreed to an English translation, although with some hesitation. My concern arose from the origins of this book—first published in 1993 in Italian, and later in German—as three separate essays written at different times between 1979 and 1993. Since 1979, however, Pompeii studies have undergone an astonishing renaissance, and more books and articles on Pompeii have appeared in the last ten years than in the previous two generations. Few areas of research exist in which international teamwork and cooperation among the various disciplines of classical studies have functioned so well. Thanks to the admirable volumes of the *Enciclopedia Italiana* entitled *Pompei: Pitture e Mosaici* and the series *Häuser in Pompeji* edited by V. M. Strocka, documentation of residential buildings in Pompeii has been substantially improved, although this applies mainly to their pictorial decoration. (At the same time, these houses have been decaying more rapidly since the earthquake of 1980, and valuable cultural artifacts are being lost forever. In view of the highly developed techniques for preservation that now exist, this situation is particularly deplorable.)

Current research at the site has acquired a new focus in contrast to earlier eras: little excavation of new buildings is under way; instead, archeologists are attempting to dig below the levels of A.D. 79, especially in residential buildings, to discover more about the history of these houses. They are looking not only at structural alterations to individual houses, but also to the development of whole architectural complexes or *insulae* (blocks). Their interest is clearly directed toward finding answers to social and economic questions.

New studies of how private and public space was used belong to the same general context. They range from new excavations and the laborious but rewarding reconstruction of the course of earlier digs (using notes and logs) to the development of new theories and analyses concerning the practical use of space and how inhabitants experienced the space in which they lived. Happily, these concerns reflect vital interests of our own time. This is particularly true of questions about different ways of forming living space, about the social and psychological implications of particular uses of space, and—in the larger context—the connections between the way in which a society is ordered and the way it orders space (see especially the works of Wallace-Hadrill, 1988–1994, Laurence, 1994, and Zaccaria Ruggiu, 1995). Researchers' emphasis on private living space as opposed to the public and political sphere also corresponds to a current trend (see Laurence and Wallace-Hadrill, 1997).

My own studies are devoted to only a small section of these larger concerns. It has been gratifying to see the questions I have pursued taken up in later studies and in some cases used as the basis for debate. Naturally, some of the conclusions I reached are in need of revision today. If I have nonetheless left the present essays largely in their original form—apart from the correction of obvious errors—it has been in order not to disrupt the logical coherence of the argument. The notes, however, have been thoroughly revised and brought up to date, so that they contain information on the most recent debates and new insights, as well as improved documentation.

On the whole my concept of four successive townscapes as reflections of a society and its outlook (originally published in 1988) and my reconstruction of certain features of late Pompeian domestic taste (1979) have stood the test of time. Significant revisions are needed, as far as I can determine, in two areas above all: the assessment of the state of the town—particularly the forum—at the time of the eruption that buried it (see chapter 2); and my attempt to link domestic taste with shifts within Pompeian society after the earthquake of A.D. 62. I have added notes in the relevant passages to alert the reader to new developments in research on these points. The first chapter, written in 1993, sketches some new ideas on the topics covered in chapters 2 and 3.

In the German edition I expressed my gratitude to a number of people for their support and assistance. In addition to them, I would like to thank Felix Pirson for his help in revising the text and notes for this edition; of course I remain responsible for any errors. J. J. Dobbins, who is currently conducting a large project on the forum in Pompeii that is expected to produce important new results, has kindly kept me informed of his progress and contributed to the success of this book. I am grateful to Deborah Lucas Schneider for her commitment to the translation, and finally, I would like to express my special thanks to Kathleen M. Coleman, who read the English text and contributed valuable suggestions.

Note

Throughout, building locations are specified by region, *insula* (block), and building; thus VII 4.57 cites region VII, *insula* 4, building 57. Figure 2 shows the distribution of the regions and *insulae*.

CIL = *Corpus Inscriptionum Latinarum*

POMPEII

Townscape and
Domestic Taste

The city is a popular topic nowadays, in classical archeology as elsewhere. Nevertheless, it would be virtually impossible for an archeologist to write a history of Greek and Roman cities comprehensive and detailed enough to satisfy modern-day interests and answer the types of questions currently being asked. The reason is simple: we know too little about how ancient cities actually looked. This may seem an odd claim given the vast numbers of surviving ruins and excavations, but it is nonetheless true.

Of course we know of countless temples, theaters, baths, amphitheaters, basilicas, circuses, and squares; sometimes we can even recognize large parts of a city's network of streets. We can describe the development of certain architectural forms (an approach that has been followed almost to excess), and even say a little about their function in the lives of the people who used them (a subject of interest mostly to specialists).[1] Only in rare cases, however, are we able to analyze the overall organization of space in a city and see it in relation to the society that inhabited it, drawing connections between the use of space and residents' particular lives, habits, and needs.

The reasons for the rarity of such instances are connected with the history of archeology and the shifting interests of excavators and their public over time. As long as excavators were primarily searching for works of art and displayed little interest in anything other than particularly impressive and well-preserved examples of ancient architecture, it rarely occurred to them to ask the types of questions that interest us today. Systematic investigations of a town as a whole, or even selected precincts, were the exception even during the heyday of large-scale digs in the nineteenth and early twentieth centuries. And in those days archeology was not yet burdened by the caution and scrupulous methods that make excavation of such vast areas all but impossible today. Over the last several decades techniques have been refined to the point where teams of specialists are necessary if a project is to appear competent in the eyes of professional archeologists. Furthermore, exhaustive documentation is demanded, in publications that require time-consuming preparations and entail high costs. The lamentable result is that even important excavations go unreported for decades.

Classical archeology, a field not noted for its progressive techniques, has taken these standards so to heart that even limited projects involving excavation of small residential neighborhoods—such as the houses on the acropolis hill at Pergamum or the terrace houses at Ephesus—consume the energies of a whole generation. These difficulties are further increased by the enormous costs connected not only with the actual excavation work, but also with designing and laying out the sites as outdoor museums afterwards. Any site that could conceivably arouse the interest of the general public must nowadays be reconstructed and presented attractively to visitors. Artificial ruins are going up on all sides as a result.

Improving the woeful state of the sources—especially with regard to our knowledge of cities as a whole and residential neighborhoods in particular—will be a very slow process, even though excavators themselves have begun to give high priority to this task. Thus for the time being there is no alternative but to revisit familiar sites and ask new questions. Because the cities around Vesuvius were virtually sealed up when the volcano erupted, they are of central importance for this type of work. The two chapters that follow, one focusing on public buildings and the townscape, the other on Pompeians' tastes as they created their domestic environments, take this approach.

Townscapes

The next chapter is devoted to the "townscapes" of Pompeii, with emphasis on the public buildings. I use this concept to describe the outward appearance of a city in the most comprehensive sense, meaning not so much the architecture of single buildings as their function within the total context of public space.[2] The focus of the inquiry is thus not the relatively narrow field of architectural history, but rather the town as a concrete instance of inhabited space. Public buildings and their setting are then viewed as a kind of performance space, a stage created by a society to meet its own needs. The public buildings, squares, streets, and monuments, together with dwellings, cemeteries, and their decorative art, represent one key way in which the inhabitants could express who they were: the city as a combination of public stage and private living space.

Seen from this point of view, a townscape also represents the framework within which urban life takes place. It not only shapes the inhabitants but is shaped by them, for the buildings and spaces, having been constructed to embody certain messages and values, continue to communicate these same messages to succeeding generations.

Pompeii

At the time of its destruction in A.D. 79 Pompeii was already an old city and had been inhabited by many generations of people from different origins, each with its own uniquely structured society. If, as is usually the case, we look only at the townscape as it happened to be preserved in A.D. 79, then what meets the eye is just the last of a series of successive townscapes. In fact for the period between the early second century B.C., when wealthy Oscan patricians built their expensive houses in the cosmopolitan Hellenistic taste of the day, and the date Pompeii was buried by Mount Vesuvius, it is possible to identify four different concepts of urban organization that left their mark on the town. I believe these different townscapes can be reconstructed, at least in outline. I will do this by investigating the interests that lay behind each construction project and promoted its realization, and then analyzing how these interests interacted as political and social changes affected the city. From the conglomeration of the city preserved by chance in A.D. 79, the outlines of four distinct townscapes emerge, each corresponding to the larger world in which its inhabitants lived.

Pompeii was by no means an important urban center; it was only one of many medium-sized country towns in Italy. But fortunately the structures of its public space and the changes observable in them are characteristic of Italian cities and the western provinces of the late Roman Republic and early Empire. This has been demonstrated by comparison with archeological evidence from other cities, many of which also expanded beyond their walls in the first century B.C. Everywhere we find imposing funerary monuments lining the main roads outside city gates; we find the rich building sumptuous villas outside the city walls, and the cultural traditions of local peoples giving way to a new and unified Roman culture. Because Pompeii lies close to the cities of Campania that came under Hellenistic influence quite early, the elementary processes of acculturation, which so thoroughly altered Roman culture after the invasion of the Greek East by the Roman armies, can be followed even more closely in Pompeii than elsewhere. The reshaping of Pompeii's public spaces in the Augustan age has parallels in many other places as well. The cult of the emperor and homage paid to him left their stamp on its forum as they did in virtually all Roman cities in the western half of the Empire. In addition, theaters were renovated and enlarged in most towns, and urban elites everywhere made similar efforts to make their city more beautiful and improve its infrastructure.

It is their very typicality that makes the various stages of these developments in Pompeii deserving of careful attention and study. Despite the fact that Pompeii is by no means entirely excavated, no other ancient city furnishes us with a picture even remotely comparable in scope and detail. And, unlike most of the excavated Roman sites in North Africa and Asia Minor, Pompeii is particularly interesting because it spans the two periods that probably saw the most profound and sweeping changes in urban structures: the last years of the Republic, when cities were growing more uniform, and the early years of the Empire, when the establishment of the monarchy embedded new values in the townscape.

The developments discussed here using the specific example of Pompeii would thus be central to any broader discussion of how the Roman cityscape evolved. They would emerge with greater clarity if considerations of space allowed for comparison with the typical Greek city of the classical or Hellenistic era on the one hand, and the cities of the middle and late Roman Empire on the other. Although my focus here is much narrower, I would like to provide at least a rough outline of the larger historical framework surrounding the townscape as it will be reconstructed for Pompeii.

Public Space in the "Democratic" Greek City

If we compare the Greek townscapes of the classical era with their Roman counterparts, it is evident how much the former were shaped by the ideals of active citizenship and political equality (of full citizens). Nowhere in Greek cities—be it in the agora, the theater (where the assembly met), or the *bouleuterion* (where the council met)—do we find the markedly hierarchical structures so prevalent in the Romans' ordering of space. In Greek cities, the sites where citizens gathered to discuss and vote on political matters, to meet one another, and to worship local divinities were integrated into a single compact public space, which also included the educational institution, the gymnasium. The only important exceptions are the temples of the various religious mysteries (and later the Oriental gods), instances governed by the concerns and needs of certain private groups.

In the fourth century B.C. the idea of democratic equality carried over even into the design of the houses. When new cities were founded such as the small country town of Priene near Miletus, citizens were assigned plots of equal size, on which they built surprisingly similar houses. This did not correspond to actual equality of wealth by any means; it was a symbolic use of space, in which the private sphere was designed to reflect the public sphere and thus politicized in a certain sense. (The fact that such idealized designs were quickly undermined by the existing unequal distribution of wealth—meaning that the rich soon bought out their poorer neighbors to enlarge their dwellings—is a different matter.) The decision to create such a democratic appearance or symbolic use of space might even run counter to the actual political organization of the city in question: the political ideals of civic equality were transferred to other spheres of life as aesthetic forms, which continued to spread in the areas of taste and outlook even when the politics did not. But even apart from the specific considerations that gave rise to these democratic cityscapes, it remains significant for the citizens' view of themselves that for centuries, well into the days of the Empire, they continued to inhabit public spaces shaped by democratic ideals. Citizens held onto the traditional design of their cities in the same way that they preserved the old political rituals embodying their ancestors' ideals (out of nostalgia, of course). This did not change until the government of Rome became a monarchy, and, in accordance with the new norms emanating from the West, political power came to be expressed in the cult of the emperor in the East as well.[3]

The Structure of Roman Cities

Roman and romanized Italic cities reflect a political structure entirely different from that of the Greek cities, even during the Republican period. Here the great noble Roman families inhabited opulent houses near or directly abutting the Forum Romanum (as in Pompeii). The people dependent on their patronage, whose numbers directly reflected the family's prestige and power, assembled in their spacious atria. Influence spread from the residences of powerful families into the public sphere and not vice versa, as was the case in Greek cities. And in the forums, too, the scene was dominated to a much greater extent than in a Greek agora by impressive public buildings often commissioned and paid for by one of the same great families. One need only think of the basilicas in the Roman forum, which were without exception named after their builders, or of the close proximity of the main temples of the state cults to certain private residences.

The forums of Roman and Italic cities were dominated by these temples to political divinities. This was not the case in Greek cities. There the chief city gods were worshiped in their own sacred precincts, whereas the agora belonged to the body of citizens as a whole. In the temples of the Roman forum, by contrast, the union of religion and the state was celebrated early on. The Dioscuri were honored as helpers in battle; Saturn watched over the sowing of crops; and Concordia was supposed to guarantee harmony within the state. The fact that the Senate frequently met in these temples was also significant. The most striking instance of the Romans' need to celebrate the unity of religion and the state, however, occurs in the *capitolia* (religious centers) of their citizen colonies. These were laid out on the axis of each forum so that overland traffic had to pass in front of them, a principle that made them very visible as symbols of the colonies' association with Rome and submission to Roman sovereignty.[4]

Whereas the compact political space used daily by citizens of Greek cities contained fully integrated educational and sports facilities as well as theaters, Roman cities initially possessed hardly any comparable structures. And when increasing Hellenization gradually led to their creation, at first they constituted a separate form of public space distinct from the political center. This circumstance reflected the fact that education and culture were not integral parts of communal life, but instead luxuries borrowed from the Greeks. The theater quarter of Pompeii demonstrates this in exemplary fashion. Indeed, even in Rome itself all the important "cultural" buildings of the late Republic were erected on the Campus Martius outside the walls of the city.

From the early days Roman cities were more open to the outside than a Greek *polis* for, unlike the latter, they belonged to an empire. This resulted in a very different relationship to space, as is evident from the way Romans built their overland roads through the centers of cities, and through the forums if possible. The extravagant funerary monuments built by rival families along these roads were intended to be seen by passing strangers, and amphitheaters were usually built at the edge of cities for the same reason. The shaping of public space (or lack of it) in the second and first centuries B.C. must be seen in this context.

The fact that in Pompeii, just as elsewhere in the West, Augustan ideology influenced the outward appearance of public space needs no additional commentary and, as noted, is reflected in no old Roman or Italic city more clearly than in Pompeii itself. Glorification of the emperor in the form of temples dedicated to him in the forum occurs in even more demonstrative fashion only in new cities such as Nîmes, Aosta, or Mérida. Here, too, we find theaters in central positions, corresponding to their significance in Augustus' program of cultural renewal, and fortified walls with elaborate gates as highly visible symbols of Roman preparedness for war.[5]

Urban Public Space in the Empire

Changes occurred in this ideologically determined townscape over the next few generations. These changes, so important in the context of cultural history, are connected with new forms of "public" space that developed gradually under the altered conditions of the monarchy. Perhaps the most significant among them are the large baths. (Pompeii is no exception in this respect, for after the major earthquake of A.D. 62 construction of a new bath complex added a striking new feature to the town's appearance.) Citizens spent many hours together at the baths, enjoying the warm water, heated air, and swimming pools. The baths offered an opportunity to spend leisure time, exercise, and care for one's appearance, activities that in the larger cities could be indulged in amid luxurious surroundings and in combination with the most varied kinds of entertainment. Those who frequented the baths were usually from the same district. The distribution of baths in various residential quarters can be documented again and again in larger towns. The sites where this type of social encounter took place thus tended to shift from the center of the city to various neighborhoods.

Subdivision by neighborhood and/or social class is a feature of public space at the height of the Roman Empire.[6] In the townscapes of the second century A.D. this development occurred not only in baths but in other types of buildings as well, principally the clubhouses of private associations, shrines to Oriental divinities, and shrines of other religious sects. As communal life shifted increasingly to these subdivided spaces and became associated with activities and pleasures previously relegated in large part to the private sphere (such as shared meals in clubhouses), the forum lost its old importance as a center of social activity. By the time it had become the site for monuments honoring the emperor and ceremonies for his worship, citizens ceased to pass through it on their daily errands, and most unscheduled activity there appears to have died out. This is certainly true for the cities of Italy and the western provinces of the Empire, where there is little sign of new construction in forums after this time. Worship of the emperor and his administration continued to be carried on there, of course, and honorary statues were erected in great numbers, but there seems to have been little spontaneous participation by citizens in these ritual demonstrations of loyalty. Indeed, the space could hardly have been filled with so many statues if large numbers of people had still been using it regularly.

As we have seen, certain functions of forums were shifted to new and geographically scattered public places like baths, clubhouses, the shrines of exclusive religious associations, and also certain particularly busy streets. The most popular meeting spots in the townscape can be identified by various features including porticos over the sidewalks, squares with pleasant fountains, and—occasionally—splendid public latrines. Strange as it may seem to us, the last-named actually became significant centers of urban communication![7]

From this time on the population could experience gatherings of the entire civic community in a new way: as spectators in the arena or at the circus. These two places thus also became the only sites where citizens could express themselves politically, either through applause or—protected by the anonymity of the crowd—through vocal protests. And in both places the emperor or other representatives of political power sat in their reserved boxes, visible to all, but inaccessible: another significant characteristic of townscapes in the imperial age!

All these developments were clearly under way in Pompeii when the city was buried: they provide striking proof of the sensitivity of townscapes to social change.

Domestic Taste and Cultural Self-Definition

Dwellings represent another fundamental component of townscapes. They mark the transition from public to private space, and they offer to their owners manifold possibilities for expressing their own personalities and identities. In speaking of the effects created by these dwellings, however, we must distinguish between the glances of casual passers-by and the impressions of people who lived there or came as invited guests. Although inhabiting a particular space is a fundamental part of daily life in every historical era, one can scarcely imagine a cultural sphere where the differences between what is familiar to us and what a Roman experienced are greater than here. Yet our ingrained assumptions make it difficult to approach the topic of houses as "inhabited space" without bias; almost inevitably we are inclined to ask the wrong questions and draw mistaken conclusions.

Residents and Visitors

Our homes are private spaces, in which we live for the most part in nuclear families, screened from the public gaze in every sense. We place great value on undisturbed privacy there; indeed, it is a right protected by law. For all but a few, little space is available to receive large numbers of guests or present an image of ourselves to the rest of society. As a rule, family dwellings are entered only by friends and relatives; hospitality has ceased to be a means of demonstrating a family's official or social position to the community at large. We tend to select home furnishings and decor to satisfy personal preferences and desires for self-expression rather than to convey to strangers a sense of who we are (Bourdieu's "distinctions" notwithstanding). Even the very wealthy, who may still open their houses for semipublic occasions in the traditional manner, are inclined to avoid ostentatious display at least on the exterior. In our society distinctions are expressed more indirectly and discreetly, for example, in choosing the location of a home or the size of a lot.

The Roman house, by contrast, was a center of social communication and pointed demonstration of the occupants' standing. As such it was located in the center of town. Even the façade and entrance offered clues to the owner's status. During the day, when the front door stood open, the lines of sight were purposely designed to allow glimpses deep into the interior of the house from the entrance. If we take the houses in Pompeii as a guide, even "middle-class" homes provided luxurious amounts of space—at least by modern standards. Much of this space, as well as all the furnishings in it, however, served to declare the owner's identity to the world.

The most important principle dictating the organization of space required clear distinction between the parts of the house devoted to socializing and display, and the purely functional areas of the infrastructure (from the kitchens to the servants' quarters). In our "servantless" households the exact opposite is the case; we have "eat-in" kitchens, and bathrooms designed to be attractive as well as utilitarian. The occupants of a Roman house "lived" only in the social space, and it alone was furnished and equipped accordingly. Pliny the Younger thus limits his detailed descriptions of villas to this area.[8] The boundaries between the two areas were open as a rule, but clearly demarcated symbolically and through visual signals. Guests could easily recognize where the service area began, for instance, from the sudden cessation of all elaborate decoration.

Modern middle-class domestic conventions are based on matching particular rooms with particular functions; our rooms tend to be dominated by specific items of furniture that make them identifiable as adults' or children's bedrooms, dining or living rooms, and so on. In Roman houses, by contrast, the elaborately decorated rooms were used for a variety of purposes. Here, where family life took place during the day—where children played, clients and visitors were received, slaves and freedmen were given their instructions—formal dinners were served to guests toward evening.

Romans had far less furniture than we do, and what they had was lighter and more portable.[9] Even the couches on which guests reclined at dinner could be carried from one room to another if necessary. Another great difference was the absence of cabinets and shelves, those symbols of our modern desire to collect objects and fill our homes with them. As a result the rooms themselves became effective as spaces and could be decorated from floor to ceiling. Pictures dominated Roman interiors in a way familiar to present-day Europeans only from baroque churches and palaces. Even ceilings and floors were treated as large surfaces to be covered systematically with bands and fields of decoration, very much in contrast to our homes, where furniture blocks most of the walls and empty spaces tend to be "filled in" with pictures more or less randomly.

The area open to visitors in a Roman house offered no privacy, and there were clearly no separate rooms for the women or children of the household, for instance, or for guests. In the central "access" spaces, the atrium and peristyle (a colonnaded courtyard), any of the people in the house might encounter one another. Their awareness of these comings and goings, the large number of adjacent rooms, and the varied tasks performed throughout the day inevitably turned the house of a large family into a site of intense social activity, which cannot be adequately described with our terms "public" and "private." It remains unclear even now whether in addition to these multifunctional rooms on the ground floor for socializing and display there were also truly private spaces such as bedrooms and children's rooms above them, since for the most part the upper stories of the houses in Pompeii were destroyed and cannot be reconstructed in detail. This uncertainty throws into sharp focus the gaps in our knowledge of the most ordinary daily activities and the specific places associated with them in Roman houses.

Houses as Indicators of Identity and Social Status

In recent years Andrew Wallace-Hadrill has offered a convincing description of the social structure of Roman houses, demonstrating the extent to which the entire space was arranged to present the identity and status of the owner to the surrounding community.[10] This is anything but a trivial observation, for the social function of a house determined both the layout of the rooms and the choice of decorative elements. Two aspects of this social function are especially characteristic, namely, the different use made of space depending on the type of visitor, and the significance of extravagant dimensions and "wasted" space as an example of what Veblen called "conspicuous consumption."[11]

The image of clients waiting in the atrium for a morning audience was used by ancient authors as a yardstick for the social status of the *patronus*. He received the more important visitors in the smaller rooms that were usually situated in the interior of the house. Confidential discussions were conducted in private, in even more secluded chambers that might also serve as bedrooms. Friends *(amici)* came to dinner in dining areas that were often located at the rear of the garden peristyle. Thus a social pecking-order was created, corresponding in spatial terms to ever-increasing access to the interior parts of the house. In the last few years it has been shown that architects took great pains when designing the peristyles of Pompeian houses of the first century B.C. to ensure that a guest would receive the most comprehensive impression of the dwelling's size and expensive decor on his way to meet his host. One way of achieving this was to place the most impressive reception rooms around the peristyle courts, so that visitors would glimpse them all, along with the garden, before reaching their goal.[12]

The number of available reception rooms played a major role in determining the rank of a house in the social hierarchy. A wealthy homeowner could choose among several settings to receive visitors, depending on their type and number as well as on the time of day or season of the year. This possibility for choice was a key status symbol. Decor also varied accordingly. Thus both architecture and interior design were employed in the competition for social status, and naturally this had an effect on stylistic developments in the various arts and crafts employed in interior decor, especially painting.

Naturally, the preceding remarks apply only to the houses of the wealthy and socially prominent. They were the only ones who needed large atria to receive clients and large dining rooms for entertaining friends (Vitruvius VI.5). But in a competitive society with relatively extensive upward mobility, the powerful create models for less wealthy and powerful contemporaries through their habits and the style in which they live, at least when they place themselves on display as ostentatiously as Roman aristocrats did. Yet creating and decorating a special part of one's house for purposes of social display was not a specifically Roman phenomenon. In Greek cities of the classical era the houses of the rich were more elaborately constructed and better furnished than those of the less affluent. A guest invited to the house of a wealthy Athenian in the fourth century no doubt expected to find a peristyle or colonnade and a pleasant room for the men's "symposium." In the houses of the Hellenistic era on Delos and elsewhere we find a separate "display" area with several reception rooms, not infrequently adorned with elaborate architectural details, floor mosaics, and walls with plaster decoration, paintings, or more mosaics. The decorative style of corresponding areas in Roman houses drew its inspiration from these Hellenistic sources, but soon acquired entirely new dimensions in the highly competitive climate of the late Republic.[13]

Living Space and Values

This discussion of the way in which the layout and decoration of rooms in Roman houses were used to communicate the owners' status and identity addresses only one aspect of these dwellings' social function. A second, no less interesting question concerns the values that received symbolic expression in such ostentatious spatial displays, and the underlying self-image of the owners. This question seems even more apposite for Roman domestic environments. Why did Romans feel a special affinity for particular architectural forms, images, and mythological figures? What thoughts, memories, wishes, and hopes were supposed to be inspired by the symbolic forms in the decor? I am referring here to everything that made up the *content* of the "discourse" in which Romans expressed their identity, for whatever a homeowner chooses to present to visitors confronts his own eyes as well. In addition to the neighbor, who looks at the home as a competitor, and the visitor who comes to compare, there are the house's occupants, who spend every day in its rooms and live with its images. The owner of a house did not see his home solely in relation to visitors on whom he wished to make an impression; he also wanted to enjoy it himself! For this to be possible, he had to be able to identify himself with it.

We have an easier time understanding this aspect of Roman houses on the basis of our own experience. Creating the environments in which we live has become a subject of enormous interest to people with disposable income, a topic of dinner-party conversation as popular as the constant talk about food. A flood of magazines, books, and catalogues offers us every conceivable model to suit our pocketbooks and our tastes, from country cottages to the last word in modern design. There is also no lack of articles by psychologists and sociologists analyzing the connections between taste in interior design on the one hand and a canon of shared values, self-definition, and social or cultural aspirations on the other. Merely by studying the floor displays of different department and furniture stores, a future historian could glean a great deal about our values and the ways we dream of spending our leisure time.

An Archeological Task

If we were to look in ancient literary sources for answers to the questions posed above, we might easily gain the impression that Romans did not give much thought to this subject. Even in the days of the Empire, when one might expect otherwise, detailed discussion of the appearance and decoration of rooms in fine houses is rare.[14] This implies not that conversation in those days excluded the subject of living conditions, but only that literature was not the primary medium for such discussions. (Because of their strong orientation toward the golden age of Greece, Roman authors only rarely occupied themselves with any aspect of contemporary life.) An intensive dialogue did, however, take place in the form of developing symbolic shapes and patterns for use within the houses themselves, for Roman householders and artisans' constant attempts to imitate, combine, and outdo previous designs are simply an ongoing discourse on the subject of refined living in a different medium.

An investigation of Pompeian tastes in domestic environments therefore presents us with a genuine archeological task, but one that has only recently been articulated. To perform this task properly new strategies must be invented, for current research tends to be limited either to the typology and dating of individual genres such as painting, terracottas, bronzes, and tools, or to the ground plans of houses and their chronological development. Once the question of taste in creating these environments has been raised, however, it is crucial to be able to reconstruct overall contexts. The ground-breaking studies of Roman houses and their interiors date from the second half of the nineteenth century. In that era Johann Friedrich Overbeck and August Mau produced their admirable books on Pompeii, in which they painstakingly assembled the knowledge then available about ancient architecture, painting, and artifacts of all kinds to give us a first impression of "the Roman house."[15] Despite their normative orientation, these books still offer a good introduction to the question of domestic environments. Nevertheless, simply recording the appearance of a house and providing an inventory of its contents from a positivist standpoint are no longer sufficient to answer the questions of interest today.[16] Domestic environments need to be studied as part of an epoch, as we study townscapes, and we need to make the same kind of attempt to create models that reflect the particular characteristics of "Roman houses as inhabited space" and combine them with insights about the processes of social and cultural change occurring at the time. This brings me to the narrower focus of the subject addressed here.

The third chapter of this book, on the villa as a model for late Pompeian taste in domestic environments, can cover no more than a small part of the history of domestic environments in the Roman Empire, for most of it still remains to be written. I have therefore concentrated on a single phenomenon, but one that is, in my view, essential if we are to understand how Romans lived at home. I take as my starting point the obvious connections between the architectural forms and decorative elements of many Pompeian houses on the one hand and those of luxury villas dating from the late Republic on the other.

The Villa: A New Way of Living

Beginning in the middle of the second century B.C., the Roman aristocracy developed an entirely new concept of "domestic environment," the *villa urbana*.[17] It was so successful that it was later adopted throughout the Roman Empire as a general style transcending class divisions. In this new concept the main rooms acquired a function above and beyond the practical needs of daily life, namely, to express a single idea in as many different ways as possible. Every element was intended to evoke the idea of Greece and its model civilization, and to symbolize the presence of Greek culture—as a kind of higher sphere—within the house.

A variety of decorative elements, both visual and atmospheric, went into realizing this aim. Courtyards, gardens, rooms, fountains, and watercourses echoed the forms of Greek architecture and were occasionally even given Greek names. Wherever one looked in a richly decorated villa, references to Greek themes met the eye. Copies of Greek sculptures in varying sizes, sometimes whole series of them, were placed around the rooms; wall paintings and floor mosaics reproduced scenes from Greek mythology, and even the furniture and tableware contained pictorial allusions to classical art and culture. Gardens recalled Greek sanctuaries. Views of the landscape were designed to correspond to the new Hellenistic experience of nature. Creating a three-dimensional enclosed representation of Greek culture was a way of claiming symbolic possession of it. Domestic environments thus became a new form of cultural memory.

Although the rich pictorial fabric of the Roman villa is in many respects comparable to the systematic pictorial decoration of Renaissance and Baroque palaces, it differs in that its elements were not chosen to complement one another or to contribute to a single thematic whole; rather, they appear to be connected loosely or not at all. What mattered was that they be artistically executed and have some association with Greece. An educated man such as Cicero, of course, attached importance to decorating a room with images that were not *inappropriate;* Dionysiac scenes would not suit a peristyle used as a study, whereas they would be fitting for dining rooms, where they are in fact often found in Pompeian houses. The same is true for the many erotic scenes with which bedrooms were decorated. Only in this very general sense can the images be related to the functions of specific rooms and houses described "topographically" as sites devoted to the pleasures of life (a description that also applies to earlier Hellenistic houses).

This fascinating new development of using domestic spaces to evoke a cultural memory had its origins in the enthusiastic adoption of Greek civilization by a portion of the Roman aristocracy beginning in the late third century B.C. The trend extended beyond classical Greek models of education and the arts to include the cultivation of *tryphe,* the luxurious and hedonistic lifestyle characteristic of the courts of Hellenistic rulers. Throughout the Greek-speaking world *tryphe* was symbolized by the figure of Dionysus. In Rome the new friends of Greek culture could not display the results of their conversion to Dionysiac values in public, for they ran counter to austere Roman traditional values and customs, and therefore came under political attack as *luxuria.* Devotees were forced to create a private world of *tryphe* at their country villas, where they could indulge in their pastimes unhampered by political considerations.

Villas became the stage sets for a new lifestyle of leisure *(otium).* Certain rituals associated with this style were sometimes enacted in reality and sometimes only in the imaginations of the villa inhabitants and their guests. They would meet and talk in the gymnasium, which they mentally trans- ported to Athens, although in fact it was in the peristyle. Or they would stroll up and down beside an artificial watercourse *(euripus),* which had associations with the hedonistic life of Alexandria, and carry on learned discussions with friends or even with real Greek philosophers who be- longed to the household and lived with the family. Or, inspired by works of sculpture in the garden, a host and his guests might converse about Greek literature, history, and art, or retire to a more secluded room for philosophical meditations.

No matter that all of this amounted to a Roman construct of Greek life, and that no such part-time, make-believe Greek intellectuals ever existed in classical Greece. Naturally, reality in Roman villas and townhouses often differed considerably from the role-players' imagined ideal as conjured up by the symbolic reminiscences of Greece in these spaces. Nonetheless, for the first time in history a distinct domestic setting had been created for cultural life, to which devotees could withdraw in their leisure time. The world of the villa and leisure was a private retreat, an antithesis to the world of business, politics, and law courts in the city.

The word "private," however, should not suggest a total withdrawal from society; the opposite was the case. The new private sphere of life was used with great frequency for social contacts. Villa owners met with friends, other members of their social class or political party, business associates, and clients. Banquets in particular—imitating Greek models—offered a new form of social communication. Here architecture, decor, and furnishings all contributed to the villa owners' efforts to display their status, becoming important tools in the competition for power, influence, and money. Possession of a luxuriously equipped villa in one of the prestigious country districts (such as on the Bay of Naples, or near Tusculum or Terracina) was indispensable for any aspirant to the highest political circles in the late Republic. From the very start, therefore, the new cultural self-definition of the Roman aristocracy became one means of display in the general competition for status. In the architecture and leisurely style of villa life two elementary needs were fused into a cultural unity.

The Romans had no desire to become Greeks, however, despite the ubiquity of Greek images and cultural rituals in their villas. They were merely expanding and revising their cultural self-definition (and, incidentally, also laying the foundations for their claims to be a great world power). The forms of their new domestic architecture gave symbolic expression to their conviction that they had absorbed the Greeks' cultural heritage, and understood how to "live" as well as how to conquer and rule, for they had adopted in equal measure the refined culture of the classical *polis* and the hedonistic, Dionysiac lifestyle of Hellenistic monarchs. The fact that in the beginning this was possible only in two separate spheres, that of public affairs in Rome and that of private leisure in country villas, reveals some of the tensions inherent in this extraordinarily fruitful process of acculturation. It is no exaggeration to say that only with the achievement of the ambitious new self-definition represented by the villa did the Romans acquire the authority in the eyes of the Greek East that military might alone would never have won for them.

The Villa and Domestic Taste in the Empire

The aristocrats' new style in domestic architecture gradually became a model for all of Roman society. The lifestyle of an elite gave rise to a general taste to which wider circles could aspire. Presumably elements of the architecture and decoration of aristocrats' townhouses in Rome were adopted first; the new style spread to the houses of the ruling class in smaller cities *(domi nobiles),* and had probably become widespread by the second half of the first century B.C.

In the third chapter we will see how various elements of the new domestic architecture and decor were imitated particularly in medium-sized and smaller residences in Pompeii in the early years of the Empire. Clearly the owners of these houses were not bothered by the fact that limitations of space permitted them to recreate these settings only in miniature, or that social life on the scale of villa owners was out of the question. Pompeians no doubt continued to lead the same modest and relatively educated or uneducated life as before. But why, in that case, did these owners expend so much money and imaginative effort to give their homes something of the flair of the great villas? What made the citizens of Pompeii want to participate in the luxurious world of their wealthy contemporaries, at least in their daydreams and imaginations?

The villas of the Roman aristocracy lay just outside the walls of Pompeii. One might easily conclude that the impetus was an urge to imitate their immediate neighbors. Whether this was actually the case, however, or whether villa imitation spread from Rome like the models for wall decoration in the second, third, and fourth styles and garden statuettes, is impossible to determine today.[18] The latter is very likely. We can say for certain only that the spread of the new style of domestic architecture and decor was a general phenomenon that prevailed throughout the entire Roman Empire until late antiquity. Or, to be more precise, we can say that the values underlying the symbolic forms associated with their style remained in force. The actual expressions these then took varied considerably over the course of generations. Nonetheless, the symbolic expression of a unified vision of culture, luxury, and pleasure, as first realized in the Roman villa, predominated throughout the era.

This form of domestic environment thus involves more than just an especially blatant case of status imitation.[19] The new taste in domestic settings became both a symbol of a concept of culture and a statement that the owner identified himself with a particular way of life.

Social Identification and Cultural Self-Definition

The individual phases of the spread of the new taste in domestic decorating have not yet been described as such. The spread of wall paintings from the second to the fourth styles, however, could be used as a paradigm. In a statistical investigation Andrew Wallace-Hadrill found that the presence and quality of wall paintings in Pompeian houses are directly related to the size and number of rooms.[20] In the early Empire the fashion of having rooms painted in the fourth style spread throughout the middle classes. As a rule, only very small houses with a total of approximately 1,000 square feet or less (small by the standards of the time!) have few wall paintings or none at all. The villa elements I have described date from the same period and are expressions of the same taste in domestic decoration. Merely by having his walls painted, a homeowner could achieve a minimum of the new look. Wallace-Hadrill observes correctly that the most rudimentary paintings, frequently of inferior quality, are intended more as demonstrations that the owners possess a certain level of culture (for the upwardly mobile, above all, in the form of "rebirth through imitation") than as displays of luxury and wealth. Given the actual conditions in the humbler houses, the latter would of course have appeared absurd. Yet simply applying terms such as "kitsch" or "lack of refinement" to the phenomenon fails to do it justice, for this approaches it too narrowly from the perspectives of imitation and cultural deficit.

A demonstration that one "belongs" in fact means more. The process by which the new style spread and was altered to fit modest dwellings was at the same time a process of its adoption and internalization by those who could afford neither luxury nor an expensive education. It was a process of abstraction or even of sublimation, in a manner of speaking, and one can see it in operation in the wall paintings themselves.

On the more ambitious or elaborate walls in the second or third style, for example, the central mythological images occasionally still refer to real picture galleries (*pinacothecae*) of wealthy collectors, which included original Greek works (as in the case of a copy of a well-known painting in the Villa Farnesina). Obviously, however, the wall paintings were not a "substitute" for a real *pinacotheca,* since they are found in even the most expensive houses. Rather, they create a symbolic system in which luxury articles actually present in many villas are combined with imagined spaces and objects. Like the villas themselves, the mural paintings in the second style evoke spaces reminiscent of Greek culture, but as abstractions, a transformation that makes them available to anyone who can afford to hire a painter, in contrast to real rooms. The process of abstraction thus set in motion rendered the images increasingly independent of the objects depicted. This process is clearly reflected in the formal changes occurring between the walls in the second style and those in the fourth (from about 80 B.C. to A.D. 79). In place of the almost palpable architecture and luxury goods in paintings from the late Republican period, we find that the architecture, objects, and people of the later paintings have become manneristic, and have been transported into an oddly unreal sphere. As we shall see, this formal removal corresponds to a process of abstraction in the underlying values. Precisely because the aim of wall paintings was to depict symbols of general values rather than concrete luxuries, even the most modest wall paintings could fulfill their intended function: namely, to give the room in which they were located a certain aura of elevated taste, and thus to express the owner's membership within a cultural circle. The message could be conveyed independent of all competition for status.

The example of mythological images shows that this need to belong was more than just pretty decor, and now had little to do with imitating wealthy villa owners' art collections. Through constant repetition (which we find occurring in other areas of contemporary cultural life as well, such as theaters, schools, and recitations) some of the myths had become so familiar that people began to associate them more and more directly with their own lives, seeing them as metaphors for situations in which they found themselves. The extent to which myths were associated with the present by a broad spectrum of the population is evident in the countless reliefs of mythological scenes on sarcophagi. For the Romans of that era, the use of myths to allude to the present seems to have been as natural as biblical references were in our own society not long ago. Ordinary people could use this relatively educated and "international" language of allusion to express their claims to membership in dominant social and cultural circles, just as they did with wall paintings. At the same time, however, the myths appear to have supplied them with models for conducting their own lives; otherwise they would not have used mythical images to express their personal sorrows and joys, hopes, and need for solace. This is what I meant earlier when I referred to the diffusion of the new taste in domestic interiors as being accompanied by a process of adoption and internalization.

The case is similar for the paradigm "luxury and the hedonistic life," which had been inseparably linked with the notions of the villa and refined domestic environments since the time of Lucullus. One could say that these "values," too, were simultaneously reflected by the symbolic forms of room decor. The most obvious trappings of luxury—such as expensive marbles and precious metals, costly fabrics and dyes, rare gems and shells, but also culinary delicacies—were present in a house, either in reality or in painted form, depending on the wealth and extravagance of the owner. At the same time the topoi of *luxuria* in the rooms' decoration were so intimately connected with scenes from myths and other highly prized emblems of classical culture that these two pillars of Hellenistic tradition always appeared together, at least in the world of symbolic forms. What had once been decried as corrupting *luxuria* was now obviously perceived, in the context of domestic space and its associated symbolic forms, as an important value, in some sense embodying abundance and enjoyment. The allusions to luxury in the decor, like the many Dionysiac images, assured beholders that they inhabited a happy world; they also corresponded perfectly to the ideological stereotypes of the *felicitas temporum* or "golden age" *(aurea aetas)* in imperial art.

In the context of the domestic environment such representational programs also contained an invitation to bring to life the allusions and reminiscences depicted in art. This occurred in the rituals of the banquet, for instance, which had as its aim the combination of pleasure with edifying conversation.

It seems likely that a connection exists between the neutralization and re-evaluation of luxury in the context of symbolic forms and its reduction in the actual lives of Roman aristocrats as social competition decreased

(Tacitus, *Annals* III, 55). In any event both the walls painted in the fourth style and the imitation of villas in Pompeian houses testify to altered perceptions of the phenomenon.

The Cult of Culture in the Empire

The fact that the new style of domestic architecture and decor gained such ground, and even advanced to become the general standard of taste in the Empire, is without doubt linked to the kinds of social change inevitably brought about by the establishment of the monarchy. One striking phenomenon in Roman art is the subordinate role that the political themes associated with the myth of the emperor played in the imagery of private homes and graves; indeed, in most houses these themes, which so dominated public monuments, do not occur at all. This suggests that, within the overall cultural framework, the Roman concept of the domestic environment functioned as a counterweight to the world of the state and politics, even after its diffusion throughout most levels of society.

The political stage was occupied by the imperial dynasty, and the awarding of public honors was controlled by the official bureaucracy. In this situation cultural activities of all kinds that had previously belonged to the private sphere acquired new significance. As the upper classes came to regard educational and cultural activities as opportunities for self-promotion and furtherance of their careers, participation in them increasingly formed a part of public life. The reason for this is simple: the fields of learning and culture were politically neutral, and therefore safe. By the time of Pliny the Younger, attendance at public or semipublic gatherings where friends and acquaintances recited their latest literary productions consumed a good part of a Roman senator's working day, as Pliny himself grumbled.[21] The huge success of the "second school" of sophists and their oratorical "performances" shows how cultural activities could lead to political office, or in any case to great prestige. In the logical culmination of this trend, ultimately even the emperor himself had to demonstrate possession of the relevant skills: not only the philosophical reflections of Marcus

Aurelius, but also Nero's aspirations as a singer should probably be seen in this context.

Through the introduction of cultural activities in the public sphere, homes designed to evoke cultural memories and the pleasures of life acquired a further significance. They became a symbol of the high level of culture afforded by the Roman Empire. Under the emperors the symbolic forms of domestic decor spread increasingly to the public sphere; one need only think of the lavish ornamentation of the main rooms in public baths, or the fountains, plantings, and sculptures in public parks. These public amenities made particularly important elements of the elite's luxury villas accessible to broader classes of people, and erased the dividing line between *privata luxuria* (private luxury) and *publica magnificentia* (public magnificence) previously demanded by the ideology of the late Republic. The alteration in the Roman definition of the public sphere mentioned above meant that the same values could be celebrated there as in private domestic settings. With this step the lengthy process of acculturation reached a kind of conclusion.

Urban Space as a
Reflection of Society

Experiences of our own "inhospitable" cities have made us more aware of the appearance of urban environments and their effect upon the people who inhabit them.★ The city as living space has become the focus of intense discussion in the past two decades, and the debate has revealed how close the connections are between a given community's economy, social conditions, health, and culture on the one hand, and the appearance of its cities on the other. In the course of only one generation the prevailing views and values have swung from one extreme to the other in Europe, from the modernization of inner cities to accommodate ever more automobiles to the creation of large car-free zones; from the heyday of commuter zones, suburbs, and city centers depopulated in the evening to their revival through construction of downtown entertainment complexes, shopping centers, and luxury apartments.

Discussion of these pressing contemporary issues has had a highly stimulating effect on historical studies. The topic of the city has been very popular for some time now, and among the many new approaches one of the most fruitful and appealing has proved to be the attempt to provide as

★ This refers to the book by the German psychoanalyst and social critic Alexander Mitscherlich entitled *Die Unwirtlichkeit unserer Städte* [The Inhospitality of Our Cities], which was published in Germany in 1965 and fostered a great deal of discussion on urban planning and modern architecture. —*Translator's note.*

complete a description as possible of a city's total appearance in a particular historical period. This approach seeks to interpret the entire physical and aesthetic configuration of a city as a reflection of the condition and mentality of the society that inhabited it. The aim is to understand how its layout, architecture, and visual imagery of all kinds work in conjunction with citizens' rituals and everyday activities to make up a single coherent structure expressive of a society's needs, values, expectations, and hopes.[1]

In cases where a substantial amount of evidence has survived, townscapes have a great deal to tell us. This is especially true where growth was organic and the city's face not created through the will of a single ruler or ideological program, for then the city represents the realization of many anonymous and in part contradictory interests. In a largely self-regulating process—as these interests interact and the participants make decisions based on specific needs, pressures, or personal preferences—inhabitants produce a configuration that becomes a self-portrait of their society, although this was by no means the intent.

Once a cityscape has been established, no historian will underestimate its effect on the mental outlook of its inhabitants. Repeated daily experience of one urban environment can be socially integrative, stabilizing, or even stimulating, while another may arouse feelings of irritation or insecurity, or undermine the citizens' general sense of well-being. In the case of ancient societies, one need only think of the antithetical vistas of late Republican and Augustan Rome, or the effect of the public monuments erected on the Athenian Acropolis in the age of Pericles, or the crumbling public edifices in the city centers of the late Empire. At the very least cityscapes understood in these terms certainly constitute an integral part of the culture of each period.

Pompeii, the best preserved Greco-Roman city, presents great difficulties to archeologists wanting to approach it in this manner, for in fact we can see only the city that was buried on August 24, A.D. 79. Since it was more than six hundred years old at the time, we are forced to imagine what the earlier buildings looked like in their original state and ask what purpose they served at the time of their construction. Many elements of former cityscapes were no longer visible in A.D. 79, yet the sheer numbers of

Figure 1   The forum, as it appeared after the earthquake of A.D. 62. The current state of the ruins is confusing, since most of the structures in the forum had not yet been re-built at the time of the eruption that buried the city. The Pompeians had cleared away the rubble and removed valuable materials such as marble slabs and decorative statuary, some of which was re-used in private houses. The fact that this public quarter with the town's most important temple and the basilica had not been rebuilt seventeen years after the quake, although construction had begun on a large new bath complex, gives an indication of the priorities set by the town council *(ordo)* at the time. Some of the valuable materials appear to have been "excavated" by the former inhabitants of Pompeii after the eruption.

buildings preserved by the eruption, both those already uncovered and those still buried, have (with a few exceptions) prevented the type of stratigraphical excavation normally undertaken at other sites.

We must also take into consideration the fact that Pompeii was not a typical ancient city. The majority of its structures, especially the public buildings, had been devastated by a severe earthquake on May 2, A.D. 62, and perhaps another in the seventies, and still lay in ruins.[2] This explains why present-day visitors find a number of buildings, particularly around the forum, so lacking in vividness and immediacy, especially in contrast to the houses that have been reconstructed (fig. 1). Not only have the forum buildings been stripped of all the carved marble decorations they displayed before the first earthquake; their present state also gives no impression of the full height of the walls or the effect of the structures as a whole.

Traditional approaches to studying Pompeii have also tended to ignore questions about historical contexts and the city's architectural evolution. From the time when excavations began in 1740, researchers' work was dominated first by aesthetic interests and later largely by the school of historical positivism. Pompeii and Herculaneum became the chief sources of our knowledge of ancient material culture, and investigators concentrated on classifying the materials they found according to genre and function.

When the remote past becomes palpable in the immediate present, the effect is fascinating, and every day thousands of visitors to the ruins gain the impression that, all in all, human beings remain basically the same throughout the ages. Pompeii is more conducive to such feelings than other sites, yet to experience the past as essentially familiar rather than as alien is a fatal error for historians.

Beginning with the standard works by Overbeck and Mau, most published studies treat Pompeii topographically, and they provide admirable examples of this approach. As a result, however, virtually no attempts have been made up to now to acquire an overview of the whole city and to distinguish the various historical layers in its fabric. The history of Pompeii continues to be written as a history of individual structures, providing little or no sense of larger connections.

In what follows, at least as far as public buildings are concerned, I shall seek to identify and differentiate three historical aggregates: the Hellenized Samnite city of the second century B.C., the period of rapid change following the founding of the Roman colony in 80 B.C., and the new townscape of the early Empire. I am grateful for a wealth of specialized archeological and epigraphical studies that have appeared in the past two decades; it is owing to their many new findings that such an attempt has become possible. The results—mainly pertaining to genres in the field of archeology and to social and economic history in epigraphy—will be evaluated for their relevance to the approach here, which is to seek a historical synchronicity of culture and mental outlook. Such an approach necessarily gives less priority to the examination of individual monuments, as the aim is rather to demonstrate that particular features common to quite different monuments can be interpreted as indicators of specific historical situations and cultural trends. I have striven to be as precise as possible, although space constraints may have led to some occasional simplification in presenting the material.

We still know very little about the first four hundred years of Pompeii's history. The most recent studies by Stefano de Caro indicate that a first wall of tufa and lava, surrounding all 157 acres of the lava plateau on which the town is situated, dates from the sixth century B.C.[3] In the early fifth century it was followed by a limestone wall, which lay outside the Samnite ramparts (end of the fourth century B.C.). The first wall might reflect an Etruscan attempt to link a number of villages and protect the strategically and economically important site at the mouth of the River Sarno from encroachment by the Greek settlers in Campania. In the course of only a few decades a small town center with the temple of Apollo (the "old city") sprang up on the site that later became the forum, and a Doric temple was built on the Triangular Forum. But by far the greatest part of the area enclosed by the walls appears to have been used for agricultural purposes.

On the basis of pottery finds scholars have inferred that a period of relative prosperity and lively trade occurred in the second half of the sixth and in the early fifth century B.C., followed by a definite decline until the end of the century. The small settlement on the arid lava spur must have languished until the Samnites emerged from their mountainous inland territories in the late fourth and third centuries and settled in the towns of the coastal plain. A portion of the surviving walls, the oldest limestone houses, and the layout of the street grid in the northern and eastern sectors of Pompeii date from this time and reflect a renewed upsurge of prosperity. No public buildings from this period have survived, however. After the Second Punic War there appears to have been a large influx of new settlers; this is suggested by the numerous simple houses without atria in region I that have been studied in recent years.

From the time of the Samnite Wars, Pompeii was an ally of Rome and required to participate in Roman military campaigns, although the town was left to manage its own internal affairs. The language spoken in Pompeii was Oscan. Not until the late second century B.C. do we have a clear enough picture of the city to gain a sense of its specific cultural identity.

The Hellenistic City of the Oscans

The Oscan city of the second century B.C. is marked by great private wealth and efforts by the upper class to acquire the Hellenistic culture that would link them to the larger Mediterranean world. Although the Romans had expanded their overseas empire into the western and eastern Mediterranean, their Italic confederates remained excluded from Roman citizenship and thus from full participation in power. These circumstances allowed the more affluent residents of the towns in central Italy and Campania to concentrate their energies on increasing their wealth. They did so mainly by increasing agricultural production and exports.[4]

From about 150 B.C. the leading families of Pompeii were clearly able to amass large fortunes, chiefly owing to the wine trade, but perhaps also to some extent to the production of oil. Amphorae and seals characteristic of the region document the export of wine by Campanian families to places as far away as Gaul and Spain. Production on this scale could be achieved on medium-sized estates by employing slave labor and using the improved methods of cultivation described by Cato. A further important factor was Campanian participation in trade with the East. Inscriptions with the names of traders from Campanian towns have been found throughout the eastern Mediterranean region and are particularly common on Delos, which was a free port from 166 B.C. and the site of auctions in which, at their peak, up to 10,000 slaves are said to have been sold in a single day.[5]

By such means members of leading circles in these towns came into direct contact with the Hellenistic world and, like their counterparts in the Roman aristocracy, were swept up in a powerful current of acculturation. Unlike the Romans and colonial aristocrats, however, the inhabitants of Pompeii encountered no political or ideological obstacles in their cult of *luxuria* and could indulge themselves to their hearts' content.[6]

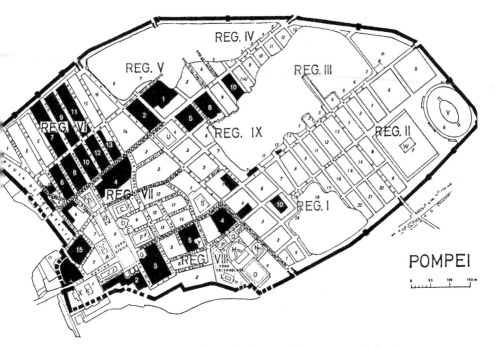

Figure 2 Distribution of elaborate residences in the second century B.C. (following H. Lauter). In this period the largest and most expensive houses were built mainly in the northern part of town (region VI), where large, regularly shaped *insulae* made construction on a grander scale possible. In the crooked lanes east of the forum (region VII) stood modest wooden structures used mostly by tradesmen and artisans.

The Old Families and Their "Palaces"

The situation described above is clearly reflected in the townscape of Oscan Pompeii, which around 100 B.C. boasted opulent private homes and impressive public buildings for both cultural and commercial purposes. By contrast, the structures with more narrowly political functions in the forum reflect only a slow advance of Hellenization with many interruptions. The leading families of this era apparently did not seek to display their status in the arena of civic affairs.

If we take the foregoing as our hypothesis, then it is appropriate to begin sketching the profile of the Hellenized town with the grand townhouses in region VI (fig. 2). They are still easily recognizable today by their façades of

Figure 3 Façades of upper-class houses in region VI. The façades of these houses from the second century B.C. can still be easily recognized today by their walls of neatly hewn tufa blocks. The entrances often have carved door frames, sometimes with elaborately sculpted capitals (compare figs. 6 and 7).

carefully hewn tufa blocks (fig. 3) and elaborate door frames, often with decorated capitals (fig. 4). The best known of these houses, the House of the Faun (fig. 5), occupies one entire *insula* of typically elongated shape, about 2,940 square meters or 31,000 square feet.[7]

A look at the floor plan of this house immediately reveals that only a small part of the enclosed area provided actual living space; two-thirds of it are taken up by two peristyle courtyards that could easily compete with the colonnades of public buildings and offer impressive proof of the family's desire for luxury and conspicuous display. As preserved today, the house shows signs of expansion and renovation in the late second century B.C. Yet even in the first half of this century it and some other houses in the town were designed as virtual palaces, boasting two atria, large rooms with high ceilings, and elaborately decorated entrances.

The new concept of luxury dictated use of space on a truly princely scale. Similar dimensions in private homes are unknown in the Italian and Greek cities of earlier times. The dwellings in newly planned Greek towns of the fourth century occupy on average only about one-tenth as much space as the House of the Faun, and the more lavish houses in the theater quarter on Delos from the second century B.C. measure about 4,300 square feet.[8] Lauter observed correctly that the only comparable structures are royal residences, such as the Palazzo delle Colonne in Ptolemais in Roman Cyrenaica (32,000 square feet) and the palaces in Pella (such as I.1, which measures approximately 56,000 square feet).[9]

This suggests that Samnite landed proprietors and exporters adopted the luxury of the Hellenistic world with the same excesses as the Roman aristocrats in their roughly contemporary villas on the Bay of Naples.[10] But unlike the Roman senators, who forced one another to show some restraint in the face of Greek *luxuria* in Rome itself, the richest citizens of

Figure 4 Reconstruction of a street in the Hellenized Oscan town of Pompeii (after F. Krischen).

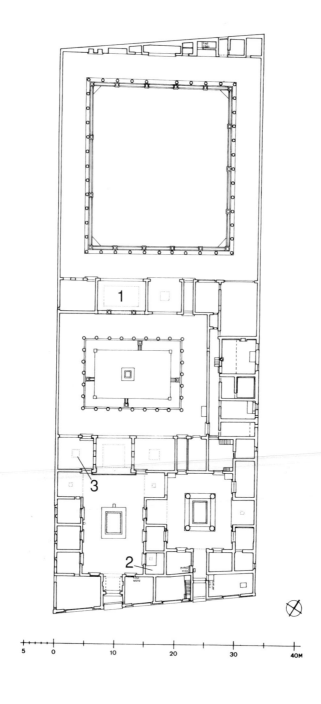

POMPEII

Pompeii apparently knew no limits—on the contrary, they proudly exhibited their newly acquired Greek cultivation. The carefully executed ornamentation of the house portals and the mosaics reveals the extent of their aspirations. This is particularly striking in the figured capitals, usually Dionysiac in theme, which some ambitious homeowners commissioned.

The capitals flanking the entrance to the House of the Figured Capitals (VII 4.57; figs. 6 and 7), directly opposite the House of the Faun, comprise virtually a full program devoted to Dionysus.[11] On the side facing the street each capital displayed a satyr and a maenad. The older satyr to the right leans drunkenly away from the maenad, whereas his counterpart on the left is clasping his partner to him. On the side of each capital facing the entrance there is displayed, in clear counterpoint to the Dionysiac couples, a decorous pair, apparently at a symposium. The men are naked to the waist, the women swathed in the usual modest robes, but their expressions and embrace make it clear that here, too, they are enjoying wine and an amorous encounter. Through this juxtaposition the owner announces in the most explicit manner his identification with the Dionysiac, hedonistic lifestyle celebrated by Oriental monarchs and characteristic of contemporary Greek cities. The portal thus proclaims his adoption of a specific form of Greek culture.

The adoption of Greek images in these and similar forms deserves careful study in conjunction with the other decorative elements of second-century Pompeian houses. Such an investigation would reveal how clearly the entire ambience was conceived as a demonstration of the Greek cult of luxury and an espousal of its values. A few examples must suffice here.

The owner of the House of the Faun increased the grandeur of his imposing atrium in the old Tuscan style by the addition of a blind second-story wall with painted Ionic columns (fig. 8).[12] In addition he tried to make an immediate impression on his visitors with elaborate architectural

Figure 5 House of the Faun, region VI 12. Ground plan (after A. Hoffmann). The house occupies an entire *insula* (approximately 31,000 square feet). The rooms are arranged around two atria and two peristyles. Such lavish use of space was unknown in townhouses of the Greek east; it is found only in palaces, like those excavated in the Macedonian royal capital of Pella.

Figures 6 and 7 Two capitals with figures that once flanked the entrance of the house named after them, the House of the Figured Capitals, across the street from the House of the Faun (now in the Pompeii Museum). On the capital to the right of the entrance the master of the

decor in the front entryway (*fauces;* fig. 9). However, the decoration about eight feet above the floor that imitates the stucco façades of two little temples is oversized for the relatively narrow passage, creating an effect that must have been more menacing than impressive. The almost forced extravagance of taste, combined with a rather haphazard placement of the various decorative elements, appears typical of upper-class outlook in Oscan Pompeii during this phase of acculturation. This mind-set called for everything to be Greek and, if possible, of first-rate quality. The plaster simulated costly marble veneer; furniture and household utensils were imported from the East; bronze statuettes from Greece and the most expensive mosaics adorned the rooms visitors were likely to see. The repertoire of the mosaics shows that the craftsmen had access to the cartoons popular throughout the Hellenistic world. One could interpret the iconography of these mosaics as the sum of everything worth striving for in the hedonistic culture of late Hellenism.[13] The immediate connection with the lives of the

house, naked to the waist, is shown at a banquet, together with his wife. Across from them are a drunken satyr and a maenad. With this type of self-depiction the owner identified himself with the cult of Dionysus and the notion of pleasure as a central value in life.

occupants of these houses becomes evident in such instances as the erotic embrace depicted in a bedroom (the *cubiculum,* in fig. 5, no. 2; plate 1) or the still life with delectable-looking fish in one of the dining rooms (fig. 5, no. 3; plate 2).

The owners of these grand houses felt entirely at home in the Greek culture of their day, which played a role even in their daily lives. This familiarity was a matter of pride and was announced to all and sundry: On the threshold to the atrium in the House of the Faun visitors crossed a broad strip of floor mosaic depicting two masks of the tragic muse and Dionysiac drums framed by an opulent garland of fruit. Classical learning constituted one element of this hedonistic lifestyle.

The most striking example of the owner's identification with Hellenistic culture, however, is the famous Alexander mosaic (fig. 10). Placed along the axis of the house so as to be visible from both peristyles, it was laid in an exedra especially designed to hold it, flanked by two Corinthian pillars on

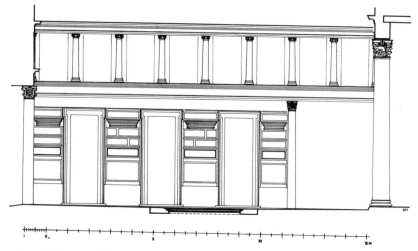

Figure 8 House of the Faun (region VI 12). Reconstruction of the west wall of the Tuscan atrium (after A. Hoffmann). The large atrium in the "Tuscan" style was the grand reception room of the house. Although the form of the room itself remained in the Italian tradition (an atrium without columns around the impluvium), the treatment of the walls used the rich vocabulary of Hellenistic architecture, including tall, carved door frames, columns, and engaged columns. The same combination of Italian and Hellenistic room forms can be found in the inclusion of two peristyle courtyards in the ground plan.

tall plinths. It is a copy, made by highly accomplished artisans, of a famous work painted about 300 B.C. by the Greek artist Philoxenos of Eretria, depicting in all likelihood the Battle of Gaugamela.[14] The mosaic dates from the same period in which the king of Pergamum had copies of famous paintings from the classical era made in Delphi. The Alexander mosaic in the House of the Faun is exhibited like a large painting in its own special room, except that the owner had it executed in the more durable form of mosaic. Perhaps his enjoyment was heightened by the technical perfection with which the craftsmen recreated the painting in the more cumbersome medium. It would be interesting to know if the exedra was used at all, or whether the extraordinary floor was only to be looked at rather than walked on. Probably the showpiece of the owner's art collection, the mosaic can be interpreted at the same time as an almost painfully blatant claim to education and a tribute to the greatest leader of the Hellenistic world. In any event one should not imagine the owner as a great connois-

POMPEII

Figure 9 House of the Faun (region VI 12). View from the atrium into the two peristyle courtyards. From the entryway and the atrium the two courtyards were visible one behind the other, so that on arrival the visitor received an immediate impression of the grand spaces in this palatial house.

seur of art, for directly in front of the Alexander mosaic lay another mosaic in a rather primitive style depicting the Nile with an amusing crocodile, a hippopotamus, and other exotic creatures.

The affluent residents with a taste for Hellenistic culture must have represented a sizable segment of the population, even though Pompeii was not a large town, and their wealth must have varied considerably.[15] This is indicated by the differing sizes of the houses in the northern quarter, which were constructed of tufa by the same painstaking method as the House of the Faun. These occupy areas ranging from one-half or one-quarter down to one-eighth of an *insula* (fig. 11). Despite the variation in their dimensions, they match the quality of the House of the Faun in construction, decorative architectural elements, and other decoration (to the extent that it has survived).

The grandest houses lay in the most important commercial thoroughfares. Rich families exploited the advantages of these sites by including

Figure 10 The Alexander mosaic from the House of the Faun, now in the Museo Nazionale, Naples (after F. Mazois). The mosaic is a copy of a famous Hellenistic painting of a battle from about 300 B.C. and was in a large exedra between the two peristyle courtyards (fig. 5, no. 1) so that it could be viewed from both sides. The owner turned his possession of a work of art into an insistent display of Hellenistic culture. By celebrating the legend of Alexander the Great, the owner of the house established his own connection with the Greek world; the transformation of the celebrated painting into a lasting floor mosaic represents a unique feat of acculturation.

space for shops on the street side of their new houses from at least the early second century B.C. Such premises often had access to a bedroom on a mezzanine floor above the shop, called a *pergula* in Latin. The phrase *natus in pergula* was used to refer to someone of humble origins. These shops were run by dependents of the wealthy owners, in most cases probably slaves or freedmen. Here the floor plans of the houses reflect the old patriarchal structures of Pompeian society.[16]

The less affluent residents must have lived in the "old town," especially in the part to the east of the forum. If we assume that their dwellings were simple wood-frame structures, it would explain the fact that no tufa houses have been found here.

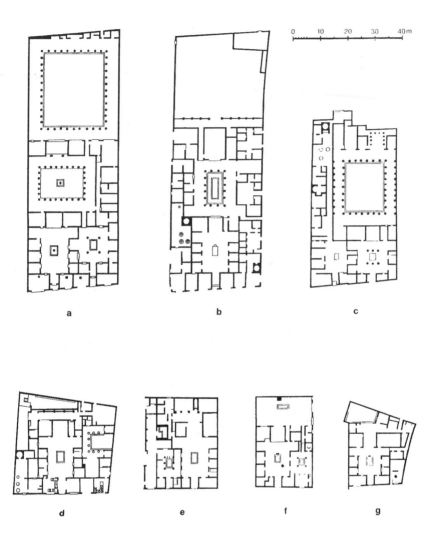

Figure 11 Comparative sizes of well-built tufa houses of the second century B.C.: (a) House of the Faun (VI 12); (b) House of Pansa with surrounding units (VI 6.1); (c) House of the Labyrinth (VI 11.10); (d) House of Sallust (VI 2.4); (e) House VI 8.20–22; (f) House VI 7.20–21; (g) House of the Surgeon (VI 1.10). The range of sizes of these houses with the same high standard of construction and decor points to a relatively large number of affluent families in the Oscan period.

Urban Space as a Reflection of Society   43

The Theater Quarter

Like the private dwellings, most public buildings from the late Samnite period reflect the Pompeians' desire to adopt Greek culture and the Greek way of life. In Pompeii it is striking, however, that the corresponding structures do not dominate the entire townscape as in comparable Greek cities of the same era, but are instead clustered away from the center, in what has come to be known as the "theater quarter" (fig. 12). In choosing a site for the theater the planners probably found the most favorable location to be the natural slope at the southern end of town, near the old Doric temple (fig. 13). Yet it is significant that within only a few decades they erected several other buildings devoted to Greek culture in the immediate vicinity of the theater.

Following the southern Italian and Sicilian practice, the builders of this first theater designed it with tiered seating facing a free-standing structure containing the stage. Campania became Hellenized earlier and more thoroughly than regions farther to the north; thus in contrast to the custom at "Latin" theaters of northern cities, the actors performed simultaneously in the orchestra pit and on the high narrow stage.[17] The reconstructed theaters in Priene and Oropus probably convey a good idea of how the original theater looked in Pompeii.[18]

Unfortunately, we do not know which plays the itinerant actors of the day presented. Undoubtedly the favorites included the type of burlesque named after the neighboring town of Atella. Performed in the local Oscan dialect, these were coarse farces with four stock characters: Maccus, the jester or fool; Bucco, a pot-bellied simpleton; Pappus, the gray-bearded cuckold; and Dossenus, the trickster. Whether Greek comedies or even tragedies were performed in Oscan translations, whether upper-class audiences knew enough Greek to attend performances of classical plays in the original language, and whether the works of Plautus and Terence were presented in Latin—these are all questions to which we would like to know the answers.[19] Later additions to the auditorium *(cavea)* also make it impossible to say how many spectators the theater originally held. For the expanded structure of the Augustan period the number has been estimated

44

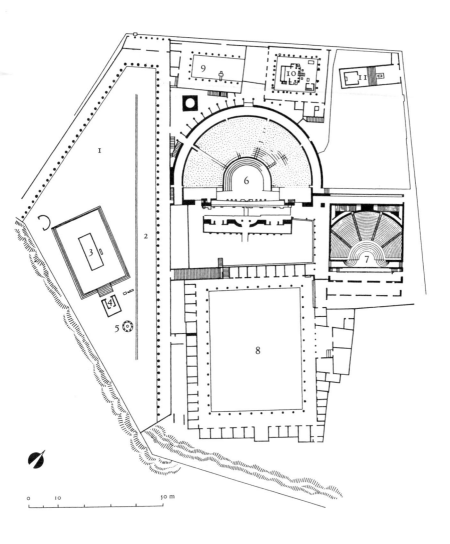

Figure 12 Plan of the theater quarter. Triangular Forum (1) with the old Doric temple (3) and (?) stadium (2); Theater (6); *Theatrum tectum* (7); Gymnasium (?) (8); palaestra (9); Temple of Isis (10); Temple of Zeus Meilichios (11). It is characteristic of the acculturation process that the new buildings associated with Hellenistic culture are not integrated into the urban fabric, but instead clustered together in a kind of cultural center on the perimeter, like an "addition" to the old town.

Urban Space as a Reflection of Society　　　　　　　　　45

Figure 13 Theater, looking toward the stage (lithograph of 1884). The excavated theater is the result of several renovations. The original building from the second century B.C. followed the model of southern Italian and Sicilian theaters and had a tall free-standing stage. After renovations in the Augustan period it could hold about 5,000 spectators (compare fig. 56).

at 5,000 (see the section "Seating by Rank in the New Marble Theater," p. 107).

In Egypt and elsewhere in the diaspora the Greeks were called "the men from the gymnasium."[20] Foreigners rightly considered education in a gymnasium, where emphasis was placed on physical fitness along with philosophy and the arts (and the atmosphere was strongly competitive), the hallmark of Greek life and culture. Extremely beautiful gymnasia were constructed of marble in the Greek cities of Asia Minor in the second century B.C. Grave stele of young men from the same period proudly record their training and achievements in the gymnasium. Given these cities' lack of political power, cultural traditions played an increasingly important role, and the gymnasium became the cornerstone of these societies' Greek identity.

The Pompeians could not have felt they truly belonged to the Greek cultural world without such an institution. In his book *Juventus* (1924), Matteo della Corte suggested that the great peristyle behind the theater

Figure 14 Large peristyle building south of the theater, perhaps originally built as a gymnasium and later used as barracks for gladiators (from an old photograph). A comparison with the plans of Greek *gymnasia* supports the hypothesis that it was constructed in the second century B.C. as a gymnasium for the boys and young men of Pompeii. There is no clear indication that it was originally planned to be used in conjunction with the theater, and its size suggests an important function in the public life of the town.

(fig. 14)[21] with its seventy-four Doric columns from the second century B.C. originally served not as a courtyard for spectators to stroll in during the intermission, but as the gymnasium of Hellenistic Pompeii. Although the study reflects a number of problematic attitudes, this particular suggestion is of interest.[22] In the period following the earthquake two stories of cells were added above the colonnade; the wall paintings and discovery of the famous helmets make it clear that the structure was used in that period as the gladiators' barracks. Della Corte's proposal has been largely ignored, probably because of the author's fascist ideology and lackluster scholarship. A comparison of the building's ground plan with Greek gymnasia suggests, however, that the hypothesis has considerable merit after all. Good parallels can be found for the peristyle's general proportions, the propylon (see fig. 18), and the exedra on the eastern side. Furthermore, the structure was clearly not designed at the same time as the theater. At no point do its outer

Figure 15 Reconstruction of the Triangular Forum with the archaic temple (after C. Weichardt, 1896). This idealized view gives an inaccurate impression of the Doric temple, which was actually a simple structure with terracotta decoration. The temple was renovated several times.

walls run parallel to the back wall of the stage building, which is separated from the presumed gymnasium by an irregularly shaped courtyard. The axis of the peristyle complex is even shifted slightly to the east relative to the theater.

By contrast a stairway, originally roofed, connects the complex with the considerably more elevated terrace of the old temple (fig. 15). This could have been the site of the gymnasium's running track and stadium, as della Corte proposed. A strip of ground corresponding to a possible track lies just in front of the eastern portico of the temple precinct, demarcated by a low wall. The track itself would have been only about half the usual length, but this does not necessarily invalidate della Corte's hypothesis. Given the fact that the Pompeians were in the process of absorbing another culture, the main point may have been to have a stadium attached to the gymnasium, its dimensions being of secondary importance. The terrain demanded some concessions, it would seem, but a widely traveled citizen might well have regarded a reduced stadium as something of an embarrassment. In this

POMPEII

connection it would be interesting to know whether the boys and young men of Oscan Pompeii participated in any serious athletic training. For the time being all these conclusions remain speculative, although stratigraphic soundings could easily provide some answers.

The "Samnite palaestra" northwest of the theater (fig. 12, no. 9) does not contradict such an interpretation of the evidence.[23] The structure's modest dimensions would have limited the amount of activity that could take place inside. It may have been a gymnasium for younger boys—cases in which the pupils were divided into two or more age groups using different facilities are documented in several Hellenistic cities—or perhaps, as has recently been suggested, it served as a clubhouse for young people from elite families *(vereiia)*.[24]

The Stabian baths (fig. 16) should also be mentioned in this context, as

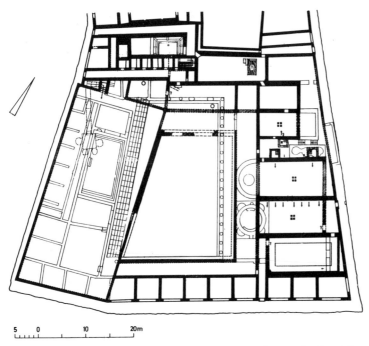

5 0   10   20m

Figure 16 Plan of the Stabian baths (after Eschebach). Roman thermae developed from the simpler baths of Greek *gymnasia*. However, the plan of these baths, the oldest in Pompeii, shows that they were designed with hardly any space for athletic exercise.

Urban Space as a Reflection of Society

Figure 17 Marble sundial from the Stabian baths, a characteristic feature of Hellenistic *gymnasia*. The inscription in Oscan indicates that it dates from the period in which the Roman colony was founded.

they were situated immediately next to the theater quarter.[25] Originally designed to provide basic hygiene in a plain setting, they were remodeled in the second century B.C. and transformed into a more luxurious establishment with separate facilities for men and women and an up-to-date heating system with hypocausts. The old courtyard was converted into a peristyle similar to those in the great tufa houses, and a more elaborate façade on the Via dell'Abbondanza advertised the new comfort and luxury of the complex. Evidence that the courtyard had superior installations at this date is provided by a sundial (fig. 17) with an Oscan inscription. (The first functioning sundial in Rome was erected in 164 B.C.) Unfortunately, we do not know much about Hellenistic baths, but there can be little doubt that this complex represents another element of Hellenistic culture. In the third century B.C., for example, the women of a Fayum village were already permitted to use the public bathhouse.[26]

The development of heated baths presumably evolved in Greek gymnasia and palaestrae. It would be interesting to know when and where baths lost their immediate association with physical exercise and athletic facilities, and became part of the cult of luxury. This process was well advanced by the time the Stabian baths were converted, in any event, for the peristyle court hardly offered enough space for serious exercise, and all the additions of this period to the main building served various stages of the bathing ritual, at least in Eschebach's reconstruction.

Returning to the theater quarter, we find that the sacred precinct containing the archaic temple also underwent renovation as part of the large-scale construction program of buildings associated with Hellenistic culture (see fig. 15).[27] Doric colonnades were added bordering the terraces on the eastern and northern sides, to a total length of about 650 feet, and the whole area was opened up toward the town by the addition of a formal propylon with six tall Ionic columns and two flanking three-quarter columns. Now partially restored, this structure is of particularly fine quality (fig. 18). It provided access not only to the newly embellished temple precinct, but also to the theater and—if della Corte's hypothesis is correct—to the new gymnasium. Thus it served as a ceremonial gateway into the world of Hellenism. In all likelihood the wall of the propylon with its

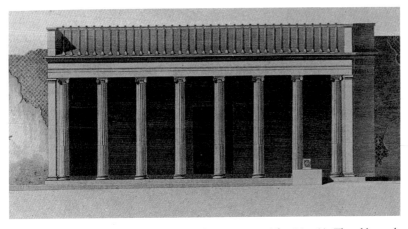

Figure 18 Propylon at the entrance to the theater quarter (after Mazois). The old temple precinct was lined with porticos when the Hellenistic cultural quarter was constructed, and fronted by a formal propylon with tall pillars on the side toward the town.

two wide openings was rebuilt after the earthquake; nevertheless, the thresholds of these passageways give an indication of their original use. The smaller entrance in the middle was intended for everyday traffic and, it is interesting to note, was angled to the left, toward the theater and what was probably the gymnasium. Presumably the wide entrance in the axis of the eastern colonnade was opened only on holidays and at performances, for processions and visitors to the theater.

The terracotta roof tiles of the old temple indicate that it was rebuilt during the second century B.C. as well.[28] The outer parts of the structure, however, were left as they were and only the *cella,* the heart of the shrine, was restored. Given the large expenditure on the colonnades at the same time, this decision seems highly significant. It reveals that the primary aim was by no means to revive the old cult; rather, the town planners were making a grand gesture in imitation of "modern" Greek cities and their aesthetically impressive architecture. This is further indicated by the fact that close parallels for the panoramic opening of the terrace toward the plain—to make the view appear like a "painted" stage backdrop—can be found in the layout of contemporary towns in Asia Minor.[29]

The archaic temple also offered the Pompeians an excellent opportunity to call attention to their city's old Greek traditions. When an elegant *tempietto* (fig. 12, no. 5) was built over the well of the old temple by the highest-ranking official of Oscan Pompeii, a *meddix* (and one from an old family that continued to be important), we may assume that he, too, was motivated more by aesthetic considerations than by a real desire to revive the old religion.

As is demonstrated by the Dionysiac images in the houses discussed above, the religious interests of the town's inhabitants in that era pointed in a different direction. It can hardly be a coincidence that among the many large building projects of the second century B.C. there is not a single major new temple for a civic cult (if we discount the renovation of the Temple of Apollo, which reduced its size), whereas a shrine to Dionysus has been found on the outskirts of town.[30] The two small religious structures in the theater quarter also deserve mention in this connection. Both the Temple of Isis (fig. 12, no. 10)[31] and the small precinct of Zeus Meilichios—or

Asclepius, as has recently been suggested (fig. 12, no. 11)[32]—date from the second century B.C. These were private shrines open only to cult members. It is highly significant that they were erected in the theater quarter, for once again they represent cultural imports, and the men who commissioned them obviously wanted them located near the town's other Greek monuments. The layout of the little shrine to Zeus Meilichios or Asclepius makes it clear that it originated from a private initiative; in the case of the Temple of Isis (see figs. 67 and 68), by contrast, we must assume some degree of public approval, for its construction rendered the theater considerably less accessible. The size of both structures indicates a relatively small number of devotees; indeed, the temple to Zeus or Asclepius strongly resembles a domestic shrine in character. Both these shrines stand in stark contrast to the imposing impression made by the public buildings reached through the propylon: the theater, presumed gymnasium, Samnite palaestra, and temple complex. The ensemble was intended to demonstrate to visitors as well as to residents the town's claims to importance, and the opening of the temple terrace toward the plain "framed" this new Greek quarter, setting it off to even greater advantage.

Extending the Forum

Whereas the construction program for public buildings for cultural purposes apparently proceeded without significant interruptions, the political zone in the center of town presents a different picture (fig. 19), although it, too, began some time around the middle of the second century B.C. with a plan for an imposing square dominated by a central temple. The inhabitants of Pompeii could take as their model the typical forum of earlier Roman colonies, over which the *capitolium* loomed as a striking and monumental symbol of allegiance to Rome. The later form of the forum in Pompeii must also have been planned in conjunction with the new temple (thought to be to Jupiter), since it lies directly along the forum's central axis, parallel to the façade of the basilica and the new wall surrounding the Temple of Apollo. This appears to be the extent of any overall architectural conception, however, for, as Lauter has shown, all other edifices from the

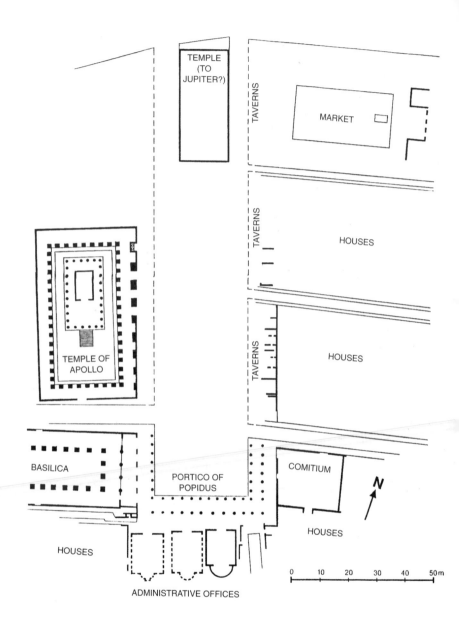

Figure 19 A sketch of the forum as it is thought to have looked before the founding of the Roman colony in 80 B.C. The Oscan elite did not promote the embellishment of the forum with the same energy they expended on the cultural quarter and their own lavish homes. The only significant building finished in a single phase was the basilica.

POMPEII

Oscan period that border the forum were separate undertakings, built virtually without reference to one another over the course of two or three generations.[33]

Of the first temple (to Jupiter?) only the podium with its heavy profile has survived. We do not know whether construction had even been completed when the building was pulled down again early in the first century B.C., to be replaced by a *capitolium* on an even grander scale. The original podium was retained in this modification, however.[34] This meant that the Hellenistic market *(macellum)*, like the building that later replaced it, stood at an angle to the forum owing to the street running along its south side. It occupied roughly the same area as the structure dating from the early Empire, although it was built on a simpler plan without a tholos, and was probably constructed at about the same time as the basilica, around 130–120 B.C.[35]

The basilica, occupying a little over 16,000 square feet, was by far the most elaborate structure in the forum (fig. 20).[36] Designed with three naves, it was constructed from start to finish by an experienced master builder and first-rate stonemasons, and served primarily as the city's commercial center, exchange, and auction house. The elaborately decorated tribunal (fig. 21) no doubt served some special function in this context, perhaps as a podium at auctions. As in the case of the cultural buildings, the leading citizens had a common interest in providing such a facility in Pompeii. With its river harbor, the town was the natural distribution point for goods from the Samnite territories inland. The site of the basilica on the west side of the forum near the harbor was dictated by its function.

Originally the portico of the basilica opened directly onto the forum. The earlier administrative offices, housed in the three small structures at the south end of the forum, also predate the colonial era; or at least the middle one and its neighbor to the east do, as Maiuri's soundings demonstrated. This includes the apse of the structure farthest to the east, so that we may imagine the highest official or officials of the Oscan town carrying out their duties from a suitably prominent position, seated in the apse.[37]

Once again it is striking, however, that these administrative buildings were clearly erected not simultaneously but one after another. As Maiuri

Figure 20 View of the basilica at the entrance from the forum, as shown in a late-nineteenth-century photograph.

noted, their northern façades facing the forum are staggered rather than aligned.[38] Only after the basilica and the small administrative buildings had been finished and work on the *comitium* (assembly) had begun (presumably in Pompeii's last years as an "independent" town) did the collection of individual structures around the forum come to seem awkward; it was then decided to hide their irregularity with a three-sided portico. The inscription commonly associated with this portico, which names a "V. Popidius q(uaestor?)" as sponsor, is in Latin, but we also know that the office of quaestor ceased to exist after Pompeii became a Roman colony. These facts could point to a construction date some time between 89 B.C. and the founding of the colony. The finished portico was not exactly a showpiece. As Lauter has shown, it was a free-standing structure that could not be integrated with the hodgepodge of buildings behind it because of their irregular alignment and varying façades. The remaining space between the colonnade and other buildings became asymmetrical "courtyards," which

POMPEII

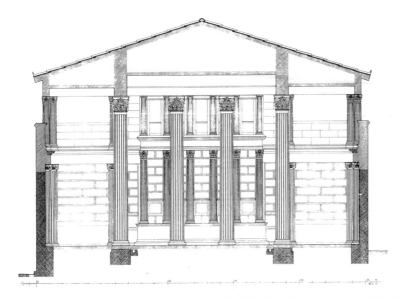

Figure 21 Elevation of the basilica as reconstructed by K. F. Ohr. This enormous roofed hall (ca. 16,000 square feet) with three naves served as a center for commerce and trade. Its position on a street leading straight to the river port opened up vast new trade opportunities for growers in the Campanian hinterland and Pompeian merchants. No wonder that strong support for construction of *this* building existed, in contrast to the forum.

must have been distinctly unpleasant to cross in wet weather and also considerably reduced the overall effect of the ambitious architecture. Furthermore, the colonnade enclosed only the southern end of the rectangle, and presumably the long side on the east had no grand public buildings at all; here two very narrow streets provided access to the forum, on either side of a motley assortment of *tabernae* (chambers; see fig. 19).

As a result the forum remained aesthetically problematic in the last phase of the Oscan city, despite the flurry of building activity, in contrast to other areas of town, such as the ensemble of cultural buildings near the archaic temple, the residential quarter in the north with its harmonious tufa façades and elaborate doorways, and even the northern city wall, punctuated by strong towers for defense. Apparently a common political will was lacking to extend the forum to comparable effect. Only in the beginning stage and during construction of the two commercial structures, the basilica and the market, do civic leaders seem to have been united by a common purpose.

Urban Space as a Reflection of Society

Figure 22 Priene (Ionia): Model of the center of this Hellenistic city as reconstructed by H. Schleif. In contrast to the organization of Oscan Pompeii, the theater and two *gymnasia* lay in the heart of town. The agora, as the center of civic life and site of festivals, was entirely enclosed by colonnades and embellished with numerous monuments.

Creation of a worthy frame for the center of the town's political life and the daily encounters of its residents commanded less interest than construction of cultural showpieces and sites for the private indulgence of luxury.

This anomaly becomes especially apparent when Pompeii is compared with other small Hellenistic towns of the same era. In Priene, for example, the most important public buildings lie directly on or near the agora (fig. 22).[39] The agora itself was framed on all sides by fine marble colonnades, which provided a congenial setting for citizens to meet, and was filled with statues honoring civic leaders. (In Pompeii, by contrast, no such monuments from pre-Roman times have been found.) The Priene council met in a well-designed *bouleuterion;* directly behind it lay the old gymnasium, and not far up the slope stood the theater, where assembly sessions took place. The Temple of Athena, the town's tutelary goddess, looked down on the agora from a dominant position, and was connected with it

POMPEII

by a set of steps. This ensemble gave fitting expression to the self-image of Priene's citizens as a democratic community that took pride in its institutions.

The peripheral location of the main cultural buildings in Pompeii, the stop-and-start construction of the forum, and the inadequacies of its final pre-Roman appearance add up to a very different picture, reflecting other social structures and the particular circumstances of an acculturation process. Here traditional patriarchal patterns prevailed, in which a few families and their clientele dominated local politics. "The people" presumably played only a small role in civic affairs. The cultural interests of the elite were relatively new, and first made their mark on private domestic space. This shared preoccupation then led to the major community projects of the theater quarter. The same holds for the elite's interest in trade and the admirable large-scale basilica.

Lauter has spoken of symbols of "self-Romanization" in connection with the construction or renovation of the temple, administrative buildings, and *comitium* in the forum; he interprets these activities as signs that the inhabitants of Pompeii expected to receive Roman citizenship shortly, the prize so long sought by the great families of Italic cities, but which the Roman Senate had stubbornly withheld. It has also been cited as further evidence of this expectation that even in Oscan times a man like the owner of the House of the Faun greeted his visitors with an inscription in the mosaic floor of his vestibule in Latin, "have," rather than in Oscan—his own language—or Greek.

Proceeding on this hypothesis, one could interpret the repeated interruptions in renovating and extending the forum, the central site of Roman political life, as a sign of disunity among the elite regarding the "self-Romanization" process. Recall that the conception of the new forum with its central temple (to Jupiter?) considerably reduced the size of the old shrine to the town's patron god, Apollo.[40] Strong interest must have been present for the Pompeians to make such a break with tradition.

It would be informative to compare the effects of Hellenization on the appearance of Pompeii with other towns in Campania and central Italy. We would probably find that the acculturation process took very different forms, depending on the location, importance, and cultural traditions of the town in question. The massive building program carried out by L. Betilienus Vaarus in the old mountain town of Aletrium in the territory of the Hernici around 100 B.C. shows tendencies similar to Pompeii.[41] Here, too, buildings with cultural or economic functions dominated the picture: *campus ubei ludunt* (palaestra?), *horologium, seedes* (theater?), *lacus balinearius* (baths?), *macelum* (market), *basilica calecanda.* The streets *(semitae in oppido omnes)* and a *porticus qua in arcem eitur* represent measures to improve the town's appearance aesthetically, most likely in ways similar to the eastern quarter of Pompeii.

By contrast Cosa, founded as a Roman colony with Latin rights in 280 B.C., could not yet boast a single ambitious cultural building by the end of the second century B.C.[42] The well-developed forum was dominated by political buildings, a category that included the temples, the curia, and the *comitium,* as well as a basilica added later. Here hardly any signs of Hellenization are to be found, apart from a few private residences.

The great terrace sanctuaries, particularly in the old towns of Latium, represent an entirely different dimension of public building.[43] In Palestrina and Tivoli the leading families were clearly interested in proclaiming the importance of their cities within the new entity of the Roman state. The case of Palestrina shows that splendid religious buildings could be connected with an ambitious renovation of the political center. In these cases the improvement and embellishment of the town's main buildings in the Hellenistic mode are designed to make an impression on the outside world. We have no reason to doubt that the aristocracy of these towns built and furnished their homes in a correspondingly modern style, but unfortunately virtually no houses comparable to the palatial House of the Faun have been found in other Italian cities.

Even this brief account should make it clear that the townscape of Oscan Pompeii as we have reconstructed it—and presumably the other old towns of Campania—had their own characteristic structure, marked by demand for a well-developed cultural quarter, an ambivalent attitude with regard to political space, and little interest in parading the town's status as an independent political entity or participating in the "rivalry" between towns that was then beginning to emerge in central Italy.

The Roman Colonists' City

Unfortunately Pompeii, in contrast to its neighbor Nuceria, was induced by the early successes of the rebels to join the Social War against the Romans. The town was besieged in 89 B.C.—the damage done by Roman artillery is still visible today in the limestone blocks of the northern city wall (fig. 23)—and probably fell to the attackers. In the war's aftermath the residents of Pompeii, like all the inhabitants of southern Italy, received Roman citizenship, in expectation of which they had built the *comitium* before the war. As participants in the uprising, however, they could not escape punishment altogether. After an interval of almost ten years Pompeii had to accept a contingent of Sullan veterans, as did other cities in Campania, and was thus turned into a Roman colony. Responsibility for planting the colony was entrusted to Publius Sulla, a nephew of the dictator

Figure 23 City wall of Pompeii, with damage caused by Roman artillery during the attack of 89 B.C. still clearly visible.

who later achieved influence in Rome. Estimates of the number of colonists vary, but it seems likely there must have been at least 2,000 veterans, to which must be added their family members and other dependents.

The redistribution of land, existing houses, and building sites in the city must have been preceded by proscription of some of the original inhabitants and confiscation of their property. The colonists were assigned their new holdings *secundum gradum militiae,* so that centurions received double and *equites* triple the portion of an ordinary soldier. The size of the basic share of a colonist in Pompeii is unknown. Thirty years later Caesar gave each man 10 *iugera* of land (about 6.2 acres) in fertile Campania. Nothing is known about the actual procedure by which property was seized in Pompeii or how rigorously it was implemented. Nonetheless, it is certain that the measure, although far-reaching, left the city's economic and social structures relatively unchanged; however, the resettlement did affect the cultural climate.

While, as Henrik Mouritsen has shown, the wealthy old families were able to preserve their influence in the long term, in the early years of the colony political life was dominated by the leaders of the new settlers. But since the older inhabitants had also become Roman citizens, they were certainly able to vote and enjoyed equal status under the law. Latin became the official language and gradually replaced Oscan as the language of daily life as well. Naturally, tensions and conflicts arose between the Oscan Pompeians and the veterans. Indeed, it should be kept in mind that after twenty years' service in the Roman army the majority of the newcomers undoubtedly had different leisure-time interests—and exhibited different social behavior generally—than their affluent, refined neighbors, who prided themselves on their Hellenistic culture.[44]

The Capitolium *and the Amphitheater*

The building activity of the next several decades shows that even though Pompeii was by no means unattractive when the colonists arrived, they made profound changes in its appearance (fig. 24). In the forum, on which the Pompeians had expended considerable effort in the preceding decades,

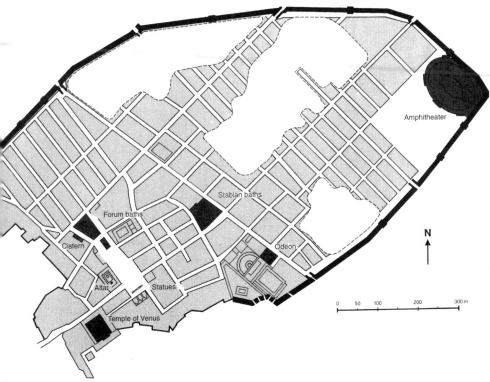

Figure 24 Plan of Pompeii with sites of public buildings erected after the founding of the Roman colony in 80 B.C. On their arrival the colonists found a town already equipped with the most important facilities. Their new construction reflects new requirements, most spectacularly a giant amphitheater far surpassing the needs of the town itself, which was financed by two rich partisans of Sulla. The location on the extreme edge of town shows that large numbers of visitors from the hinterland were expected. Some of the colonists were presumably settled in the surrounding countryside, where numerous farmyards have been discovered.

the veterans found little in need of improvement. Naturally, they completed construction of the *comitium* and began using it. Presumably the forum then began to play a larger role in public life. It seems highly likely that the two matching plinths in front of the magistrates' buildings held statues honoring leading civic officials, of the type that became customary in the course of the following decades.

The most significant alteration to the forum, however, was the conversion of the temple into a *capitolium,* an event I would place in the early

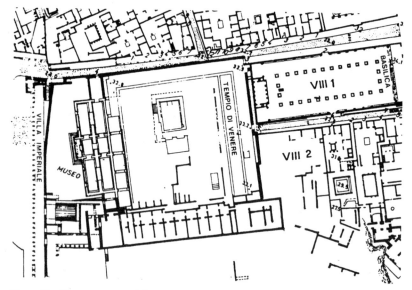

Figure 25 Western sector of Pompeii with the Temple of Venus and the town villa of M. Fabius Rufus. The temple was erected as a symbol of the *Colonia Cornelia Veneria Pompeianorum* in honor of the town's new patron goddess. Venus was also the deity who protected the general and dictator P. Cornelius Sulla, whose veterans were settled in Pompeii. The land sloped sharply downward from the city wall, making the temple visible from a great distance on the plain to the south.

years of the colony (in contrast to Lauter; see above). In the new construction on the old podium, the temple cella was fronted by immense two-story columns, and the interior was decorated with mosaic floors and wall paintings in the second style. Images of the three divinities Jupiter, Juno, and Minerva stood on top of a high podium, each in its own aedicula.[45] The aim here was to celebrate the city's status as a *colonia* in a suitably elaborate display, although from an aesthetic point of view it does give the impression that the Pompeians went a bit overboard. The city's presentation of itself as a new *colonia* was served further by the construction of a temple to Venus on the southern slope between the Marine Gate and the basilica (fig. 25).[46] The veterans had formally renamed the city *Colonia Cornelia Veneria Pompeianorum* in honor of their commander Sulla and his patron deity. Dominating the river valley from its hillside, the temple of the city's new tutelary goddess greeted passers-by and visitors on their arrival, and should be seen in the context of the large new terrace sanctuaries of central Italy, whose extravagant character has already been mentioned. But with the building of this temple to its patroness the new *Colonia Cornelia Veneria* also stated its own aspirations, announcing—albeit in the context of its modest resources—its entry into the competition for prestige among Italian cities.

It is also possible, however, to view the Temple of Venus as a companion piece to the archaic temple near the theater, which has a similar geographical orientation. In a self-confident gesture, the settlers now set the new identity of the city as a Roman *colonia* against the Greek traditions of old Pompeii. Hardly any of this Sullan edifice has survived apart from the foundations and parts of the portico, so that very little impression of the original structure can be gained on site nowadays. But the one published ground plan shows a precinct laid out on a different axis from that of its successors, with a three-sided colonnade and an outer wall fronting the street in line with the north wall of the basilica (compare fig. 20).

The *capitolium* and the Temple of Venus were of course built to compete with the Temple of Apollo, the old patron deity of the city. It is therefore noteworthy that in one of the first years after the colony was founded the two duumviri and two aediles donated a new altar to the Temple of Apollo. One of the duumviri was the same M. Porcius who was soon to become a dominant figure in the new colony. Since this temple had been completely renovated only shortly before, in 100 B.C., and was certainly not lacking an altar, the dedication of a new altar and removal of the old one had symbolic significance (fig. 26). The Latin inscription of the new altar names the donors and the city council's decree authorizing its construction, thereby underlining the intention of the city's new masters to appropriate the religious traditions of the old inhabitants for their own use, or—viewed from the latter's perspective—to eradicate important emblems of their previous identity.[47]

Construction of the roofed theater *(theatrum tectum)* next to the large theater was also begun in the early years of the colony (fig. 27).[48] Strangely enough, no one has yet asked why the colonists should have chosen to erect an odeon, as this type of building came to be known during the

Figure 26 Dedicatory inscription on the new altar in the sanctuary of Apollo. As soon as the new political structure had been instated after the colony's founding, the four highest officials *(quattuorviri)* dedicated a new altar in the old Temple of Apollo next to the forum. The dedication in Latin represents a symbolic act of appropriation of the old civic cult by the colonists.

Empire, so soon after their arrival. One must assume that it served some necessary function. Yet, given the veterans' probable cultural interests, they are scarcely likely to have been in urgent need of a lecture hall for small-scale recitations and musical performances (as is occasionally claimed). Since the structure's architecture and size recall the *bouleuteria* of Hellenistic cities, might the building, which would have accommodated between 1,500 and 2,000 people, not perhaps have served as a meeting place for the veterans? They were living as a minority among "fellow citizens" who must have regarded them with some suspicion, at least at the beginning. Their need for contact with one another and a sense of community must have been very great, and the new settlers are also likely to have faced certain practical problems in common during the early years.[49]

Construction of the roofed theater was directed (and probably paid for as well) by Quinctius Valgus and Marcus Porcius, the duumviri who a few years later also sponsored construction of the large amphitheater (plate 3.1). These two men, who had amassed fortunes from Sulla's campaigns, were familiar with the veterans' needs.[50] They hired a firm of experienced local stone cutters to do the work, and the similarity between the supporting figures at the roofed theater (plate 4) and those on the *analemmata* (enclosing walls) of the slightly earlier theater in Pietrabbondante has rightly been pointed out. Because this type of building had long been known in the Hellenistic world, and because the combination of a large theater with a small roofed assembly room is known to have existed in Sicily and even in the neighboring city of Neapolis (Statius, *Silvae,* III 5.91), scholars have

Figure 27 The Odeon *(theatrum tectum).* Able to hold 1,500 to 2,000 people, this small "theater" is reminiscent of Greek *bouleuteria,* where city councils met, and was presumably built as a meeting place for the colonists.

conjectured that the colonists merely carried out a previously conceived plan.[51] The way in which the roofed theater is joined to the large theater and its location on the street make this seem improbable, but that the colonists should have turned to the superior cultural traditions of Campania in choosing a type of architecture for their building is not surprising.

The same holds true for the public baths, which were already common in Campania, although still rare in central and northern Italian cities at that time. A further project undertaken by the settlers in the early days of the *colonia* was a second public bath complex with a huge cistern, erected in the immediate vicinity of the forum.[52] The residents of the adjacent quarter of town were thereby spared the rather long trip to the older Stabian baths. The new role the forum was intended to play may also have influenced the choice of site. The forum baths presumably filled a pressing need of the new settlers, some of whom, as Zevi has suggested, may have lived in the countryside to the north of the town. Significantly, the dedicatory inscription of this structure mentions explicitly that it was financed *ex pequnia publica,* in contrast to all the other public buildings with surviving inscriptions that date from the early period of the *colonia*.[53] At about the same time the Stabian baths appear to have been renovated and equipped with a *laconicum* (sauna) and *destrictarium*. Clearly the renovations had the aim of offering visitors to both establishments the same amenities.[54]

But by far the largest public building of the early colonial period was the amphitheater. At the time it did not yet go by this rather high-sounding Greek name, and was instead appropriately known as *spectacula* (the term used in its dedicatory inscription). Its two sponsors, Quinctius Valgus and Marcus Porcius, made it known in the inscription that the funds for it had come *de sua pequnia*. The amphitheater was erected during their term as *quinquennales,* that is, when they had reached the summit of their careers in local government, in about 70 B.C.[55]

It was a very sizable gift, out of proportion in every respect for a medium-sized country town. But then the donors' money had not been earned there either, at least not Quinctius Valgus' fortune: he had profited from Sulla's proscriptions and may be considered one of the dictator's followers.[56] Valgus' main activities were concentrated in Hirpinian territory to the north of Pompeii, where he held the highest municipal office in several towns and endowed large public works in all of them. In one town (not yet identified) where he was made *duumvir quinquennalis,* he donated money for the walls and their gates, a forum with porticos, the curia, and a cistern (presumably for the baths), that is to say, for every edifice contributing to the settlement's new identity as a city, apart from the sacred buildings. In Aeclanum he served as a *patronus municipii* and counted among the sponsors of the "walls with towers and gates."[57] M. Porcius may be identical with a large wine producer of the same name whose amphorae have been found in Gaul and Hispania Tarraconensis. In any event he must have had a similarly large fortune at his disposal. M. Porcius remained loyal to the *Colonia Cornelia Veneria.* His monumental tomb occupying the best site outside the Herculaneum Gate is evidence that he was honored by the community almost like a founding hero.[58] The aim of these huge endowments in various cities was to acquire the largest possible following for a political career in Rome.

As a site for the amphitheater (*spectacula;* fig. 28, plate 3.2) the two donors chose the southeastern corner of town, a particularly suitable location for two reasons: first of all, the wall surrounding the city could be used to support part of the huge structure (approximately 455 by 340 feet), reducing the need for a massive foundation and other retaining walls. And second, a site on the edge of town with few other buildings nearby could more easily accommodate the arrival and departure of large crowds on days when shows were presented. The plan for seating for 20,000 spectators shows that visitors from the surrounding communities were expected. Originally, perhaps, the planners reckoned first and foremost with other Sullan veterans from nearby settlements such as Abellinum or Nola.[59]

This type of structure was new at the time. Presumably few other cities in Campania possessed such an arena, and in any event the amphitheater in Pompeii is the oldest of its kind. It is evident from the construction that, unlike the case of the roofed theater, the architect had no previously tested models to follow. To avoid having to build an elaborate foundation he set

Figure 28 Aerial view of the amphitheater, known as *spectacula*. Donated by the town's two highest officials around 70 B.C., it could hold some 20,000 spectators and was the setting for gladiatorial combat and *venationes* (combat between men and beasts). Clearly many spectators from neighboring towns were expected. The thirty-five rows of seats are divided into three raised sectors by tall podia. Did the veterans perhaps originally take their seats according to the military rank they had achieved? The Pompeii arena is one of the oldest known amphitheaters. It points to a radical change in the cultural climate of the city.

the floor of the arena and part of the building below ground level. In addition the entrances and logistics of the circulation system are quite primitive in comparison with later amphitheaters (fig. 29).

All the same the Pompeians could pride themselves on being among the first to be presented with such a splendid structure: it is no accident that the sponsors included in the inscription the fact that they had erected it *coloniai honoris caussa*.[60] They also dedicated the building expressly to the colonists: *coloneis . . . in perpetuom*. Understood in a legal sense this phrase certainly refers to all the citizens of Pompeii, although repeated use of the terms *colonia* and *colonei* as beneficiaries gives one pause. As late as 62 B.C. representatives of the "townsfolk" *(municipes)* and "colonists" *(colonei)* appeared separately in court in Rome to testify on P. Sulla's behalf at his trial (Cicero, *Pro Sulla* 21, 60–62). At any rate the inscription lays great stress on what a blessing the founding of the colony had been and con-

Figure 29 Amphitheater: staircase to the *summa cavea*. The plan and execution of the Pompeii arena (unlike those of later amphitheaters) reveal that the architect had no tested models to follow. This is particularly apparent in the location of entrances and access to seats, and the awkward position of the staircases.

tinued to be for the city, a sentiment that is unlikely to have sat well with the older inhabitants.

Such an amphitheater must have primarily served the needs of the veterans, although this does not mean that the precolonial residents necessarily turned up their noses at the gladiators and wild animals, for all their pretensions to Hellenistic culture. The old soldiers could sit with their former comrades from nearby towns, probably divided by military rank, as the thirty-five rows of seats are divided into three sections by high retaining walls *(pulpita)*. One cannot help wondering whether the townsfolk really had any chance of obtaining good seats in the early days. It is probably no accident that one of the earliest amphitheaters was built for a veterans' colony: the soldiers may have needed this type of spectacle as an outlet for their aggressions more than other people. At any rate it is certain that their preferences played a decisive role in determining the kind of spectacle that became firmly established in the arena at Pompeii. The enormous popularity of the gladiators' contests can still be deduced from the numerous graffiti on walls throughout the city. More than any other of the colonists' innovations, the amphitheater altered the cultural climate in the town.

Display and Self-Promotion in Houses and Tombs

Unfortunately, no attempt has ever been made to identify which houses in Pompeii were owned by colonists. Since we may assume that at least those members of the elite with friendly feelings toward Rome retained their elegant homes in the northern part of town, and that the established inhabitants—who had become Roman citizens, after all—could not simply be driven out, it was necessary to build many new houses and remodel many others. In this connection I at first considered the one-family dwellings studied by A. Hoffmann as a possible "colonists' quarter,"[61] but in the meantime several scholars have advanced convincing arguments for dating them to a considerably earlier period.[62] Future studies might take as starting points the consolidation of several houses to make a lavish complex in I 4.5 and 25 and the façade of IX 1.20, both described by H. Lauter.[63] Without more thorough investigation, however, these scattered observations remain too hypothetical. In our particular context it is more important to note that despite the influx of new residents the overall appearance of the existing residential quarters did not undergo marked alteration. The tufa façades of the second-century houses continued to set the tone in the grander neighborhoods. New construction was limited largely to the eastern end of town, but even there builders followed the established style. Fausto Zevi has recently advanced plausible arguments for the view that the veterans lived on the estates and in the villas to the northwest along the Via dei Sepolcri outside the Herculaneum Gate, while the old inhabitants remained in their houses in town. He regards the wall decorations in the late Hellenistic first style as evidence that these dwellings belonged to the old Oscan families.

In any event, however, entirely new "townscapes" arose over the course of the first century B.C. on the hillsides to the west and south and outside the gates (fig. 30). Previously, the families constituting the old Pompeii

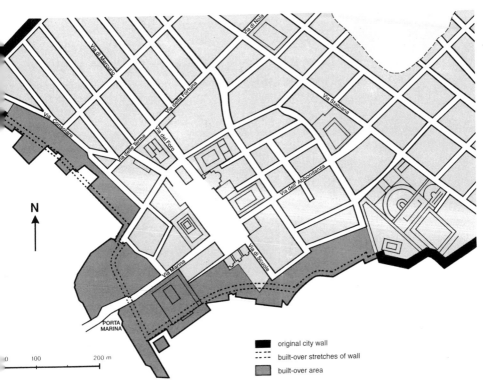

Figure 30 Pompeii, construction on top of the city walls. During the first century B.C. the city walls were built over with large terrace villas on the sites with the best views. The luxurious villas built around the Bay of Naples by Romans beginning in the preceding century had clearly influenced the taste of wealthy Pompeian families.

Urban Space as a Reflection of Society

elite had lived in the middle of town and were fully integrated in day-to-day life there through their dependents and clients; one need only recall the number of houses containing shops facing the street. But in the ensuing period more and more affluent residents took their cue from the new taste established by the owners of Roman villas.[64] In the mid–second century B.C. Roman aristocrats began building such country retreats overlooking the most beautiful spots on the Bay of Naples—within view of Pompeii, whose inhabitants soon took to imitating them. Some Pompeians built small villas just outside the Herculaneum Gate, while others tried to combine the comfort and sea view of the Romans' houses with the convenience of a townhouse. The preferences of this second group led to construction of terrace houses on the site of the southwestern portion of the city wall, now clearly no longer required for purposes of defense. They altered the town's appearance spectacularly.[65] The largest of these complexes, the House of Fabius Rufus in the Insula Occidentalis (fig. 31), compares in square footage with the House of the Faun, but differs in that it is entirely closed off from the street.[66] This residence has turned its back on the town. Of course, one must keep in mind the possibility that old entryways may have disappeared as the complex grew. Yet the smaller houses in the theater quarter reveal essentially the same structure, with closed fronts on the street side and terraces opening out onto the landscape; inside, the rooms are arranged not around the atrium in a strict pattern, but rather to conform to the sloping terrain.

The new situation is characterized by the make-up of the affluent class interested in building in the "new taste": it is broader and culturally far less homogeneous than the Hellenized elite of Oscan Pompeii. A study of the distribution of wall paintings in the second style around the city might be highly revealing; in the process it would be important to note the occurrence of room forms used in villa architecture and the relationship of such villa elements to the rest of the house. The House of the Cryptoporticus, joined with the House of the Trojan Shrine as a single dwelling (I 6.2 and 4), seems representative: in the mid–first century B.C. the owner had a large *cryptoporticus* (underground portico) with baths built in his garden and painted with literary motifs at enormous expense. Although the quality of

74

Figure 31 House of Fabius Rufus (Insula Occidentalis), view from the south, compare fig. 30. This house, excavated only in the past two decades, is comparable in size to the grandest townhouse of the second century B.C., the House of the Faun (see fig. 5). But, by contrast, this house is closed off on the side facing the town and possesses neither shops nor a large atrium. These are all indications that the owner's social behavior was also different.

the painting is superb, the owner's showy gesture and cultural aspirations stand in striking contrast to his modest dwelling and social status.[67] When the house was later divided in two, the contrast became even more striking.

In the case of the palatial tufa houses of the second century B.C., by contrast, the proportions had been correct. The Oscan landowners and merchants who built them were newcomers to Hellenistic culture, but nonetheless full participants in it, indistinguishable from the Greeks of the mother country and Asia Minor except perhaps for a slight degree of excess. When their successors began taking the great Roman aristocrats' villas as their point of orientation, however, Pompeii lapsed into cultural provincialism.

The role played by extravagant display in the altered cultural climate can be particularly well observed in the tombs of this epoch flanking the roads out of town.[68] Large funerary monuments were unknown to the inhabitants of Oscan Pompeii. Even the great families buried their dead in the enclosed cemeteries situated away from the road. It was the colonists who first erected grand tombs along the main roads, a custom they had observed in Rome and other cities of the Roman world. Soon various types of ostentatious monuments were ranged next to one another, for the most part altar tombs and aediculae on tall plinths. The intent was to give prominent display to the achievements and wealth of the deceased, but above all to their political and social rank.

The community gave a political leader like M. Porcius a place of honor outside the Herculaneum Gate in the *pomerium* (sacred zone), which extended a hundred feet out from the town walls. His tomb in the form of an enormous altar with a Doric frieze resembles a monument to a hero. With the passage of time these graves came to reflect the competition for—and nuances of—rank and status within the town more and more clearly. An important element of this competition was that it was open to anyone with the requisite funds: if the town did not vote you an honorary statue in the forum, your relatives could simply commission one and place it in an aedicula on your tomb. And if they could not afford that, they could join forces with others in the same position and share the cost of a monument. The freed slaves of the Flavii, for example, erected a tomb for themselves at the crossroads by the Nucerian Gate that resembled a kind of apartment house—and in an exclusive neighborhood, too, next to the monuments of several citizens of vastly higher rank, from the colony's first families.[69]

Such "streets of tombs" (plate 5) were created all over Italy during the first century B.C. These displays by urban dwellers of their own wealth and importance were placed outside the gates of their towns in order to impress passers-by as well as fellow citizens. Travelers through Italy could now make comparisons and assess the consequence of a city even before they entered it; they could also learn the identity of the most prominent local households, the *domi nobiles*. Here again the point of orientation was Rome, the capital that politically ambitious men from every town aspired to reach.[70] Although this alteration of the townscape was not specific to Pompeii, it acquired a unique dimension by departing so radically from previous burial customs. At least in the early days of the colony, every time the older inhabitants of the town took a stroll out past the gates, the sight of the new ostentatious tombs would have reminded them who now ran the town. The shift of language from Oscan to Latin was not the only change Pompeii witnessed.

If we try to sum up the total effect of these separate and quite heterogeneous phenomena, we cannot help concluding that the half-century from 80 to 30 B.C. represented a period of significant transformation.[71] Although the Hellenistic appearance of the town was preserved on the whole, the major new buildings shifted the accents. No coherent construction program developed similar to the one that had taken place in the previous century, for in Pompeii the colonists had encountered a town with excellent modern facilities, in contrast to most of the cities in central and northern Italy. They erected a number of public buildings in the first decade after their arrival, but these structures were separate projects; they served less as a response to the new inhabitants' basic needs than as a means of cementing Pompeii's new identity as a colony and adding to its attractions. But the political and ideological motives behind them were new. From then on sponsors and donors had more in mind than simply the effect of their gifts on their fellow citizens; their gaze was fixed on places farther afield, especially Rome. The resulting spirit of competition then spread from the elite to all strata of society. On all sides we see the need for exhibition and self-promotion growing, reflected in public statues and private tombs, and by a new taste in domestic decor visible in more modest houses as well as in those of the rich.

The perspective opened up by the new orientation toward Rome and other Roman towns altered the cultural climate and townscapes profoundly in the first century B.C. The catchphrase according to which every citizen had two *patriae,* his own city and the Roman state as a whole, found direct and material expression in the extravagant outward display observable everywhere in urban vistas and funerary monuments.

Townscape and Ideology in the Age of Augustus

Another set of major alterations to the townscape of Pompeii occurred in the early years of the Empire. Almost all public building from about 20 B.C. was undertaken, either directly or indirectly, as a result of Augustus Caesar's establishment of a monarchy and his policies of religious and cultural renewal. Like the urban elite throughout Italy and the western provinces, the most influential families in Pompeii identified themselves with the cultural aims of the *princeps* and the cult developing around his person. It was these families, the *domi nobiles*, who interpreted the signs of the new era for their fellow citizens and attempted to imitate the exemplary actions of the ruler in their own cities. After the chaos of the Republic's final years, marked by civil wars, proscriptions, and expropriations of property, the elite class found itself able to arrive at a new self-definition by adopting his prescribed code of conduct. The prerequisite for this step was the return of peace and personal security, followed by a significant economic upswing in the first half of Augustus' reign.[72]

The most important leitmotif of Augustus' new policy was *pietas* (piety). The return to the old faith in the gods would, he hoped, lead to a renewed flowering of virtue and morality, and halt the decline in cultural activity. From 28 B.C. Augustus had taken the lead in reviving piety in Rome. He had renovated all the crumbling temples and built magnificent new shrines for his special protectors Venus, Apollo, and Mars.

Renovating the Temples, Reviving the Cults

All the great donors and benefactors of early Augustan Pompeii held priestly offices. Like their ruler, they both restored and embellished the old temples, and also built new ones. (Not all these temples date from Augustus' reign, however; presumably some of them required decades for their completion.) The city's two patron divinities, Apollo and Venus, gave the Pompeians a special connection with the new era and a particular reason to welcome it, for the emperor was descended from Venus, and he ascribed his success at Actium to Apollo's intervention. Enormous temples to both had been erected in Rome, and in Pompeii the old Sullan temple to Venus was no longer regarded as sufficiently grand. Perhaps, too, its negative associations with the dictator Sulla and the unhappy period of the colony's founding were considered serious disadvantages. In any event the council ordered work begun on a new temple—at an unknown date, unfortunately, since the structure still awaits detailed investigation—which was presumably not yet completed when the earthquake struck in A.D. 62. In order to enlarge the site for the new Temple of Venus, substructures were built on the southern side; they were so extensive that a part of the "Villa Imperiale" had to be sacrificed to make room for them. A stairway that led from the substructures directly up to the temple forecourt is reminiscent of the link between the house of Augustus and the Temple of Apollo on the Palatine in Rome. Possibly the owners of the Villa Imperiale wished to imitate Augustus in this respect as well, or perhaps the priestess of one of the civic cults *(sacerdos publica)* actually lived there. The latter possibility is no more than speculation, of course. But several details show that the enlargement of the sanctuary of Venus represented a symbolically charged and highly important act; moving the northern wall of the sacred precinct one yard farther north required that the entire sidewalk along the street running from the Marine Gate to the forum be sacrificed to the goddess, yet it was done! The aim was to transform the old shrine into a lavish marble temple with double colonnades on the eastern and western sides and a broad terrace with a view toward the sea to the south. A decision to make such sweeping changes is most easily comprehensible in the context of the grand innovations of the Augustan age.

Apollo received renewed attention as well (figs. 32 and 33, plate 6). Sometime shortly before 3/2 B.C. the town council granted the two duumviri the right to construct a new wall on the western side of the god's shrine, which obstructed an existing window of the house next door (VII 7.2; *CIL* X 787). One of them was M. Holconius Rufus, the man later awarded the honorary title "benefactor of the colony" *(patronus coloniae)* for undertaking the costs of renovating the theater. Two other duumviri erected a sundial in front of the Temple of Apollo (*CIL* X 802). The wall and the sundial were of course relatively modest tributes to the town's

Figure 32 Reconstruction of the Temple of Apollo (after Mazois). As in Rome and many other Roman cities, the sanctuaries and temples of Pompeii were renovated and richly embellished during the reign of Augustus. The emperor's program of encouraging religion included revival and lavish observance of the temple festivals. Some parts of the Games of Apollo *(ludi Apollinares)* were celebrated in the forum, which had a direct connection to the temple.

traditional patron deity. An inscription from the Augustan period, however, conveys an impression of the munificence with which the Games of Apollo *(ludi Apollinares)* were celebrated in that era. As we learn from the inscription on the tomb of Aulus Clodius, not only was he duumvir for three terms, *quinquennalis,* and *tribunus militum a populo,* but he also financed the procession *(pompa)* in the forum, and bulls, bullfighters and their attendants, three pairs of *pontarii* (gladiators), a team of boxers, individual boxers, and various stage performers for the games (*CIL* X 1074).[73]

The rituals and some of the performances listed on his tomb took place in the forum, which was directly connected with the Temple of Apollo through great gateways opened on festival days. In recent years various scholars have rightly stressed the importance of visualizing the architecture in combination with such rituals if we are to assess its full effect properly.[74] The inscription containing information on how the Games of Apollo in Pompeii were celebrated provides one valuable opportunity to do so.

Figure 33 Model of the Temple of Apollo and the forum (Pompeii Museum). The forum was lined on three sides by religious buildings. Several structures devoted to the cult of the imperial family were added on the long eastern side in the early years of the Empire, joining the older precinct of Apollo and the Temple of Jupiter, which dominated the square.

The Cult of the Emperor

Augustus' program of *pietas* in Rome was intended to honor the full pantheon, but the gods most closely associated with him naturally received the greatest reverence. It was to their cults above all that the magnificent new marble temples were devoted. In Rome Augustus limited the cult of his own person to an indirect manner; his *genius* could be honored only in combination with the Lares. However, he clearly had no objection if the designation *augustus* was added to the names of certain divinities, especially those who personified the virtues being so vigorously promoted. Magistrates in smaller towns throughout Italy followed his lead. A large majority of the many new shrines and temples built in the early Augustan age were intended to honor the emperor in this indirect manner. And it was possible to celebrate the superhuman attributes, indeed the divine nature of the ruler's power, far more openly in the provinces than in Rome itself, in the emperor's own presence. One could even go so far as to say that the official elites of Roman towns in the western half of the Empire found a new source of identity for themselves in the many gifts they made to honor the imperial dynasty. Because of the large number of inscriptions and monuments preserved there, Pompeii offers the best example of this development.

The first sanctuary built in Pompeii to honor the emperor in this broad sense is the Temple of Fortuna Augusta (figs. 34–36).[75] It was erected by M. Tullius, one of the town's most influential citizens, who was probably at the height of his career in the earlier part of the Augustan era (25–5 B.C.?) and served as duumvir for several terms, as *quinquennalis,* and as *tribunus militum a populo;* he also held a lifetime appointment as augur.[76] The post of tribune was an honorary one, awarded by the emperor to nominees proposed by the civic leaders of Italic cities. M. Tullius, along with the M. Holconius Rufus who sponsored the renovation of the theater, numbered among the Pompeian officials who were elevated to the nobility in this fashion and were thereby able to enter into direct contact with the imperial dynasty.

M. Tullius sponsored construction of the marble-faced Temple of Fortuna Augusta on his own land and at his own expense *(solo et pecunia sua).* For its site he chose a location just north of the forum, at the intersection of two of the town's most important streets. The podium of the pseudoperipteral temple jutted out into the street. Later an attempt was made to integrate it with the forum by adding a narrow portico. Most likely its construction was prompted by Augustus' safe return from a journey, either to the East in 19 B.C. or to the West in 13 B.C. Altars and shrines to Fortuna Redux were built in Rome and many other cities at that time, and in addition the Corinthian style of the marble capitals (plate 7) argues for such an early date.[77]

We may well ask why M. Tullius did not build his temple in the forum itself. Was he unable to acquire a lot on the forum's long eastern side, the only location still available for this purpose? Or were the buildings associ-

tes 1 and 2   Two mosaics from the House of the Faun (VI 12). In the Oscan era the taste of the
,an elite' in Pompeii was decisively influenced by the culture of Hellenistic cities in the eastern
,diterranean. Furniture, implements, and works of art—such as the bronze statuette of the "dancing
,n" after which the house is named—were imported or commissioned from itinerant Greek arti-
,s. The mosaics in grand reception rooms also bear a close resemblance to those found on Delos and
,other Greek cities. Erotic scenes with satyrs and nymphs were one of the most popular subjects of
, Hellenistic art, as in this floor mosaic from a bedroom off the Tuscan atrium (fig. 5, no. 2).

Plate 2   Mosaic depicting fish and other sea creatures. Like most of the motifs in the mosaics of the House of the Faun, it is based on a famous model, in this case one thought to have been in the Museum, the center of learning at the court of Alexandria. The careful depiction of the creatures reflects an interest in natural phenomena; at the same time, however, many of the fish shown were culinary delicacies, so that the motif would have been suitable for a dining room (fig. 5, no. 3).

Plate 3.1   Dedicatory inscription of the Odeon *(theatrum tectum)*. The two chief officials of Pompeii, the duumviri C. Quinctius Valgus and M. Porcius, supervised construction of the building, which had been commissioned by the town council, and carried out the final inspection: *C. Quinctius C. Valg(us), M. Porcius M. f.. duovir(I) dec(urionum) decr(eto) theatrum tectum fac(iundum) locar(unt) eidemq(ue) prob(arunt)* (Degrassi, vol. 1, no. 646).

Plate 3.2   Aerial view of the amphitheater *(spectacula),* showing clearly how the city wall was used as a support on one side. To the left is the field enclosed with colonnades in the Augustan period, perhaps as a *gymnasium,* a sports ground for the boys and young men of Pompeii (cf. figs. 59, 60).

C·QVINCTIVS·C·F·VA[...]
M·PORCIVS·M·F
DVO·VIR·DEC·DECR·
THEATRVM·TECT·VN
FAC·LOCAR·EIDEMQ·PROB

ate 5 Tombs along the road outside the Nucerian Gate. The custom of self-promotion in the form
exhibitionist funeral monuments was brought to Pompeii by Roman colonists. The size and cost
the tombs were intended to reflect the prestige and rank of the deceased and their families, and it
was also important to secure a good site (as close as possible to one of the heavily traveled roads near
city gate). Dimensions and artistic embellishment of the monuments were key criteria as families
ed to outdo one another.

ate 4 Odeon (*theatrum tectum:* cf. fig. 27). One of the two satyrs whose backs support the walls
halemmata) surrounding the auditorium *(cavea)*. The same stonemasons appear to have built the the-
er in Pietrabbondante, where the Samnites living in the mountains used to assemble.

Plate 6   View of the reconstructed portion of the colonnade, Temple of Apollo. The temple unde[r]
went extensive renovation in the Augustan period, and many embellishments were added. Two co[st]
ly bronze statues, representing Apollo (see photo) and Diana as archers, were probably votive offi[er]
ings dedicated in that period. The style and rather inferior craftsmanship suggest that they date fr[om]
the late first century B.C.

Plate 7   Two marble capitals from the Temple of Fortuna. The architectural decoration in the n[ew]
cult buildings of the Augustan Age reflects a quality of execution never before achieved by Italic sto[ne]
cutters. Models from Rome played a key role in raising the level of skill and sophistication.

Plate 8.1 A water tower *(castellum aquae)* near the Vesuvian Gate. Water brought from the mountai[ns?]
by aqueduct was fed into large tanks like this and later piped to different parts of the town.

Plate 8.2 *Campus,* known as the palaestra. Consisting of three very long porticos surrounding a lar[ge]
grassy area, it was built in the Augustan period primarily as a sports and recreational center for t[he]
youth of the town. In the foreground are visible the hollows left by the root systems of the large tr[ees]
that once stood there.

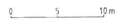

0   5   10 m

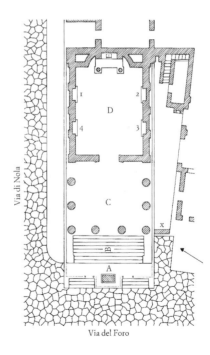

Figures 34–35 Ruins and ground plan of the Temple of Fortuna Augusta. Early in Augustus' reign M. Tullius, one of the leading citizens of Pompeii, privately sponsored the construction of this first temple dedicated to the cult of the emperor. Like many civic leaders elsewhere, he thereby followed the example of the Roman Senate, which had erected marble altars to honor the emperor's Fortuna Redux. The ground plan and lavish ornamentation are also modeled upon Augustus' new marble buildings in Rome.

Urban Space as a Reflection of Society

Figure 36 Idealized reconstruction of the Temple of Fortuna Augusta and its surroundings (after C. Weichardt, 1896).

ated with the cult of the emperor and the building of Eumachia already in the planning stage? Were the Pompeians not yet willing to sacrifice the shops south of the market for a project connected with a political cult in the early days of the principate? It is to be hoped that J. J. Dobbins's "Pompeii Forum Project" will provide some answers to these questions.

The temple's form and manner of construction show that the builder and architect were familiar with the new principles of sacred architecture in Rome, although no specific models existed as yet for them to imitate. The costly white marble reflected the lavishness fitting for the gods, and also measured up to new standards of craftsmanship and aesthetics. The emphasis of the façade with podium and integrated altar (fig. 35, A) matched the highly effective symbolism of the *aurea templa* in Rome.[78] The long sides of the *cella* were designed to contain niches for statues of the benefactor and his family, and perhaps also members of the imperial house (1–4). The statue of a toga-clad figure from the Augustan era found here might possibly depict M. Tullius, while a female figure might represent a member of the dynasty upon whom the sentence of *damnatio memoriae* was later pronounced, perhaps Julia, since the original face was destroyed and replaced by another. Construction of new temples for the cult of the emperor provided local officials with effective opportunities to draw attention to themselves and promote their own careers.[79] Just like the members of the imperial family, whose statues were now placed everywhere in temples both old and new, so too these local dignitaries acquired something of the aura of the ruler and of the divinities associated with his cult.

We find the same kind of self-promotion in the aedicula of the market (figs. 37 and 38).[80] This was a recess containing steps up to a raised platform, which was created at the eastern end of the new market building. (To the left was a meeting room for officials of the cult; to the right was the fish market.) At the time of the earthquake the recess contained a statue of the emperor, of which unfortunately only one arm has been found. (The globe held in the hand shows that the emperor was seated, like the frequently depicted "Jupiter on his throne.") The two statues found in the niches to the right, from the reign of Nero, no doubt honor officials who had performed valuable services on behalf of the market. The man (fig. 39), probably already deceased, is shown naked except for a drape around his hips, in the heightened heroic pose of rulers and princes, while the woman (fig. 40) is depicted in the robes of a priestess, wearing a wreath on her head and holding a small box of incense. She may have been one of the public priestesses *(sacerdotes publicae)* who played such a large role as civic benefactors in Pompeii in the early years of the Empire.[81]

To the south of the market, the old shops were razed to make room for two new buildings associated with the cult of the emperor. The Sanctuary of the Lares (figs. 41 and 42) presumably dates from the period between the death of Augustus and the earthquake.[82] It was not still under construction, as Maiuri thought; instead the shrine was stripped of its valuable marble facing by robbers during the long period when the forum lay in ruins. One good indication for the validity of this hypothesis is the discovery of the remnants of a marble floor during excavation. The Sanctuary of the Lares is an unusual structure, with a central apse that is flanked by square exedrae and has many niches for statues. Whether the sanctuary was roofed or open to the elements remains a matter of controversy. It also had its own portico,

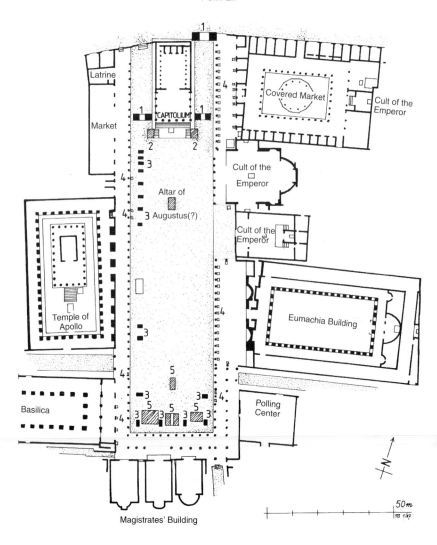

Figure 37 The forum as it appeared in the early Empire. Some elements of the plan are speculative. By this time the space had become entirely dominated by monuments to the imperial family. Presumably an altar to Divus Augustus stood in the center opposite the two small temples for the cult of the emperor.

1: Arches. 2: Equestrian statues of imperial princes (?). 3: Equestrian statues of local magistrates. 4: Honorific portrait statues. 5: Imperial monuments.

Figure 38   The market with an exedra for the cult of the emperor. In the Augustan era even the market building had a chapel added to it for the cult of the imperial family. A statue of the seated emperor, modeled on similar statues of Jupiter, stood in the center.

which was open at both ends and used as a passageway along the forum. From the beginning this building's main purpose appears to have been to display a large number of statues, most likely members of the imperial family, similar to the collections found in so many cities of Italy and the western provinces. An altar stood in the center, where citizens could pay homage to the Lares of the city, as well as to (obviously) the emperor. Recently, J. J. Dobbins has dated the building in the period after the earthquake of A.D. 62, proposed that it had an elaborate dome, and connected the construction with a workshop of Roman stonemasons.

Several features of the Temple of Vespasian (fig. 43), located to the right of the Sanctuary of the Lares, suggest that it was constructed during the Augustan period.[83] The niches on the inside of the surrounding wall exhibit motifs similar to those on the southern façade of the Eumachia Building, providing a rough indication of their date. The appearance of the altar,

Figures 39–40 Marble statues from the market. These statues of two members of a leading Pompeian family flanked the larger-than-life-size statues of the imperial family; probably the man and woman depicted belonged to the family that donated the new chapel. The woman's

wreath and box of incense mark her as a priestess, while the man is shown in a heroic pose also used for members of the ruling dynasty. On the basis of the hairstyles the statues can be assigned to the period around A.D. 60.

Urban Space as a Reflection of Society

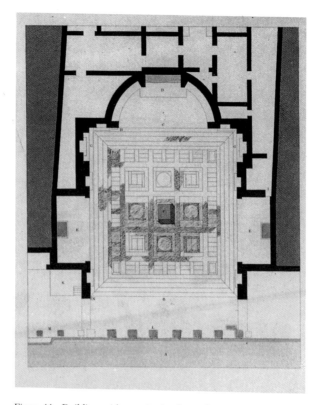

Figure 41 Building with apse in the forum known as the Lararium, with a reconstruction of the tile floor (after Mazois). The many niches of this singular structure suggest that it was designed to hold a gallery of statues of the imperial family, such as are known to have existed in many other towns. The floor tiles of various colored marbles, some of them imported from great distances, offer a good example of the costly fittings used in such ceremonial buildings.

which was renovated and partially replaced after the earthquake, also agrees with this dating (fig. 44).

The shrine consists of a forecourt, an altar, and a small peristyle temple with four columns on a tall podium, accessible by a staircase on either side. The motifs on the altar—a shield *(clipeus virtutis)*, an oak wreath *(corona civica)*, garlands of laurel, and the sacrifice of a bull—document the shrine's connection with the cult of the emperor.[84] In the nineteenth century Fiorelli connected the well-known inscription of Mammia with this build-

Figure 42 Building with apse in the forum (Lararium). Reconstruction of the elevation (after Mau, 1902).

Figure 43 Shrine for the cult of the emperor, with altar and temple known as the Temple of Vespasian. The small shrine, presumably dedicated to the genius of Augustus, is thought to have been first erected in the Augustan era; it was repaired after the earthquake. The little temple with four columns in front stands on a tall podium accessible only from the sides.

Urban Space as a Reflection of Society

Figure 44 Marble altar in the precinct for the cult of the emperor. The relief shows a bull being sacrificed, a frequent ceremony in the cult. A temple with four columns can be seen in the background below the drapery; on the pediment is the *clipeus virtutis* characteristic of worship of the emperor.

ing. This inscription on a marble epistyle, now in the Museo Nazionale in Naples, reads: *M[a]mmia P. f. sacerdos public(a) Geni[o Aug(usti) s]olo et pec[unia sua].*[85] It was soon recognized that this dedicatory inscription on the temple should probably be seen in connection with the homage paid to Augustus in the shrines to the Lares in the different districts of Rome from 7 B.C., and the date of the Pompeian temple reckoned accordingly.

Mammia belonged to an old established family in Pompeii.[86] She must have earned the city's gratitude, for the town council honored her after her death with a burial plot inside the *pomerium* directly in front of the Herculaneum Gate and next to the tomb of M. Porcius.

The largest building by far to be constructed in the forum in the Augustan age was also the work of a public priestess (figs. 45 and 46).[87] Eumachia dedicated it to Concordia Augusta and Pietas in her own name and in the name of her son, M. Numistrius Fronto, who is probably identical with the duumvir of A.D. 2/3 (*CIL* X 810). This suggests that we should understand the large gift to the town in the context of his election campaign. Architecturally the structure is a somewhat strange combination of the heterogeneous elements listed individually in the inscription: *chalcidicum, crypta, porticus.* The inscription itself was carved in giant letters on the frieze above the short Doric columns of the façade and below a presumed second order of Ionic columns.

The term *chalcidicum* refers to the portico. It is as deep as the double colonnade in front of the *comitium,* but it did not serve as an extension of the latter, since the southern end was blocked by a statue base and a metal grating. It thus appears that the donor wished to have the building stand on its own as a single, unconnected entity that could be entered only from the side facing the forum. The interior, faced with the most expensive kinds of marble, must have been impressive, but unfortunately most of it was plundered after the earthquake.

Surviving traces indicate that the decor alluded to some of the lofty themes of Augustan ideology; these include the two laudatory inscriptions *(elogia)* to Romulus and Aeneas set into the wall below the small niches on the sides of the semicircular exedrae. They represent "quotations" from the program of images and inscriptions of the *summi viri* in the Forum of

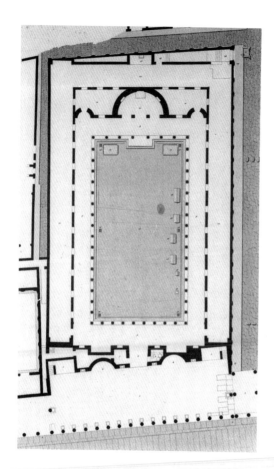

Figure 45 Ground plan of the Eumachia Building in the forum. Eumachia, together with her son, dedicated this very lavish building to Concordia Augusta and Pietas. The building consists of various parts, which presumably served different functions. There was a gallery of statues in the portico. The cryptoporticus and garden may have served as a meeting place and center for recreation, as in Rome. The cult statue stood in the exedra.

Augustus.[88] One would like to know whose statues stood in the two niches on the right. A further odd feature of the building consists in the two rectangular exedrae, each containing a flight of steps (though only the flight on the left actually gives access to the podium). Were these *podia* meant as auctioneers' platforms, as has been supposed, or is it not more likely that they represented platforms for commemorative oratory on festival days honoring the emperor (and that the one on the left was actually used for this purpose)?

The grand style of the *chalcidicum* is revealed by the long row of identical statue bases behind the columns. They must have held a gallery of honorific statues similar to those in the forecourt of the market. Were they

Figure 46 Portico of the Eumachia Building, with a view of the doorway. This door frame, made of marble slabs with the well-known acanthus scroll motif, was reconstructed after excavation.

perhaps *summi viri* modeled after those in the Forum of Augustus, or were they memorials to deserving former municipal officials? The best clue we have to the donor's extravagance is the magnificent door frame with carved acanthus scrolls (fig. 47). It resembles the reliefs of the Ara Pacis so closely and is of such high quality that it may be justifiably assumed to have

Figure 47 Detail of the marble door frame (?) in the Eumachia Building. The style and quality of the scroll frieze make it comparable to the Ara Pacis in Rome. The donor probably commissioned it from a Roman workshop. Later the door frame was joined to the building for the cult of the emperor to the left of the Eumachia Building.

come from a workshop in Rome. As it does not fit the opening in the wall exactly, K. Wallat has recently suggested that it may originally have adorned the entrance to the Temple of Vespasian.

The interior of the building consists of a four-sided colonnade *(porticus)* around a central courtyard, with a large apse devoted to Concordia

POMPEII

Augusta at the rear, flanked by two small semicircular exedrae. Behind this colonnade lay the three-sided *crypta* (covered gallery); from the short side behind the apse one could look from the *crypta* onto the two small spaces on either side of the apse that were planted as gardens. From the way in which various architectural elements are combined, it is apparent that this lavish building served a variety of leisure-time purposes. Clearly Eumachia wanted her building in the forum to bring a touch of urban flair to Pompeii. As the flat terrain in no way necessitated the construction of a cryptoporticus, it seems that the donor was motivated by the Augustan theme of *publica magnificentia,* and wished to create a particularly impressive example of it. In such a context the combination of a *porticus* with a *crypta* and gardens had far more dash than a simple colonnade.

Eumachia's gift to the town appears to have been inspired by the Porticus Liviae in Rome, a form of "community center" built by Livia and her son in the densely populated area of the Subura. The latter was dedicated in 7 B.C. and also consecrated to Concordia Augusta. Eumachia probably followed Livia's example only a few years later, whereby her chief aim seems to have been not so much to imitate the Roman building's celebrated architecture as to rival Livia's civic-mindedness and piety.[89]

Of course in this instance the piety was directed toward the imperial family itself. In the large apse of Eumachia's building stood an elaborately carved statue of Concordia with a gilded cornucopia (fig. 48). The goddess was probably depicted with Livia's features, a frequent form of homage. This is suggested by the simple relief on the fountain facing the side entrance to the building, which shows Concordia with Livia's fashionable hairstyle (fig. 50).[90]

Eumachia offers another instance of a donor's using a building for direct self-promotion. A statue of her was found in the *crypta* in a niche directly behind the chapel to Concordia. Presumably Eumachia arranged to have this statue, space for which was included in the original plan of the building, dedicated to her by the *fullones,* the cloth fullers and dyers; obviously they owed her a particular debt of gratitude. It depicts her as a priestess and holy woman, with her head covered (fig. 49), and was executed in the classical style.[91] This is noteworthy, because the sculptor was not a particularly skilled craftsman. Both face and body are depicted entirely in the

Figure 48 Statue of an Augustan divinity with the features of Livia (Ny Carlsberg Glyptotek, Copenhagen). Several indications suggest that the cult statue in the Eumachia Building must have resembled it (compare figure 50). The imperial family is here celebrated as the source of all prosperity, in the form of a goddess with a cornucopia.

Figure 49 Statue of Eumachia (Museo Nazionale, Naples). The statue of the benefactress was found in the niche behind the large exedra for the cult statue. It was donated by the *fullones,* the cloth fullers and dyers; Eumachia may have been their employer. The veil over her head alludes to her piety and to her office as civic priestess *(sacerdos publica).* The two statues of the goddess/empress and the local benefactress were thus placed in relation to each other, despite their separation by a wall.

Figure 50 Fountain at the side entrance to the Eumachia Building. The rather crude relief made by a local stone carver is presumed to be an imitation of the lost cult statue of Concordia Augusta inside.

idealized forms of the late classical epoch. The movement of the body expresses reserve and grace *(charis)* in equal measure, and the rendering of the face reflects no attempt to portray the real Eumachia, whose appearance must have been familiar to all. The statue's features are completely idealized. This classical vocabulary had ethical connotations for Augustan ideology, associations with which the Pompeians who commissioned the work must have been acquainted.[92] But visitors to the splendid building no doubt felt that this exalted language of form, familiar to them from statues of the imperial family, elevated and ennobled their neighbor Eumachia. Thus we see that even the few finds from the priestess's building offer important evidence showing how the new visual symbolism of the Roman state was absorbed and reworked on different levels.

In the course of only a few decades four imposing buildings (or perhaps only three, if Dobbins's theory is confirmed) were added to the eastern side of the forum, all faced at least in part with marble, and distinguished by their elaborate decoration and light travertine façades. These features gave them a certain substance in comparison with the older buildings made of tufa. Even more important, however, each of these new structures had direct or indirect ties to the worship of the emperor and his family; again and again, the particular rituals and festivals associated with each one drew the inhabitants' attention to the buildings and their cults.

New research has shown that the forums of many cities underwent similar profound changes in appearance in the early years of the Empire. Many such buildings were erected during Augustus' reign, others during the reigns of his immediate successors. The location, size, and decoration of these shrines varied from place to place, for they were built by local officials to demonstrate their loyalty. In this instance townscapes offer a unique reflection of the political changes that were occurring, and prove the extent to which society identified itself with the new system. In many cities builders and architects were able to create far more impos-ing ensembles than in Pompeii; indeed, in cities founded in this era the buildings associated with the cult of the emperor dominate all the rest.[93] The case of Pompeii is particularly valuable, however, because here we are able to gather some impression of how the transformation pro-ceeded.

It is significant that each such building resulted from individual initia-tive. There was no overall plan, not even for integrating the new structures into the existing ensemble. Although this seems amazing, we know it is the case, since not one of the façades is flush with any of the others. In conse-quence there was also no continuous portico on the eastern side of the forum; instead the forecourt of the market, the Sanctuary of the Lares, and the Eumachia Building all presented the square with façades of differing sizes and styles.

Honorific Monuments in the Forum

The area of the forum itself acquired new features in the early Empire.[94] After the colony was founded at Pompeii, it appears that equestrian statues of a certain size came into fashion as tributes to the town's highest officials; this is suggested by the old pedestals on the western side of the forum and in front of the municipal offices to the south (fig. 51). Some of these were removed as early as the Augustan era, however, to make room for an arch, which may have been surmounted by a statue of the emperor driving a four-horse chariot *(quadriga)* like the famous one in the Forum of Augustus in Rome. Later two enormous monuments on rectangular plinths were added flanking the arch, probably also *quadrigae,* as well as a colossal equestrian statue farther toward the center of the forum on its long axis. Presumably the equestrian statues that had previously been lined up at the southern

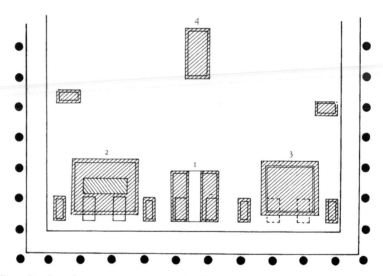

Figure 51 Bases for statues on the south end of the forum (after Mau). Originally there was a row of equestrian statues there, but most of them were taken down to make room for monuments to the imperial family on three huge bases (1–3).

end were removed and re-erected elsewhere in the square, but the overall effect in creating the new monuments—which doubtless honored members of the imperial family—was to marginalize the town's most illustrious citizens; their lesser significance was also reflected in the figures' relative size.[95]

The position directly in front of the main town offices at the forum's southern end clearly had the highest status; this probably came about because it was the busiest part of the square. It does in fact appear as if the imperial monuments were aligned facing the path that would have been taken by traffic between the Via dell'Abbondanza and the Marine Gate. The long western side conveyed less prestige, as is obvious from the smaller size of the pedestals. The few statues of standing figures along the steps of the portico would have been completely overshadowed. The surviving inscriptions indicate that these were honorific statues of local officials. It thus emerges that a clear hierarchy existed in the location of imperial and municipal monuments.

The north end of the forum was dominated by more monuments to the imperial family no less impressive than those to the south. Two arches were erected, one on either side of the *capitolium*, modeled on those on the east side of the Forum Romanum and in the Forum of Augustus; they presumably honored princes of the imperial house (fig. 52). Later the arch on the right was moved all the way back to the street running behind the *capitolium*, both to keep it from blocking the new forecourt of the market and to create a better visual link to the Temple of Fortuna Augusta and the portico leading to it. When still later a further arch was built next to this temple in the line of sight from the forum arch, it created an effective receding vista reminiscent of far larger cities (see fig. 54).

The arches' proximity to the temple façade elevated to the religious sphere the statues of the family members thus honored; they also drew the old *capitolium* into the ensemble, virtually making it part of the encomium to the emperor. This effect was increased by placing equestrian statues on both sides of the steps, as shown on the relief in the lararium of the house of Caecilius Iucundus (fig. 54a).[96] No doubt these, too, honored members of the imperial dynasty.

Figure 52 A reconstruction of the north end of the forum (after D. Scagliarini Corlàita). This side of the square was also dominated by monuments to the ruling dynasty. As in the fora of other Italic cities, they were displayed in two places: flanking the steps to the Temple of Jupiter, and on top of the two triumphal arches adjoining the temple.

The forum itself was repaved with travertine, probably in the early imperial period; the new surface must have created a far grander impression than the old blocks of tufa that it replaced.[97] An inscription set in the pavement near the *suggestum* (platform) and running the width of the forum named the donor. It is reminiscent of the inscription in the Forum Romanum naming the Praetor Surdinus and similar pavement inscriptions in other Italic cities. Unfortunately, only a few letters of this bronze inscription can be reconstructed, but even this much suffices to show that the donor was as little inclined to modesty as Eumachia. The lettering is larger than in Surdinus' inscription in Rome! The occasion of the repaving may have been used to arrange the commemorative statues in a more systematic way. Perhaps the town magistrates decided then to remove all the pedestrian statues from the forum and reassemble them in the *chalcidicum* of the Eumachia Building and the forecourt of the market (see fig. 53). The identical bases in both places suggest a kind of portrait gallery, similar to the *summi viri* in the Forum of Augustus in Rome.

If we now turn our attention to the effect created by the forum as a whole, we see that the space in the center was kept free of honorific monuments. But at about the height of the two buildings devoted to the cult of the emperor are the remains of a tall rectangular base on the long axis of the square (see fig. 37). Its dimensions have led to speculation that it was an altar, and I believe this is correct. It could not have belonged to the *capitolium,* however, for its altar, once located in the forum but closer to the temple, was moved to the temple podium in the Augustan era, as it is shown in the lararium relief of the House of Caecilius Iucundus (see fig. 54a). There is good reason to suppose that the base in the center of the forum represents the remains of an altar dedicated to the emperor, which would then have been surrounded on three sides by buildings for his cult or monuments in his honor. The altar's orientation with regard to the cult buildings would then seem to indicate a shift of focus in the forum, in a

Figure 53 A reconstruction of the portico in front of the market (*macellum;* after Weichardt, 1896). A series of similar statue bases stood in front of the market and in the portico of the Eumachia Building. Perhaps the earlier statues of civic leaders of Pompeii were re-erected here after the places of honor in the forum were appropriated for monuments to the emperor and his family. In reality, however, the effect created by these porticos was not quite as grand as was imagined by this illustrator in the late nineteenth century!

Urban Space as a Reflection of Society

Figure 54 A view from the forum to the arch adjoining the Temple of Fortuna Augusta (A. Gaeta). Later on a small triumphal arch that served to distribute water as well was erected next to this temple. The vista gives an impression of the impact made by the new ceremonial buildings and honorific monuments.

Figure 54a Relief from the lararium in the House of Caecilius Iucundus (V 1.26) showing the Temple of Jupiter during the earthquake, with the presumed altar for the cult of the emperor to the right and an honorific arch to the left.

POMPEII

manner of speaking, toward the grand new structures associated with the emperor. We may then consider whether the large altar shown in the center of the lararium relief may not in fact represent this very monument.

Seating by Rank in the New Marble Theater

> M(arcus et) M(arcus) Holconii Rufus et Celer
> cryptam tribunalia theatrum s(ua) p(ecunia)

The above inscription (*CIL* X 833–34), several copies of which survive, refers to the large-scale renovation of the Hellenistic theater in the Augustan era (figs. 55, 56).[98] It was placed above both side entrances *(parodoi)* and probably on the façade of the stage-building as well, where audiences would have in view a constant reminder of the generosity of the Holconii. The word *crypta* refers to a considerable enlargement of the curving cov-

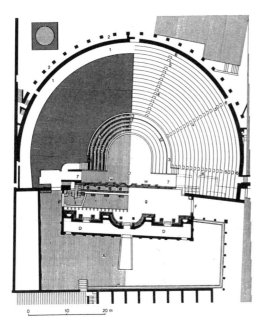

Figure 55 A plan of the theater after its renovation in the Augustan era.

Figure 56 Reconstruction of the large theater after its enlargement and embellishment in the Augustan era (after de Franciscis). In the later part of Augustus' reign the original theater from the second century B.C. was enlarged and refurbished by the Holconii brothers. The renovation reflected not only the general desire for impressive public buildings, but also the increased emphasis on social distinctions in the Empire. Spectators now sat in clearly demarcated sections according to their social rank, and the official sponsors sat in prominent view on newly installed tribunals. Presumably the façade of the stage-building was decorated with statues of the imperial family, as in many other cities.

ered gallery around the auditorium; after the renovation it became a passageway dividing the old seats in the lower rows from the new, more closely spaced rows on top (*summa cavea;* see fig. 55, no. 1). The word *theatrum* must refer among other things to the renovation of the auditorium—so substantial it must have almost amounted to complete reconstruction—that was necessary before the steps and seats could be faced with marble (see fig. 55, nos. 3 and 4).

The side entrances had been covered with vaulting in the Sullan period; now, with the addition of two seating platforms (*tribunalia,* no. 7) above them—also faced with marble, of course—the old theater from the second century B.C. had become thoroughly Roman in appearance. It enabled the magistrates sponsoring the performances to be seated in elevated boxes, as befitted their rank and dignity, where they could be seen by everyone in the theater. The general renovation must have included facing the stage-building or *saenae frons* with marble as well. The many theaters of the early Empire and their stage walls with two- and three-story orders of columns are well known. Unfortunately, very little of the marble facings survived in the theater at Pompeii, and it has not been possible to reconstruct the exact appearance of the stage reliably.[99] Perhaps we may imagine it as similar to the one in the theater at Herculaneum. In any event we may safely assume that some of the statue bases found in the theater once stood between the columns of the stage front, which in Pompeii may also have contained statues of the emperor and his family in the center. The customary hierarchy of rank would dictate that these were flanked by portraits of the Holconii, at least three of which have been positively identified.

M. Holconius Rufus was the leading citizen of Pompeii in the middle and late Augustan era (compare fig. 58).[100] He was descended from an old family that produced excellent wine and even had a type of grape named after them. M. Holconius Rufus' political career must have begun about 20 B.C., for at the time the theater was built in 3/2 B.C. he had already served as duumvir four times, as *quinquennalis* once, and been awarded the honorary title of *tribunus militum a populo* by the emperor. In addition he held the office of priest in the cult of the emperor *(sacerdos Augusti)*. He later received the title of "patron of the colony" *(patronus coloniae)*, the highest honor that the town of Pompeii could bestow.

The relative by the name of Celer mentioned together with M. Holconius Rufus in the inscriptions must have been considerably younger: he was not chosen duumvir until A.D. 13/14, although by that time he was *quinquennalis* designate and *sacerdos Augusti*. Still later he became *sacerdos divi Augusti*. Probably he was Rufus' son. As in the case of Eumachia's splendid donation, this gift was intended, among other things, to advance the career of a younger member of the family and thus help to maintain a leading family's status.

Like construction of the buildings for the cult of the emperor, the extensive renovations in the theater offered the sponsors ample opportunity for self-promotion. The honorific monuments placed there by the citizens should once again be seen in the living context of festivals and performances. Members of the *gens Holconia* occupied places of honor not only at the dedication of the refurbished theater, but later on as well; as magistrates or priests of the emperor's cult they would have had places in the seats reserved for officials, or on the new seating platforms as sponsors of performances. The particular prestige M. Holconius Rufus enjoyed in Pompeii is revealed above all by a monument that stood on the lowest step of the middle tier along the central axis of the auditorium, accompanied by an inscription listing his complete *cursus honorum* (fig. 57). The pattern of the holes drilled in the step to attach the monument suggests it may have been a bronze curule chair *(sella curulis)*, a form of honorific monument later documented for members of the imperial family.[101] In this way audi-

Figure 57 Inscription honoring the benefactors, the Holconii brothers, in the center of the seating area in the *cavea.*

POMPEII

Figure 58 Honorific statue of M. Holconius Rufus. Citizens honored Pompeii's most important political figure in the late Augustan era with this monument showing him in armor. It stood outside the Stabian baths on one of the busiest streets in town. The military nature of the statue refers to Holconius' status as *tribunus militum a populo*, an honorary title bestowed by the emperor on leading citizens of Italic cities who had performed some outstanding service (*CIL* X 830).

ences would have had before their eyes a conspicuous reminder of the honorand's outstanding career in office.

The case of the Holconii offers us unusually good insights into the process by which the prominent families in Roman cities functioned as intermediaries. It was these leading families who led the campaign for Augustus' program of cultural renewal and created corresponding symbols with their donations. Like M. Holconius Rufus, most of them had direct political connections with Rome, and even with Augustus himself. They were certainly very well informed about the new political guidelines and prepared to identify with them. Political leadership, observance of the cult of the emperor, and interest in improving the appearance of their home towns went hand in hand. M. Holconius Rufus is the first securely documented instance of a priest of Augustus (without the slightest euphemism in his title, incidentally: *Augusti sacerdos*). The emperor had honored him personally, awarding this man with no military connections the high-sounding title of *tribunus militum a populo*. Among other privileges, this entitled Holconius to a particularly prominent seat among the *equites* on his visits to the theater at Rome. When the citizens of Pompeii erected a statue to him at a busy intersection in front of the Stabian baths, they commissioned it from a workshop in Rome. It is likely that Holconius, who knew Rome well, also had a hand in this selection. The type of monument chosen—a copy of the cult statue of Mars Ultor from the Forum Augustum—provided Pompeii with a further important portrait. It gave the highly honorific title a concrete pictorial form, while at the same time proclaiming the importance of manliness and the military.[102]

By refurbishing the theater in marble, M. Holconius Rufus contributed substantially to Pompeii's appearance—another case in which public magnificence was the main theme. New theaters on an ambitious scale were going up everywhere in Roman cities at that time, in central locations inside the walls. In Rome Augustus himself had acted as the sponsor. One function of such institutions was to embody and express the cultural aspirations of the new era. At the same time the members of the upper class in the cities wished to create appropriately elegant settings where they could gather and enjoy themselves. This aim was furthered by the theaters' elaborate and costly decoration with marble, columns, and ornamental statuary, and also by the fact that citizens were expected to wear their best clothes when attending.[103]

One might ask why the Pompeians, who had had two attractive theaters at their disposal for some time, did not consider them sufficient to fulfill this aspect of Augustus' program. Presumably the problem was the lack of marble, which rendered the old theater ugly in their eyes in comparison with the new buildings going up elsewhere. The renovations resolved this difficulty, but the inscription on the refurbished theater reveals that the Holconii had specific sociopolitical aims in view as well. The new *crypta* created additional seating for the lowest-ranking members of the audience (visitors, slaves, the poor, and possibly also women), but was constructed so as to keep them apart from the rest. These seats in the highest tier were accessible only by staircases—quite crude ones, incidentally—leading up directly from outside the building, and there was no connection with the middle tier, where the middle classes sat, preventing this section of the audience from mingling with the others. Such an arrangement reflects perfectly the political concept behind Augustan regulations regarding the theater: the number of those privileged to attend was meant to be increased—to include deserving slaves, for instance—but at the same time distinctions of rank were to be made clearer than ever.

In this connection reconstruction of the *crypta* served a second important purpose, namely, altering access routes to the middle tiers of seats. Thanks to the new *crypta,* there was now separate access to the middle and the bottom tiers *(ima cavea).* The free citizens of the town could reach the twenty rows of seats allotted to them in the middle tier by six staircases leading down from doors in the *crypta;* this allowed the orchestra entrance to be reserved for the aristocrats, who sat in the bottom tier closest to the stage. Probably further divisions existed within the middle tiers for special groups such as members of youth brigades or the army, and in all likelihood the provisions of the *lex Iulia theatralis* created additional categories of privilege and exclusion, as they did in Rome and elsewhere.[104] The only seating divisions preserved in Pompeii are the lines (with matching numbers) on the marble seating indicating that the width allotted per seat was a little over fifteen inches. In sum, it is evident that thanks to the efforts of the Holconii the theater in Pompeii, too, became a setting in which the members of society could experience their own hierarchical order repeatedly and in an enduring fashion, just as their emperor desired.

An "Athletic Field" for Young Men

One further public building in Pompeii from the Augustan era demonstrates the citizens' eagerness to follow the example of the emperor in Rome: the large palaestra next to the amphitheater (figs. 59 and 60).[105] Improving the physical and moral condition of young men in the upper classes was one of Augustus' main concerns; as a means of reaching this goal he promoted equestrian sports, parades, and an annual inspection *(probatio equitum)*. The Troy Games had been revived, and the young men of Rome practiced for them in public view on the Campus Martius. When Augustus' adopted sons Gaius and Lucius were awarded the honorary titles *principes iuventutis* and took on leading roles in the games, these activities acquired even greater significance. The Roman example had an invigorating influence on other towns, where organizations for young men were revitalized and began to sponsor similar competitions. The provision of new training grounds showed how seriously the matter was taken.[106]

The large palaestra is without doubt Pompeii's version of the athletic field. It consists of a very large park-like area (458 by 347 ft.) surrounded on three sides by a colonnade. The front side, which faced the amphitheater, had three entrances surmounted by pediments, with merlons along the walls (fig. 60). The last feature alluded to the structure's function, in theory

Figures 59–60 Ground plan and front view of the *campus* known as the "palaestra." This sprawling sports ground for boys and young men reflects another aspect of Augustus' program of cultural renewal. The park-like area was surrounded by a front wall with three gates and a three-sided colonnade, and had a large swimming pool in the center. The decorative merlons on the wall are an architectural allusion to the underlying ideology of preparedness for battle. In fact, however, under Augustus young men were no longer required to give proof of their fitness for military service, since battles were fought by the professional troops of the Empire.

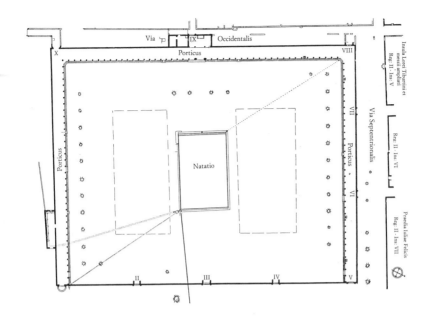

at least: the sponsors—whose identity is unfortunately not known—intended it as a site where the young men of the town could be trained in the basic military arts and keep physically fit. In practice, however, young men in Italy were hardly ever called upon to serve; increasingly, the emperor relied on professional soldiers and barbarian auxiliaries to defend the borders of the Empire. If the donor of the training ground *(campus)* nonetheless insisted on giving it a touch of the fortress, architecturally speaking, it was to serve as a reminder of the cult of *virtus* ("manliness"). A militarization of imagery can be observed in various areas in the early Empire. It both expressed and served to stabilize an outlook that had spread throughout Italy as a result of Augustus' cultural policies, the awareness of being a ruling power.

In actual fact the *campus* was used for a variety of leisure-time activities. There was a large swimming pool *(natatio)* that must certainly have been welcome in the summer, and two rows of plane trees that offered cool places in the shade to rest in between dips. The thick roots of these trees provide an important clue to the age of the structure.[107] At the time of Pompeii's destruction the trees were almost 100 years old (plate 8.1), so that the *campus* dates from the early years of Augustus' principate.

The colonnade, measuring 1,160 feet in total length, has no annexes except for a latrine on the south side and a small shrine, perhaps for the cult of the emperor, in the middle of the long western side. From this we know that no institution such as a *collegium* was permanently established there. However, evidence that the palaestra was actually used as a site for games and athletic contests does exist in the form of several graffiti. Most of these scrawled comments reflect other activities, such as the verses written by a schoolmaster complaining that he has not been paid. Others wrote lines of poetry they had memorized, and of course many graffiti refer to the gladiators' contests that took place next door in the amphitheater. The palaestra was probably heavily frequented by spectators during breaks in the games. And there is no lack of other messages—such as price lists, recommendations for barbers, and naturally the ubiquitous obscenities—indicating that, fortunately, everyday life often diverged greatly from the austere ideals of the reigning ideology.

POMPEII

Small Amenities around Town

After Augustus transformed Rome into a "city of marble," even smaller towns in the western part of the Empire put up expensive public buildings with marble facing. For his contemporaries marble was more than just a means to improve the appearance of their cities; it became a symbol of the new era and acquired a variety of connotations. Buildings made of marble proved that Romans need no longer fear comparison with the beautiful Greek cities of the East. It also stood for a new political culture and morality. In the past only the palaces and villas of the wealthy had been adorned with marble, but now civic buildings were gleaming white, too. The emblem of private luxury was transformed into a symbol of public magnificence, reflecting the priority of communal interests over individual self-indulgence. The new buildings proclaimed the solidity of the new order, from which each citizen's personal security was derived.

Of course not every community could afford marble. Sometimes people had to make do with the lighter shades of limestone or artful stucco work. The Pompeians often fell back on such substitutes, as in the case of the columns for the large palaestra, which were made of stucco-covered bricks. But the values behind the symbol remained potent, and for this reason even small marble embellishments or decor imitating marble had great significance. They accented the appearance of streets and buildings, functioning as encapsulated references to the larger phenomenon of "cities of marble." Pompeii was full of such minor allusive embellishments.

Some were purely small amenities, such as the two marble sundials in the courtyard of the Temple of Apollo and the sacred precinct near the theater. The temple sundial stood on a short column, while the one at the archaic temple was combined with a semicircular bench (schola).[108] In the covered theater the duumvir M. Oculatius donated a new floor in the orchestra made of variegated marble paving.[109] Probably the tribunalia and the marble veneer of the scaenae frons also date from this time. Over a period of years a number of magistrates donated new rows of seats in the amphitheater.[110] In contrast to those in the theater, however, these were made only of tufa. In the Augustan age the amphitheater ranked far below the other entertainment sites in cultural importance. The two public baths also underwent renovation and had improvements added. In the forum baths, for instance, the duumviri of the year A.D. 3/4 donated a large marble basin (*labrum,* fig. 61).[111]

These examples show that men and women chosen for public office were virtually required to become donors as well. Especially wealthy officials could afford to attach their names to entire structures, like Eumachia and the Holconii, but also M. Tullius and Mammia. But the less affluent could still commemorate themselves in marble in some smaller way. As a result the townscape presented itself to the eye as a communal achievement, but one in which distinctions of social and political rank were preserved all the same. The overall impression must have been one of manifold and ceaseless activity; the citizens felt the town was "on its way up," and everyone contributed to the general effort.

Supplying Water to the Town

Improvements to the infrastructure greatly affected people's outlook. In Pompeii, as in many other places in Italy at this time, streets were repaired and the sewage system was improved.[112] Above all a constant supply of fresh running water was made available to the town's inhabitants. This is thought to have occurred early in Augustus' reign.[113] Unfortunately, we do not know much about how this ambitious project was carried out. The main aqueduct carrying water to the naval port of Misenum had a branch that supplied Pompeii; the water was fed into the main tank standing at the highest point in town, next to the Vesuvian Gate (plate 8.2). From there three large pipes carried it to different neighborhoods. The sloping terrain created considerable water pressure, which was regulated in columnar water towers up to nineteen feet tall.[114] To date fourteen such secondary tanks (*castella secundaria*) have been found; they can be spotted all over town, sometimes standing on sidewalks, and supplied the immediate vicinity with fresh water. It is astonishing to see how many houses were connected to the system and had running water; a large portion of the population profited directly from the new convenience. The supply was also

Figure 61 Marble basin in the caldarium of the forum baths, donated by the two duumviri who served in A.D. 3/4. The basin is one of the small amenities typical of urban improvements in the Augustan period.

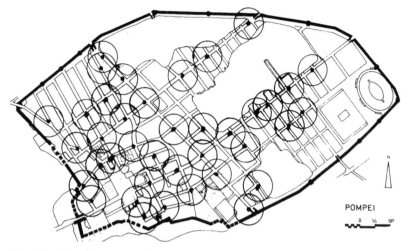

Figure 62 Sites of fountains with running water in Pompeii (after Eschebach). Piped water and a sewage system were standard facilities in the modernized infrastructure of Roman towns. The equal distribution of water pipes throughout the town improved the quality of life of all the citizens. Filled dots indicate street fountains; circles around them show supposed range of supply.

abundant; in the houses of the more affluent we find decorative basins *(nymphaea)* and fountains everywhere, and even some private baths *(thermae).*

But even those too poor to have their houses connected to the city system could enjoy fresh water piped from the mountains, for no fewer than forty public fountains have been discovered in all parts of the town (fig. 62).[115] They tend to be of a standard shape and dimensions, but the details can vary considerably, especially the pretty decorative reliefs carved by unassuming local craftsmen (compare fig. 50). Most of these fountains are made of lava slabs, with a few exceptions fashioned of carved travertine or marble. The more elaborate ones may have been financed by private donations (fig. 63).

When we recall that before introduction of this system the Pompeians were dependent on deep wells and rain-collecting cisterns for their water, it is easy to imagine their joy over the new amenity, which truly represented a substantial improvement in their quality of life.

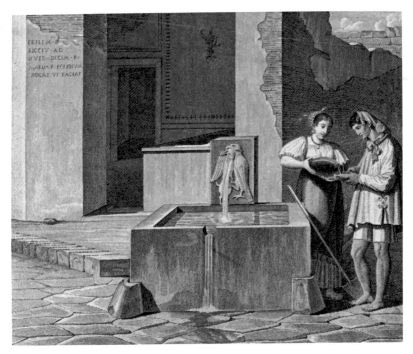

Figure 63 Fountain with running water at a street corner (after Mazois, around 1830). The spouts of such fountains were usually decorated with simple reliefs: compare figure 50.

While the general assumption is correct that the aqueduct going to Pompeii was a subsidiary branch of the imperial aqueduct that carried water to the new harbor facilities and the fleet in Misenum, the townspeople had the emperor to thank personally for authorizing the diversion of part of the supply. Augustus also had aqueducts built to supply many other towns, or contributed toward their construction.[116] Agrippa had set an example with his renovation and expansion of the water supply system in Rome beginning in the late 30s. The Pompeian installations must also be seen in this context; the Roman example was followed everywhere, down to the decorations on the public fountains. And, as in Rome, the new water supply led to increased luxury in the public baths. Here and in other instances of improvements paid for by the Pompeians themselves, the new aqueduct led them to associate such benefits with the emperor. In the last

Urban Space as a Reflection of Society

analysis, or so it must have seemed to them at the time, it was he who was responsible for the fact that life was getting better.

Honorific Tombs as Expressions of Civic Pride

In concluding this survey of Pompeii in the age of Augustus, we must look at an area outside the walls, where Augustan ideology led to another alteration in the townscape: the tombs in the form of benches *(scholae)* studied by V. Kockel (fig. 64).[117] Thus far eight of these unusual tombs, consisting of a semicircular bench made of tufa, have been found outside the Herculaneum, Vesuvian, Nolan, and Stabian Gates.

They were honorific tombs for former duumviri or their relatives, to whom the town council had given special permission to build within the

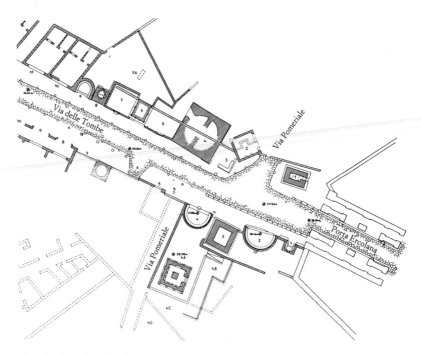

Figure 64   Tombs lining the road outside the Herculaneum Gate (after Kockel/Weber). The most meritorious citizens were honored with grave monuments in the form of exedra near the town gates.

POMPEII

Figure 65 Tomb of the priestess Mammia outside the Herculaneum Gate (painting by Jacob Philipp Hackert, 1793; Goethe Museum, Weimar). During the Augustan era a new form of roadside tomb for distinguished families came into fashion, in the form of a large, exedra-shaped bench on which passers-by could rest. The tomb honoring an individual thus served simultaneously as a decorative amenity for the town. Its worn steps reveal how much it was used by both residents and travelers.

ninety-foot-wide sacred perimeter *(pomerium)*. Honorific monuments of a related type have been found in Greek sanctuaries, but Pompeii is the only place known where they serve as tombs. Some of the *schola* tombs, like the Greek monuments, enclose a base in the middle to support a column or altar. Since no burials have been found at the site, it seems likely that the column or altar held an urn with the ashes of the deceased.

All the people for whom these tombs were built belonged to the leading families of Pompeii. Mammia's name was chiseled into the backrest of her *schola* tomb in huge letters (fig. 65). The group that allowed itself to be honored in this manner for its achievements was a closed social circle. Whoever had the opportunity to compare these commemorative monuments with the flashy tombs of the "colonial era," particularly the altar graves and aedicula graves, some of them in marble, could not help being struck by their simple dignity. In addition, a special effect was created by

Urban Space as a Reflection of Society   123

the fact that these civic leaders designed their graves as places for fellow citizens to sit and rest, an unusual idea fully in keeping with the spirit of Augustan reform. The worn steps of Mammia's grave reveal how often people sought out the semicircular benches. The slightly raised seats of the *scholae* offer a good view of passing traffic; in addition to providing travelers with a convenient resting spot, they must have been the site of countless conversations, where Pompeians could keep an eye on all that was going on and pass along the latest news.

Most of the building activity observable in Pompeii in the early decades of the Empire has parallels elsewhere. Many cities in Italy and the western provinces did not acquire their major monuments until the reigns of Augustus or his immediate successors. The smaller towns especially tended to retain this appearance with few or no major changes down to late antiquity.[118] The high concentration of lavish public building in this epoch would have been incomprehensible without the impetus provided by Augustan cultural policies.

In many places the new buildings were more elaborate and architecturally more interesting than in Pompeii. But nowhere else can we distinguish so many separate initiatives or learn the identities of so many important benefactors. Pompeii also offers us a unique opportunity to observe in detail the social interaction that made it possible to carry out Augustus' policies with the limited means available to smaller cities.

The City's Final Years

We must now turn briefly to the state of the town after the devastating earthquake of A.D. 62 (fig. 66). In A.D. 79 many parts of Pompeii still lay in ruins, despite all the efforts of the intervening years.[119] The inhabitants seem to have been left on their own, without any significant assistance from Rome. They concentrated on making those repairs that were absolutely necessary, and beyond that clearly chose to rebuild the places with the greatest significance for them. To obtain a picture of this period we should start with the shops, workshops, and dwellings, for this was the area in which reconstruction was furthest along. We have a far more compre-

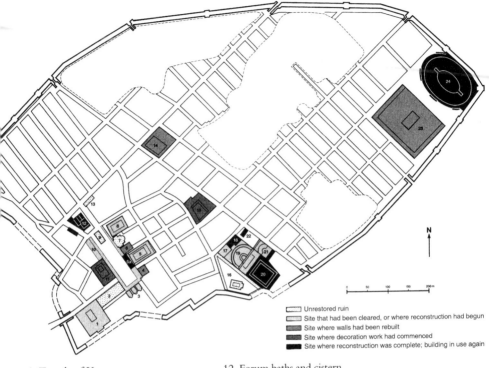

Unrestored ruin
Site that had been cleared, or where reconstruction had begun
Site where walls had been rebuilt
Site where decoration work had commenced
Site where reconstruction was complete; building in use again

1. Temple of Venus
2. Basilica
3. Administration building
4. Comitium
5. Eumachia building
5a. Chalcidicum
6. Building for the imperial cult
   (Temple of Vespasian)
7. Forum exedra (Lararium)
8. Market
9. Capitolium
10. Produce market *(Forum holitorium)*
11. Temple of Apollo
12. Forum baths and cistern
13. Temple of Fortuna Augusta
14. New central baths
15. Stabian baths
16. Triangular forum and archaic temple
17. "Samnite" palaestra
18. Temple of Isis
19. Large theater
20. Presumed gymnasium
21. Covered theater
22. Temple of Zeus Meilichios
23. Campus
24. Amphitheater

Figure 66 Public building activity in Pompeii after the earthquake of A.D. 62. New priorities are reflected in the order of projects chosen for rebuilding. Compared with earlier times, the main political centers, including temples connected with the cult of the emperor and the old civic temples, have declined in importance, while centers of leisure activity such as baths and the amphitheater are given top priority, along with the temples of private cults.

hensive picture of Pompeii in its last phase—when its political and cultural life was dominated by a large and very homogeneous "middle class"—than for any other ancient city. Many of the restored houses had been decorated in a distinct style. Everywhere, even in the smallest dwellings, we encounter elements of the luxury associated with villas, usually on a reduced scale and often only as pictorial allusions.[120] Unfortunately, we are not able to compare the late Pompeian houses with contemporary dwellings in other towns. But it appears that being surrounded by piles of rubble after the earthquake inspired the inhabitants to make their houses as beautiful and their lives as pleasant as possible.

The center of daily activity had shifted from the badly damaged forum to certain streets, mainly the Via Stabiana, Via dell'Abbondanza, and the Via degli Augustali. The stretch of the Via dell'Abbondanza that widens almost into a square in front of the Stabian baths seems to have become an important focal point of city life.

In contrast to private dwellings, on which reconstruction work was well advanced, a number of important public structures still lay in ruins seventeen years after the earthquake. Repair work had begun on some, and others were nearly finished, but only a few were back in full use again. Their state of repair clearly reflects the priorities that had been established by the inhabitants of the town (see fig. 1).

Although the numerous shrines to the Lares and altars in and adjoining private homes show that the inhabitants remained basically religious, not one of the old municipal sanctuaries had been fully restored. Little or no work had been done on the *capitolium,* the Sanctuary of the Lares, the chapel in the Eumachia Building, or the Temple of Venus. The smaller of the two structures in the forum dedicated to the cult of the emperor had been rebuilt, but it was not yet redecorated. The only structure where repairs were already far advanced was the Temple of Apollo, indicating that Pompeians attached greatest importance to their oldest religious tradition, veneration of the town's tutelary god, Apollo. The fact that the Temple of Isis was fully restored is not surprising, given that the initiates of her cult constituted a closely knit and intensely devoted group (figs. 67 and 68). The wealthy freedman N. Popidius Ampliatus assumed the cost of the

Figures 67–68   View of the Temple of Isis and dedicatory inscription. The shrine to Isis, first erected in the second century B.C., was rebuilt immediately following the earthquake, in contrast to the capitolium in the forum. It is significant that the cost was assumed by a wealthy freedman, N. Popidius Ampliatus, who achieved in return the election of his six-year-old son to the city council.

work in the name of his six-year-old son Celsinus.[121] In gratitude for this generous donation the town council elected the boy a member. In this manner the father achieved for his son, at least, the social advancement denied to himself as a former slave. However, the honor also shows the political influence wielded by devotees of Isis in the town at this date.

The small temple of Zeus Meilichios or Asclepius was in serviceable condition again, although this did not require very much effort. It is likely, incidentally, that the somewhat oversized statue of Juno and a bust of Minerva found there—both late Hellenistic works in terracotta—were

Urban Space as a Reflection of Society

Figure 69 Election slogans on the façade of a house. The colorful painted graffiti reflect the active political life of the town, which remained restricted to local affairs. The emperor and Empire had ceased to play a significant role. The religious drawings honor the old household divinities, the Lares, who were generally worshiped in the form of snakes. Apart from elections, gladiatorial contests are the only public events mentioned in wall graffiti.

placed alongside the clay statue of the foreign god in the early days after the colony's founding, in order to increase his resemblance to Capitoline Jupiter.[122]

The state of repair of other public buildings offers a highly revealing picture as well. Of the three structures devoted to shows and entertainment, only the amphitheater was in viable condition. Extensive damage there, especially to the vaulted passages, seems to have been repaired with donations from the two C. Cuspii Pansae, father and son, who were rewarded with honorary statues in new niches added on either side of the main gate.[123] The large outdoor theater and small covered theater remained unsuitable for use, although work was proceeding on a new marble stage front at the former. Obviously, however, the gladiators' contests in the amphitheater had absolute priority. It was for their sake, too, that the large palaestra next door, presumably part of the former gymnasium, was also remodeled into barracks housing. The many small rooms behind the colonnade were all added after the earthquake.

The citizens were prepared to spend even more money on rebuilding the baths. Both the forum baths and the Stabian baths were completely restored and refurbished with elaborate plaster decoration and wall paintings. At the Stabian baths the central water system was still not repaired, but the forum baths were open for business again—at least for male clients, who used water from the large cistern nearby. It is noteworthy, however, that repairs to the women's facilities were still not finished.

Even more revealing than these renovation projects is the construction of a third large public bath in region IX (fig. 70).[124] Here an *insula* previously occupied by private houses was turned into a bath complex modeled on one in Rome, with the same high windows designed to flood it with sunlight. The shell of the building was already complete, and the workmen had just begun putting up expensive marble columns at the time of the eruption.

This example shows that the town itself or its private benefactors were able to finance expensive projects. That makes it all the more surprising to find little evidence of interest in repairing the forum and the symbolic public buildings fringing it. The square itself had been more or less cleared

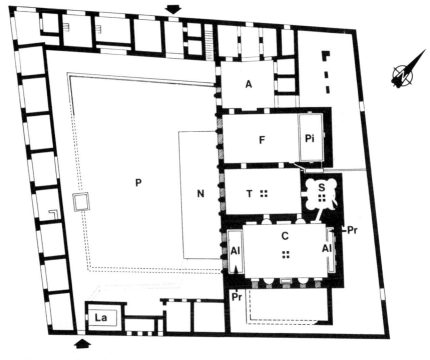

Figure 70 Plan of the central baths, as they were built following the earthquake. The architect based his plan on models from Rome, using windows high up the walls and marble columns. The result suggests that the town had no interest in cost-cutting here.

of debris, but that was all. Most of the statues had toppled off their plinths, which had themselves been stripped of their marble facing. The ruins of the *capitolium,* the Sanctuary of the Lares, and the colonnades around the forum must have been a depressing sight, surrounded by other buildings encased in scaffolding, on which work was proceeding only sporadically. Essential festivals in honor of the emperor must have taken place in the Temple of Vespasian, which had been hastily patched together. The municipal building with an apse (the office of the duumviri) was in use again, while work was going forward on the *comitium* and the two other municipal offices.

Even this rough sketch shows how much the emphasis had shifted. The low levels of interest in the town's political center and state cults combined with the great efforts made to repair structures used for entertainment and pleasure stand in stark contrast to the building boom of the early Empire. The lively campaign slogans painted on house walls show that Pompeian political life remained vigorous in the city's final years, but it was entirely restricted to local affairs.[125] The Pompeians, who had been left to pick up the pieces after catastrophe struck, must have felt abandoned by the emperor, who—understandably—was seen as a more remote figure than in earlier years. It is possible that a number of the great families—those with estates in other areas and ambitions for careers in the imperial administration—had left the city long before the eruption, leaving freed slaves to manage their property in the struggling and still endangered city. And although extraordinary efforts had been made, Pompeii's limited ability to function is evident from the breakdown of the water supply system, which had still not been restored. In all probability the earthquake had destroyed the aqueduct originally financed by the emperor, and there was no money to repair such a large-scale project. A few wealthy individuals, unwilling to give up the fountains in their courtyards, had private water supplies connected to their houses, but the source from which they drew the water has not been established.

Despite the pressures created by the exceptional circumstances, however, the priorities of the "reconstruction program" in Pompeii reveal a clear general trend. After the heady atmosphere of Augustus' campaign for cultural renewal had faded, even in the later years of his own reign, his cult and its accompanying ideology of the state had quickly become a matter of routine. Wealthy towns continued to erect temples to the emperor on an ever grander scale, but they tended to put them at ceremonial sites away from the centers of people's daily rounds. What really counted in the Flavian-Antonine era, and what determined the appearance of its cities, was a desire to enjoy the pleasures of life, be it in sumptuous houses with marble colonnades, at shows in the arena and the theater, or in lavishly decorated baths that developed into centers of leisure-time activity.

Since I originally developed this view of Pompeii, which is reflected in figure 66, new interpretations of the evidence have been proposed; investigations of the relevant structures at the site are also in progress (although not by any means complete). As a result, the picture of the town developed above may require some adjustment or refinement. The new observations are related to two areas in particular, the first being the forum. Here a number of indications suggest that immediately after the town was buried by the eruption a more or less systematic search was made to retrieve building materials for re-use. That these actions were carried out in a planned manner under the direction of a commission sent from Rome comprising *curatores Campaniae restituendae* (ministers for the restoration of Campania), as has recently been suggested, seems rather unlikely.[126]

The second area concerns the state of buildings after the earthquake of A.D. 62, and/or at the time of the eruption. Our understanding of their condition used to be derived mainly from Maiuri's investigations; now the research efforts of John Dobbins and Kurt Wallat are providing new data, which do not, however, always point to the same conclusions. Dobbins is the initiator of the large-scale "Pompeii Forum Project," which has as its goal a close examination of the buildings on the east side of the forum. At the present time, only preliminary results are available, and in my view the theories to which they have given rise require confirmation from further excavations. According to the new view, construction was undertaken along the whole east side after the earthquake, and the result was a more imposing façade than before. And whereas the *macellum,* the Temple of Vespasian, and the Eumachia Building, which pre-dated the earthquake, were only to be restored or embellished, the structure identified as the Sanctuary of the Lares was not designed and built until after A.D. 62. If these theories should prove true, then we would have to recognize that the inhabitants of Pompeii made a far more determined attempt to restore their forum than I previously assumed. In the context of my own proposals, it would be important to know how far construction on these buildings had progressed after seventeen years. Modern excavators have discovered hardly any traces of interrupted construction work. Was such work indeed interrupted by a second quake, as several scholars have assumed? Furthermore, it remains accepted that the two largest structures in the forum, the *capitolium* and the basilica, had undergone no renovation at all. Such findings would make no essential difference as regards the appearance of

the forum in the Augustan or early imperial period. However, the elaborately decorated Sanctuary of the Lares, should it prove in fact not to have
been built until after A.D. 62, would be evidence of considerable commitment to the cult of the emperor. Nevertheless, in the light of all we know
about the forms of official involvement by the Senate or the emperor, I do
not consider it possible that the sanctuary was financed by the imperial
family itself.[127]

The Domestic Arts
in Pompeii

The Roman villa has long epitomized an elegant and luxurious refuge, a haven removed from the commotion of everyday life. Even in ancient times the word conveyed felicity; since the fifteenth century these associations have brought villas back into fashion again and again. In our own day the word "villa" is still used in England, for example, to suggest a touch of elegance, to imply that a house is a "residence of a superior type," when in fact the opposite is often the case.

For Romans in the late Republic and the Empire, villas and time spent at villas were synonymous with pleasure, wealth, and leisure. This was as true for broad segments of the population as it was for the fortunate few who actually owned villas; the claim applies to the Pompeians, at any rate, if the evidence of the architecture and decor of their homes is anything to go by.

In the very extensive archeological literature on Pompeian houses,[1] however, this phenomenon has received scarcely any attention.[2] Scholars, of course, frequently make mention of the villa as a model for individual elements of architecture or decor, but to my knowledge the comprehensive taste that prevailed, particularly in the final decades of the city's existence, has never been analyzed in detail. Pompeian houses represent a unique historical source for answers to such questions of taste, allowing us to draw important conclusions about the values and aspirations of a large segment of the population in the early years of the Empire that emerge only sketchily from literary and epigraphic sources.

In a study such as this, the wealth of material is best illustrated through the use of significant individual examples, entailing references to many familiar paintings and objects. In each case, the choice was dictated by the relationship each example has in common with the overall context under investigation.

The Origins of the Roman Villa

The complex origins of the Roman villa have been little studied to date.[3] The villa represents far more than an architectural category, fascinating though its variety may be. In fact it is a key phenomenon in the adoption of Hellenistic culture by upper-class Romans. At the outset I would like to sketch in the background of this process.

When Rome expanded its rule into the western and eastern Mediterranean, Roman aristocrats, who in some respects had retained their traditional simple customs, were brought into direct contact with the opulent style of life in the Hellenistic world, particularly in the dwellings and habits of Eastern potentates. They began to desire lavish surroundings to match their sense of power and dominance. In Rome itself, however, old Republican traditions blocked or hindered open espousal and display of Hellenistic luxury. Isolated country estates offered an escape, so to speak, where aristocrats could spend their leisure time in a completely private sphere. And even Cato the censor recommended adding urban amenities to simple villas on agricultural estates, in order to make the necessary inspection visits more attractive for the proprietor (*De Agri Cultura* 4). Soon afterward Romans began building country retreats in the most beautiful parts of Campania and Latium, for purely recreational purposes.[4]

This new way of life called for opening the house to the landscape and including gardens and parks in the inhabited space. Early villas tended to be built on slopes with expansive and beautiful views.[5] After Pompey's campaign rid the area of pirates, sites directly on the coast came to be preferred (Plutarch, *Lucullus* 39). Even though the ruins of many such dwellings have been excavated and become well known, they can convey only a very inadequate notion of the great villas' size and rich decoration. The best impression of the sequence of rooms and their dimensions can be gained today from the Getty Museum in Malibu, California, a reconstruction of the relatively modest Villa of the Papyri in Herculaneum,[6] and from the great villa of Oplontis (Torre Annunziata).[7] The numerous depictions of villas in Pompeian wall frescos—often in imitation of a panel painting *(pinax)*—are a valuable source for seeing how the estates were embedded in the landscape.[8]

The intent to include gardens and the landscape in the inhabited space is a consequence of the Hellenistic experience of nature. Not infrequently public buildings in the agora or in sanctuaries had colonnades and terraces that served to frame vistas (as at Pergamum, Samothrace, Lindos, and Rhodes).[9] The latest example comes from a residence, albeit a royal one, namely, the Macedonian palace of Palatitsa, which a growing amount of evidence places in the late fourth century. There a veranda with a view across the plains has been documented.[10] Hellenistic building complexes may also have inspired the ground plans of large villas; for the *villa maritima* one might think of the royal palace quarter in Alexandria, for example, whereas the fortress-like villas of Marius, Pompey, and Caesar in Baiae (Tacitus, *Annals* 14.9.3; Seneca, *Epistles* 51.11), which dominate their sur-roundings, are reminiscent of the palace at Demetrias.[11] Although at the present time we can only speculate about influences in specific cases, the dominant role of large peristyles and the new use of atria (occasionally redecorated in the Greek manner) speak for themselves. Yet however great or small a role one ascribes to the influence of Hellenistic models on the development of the ground plans of early Roman villas, one thing is clear: the clever orientation of porticos, dining rooms, and bedrooms to take advantage of particular vistas shows that Roman aristocrats and their archi-tects consciously included nature and the landscape in their designs to enhance them and add a new dimension to the inhabitants' enjoyment. This takes the Hellenistic approach to an extreme.

Nature was included in another sense as well. The largest villas were often located on landed estates; in such cases, the owner had plenty of space to create sweeping parks and game enclosures, and thus live like a king.

For the imposing architectural forms of their interiors, the early villas once more probably owed most to Hellenistic courts, for there the owners' emphasis lay on creating magnificent displays. The real structural architecture of lavish Corinthian, tetrastyle, Egyptian, and Cyzicene reception rooms (*oeci:* Vitruvius VI 3.143)[12] was complemented by the architectural wall paintings of the second style.[13] These increased the effect with painted vistas showing imposing façades, palace courtyards, shrines, and luxurious parks of a royal character. Such paintings served not only to enlarge the actual space, but also to conjure up associations of magnificent surroundings. Characteristically, the owners showed little or no concern with making these vistas spatially logical or consistent in content. What mattered was to have a great variety of scenes, each one full of interesting detail. Small villas in particular often displayed the most disparate views next to one another in confined spaces. One of the best examples of this is to be found in a *cubiculum* (bedroom) of the villa at Boscoreale. Sanctuaries and sacred precincts occur with great frequency in these paintings, reflecting the religious character of gardens around the palaces of Hellenistic rulers.[14]

Hellenistic courts provided models for the furnishings of Roman villas as well. It is hardly accidental that Cicero accused Verres of trying to match the aspirant to the throne of Syria in this respect (*In Verrem* II 4.61ff.). Verres was hardly the exceptional figure Cicero made him out to be; he surpassed some of his rich friends only in the degree of his obsession and the extremes to which he was prepared to go to acquire objects he fancied.[15]

Congenial company was a requisite of villa life.[16] Cicero's letters offer us a picture of the great figures of Roman society visiting one another when the law courts were not in session, at their large estates in the hills near Tivoli or, above all, on the Bay of Naples, that "charming bowl" (*crater delicatus: Letters to Atticus* II 8.2) where they vied to outdo one another in the luxury of the accommodations and the banquets (Plutarch, *Cicero* 7). Of course, in order to enjoy the various landscapes and climates (Plutarch, *Lucullus* 39)—and also not to miss out on what others were doing—one needed to own several villas.[17] Cicero himself, who was not a particularly wealthy man but liked to keep abreast of developments, had no fewer than seven.[18]

POMPEII

For those wishing to occupy themselves with philosophical, historical, literary, or artistic matters, villas were more suitable than townhouses,[19] for at one's leisure, far from the press of business, it was possible to feel liberated from the official schizophrenic attitude toward Greek culture.[20] When Roman aristocrats conversed informally with philosophers and poets at their villas, and indulged in their own dilettante pursuits of art and literature, they were following the tradition of Hellenistic rulers, whose portraits they occasionally displayed in their colonnades next to the great Greek intellectuals. Cultural interests were deemed such an integral part of villa life that libraries and *pinacothecae* were standard amenities (Vitruvius VI 5.2), regardless of the owner's actual interests or preferences.[21] Petronius later had his satirical character Trimalchio, the self-made man, boast of the Greek and Latin works in his library (Petronius, *Satyrica* 48). It was fashionable to refer to colonnades or parts of the garden as the "gymnasium" or the "palaestra," or to name them specifically after famous sites of classical learning. Greek names were sometimes given even to lesser rooms (Varro, *Res rusticae* II 2). Collections of statuary and other decor increased the associations with classical culture, making the appellations of these rooms clear to all. The average villa owner, however, certainly did not go to the lengths Cicero did to make his surroundings match his own broad intellectual horizons; many owners were no doubt content to purchase the standard furnishings available on the market.[22] The memory of famous cities and tourist spots in the Greek world was cultivated by the names given to individual parts of the villa, along with the corresponding decoration. Hadrian's villa is the latest and richest example of this form of cultural reminiscence, a *Bildungslandschaft* ("educative landscape").[23] External similarities were not always required; any pond, watercourse, or stream could be transformed at will into one of the popular imitations of the Euripus, the strait between Euboea and Boeotia, or the Nile (Cicero, *On Laws* II 2), or a natural grotto such as the one in Sperlonga could be turned into the cave of Polyphemus.

In sum, the adoption of Greek culture by the Roman upper class manifests itself in the late Republican villa. The leisure *(otium)* associated with villas embraces a whole sphere of life in which architecture and decor were inseparably connected with certain styles, habits, and intellectual pursuits. The painted vistas must be seen in relation to furniture, other furnishings, the silver on the table, and last but not least the exquisite food served there. A herm of Aristotle in the peristyle, for instance, points beyond the specific locale and style of furnishings that may have been used; for one owner it might have served to stimulate or recall to mind a variety of educational experiences, while for another it merely demonstrated that he kept up with current fashions.

The experience of architecture and villa surroundings in connection with an extensive and multifaceted network of associations reflects the villa owners' new and ambivalent sense of identity. Their awareness of their own power and status demanded appropriately princely settings, yet at the same time the dominant Greek cultural tradition was present in every room, inspiring occupants not just to congratulate themselves on how educated they were, but also to continue learning, and to meditate on the past.

Naturally, the unbridled competition for offices, wealth, and prestige so characteristic of the late Republic had a noticeable effect in the area of domestic luxury. After the Social War, participation in an elite culture was open to a large class on the top rungs of the social ladder, including the prominent office-holding families of Italic cities and rich merchants as well as Roman aristocrats.[24] Their levels of affluence and education varied, but all felt the same need for self-promotion and display. Thus we find villas of the Republican era across a correspondingly broad spectrum, ranging from enormous complexes resembling little self-contained cities (Sallust, *Catiline* 12–13) to the compact villas just inside Pompeii's southern wall (compare fig. 71). In the first century B.C. such luxurious country estates—referred to euphemistically as "gardens" *(horti)*—had crept up to the old walls of Rome, and the lifestyle cultivated at country villas had become the norm among the upper classes in the city, too. Exploiting Rome's geography, the elite built themselves little urban villas with their own views on the Palatine and Aventine hills.[25]

The degree to which villas had come to epitomize wealth and luxury is revealed by an episode in the campaign of the tribune A. Gabinius against

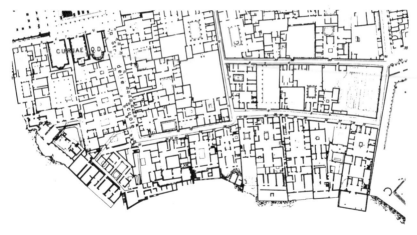

Figure 71   Terrace houses in the theater quarter, region VIII 2 (after Noack and Lehmann-Hartleben). The original atrium houses with an orientation toward the street were expanded in the course of the first century B.C. to provide a view across the plain to the sea.

Lucullus. To turn popular opinion against his opponent, Gabinius had a picture of Lucullus' famous villa at Tusculum shown from the rostra (Cicero, *Pro Sestio* 93). During proscriptions, possession of a beautiful villa could seal a man's doom (Plutarch, *Sulla* 31.4).

The example set by the wealthiest and most prestigious aristocratic families in the second century B.C., when they began to adopt Greek culture, had enormous influence in the later climate of competition, when everything the upper classes did was imitated. The phase of discriminating individual selection was thus followed swiftly by one in which the market offered standardized "Greek" house and decor plans suited to every pocketbook.

This cultural and historical setting explains some key features of Roman villas, such as the haphazard assembly of decorative elements, the frequent disregard of organic harmony and proportions, exaggeration in scale and motifs, and excessive use of expensive materials (or imitations of them). This is true not only for lesser villas; even the huge collection of bronze sculptures at the Villa of the Papyri in Herculaneum and the wall frescos at the recently excavated Villa of Oplontis (Torre Annunziata) display such features.[26] The lifestyle associated with the villa proves to have been a grand and vital mixture of Greek cultural elements that formed different amalgams in each house, depending on the temperament and education of its owner.

Two Forms of Living Space

The Samnite growers and merchants[27] in the area around Pompeii had learned about Greek homes and interior decor along with the Romans, either directly, through travel in the East along Roman trade routes, or indirectly, through gradual adoption of trends from Rome, the center of Hellenism in Italy from the second century.[28] In contrast to aristocrats in Rome itself, the Samnites had no traditions hostile to indulgence in luxury. There was nothing to prevent them from investing their new wealth in large townhouses. It is characteristic of the richest families in Pompeii that they clearly identified themselves not with middle-class Greeks, such as the merchants and traders who built houses on Delos, for example, but rather with aristocrats and their opulent residences. H. Lauter has offered convincing evidence of a resemblance between the largest of the early houses, the House of the Faun (VI 12), which occupies an entire *insula* measuring roughly 31,000 square feet, and the urban palaces of the Macedonian aristocracy excavated in Pella.[29] The Italic atrium is retained in reduced form, as in the early villas, but its original function as the central living space has usually been lost in Pompeian houses. In some instances the whole ground plan is dominated by peristyle gardens. The free combination of atria and peristyles in different sizes is also characteristic of large Pompeian houses. However, in contrast to the palaces of the nobility at Pella, which are even larger than the House of the Faun, the latter contained peristyles that were surrounded by only a few large rooms: the owner of the House of the Faun in fact required far less living space than a Macedonian prince. The second peristyle in his house, for example, had no function beyond creating an impression of grandeur.[30]

Thus the House of the Faun, although not derived from the villa, contains essential elements of villa architecture, such as peristyle gardens with fountains, extensive rooms with costly mosaics (for example, the exedra containing the Alexander mosaic), and even a small bath complex.[31] This elegant, completely inward-looking house provided its occupants with the Hellenistic sense of extensive space and shifting vistas through zones of shade and light in the successive peristyles, much like a villa.

The rooms in other great Pompeian houses built around 100 B.C. display even richer forms of Hellenistic interior design. The opulent living or dining rooms *(oeci)* were probably inspired by villas, that is to say, they were one step removed from Greece; the elaborate painted architectural vistas support this view.[32] In the Corinthian room *(oecus corinthicus)* of the House of the Labyrinth (VI 11.10; fig. 111b), for example, a wall painting showed a view of a palace courtyard with a small, round Hellenistic temple in the center.[33] Ptolemy IV once enjoyed a similar view—in actuality, not painted—from the Corinthian salon of his Nile ship, which was itself constructed as a floating palace.[34] The two-story arrangement of columns explodes the spatial dimensions of the Pompeian dining room: interior architecture originally intended for a large hall or banquet room was reproduced in such drastically reduced form that the real function of the room as a dining area was considerably restricted.[35]

In the second century B.C. the wealthy Samnite elite constructed their houses clustered together in the center of town, completely closed off from the landscape. After the Roman colony was founded and the city walls ceased to have any defensive function, however, affluent Pompeians in the first half of the first century began to build on the southern slopes of town, which offered a beautiful vista across the bay to the Sorrento Peninsula. The plan of the town shows that the sites on the southwestern slopes were especially sought after. It is here that the largest houses were built, not much smaller in total area than the House of the Faun (Insula Occidentalis 19–26; see figs. 30 and 31).[36] These complexes display the same orientation toward panoramic views as the villas outside the Herculaneum Gate. While the entry area remains connected with the street, the living area extends out to elaborate terraces on different levels, opening the house to the landscape. A present-day visitor can gain a sense of the size of different areas in these new "urban villas" from the portico of the Villa Imperiale next to the Marine Gate below the old museum (VIII 1).

More modest houses were added to and remodeled, spreading down the southwestern slopes toward the theater quarter (VIII 2; see fig. 71). K. Lehmann-Hartleben's study of these houses, based on Noack's notes and published in the 1930s, is a model analysis still of considerable interest for social historians today.[37] His research shows that the early first century B.C., the peak period of villa construction in Campania, was also the time when most of these houses were rebuilt as villas to take advantage of the view. Lehmann-Hartleben's drawings of them as they must have looked convey an impression of the sides facing the sea, with staggered porticos and balconies on different stories (fig. 72).[38] The extensive excavation and foundation work required for the additions suggests once again that the owners of these houses were well-to-do, but nonetheless they are clearly smaller in scale and less ambitious than the large villas on the western slopes. Although they could not compete with the type of villa that spread out into

Figure 72 Reconstruction of a terrace house in the theater quarter (after Noack and Lehmann-Hartleben). The architecture of the additions at the rear imitates the terraces and withdrawing rooms of Roman villas.

POMPEII

the landscape, these mini-villas nevertheless provided their occupants with an essential element of the new style, namely, a beautiful view.[39]

In a few houses in the town center we find renovations and additions dating from the late second and first centuries B.C., showing that here, too, the villa served as a model for cultivated living. They include such features as the bath complex and cryptoporticus in the House of the Cryptoporticus (I 6.2–4),[40] and the small bath complex and exedra with two apses in the peristyle of the House of Menander (I 10.4; fig. 111c).[41]

A Miniature Villa in the Town

As we have seen, the imitation of villa architecture in Pompeii in the first century B.C. was mainly limited to exploitation of sites with the best views on the surrounding slopes and isolated cases of luxurious interior renovation in the grandest houses in town. In the last decades of Pompeii's existence, however, the effect of villas and the decor and lifestyle associated with them spread to a very broad segment of the town's inhabitants. We find many different elements of villa architecture and decor in houses restored or remodeled[42] after the earthquake of A.D. 62,[43] although some of these features might not be recognizable at first glance as having been derived from this source.

As a rule the renovation or remodeling work was limited to the houses' gardens and peristyles. Let us begin by looking at a well-known house in the Via dell'Abbondanza (II 2.2; figs. 73 and 74) named after Loreius Tiburtinus, a fictional character.[44] The sloping lot covers almost an entire *insula,* more than two-thirds of which is taken up by the garden. When viewed from the bottom of the garden, the living quarters appear mounted on a platform reminiscent of a *basis villae* (foundation wall; Cicero, *Letters to Quintus* 3.1.5). The structure is an instance of renovation in an older, medium-sized atrium house, which in the final period of the town's existence had a tavern occupying the front section. After the earthquake the house underwent extensive remodeling, most of it concentrated on the garden and the rooms adjacent to it. This work was not yet completed at the time of the eruption.[45]

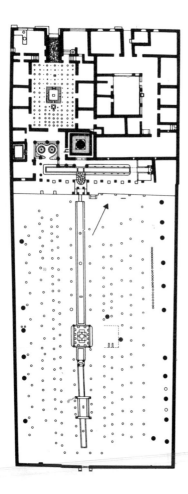

Figure 73 Plan of the "miniature villa" in the Via dell'Abbondanza (II 2.5). The garden of the relatively small atrium house was redesigned to imitate the grounds of a villa in miniature, with pergolas, fountains, porticos, and so on.

The main room or *tablinum* behind the atrium was replaced by a kind of truncated peristyle, leading to a large, almost square dining room (*triclinium*, with three couches) on the left, and to two smaller rooms, one containing a shrine (*sacellum*), to the right. The plaster-covered columns of varying diameters stand at irregular intervals determined by the adjoining rooms. This truncated peristyle connects—but also collides and competes—with two further rows of roof supports, bringing utter confusion into the ground plan. A regular porch (*pronaos*) in front of the shrine has two columns between piers with engaged columns. The pier on the garden side is flush with a row of sturdy brick supports for the more than sixty-five-

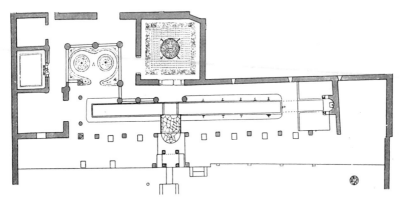

Figure 74 Plan of the terrace at the "miniature villa." Several elements of villa architecture are combined here in such a small space that they partly overlap.

foot-long pergola extending across the rear of the house (fig. 75). The pergola shades a small ornamental canal, only about three feet wide, which runs along the axis of the shrine; it is spanned by two bridge-like structures and ends in a *biclinium* (dining area with two couches) with a fountain at the other end of the terrace.[46] We know from the collection of statues found here that the ensemble re-created in miniature the type of water-course *(euripus* or *nilus)* already popular in the villas of Cicero's era.[47] A surviving example on a monumental scale is the Canopus at Hadrian's Villa.[48]

A total of five elements derived from villa architecture and reduced to miniature size are thus combined and compressed, sometimes one inside the other, onto a terrace that is only twenty-two feet wide: (1) the trun-cated peristyle with the *triclinium* and day rooms *(diaetae);* (2) the shrine; (3) an aedicula to Artemis behind the fountain and above a *nymphaeum* (dis-cussed below); (4) the watercourse associated with the pergola; and (5) the *biclinium* with the fountain-aedicula (fig. 76). All five are components of the expansive type of villa that opened up the house to the surrounding views and landscape and had become popular by the mid–first century B.C. at the latest.[49] The villas of Pliny the Younger are good examples of this type, as are some of the excavated houses in Campania and those depicted in wall paintings at Pompeii.[50] On the terrace of this particular house,

Figure 75 An old photograph of the terrace at the "miniature villa," showing the collection of garden statuettes (now missing) lined up along the watercourse *(euripus)* spanned by a little bridge. The whole terrace is surmounted by a pergola stretching from a small shrine to Isis at one end to two masonry couches at the other. The paths are too narrow to permit two people to stroll side by side or in groups, an integral feature of the Roman villa.

however, the various components are squeezed into such a small space that two people cannot walk next to each other under the pergola without running up against a fountain, little bridge, pillar, or post at every turn, or tripping over the statuettes in the grass. A portion of the architecture has lost its original function.

The sense of constriction is increased by the excess of decorative painting and statuary. In the large *triclinium* there are two friezes above a wide panel painted to look like expensive multicolored marble incrustations.[51] A raised curtain painted in at the top of the picture is intended to heighten the illusion that the friezes are valuable Greek originals, and it gives the room the aura of a *pinacotheca* (fig. 77). The upper frieze (approximately two and a half feet tall) shows the labors of Hercules—probably following a Hellenistic model; the smaller frieze below contains scenes from the *Iliad*.

POMPEII

This room, distinguished from others in the house by its very elaborate decoration, offered occupants a view through the Artemis aedicula and the lower part of the garden to the city and mountains beyond (plate 9). The *sacellum,* set off by two columns between piers with engaged columns, is also painted elaborately in the fourth style, this time depicting a wall. The figure of a priest of Isis on one of the inner walls and the diptych of Diana and Actaeon on the façade (along with the Egyptian terracottas found in the little garden in front of it) all suggest that the shrine was devoted to Isis/Diana. Her image probably stood in the niche on the back wall.[52] The architect had to dispense with a gable for the shrine, however, since it would have interfered with the pergola.

Small shrines, sometimes located in a garden, were quite common at

Figure 76 Masonry couches at the "miniature villa," with a "view" over the *euripus.* In the foreground one can see the slanted surfaces on which mattresses were placed. Behind them are an aedicula and two frescos with mythological motifs designed to look like framed paintings.

Figure 77 Wall painting in the reception room opening onto the terrace at the "miniature villa" (after Spinazzola; compare fig. 74). This *triclinium* was the most opulently decorated room in the house, and the owner could display his taste and learning in the frescos. The lower part of the wall imitates costly multicolored marble; it is surmounted by a frieze with scenes from Homer's *Iliad*. The main zone depicts the labors of Hercules. A painted raised "curtain" above these scenes is intended to suggest that they are valuable "paintings" that need to be protected from light, just as in some modern museum displays.

larger villas; one need only think of the "Amaltheion" that Cicero so admired on the country estate of his friend Atticus in Epirus.[53] In the house we are concerned with here, the shrine was used as a kind of gazebo, from which one could look out the door toward the terrace and the watercourse, or through the window on the other side toward the lower part of the garden.

The statuary along the "banks" of the watercourse was adapted to the small format of the architecture.[54] The muses mounted on bases (fig. 78) are of normal statuette size—although there was apparently never a complete set—but the various figures in a seated or recumbent position and scattered about the grass are definitely miniatures (see fig. 75). They are

POMPEII

also associated with a variety of different themes. The recumbent river god and the Sphinx are part of the usual watercourse decor; the herms were usually placed along garden paths. The little seated satyr belongs in a Dionysiac park, while the two sets of figures depicting hounds and quarry belong in a *paradeisos* (preserve for wild animals). The statuettes of the muses themselves belong in a *museion* (museum) of the type so frequently found at villas.[55] To this collection we should also add the little satyr in the

Figure 78   Statuettes of two muses that stood along the *euripus* at the "miniature villa." They are copies of two statuettes from a famous Hellenistic group of all nine muses. As in the case of copies of paintings, such decorative statuary was intended to awaken associations of "Greek sculpture" and "art collections" in visitors.

pose of Atlas supporting the fountain, and there must have been a statue of Artemis/Diana intended as a cult image for the aedicula, since its gable bears a portrait of her (fig. 79).

In addition to these numerous sculptures there was no lack of wall paintings. The fountain aedicula, lined with pumice stone, is flanked by two large mythological scenes, one depicting Pyramus and Thisbe and the other a seated Narcissus (plates 10.1 and 10.2).[56] An artist named Lucius proudly signed his name to them, although their quality is undistinguished. These frescos in the manner of panel paintings call to mind the passionate art enthusiast and collector Hortensius, who at his villa Tusculum made a shrine *(aedem fecit in Tusculano suo)* for Kydias' painting of the Argonauts (Pliny, *Natural History* 35.130). And there was still more: the entire length of the wall (over twenty-three feet long) to which the pergola was attached was covered with frescos depicting a variety of scenes—Orpheus charming the beasts, a hunting scene in a *paradeisos,* and Venus hovering above a shell on the sea.[57] These paintings and the statues of the muses on elaborate plinths were intended to give the airy pergola the flair of a lavish portico.

All this decoration and elaboration, however, represents only the upper level of the plan. From the terrace a flight of steps led down to the garden some three feet below, which measured approximately 180 by 95 feet. It was enclosed by a high wall and, like the terrace, bisected by a type of *euripus.* Pergolas and rows of shrubs and trees were arranged parallel to it. Similar paths ran along the brook on Varro's estate near Casinum (*Rustica* 3.9). The remains of a marble table indicate that there was a round seating area, and a recumbent hermaphrodite must be the sole remnant of a group of sculptures placed in the borders.[58] As mentioned above, the *euripus* ran not down the middle of the garden but rather along the axis of the large dining room decorated to look like a *pinacotheca.* This canal was interrupted or spanned by several structures, and was also linked to the terrace pergola by a hybrid two-story construction, the upper portion of which we have already encountered as the Artemis aedicula. The lower story contained a miniature *nymphaeum*[59] with a fountain connected to two water spouts: a mask of Oceanus and an Eros with masks sitting above the steps down which the water flowed.[60] There were also fish painted on the upper basin.

Figure 79 Aedicula with a *nymphaeum* in the garden of the "miniature villa." The aedicula, which was accessible from the garden terrace, originally contained a statue of Artemis, the goddess of hunting. The goddess was placed there in part as an allusion to the hunting preserves connected with great landed estates. The lower story of the structure, accessible only from the garden, is fitted out as a miniature *nymphaeum*. Such a composite, multipurpose structure is characteristic of the overall architectural and decorative style of the house.

The Domestic Arts in Pompeii

To one side of the fountain Actaeon is shown watching Diana bathing, and as if all these were not enough mythological trimmings for one small fountain, on the narrow sides the artist added some small framed landscape scenes with shrines to Apollo and Diana. The room itself measures only about 9.7 by 3.2 feet, and with the fountain in it does not have space for even one couch.

At about the same time that this house was being remodeled, an owner of one of the terrace houses in the theater quarter (VIII 2.28) was building a *nymphaeum* on his property, in the form of a grotto just large enough to use and carefully placed to take advantage of the mountain view across the bay.[61] Thus, the borrowing of elements from villa architecture proceeded in steps, and models for some features could already be found within the town.

To return to the miniature villa: the more than 160-foot-long watercourse below the *nymphaeum* is divided into several sections. The water flowed first into a channel approximately 80 feet long with three jets of water spaced along it. Below this was a large pool lined with marble containing a square fountain in the middle, with steps on each side for the water to flow over and bases for twelve statuettes or vases around the edges (fig. 80).[62] Only 12 feet further on the channel is spanned by a decorative baldachin bridge, much too small for actual use. Below the bridge the watercourse then shifts direction slightly to point toward the gate in the wall at the bottom of the garden. Clearly there was already a path up to the house from this gate, and the watercourse was designed to run alongside it. By continuing his watercourse down this far, the owner also enabled passers-by to catch a glimpse of it through the gate. The lower channel below the canopied bridge is interrupted once, too, by a wider basin. Both it and the square pool higher up were probably shaded by arbors.

Thus the watercourse actually consisted of a series of separate pools of varying sizes connected by overflow troughs.[63] Once this has been recognized, the function of the pools becomes clear: they were fish ponds of the type popular at large seaside villas. Most likely they were painted in distinctive colors.[64] Varro and Cicero mention both the profits that could be made by raising fish and also the grotesque excesses to which some of these

Figure 80 Marble fountain in the lower part of the watercourse at the "miniature villa" (compare fig. 74). This fountain interrupts the flow of the *euripus* and is too large in proportion to the other elements of the garden architecture. In the background a further aedicula is visible.

piscinarii were led by their passion for their favorite breeds.[65] Fish ponds represent another feature of villa life imported from the courts of Eastern potentates.[66]

In the case of the miniature villa in Pompeii, the clever arrangement of the fish ponds gave the owner a second watercourse! As we have seen, this excess was characteristic of the villa owner. We find the same principle of overkill with some miniaturized elements of villa architecture in the garden as on the terrace; in both places too many separate structures have been crammed into too small a space. Instead of distributing the decorative features around his garden—as the villa model would have suggested and his good-sized lot allowed—he first turned his fish ponds into a *euripus* and then added the *nymphaeum,* marble fountain, baldachin bridge, and pergola. His method did have one advantage, of course: it enabled him to survey the full complement of architectural splendors in his garden from

The Domestic Arts in Pompeii

the door of his dining room. Furthermore, the perspective made the entire layout seem larger than it was (although perhaps too much emphasis has been placed on such effects in recent studies).[67]

In this manner a country villa was re-created in miniature in Pompeii during the last decade of the town's existence. Perspectives actually intended for wider views are cunningly inverted—architectural elements borrowed from villas in the country or by the seaside are crammed together into a Walt Disney world. The elaborate garden is wholly out of proportion to the quite modest size of the actual living quarters; the remodeled section of the house is also characterized by a poor sense of proportion and a low level of artistic skill, in contrast to the "Neronian" wall paintings in the fourth style in the older section. The owner, eager to imitate the lavish world of villas he so clearly admired, preferred quantity over quality.

A Courtyard with a Large Marble Fountain

The miniature villa with the features discussed above is by no means unique to Pompeii; it is only the richest and best preserved example of a widespread taste in domestic environments. Proof that it is no exception is offered by another instance of remodeling in the last decades before the eruption, in a smaller house with a far less advantageous site that appears to have been acquired in bits and pieces. The House of Apolline, located directly in front of the town wall (VI 7.23; fig. 81), was excavated between 1810 and 1840 and, like most of the houses discussed here, is in deplorable condition today.[68] The marble fittings discovered by the excavators have now virtually all disappeared, and if the team had not jotted down at least a few notes we would not be able to interpret the site today. A small atrium without *alae* (wings) leads to the main room, which in turn gives onto a narrow courtyard almost filled by an elaborate marble fountain similar to the one above the lower watercourse at the miniature villa (fig. 82).[69] Around the fountain the excavators found double herms and marble vases decorated with reliefs; we should picture these arranged on the surrounding ledge. The scale of the whole ensemble was completely out of propor-

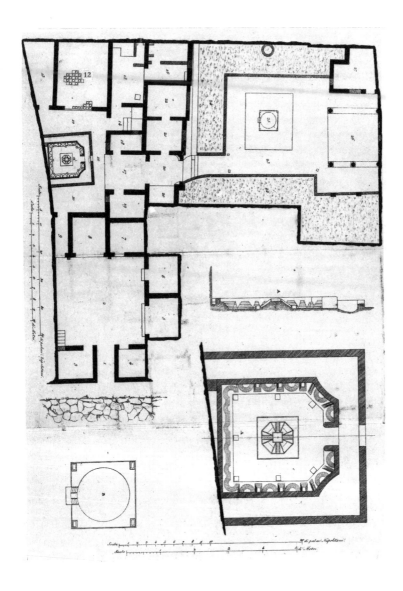

Figure 81 Ground plans of the House of Apolline (VI 7.23) and its two fountains. This is another case of a modest atrium house combined with a large garden, some of which was bought up and added to the property at a later date. The very large reception room at the western end (12) opens onto a court with a large fountain. The actual villa garden was enclosed by porticos and contained a *nymphaeum* and enclosures with couches.

The Domestic Arts in Pompeii 157

Figure 82 Marble fountain in the courtyard of the House of Apolline. The fountain was originally decorated with double herms and marble vases carved in relief. The wall at the left was decorated with a large painting depicting a villa garden.

tion to the small courtyard (off which lay a rather large dining room, the kitchen area, and two further rooms in addition to the main room). On the wall behind the fountain the owner commissioned a large painting of a garden scene, no doubt to give the illusion of greater space. Its depictions of a park with many different kinds of birds, a fish pond, and a statue of Diana were no doubt intended to call up associations with villas.[70]

The real garden, as opposed to a painted one, is located on a plot of ground to the north that was probably acquired after the house was built and measures only a little over 3,000 square feet. Passing through what used to be two rooms in between, one comes down a few steps into the garden, which was enclosed by a kind of terrace on three sides. The terrace, which varies in width, lies about three and a half feet above the ground and hides a cistern beneath it on the western side. The paintings and mosaic on the walls behind make it seem likely that an arbor ran the entire length of the terrace.[71] The "sunken" garden had a second marble fountain in the middle, this time round in shape, but like the courtyard fountain it was surrounded by marble herms. The figure in the center and a flight of marble steps face to the north, where on the far wall three intersecting structures were squeezed together (fig. 83).[72] The middle structure was open on each side, where two columns and one engaged column supported an architrave. The line of its roof is still visible in the garden wall. The wall contained three niches for statuettes; both it and the outside wall of the *cubiculum* to the left had a pumice-stone facing above and marble veneer below, while the columns were decorated with mosaic and shells in elaborate patterns. All these features indicate that the structure was conceived as a kind of open *nymphaeum*.[73] The few fragments found at the site suggest that it was lavishly fitted with marble, herms, and the like.

To the right of the *nymphaeum* two posts show that there was probably a deck under a pergola. To the left a door led to a "summer room" lit by two windows and containing two alcoves for beds. This charming room is a modest imitation of the tiny garden houses described by Pliny the

Figure 83   View of the *nymphaeum* and garden rooms at the House of Apolline (from an old photograph). The roof line of the *nymphaeum* can still be discerned in the bricks of the rear wall, whose three niches were designed to hold statues.

Younger, located in the grounds of large villas away from the bustle of the main house (*Epistles* II 17.20).[74] It seems odd today that a space designed for withdrawal and contemplation should have walls covered with large perspective paintings of stage sets. These are so out of proportion to the room's actual dimensions that the overall effect is disorienting.[75] Just as in the case of the miniature villa, allusions to Greek culture formed part of the standard decorative repertoire. The same applies to two statues of philosophers, now lost, which stood somewhere in the garden.

A Garden as Sanctuary

The discrepancy between a householder's ambitions and the actual possibilities for realizing them is particularly striking in cases where the goal was to re-create the atmosphere of a grand and sprawling villa in a very confined space. Another owner of a medium-sized house achieved a far better effect by limiting his borrowing to a single villa element, but then incorporating it into his property on a lavish scale. The foundations of the House of the Black Anchor (VI 10.7; figs. 84, 85, and 112c)[76] date back to the first century B.C. At the time of the eruption the owner was in the process of constructing a very grand two-story peristyle to replace the former garden or courtyard at the bottom of the property; work on it was not quite complete (fig. 85 and plate 11.1). The builder had found a clever way to compensate for the difficult sloping terrain. The garden, only about 1,000 square feet in size, lay off a small atrium and down a staircase; originally it was enclosed by a vaulted arcade. Later the arched openings of this arcade were bricked up, creating a cryptoporticus. This was then lined with a series of stout square pillars, two stories high. In the upper story these pillars alternate with brick columns on the two long sides, whereas on the southern side, at the far end from the house, there are only round columns. The two phases of construction appear to have followed one another in quick succession.[77]

It is evident that the owner did not have the services of a first-rate builder or architect, but he clearly wished the final impression to be very imposing: pedestals reveal that the blind arches were to contain statues or

160

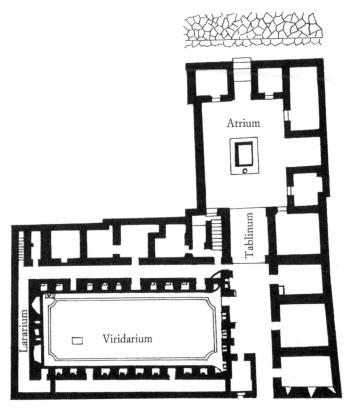

Figure 84 Ground plan of the House of the Black Anchor (VI 10.7; after W. Zahn). Here the small atrium house has a garden in the form of a sanctuary. The reception rooms lay to the north with the best view of the garden architecture.

ornamental vases. The southern end is designed as an ornate façade, with two oversized fountain aediculae[78] flanking an aedicula to Fortuna or Venus Pompeiana framed by stucco rudders.[79] This central aedicula, which is proportionately too small, gives the garden the character of a sacred precinct. When the occupants and their guests gathered in the only large room of the house, this is the façade that lay in view on the far side of the peristyle. Owing to the modest size of the house, however, this *triclinium* was situated above the stable and the rear gate, where carts pulled up to load and unload. Comparably grand peristyles would have been found only in opulent villas like Hadrian's. The evidence of landscape paintings in the

Figure 85 View of the garden at the House of the Black Anchor. The garden peristyle was two stories high, with a cryptoporticus behind the pillars on the ground floor. Only a few remnants of the masonry and plaster columns on the second story remain.

second style shows that the combination of a two-story peristyle with a shrine was once again originally derived from Hellenistic palace court-yards.[80] By contrast, the "sunken" peristyle and the orientation of the garden to make it visible from one main room in the house can be considered typical elements of villa architecture.[81] The Villa of Diomedes, only a few minutes away outside the Herculaneum Gate, may serve as an example; its garden area as a whole is comparable, although the design is far simpler.[82]

The enormous size of the garden peristyle in relation to the rest of the House of the Black Anchor, with its few modestly proportioned rooms, shows how much significance the owner attached to the impression made on guests, and the expense he was prepared to incur to this end.

As in the case of the tiny villa on the Via dell'Abbondanza, the miniaturization of some of the borrowed architectural elements robs them of

te 9 View from the door of the main reception room of the "miniature villa" in the Via
l'Abbondanza (compare fig. 73). The various elements of the garden architecture are strung like
:ads" along the observer's line of vision, producing a more impressive view than if they had been
ttered throughout the garden.

Plates 10.1 and 10.2

Two "framed" paintings from the wall behind the *biclinium* on the terrace of the "miniature villa." They show Narcissus admiring his own reflection and the unhappy lovers Pyramis and Thisbe. The paintings are reminiscent of the Greek panel paintings that hung in the villas of the wealthy and, despite their modest quality, are intended to evoke the flair of literacy and aesthetic culture.

e 11.1   View of the garden at the House of the Black Anchor (VI 10.7). The garden of this small ...se was designed as a miniature sanctuary with elaborate architecture (compare fig. 84).

te 11.2   Painting of frescos at the House of Sallust (VI 2.4; watercolor by F. Morelli, 1809). These ...scos discovered by excavators on the back wall of the garden have now been completely destroyed ...ough exposure. They extended the relatively small garden by opening a vista into a park inhabited ...rare birds. The painted architecture suggests an open hall decorated with festive garlands.

Plate 12   Garden at the House of the Small Fountain (VI 8.23–24). Note the current state of the large landscape painting next to the fountain (compare fig. 104 for the original effect).

Plate 13   Fountain at the House of the Large Fountain (VI 8.22), completely covered with mosaic decoration. The water splashed down the marble steps into the pool. Originally there was a theatrical mask on each side of the fountain. The missing mask depicted a tragic hero; the mask on the right shows Hercules wearing a lion's skin over his head. Both were intended as allusions to "classical education."

Plate 16 Fresco imitation of a small panel painting in the *tablinum* of the House of M. Lucretiu
Fronto (V 4.11), showing a seaside villa. Depictions of luxurious villas are ubiquitous in Pompeia
houses as symbols of a moneyed and cultivated lifestyle. Constant allusion to the world of the ver
rich remained characteristic of domestic decoration in Pompeii throughout the imperial era.

Plate 14.1 Painting of a fresco at the House of the Amazons, now destroyed (VI 2.14; watercol
by F. Morelli, 1812). The illusionist character of the fresco is strengthened by the vista of island vill
in the background. In the foreground between palm trees is an aedicula with statues of the Egyptia
deities Isis and Osiris.

Plate 14.2 Fresco from the House of Orpheus (VI 14.20), from a lithograph of 1875 that distor
the colors. The view of a game park is combined here with the myth of Orpheus, who enchante
wild beasts with his playing. The insets on either side are views of villa gardens. The juxtaposition o
different motifs in one picture is characteristic of late Pompeian wall painting. Here again the aim wa
not so much to create a surprising illusion as to evoke many different associations in the mind of th
viewer.

Plate 15 Fresco in the garden of the House of Venus (II 3.3). View of a park with a marble statu
of Mars or a military hero.

their function: the cryptoporticus was not much more than three feet wide, and even before its completion the northeast wing had been subdivided to make storage space.

A Parlor Overlooking Diana's Sacred Grove

Another form of garden shrine was achieved at far less expense by a wine merchant at the edifice known as the House of the Moralist (III 4.2; figs. 86 and 87).[83] These premises housed both a dwelling and a shop and had been made by joining two older houses together; behind them the owner turned the courtyard of just over 3,000 square feet into a kind of grove sacred to Diana (*lucus* or *silva Dianae*). From the surviving roots of young trees all oriented around a central point we may deduce that the garden had been laid out not long before. Between the roots the excavators found a statuette of Diana and a bronze incense burner (see fig. 87).[84] Wall paintings and literary sources tell us that such "woods" (*silvae*) and "sacred groves" were often created on the grounds of large villas.[85] Our wine merchant also appears not to have been the only Pompeian to lay out a miniature woods for himself.[86] The rear of the house was opened toward the garden by means of large windows and balconies (fig. 88). The dining room on the ground floor where the wine merchant entertained his guests has been preserved. The familiar maxims and adages painted on the walls illuminate the moral principles and rules of conduct he wished to impress upon them.[87]

Each of the houses discussed above imitated villa style in a different way. Of course the selection of architectural components depended on the possibilities offered by the lot, the existing structure, and the owner's means. Both owners and "architects" may have been inspired by the great variety of models in the immediate vicinity. When one considers the limited space available, the amount of inventiveness they displayed seems astonishing. And while the majority of homeowners had too little space to add new architectural elements, this by no means forced them to forgo the aura of a villa altogether.

Porticos and peristyles both represented elements of a villa, and their

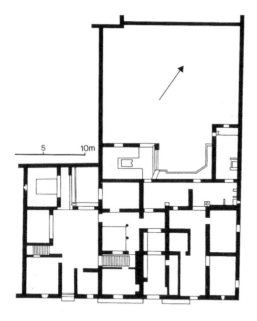

Figures 86–87 Ground plan of the House of the Moralist (III 4.3) and view of its garden after excavation. This building owned by a wine merchant combined a residence and a shop. Two originally separate atrium houses were combined, and a garden was added in the style of a sanctuary. The remains of tree roots suggest how it was once planted. The small shrine was presumably dedicated to Diana, for a statue of the goddess was found in the garden.

Figure 88 Reconstruction of the House of the Moralist (after Spinazzola). The reception rooms had large windows overlooking the garden. In most houses such a view did not exist in reality, and had to be supplied by a wall painting. The wine merchant who owned this house could at least offer his guests views of real trees, like the owner of a villa.

combination with the appropriate types of room brought out even more of the villa character in the later houses. In this connection a large and imposing dining room played a key role, and we find one in virtually all the houses discussed thus far.[88] Whenever possible, the dining room was placed so as to afford a view of the garden. In the grand houses these *triclinia* became real dining halls; the House of Menander possessed the largest in Pompeii, dating from the Augustan era (I 10.4; fig. 111c). After A.D. 62 formal dining rooms on this scale were created in the House of Pansa (VI 6.1), the House of Castor and Pollux (VI 9.6–7), the complex of dwellings joined together that is known as the House of the Citharist (I 4.5), and the House of the Golden Cupids (VI 16.7).[89]

But summer rooms and exedrae also had porticos added to them. The "truncated peristyle" added to the venerable House of Sallust in the late era is a particularly good example (VI 2.4; fig. 89).[90] The two porticos at the sides end in two small rooms that are open to the small peristyle garden through disproportionately large windows. In the room to the right two pictures of lovers from mythology of the type frequently found in bedrooms can still be made out, despite the damage incurred during the Second World War.[91] Clearly these little rooms represent imitations of the day room located on the grounds of large villas at points with especially fine views, of the type to which Pliny the Younger liked to withdraw (*Epistles* 2.17.20ff.). Two comparable rooms on the scale appropriate to a small suburban villa can be found in a Flavian house at the edge of Herculaneum overlooking the sea.[92] By contrast, the only view from the day room of the House of Sallust was of the flower beds in the little garden and a wall decorated with a mythical landscape (fig. 90 and plate 11.2). This visual opening is flanked by two pedestals with marble statues of nymphs.[93] In this manner a villa garden was created with an architectural element largely stripped of its function, for the little rooms hardly offered much accommodation. Perhaps they soon found a use as tool sheds or storerooms. A

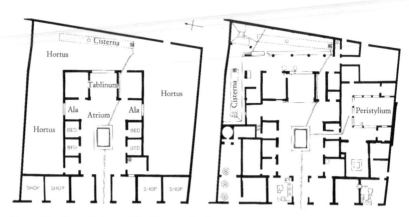

Figure 89 Ground plans of the House of Sallust before and after renovation (VI 2.4; after J. B. Ward-Perkins). This example shows how the orientation of the house was shifted away from the interior and toward the garden. The house was embellished with various elements of villa architecture.

Figure 90 View of the fresco on the garden wall in the "peristyle court" built on to the House of Sallust. The painted "marble" statues create an illusionist transition from the little garden to the mythical landscape in the large fresco, which depicts Actaeon being torn apart by hounds after surprising Artemis at her bath. In the wall to the right a window of one of the two small garden rooms *(diaetae)* is visible.

The Domestic Arts in Pompeii

similarly placed room in the House of the Epigrams (V 1.18) shows that the arrangement was not unique.

Large windows were used to provide other rooms with a "vista" of a portico, or a tiny courtyard with a miniature garden or paintings of a garden.[94] We should also view in this same context the numerous *tablina* (main rooms) separated from garden courtyards only by a low wall, which thus turned them into "garden rooms" reminiscent of country villas.[95] This phenomenon, too, is most frequently associated with houses from the late period.

Gardens Filled with Sculptures

For the owner of a house with a sizable peristyle courtyard, the obvious next step was to plant a garden in it. Some of these gardens acquired an aura of luxury through the use of expensive plants and decorative objects such as fountains, sculptures, and other marble pieces. Once overloaded with such fixtures, they were intended more to be looked at than actually used. There can be little doubt that their design imitated the gardens and parks around villas, some notion of which is conveyed both by paintings and by literary sources. The rather strange fashion of filling in the spaces between columns with walls waist-high, which we encounter in a number of late houses, seems to be a feature of this imitation. The side of the wall facing the garden is always painted with more scenes of beautiful gardens, thereby expanding the associations suggested by the garden itself (fig. 91).[96] Since almost nothing remains of the original gardens at large villas, the imitations in Pompeii and Herculaneum represent modest but nevertheless useful sources of information about them.

The House of the Golden Cupids (VI 16.7; fig. 92), which has been described in detail in an excellent recent publication, offers a particularly important example of a lavish peristyle garden.[97] Despite its small size, it is reached by a broad staircase from the raised portico on its western side. The façade of the "Rhodian peristyle" (Vitruvius 6.7.3) is rendered even more impressive by the combination of a flight of steps and a gable (figs. 93 and 94).[98] It creates a grand front for the dining room behind it, but a front completely out of proportion to the small garden. In the middle of this

Figure 91 Peristyle in the House of Menander (I 10.4). In later houses the spaces between the columns were filled in with a low wall that was decorated with paintings on the side toward the garden. They were designed to heighten the effect of the garden as an independent element in the decor of the house. Such gardens were meant to be looked at rather than walked in.

garden there is a pool, as we so often find; this one is very large and once had a statue on its rim. It was encircled by a tiny path dotted with sculptures and marble pieces.

Dominating the borders of the garden is a series of tall pillars distributed more or less evenly, surmounted by heads and reliefs of Dionysiac masks (see fig. 94). Most of these herms are representations of Dionysus or one of the figures associated with him, including Eros; there is also one of Jupiter Ammon. The large and small masks *(oscilla)* hanging between the columns further emphasize the basic Dionysiac theme, but other types of decoration frequently found at villas are present as well. A tiny statue of Omphale next to the steps serves as a "reference" to Greek art and mythology. The reliefs set into the eastern wall, including a Hellenistic votive relief, are perhaps intended to imitate an art collection.[99] A herm with an almost unrecognizable portrait of Menander alludes to the gallery of great Greeks—statesmen, philosophers, and poets—so popular with villa owners.[100] The sculptures in the grass around the garden fountain included various animals and a group of hounds pursuing a boar; we may consider these "excerpts" from a "marble *paradeisos*," so to speak. There is even an allusion to the theme of the palaestra. Thus in addition to the dominant Dionysiac theme we find all the major categories of villa statuary represented, even if by only a single piece in some cases.[101] Smaller marble objects stood among all these statues as well, including tables, the fountain basin, the remains of a candelabrum, and a sundial.

Just like the architectural elements, this entire diversified inventory of objects had to be squeezed into an extremely small space; as a result, while the position of some could be chosen for effect, that of others was purely arbitrary.[102] In this instance, too, the ruling principle appears to have been simply to display a great quantity of objects, and discrepancies with regard both to size and to artistic quality were no more disturbing to the owner of the house than to the owner of the collection at the miniature villa in the Via dell'Abbondanza (see figs. 75 and 78). The owner of the House of the Golden Cupids apparently had no scruples about converting a Dionysus herm into a fountain with a water spout or taking some expensive tall

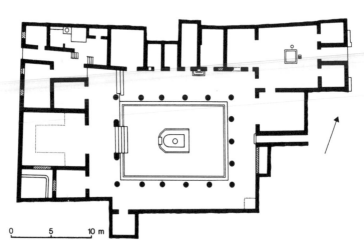

Figure 92 Ground plan of the House of the Golden Cupids (VI 16.7). After being "Hellenized," Roman houses ceased to be oriented around their central atrium, the heart of the inward-looking design. In many houses such as this one the atrium has been abandoned entirely in favor of a peristyle. All the reception rooms here are oriented toward the garden, which has been fitted out according to its new function as a central area of communication, in imitation of villa life.

170

Figures 93–94 Two views of the little villa garden at the House of the Golden Cupids. A broad set of steps leads down from the hall of the "Rhodian" peristyle into the garden. Marble herms, reliefs, and other sculptures were placed along the paths, and round masks *(oscilla)* hung between the columns. The garden decor was intended to evoke or even create a little sanctuary of Dionysus.

The Domestic Arts in Pompeii

pilasters decorated with fine reliefs—clearly intended for a larger garden—and sawing them in half to make supports for two more reliefs.[103]

We observed a sculpture collection with a similar mixture of themes crammed into a tiny space along the watercourse of the miniature villa in the Via dell'Abbondanza. Whereas there the statues of the Muses along the little watercourse may have created a nice effect on their tall pedestals, the sphinx and the young "Heracles" with a goose look distinctly incongruous among the Dionysiac herms. Taken together they can be understood only as an attempt to imitate larger garden layouts with sculptures haphazardly assembled from a variety of the available thematic sets.[104] A statue that may have had a meaningful connection with its setting at a large villa could sink to the level of mere decoration when it was miniaturized and placed in the context of a small Pompeian peristyle, where its main function was simply to add a touch of class. Often enough the selection of objects for the collection may have been dictated by what local merchants happened to have on hand. I believe it would not be difficult to collect material demonstrating that, during the period just before the eruption, studios specializing in production for this market existed in Campania and elsewhere.[105] Yet, despite the random nature of much of the repertoire of imitation villa statuary in Pompeii, it appears that certain thematic preferences did exist. It is striking, for example, that, in contrast to villa decor, portraits of famous Greeks, including rulers, and statues related to themes from myth and the palaestra occur only rarely and in the most selective detail.[106] On the other hand, if a Pompeian house has any sculptures at all, one will almost certainly find groups of animals and works related to Dionysiac themes.

The most beautiful and unified collection of sculptures on these two themes so popular with Pompeians is to be found in the little garden in the house of M. Lucretius (IX 3.5; figs. 95–97), although it still contains a few inconsistencies.[107] The garden is located in a central courtyard and is visible from the main rooms of the house. Sculptures of all kinds of animals appear to be lying or ambling around a circular basin in the middle, including an Egyptian ibis; the basin itself also has two dolphins with cupids. Between the animals one finds a young satyr shading his eyes from the sun as if looking for something, while another is attempting to remove a thorn from the foot of his friend Pan. A goat standing on its hind legs sniffs at yet

Figures 95–96 Ground plan and view of the reconstructed garden at the House of M. Lucretius (IX 3.5; from an old photograph). In this instance the small garden area lies at the junction between the front portion of the house and the raised wing at the rear. All the main reception rooms had a view of the garden, which was filled with sculptures related to Dionysiac themes in a manner reminiscent of a nativity scene. The figures were placed around a cascade and a circular pool.

The Domestic Arts in Pompeii

Figure 97　View from the *tablinum* toward the elevated garden at the House of M. Lucretius (IX 3.5; from an old photograph).

another satyr, frozen in the form of a herm. The juxtaposition of "lifelike" and more stylized works, especially the herm, suggests that this must have been one of the chief charms of late Hellenistic garden sculpture in Roman villas.

The central position of the statuary garden in the house of M. Lucretius allowed for one further special effect. Thanks to the rising terrain, the garden behind the main room lay on a higher level than the street, so that to a guest arriving at the front door it must have appeared like a stage set. Thus the most expensive decorative feature of the house was made to serve the function of impressing visitors.[108]

Dining under the Stars

Even in smaller houses, especially ones with no peristyle, two features we have already encountered were extremely popular, namely, outdoor tables with two or three masonry couches (*bi-* or *triclinia*) shaded by a pergola, and fountains. Both had the advantage of retaining their pleasure-giving function even in the smallest garden, and of evoking something of the aura of a villa even in the humblest surroundings, either alone or in combination.

Almost all of the many stone or brick couches (usually shaded by pergolas) that we find in Pompeian gardens seem to date from the last decades of the city's existence.[109] Although they are found in even the simplest houses, they are not a universal feature of life in a Mediterranean climate, as we might tend to assume. This is shown not only by their late appearance on the scene, but also by their close connection with other villa features, especially fountains and wall paintings alluding to villa life. The House of Sallust referred to above (VI 2.4; see figs. 89 and 90) shows how both fountains and frescos were used in a vacant area behind the main room and portico to give even a "left-over" corner of the property a touch of villa flair. The dining area was built at the narrowest point. A faded illusionist painting on the outer wall expanded the real architecture of the old portico into a kind of peristyle, where between painted pillars vistas of a park filled with rare birds can be glimpsed (figs. 98 and 99).[110] In three of these spaces fountain basins were depicted in niches surrounded by lattices. A fourth fountain beside the dining area contained real running water, creating a further link between reality and illusion.[111]

In region I a man by the name of Cornelius Tages, a member of a family of freedmen who probably made his money as a wine merchant, bought up no fewer than four separate houses and joined them into a single complex (I 7.11; figs. 100 and 101).[112] Since he had no grand atrium, he admitted visitors through a special door (no. 12) directly into the garden and the adjacent rooms, which constituted the showpiece of the house. A masonry base for two dining couches (p) stood in the center of his irregularly shaped garden, with four columns supporting a pergola above it. Behind this structure stood an aedicula containing a fountain with a cascade, adorned by a bronze nymph.[113] The water collected between the couches and may have given the occupants the feeling of reclining on a small island (see fig. 101)—a possibility that could actually be realized by owners of villas like the one at Sperlonga. The illusion was heightened by the paintings on the couches' bases, which depicted scenes along the Nile with the most varied inventory of architecture and actors and ran the thematic gamut from the

POMPEII

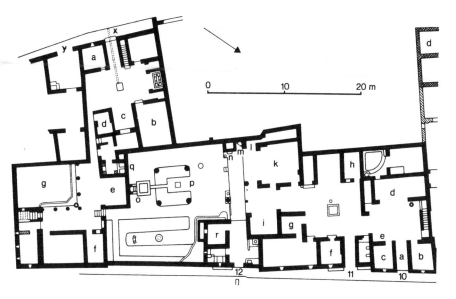

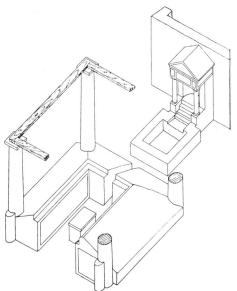

Figures 100–101 Ground plan and reconstruction of the garden architecture, fountain, and masonry couches at the House of the Ephebe (I 7.10–12). The presumed owner of the house, a freedman named Cornelius Tages, bought up several small houses and designed the garden to be the main reception area. The couches were connected with a fountain, and the desired illusion—that one was lying beside a little stream or on an island—was heightened by corresponding paintings.

Figures 98–99 Portico and garden behind the House of Sallust (VI 2.4). The drawings show them after excavation in the early nineteenth century (Gell) and in a reconstruction (Overbeck). The wall paintings and architecture complement one another in the effort to create the richest possible evocation of a villa atmosphere. The masonry couches were placed at the narrow end of the garden, in order to maximize the "vista" (compare fig. 90).

The Domestic Arts in Pompeii

177

sacred to the erotic. Nearby stood the pride of the owner's art collection: the well-known classicizing bronze statue of a youth *(ephebos)* on a round base holding a candelabrum in the form of a vine (now in the Museo Nazionale in Naples; fig. 102).[114] A dinner guest might well have felt transported to the distant banks of the Nile or one of the luxurious retreats on the shores of the Euripus. In a manner of speaking, the valuable bronze statue anchored such reveries in the wealth of the present.

The "Egyptian" picnic spot was surrounded by imitations of villas and their parks. Immediately to the left, four small marble herms framed a corner of the garden[115] that probably contained three marble statuettes: a figure of Pan carrying a basket of flowers and treading on a krupezion (an instrument resembling a castanet, worked by the foot), a recumbent satyr, and a doe nursing her young.[116] Surely we would not go far wrong if we were to imagine the wall at the back to have been painted with a view of a park. Opposite this "mythological" garden populated by figures associated with Dionysus, and to one side of the fountain aedicula, stood a painting of a game park. In a moment I shall return to this motif and its connection with villas, but first it should be noted that once again we find the characteristic painted and gilded statues of heroes or Mars standing on tall pedestals in front of the picture frame.[117] We have already encountered similar painted statues at the House of Sallust (see fig. 90), and they are frequently found next to vistas of gardens or game parks. They replace real marble in the decoration of the garden and are typical of late wall frescos in garden environments (compare figs. 90 and 106).[118] In this case the painted statues

Figure 102   Bronze statue of a servant holding a candelabrum found in the garden at the House of the Ephebe (Naples, Museo Nazionale). It originally functioned as a "dumb waiter," standing on a round base next to the couches under a pergola in the garden and adding grace to the whole ensemble. The classic lines emphasized the artistic character of the work and recalled works of art in large villas. The statue was produced by an eclectic workshop in the Augustan era. For the body the sculptor used a classical statue of a boy in the style of Polyclitus, but he placed a girl's head of early classical type on top of it. The homoerotic charm of this "dumb waiter" may well have constituted no small part of the viewers' enjoyment of this quite valuable work of art, which probably belonged to the collection of a wealthy villa owner before its arrival at the rather modest home of Cornelius Tages.

connect the *paradeisos* image with a richly furnished villa interior. The dining room (k), which affords a view of the garden, represents at least an imitation of such an interior, with its costly paving of different kinds of marble known as *opus sectile* ("cut work"),[119] gilded decoration, and Alexandrian fittings.[120]

Steps lead down from the garden containing the fountain and dining area to the peristyle (g) of a small house (I 7.19) that was apparently a later acquisition joined to the owner's original property. Its entrance lies on the opposite side of the *insula*. Here the truncated peristyle is "completed" by painted Ionic columns, with a scene of a park between them, similar to the scene in the House of Sallust. This time the niches separated from the park by a lattice contain a statue of Venus in addition to a marble vase and a fountain basin.[121] Finally, from the tiny main room (c) of this extended house a large "window" looked out onto what may well have been the smallest *trompe l'oeil* garden in Pompeii: in the narrow light-well traces of the typical painted garden lattice and trees were found.

Two aspects of Cornelius Tages' house are of particular significance here: first, the direct juxtaposition of costly decorative objects and fittings (such as the bronze statue and the floor in *opus sectile*) on the one hand and the very limited living space on the other; and second, the characteristic framing of genuine villa elements with painted vistas and illusions. The *paradeisoi* and banks of the Nile, which remained out of reach in reality, lay probably no further away in the owners' imaginations than villa gardens, parts of which could be imported into their actual living space in the form of outdoor dining areas, fountains, and garden sculptures.

In both its technical design and its artistic decor the fountain dining room at the House of the Ephebe (or House of Cornelius Tages) is modeled after similar arrangements at villas or large gardens *(horti)* in Rome. Proof of this is offered by the far grander grotto dining room in the "clubhouse" of Julia Felix (II 4).[122] There water also collected in a pool between the couches after trickling over a set of steps. And like Cornelius Tages' guests, the diners looked at a Nilotic landscape. In the House of Julia Felix, the dining area is on a true villa scale. Rakob has pointed out the frequency with which this type is found, and its connection with fountains or grotto dining areas in the imperial Domus Aurea and Transitoria. In such a case as this it becomes apparent how we should picture the adoption of various villa elements as occurring in a number of steps. We have already encountered a similar example in the rooms with a view of the sea at the little terrace villa in Herculaneum.

If space was too limited to place free-standing masonry couches around a fountain, many Pompeians could at least manage to have a fountain, which might, for instance, be set into the back wall of the house. Along with permanent dining areas, this seems to have been a feature characteristic of late houses in particular.[123] The most impressive solution is found in connection with a "truncated portico" at the House of the Bull (V 1.7).[124] It appears to have been inspired by façades of imposing urban buildings. The "frames" of such fountains are usually decorated with mosaics and occur in a wide variety of sizes. But even the largest of them give the impression of miniature imitations of the great garden fountains in luxurious parks. Not too long ago the remains of one were found on the Quirinal.[125]

Two of the most beautiful mosaic fountains in Pompeii are located next door to each other, in the houses named after them: the House of the Large Fountain (VI 8.22; figs. 105, 113b, and plate 13) and the House of the Little Fountain (VI 8.23; fig. 104 and plate 12).[126] Each fountain is aligned with the axis of the front door, like a costly piece of furniture, so that the gaze of someone entering the house would fall on it immediately.

From their setting amid painted illusions of villas and landscapes symbolizing felicity we can deduce that these fountains also stood for everything implied by the word "villa." Another good example of this is provided by the tiny House of the Grand Duke (VII 4.56).[127] This dwelling stands on a narrow, poorly proportioned strip of land and consists of only a few rooms grouped around a cramped atrium. Here, too, the little fountain stands in the courtyard in the line of sight from the entrance. Three columns and one engaged column attempt to give the space at least the aura of a peristyle (fig. 103). The *tablinum* has been made into a "garden room" by widening the opening, and another room has been given a large window opening onto the same "villa area." The pool in front of the fountain is divided into

Figure 103 View of the fountain and a portion of the "colonnade" at the House of the Grand Duke (VII 4.56). If a small house offered scant space for an extensive garden, a fountain with elaborate mosaics surrounded by landscape paintings often provided the only reminiscence of villa life.

three parts; once again they must be ponds for different types of fish, as in the garden of the miniature villa. However, the most important aspect of the decor in determining the overall impression is the walls, which were covered with paintings of ornamental topiary gardens. Above a waist-high lattice-work fence are scenes of a park landscape. Here, too, a small marble table helps to bridge the transition between illusion and reality.

At another very small dwelling with a similarly irregular ground plan, the House of the Bear (VII 2.45; fig. 113f), the courtyard was designed in much the same way, with a room opening onto it.[128] No space remained for columns, but as if to make up for this the fountain was given broader proportions and the walls even richer decoration. A fountain supported by a nymph once stood in front of the garden vista (as at the House of Sallust), and the water spout was shaped like a sphinx. Farther up was a group of animals, and above the fountain Venus and her shell. These large-format wall paintings merit separate discussion.

POMPEII

Figure 104 Reconstruction of the portico with fountain and frescos at the House of the Small Fountain (VI 8.23–24; after Gell, 1832). During the last few decades before Pompeii's destruction, a fashion developed for large paintings that often covered the entire surface of the garden walls. Not unlike travel posters of exotic places in our own day, they suggested lush gardens, rare plants, birds, and costly marble sculptures, or game preserves such as actually existed on great estates. Such garden paintings became highly popular again in Europe in the neoclassical period. In the reconstructions of the early nineteenth century, the modest spaces take on a festive character.

Figure 105 Depiction of the garden, with fountain and paintings, at the House of the Large Fountain after excavation (VI 8.22; after Gell, 1832).

The Domestic Arts in Pompeii

Large Pictures for Small Dreams

Large frescos of the type we first encountered at the House of the Ephebe are common in Pompeii. Usually covering entire walls, they repeat the same motifs again and again, in apparently arbitrary combinations: gardens lavishly adorned with pergolas, fountains, and sculpture; landscape vistas containing seaside or country villas; *paradeisoi* and the type of scene known as a "sacred" or Nilotic landscape.[129] Particularly good examples are found at the House of the Small Fountain (see fig. 104, plate 12) and the House of the Large Fountain (see fig. 105, plate 13).[130]

Such large-format pictures have been found mainly in small houses where there were few or no architectural or other decorative villa elements. They served as the most inexpensive form of villa imitation. It is once again striking that they were used almost exclusively in the garden area, either alone or to decorate part of a peristyle.

In the medium-sized House of Romulus and Remus (VII 7.10) the wall at the end of the small "truncated peristyle" was covered with a fresco of a park filled with sculptures, including the already familiar fountains supported by nymphs, a statue of Silenus, and a large marble bowl (fig. 106).[131] In the adjoining portico the wall opens up with a view of a tranquil game park. At the tiny House of the Ceii (I 6.15; see fig. 113e), however, there was no room for even the most shrunken peristyle in the courtyard, so the walls were decorated with large frescos of a Nilotic landscape, an "Egyptianizing" sacred landscape, and a large *paradeisos* against a dark background.[132] In the foreground we once again find painted marble fountains, here in the form of shallow basins supported by sphinxes. The courtyard is surrounded by a narrow channel that was intended to catch and hold rainwater and was apparently treated as a miniature watercourse. One sees how directly the paintings were connected with the real, three-dimensional garden from the fact that a painted marble fountain nymph appears to be pouring painted water into the actual channel below. A tiny room in a corner of the courtyard was conceived as a garden room with a large window opening onto this miniature villa idyll, but in the last year of the town's history it served as a storeroom.

Figure 106 Paintings in the truncated peristyle at the House of Romulus and Remus (VIII 7.10): on the left a villa garden with a marble urn and rare animals; on the right a "game preserve" with a collection of exotic animals that could hardly have existed peaceably together in reality. The juxtaposition of the pictures shows that the aim was not to create a visual illusion, but rather to conjure up attractive scenes of prestigious and desirable ideals.

Large wall frescos first made their appearance in Pompeii during the reign of Vespasian, as Schefold has correctly observed. In the wall designs of the second to fourth styles, comparable subjects were depicted only in friezes or painted panels *(pinakes)*. Nevertheless, however well large-scale pictures fit our notions of Flavian style, they are not an innovation of this period. From Vitruvius we know that in his time and even earlier long promenades *(ambulationes)* were painted with scenes of harbors, hills, coastlines, rivers, springs, straits, shrines, woods, mountains, herds of animals, and shepherds (7.5.2); in the era of Augustus it was chiefly a certain Ludius (?), according to Pliny, who added to this Hellenistic repertoire new themes typically associated with villa life: "villas and porticos, gardens, groves, woods, hills, fish ponds, watercourses, rivers, shores, and whatever else one might wish, such as various ramblers or travelers, on sea or land, mounted on donkeys or riding in carriages to their country houses, also fishermen, bird catchers, hunters, and vintners" (*Natural History* 35.116).

The text reveals that Ludius painted not panel pictures but frescos.[133] Such depictions were first placed in actual villa porticos as "vistas," and later imitated in more modest villas and houses as replacements "for a very beautiful view at minimal cost" (ibid., 35.117). The fact that a contemporary of Pompeian householders mentions heightening the beauty of real living conditions, *qualia quis optaret,* is worth stressing. The late appearance of such pictures in Pompeii can be explained on the one hand by the unusually extensive building activity after the earthquake of A.D. 62, and on the other hand by the dominant style, which took its orientation from villa decor. It demonstrates once more how problematic it can be to deduce "stylistic developments" from derivative works of art.

In a number of cases the "vista" character of wall paintings becomes evident from the way they are framed. We have already encountered examples of this at the House of the Ephebe, the House of the Small Fountain, and the House of the Ceii. Another example is offered by a wall in the House of the Amazons (VI 2.14; plate 14.1).[134] Behind a marble balustrade, on which we once again find perched the birds that were such a popular motif, lie a park and in the distance the sea, with no fewer than three island villas. An aedicula with Egyptian divinities in the foreground recalls the character of gardens as sacred groves. The whole vista is framed by garlands of ivy.

The connection between depictions of *paradeisoi* and villa life is documented by accounts of game parks on great country estates.[135] Having originated in the Orient, they arrived in Italy by way of the royal game parks of Hellenistic potentates.[136] Polybius mentions that the young Scipio indulged his passion for hunting in the royal game preserves of Macedonia (32.15). A marble relief in the Vatican that may once have formed part of a balustrade gives an indication of what the transition between a Roman garden and a *paradeisos* may have looked like (fig. 107).[137] The wild animals' range is demarcated by a fence interrupted at intervals by overgrown niches that hold statues of cupids and are flanked on top by herms. Thanks to a

Figure 107 A marble relief in the Museo Chiaramonti at the Vatican. It shows a view of a game preserve from a villa garden. Herms with busts of famous Greeks numbered among the standard decorative objects in villa gardens and represented the values of classical education and culture. Such herms were a great rarity, however, in the middle-class houses of Pompeii.

passage in Varro, even the painting of a mythologically enhanced *paradeisos* in the House of Orpheus (VI 14.20; plate 14.2) can be directly linked with the villa life of great families; it is immaterial whether the Pompeian house-holder was himself aware of such a connection or not.[138] Varro reports that Q. Hortensius Hortalis was in the habit of entertaining guests in the game preserve at his villa at Ostia, where a slave dressed up as Orpheus would attract the animals with his music.[139] The huge fresco at Pompeii covers the entire rear wall of the little house and, like the fountains mentioned above, is visible to visitors arriving at the front door. Here, too, two garden vistas—from grotto *nymphaea*—cement links with the villa.

Clearly, a picture placed to catch the eye in this manner is more striking than a smaller one forming part of a series in a long *ambulatio*. The artistic quality of such large frescos, designed to awaken associations rather like a travel poster, is correspondingly crude. The same stereotyped animals oc-cur repeatedly, obviously copied from models in the painters' pattern books and assembled *ad hoc,* with the result that their juxtaposition often appears senseless or absurd.[140] One finds, for instance, hunting scenes and groups of animals in combat next to assemblages of peaceful creatures, as in the rocky landscape at the House of the Ancient Hunt (VII 4.48; fig. 108).[141] It is likely that patrons' ideas of a *paradeisos* were not infrequently overlaid with associations from the world of gladiatorial and animal com-bat. Characteristically, the "Gladiators' Barracks" in Pompeii (V 5.3) con-tains a *paradeisos* fresco.[142]

The scenes painted on the bases of the masonry couches at the House of

Figure 108   Nineteenth-century sketch of a painting at the House of the Hunt (VII 4.48; by an anonymous artist). The idea of game preserves at great villas was frequently conflated with scenes of hunting and animal combat in the arena.

the Ephebe are an important clue to understanding the vistas of exotic landscapes, especially views of Egypt. We know this clue is accurate because the same theme occurs in large-format frescos almost exclusively in connection with fountains or watercourses. We saw that *euripi* were also included among the themes of villa paintings by Ludius, and at the miniature villa in the Via dell'Abbondanza we encountered a reflection or derivative of a villa watercourse in combination with a collection of Egyptian statuary. The main point of such Egyptian landscapes appears to be to increase the sense of well-being already created by reminiscences of villa life such as architecture, furnishings, and decor; to these cues suggesting felicity the paintings added allusions to famous landscapes associated with the good life. It is no accident that Seneca equates Baiae and Canopus in epitomizing the height of luxury—and decadence (*Epistles* 51.3).[143]

The large-format paintings of bucolic, mythological, and sacred landscapes must no doubt have served the same purpose. They would also provide inviting locales to which the owner's thoughts could stray as he enjoyed his little garden. Once again the world of royalty offers a comparison. After Nero had created a game park and acres of bucolic landscape around his Golden House (Domus Aurea), he said that he was "at last beginning to be housed like a human being."[144]

The Pompeians who renovated their houses after the earthquake typically attached little or no importance to creating a logical architectural context for the large-format vistas they had painted on their walls; indeed, they often dispensed with even the suggestion of a frame that would have brought the painting into some relation with the room in which it was located. The spatial relationships between paintings in a room was apparently also a matter of indifference: it did not matter whether they existed side by side, one above the other, or in any particular order. What counted was size—namely, as large and conspicuous as possible—and the quantity of associative motifs. The aim was to render as realistically as possible the objects and settings the owner wished to have conjured up.

A typical example of this can be found in the *nymphaeum* at the House of the Centenarian (IX 8.6; fig. 109).[145] The lower part of the wall, which has a stripe all the way around it, is presented as a garden balustrade hung with ivy; at its foot are various birds and lizards. Above it, however, one finds ponds containing a rich assortment of fish, while to the sides there are garden scenes with the now familiar fountain bases supported by sphinxes.[146] Finally, the wall at the entrance and the door at the end are covered with scenes of game parks, even though in the middle of the latter there is a real fountain, painted to look as if it were built of rare marble. The water runs down a flight of marble steps into a large basin. The link between architecture and painted decor in this room is once again the world of the luxury villa and its gardens. Each separate motif recalls a different aspect of this world, but as a whole the room is—to our modern eyes—a grotesque potpourri. Here it becomes obvious that the owners of such a retreat were interested first and foremost in having a great variety of images to help them pretend they had been transported to the world of their imagining. We can only conclude that they must have had mental

Figure 109 *Nymphaeum* in the garden at the House of the Centenary (IX 8.6). The paintings surrounding the fountain have no "realistic" association whatsoever. It is characteristic, for example, that the depiction of a fish pond is placed directly above a garden scene. This indicates that such paintings were "read" in quite arbitrary succession, corresponding to their function as evocations of a whole series of different associations.

powers of association that allowed them to overlook striking contradictions in their immediate surroundings!

We now come to the wall paintings in the principal reception rooms of important houses modernized in the town's final decades. Pompeians began borrowing their wall decor schemes from the homes of the aristocracy in Rome in the first century B.C. In both cities subdivision of space by means of architectural elements and landscape vistas remained very popular all the way down to the fourth style, at least in the more important rooms. But although later walls may have a more unified character, their vistas and glimpses of fancifully imagined architecture still lent them a dimension of unreality. The original inspiration behind them, namely, the grandiose architecture of royal palaces, continued to play a role here, too, even if the homeowners were no longer aware of the source.

In the very last houses, however, we find that one element has come to the fore with a very specific connection to villa life: the designs that Schefold has so convincingly described as imitation *pinacothecae*.[147] As is well known, impressive examples from the reign of Vespasian can be found in the freedmen's dwelling at the House of the Vettii (VI 15.1; fig. 110)[148]—which also contains an important example of villa imitation in the form of a "sculpture garden"—and at the House of the Tragic Poet (VI 8.3).[149] Comparative analysis has demonstrated the degree to which the selection of "pictures" for these "galleries" was determined by the standard pattern books available to the painters.[150] The Pompeians' overfondness for this type of decor and their tendency to turn even the tiniest room into a *pinacotheca* are familiar to every visitor to the site. Their increased ambitions in this regard are accompanied by a decline in the quality of the older architectural form of wall decoration. We can observe this in a number of

Figure 110 Reception room with wall paintings in the fourth style (ca. A.D. 60–70) at the House of the Vettii (VI 15.1). The large-format mythological pictures were intended to provide evidence of the owner's education and at the same time recall actual *pinacothecae* containing original Greek paintings.

details in the very last wall paintings. A room in the House of the Vettii contains a good example: a frieze with a fish motif that is far too large in proportion to the other elements of the design.[151] The families that commissioned such work had a preference for realistic depictions of certain motifs, but they also liked regular "wallpaper" patterns in strong contrasting colors.[152] These qualities can be directly linked with the "framed" giant frescos in the gardens and understood as elements of the new style.

It is difficult to avoid overemphasizing the importance of Pompeian painting because it is so well preserved. This is true not only with respect to its quality—especially in the late houses and in connection with its figured compositions—and the information it provides on lost masterworks of Greek panel paintings, but also for what it reveals about the function and meaning of the world it depicts within the overall context of Neronian and Flavian culture and the Pompeians' daily lives. As in the case of the sculptures and decorated fountains in their gardens, the owners' principal aim in decorating their walls must have been to achieve as grand and impressive an effect as possible. The late wall paintings thus represent a phenomenon similar to the painted vistas in the second style at nearby villas. If we regard Pompeian wall paintings of the last two decades, at least, as one element of a derivative domestic taste acquired at second and third hand from aristocratic neighbors, then we will take a more skeptical view of claims for them as direct expressions of profound learning and piety. But this is a broad and complex field of inquiry better addressed elsewhere.

Domestic Taste and Cultural Identity

The examples of Pompeian architecture we have looked at thus far have ranged from the many-faceted miniature villa and houses incorporating one or more villa elements to architectural "garden furniture," collections of decorative statuary, and finally to large-scale wall paintings and *pinacothecae*. In this survey architecture has been treated more extensively than other elements because it made the greatest demands on owners in terms of expense, planning, and *engagement*. Here we can be sure it is not a question of decor adopted simply because it happened to be in fashion. Anyone undertaking the various forms of construction considered here must have had a particular set of ideas in mind. The fact that a close connection exists between the buildings themselves and the other decorative elements enabled me to include the latter in this analysis, thereby expanding its scope and increasing the amount of information to be drawn from the evidence.

The resulting picture is unambiguous: although the owners of these houses made use of different forms—and achieved differing degrees of success—they all shared the same aim, namely, to create the illusion of a villa. They all envisaged their ideal as a world of luxury. And everywhere we find the same characteristic taste, derived from models that have been heaped one upon the other and jumbled together until the sense of their original meaning and function is largely lost. It is the taste of a broad class of comfortable to well-to-do Pompeians who took their orientation entirely from the values and style of the very rich and imitated them as their pocketbooks allowed.

This becomes apparent when we compare the ground plans of the most important houses we have discussed. The most interesting and "original" architectural forms of villa imitation are to be found in houses of medium size (figs. 112a–e). They enclose much less space than the great Hellenistic houses of the Samnite elite and the largest houses of the first century B.C., such as the Insula Occidentalis or the House of Menander (fig. 111c). The miniature villa in the Via dell'Abbondanza (fig. 112a) falls into this category along with the Houses of Apolline, the Black Anchor, the Ephebe, the Moralist, and the Golden Cupids. Its sole advantage over similar houses lies in the large size of its garden—and in this connection we should not forget that perhaps prices for lots were lower in this less thickly populated quarter. The dimensions of the rooms in these medium-sized houses are quite comparable as well. Their owners clearly belonged to a well-to-do "middle class," which seems to have been particularly keen on adopting the kind of taste oriented toward villa imitation.

The same style also predominates in some smaller houses, however, including some of the very smallest, which frequently consist of not much more than several small rooms off a cramped atrium, with a courtyard only a few yards square. Sometimes, but not always, a few elements of a portico,

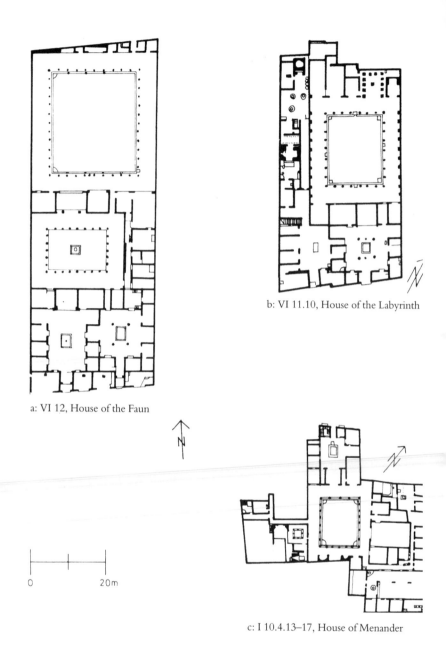

a: VI 12, House of the Faun

b: VI 11.10, House of the Labyrinth

c: I 10.4.13–17, House of Menander

0   20m

Figure 111a–c   Comparative ground plans I

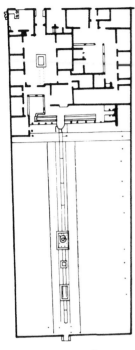

b: VI 7.23, House of Apolline

a: II 2.5, House of Loreius
Tiburtinus

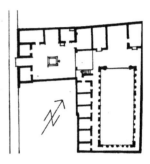

c: VI 10.7, House of the Black
Anchor, upper story

d: III 4.3, House of the
Moralist

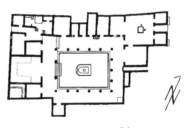

e: VI 16.7, House of the
Golden Cupids

Figure 112a–e   Comparative ground plans II

a: IX 3 + 24, House of M. Lucretius

b: VI 8.22, House of the Large Fountain

c: I 7.10–12.19, House of the Ephebe

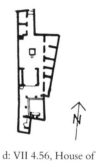

d: VII 4.56, House of the Grand Duke of Tuscany

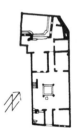

e: I 6.15, House of the Ceii

f: VII 2.45, House of the Bear

Figure 113a–f Comparative ground plans III

reduced in size, can be found in such courtyards. We have encountered examples of this type in the houses of the Grand Duke, the Ceii, and the Bear (fig. 113a–f). Thanks to the characteristics described above, the new style could be realized in almost every type of space and could fit virtually every pocketbook. Since the owners of the smallest houses had to limit themselves to wall decoration for the most part, the manifestations of the new taste appear more stereotypical and less varied than in the houses that could accommodate villa elements in the architecture.

At the same time the new style spread even into the large older houses. We saw examples of this at the House of the Centenarian (see fig. 109) and the House of Sallust (see fig. 90). Yet here—apart from the occasional fountain, *piscina,* or large *triclinium*—the absence of larger elements is striking; we meet with the clearest manifestations of the new taste in the wall paintings in individual rooms.[153] Some of the old Samnite *domus* like the House of the Faun have virtually nothing in the new style, and here and there old paintings appear to have been carefully repaired. This does not invalidate the general argument, however, since we must take into account that as a rule the owners of small and medium-sized houses put much more effort into rebuilding after the earthquake than the great families did. This difference may well be due to the fact that the lesser property-holders earned their living in Pompeii and thus stayed on after the earthquake, whereas those few very rich families still in residence probably moved away (cf. Seneca *Nat. Quest.* VI 1.1).[154] Thus, unfortunately, we are not in a position to say much about their domestic taste.

The picture assembled here matches the results Castrén obtained from his study of the town council *(ordo)* in Pompeii. He concluded that the composition of the council and the social class of other office-holders showed signs of shifting in the Claudian period, shifts that became manifest in the years between the earthquake and the destruction of the city. In those years political influence was achieved by large numbers of Pompeians whose families had been either unknown earlier or not represented in the council for decades. Simultaneously, the names of those families who had been able to maintain their hold on both political and social leadership from the early Augustan period down to Claudian times disappear. Castrén observes, "The rise of the new families and of the descendants of freedmen is a proof of a gradual replacement of the landed aristocracy in the administration of the municipalities, a development that becomes visible already during the reign of Claudius."[155] In Pompeii (as in other Italic cities) many members of the new plutocracy were descended from freedmen. As the city gradually recovered, builders, brokers, traders, and craftsmen became the people in demand; the economic and social situation must have favored members of this group more in Pompeii than elsewhere, and no doubt some of the owners of the medium-sized, freshly renovated houses discussed here numbered among them.[156] We have come across several homes built or renovated by owners who apparently had made their money in commerce or a trade, some of them in a relatively short time. The best example was the House of Cornelius Tages, named after a man who appears to have bought up the properties next to his original small house one after the other and connected them (see figs. 100 and 101).[157]

Membership on the town council cannot be documented for any owners of the houses we have discussed. But even if they failed to advance to such a position, they surely numbered among the leaders in the town's economic life, and worked closely with council members, as the wax tablets of Caecilius Iucundus demonstrate.[158] And although these families may not have succeeded in placing one of their members on the council, they shared the same aspirations as the families who did; this is demonstrated by the grave of the young aedile Vestorius Priscus, who died while in office (probably in A.D. 75/76).[159] On his tomb his family placed depictions of the deceased that showed him in his role as an official and recalled the gladiatorial games he had sponsored, but—characteristically—they also added paintings of the grand entrance to his house, his fine collection of silverware, a luxurious garden, and a *paradeisos*.[160]

In a recent study Henrik Mouritsen, using a new method, has reached results different from Castrén's; Mouritsen believes that the old families continued to set the tone in the political order and social life of the town even in the late period. Such conclusions have in principle little effect on my thoughts concerning domestic taste. What I have been able to show with my examples is a specific way of creating private living space that is found above all in medium-sized houses. It would be entirely mistaken, however, to connect this taste with a particular social stratum definable in terms of legal or economic status. People with very small dwellings may have had the same taste as those with larger homes, but lacked the physical space in which to express it. Regarding the spread of the new style among the elite, Fausto Zevi suggests that, for the period following the founding of the colony, a group of families continued to reside in their old houses with walls decorated in the first style and rejected any notion of altering the style in which their forebears had lived. In fact it is striking how many owners of relatively large old houses, including those with paintings in the second style, did *not* introduce miniaturized elements from villa architecture or large, poster-like landscape paintings into their homes.[161]

We see many inhabitants of late Pompeii captivated by thoughts of the luxury in which the Roman upper classes lived, however, and full of desires to imitate it. The garden architecture, "sacred" groves, fountains and picnic spots, *pinacothecae,* painted sculptures, landscape vistas and *paradeisoi,* the costly materials and imitations of them—all these testify to a need to participate in some form of luxurious villa life. The residential sphere is dominated by architectural or artistic imitations of a world with which, as a rule, the occupants had no direct links at all through their own traditions or experience. And very few of them could have gained access to this world of Greek culture and literature through education. Almost nothing in their homes reflects their own everyday world or religious ties and beliefs, apart from the household shrines to the Lares, and these tend to seem unconnected to the rest of their surroundings. On all sides we find the same elements repeated in the decor; the choice of fresco motifs is so limited and repetitious as to be depressing.

All the same, the architectural elements in particular reflect the love and attention people lavished on their little imitation villas, and the importance of this decorative vocabulary in their daily lives. It is significant that the Pompeians were not satisfied with imaginary painted scenes; they needed to come into contact with some three-dimensional, *physical* re-creation of a villa. There can be no doubt that this reflected splendor somehow made them happier, enhancing their lives. This heightened quality of life was not internalized but designed to impress visitors and passers-by. The aim was to demonstrate that one had arrived, that one could afford the very best—or at least a picture of it.

If these considerations point in the right direction, then they must of necessity affect our understanding of late Pompeian culture. It becomes impossible to interpret the gardens and tiny courtyards of Pompeii as touching reflections of the old Italic sense of nature; nor could one conclude from the architecture and painting that the last inhabitants were imbued with religious piety and a deep appreciation for Greek education and culture.[162] On the contrary, the late houses must be seen as evidence of the materialistic values that dominated Roman society in the early Empire.

We lack firm archeological evidence that would tell us how widespread this domestic style was in Italy. Pompeii itself happened to lie in a landscape dotted with villas that could provide direct inspiration. The house lots also tended to be larger than in many other towns, giving the Pompeians more room to renovate and add on to their dwellings as fashions changed. Property owners at Pompeii were familiar with the world of villas not only from the surrounding district, but also from the town itself, where owners of the great houses in the center and terrace houses on the periphery adopted elements of villa style early on. The villa character of the corresponding houses in Herculaneum is particularly striking (and indeed many of the phenomena we have observed in Pompeii can also be found there in even more lavish variations).[163] These imposing "town villas" and the lesser villas just outside the walls doubtless played an important role in mediating local development of the new taste. The towns on the Bay of Naples and near other centers of villa culture certainly occupy a special position in this respect.

Nevertheless, social and economic conditions in other romanized parts of the Empire cannot have been very different, at least in the essentials. Scattered archeological findings in the area of ornate garden tombs and tomb paintings reflecting visions of earthly happiness suggest that similar forms of expression also occurred elsewhere.[164]

P. Veyne has shown that Trimalchio's lifestyle, outlook, and values make Petronius' grandiose, overblown character the prototype of a figure common in the early Empire, namely, the independent freedman *(libertus)*.[165] The guests at his feast are freedmen of the same stamp as the host. Like him, they had a chance to try their luck as independent craftsmen or merchants, unhampered by obligations to a patron. Trimalchio differs from them only in his immense degree of success, which Petronius used as the basis for a caricature, portraying the fatal consequences of such a lifestyle and outlook.

Although freedmen of this kind could quickly achieve a measure of affluence and occasionally even great wealth, they could not aspire to a career in public life or social recognition. The resulting tensions found expression in the unregulated area of self-display, which offered many possibilities. Trimalchio is sharp and lucky enough to have made a fortune, and with it he buys an enormous country estate. Withdrawing from business affairs, he sets out to imitate the leisurely life of a landed aristocrat, although without the same opportunities to serve as a magistrate or participate in politics. Within the sharply defined social categories of the day, he has arrived at the top of his particular heap, and he must try to enjoy his good fortune with the assistance of others in the same position.

Material wealth and possibilities for displaying it offered some compensation in the face of a rigidly inflexible social order. The extent to which these rules governed life in Pompeii, even in the circle of freedmen, has been demonstrated by Andreau in his analysis of Caecilius Iucundus' wax tablets and the way in which the names on them are listed.[166]

The Pompeians whose houses we have examined were well off; they had no enormous wealth like Trimalchio, but they could have been his guests. They, too, were engaged in imitating the world of the Roman aristocracy—with the means at their disposal. While they were perhaps convinced that they had achieved a degree of real upper-class living in at least one little corner of their homes, Trimalchio's success appears to have given him full access to its glory. Petronius' satire reveals this "good fortune" as a great illusion, however. Like the Pompeian homeowners, Trimalchio cannot alter who he is. His habits, thoughts, feelings, and intellectual horizons appear thoroughly out of place in the domestic setting and lifestyle he is intent on copying.

Trimalchio's friends are ideal representatives of Pompeians who adopted the style we have encountered at the "House of Trimalchio" and in late Pompeii in general. And while it must be stressed that this taste was by no means limited to freedmen's circles, a good deal of evidence suggests that the freedmen families who were engaged in crafts and trade took the lead in spreading it, especially in provincial Italian towns.[167]

As we have seen, this style derives from the desire not just to imitate the decor of aristocrats' houses, but also to share their world, to participate in the good life and the happiness it brings—through the creation of illusions, if need be. The Flavian emperors, aware of the existence of these desires and aspirations in broad segments of the population, seem to have taken them into account in their policies, with highly effective public projects and entertainment programs. It is instructive to read certain passages in the *Silvae* in this connection, for example, passages in which the poet Statius depicts ordinary people (I.6), or the emperor's invited guests with the emperor as a new Jupiter (IV.2), in a heaven eclipsing everything they have experienced before, a heaven that manifests itself in material form. In these instances the illusion is intentionally staged.[168]

The villa culture of the Roman aristocracy in the late Republic was well suited to serve as a model for the domestic taste of a broad "middle class," since this culture was itself composed of many disparate, loosely associated elements borrowed from other cultures. Even before the villa style began to spread it was marked by striking disjunction between, for example, the design of particular rooms and the way they were actually used, or between old and new forms of decorative elements and furnishings. But although the general domestic taste in late Pompeii retained many of the basic elements that had constituted upper-class style in the late Republic, one decisive difference existed: the aristocratic exponents of villa culture in the second and first centuries B.C. had a first-hand knowledge of Greek civilization through their education, and were thus able to create new meanings for the formal elements they adopted.

It remains for future investigators to study Pompeian domestic taste within the broader context of the Neronian-Flavian period and its prevailing styles. In Pompeii itself there seems to be a connection between shifts occurring in the social structure of the population and new forms of domestic architecture and decor. This link points the way toward further interesting questions, such as the causes behind the profound changes in style observable in all genres of art and architecture after the Julio-Claudian era, causes which are far from self-evident.[169]

Abbreviations

Notes

Illustration Credits

Index

Abbreviations

AA	*Archäologischer Anzeiger*
ADelt	*Archaiologikon Deltion*
AJA	*American Journal of Archaeology*
AM	*Mitteilungen des Deutschen Archäologischen Instituts. Athenische Abteilung*
ANRW	*Aufstieg und Niedergang der Römischen Welt* (Berlin: 1972)
AttiPalermo	*Atti dell'Accademia di scienze, lettere e arti di Palermo*
BdA	*Bollettino d'arte*
BJb	*Bonner Jahrbücher des Rheinischen Landesmuseums in Bonn und des Vereins von Altertumsfreunden im Rheinlande*
BullCom	*Bulletino della Commissione archeologica comunale di Roma*
CIL	*Corpus Inscriptionum Latinarum*
DArch	*Dialoghi di Archeologia*
EAA	*Enciclopedia dell'Arte Antica* (Rome: 1958–)
JdI	*Jahrbuch des Deutschen Archäologischen Instituts*
JRA	*Journal of Roman Archaeology*
JRS	*Journal of Roman Studies*
MarbWPr	*Marburger Winckelmannsprogramm*
MEFRA	*Mélanges de l'École française de Rome, Antiquité*
MemAccLinc	*Memorie. Atti dell'Accademia nazionale dei Lincei, Classe di scienze morali, storiche e filologiche*
MemAmAc	*Memoirs of the American Academy in Rome*
MonPitt	*Monumenti della pittura antica scoperta in Italia* (Rome: 1937)
NSc	*Notizie degli Scavi di antichità*
ÖJh	*Jahreshefte des Österreichischen Archäologischen Institute in Wien*

OpRom	*Opuscula Romana*
PBSR	*Papers of the British School at Rome*
PP	*La Parola del Passato*
PPM	*Pompei. Pitture e mosaici* (Enciclopedia Italiana, Rome: 1990)
RAC	*Reallexikon für Antike und Christentum* (Stuttgart: 1950)
RE	*Pauly's Realencyclopädie der classischen Altertumswissenschaft,,* rev. ed. (Stuttgart: 1894)
RenAccNap	*Rendiconti dell'Accademia di Archeologia, Lettere e Belle arti di Napoli*
RM	*Mitteilungen des Deutschen Archäologischen Instituts. Römische Abteilung*
YaleClSt	*Yale Classical Studies*

Notes

Townscape and Domestic Taste

1. Compare, however, Y. Thébert, "Private Life and Domestic Architecture in Roman Africa," in Paul Veyne, ed., *History of Private Life* (Cambridge, Mass.: 1987); J.-A. Dickmann, "Strukturen des Raumes und repräsentatives Wohnen am Beispiel pompejanischer Stadthäuser" (Ph.D. diss., University of Munich, 1992).

2. This concept is discussed at greater length in Walter Trillmich and Paul Zanker, eds., *Stadtbild und Ideologie: Die Monumentalisierung hispanischer Städte zwischen Republik und Kaiserzeit. Kolloquium Madrid 1987, Abhandlungen der Bayerischen Akademie der Wissenschaften,* vol. 103 (Munich: 1990), pp. 9ff., and in the section on the Pompeian townscape in this book.

3. W. Hoepfner and E. L. Schwandner, *Haus und Stadt im klassischen Griechenland* (Munich: 1986); W. Schuller et al., eds., *Demokratie und Architektur* (Munich: 1989); T. Hölscher, "The City of Athens: Space, Symbol, Structure," in A. Molho et al., *City-States in Classical Antiquity and Medieval Italy* (Ann Arbor: 1991), pp. 355–380.

4. See P. Gros and M. Torelli, *Storia dell'urbanistica: Il mondo romano* (Rome: 1988), which contains a copious bibliography.

5. P. Zanker, *The Power of Images in the Age of Augustus* (Ann Arbor: 1988), trans. Alan Shapiro, pp. 316–333; M. Pfanner, "Modelle römischer Stadtentwicklung am Beispiel Hispaniens und der westlichen Provinzen," in Trillmich and Zanker, *Stadtbild und Ideologie,* pp. 59ff.

6. These aspects are discussed more fully in P. Zanker, "Veränderungen im öffentlichen Raum der italischen Städte der Kaiserzeit," in *L'Italie d'Auguste à Dioclétien: Colloque internationale Rome 1992* (Rome: 1994), pp. 259–284.

7. For more on this subject see R. Neudecker, *Die Pracht der Latrine: Zum Wandel öffentlicher Bedürfnisanstalten in der kaiserzeitlichen Stadt* (Munich: 1994). For "street activity and public interaction," compare the new approach by R. Laurence, *Roman Pompeii: Space and Society* (London: 1994).

8. R. Förtsch, *Archäologischer Kommentar zu den Villenbriefen des jüngeren Plinius* (Mainz: 1993).

9. S. T. A. M. Mols, *Houten Meubels in Herculaneum* (Nijmegen: 1994).

10. A. Wallace-Hadrill, "The Social Structure of the Roman House," *PBSR,* 56 (1988): 43–97; "Elites and Trade in the Roman Town," in J. Rich and Wallace-Hadrill, eds., *City and Country in the Ancient World* (London: 1991); and *Houses and Society in Pompeii and Herculaneum* (Princeton: 1994). For a recent discussion on the problem of the "private" and "public" spheres, see M. Grahame, "Public and Private in the Roman House: Investigating the Social Order of the *Casa del Fauno,*" in R. Laurence and A. Wallace-Hadrill, eds., *Domestic Space in the Roman World: Pompeii and Beyond, JRA* Supplement 22 (1997): 137–164. In this essay Grahame applies a theory developed by Hillier and Hanson in order to determine the degree of "privacy" existing between friends or visitors on the one hand and inhabitants of the house on the other. See also Annapaola Zaccaria Ruggiu, *Spazio privato e spazio pubblico nella città Romana,* Collection de l'École Française de Rome 210 (Rome: 1995).

11. T. Veblen, *The Theory of the Leisure Class* (New York: 1899).

12. J.-A. Dickmann, "Strukturen des Raumes und repräsentatives Wohnen am Beispiel pompejanischer Stadthäuser" (unpublished dissertation, University of Munich, 1992); "The Peristyle and the Transformation of Domestic Space in Hellenistic Pompeii," in Laurence and Wallace-Hadrill, eds., *Domestic Space,* pp. 121–136.

13. Raeder, "Vitruv, *De Architectura* VI 7 *(aedificia Graecorum)* und die hellenistischen Wohnhaus- und Palastarchitekturen," *Gymnasium,* 95 (1988): 316–368.

14. R. Förtsch, *Archäologischer Kommentar zu den Villenbriefen.*

15. J. Overbeck and A. Mau, *Pompeji,* 4th ed. (Leipzig: 1884).

16. P. M. Allison, *The Distribution of Pompeian House Contents and Its Significance* (Ph.D. diss., University of Sydney, 1992); "Artefact Distribution and Spatial Function in Pompeian Houses," in B. Rawson and P. Weaver, eds., *The Roman Family in Italy* (Canberra and Oxford: 1997); J. Berry, "Household Artefacts: Towards a Re-interpretation of Roman Domestic Space," in Laurence and Wallace-Hadrill, eds., *Domestic Space,* pp. 183–195.

17. Summary in H. Mielsch, *Die römische Villa: Architektur und Lebensform* (Munich: 1987); R. Neudecker, *Die Skulpturenausstattung römischer Villen in Italien* (Munich: 1988), with review by R. Förtsch, *Gnomon,* 64 (1992): 520–534.

18. The so-called four styles of Pompeian wall painting are categories determined by scholars on the basis of developments perceptible in extant paintings: down to the early first century B.C., painting is characterized by molded plaster relief imitating masonry and marble, sometimes with pictures inserted in a frieze at eye level (first style, an Italian version of a Hellenistic style; also known as the masonry style); from the early first century B.C. until c. 15 B.C., plausible architectural forms were reproduced by purely pictorial means, and sometimes these architectural motifs were used to "frame" figured paintings (second style); from c. 15 B.C. until A.D. 50, architectural forms became increasingly insubstantial and imaginative, and the wall reverted to a flat plane surrounding a central pictorial motif, sometimes very large (third style); after A.D. 50, the central panels became smaller and were combined with unreal architecture, while borders were added to contribute a sense of depth (fourth style).

19. In this respect my essay in 1979 did not lay sufficient emphasis on the phenomenon as part of an overarching cultural program.

20. Wallace-Hadrill, "Elites and Trade in the Roman Town."

21. See L. Friedländer, *Darstellungen aus der Sittengeschichte Roms,* 10th ed. (Leipzig: 1923), vol. 2, pp. 191ff., especially p. 228.

Urban Space as a Reflection of Society

1. As it would be impossible to list the vast literature on traditional urban studies here, I will mention only a few studies that stimulated my own thinking: K. Lynch, *The Image of the City* (1960); G. Cullen, *The Concise Townscape* (1961); L. Mumford, *The City in History: Its Origins, Its Transformations, and Its Prospects* (1961); L. Benevolo, *Storia della città* (1975); W. Braunfels, *Abendländische Stadtbaukunst: Herrschaftsform und Baugestalt* (1976), and *Mittelalterliche Stadtbaukunst in der Toskana,* 4th ed. (1979); Mark Girouard, *Cities and People: A Social and Architectural History* (1985).

2. Jean Andreau, "Histoire des séismes et histoire économique. Le tremblement de terre de Pompéi (62 ap. J.-C.)," *Annales: Economies, sociétés, civilisations,* 28 (1973): 369–395. Since the postulation of a second earthquake, principally by K. Schefold, *RM,* 64 (1957): 152–153, new observations have been made by the research group associated with V. M. Strocka; see V. Kockel, "Archäologische Funde und Forschungen in den Vesuvstädten II," *AA* (1986): 543. See also *Archäologie und Seismologie. La regione vesuviana dal 62 al 79 d.C. Problemi archeologici e sismologici. Colloquium Boscoreale 1993* (Munich: 1995).

3. S. De Caro, "Saggi nell'area dell' tempio di Apollo a Pompei," *Annali dell'Istituto Orientale di Napoli,* 3 (1986): 19ff. For a survey see De Caro, "La città sannitica,"

in Zevi, ed., *Pompei*, vol. 1, pp. 23–46, and M. Cristofani, "La fase 'etrusca' di Pompei," in Zevi, ed., *Pompei*, vol. 1, pp. 9–22.

4. For this epoch of the town's history see S. C. Nappo, "Urban Transformation at Pompeii in the Late Third and Early Second Centuries B.C.," in Laurence and Wallace-Hadrill, eds., *Domestic Space*, pp. 91–120.

5. P. Castrén, *Ordo populusque Pompeianorum: Polity and Society in Roman Pompeii (Acta Instituti Romani Finlandiae,* 8) (Rome: 1975), pp. 38 ff.; F. Coarelli, D. Musti, and H. Solin, eds., *Delo e l'Italia (Opuscula Instituti Romani Finlandiae,* 2) (Rome: 1982).

6. See P. Zanker, *The Power of Images in the Age of Augustus* (Ann Arbor: 1988), pp. 5–8. Since 1988 much has been published on this topic; E. S. Gruen offers a survey in *Culture and Identity in Rome* (Ithaca, N.Y.: 1992).

7. For the tufa block façades, see A. Hoffmann, "Elemente bürgerlicher Repräsentation: Eine späthellenistische Hausfassade in Pompeji," in *Akten des XII. Internationalen Kongresses für Klassische Archäologie in Berlin 1988* (Berlin: 1990), pp. 490ff.; B. Gesemann, *Die Straßen der antiken Stadt Pompeji: Entwicklung und Gestaltung* (Frankfurt a.M.: 1996); F. Pirson, *Mietwohnungen in Pompeji und Herkulaneum: Untersuchungen zur Architektur, zum Wohnen und zur Sozial- und Wirtschaftsgeschichte der Vesuvstädte* (Ph.D. diss., University of Munich, 1996); and F. Pirson, "Rented Accommodation at Pompeii: The Evidence of the *Insula Arriana Polliana* VI 6," in Laurence and Wallace-Hadrill, eds., *Domestic Space,* pp. 165–181. For the House of the Faun, see A. Mau, *Pompeji in Leben und Kunst,* 2nd ed. (Leipzig: 1908), pp. 300ff.; J. Overbeck and A. Mau, *Pompeji,* 4th ed. (Leipzig: 1884), pp. 346ff. See also A. Hoffmann, "Elemente bürgerlicher Repräsentation," and review of P. Zanker, *Pompeji: Stadtbilder als Spiegel von Gesellschaft und Herrschaftsform* in *Gnomon,* 64 (1992): 426–433. Recent publications by Fausto Zevi have revealed the central importance of the House of the Faun and its owner for the history of Pompeii: see F. Zevi, "La città sannitica. L'edilizia privata e la Casa del Fauno," in Zevi, ed., *Pompei,* vol. 1, pp. 47–76; "Sul tempio di Iside a Pompei," *PP,* 49 (1994): 40ff.; "La Casa del Fauno," in *Pompei. Abitare sotto il Vesuvio* (exhibition catalogue; Ferrara: 1996), pp. 36ff. Some of the artefacts found in the house are shown in the catalogue, pp. 207–214. For the double atrium and the porticos, including their use as *ambulationes,* see Dickmann, "The Peristyle and the Transformation of Domestic Space." Dickmann correctly stresses the function of public buildings in Hellenistic cities as models for the introduction of peristyles into Pompeian domestic architecture. For the history and decoration of the House of the Faun, see also the works cited in note 30 of chapter 3 below.

8. Hoepfner and Schwandner, *Haus und Stadt,* pp. 50, 108, 169.

9. H. Lauter in B. Andreae and H. Kyrieleis, eds., *Neue Forschungen in Pompeji*

(Recklinghausen: 1975), p. 148. For Pella, see C. Makaronas, *ADelt,* 16 (1960), Meletes 74, fig. 1 and plates 48–49, 67ff.

10. J. H. D'Arms, *Romans on the Bay of Naples: A Social and Cultural Study of the Villas and Their Owners from 150 B.C. to A.D. 400* (Cambridge, Mass.: 1970); H. Mielsch, *Die römische Villa,* pp. 37ff.

11. See E. von Mercklin, *Antike Figuralkapitelle* (Berlin: 1962), pp. 70ff., for the House of the Figured Capitals (VII 4.57), no. 188, a and b, figs. 351–357. Compare also Margareta Staub-Gierow, *Casa del Granduca VII 4, 56. Casa dei Capitelli figurate VII 4, 57* (Munich: 1994).

12. Compare the diagram of the wall in the exhibition catalogue *Pompei. Abitare sotto il Vesuvio,* following page 47.

13. E. Pernice, *Pavimente und figürliche Mosaiken: Die Hellenistische Kunst in Pompeji,* vol. 6 (Berlin: 1938); M. E. Blake, "The Pavements of the Roman Buildings of the Republic and Early Empire," *MemAmAc,* 8 (1930): 7ff.; M. de Vos, in F. Zevi, ed., *Pompei 79: Raccolta di studi per il decimonono centenario dell'eruzione Vesuviana,* 2nd ed. (Naples: 1984), 161–179.

14. B. Andreae, *Das Alexandermosaik aus Pompeji* (Recklinghausen: 1977); T. Hölscher, *Griechische Historienbilder* (Würzburg: 1973), pp. 122–162. For a recent interpretation of the Alexander mosaic, see F. Zevi, "La Casa del Fauno," in the exhibition catalogue *Pompei. Abitare sotto il Vesuvio.*

15. H. Lauter, in Andreae and Kyrieleis, eds., *Neue Forschungen,* p. 148.

16. For habitation in *tabernae* and the social and economic use of real estate in the town, see Pirson, *Mietwohnungen in Pompeji und Herkulaneum* and "Rented Accommodation at Pompeii."

17. H. Lauter, in Zanker, ed., *Hellenismus in Mittelitalien,* pp. 415ff.; W. Johannowsky, ibid., p. 272; Kockel, "Vesuvstädte II," pp. 465–466.

18. M. Bieber, *The History of the Greek and Roman Theater* (Princeton: 1961), pp. 108ff.

19. See E. Rawson, "Theatrical Life in Republican Rome and Italy," *PBSR,* 53 (1985): 97–113, later published in *Roman Culture and Society* (Oxford: 1991), pp. 468–487.

20. J. Delorme, *Gymnasion: Étude sur les monuments consacrés à l'éducation en Grèce* (Paris: 1960); see also the entry under "Gymnasium" by Delorme in *RAC,* 13 (1986): 155ff.

21. The "theater peristyle" is discussed by Overbeck and Mau, *Pompeji,* pp. 193ff.; Mau, *Pompeji in Leben und Kunst,* pp. 164ff.; La Rocca, M. de Vos, and A. de Vos, *Pompei,* 2nd revised ed. (Milan: 1994), pp. 158–161; and A. de Vos and M. de Vos, *Pompei, Ercolano, Stabia: Guida archeologica Laterza* (Rome: 1982), pp. 67ff.

22. The suggestion had previously been advanced by Petersen, *RM,* 14 (1899): 103–

104. Recently, Dickmann has taken a critical view, "The Peristyle and the Transformation of Domestic Space," p. 125.

23. The palaestra is discussed by Overbeck and Mau, *Pompeji*, pp. 150ff.; Mau, *Pompeji in Leben und Kunst*, pp. 171ff.; La Rocca et al., *Pompei*, pp. 165–166; de Vos, *Guida archeologica*, pp. 71ff.; Kockel, "Vesuvstädte II," p. 464. An Oscan inscription found at the site mentions that the building was constructed for the *vereiia*, the young people. This was originally a military institution of the aristocracy, which is also documented in other Samnite communities. See S. De Caro, "La città sannitica," in Zevi, ed., *Pompei*, vol. 2, p. 37; F. Zevi, "Sul tempio di Iside a Pompei," *PP*, 49 (1994): 45.

24. *RAC*, 13 (1986): 163ff. See the entry under "Gymnasium" (J. Delorme).

25. See H. Eschebach, *Die Stabianer Thermen in Pompeji* (Berlin: 1979), and the review by V. Kockel in *Gnomon*, 54 (1982): 178–179; and most recently Kockel, "Vesuvstädte II," p. 467.

26. A. S. Hunt and C. C. Edgar, eds., *Select Papyri*, vol. 2 (1934), pp. 234ff., no. 269.

27. The Triangular Forum is discussed by Overbeck and Mau, *Pompeji*, pp. 75ff.; Mau, *Pompeji in Leben und Kunst*, pp. 133ff.; La Rocca et al., *Pompei*, pp. 146–151; de Vos, *Guida archeologica*, pp. 60ff.; and Kockel, "Vesuvstädte II," p. 462.

28. See Kockel, "Vesuvstädte II," pp. 462–463.

29. See the most recent remarks by H. Lauter, *Die Architektur des Hellenismus* (Darmstadt: 1986), pp. 64ff.

30. A. Maiuri, *Bicentenario degli scavi di Pompei* (Naples: 1948), p. 28; D. Elia and G. Pugliese, "Caratelli, Il santuario dionisiaco di Pompei," *PP*, 34 (1979): 442–481; Kockel, *AA* (1985): 568–569.

31. Temple of Isis: Tran Tam Tinh, *Essai sur le culte d'Isis à Pompéi* (Paris: 1964), pp. 30ff.; Kockel, "Vesuvstädte II," pp. 464ff. On the dating of the Hellenistic structure see H. Lauter-Bufé, *Die Geschichte des sikeliotisch-korinthischen Kapitells* (Heidelberg: 1987), pp. 36–37, plate 26 (soon after 150 B.C.), and *Alla Ricerca di Iside: Analisi, Studi e Restauri dell'Iseo pompeiano nel Museo di Napoli* (Naples: 1992); also various contributions in *PP*, 49 (1994).

32. See Overbeck and Mau, *Pompeji*, pp. 110ff.; Mau, *Pompeji in Leben und Kunst*, pp. 188ff.; La Rocca et al., *Pompei*, pp. 171–173; de Vos, *Guida archeologica*, pp. 78–79. Compare the recent monograph by D. Russo, *Il tempio di Giove Melichio a Pompei* (Naples: 1991). For the cult statue see H. Von Rohden, *Die Terracotten von Pompeji* (Stuttgart: 1880), pp. 20–21, 42–43; A. Levi, *Le terrecotte figurate del Museo Nazionale di Napoli* (Florence: 1925), p. 186, plate 11; W. Johannowsky, in Zanker, ed., *Hellenismus in Mittelitalien*, p. 287. The walls around the precinct of Zeus Meilichios may have come later. It is possible that the shrine was originally wider, and the altar not placed at an angle until later. For the identification with Asclepius, see S. De Caro, in *PP*, 49 (1994): 9–10.

33. H. Lauter, *JdI*, 94 (1979): 416ff. For the extension of the forum see the soundings taken from the area between the Temple of Apollo and the basilica, discussed by P. Arthur in the *Antiquarian Journal*, 66 (1986), pp. 29ff., and Hoffmann, *Gnomon*, 64 (1992): 428.

34. The date of the temple's renovation is a matter of controversy. Lauter assigns the more elaborate structure to pre-Roman times, but I do not find his arguments entirely convincing. Also skeptical are Kockel, "Vesuvstädte II," pp. 454ff.; and F. Zevi, "Pompei della città sannitica alla colonia sillana: per una interpretazione dei dati archeologici," in *Les Élites municipales de l'Italie péninsulaire des Gracques à Néron. Colloquium Clermont-Ferrand 1991* (Naples and Rome: 1996), pp. 125–138. For a recent discussion of the statue of Jupiter, see H. G. Martin, *Römische Tempelkultbilder* (Rome: 1987), pp. 142ff. and 222ff.

35. For discussion of the *macellum* see H. Lauter, *AA* (1971): 59–60, and *JdI*, 94 (1979): 429 and 434; Kockel, "Vesuvstädte II," p. 456.

36. K. F. Ohr and J. J. Rausch, *Die Basilika in Pompeji* (Berlin: 1991); H. Lauter, *JdI*, 94 (1979): 430; Kockel, "Vesuvstädte II," pp. 459–460; Lauter-Bufé, *Die Geschichte des Kapitells*, p. 38.

37. Lauter, *JdI*, 94 (1979): 435–436.

38. A. Maiuri, *NSc* (1941): 371ff.

39. M. Schede, *Die Ruinen von Priene*, 2nd ed. (Berlin: 1964); Hoepfner and Schwandner, *Haus und Stadt*, pp. 141ff.

40. For a discussion of the Temple of Apollo in the Hellenistic period see De Caro, "La città sannitica," pp. 25–26. The capitals (circa 110–100 B.C.) are discussed by Lauter-Bufé, *Die Geschichte des Kapitells*, p. 39; for the dating see also Lauter, *JdI*, 94 (1979): 427, and Kockel, "Vesuvstädte II," pp. 454–455.

41. F. Zevi in Zanker, ed., *Hellenismus in Mittelitalien*, pp. 84ff.; A. Degrassi, *Inscriptiones Latinae Liberae Rei Publicae*, vol. 2 (Rome: 1963; reprinted 1972), pp. 56–57, no. 528.

42. F. E. Brown, *Cosa: The Making of a Roman Town* (Ann Arbor: 1980).

43. P. Gros, *Architecture et Société* (Brussels: 1978), pp. 51 and 88; F. Coarelli, in *Les "Bourgeoisies" municipales aux IIe et Ier siècles av. J.-C. Colloque 1981* (Paris: 1983), pp. 217ff.

44. For recent discussions of the founding of the Roman *colonia* at Pompeii and its constitution, with citations of the earlier literature, see E. Lo Cascio, in *Les Élites municipales. Colloquium Clermont-Ferrand*, pp. 111–124; H. Mouritsen, *Elections, Magistrates and Municipal Elite: Studies in Pompeian Epigraphy*, Analaecta Romana Supplement 15 (Rome: 1988), pp. 87–88, 116–117; H.-J. Gerke, *Hermes*, 111 (1983): 471–490. The question of the Sullan colonists and their importance for the cultural life of the town is discussed by V. Kockel in H. von Hesberg and P. Zanker, eds., *Römische Gräberstraßen: Selbstdarstellung, Status, Standard. Kolloquium*

1985 (Munich: 1987), pp. 185ff. For the economic consequences of the transformation, see J. Andreau, *Revue des Études Anciennes,* 82 (1980): 183ff. See also S. Adamo Muscettola, "La trasformazione della città tra Silla e Augusto," in Zevi, ed., *Pompei,* pp. 75–114; Zevi, "Pompei della città sannitica alla colonia sillana."

45. For the *capitoleum,* see Zevi, "Pompei della città sannitica alla colonia sillana," p. 126; Lauter, *JdI,* 94 (1979): 430ff.; La Rocca et al., *Pompei,* pp. 132–135. For the cult statue, see Martin, *Römische Tempelkultbilder,* pp. 142–143 and plates 21 and 22; Kockel, "Vesuvstädte II," pp. 455ff.

46. For discussions of the Temple of Venus see Mau, *Pompeji in Leben und Kunst,* pp. 120–121, and *RM,* 15 (1900): 270–308 and plates 7 and 8; A. Maiuri, *Saggi di varia antichità* (Naples: 1954), pp. 241ff., and *BdA,* 45 (1960): 173–174; A. Hoffmann, "L'Architettura," in Zevi, ed., *Pompei 79,* pp. 102–103; de Vos, *Guida archeologica,* pp. 26–27; Kockel, "Vesuvstädte II," pp. 461–462; Adamo Muscettola, "La trasformazione della città tra Silla e Augusto," pp. 77–78; Zevi, "Pompei della città sannitica alla colonia sillana," pp. 128–129. For the role of the goddess Venus in election propaganda soon after the founding of the colony, see Castrén, *Ordo populusque Pompeianorum,* p. 86.

47. For the Temple of Apollo see Zevi, "Pompei della città sannitica alla colonia sillana," p. 128; De Caro, "La città sannitica," p. 25; *CIL* X 800; Degrassi, *Inscriptiones Latinae Liberae Rei Publicae,* vol. 2, p. 107, no. 644.

48. For discussions of the *theatrum tectum* see Overbeck and Mau, *Pompeji,* pp. 171ff.; Mau, *Pompeji in Leben und Kunst,* pp. 160ff.; de Vos, *Guida archeologica,* pp. 69–70; R. Meinel, *Das Odeion* (Frankfurt: 1980), pp. 36ff., 180ff., 205ff; Kockel, "Vesuvstädte II," p. 466; M. Fuchs, *Untersuchungen zur Ausstattung römischer Theater* (Mainz: 1987), pp. 46–47. For inscriptions, see J. Bauer, "Munificentia Privata Pompeiana," unpublished master's thesis (University of Munich, 1988), pp. 15–16 and 40–41. Compare the discussion of the construction under the aspect of two *genera civium* in Zevi, "Personaggi della Pompei sillana," *PBSR,* 63 (1995): 1–24; and "Pompei della città sannitica alla colonia sillana," p. 130.

49. Compare F. Kolb, *Agora und Theater: Volks- und Festversammlung* (Berlin: 1979). My interpretation does not exclude use of the new building as a theater; compare Zevi, "Personaggi della Pompei sillana."

50. For more on the two donors, see Castrén, *Ordo populusque,* pp. 209–210 and 212.

51. Compare H. Lauter, *Die Architektur des Hellenismus,* p. 173.

52. For the forum baths see Overbeck and Mau, *Pompeji,* pp. 200ff.; Mau, *Pompeji in Leben und Kunst,* pp. 20ff.; de Vos, *Guida archeologica,* pp. 49ff.; Kockel, *AA* (1986): 467, and in von Hesberg and Zanker, eds., *Römische Gräberstraßen,* p. 185; L. Eschebach, *Antike Welt,* 22 (1991): 257–287.

53. *CIL* X 819; Degrassi, *Inscriptiones Latinae,* vol. 2, pp. 105–106, no. 641.

54. *CIL* X 829; Degrassi, *Inscriptiones Latinae,* vol. 2, pp. 108–109, no. 648; H. Esche-bach et al., *Die Stabianer Thermen in Pompeiji* (Berlin: 1979); H. Eschebach, *RM,* 80 (1973): 235ff. Compare Zevi, "Pompei della città sannitica alla colonia sil-lana," p. 129.

55. For discussions of the amphitheater see Overbeck and Mau, *Pompeji,* pp. 176ff.; Mau, *Pompeji in Leben und Kunst,* pp. 216ff.; de Vos, *Guida archeologica,* pp. 150–151 and 362; R. Graefe, *Vela erunt* (Mainz: 1976), pp. 67ff., 104ff., and plates 77ff.; Kockel, *AA* (1986): 466, and in von Hesberg and Zanker, eds., *Römische Gräberstraßen,* p. 185; Zevi, "Pompei della città sannitica alla colonia sillana," pp. 131–132.

56. H. Dessau, *Inscriptiones Latinae Selectae* (1892–1916), no. 5318.

57. Castrén, *Ordo populusque,* pp. 88–89; Gehrke, *Hermes,* 111 (1983): 488, note 87; Bauer, *Munificentia Privata,* pp. 59–60. For Aeclanum see Degrassi, *Inscriptiones Latinae,* vol. 2, pp. 54–55, no. 523 with commentary.

58. V. Kockel, *Die Grabbauten vor dem Herkulaner Tor in Pompeji* (Mainz: 1983), pp. 53ff.

59. For the founding of other Sullan colonies see E. Gabba, *Athenaeum Pavia,* 29 (1951): 270–271.

60. Degrassi, *Inscriptiones Latinae,* vol. 2, pp. 107–108, no. 645. For the inscription see Gehrke, *Hermes,* 111 (1983): 488; Mouritsen, *Elections, Magistrates and Municipal Elite,* p. 88.

61. A. Hoffmann in *Wohnungsbau im Altertum: Bericht über ein Kolloquium, Diskussionen zur archäologischen Bauforschung,* vol. 3 (Berlin: 1978), p. 162; A. Hoffmann, *Architectura,* 10 (1980): 1–14; and "L'Architettura," in Zevi, ed., *Pompei 79,* pp. 97ff.; and most recently his review in *Gnomon,* 64 (1992): 430.

62. Compare Nappo, "Urban Transformation at Pompeii."

63. H. Lauter in Andreae and Kyrieleis, eds., *Neue Forschungen,* p. 121. Lauter has kindly communicated to me his belief that the dating of house IX 1.20 needs to be reconsidered.

64. See the section "Two Forms of Living Space" below.

65. For information on new excavations in the *Insula Occidentalis,* see Kockel, "Vesuvstädte II," pp. 507ff.

66. Ibid., pp. 508ff.

67. V. Spinazzola, *Pompei alla luce degli scavi nuovi di via dell'Abbondanza,* 3 vols. (Rome: 1954), vol. 1, pp. 437ff.; vol. 2, pp. 869ff.; *PPM,* vol. 1, pp. 193ff. (with a good analysis of the houses); Dickmann, "The Peristyle and the Transformation of Domestic Space," p. 134.

68. Kockel, *Die Grabbauten vor dem Herkulaner Tor,* pp. 9–10, notes 77 and 11, and in von Hesberg and Zanker, eds., *Römische Gräberstraßen,* pp. 187–188.

69. For the most recent discussion see Kockel, "Vesuvstädte II," pp. 556–557, and in von Hesberg and Zanker, eds., *Römische Gräberstraßen,* p. 192.

70. Compare H. von Hesberg and P. Zanker in *Römische Gräberstraßen,* pp. 9ff.

71. Kockel's survey of the colonists' construction (ibid., pp. 183ff.) emphasizes different points, in particular the new residents' highly interesting adoption of specific burial forms so far documented only in Pompeii.

72. For an earlier discussion of the issues in the section that follows, compare Zanker, *The Power of Images,* especially Chapter 8; on public buildings in Pompeii see also De Caro, "La città in età imperiale," in Zevi, ed., *Pompei,* vol. 2, pp. 11–38.

73. De Caro, "La città sannitica," p. 25; R. Etienne, *La vie quotidienne à Pompei,* 2nd ed. (Paris: Hachette, 1977), p. 333.

74. Compare S. R. F. Price, *Rituals and Power* (Cambridge: 1984); M. Wörrle, *Stadt und Fest im kaiserzeitlichen Kleinasien* (Munich: 1988).

75. For the Temple of Fortuna Augusta see Overbeck and Mau, *Pompeji,* pp. 114ff.; Mau, *Pompeji in Leben und Kunst,* pp. 129ff.; La Rocca et al., *Pompei,* pp. 141–143; de Vos, *Guida archeologica,* pp. 52–53. A more recent discussion with citations of further literature can be found in H. Hänlein-Schäfer, *Veneratio Augusti: Eine Studie zu den Tempeln des ersten römischen Kaisers* (Rome: 1985), pp. 105–106; De Caro, "La città in età imperiale," pp. 20ff. For the inscription, see *CIL* X 820. For *Ministri Fortunae Augustae,* see Castrén, *Ordo populusque,* pp. 76–77.

76. For more on M. Tullius M. F., see Castrén, *Ordo populusque,* pp. 96–97, and p. 231, no. 420, 4.

77. H. Heinrich comes to this conclusion in his unpublished dissertation on series of capitals in Campania (Munich).

78. P. Gros, *Aurea Templa* (Rome: 1976), with review by H. von Hesberg, *Göttingsche Gelehrte Anzeigen,* 223 (1981): 218ff.

79. For the statues in the Temple of Fortuna, see G. Fiorelli, *Pompeianarum Antiquitatum Historia,* vol. 3 (Naples: 1864), pp. 48–49; A. Ruesch, *Guida illustrata del Museo Nazionale di Napoli* (Naples: 1908), p. 260, no. 1095; A. De Franciscis, *Il ritratto romano a Pompei* (Naples: 1951), p. 34, fig. 21; P. Cain, *Männerbildnisse neronisch-flavischer Zeit* (Munich: 1993), p. 175, where the statue is dated after A.D. 62.

80. For the *macellum* see Mau, *Pompeji in Leben und Kunst,* pp. 90ff.; Overbeck and Mau, *Pompeji,* pp. 128ff.; La Rocca et al., *Pompei,* pp. 128–132; de Vos, *Guida archeologica,* pp. 43ff.; Kockel, "Vesuvstädte II," p. 456; J. J. Dobbins, "Problems of Chronology, Decoration, and Urban Design in the Forum of Pompeii," *AJA,* 98 (1994): 629–694.

81. For the two statues from the *macellum* (nos. 6044 and 6041 in the inventory of the Museo Archeologico Nazionale, Naples), see De Franciscis, *Il ritratto romano,*

pp. 70–73, and Zanker in Zevi, ed., *Pompei 79,* p. 194.

82. For the Sanctuary of the Lares, see Mau, *Pompeji in Leben und Kunst,* pp. 98ff.; Overbeck and Mau, *Pompeji,* pp. 128ff.; La Rocca et al., *Pompei,* pp. 127–128; de Vos, *Guida archeologica,* pp. 43ff.; Kockel, "Vesuvstädte II," p. 456; De Caro, "La città in età imperiale," pp. 15–16. For the galleries of statues of the imperial family see C. B. Rose, *Dynastic Commemoration and Imperial Portraiture in the Julio-Claudian Period* (Cambridge: 1997). For the dating see J. J. Dobbins, "The Imperial Cult Building on the Forum of Pompeii," in *Subject and Ruler,* ed. A. Small, *JRA* Supplement 17 (1996), 96–114.

83. For the Temple of Vespasian, see Mau, *Pompeji in Leben und Kunst,* pp. 102ff.; Overbeck and Mau, *Pompeji,* pp. 117–118; La Rocca et al., *Pompei,* pp. 125–127; de Vos, *Guida archeologica,* pp. 41ff.; Kockel, "Vesuvstädte II," p. 457 (who argues for dating it in the Augustan period); De Caro, "La città in età imperiale," pp. 14–15. Recently J. J. Dobbins has argued that the present form of the temple dates from the Augustan period, but he assumes that much of it was rebuilt after the earthquake of A.D. 62; see "Problems of Chronology in the Forum of Pompeii," pp. 661–668.

84. B. M. Felletti Maj, *La tradizione italica nell'arte Romana* (Rome: 1977), pp. 337ff.; J. J. Dobbins, "The Altar of the Genius of Augustus in the Forum of Pompeii," *RM,* 99 (1992): 251–263.

85. *CIL* X 816; Hänlein-Schäfer, *Veneratio Augusti,* pp. 133ff., plate 9a (with citation of earlier literature). Compare also I. Gradel, "Mammia's Dedication, Emperor and Genius: The Imperial Cult in Italy and the *Genius Coloniae* in Pompeii," *Analecta Romana,* 20 (1992): 43–58, whose divergent interpretation is correctly rejected by Dobbins, "Problems of Chronology in the Forum of Pompeii," pp. 662–663.

86. Castrén, *Ordo populusque,* pp. 71, 96, and 188, no. 237; Kockel, *Die Grabbauten vor dem Herkulaner Tor,* p. 59. Compare Mouritsen, *Elections, Magistrates and Municipal Elite.*

87. For the Eumachia Building, see Mau, *Pompeji in Leben und Kunst,* pp. 106–107; Overbeck and Mau, *Pompeji,* pp. 131–132; La Rocca et al., *Pompei,* pp. 121–125; de Vos, *Guida archeologica,* pp. 39–40; Kockel, "Vesuvstädte II," pp. 457–458; Zanker, *The Power of Images,* pp. 320–323; Bauer, *Munificentia Privata,* pp. 47ff. and 63ff.; De Caro, "La città in età imperiale," p. 16; Dobbins, "Problems of Chronology in the Forum of Pompeii," pp. 647ff. K. Wallat, in *AA* (1995): 345–373, has recently identified the marble door frame with the temple for the imperial cult.

88. For laudatory inscriptions, see *CIL* X 808, 809; for the most recent discussion of the Forum of Augustus, see J. Ganzert and V. Kockel, in *Kaiser Augustus und die*

verlorene Republik (exhibition catalogue, Berlin: 1988), pp. 149ff. For more on the links between the Forum of Augustus and the decor of the *chalcidicum,* see H. Döhl, in Zevi, ed., *Pompei 79,* pp. 185–186.

89. Compare Zanker, *The Power of Images,* pp. 135–139, and H. von Hesberg in *Kaiser Augustus und die verlorene Republik,* pp. 93ff.

90. This was observed by Kockel, "Vesuvstädte II," p. 458.

91. De Franciscis, *Il ritratto romano,* p. 53, figs. 52–54. There is a good photograph of a detail of the statue in T. Kraus and L. von Matt, *Lebendiges Pompeji: Pompeji und Herculaneum* (Cologne: 1973), pp. 40–41.

92. Zanker, *The Power of Images,* pp. 239–245.

93. Compare Hänlein-Schäfer, *Veneratio Augusti,* passim, and Zanker, *The Power of Images,* p. 307.

94. H. Döhl, in Zevi, ed., *Pompei 79,* pp. 185ff.; J. Bergemann, *Römische Reiterstatuen* (Mainz: 1990), pp. 17, 19, 37.

95. A. Mau, *RM,* 11 (1896): 150–156.

96. Maiuri offers a detailed interpretation, *L'ultima fase edilizia di Pompei* (Rome: 1942), pp. 10ff.

97. Ibid., pp. 27–28.

98. Kockel, "Vesuvstädte II," pp. 465–466; Graefe, *Vela erunt,* pp. 36ff.; Fuchs, *Untersuchungen zur Ausstattung römischer Theater,* pp. 44ff.; De Caro, "La città in età imperiale," pp. 25–26.

99. See Fuchs, *Untersuchungen zur Ausstattung römischer Theater,* passim.

100. Castrén, *Ordo populusque,* p. 176, nos. 197, 9, and 15; D'Arms, *Romans on the Bay of Naples.* There are good observations on the *cursus honorum* in Bauer, *Munificentia Privata,* pp. 66ff. Compare Mouritsen, *Elections, Magistrates and Municipal Elite.* On the title *tribunus militum a populo,* cf. C. Nicolet in *MEFRA* 79 (1967), pp. 29–76.

101. Bauer presents a convincing argument for this interpretation, *Munificentia Privata,* pp. 52–53.

102. Zanker, *AA* (1981): 349ff.

103. Zanker, *The Power of Images,* pp. 147–153.

104. E. Rawson, "*Discrimina ordinum:* The *lex Julia theatralis,*" *PBSR,* 55 (1987): 83–114, republished in *Roman Culture and Society,* pp. 508–545.

105. For more on the *campus,* see A. Maiuri, *NSc* (1939): 165–238; Etienne, *La vie quotidienne,* pp. 361–363; La Rocca et al., *Pompei,* pp. 254ff.; de Vos, *Guida archeologica,* pp. 147ff.; Wilhelmina F. Jashemski, *The Gardens of Pompeii, Herculaneum and the Villas Destroyed by Vesuvius,* vol. 2 (New Rochelle, N.Y.: 1993), pp. 91–92; De Caro, "La Città in età imperiale," p. 27.

106. For literature on the training of youth and fitness in the Augustan era, see

D. Kienast, *Augustus* (Darmstadt: 1982), pp. 153–154. For the architecture and functions of the *campus,* see H. Devijver and F. van Wousterghem, *Acta Archaeologica Lovaniensia,* 20 (1981): 33–68; and 21 (1982): 93ff.

107. W. F. Jashemski, *The Gardens of Pompeii,* vol. 1 (New Rochelle, N.Y.: 1979), pp. 160–161.

108. For inscriptions relating to the sundials, see *CIL* X 802 (Temple of Apollo) and 831 (archaic temple and bench).

109. For the marble floor in the odeon see *CIL* X 845. Another gift of the same magistrate is mentioned in *CIL* X 955. See further O. Puchstein, *AA* (1906): 302–303; Bauer, *Munificentia Privata,* p. 41.

110. *CIL* X 853–857d; Bauer, *Munificentia Privata,* pp. 30ff.

111. *CIL* X 817; compare Castrén, *Ordo populusque,* p. 102.

112. *CIL* X 1064; Bauer, *Munificentia Privata,* p. 34. Compare Gesemann, *Die Straßen der antiken Stadt Pompeji.*

113. For more on the water supply, see the article by van Buren in *RE,* vol. 21, part 2 (1952), under "Pompeji"; H. Eschebach, *Cronache Pompeiane,* 5 (1979): 24–60, and *Antike Welt,* 10, part 2 (1979): 3ff.; Kockel, "Vesuvstädte II," pp. 551–552; De Caro, "La città in età imperiale," p. 29. For the most recent research results see *Cura Aquarum in Campania. Proceedings of the Ninth International Congress on Water Management and Hydraulic Engineering in the Mediterranean Region 1994,* ed. Nathalie de Haan and Gemma C. M. Jansen, *Bulletin Antieke Beschaving* Supplement 4, 1996.

114. J. Dybkjaer Larsen, *Analecta Romana Instituti Danici,* 11 (1982): 41ff.

115. H. Eschebach and T. Schäfer, *Pompeii Herculaneum Stabiae: Bolletino,* 1 (1983): 11–40; Laurence, *Roman Pompeii: Space and Society;* Gesemann, *Die Straßen der antiken Stadt Pompeji.*

116. For more on the construction of aqueducts in the Augustan era see W. Eck in *Die Wasserversorgung antiker Städte: Pergamon, Geschichte der Wasserversorgung,* vol. 2 (Mainz: 1987), p. 72.

117. Kockel, *Die Grabbauten vor dem Herkulaner Tor,* pp. 18ff, and in von Hesberg and Zanker, eds., *Römische Gräberstraßen,* p. 188.

118. Compare Trillmich and Zanker, eds., *Stadtbild und Ideologie,* passim.

119. The fundamental accounts of this period are Maiuri, *L'ultima fase di Pompei,* and Castrén, *Ordo populusque,* pp. 108ff. See Dobbins, "Problems of Chronology in the Forum of Pompeii."

120. Zanker, *JdI,* 94 (1979): 460ff.

121. See Maiuri, *L'ultima fase di Pompei,* pp. 68ff. For the inscription: *CIL* X 846; Zevi, ed., *Pompei 79,* p. 43 (illustration). For the temple statuary: H. Döhl in Zevi, ed., *Pompei 79,* pp. 183–184. For the benefactor: Castrén, *Ordo populusque,*

pp. 114 and 209, nos. 318, 11, and 12. Compare *Alla ricerca di Iside;* Zevi, "Sul tempio di Iside a Pompei"; P. Hoffmann, *Der Isistempel in Pompeji* (Münster: 1993).

122. H. Döhl in Zevi, ed., *Pompei 79,* p. 182; S. De Caro in *PP,* 49 (1994): 9–10.

123. *CIL* X 858 and 859; Maiuri, *L'ultima fase di Pompei,* p. 86.

124. For more on the new baths, see Mau, *Pompeji in Leben und Kunst,* pp. 212ff.; Overbeck and Mau, *Pompeji,* pp. 233ff.; La Rocca et al., *Pompei,* pp. 318–320; de Vos, *Guida archeologica,* pp. 206–207. Compare also I. Nielsen, *Thermae et Balnea: The Architecture and Cultural History of Roman Public Baths,* II (Copenhagen: 1991), p. 8, no. C47, fig. 79; P. Bargellini, "Le terme centrali di Pompei," *Les thermes romains,* proceedings of a conference held in Rome in 1988 (Rome: 1991). Two more small baths dating from the same period have recently been excavated or investigated: L. Jacobelli, *Le pitture erotiche delle terme suburbane a Pompei* (Rome: 1995); A. Koloski Ostrow, *The Sarno Bath Complex* (Rome: 1990).

125. J. L. Franklin, Jr., *Pompeii: The Electoral Programmata Campaigns and Politics,* A.D. 71–79 (Rome: 1980), with reviews by T. Pekary, H.-J. Gehrke, and H. Galsterer (see Kockel, "Vesuvstädte II," p. 537). Compare Mouritsen, *Elections, Magistrates and Municipal Elite.*

126. For the excavation and recovery efforts after the eruption in A.D. 79, see Zevi, "Sul tempio di Iside a Pompei," pp. 51ff.; Zevi, "Il terremotò del 62 e l'edilizia privata," in *Pompei,* vol. 2, pp. 44–45.

127. See Dobbins, "The Altar of the Genius of Augustus," "Problems of Chronology in the Forum of Pompeii," and "The Imperial Cult Building on the Forum of Pompeii"; K. Wallat, "Der Zustand des Forums von Pompeji am Vorabend des Vesuvausbruchs 79 n. Chr.," in *Archäologie und Seismologie,* pp. 75–92, and the other contributions to that volume.

The Domestic Arts in Pompeii

Note. Andrew Wallace-Hadrill offers a good overview of the issues connected with domestic environments as indicators of identity and social status in his essays "The Social Structure of the Roman House" and "The Social Spread of Roman Luxury" (*PBSR,* 56 [1988]: 43–97, and 58 [1990]: 145–192, respectively). The situation in Pompeii in the early imperial period is discussed by H. Mouritsen in *Elections, Magistrates and Municipal Elite,* where he revises some of Castrén's conclusions in *Ordo Populusque,* on which I draw here. This and other recent evidence, including J.-A. Dickmann's unpublished dissertation from 1992, "Strukturen des Raumes und repräsentatives Wohnen am Beispiel pompejanischer Stadthäuser," suggest that late Pompeian taste in domestic interiors should be seen as a general phenomenon and not be linked quite so directly with the specific outlook of freedmen, as I conclude in the present work. Compare also the section "Social Identification and Cultural Self-Definition" in chapter 1.

1. Older works on the subject of the Pompeian house include, in addition to the works cited below in note 3, Overbeck and Mau's *Pompeji*, 4th ed. (Leipzig: 1884), and Crema, *L'architettura romana* (Torino: 1959). Compare T. Kraus and L. von Matt, *Lebendiges Pompeji: Pompeji und Herculaneum* (Cologne: 1973); Robert Etienne, *La vie quotidienne à Pompéi*, 2nd ed. (Paris: Hachette, 1977); E. La Rocca, M. and A. de Vos, and F. Coarelli, *Guida archeologica di Pompei*, 2nd ed. (Rome: 1976); J. B. Ward-Perkins, *Pompeii A.D. 79* (New York: 1978); B. Tamm, *OpRom*, 9 (1973): 53ff.; J. R. Clarke, *The Houses of Roman Italy, 100 B.C.–A.D. 250* (Berkeley: 1991); E. de Albentiis, *La casa dei Romani* (Milan: 1990); and the extensive bibliography on house decoration in the exhibition catalogue *Pompei. Abitare sotto il Vesuvio* (Ferrara: 1996), pp. 291–298.

2. Valuable observations of some of these phenomena were made for the first time by K. Schefold, however, to whose work I am indebted despite our differences in interpretation and evaluation of the material. See especially *Neue Beiträge zur klassischen Altertumswissenschaft: Festschrift B. Schweitzer* (Stuttgart: 1954), pp. 297ff.; *Pompejanische Malerei: Sinn und Ideengeschichte* (Basel: 1952); *RM*, 60/61 (1953–54): 107ff.; and his essay in Andreae and Kyrieleis, eds., *Neue Forschungen in Pompeji* (Recklinghausen: 1975), pp. 53ff.; *ANRW*, I, 4 (1974), pp. 945ff.

3. Compare the observations of H. Drerup in *MarbWPr* (1959), 1ff. Later discussions include D'Arms, *Romans on the Bay of Naples*; A. Boethius and J. B. Ward-Perkins, *Etruscan and Roman Architecture* (Harmondsworth: 1970); P. Grimal, *Les jardins romains*, 2nd ed. (Paris: 1969); A. G. McKay, *Houses, Villas and Palaces in the Roman World* (London: 1975); H. Mielsch, *Die römische Villa: Architektur und Lebensform* (Munich: 1987); and S. De Caro in the exhibition catalogue *Pompei. Abitare sotto il Vesuvio*, p. 21.

4. A fragment by Cato mentions luxurious villas as early as 152 B.C.: E. Malcovati, *Oratorum Romanorum Fragmenta*, 2nd ed. (Torino: 1955), no. 185. Compare D'Arms, *Romans on the Bay of Naples*, pp. 10–11.

5. Compare the ancient sources and the archeological evidence in F. Noack and K. Lehmann-Hartleben, *Baugeschichtliche Untersuchungen am Stadtrand von Pompeji* (Berlin and Leipzig: 1936).

6. For more on this consult the guidebook, *The J. Paul Getty Museum* (Malibu: 1975).

7. A. de Franciscis, in Andreae and Kyrieleis, eds., *Neue Forschungen*, pp. 9ff., and *The Pompeian Wall Paintings in the Roman Villa of Oplontis*, trans. Rosemary Kunisch (Recklinghausen: 1975). For the decoration (with new literature), see the exhibition catalogue *Pompei. Abitare sotto il Vesuvio*, pp. 135ff. and 266ff.

8. M. Rostowzew, *JdI*, 19 (1904): 103ff., and *RM*, 26 (1911): 1ff.; G. D'Anneo, *AttiPalermo*, 18 (1940): 236ff.; W. J. P. Peters, *Landscape in Romano-Campanian Mural Painting* (Assen: 1963); B. Förtsch, *Archäologischer Kommentar zu den Villenbriefen des jüngeren Plinius* (Mainz: 1993), p. 201 (catalogue of the descriptions of villas).

9. B. Fehr, *MarbWPr* (1969), pp. 31ff.

10. D. Pandermalis, in P. Zanker, ed., *Hellenismus in Mittelitalien, Abhandlungen Göttingen,* series 3, no. 97 (Göttingen: 1986), vol. 2, pp. 387ff.

11. Compare M. Leppert's unpublished dissertation on imperial Roman villas (University of Freiburg, 1974); Zanker, in Zanker, ed., *Hellenismus in Mittelitalien,* pp. 377–378. For the current state of Demetrias see V. Milojcic and D. Theocharis, *Demetrias,* vol. 1 (Bonn: 1976), pp. 75ff.

12. Vitruvius VI 3.8–10; F. Mazois, *Le palais de Scaurus,* 3rd ed. (Paris: 1859); Crema, *L'architettura Romana,* pp. 115–116 and figs. 106–109; Boethius and Ward-Perkins, *Etruscan and Roman Architecture,* p. 156; Förtsch, *Archäologischer Kommentar zu den Villenbriefen,* passim.

13. For more on the second style, see Roger Ling, *Roman Painting* (Cambridge: 1991), pp. 23–51; for the view expounded here, see K. Fittschen in Zanker, ed., *Hellenismus in Mittelitalien,* pp. 539ff.; P. Williams-Lehmann, *Roman Wall Paintings from Boscoreale in the Metropolitan Museum* (New York: 1953), pp. 82ff. Compare also R. A. Tybout, *Aedificiorum figurae: Untersuchungen zu den Architekturdarstellungen des frühen zweiten Stils* (Amsterdam: 1989), with review by B. Wesenberg, *Gnomon,* 64 (1992): 433–438; Clarke, *The Houses of Roman Italy,* pp. 78–123.

14. Associated with the relatively modest palace at Pergamum was the precinct of Athena with its colonnades, library, and works of art. The actual residence of the ruler formed only the smaller part of a typical Hellenistic "palace"; the larger part was composed of different sacred precincts. Compare K. Schefold, *Pompejanische Malerei,* p. 21, and A. Boethius, *The Golden House of Nero* (Ann Arbor: 1960), pp. 96ff. For Hellenistic palace gardens, compare Grimal, *Les jardins romains,* pp. 76–77; V. M. Caroll-Spillecke, *Kepos. Der antike griechische Garten* (Munich: 1989), especially pp. 51ff.

15. G. Zimmer, *Gymnasium,* 96 (1989): 493–520.

16. For more on villa life in this period, compare G. Hahn, "Der Villenbesitz der römischen Großen in Italien zur Zeit der Republik" (Ph.D. diss., University of Bonn, 1922); W. Kroll, *Die Kultur der ciceronischen Zeit* (Leipzig: 1933). For later discussions, compare J. H. D'Arms, in *I Campi Flegrei nell'archeologia e nella storia. Acc. Linc. Atti Convegni,* 33 (1977), pp. 347ff.; R. Neudecker, *Die Skulpturenausstattung römischer Villen;* Mielsch, *Die römische Villa.*

17. Lucretius sketches a nice picture of the villa owners restlessly traveling back and forth in *De Rerum Natura,* III 1060ff.

18. O. E. Schmidt, *Neue Jahrbücher für Antike und deutsche Bildung,* 2 (1899): 328ff. and 466ff. (Cicero's villas), reprinted and edited by H. G. Niemeyer and E. Thomas in the series of the Wissenschaftliche Buchgesellschaft: *Libelli,* vol. 324 (Darmstadt: 1972). Compare M. A. Sollmann in *Studies D. M. Robinson,* 2 (1953), pp. 1238ff., and Wallace-Hadrill, "The Social Structure of the Roman House."

19. Compare, for instance, the group that Cornelia, the mother of the Gracchi, gathered around her at her villa; Plutarch, *C. Gracch.* 19.1.2.

20. E. S. Gruen, *Culture and National Identity in Republican Rome* (Ithaca, N.Y.: 1992). For the archeological aspect of the subject, compare especially H. Jucker, *Vom Verhältnis der Römer zur bildenden Kunst der Griechen* (Frankfurt a.m.: 1950); J. M. André, *L'Otium dans la vie morale et intellectuelle romaine* (Paris: 1966); and most recently Mielsch, *Die römische Villa.*

21. Compare Hahn, *Der Villenbesitz der römischen Großen,* p. 12. One of the first libraries was probably that of Perseus V of Macedonia, which Aemilius Paullus gave to his sons: Plutarch, *Aemilius Paullus* 28. For libraries in villas, see R. Neudecker, *Die Skulpturenausstattung römischer Villen in Italien* (Munich: 1988), p. 70.

22. See Cicero's Letters to Atticus I 1.5, 4.3, 5.6, 6.2, 7.1, 8.2, 9.2, 10.3, 11.3, 16.15 and 18; Letters to Friends VII 23.2–3. Compare also Neudecker, *Die Skulpturenausstattung römischer Villen,* and the relevant contributions (especially those of H. Galsterer, G. Zimmer, and T. Hölscher) in *Das Wrack. Der antike Schatzfund von Mahdia. Katalog Ausstellung Bonn* (Cologne: 1994), vol. 2.

23. S. H. A. (Spartianus), *Vita Hadriani* 26. Compare Jucker, *Vom Verhältnis der Römer zur bildenden Kunst,* pp. 37–38; B. Kapossy, *Gymnasium,* 74 (1967): 38ff.; Zanker, in W. Helbig, *Führer durch die öffentlichen Sammlungen klassischer Altertümer in Rom,* 4th ed., H. Speier, ed., vol. 4, pp. 155–156; C. S. Sweet, *AJA,* 77 (1973): 229; J. Raeder, *Die statuarische Ausstattung der Villa Hadriana bei Tivoli* (Frankfurt and Bern: 1983). For a recent discussion of the Greek terms, see R. Förtsch, *Archäologischer Kommentar zu den Villenbriefen des jüngeren Plinius* (Mainz: 1993).

24. Compare F. Coarelli, *DArch,* 4/5 (1970/71): 476ff.

25. See the entry under *"hortus"* by Lugli in De Ruggiero, *Dizionario epigrafico di antichità romane,* rpt. (Rome: 1961); S. Platner-Ashby, *A Topographical Dictionary of Ancient Rome* (Oxford: 1929), pp. 264ff. Compare also Noack and Lehmann-Hartleben, *Baugeschichtliche Untersuchungen,* pp. 202ff., and Grimal, *Les jardins romains,* pp. 107ff. For discussions of *domus* and *horti* at Rome in the recent literature, see C. Häubler, in *Das Wrack,* vol. 2, pp. 911–926.

26. Neudecker, *Die Skulpturenausstattung römischer Villen,* pp. 147ff.; M. R. Wojcik, *La villa dei Papiri ad Ercolano* (Rome: 1986); D. Pandermalis, *AM,* 86 (1971): 173ff.; W. Trillmich, *JdI,* 88 (1973): 256ff.

27. For the sources of their wealth, see Castrén, *Ordus populusque,* pp. 37ff.

28. For more on the problems discussed here, see Zanker, ed., *Hellenismus in Mittelitalien*, pp. 14ff. and passim. Compare also K. Schefold, in *Neue Beiträge: Festschrift B. Schweitzer*, pp. 297ff.

29. H. Lauter, in Andreae and Kyrieleis, eds., *Neue Forschungen*, p. 148. Compare also H. Gabelmann, *BJb*, 176 (1976): 468–469, where he notes correctly that the width of *insulae* already assumes houses will be of the expanded atrium type.

30. For the House of the Faun, compare Kockel's summary of Hoffmann's research in "Vesuvstädte II"; unfortunately, Hoffmann's manuscript remains unpublished, although it was completed years ago. Compare A. Hoffmann, "Ein Rekonstruktionsproblem der Casa del Fauno in Pompeji," *Bericht über die 30. Tagung für Ausgrabungswissenschaft und Bauforschung. Colmar 1978* (Bonn: 1980): 35–41; "Elemente bürgerlicher Repräsentation"; and review in *Gnomon*, 64 (1992): 433–438; Zevi, "Pompei della città sannitica alla colonia sillana"; Zevi, "Sul tempio di Iside a Pompei," *PP* 49 (1994): 37–56.

31. These gardens were also taken over from Hellenistic models; see H. Lauter-Bufé, in Andreae and Kyrieleis, eds., *Neue Forschungen*, p. 169, and Fittschen, in Zanker, ed., *Hellenismus in Mittelitalien*, p. 547.

32. Fittschen, in Zanker, ed., *Hellenismus in Mittelitalien*, pp. 545ff. See also the discussion there on the problems connected with dating vista paintings in the second style (p. 543). Even if the later dates apply to the paintings in Pompeii, this style may have been popular in Italy before the Sullan era. Compare Tybout, *Aedificiorum figurae,* and the review by B. Wesenberg, *Gnomon*, 64 (1992): 433–438; Ling, *Roman Painting*, pp. 23ff.

33. See K. Schefold, *Vergessenes Pompeji* (Bern: 1962), which also has a color plate of this painting, pp. 36–37, 41ff., plates 3.2 and 20.

34. F. Studniczka, *Das Symposion Ptolemaios' II, Abhandlungen der philologisch-historischen Klasse der Königl. Sächsischen Gesellschaft der Wissenschaften*, vol. 30, no. 2 (Leipzig: 1914): 31–32; F. Caspari, *JdI*, 31 (1916): 42ff.

35. The structure known as the Palazzo delle Colonne in Ptolemais (Roman Cyrenaica) comes to mind: H. Lauter, *JdI*, 86 (1971): 149ff. For the connection with palace architecture (Nile ships of the Ptolemies), see M. Nowicka, *Bibliotheca Antiqua*, 9 (1969): 154ff.

36. Eschebach, *Die städtebauliche Entwicklung des antiken Pompeji, RM,* Ergänzungsheft 17 (Heidelberg: 1970), foldouts 2 and 3; La Rocca et al., *Guida archeologica di Pompei*, p. 326. Sadly, there is to date no publication available on the complex of buildings.

37. Noack and Lehmann-Hartleben, *Baugeschichtliche Untersuchungen.*

38. Compare Boethius and Ward-Perkins, *Etruscan and Roman Architecture*, p. 157 and fig. 82.

39. Back in the 1930s Noack and Lehmann-Hartleben noted the resemblance of these small villas to hillside houses in Rome, *Baugeschichtliche Untersuchungen*, pp. 202ff.

40. V. Spinazzola, *Pompei alla luce degli scavi nuovi di via dell'Abbondanza* (Rome: 1953), vol. 1, pp. 435ff.; K. Schefold, *Die Wände Pompejis* (Berlin: 1957), pp. 17ff.; La Rocca et al., *Guida archeologica di Pompei*, pp. 199ff. See the section "Display and Self-Promotion in Houses and Tombs," chapter 2.

41. A. Maiuri, *La casa del Menandro* (Rome: 1933); Schefold, *Die Wände Pompejis*, pp. 38ff.; La Rocca et al., *Guida archeologica di Pompei*, pp. 175ff.; Roger Ling, *The Insula of the Menander at Pompeii*, vol. 1 (Oxford: 1997). The phenomenon can be documented elsewhere in the later first century B.C. Compare the well-excavated house (*domus* III) in Bolsena, as shown in A. Balland et al., *Bolsena II: Les architectures* (Rome and Paris: 1971), pp. 234–235 and plate 9; and the loggia in the SUNY house in Cosa, as described by V. J. Bruno, *Archeology*, 23 (1970): 233ff. Compare also R. Ling, "The Insula of Menander at Pompeii: Interim Report," *Antiquarian Journal*, 63 (1983): 34–57.

42. I have based the dating principally on Maiuri, *L'ultima fase edilizia di Pompei* (Rome: 1942), passim, but his conclusions must now be considered outdated in part. Compare the critique by J. Andreau, "Le tremblement de terre de Pompéi," pp. 369ff.; and F. Zevi, "Il terremotò del 62 e l'edilizia privata," in Zevi, ed., *Pompei*, vol. 2 (Naples: 1992).

43. For recent studies on the dating of the earthquake, see Étienne, *La vie quotidienne*, pp. 15–16; J. P. Adam in F. Guidoboni, ed., *I terremoti prima del Mille in Italia e nell'area mediterranea* (Bologna: 1989), pp. 460–474; *Archäologie und Seismologie: La regione vesuviana dal 62 al 79 d.C. Problemi archeologici e sismologici. Colloquium Boscoreale 1993* (Munich: 1995).

44. For more on the subject see Spinazzola, *Pompei alla luce degli scavi nuovi*, vol. 1, pp. 369ff; A. Maiuri, *La casa di Loreio Tiburtino e la villa di Diomede in Pompei, I monumenti italiani*, ser. 2, fasc. 1 (Rome: 1947). The voluminous literature includes E. D. van Buren, *MemAmAc*, 12 (1935): 151–152; Jucker, *Vom Verhältnis der Römer zur bildenden Kunst*, pp. 28ff.; Schefold, *Die Wände Pompejis*, pp. 50ff.; H. Drerup, *RM*, 66 (1959): 164–165, and *MarbWPr* (1959), p. 14; H. Kähler, *Rom und seine Welt* (Munich: 1960), pp. 217ff.; F. Rakob in T. Kraus, ed., *Das römische Weltreich* (Berlin: 1967), pp. 184–185 and no. 85; Boethius and Ward-Perkins, *Etruscan and Roman Architecture*, pp. 315–316; McKay, *Houses, Villas and Palaces*, pp. 44–45; Castrén, *Ordo populusque*, p. 184; La Rocca et al., *Guida archeologica di Pompei*, pp. 240–241. Compare Jashemski's detailed discussion (with good documentation of the sculptures), *The Gardens of Pompeii*, vol. 1 (New Rochelle, N.Y.: 1979), p. 45; vol. 2 (New Rochelle, N.Y.: 1993), pp. 78–83. If the seal found in the first *cubiculum* to the left of the entrance (Spinazzola, *Pompei*

alla luce degli scavi nuovi, vol. 1, p. 369 and fig. 414) is any indication, the house could have belonged to a D. Octavius Quartio, of whom nothing else is known (Della Corte, *Case e abitanti di Pompei,* 3rd ed. [Rome: 1965], pp. 370–371, no. 800, with fantastic combinations based on the inscriptions on the walls; Castrén, *Ordo populusque,* p. 199, no. 285); F. B. Sear, *Roman Wall and Vault Mosaics, RM,* Ergänzungsheft 23 (Heidelberg: 1977), p. 93. F. Jung, "Gebaute Bilder," *Antike Kunst,* 27 (1984): 106ff.

45. Maiuri, *L'ultima fase di Pompei,* pp. 152ff.

46. Paintings of villas suggest that such miniature bridges were extremely popular on the grounds. A watercourse *(euripus)* almost large enough for a villa is found at the Praedia of Julia Felix (II 4.3). Schefold, *Die Wände Pompejis,* pp. 53–54; La Rocca et al., *Guida archeologica di Pompei,* p. 244, with ground plan; H. Döhl, *Plastik aus Pompeji* (unpublished *Habilitation,* University of Göttingen, 1976), p. 101.

47. Cicero, *Ad Quintum fratrem* 3.7.7 and *De Legibus* 2.2. Grimal, *Les jardins romains,* pp. 296ff. The Villa of the Pisones in Herculaneum offers two examples; see Crema, *L'architettura Romana,* p. 232, fig. 251; D. Mustilli, *RenAccNap,* new series, 31 (1956): 77ff.; Drerup, *MarbWPr* (1959), p. 3. Further examples can be found in Rakob, *RM,* 71 (1964): 182ff., especially fig. 9.

48. S. Aurigemma, *Villa Adriana* (Rome: 1961), pp. 100ff.; Rakob in Kraus, ed., *Das römische Weltreich,* pp. 190ff. on fig. 30. Compare W. L. Macdonald, *Hadrian's Villa and Its Legacy* (New York and London: 1995), pp. 108ff.

49. Noack and Lehmann-Hartleben, *Baugeschichtliche Untersuchungen,* pp. 205–206; D. Mustilli, *RenAccNap,* 31 (1956): 91ff.; Drerup, *MarbWPr* (1959), p. 9, where the typological "development," however, is in my view given too much emphasis. Clarke, *The Houses of Roman Italy,* p. 19; Mielsch, *Die römische Villa,* pp. 49ff.

50. Pliny, *Epistulae* 2.17 and 5.6; Förtsch, *Archäologischer Kommentar zu den Villenbriefen.* Compare K. Lehmann-Hartleben's edition with commentary, *Lettere scelte con commento archeologico* (Florence: 1936), pp. 42ff.

51. Spinazzola, *Pompei alla luce degli scavi nuovi,* vol. 1, p. 390, fig. 443; vol. 2, pp. 973ff., plates 90–96. Compare Jucker, *Vom Verhältnis der Römer zur bildenden Kunst,* p. 28.

52. Spinazzola, *Pompei alla luce degli scavi nuovi,* vol. 1, p. 383, figs. 432ff.

53. Cicero, *Att.* 1.16.15 and 17; 1.13.1; *De Legibus* 2.3.7. Compare the shrine to Hercules in the villa of Pollus Felix near Sorrento: Statius, *Silvae,* 3.1. For excavated villas, such as the villa on Brioni, see A. Gnirs, *ÖJh,* 18 (1915): insert, 99ff. For the use of a shrine as a day room *(diaeta)* compare P. Williams-Lehmann, *Roman Wall Paintings from Boscoreale* (New York: 1953), p. 107, with further examples of "shrines" at villas on p. 123.

54. Spinazzola, *Pompei alla luce degli scavi nuovi,* vol. 1, pp. 396ff., figs. 454–457, and

461; Döhl, *Plastik aus Pompeji,* pp. 149–150. The "boy with a goose" that has been turned into a *herakliskos,* or "little Hercules," is an interesting example of a change of taste on the part of the owner. The simple and familiar myth made the content of the Hellenistic masterpiece accessible. The bronze head between the claws of the Sphinx, which serves as a water spout, also creates a mythological link. Compare *Aquileia e Milano: Antichità Altoadriatiche,* vol. 4 (Udine: 1973), pp. 105ff., fig. 7; *Arte e civiltà nell'Italia settentrionale,* vol. 1 (Bologna: 1964), plate 28, no. 62; vol. 2 (Bologna: 1965), p. 146, no. 224 (I am indebted to H. Pflug for this reference).

55. Compare the "museum" in the park of Varro's villa near Casinum, which one should probably imagine as no more than a porticus decorated with the appropriate statues: Varro, *Res rusticae* 3.5.8. Compare also K. Schefold, *Pompejanische Malerei* (Basel: 1952), where the term is, however, understood in a very broad sense. I am indebted to R. Neudecker for pointing out to me a small poem found on the shaft of a herm that announces the equipping of such a garden "museum" at a villa on the Via Appia: see R. Paribeni, *NSc* (1926): 284.

56. Spinazzola, *Pompei alla luce degli scavi nuovi,* vol. 1, pp. 402ff., figs. 458ff.

57. Ibid., p. 391, figs. 444, 445; Schefold, *Die Wände Pompejis,* p. 53, no. 1. Compare also the section "Large Pictures for Small Dreams" below.

58. Spinazzola, *Pompei alla luce degli scavi nuovi,* vol. 1, p. 411, figs. 470 and 478. (Figure 80 of this book shows the sculpture as placed by the excavators in a decorative but false position.) This is reminiscent of the ivy-covered statues that resemble gardeners at the villa of Cicero's brother (Cicero, *Ad Quintum fratrem* 3.1.5). Compare Jucker, *Vom Verhältnis der Römer zur bildenden Kunst,* p. 43, and M. Kunze, "Griechische Einflüsse auf Kunst und Gesellschaft im Rom der späten Republik und der frühen Kaiserzeit," in E. C. Weiskopf, ed., *Hellenistische Poleis,* vol. 3 (Berlin: 1974), p. 1611.

59. Spinazzola, *Pompei alla luce degli scavi nuovi,* vol. 1, p. 409, figs. 467–468.

60. For the fountain figures compare B. Kapossy, *Brunnenfiguren der hellenistischen und römischen Zeit* (Zurich: 1969), pp. 40 and 60. For more on the popularity of *nymphaea* at villas, see Grimal, *Les jardins romains,* pp. 304ff.

61. Noack and Lehmann-Hartleben, *Baugeschichtliche Untersuchungen,* pp. 70ff., 186, and 221ff.; N. Neuerburg, "L'architettura delle fontane e dei ninfei nell'Italia antica," *RenAccNap,* 5 (1965): 31, no. 35 and fig. 49.

62. Spinazzola, *Pompei alla luce degli scavi nuovi,* vol. 1, pp. 410ff.

63. Ibid., p. 412, fig. 472.

64. Compare the basin painted with fish in the House of Epidius Sabinus discussed by Schefold, *Die Wände Pompejis,* p. 237.

65. See the entry under "piscina" in *RE,* vol. 20, part 2 (1950). Archeological exam-

ples are cited by G. Schmidt, *Il livello antico del Mar Tirreno* (Rome: 1972); Mielsch, *Die römische Villa*, pp. 23ff.

66. D'Arms, *Romans on the Bay of Naples*, p. 41.

67. In my view Drerup and Rakob overestimate the aesthetic component by interpreting the rigid perspectival arrangement as a stylistic phenomenon. If one imagines the aedicula filled by a statue or even a statuette similar in size to the two muses, then it would surely have blocked the view of the more distant elements in the series. And the fact that the lower part of the garden *euripus* is angled makes one even more skeptical: Drerup, *RM,* 66 (1959) and *MarbWPr* (1959); Rakob, in T. Kraus, ed., *Das römische Weltreich* (Berlin: 1967).

68. The only detailed description of the house is found in an unpublished manuscript by T. Warscher in the library of the German Archeological Institute in Rome: "A Key to the 'Topographischer Index für Pompeji' of Helbig," vol. 1 (1954), 63–83 (reference number: Ib Pompeji 5269). Warscher cites the most important earlier descriptions, including E. Breton, *Pompeia décrite et dessiné,* 2nd ed. (Naples: 1855), p. 271; G. Fiorelli, *Descrizione di Pompei* (Naples: 1875), pp. 115–116; Mau, *Pompeji in Leben und Kunst,* 2nd ed. (Leipzig: 1908), p. 368; Schefold, *Die Wände Pompejis,* pp. 102ff.; E. La Rocca et al., *Guida archeologica di Pompei,* pp. 287–288; Döhl, *Plastik aus Pompeji,* pp. 104ff. (with an evaluation of the finds relating to the marble decoration); Jashemski, *The Gardens of Pompeii,* vol. 2, pp. 130ff.; E. B. Andersson, "Fountains and the Roman Dwelling: Casa del Torello in Pompeii," *JdI,* 105 (1990): 234. Compare also the extensive documentation in *PPM,* vol. 4., pp. 470ff. The old identification of the house's owner (first proposed by Fiorelli) as a certain A. Herennuleius Communis, whose name also appears on the wax tablets of Caecilius Iucundus (Castrén, *Ordo populusque,* p. 175, no. 192; J. Andreau, *Les affaires de Monsieur Jucundus* [Rome: 1974], pp. 191 and 217), has been shown by Döhl to be erroneous. Surgical instruments were found in the house.

69. A picture of the fountain, now in a state of extreme disrepair, can be found in A. Ippel, *Pompeji* (Leipzig: 1925), p. 100, fig. 103.

70. W. Helbig, *Die Wandgemälde der vom Vesuv verschütteten Städte Campaniens* (Leipzig: 1868), p. 68, no. 240.

71. "Les murailles de la terrasse étaient couvertes de peintures peu soignées représentant des arbustes, des oiseaux et plusieurs figures qui semblent être des esclaves apportant des plats," Breton, *Pompeia décrite,* p. 272. Compare Döhl, *Plastik aus Pompeji,* pp. 111–112.

72. Compare the distribution of space at the rear wall of house III 2.1 ("House of Trebius Valens"), Spinazzola, *Pompei alla luce degli scavi nuovi,* vol. 1, pp. 281ff.; Schefold, *Die Wände Pompejis,* pp. 56–57; Rakob, *RM,* 71 (1964): 183. The fountain and *piscina* also correspond to the distribution at the House of Apolline: see Sear, *Roman Wall and Vault Mosaics,* pp. 68–69.

73. Döhl (*Plastik aus Pompeji*, p. 109) correctly points out the affinity with the House of the Mosaic of Neptune and Amphitrite in Herculaneum (V 6.7; Maiuri, *Ercolano*, vol. 1 [Rome: 1958], pp. 393ff.). Such artificial grotto elements can be found quite frequently in the later period of Pompeii's history. For their connection with villas, see Rakob, *RM*, 71 (1964): 185.

74. For further references to villa *diaetae*, see Förtsch, *Archäologischer Kommentar zu den Villenbriefen*, pp. 48ff.

75. P. Hermann, *Denkmäler der Malerei des Altertums* (Munich: 1904–1950), plates 224–228; further literature is cited by Schefold, *Die Wände Pompejis*, p. 103. Compare the good documentation in L. Caso, *Rivista di Studi Pompeiani*, 3 (1989): 111–130.

76. G. Fiorelli, in *Pompeianarum Antiquitatum Historia* (Naples: 1860–64), vol. 2, pp. 237ff., and *Descrizione di Pompei*, pp. 142–143; Mau, *Pompeji in Leben und Kunst*, pp. 368–369, and "Anhang" (1913), p. 49; T. Warscher, "Codex top. Reg. VI 10.1" (1936), nos. 90–120a, and "A Key to Helbig," vol. 4, nos. 409–418 (both works are unpublished manuscripts in the German Archeological Institute in Rome); Schefold, *RM*, 60/61 (1953–54): 111–112 ("Konkretisierung der Illusionsarchitektur"), and *Die Wände Pompejis*, p. 123; Grimal, *Les jardins romains*, p. 227; Sear, *Roman Wall and Vault Mosaics*, pp. 56–57; Jashemski, *The Gardens of Pompeii*, vol. 1, p. 45; vol. 2, p. 141. Compare also *PPM*, vol. 4, pp. 1050ff.

77. A reliable assessment of the various phases of construction is not possible without further detailed study. But for our purposes it is immaterial whether the house already possessed a simple garden arcade in the first century B.C.; the decisive final phase of remodeling dates without doubt from the last decade of the town's existence. See Sear, *Roman Wall and Vault Mosaics*, p. 58.

78. Grimal, *Les jardins romains*, p. 241, plate 16.2; Neuerburg, "L'architettura delle fontane," pp. 62, 75, 125–126, and plate 132; H. Lauter-Bufé, in Andreae and Kyrieleis, eds., *Neue Forschungen*, p. 171.

79. For depictions of Venus Pompeiana with a rudder, compare Spinazzola, *Pompei alla luce degli scavi nuovi*, vol. 1, pp. 191, fig. 222, and p. 215, fig. 243.

80. Compare the "sacred precinct" in the frescos at Oplontis; A. de Franciscis, in Andreae and Kyrieleis, eds., *Neue Forschungen*, figs. 23ff., and *Die pompejanischen Wandmalereien in der Villa von Oplontis* (Recklinghausen: 1975).

81. Noack and Lehmann-Hartleben, *Baugeschichtliche Untersuchungen*, p. 198.

82. Overbeck and Mau, *Pompeji*, pp. 369ff.; Mau, *Pompeji in Leben und Kunst*, pp. 376ff.; Sogliano, *RenAccNap*, 8 (1924): 136ff.; A. Maiuri, "La casa di Loreio Tiburtino"; Maiuri, *L'ultima fase di Pompei*, p. 157; Drerup, *MarbWPr* (1959): 12–13; Jashemski, *The Gardens of Pompeii*, vol. 1, p. 110; vol. 2, pp. 280ff. Compare also Williams-Lehmann, *Roman Wall Paintings*, pp. 104–105.

83. Spinazzola, *Pompei alla luce degli scavi nuovi*, vol. 2, pp. 727ff.; Schefold, *Die Wände*

Pompejis, p. 58; Jashemski, *The Gardens of Pompeii*, vol. 2, p. 102; *PPM*, vol. 3, pp. 406ff. For more on the owner, see Della Corte, *Case e abitanti di Pompei*, p. 358; Andreau, *Les affaires de Monsieur Jucundus*, pp. 244–245, and p. 268; Castrén, *Ordo populusque*, p. 165; La Rocca et al., *Guida archeologica di Pompei*, pp. 236ff.

84. Spinazzola, *Pompei alla luce degli scavi nuovi*, vol. 2, pp. 759–760, figs. 740 and 741.

85. Vitruvius 6.5.2ff.; Cicero, *Ad Quintum fratrem* 3.1.3; Horace, *Carmina* 3.22; *Epistulae* 1.10.12; Pliny the Elder, *Naturalis Historia* 31.6. Compare Förtsch, *Archäologischer Kommentar zu den Villenbriefen*, p. 77; Williams-Lehmann, *Roman Wall Paintings*, pp. 98ff.; F.-M. Pairault, *MEFRA*, 81 (1969): 425ff.

86. House I 2.17–19 has a small garden with an aedicula containing a statue of Aphrodite (Döhl, *Plastik aus Pompeji*, pp. 68ff.). House II 8.6 has a structure honoring Hercules in a large flower garden used for commercial purposes (W. F. Jashemski, *Antike Welt*, 8, part 4 [1977]: 7ff.). House VII 6.28 has a tree and altar in the peristyle, and fine paintings of gardens on the north wall of the peristyle (*NSc* [1910], p. 467, figs. 9 and 9a). House VIII 3.14 has what Fiorelli describes as "una statua di Diana ed innanzi un thymiaterion entrambi di marmo," *Descrizione di Pompei*, p. 326.

87. *CIL* IV suppl. 3, no. 6798; Spinazzola, *Pompei alla luce degli scavi nuovi*, vol. 2, pp. 754ff.

88. Förtsch, *Archäologischer Kommentar zu den Villenbriefen*, pp. 100ff.; Noack and Lehmann-Hartleben, *Baugeschichtliche Untersuchungen*, p. 222.

89. Étienne, *La vie quotidienne*, p. 255.

90. Mau, *Pompeji in Leben und Kunst*, pp. 294ff., with literature cited in the appendix of the second edition of 1913, p. 46; Maiuri, *L'ultima fase di Pompei*, pp. 98–99, and *MemAccLinc*, 8, 5 (1954): 450–451; Schefold, *Die Wände Pompejis*, pp. 93–94; La Rocca et al., *Guida archeologica di Pompei*, pp. 326–327; J. B. Ward-Perkins, *Pompeii A.D. 79* (New York: 1978), p. 46, with the plan reproduced here; Jashemski, *The Gardens of Pompeii*, vol. 1, p. 168; vol. 2, p. 121. See also *PPM*, vol. 4, pp. 87ff.

91. *PPM*, vol. 4, pp. 136ff. Schefold describes these paintings as "probably from the reign of Vespasian," *Die Wände Pompejis*, pp. 93–94.

92. A. Maiuri, *Ercolano*, vol. 1, pp. 302ff. See also Rakob in Kraus, ed., *Das römische Weltreich*, p. 185, no. 86.

93. C. M. Dawson, *Yale ClSt*, 9 (1944): 96–97, no. 35 and plate 13; Schefold, *RM*, 60/61 (1953–54): 117–118, and *Die Wände Pompejis*, p. 93.

94. Compare, for example, Spinazzola, *Pompei alla luce degli scavi nuovi*, vol. 2, p. 688.

95. Compare the House of M. Lucretius discussed in the section below, and the House of the Ephebe in the section "Dining under the Stars"; Spinazzola, *Pompei alla luce degli scavi nuovi*, vol. 1, pp. 281ff.

96. Maiuri discusses the good examples in the House of Menander, *La Casa del Menandro* (Rome: 1933). These small garden scenes, usually on dark backgrounds, are also freqently found on lower wall panels in other rooms. There is a particularly beautiful example in the *tablinum* of the House of Lucretius Fronto (V 4.11: see Jashemski, *The Gardens of Pompeii*, vol. 1, p. 35; vol. 2, pp. 153–156); see Schefold, *Die Wände Pompejis*, p. 85; A. Sogliano, *NSc* (1901), p. 153; *PPM*, vol. 3, pp. 1011, 1016.

97. Sogliano, *NSc* (1907), pp. 549ff.; Mau, *Pompeji in Leben und Kunst*, pp. 371–372; Maiuri, *L'ultima fase di Pompei*, pp. 113–114; Schefold, *Die Wände Pompejis*, pp. 153–154; La Rocca et al., *Guida archeologica di Pompei*, pp. 282ff.; Döhl, *Plastik aus Pompeji*, catalogue 26ff.; *PPM*, vol. 5, pp. 714–864. The arguments for a connection between the house and the family of the empress Poppaea are insufficient, and Della Corte's even more far-ranging interpretations are pure speculation, *Case e abitanti di Pompei*, pp. 76ff.; compare Castrén, *Ordo populusque*, p. 209. Compare also the extensive documentation of the entire sculpture collection in F. Seiler, *La Casa degli Amorini Dorati* (Munich: 1992), figs. 529ff.

98. Schefold, *RM,* 60/61 (1953–54): 111.

99. Seiler, *La Casa degli Amorini Dorati*, catalogue p. 38, fig. 614. Compare the classical Greek votive relief in house V 3.10, illustrated in Kraus and von Matt, *Lebendiges Pompeji*, p. 193, no. 266.

100. Seiler, *La Casa degli Amorini Dorati*, catalogue p. 29, figs. 590–593; G. Richter, *The Portraits of the Greeks*, vol. 2 (Oxford: 1965), p. 230, no. 14, figs. 1561 and 1563. Compare also the more recent studies by Neudecker, *Die Skulpturenausstattung römischer Villen*, and E. Bartman in E. K. Gazda, ed., *Roman Art in the Private Sphere: New Perspectives in the Architecture and Decor of the* Domus, Villa, *and* Insula (Ann Arbor: 1991), pp. 71ff.

101. Neudecker, *Die Skulpturenausstattung römischer Villen.*

102. Thus a fountain stood at each end of the south portico, for example, while a herm with a child (Eros?) stood at each end of the north portico.

103. *NSc* (1907), pp. 568ff.

104. Compare Döhl, *Plastik aus Pompeji*, p. 150.

105. Interesting in this context, for instance, are the corresponding statuettes from the *Isola sacra* found in Ostia, which are, however, of superior craftsmanship; R. Calza and M. F. Squarciapino, *Museo Ostiense* (Rome: 1962), p. 38, figs. 21 and 22; Helbig, *Führer durch die öffentlichen Sammlungen*, vol. 4, pp. 3037–3038. Part of the material has been assembled in Kapossy, *Brunnenfiguren.*

106. House VI 14.43. Döhl, *Plastik aus Pompeji*, catalogue 71.

107. Overbeck and Mau, *Pompeji*, p. 314; Mau, *Pompeji in Leben und Kunst*, pp. 372–373 (see also appendix to second edition of 1913 with list of earlier literature); Maiuri, *L'ultima fase di Pompei*, p. 128; Schefold, *Die Wände Pompejis*, pp. 246ff.;

Jashemski, *The Gardens of Pompeii*, vol. 1, pp. 42–43; vol. 2, pp. 231–233. For more on the garden, see Neuerburg, "L'architettura delle fontane," p. 131, no. 36; Kapossy, *Brunnenfiguren*, pp. 59 and 77–78; Döhl, *Plastik aus Pompeji*, pp. 141ff., catalogue 52–53. For the owner, see J. Day, *YaleClSt*, 3 (1932): 206ff.; M. Della Corte, *RM*, 57 (1942): 33–34, and *Case e abitanti di Pompei*, pp. 161–162. Andreau correctly argues that the case for identifying the owner as a wine merchant cannot be proved, *Les affaires de Monsieur Jucundus*, pp. 226 and 230. Unfortunately, it is equally impossible to prove whether M. Lucretius, "priest of Mars" *(flamen Martis)*, who appears as the recipient of a letter in a fresco with an *instrumentum scriptorium*, is the name of the owner of the house. This priesthood is not otherwise documented in Pompeii: Sear, *Roman Wall and Vault Mosaics*, p. 93. Compare also the more recent essay by E. Dwyer, in Gazda, ed., *Roman Art in the Private Sphere*, pp. 71ff.

108. We previously encountered the same phenomenon of "staging" part of a domestic environment's decor at the miniature villa in the Via dell'Abbondanza. We will find it again in the mosaic fountains and dining couches discussed below in the section "Large Pictures for Small Dreams," and in large wall frescos.

109. P. Soprano, "I triclini all'aperto di Pompei," in *Pompeiana: Raccolta di studi per il secondo centenario degli scavi di Pompei* (Naples: 1950), pp. 288–310.

110. For sketches of the garden paintings see F. Mazois, *Les ruines de Pompei* (Paris: 1824), vol. 2, plate 37; and W. Gell, *Pompeiana* (London: 1832), plate 32; *PPM*, vol. 4, p. 120. For this type of painting compare the frescos in the "auditorium" of Maecenas, *BullComm*, 2 (1874): plates 14–16. One should not, however, deduce an early date from this. In many houses in Pompeii the context reveals that such large garden scenes on walls in the peristyle or courtyard were painted almost without exception during the very last period of the town's history, when the houses were being remodeled and fitted out as miniature villas.

111. Compare Overbeck and Mau, *Pompeji*, p. 301, fig. 165 (plan), and p. 304, fig. 167 (reconstruction); Rakob, *RM*, 71 (1964): 182 and plate 51.2.

112. See A. Maiuri, *NSc* (1927): 52ff. and (1929): 365ff.; *MonPitt Pompei*, vol. 2 (1938), pp. 13ff.; *MemAccLinc*, 8, 5 (1954): 459–460. See further Schefold, *Die Wände Pompejis*, pp. 31–32; Rakob, *RM*, 71 (1964): 182–183; Neuerburg, "L'architettura delle fontane," p. 117, no. 18; Grimal, *Les jardins romains*, pp. 444–445; La Rocca et al., *Guida archeologica*, pp. 212ff. (with the ground plan reproduced here). Compare *PPM*, vol. 1, pp. 619ff. For more on the owner, his business, and his social status, see Della Corte, *Case e abitanti di Pompei*, pp. 325ff. and no. 647. For a more recent discussion see Andreau, *Les Affaires de Monsieur Jucundus*, especially pp. 259 and 158, and nos. 129 and 41.

113. For this type, which was used in several places in conjunction with fountains, see Kapossy, *Brunnenfiguren*, pp. 12–13.

114. For a recent discussion of this work see H. Sichtermann, in Kraus, *Das römische Weltreich*, p. 246, no. 261; compare P. Zanker, *Klassizistische Statuen* (Mainz: 1974), pp. 77 and 87.

115. For the "fence" of herms, see H. Wrede, *Die spätantike Hermengalerie von Welschbillig* (Berlin: 1972), p. 126, no. 3.

116. Döhl, *Plastik aus Pompeji*, catalogue, 4–5.

117. Maiuri, in *MonPitt Pompei*, vol. 1, fig. 20.

118. Compare Schefold, *RM*, 60/61 (1953–54): 122.

119. E. La Rocca et al., *Guida archeologica di Pompei*, p. 214 with color illustration.

120. See *NSc* (1927): 75ff.

121. *MonPitt Pompei*, vol. 1, fig. 27; *NSc* (1929): 354ff., plate 20; Schefold, *Die Wände Pompejis*, p. 36 (where his dating of the picture as "early third style," however, is in my view incorrect). For more on such "truncated peristyles" with garden paintings, see Grimal, *Les jardins romains*, p. 209 and appendix I, p. 457.

122. *PPM*, vol. 3, pp. 184–309. On the grotto *triclinium* see F. Rakob, *RM*, 71 (1964): 182–183. Proof of the popularity of *triclinia* surrounded by flowing water is also offered by the clubhouse of the *pagus maritimus:* O. Elia, *BdA*, 46 (1931): 200ff., and K. Schauenburg, *Gymnasium*, 69 (1962): 521ff.

123. For a recent discussion of the dating, see H. Lauter-Bufé in Andreae and Kyrieleis, eds., *Neue Forschungen*, p. 170. I believe, however, that the argument made there for a "developing" fountain architecture does not hold up, at least not in the case of Pompeii. The existence of imitation in a second-rate town of this period seems to me largely accidental; the various "types" were probably all available in merchants' stock simultaneously. See also E. B. Anderson, "Fountains and the Roman Dwelling: Casa del Torello in Pompeii," *JdI*, 105 (1990): 207–236.

124. *PPM*, vol. 3, pp. 481ff.; Lauter-Bufé, in Andreae and Kyrieleis, eds., *Neue Forschungen*, p. 171, with illustration in Maiuri, *L'ultima fase di Pompei*, p. 45; Neuerburg, "L'architettura delle fontane," pp. 121–122, no. 23, fig. 153; Sear, *Roman Wall and Vault Mosaics*, pp. 60–61. See also Anderson, "Fountains and the Roman Dwelling," pp. 208–209.

125. Rome, Region VI, on the Via 22 Settembre under the Caserna dei Corazzieri: *EAA*, Supplement (1970), p. 662, see under "Roma, Reg. VI" (Coarelli); W. von Sydow, *AA* (1973): 554–555. Compare also the remains of a *nymphaeum* found under the Bibliotheca Hertziana in Rome: W. von Sydow, ibid., pp. 557ff.; Sear, *Roman Wall and Vault Mosaics*, pp. 79 and 81.

126. *PPM*, vol. 4, pp. 613ff., 621ff.; Neuerburg, "L'architettura delle fontane," pp. 121ff., nos. 25 and 16; Sear, *Roman Wall and Vault Mosaics*, pp. 73 and 75. For a recent study of the House of the Small Fountain see Thomas Fröhlich, *Casa della Fontana piccola VI 8, 23.24* (Munich: 1996).

127. Staub-Gierow, *Casa del Granduca VII 4, 56. Casa dei Capitelli figurati VII 4, 57* (Munich: 1994); Neuerburg, "L'architettura delle fontane," pp. 129–130, no. 32 and fig. 115; Schefold, *Die Wände Pompejis,* pp. 185–186; Sear, *Roman Wall and Vault Mosaics,* p. 67.

128. W. Erhardt, *La Casa dell'Orso VII 2, 44–46* (Munich: 1988); Neuerburg, "L'architettura delle fontane," pp. 128–129, no. 31 and fig. 117; Schefold, *Die Wände Pompejis,* pp. 174–175; Maiuri, *L'ultima fase di Pompei,* p. 126; Sear, *Roman Wall and Vault Mosaics,* p. 77.

129. Schefold, *RM,* 60/61 (1953–54): 117–118, and *Vergessenes Pompeji,* pp. 146–147. There is a list of *paradeisoi* and Nilotic scenes in the index of Schefold, *Die Wände Pompejis,* and a list of "topia" paintings in Grimal, *Les jardins romains,* pp. 457ff. Compare further D. Michel, *La Casa dei Cei* (Munich: 1990), and M. T. Andreae, "Tiermegalographien in pompeianischen Gärten," *Rivista di Studi Pompeiani,* 4 (1990): 45–124.

130. Compare note 126. The two engravings reproduced in figs. 104 and 105 are taken from W. Gell, *Pompeiana* (London: 1832), vol. 1, p. 194, plate 53, and vol. 2, p. 4, plate 56. Concerning the House of the Large Fountain Gell observes, "The high wall was, at the time of its excavation, perfect; and this drawing is probably now the only record of its existence, the author having been fortunate enough to copy it before the painting fell," p. 125.

131. Schefold, *Die Wände Pompejis,* pp. 194–195, and *Vergessenes Pompeji,* fig. 151.2.

132. D. Michel, *La Casa dei Cei* (Munich: 1990); Spinazzola, *Pompei alla luce degli scavi nuovi,* vol. 1, pp. 257ff.; Schefold, *Die Wände Pompejis,* pp. 26ff.; La Rocca et al., *Guida archeologica di Pompei,* pp. 189ff., with a ground plan and color plate of the *paradeisos.*

133. For a recent interpretation of this much discussed passage, see Grimal, *Les jardins romains,* pp. 92–93; R. Ling, *JRS,* 67 (1977): 1ff.

134. *PPM,* vol. 4, p. 168; Grimal, *Les jardins romains,* p. 485, plate 3.2; Tran Tam Tinh, *Essai sur le culte d'Isis a Pompéi* (Paris: 1964), p. 51.

135. See, for example, Varro, *Res rusticae* 3.13.2–3; Appian, *Bell. civ.* 1.104 (Sulla).

136. *RE,* vol. 7 (1912), col. 838, see under "Gartenbau" (Olek); *EAA,* vol. 3 (1960), p. 883, see under "giardino" (L. Guerrini); Grimal, *Les jardins romains,* pp. 79ff.; J. Borchhardt, *Istanbuler Mitteilungen,* 18 (1968): 166ff.; J. Aymard, *Essai sur les chasses romaines des origines à la fin du siècle des Antonins (Cynegetica)* (Paris: 1951).

137. Vatican, Museo Chiaramonti. Amelung, *Vat. Cat.,* vol. 1, pp. 679–680, no. 550 and plate 73; Helbig, *Führer durch die öffentlichen Sammlungen,* vol. 1, p. 252, no. 327 (E. Simon); H. Wrede, *Die spätantike Hermengalerie von Welschbillig,* p. 139, plate 78.1.

138. *PPM,* vol. 5, pp. 264–307. The fresco of Orpheus has suffered considerable dam-

age since its discovery. See E. Presuhn, *Die pompejanischen Wanddekorationen* (Leipzig: 1882), plate 23 (the same fresco appears here in plate 14, with contemporary tints!); P. Hermann, *Denkmäler der Malerei des Altertums,* vol. 2, pp. 61ff., fig 21, and plate 240; Schefold, *Die Wände Pompejis,* p. 132. The same theme together with a large painting of a hunt (*PPM,* vol. 5, p. 106) is depicted on the terrace wall at the miniature villa (II 2.2–5). Schefold, ibid., p. 53.

139. "At Quintus Hortensius's place near Laurentum . . . there was a forest which covered, he said, more than fifty *iugera;* it was enclosed with a wall and he called it, not a warren, but a game-preserve. In it was a high spot where was spread the table at which we were dining, to which he bade Orpheus be called. When he appeared with his robe and harp, and was bidden to sing, he blew a horn; whereupon there poured around us such a crowd of stags, boars, and other animals that it seemed to me to be no less attractive a sight than when the hunts of the aediles take place in the Circus Maximus," Varro, *Res rusticae* 3.13.2–3, trans. W. D. Hooper, Loeb Classical Library.

140. Andreae, "Tiermegalographien." The individual animal types are perhaps derived in the last analysis from Hellenistic models, presumably small in format *(pinakes?).* The well-known mosaics from Hadrian's Villa could represent a modest reflection of them (compare Helbig, *Führer durch die öffentlichen Sammlungen,* vol. 1, pp. 106 and 203 [Parlasca]).

141. Schefold, *Die Wände Pompejis,* pp. 180ff.; La Rocca et al., *Guida archeologica di Pompei,* p. 268.

142. *PPM,* vol. 5, pp. 1069–1098; Schefold, *Die Wände Pompejis,* p. 89.

143. For more on the popularity of travel to Egypt and the opulent lifestyle of Alexandria and its surroundings, see L. Friedländer, *Darstellungen aus der Sittengeschichte Roms,* 10th ed. (1922), pp. 423ff.

144. Suet. *Nero* 31, quoted from *Lives of the Caesars,* trans. J. C. Rolfe, Loeb Classical Library, vol. 2, p. 137: "in the grounds of the Golden House there was also a pond, surrounded with buildings representing cities, as well as fields, vineyards, meadows with livestock, and woods with wild animals of all kinds"; compare Tacitus, *Annales* XV 42.

145. Overbeck and Mau, *Pompeji,* p. 355; Mau, *Pompeji in Leben und Kunst,* p. 39, fig. 6; Schefold, *RM,* 60/61 (1953–54): 117–118, plate 50.2, and *Die Wände Pompejis,* p. 277 (in the style of the Vespasianic era); Neuerburg, "L'architettura delle fontane," pp. 133–134 (with bibliography) and fig. 116; Sear, *Roman Wall and Vault Mosaics,* p. 84.

146. A similar frieze, also unrelated to the rest of the wall decoration scheme, can even be found at the House of the Vettii: see Schefold, *Vergessenes Pompeji,* fig. 138.

147. K. Schefold, *Pompejanische Malerei,* pp. 32ff. (with earlier literature and ancient

sources listed on p. 180, note 32), and *La peinture pompéienne,* Coll. Latomus, vol. 108 (1972), pp. 50ff.; H. Jucker, *Vom Verhältnis der Römer zur bildenden Kunst,* pp. 29 and 35–36.

148. Hermann, *Denkmäler der Malerei,* vol. 1, pp. 29ff. and plates 20–48. The earlier literature is cited by Schefold, *Die Wände Pompejis,* p. 139; Kraus and von Matt, *Lebendiges Pompeji,* pp. 70ff.; La Rocca et al., *Guida archeologica di Pompei,* pp. 269ff.; *PPM,* vol. 5, pp. 468–572. For more on the man presumed to be the last owner, A. Vettius Conviva, see Andreau, *Les Affaires de Monsieur Jucundus,* pp. 172, 190, 194, 205, 267, 277, and Castrén, *Ordo populusque,* pp. 239–240. Given all that has been learned about the Augustales, it can be viewed as certain that the Augustalis A. Vettius Conviva came from a family of freedmen. As we know, they were at the top of the "second" local oligarchy. For the "program" of the *pinacothecae* see T. Wirth, "Zum Bildprogramm der Räume n und p in der Casa dei Vettii," *RM,* 90 (1983): 449–455; for the sculpture garden see Döhl, *Plastik aus Pompeji.*

149. *PPM,* vol. 4, pp. 527–608. Compare N. Wood, *The House of the Tragic Poet: A Reconstruction* (London: 1996); B. Bergmann, in *Art Bulletin,* 76 (1994): 225–256.

150. Schefold, *Vergessenes Pompeji,* pp. 186ff.

151. Ibid., plate 138.

152. For more on these symptoms of "decay," see O. Elia, *NSc* (1934): 278ff.; Schefold, *RM,* 60/61 (1953–54): 113ff.

153. Compare the House of Meleager (VI 9.2), in La Rocca et al., *Guida archeologica di Pompei,* pp. 268–269; the House of the Citharist (I 4.5.25.28), ibid., p. 167, and Döhl, *Plastik aus Pompeji,* pp. 77ff.; and some of the terrace houses in the theater quarter, Noack and Lehmann-Hartleben, *Baugeschichtliche Untersuchungen,* pp. 224–225.

154. Compare Seneca, *Naturales Quaestiones* VI 1.1. For the economic consequences of the earthquake, see J. Andreau, "Le tremblement de terre de Pompéi," pp. 369ff.

155. Castrén, *Ordo populusque,* p. 121. Castrén's conclusions, to which I refer here, must now be revised in part as proposed by Mouritsen in *Elections, Magistrates and Municipal Elite,* and "Order and Disorder in Late Pompeian Politics," in *Les Élites municipales de l'Italie péninsulaire des Gracques à Néron. Colloquium Clermont-Ferrand 1991* (Naples and Rome: 1996), pp.139–144; and also by W. Jongman, *The Economy and Society of Pompeii,* Dutch Monographs on Ancient History and Archaeology, 4 (Amsterdam: 1988).

156. See Andreau, "Le tremblement de terre de Pompéi," and *Les affaires de Monsieur Jucundus,* pp. 163ff.

157. Consider also the case of the wine merchant who owned the House of the Moralist and the tavern in the "miniature villa." See Andreau, *Les affaires de*

Monsieur Jucundus, pp. 223ff., for more on the social and economic situation of this group in Pompeii.

158. See Andreau, ibid., passim.

159. G. Spano, *NSc* (1910): 400, fig. 11 (plan), and 402 (inscription); M. Della Corte, *Memoire dell'Accademia di archeologia di Napoli,* 2, 2 (1913): 185–188 (dated to the reign of Vespasian); G. Spano, *MemAccLinc,* 7, series 3 (1943): 237–315; J.-M. Dentzer, *MEFRA,* 74 (1962): 533–594; V. Weber, *Historia,* 18 (1969): 377–380 (before 62, but after Claudius [coins]); Castrén, *Ordo populusque,* p. 239, no. 453.1 (aedile 75/76, dies in office [?]); H. Mielsch, *RM,* Ergänzungsheft 21 (1975), pp. 55–56, and p. 139, cat. no. 50, plates 44–45 (from the reign of Vespasian). All the archeological evidence clearly suggests an earlier date, as Weber surmises. V. Kockel assumes the construction occurred in two phases, a phenomenon he has observed at graves outside the Herculaneum Gate. In my view, the tomb's affinity with the late domestic taste comprehensively excludes any allegorical interpretation with supposed allusions to the afterlife.

160. There is a color plate of the silverware in R. Bianchi-Bandinelli, *Roma: L'arte romana nel centro del potere* (Rome: 1969), p. 42.

161. Mouritsen, *Elections, Magistrates and Municipal Elite;* "A Note on Pompeian Epigraphy and Social Structure," *Classica et Mediaevalia,* 41 (1990): 131–149; and "Order and Disorder in Late Pompeian Politics." See also Zevi, "Pompei della città sannitica alla colonia sillana."

162. Such conclusions are frequently drawn, and are supposedly based on the conclusions of Grimal in *Les jardins romains.* However, Grimal himself takes a quite different view and has attached great importance to the influence of Hellenism.

163. A. Maiuri, *I nuovi scavi di Ercolano,* vol. 1 (Rome: 1958).

164. For cepotaphs see the entry under "cepotaphium" by Samter in *RE,* vol. 3 (Rome: 1899), col. 1966; J. M. C. Toynbee, *Death and Burial in the Roman World* (London: 1971), with a bibliography; H. Wrede, *RM,* 78 (1971): 127. Compare also H. Wrede, *Consecratio in formam deorum* (Mainz: 1981); W. F. Jashemski, *Classical Journal,* 66 (1970): 97ff. Compare further the statuettes mentioned in note 105 above from the cemeteries in Ostia. A collection of bucolic statues also belonged to the tomb of the Haterii: see A. Giuliano, *MemAccLinc,* 8, series 13, 6 (1968): plate 1 and fig. 21. Vistas of luxurious gardens continued to play a role in later tombs as well: see H. Wrede, *Die spätantike Hermengalerie von Welschbillig,* pp. 132–133, plates 76 and 77.

The continued use of elements from villas in later domestic architecture would be worth investigating; one only has to think of the well-preserved houses at Bulla Regia with their peristyles and fountains and corresponding *triclinia* and spots for rest and recreation: see A. Beschaouch, *Les ruines de Bulla Regia* (Rome:

1977). For the small *piscina* at the villa belonging to the Venantii family, with the inscription *Venantiorum Baiae,* see ibid., 78, fig. 74.

165. P. Veyne, *Annales: Économies, sociétés, civilisations,* 16 (1961): 213ff. See also the section "The Villa and Domestic Taste in the Empire" in chapter 1. I now believe that my description in this section tends to interpret the phenomenon too narrowly as the taste of freedmen.

166. Andreau, *Les affaires de Monsieur Jucundus,* pp. 170ff.

167. The need to distinguish between Rome and the provinces, and especially between imperial freedmen and others, is well known. For more on the view taken of themselves by the imperial *liberti,* who served as officials in the administration of the Empire, see the thoughtful essay by G. Lotito, *DArch,* 8 (1974/75): 275ff. That the taste and values of the Pompeians were not unknown to broad segments of the population of Rome is in my view demonstrated by the iconography of numerous Flavian marble urns: F. Sinn, *Stadtrömische Marmorurnen* (Mainz: 1987).

168. Cf. K. M. Coleman, ed., *Statius Silvae IV* (Oxford: 1988); H. Cancik, *Untersuchungen zur lyrischen Kunst des P. Papinius Statius,* Spudasmata, 13 (1965): 65ff. and 100ff.

169. Compare V. M. Strocka, ed., *Die Regierungszeit des Kaisers Claudius (41–54 n. Chr.): Umbruch oder Episode?* (Mainz: 1994).

Illustration
Credits

Figures

Alinari: 1, 9, 14, 34, 44, 76, 80, 91, 96

Anderson: 20, 83, 90, 94, 109

B. Andreae and H. Kyrieleis, eds., *Neue Forschungen in Pompeji* (Recklinghausen: 1975): 2

O. Brendel, *Introduzione all'arte romana* (Turin: 1982): 110

A. Degrassi, *Imagines* (Berlin: 1965): 26

H. Eschebach, *Antike Welt*, 10 (1979): 62

H. Eschebach, *Pompeji* (Leipzig: 1978): 27, 29, 58

H. Eschebach, *Die Stabianer Thermen* (Berlin: 1979): 16

H. Eschebach, *Die städtebauliche Entwicklung des antiken Pompeji, RM,* Ergänzungsheft 21: 11, 12, 25, 92

L. Eschebach: 17

Fotocielo: 28

W. Gell, *Pompejana* (London: 1832): 98, 104, 105

German Archeological Institute, Rome; InstNegRom: 3, 6, 7, 35, 39, 40, 50, 54, 93, 102, 106, 108

R. Graefe, *Vela Erunt* (Mainz: 1979): 56

H. Heinrich: 47

A. Hoffmann: 5, 8

Istituto Centrale per il Catalogo e la Documentazione: 31, 85

V. Kockel, *Die Grabbauten vor dem Herculaner Tor* (Mainz: 1983): 64, 65, 111, 112, 113

F. Krischen, *Die griechische Stadt* (Berlin: 1938): 4

E. La Rocca and M. and A. de Vos, *Pompeji* (Bergisch Gladbach: 1979): 35, 55, 73, 100

A. Maiuri, *NSc,* 17 (1939): 59, 60

A. Maiuri, *Pompei* (Naples: 1956): 46, 49, 61

A. Maiuri, *L'ultima fase edilizia di Pompei* (Rome: 1942): 68

Mau, *Pompeji in Leben und Kunst,* 2nd ed. (Leipzig: 1908): 42

Mau, *RM,* 11 (1896): 51, 67

F. Mazois, *Les ruines de Pompéi dessinées et mésurées,* vol. 3 (Paris: 1838): 18, 41, 45, 63; vol. 4: 10, 32

MemAmAc, 5 (1925): 23

Museum für Abgüsse Klassischer Bildwerke, Munich: 38, 43, 97

I. Nielsen, *Thermae et Balnea,* vol. 2 (Copenhagen: 1991): 70

F. Noack and K. Lehmann-Hartleben, *Baugeschichtliche Untersuchungen am Stadtrand von Pompeji* (Berlin and Leipzig: 1936): 71, 72

K. Ohr, *Die Basilika in Pompeji* (Berlin: 1991): 21

J. Overbeck and A. Mau, *Pompeji,* 4th ed. (Leipzig: 1884): 13, 99

Real Museo Borbonico (Naples: 1824–1857): 81, 95

D. Scagliarini Corlaita, *Studi sull'arco onorario romano* (Rimini: 1977): 52

M. Schede, *Die Ruinen von Priene* (Berlin: 1960): 22

R. Senff: 57

P. Soprano, *Pompeiana* (Naples: 1950): 101

V. Spinazzola, *Pompei alla luce degli scavi nuovi di via dell'Abbondanza* (Rome: 1953): 69, 74, 77, 79, 86, 87, 88

K. Stemmer: 103

V. Tran Tam Tinh, *Le culte d'Isis à Pompei* (Paris: 1964): 75, 78

Vatican, Museo Chiaramonti: 107

J. B. Ward-Perkins, in *Pompei AD 79,* exhibition catalogue (London: 1976): 89

C. Weichhardt, *Pompei vor der Zerstörung* (Munich-Leipzig: 1896): 15, 36, 53

W. Zahn, *Die schönsten Ornamente* (Berlin: 1828): 84

P. Zanker, *The Power of Images* (Ann Arbor: 1988): 48

P. Zanker and M. Pfanner: 19, 37

P. Zanker and von Harsdorf: 24, 30, 66

F. Zevi, ed., *Pompei 79: Raccolta di studi per il decimonono centenario dell'eruzione Vesuviana,* 2nd ed. (Naples: 1984): 40, 54a

Color plates

B. and D. R. Brothwell, *Manna und Hirse* (Mainz: 1994): 2

M. Carroll-Spillecke, *Der Garten von der antike bis zum Mittelalter* (Mainz: 1992): 9

V. Kockel: 3.1, 4, 5, 8.1, 12, 15, 16

F. P. Maulucci, *Pompei* (Naples: 1987): 3.2

PPM, 4, 1: 11.2, 14.1

E. Preshuhn, *Pompeji: Die neuesten Ausgrabungen von 1874–1881* (Leipzig: 1882): 14.2

P. Quignard, *Le sexe et l'effroi* (1994): 1

P. Zanker: 7, 8.2, 10.1 and 2, 11.1, 13

F. Zevi, ed., *Pompei* (Naples: 1991), vol. 1: 6

Index

REVOLUTION

European Radicals from Hus to Lenin

REVOLUTION

European Radicals from Hus to Lenin

Charles H. George

Northern Illinois University

Scott, Foresman and Company
Glenview, Illinois   London

Acknowledgements (listed in order of appearance of selections)

From *Epistola De Insula Nuper Inventus* by Christopher Columbus, translated by Frank E. Robbins. Reprinted by permission of the William L. Clements Library.

From *Great Problems in European Civilization*, p. 170 in "Du Bois." Kenneth M. Setton & Henry R. Winkler, Editors, *Great Problems in European Civilization* © 1954. Reprinted by permission of Prentice-Hall, Inc., Englewood Cliffs, New Jersey.

From *An Anthology of Czechoslovak Literature* edited by Paul Selver, p. 36 in "Comments of Peter Chelcicky." Copyright 1929. Reprinted by permission of Routledge & Kegan Paul Ltd.

From pp. 240, 244–246 in "Fragments" from *Meister Eckhart: A Modern Translation* by Raymond Bernard Blakney. Copyright, 1941 by Harper & Row, Publishers, Inc. Reprinted by permission of Harper & Row, Publishers.

From *The Praise of Folly,* by Desiderius Erasmus, translated by Hoyt Hopewell Hudson (copyright 1941 © 1970 by Princeton University Press: Princeton Paperback, 1970), pp. 56–59, 76–79, 85–89. Reprinted by permission of Princeton University Press.

From *Luther's Works* edited by Robert C. Schultz and Helmut T. Lehmann, Vol. 46, pp. 49–55, 51–52, 53–54. Copyright 1967. By permission of Fortress Press.

From *The Pursuit of the Millenium* by Norman Cohn, p. 267 in "Müntzer," pp. 365–367 in "Coppe." Copyright 1957. By permission of Oxford University Press.

From *The Leveller Tracts, 1647–1653* edited by Haller and Davis, pp. 52–56, 318–328. Copyright 1944. Reprinted by permission of Columbia University Press.

From *The Works of Gerrard Winstanley*, pp. 315–317, 566–570, 576–581, 596–597. Reprinted from George H. Sabine (editor): *The Works of Gerrard Winstanley.* Copyright, 1941, by Cornell University. Used by permission of Cornell University Press.

From *A Documentary Survey of the French Revolution*, pp. 87, 113–115, 305–306. Reprinted with permission of The Macmillan Company from *A Documentary Survey of the French Revolution* by John Hall Stewart. Copyright 1951 by The Macmillan Company.

From *Rousseau: Political Writings* translated and edited by Frederick Watkins, pp. 277–286. Copyright 1953. Reprinted by permission of Thomas Nelson & Sons Ltd., Publishers.

From *Collected Works of V. I. Lenin,* Vol. 4 Book 2, pp. 109–110, 136, 149–152, 153–154, 157–162, 165; Vol. 20 Book 1, pp. 106–110. From *Collected Works of V. I. Lenin,* reprinted by permission of International Publishers Co., Inc. Copyright © 1929.

From *The War and the Second International,* pp. 56–58. From *The War and the Second International* by V. I. Lenin. Reprinted by permission of International Publishers Co., Inc. Copyright © 1932.

From *The Dictatorship of the Proletariat* by Karl Kautsky, pp. 1–3. Copyright 1964. Reprinted by permission of The University of Michigan Press and George Allen & Unwin Ltd.

From *The Great Purge Trial*, pp. 514–518, 656–659, 664–668. Reprinted from *The Great Purge Trial*, edited by Robert C. Tucker and Stephen F. Cohen. Copyright © 1965 by Grosset and Dunlap, Inc. Published by permission of Grosset and Dunlap, Inc.

From pp. 98–113 in "Ignazio Silone" from *The God That Failed*, edited by Richard Crossman. Copyright, 1949 by Ignazio Silone. Copyright © 1950 (Hamish Hamilton, London). Reprinted by permission of Harper & Row, Publishers and Hamish Hamilton, London.

From *The New Class: An Analysis of the Communist System* by Milovan Djilas, pp. 1–14. Copyright 1957. Reprinted by permission of Frederick R. Praeger, Inc., and Thames and Hudson Ltd.

To David, Claudia,
Laurie, Andi,
and Jessica

Preface

We of the twentieth century have grown up in a brutalizing atmosphere of war and revolution. Americans in particular are repelled and frightened by the word "revolution." This mood of fear has distorted our perceptions of our own past, and in a world alive with novelty and wonder, has left us cowed, desiring only to be passed by its rapid changes and left half-made and at peace.

Here is a book to revive life, to stimulate a sense of *being*. Here is the record of the radicals. I want you to share my feeling that they are a wonderful crew, and that they represent not some sinister aspect of our tradition, but rather the best stuff that is in us. You will see in the organization and argument of the book that I regard the European revolution not as a recent aberration of commissars and bearded Cubans, but as the characteristic genius of our civilization. Some of our greatest radicals were born before Karl Marx—or so I hope to convince you. I don't wish to imply that creative radicalism is dead: yet the essential tradition of the men who have struggled for identity, dignity, and justice against a civilization built of superstition and force is dying.

Every civilization celebrates the successful: the compromisers and the clever, the manipulators of opportunity within the prescriptions of propriety, the tribal chiefs and their wise men. I find the greatness of Europe in its history of brilliant failure. Radicalism from the fourteenth to the twentieth century has attempted in a unique way to close the gap between ideal and practice, to increase the works of the imagination while demanding honesty of society. It has been a positive, specific, sensual, immediate, and utopian history. The beauty of radicalism in its traditional forms is threatened in our own time less by the forces of inertia than by internal weakness. Precisely because advanced radical ideologies have fi-

nally won political victories after five hundred years, radicals have been alienated by the fact that their cherished goals have been altered and sometimes destroyed in the crucibles of organized socialist power; they have therefore diverted their energies into exculpating their ideals of socialism from the crimes of its real and imagined past. The major existing socialist societies in the West have failed to inspire recent generations with admiration, or even, more seriously, with a desire to understand the history of revolutionary efforts.

Instead, the majority of revolutionary young are deluded by fantasies about the mystical "Third World" of races and cultures (in Africa, Latin America, and Asia) whose destiny is to solve the problems created by the mighty capitalist empires and socialist powers. They seem unwilling to accept the challenge to learning and thought imposed by the problems of twentieth-century capitalism or those revolutionary forms of socialism which betray libertarian ideals. In short, they have failed to understand the realities of revolution as history. The rest of the young are in still greater need of the radical record of western culture; for they threaten to lead us along the deadening paths of conformity.

This collection, then, is *engaged*. That is, I want to challenge the student of whatever ideology to look to the origins and development of those protests, radical activites, and intellectual revolts which have confronted feudal, capitalist and progressive culture in the West from late medieval times to these present years of crisis.

Now on with the tale of our out-of-step ancestors. What follows is centered upon a small group of people, often people of genius, who represent a responsive outgrowth of a consciousness of social cataclysm. The social cataclysm is that first adequately analyzed by Karl Marx as a transformation in Western Europe from feudal to capitalist society, the basis of which was the revolutionizing of the material, economic complex of technology, institutions and social relations which Marx called the "mode of production." I cannot even illustrate, let alone relate that massively consequential shifting in the social foundations of Western culture. But the process of change is nevertheless most fully revealed in the documents which reflect the social consciousness of modern Europeans. That consciousness, particularly in its more critical and creative forms, is the principal subject of this book. I hope, however, that a greater subject—the revolutionized civilization of the West—is also illuminated by my presentation of its revolutionaries.

C. H. George
Dekalb, Illinois

Table of Contents

x

List of Major Documents

1 The Crater in the Volcano

Where should our story begin? This is not an unimportant question for the serious historian of the modern world. Periodization in writing history is one of the crudest necessities of the trade for nothing "begins" in the historical sense; everything is contingent upon a specific past; and behind every event there is an antecedent and related event. Still, one cannot perpetually retell the history of the world; the seamless robe must be rent. The crucial decision is to determine—and it is always a subjective choice reflecting the interests and perceptions of the particular historian—at what coordinates of time and place the onrushing process of human social and cultural life takes on special meaning; at what moments and situations all of the raw, intricate mass of the past seems the stuff great stories are made of. The creativity of the historian must begin with this undifferentiated sense of meaning amidst the debris of the dead; it should end in the art of relating a refined perception of what happened in terms of the sympathies and curiosity of the writer.

My own sense of the past makes it hard for me to begin the story of modern Europe even though I have a very strong feeling that the history of European man took on a special dimension of revolt and rapid discovery that must be radically distinguished as a whole from the earlier pattern of life in Europe. However, I find myself just as interested in tracing back in time, and outward from Europe, the genesis of the elements of revolt and novelty as in describing the syndrome of events and persons that constitute the process of modernity itself. Further, it should be noted that when one "begins" an account of historical processes there is never any justification for the hideous textbook fixation on key dates—the dating of significant change can never be precise, and it is usually misleading. How can one learn to think historically if the Ottoman conquest of Constantinople in 1453 is taught as the key date in the development of modern Europe? Nor is the search for more appropriate dates good exercise in historical logic. Human culture, the essential subject of all general histories, absolutely defies such analysis: what one must learn to search out are *relationships* among a complex of events, the accumulations of activities, nuances of intellectual and emotional change—all of the multifactorial

shifts in ethos and social structure which can only occur in a complicated time sequence. Thus it is possible to date the trial of Joan of Arc, or the Statute of Mortmain, or Columbus' voyages of exploration, or the wars of Louis XIV, or even Descartes' invention of analytical geometry —but never can one date the beginnings of modern Europe, nor any of the major cultural and social features which distinguish that modernity.

Let me illustrate something of the complicated nature of our endless past with a brief excursion into the late centuries of medieval civilization to find some patterns of life which suggest the drift of European society toward those radical innovations we now characterize as modern. What I should like to emphasize is that medieval Europe was developing forms of organization, thought, and sentiment that have remained a living part of the western tradition: often these forms (and the people who give them life) are medieval simply in that they were not then predominant. There are at least three major categories of activities in medieval Europe which seem to me most significantly the basis of that modern revolutionary culture I hope to describe. First, the economic energy and organization of European entrepreneurs. Second, the beginnings of the modern national state. And, third, the varieties of popular uprisings and individual alienation which fill the history of the fourteenth and fifteenth centuries. This medieval subculture begins our story.

Medieval Economic Creativity

The economic activities of Europeans in the generations that followed the failure of the Roman imperium in the West were astonishingly varied and interesting. The stereotypes of medieval economic life as manorial humdrum involving primarily the dreary arithmetic of two-field or three-field planting schedules are far from the truth. From the 1100's on, Europeans were doing very exciting and original things as producers and distributors of economic goods outside the confines of village grain production (not to slight the earthy achievements of the monkish agronomists, of the bold frontiersmen in south-central France and eastern Germany, and the technological advances of horse collar and heavy plowshare). In many ways, the twentieth-century merchant and industrialist is a less imaginative and creative fellow than his counterpart in the brawling, bustling new capitalism of the twelfth century. Starting from the devastation and dearth of the tenth century, a brilliant, free-wheeling group of entrepreneurs in market towns, fair towns, old Roman cities, new city foundations, in the sees of bishops and the courts of kings, began aggressively to reconstitute the techniques and to rekindle the fires of energy upon which civilization depends. The European capitalists of the Middle Ages were working against staggering odds compared to their historic cousins in the eastern Mediterranean—their communities were a geographic outpost of the trading world, their transportation and communication problems were multiplied by the political localism of feudal governments, there

was almost no investment capital from public sources, the institutions of baronial and ecclesiastical rule were miserably inappropriate to serve the needs of sophisticated cupidity and predation, and the ideologies of European aristocrats, from chivalry through saintliness, were obstructive. Yet before Thomas Aquinas was in his grave the townsmen surmounted all, and in staccato bursts of energy turned the old, moribund western provinces of the former Roman Empire into the most productive industrial and commercial polity in the world.

The rise of the merchants from the twelfth to the fourteenth century is in one important historical sense revolutionary: it is the base upon which much of the political, social, and cultural revolution—the conscious revolution, as it were—of the modern European is constructed. If one asks why the world of the *chansons de geste,* the Rule of St. Benedict, the ordinances of King Louis IX, the epic of Dante, and the summae of St. Thomas—why it should have finally fallen before the anger and power of dissidents and revolutionaries, one may very well begin to look for answers within the town walls. Theoretically, and for a long time practically, the townsmen fitted nicely enough their relegated niche in the higher and controlling communities of barons. Medieval sources are full of platitudes about the "good merchant"; kings found them superb sources of quick revenue, and the more enterprising lords encouraged town settlements as a boon to the value of their feudatories. It was even possible for great merchants to derive from their subordinate role in the power structure of medieval Europe some sense of pride and public status—greater perhaps than that of the same group in the aristocratic society of Rome. Though berated in a thousand sermons for the sin of usury, for "fraud in buying and selling," even for turning a handsome profit, the merchant oligarchs could look to the satisfaction of power within their own institutions of guild and town.

On the other hand, much that developed within the towns was so new and vital, so obviously a function of the specialized self-interest of commercial and industrial entrepreneurs, that the dominant forms of medieval organization and thought were challenged or undermined. A thirteenth-century Venetian merchant named Marco Polo had expressed the adventurous, daring, ultimately subverting spirit of the citizen class when in the Prologue to his *Travels* he vaunted "that from the creation of Adam to the present day, no man, whether Pagan, or Saracen, or Christian, or other, of whatever progeny or generation he may have been, ever saw or inquired into so many and such great things as Marco Polo. . . ." Here is one of the earliest glimmerings of that peculiar individualistic verve which is alien to the status ideologies of medieval societies, and when raised to the intensity of genius, is the basis of Renaissance humanism and art. But curiosity and dash are only the finest flowers of the medieval European towns—almost as remarkable is the proliferation of organizations and skills. Florence in the year 1316 listed for tax purposes the existence within the town of some seventy-three kinds of business enterprise. The great export industries, the cloth industry above all, became amazingly intricate operations of organizational innovation and of financial and legal inventions which the usual

descriptions of guild economics (inherited from the reforming preoccupations of mercantilist and classical economists and bureaucrats of a much later age) badly misrepresent. Currently there rages a scholar's debate over the nature of business prosperity in the later Middle Ages. Professors Labande and Lopez argue convincingly that in Italy there was a general economic decline in the fourteenth and fifteenth centuries. But whether or not there was a falling off in the period of the Renaissance from the high rate of demographic and economic growth of the twelfth century, the total impact of the urban communities upon the traditional (that is, feudal, manorial, clerical) institutions and consciousness of Europe is assuredly the proper focus of attention for the student of modern revolutions. It was the city men, for all the provincial, cynical, self-seeking nature of their oligarchies, who were restless within the feudal status system and whose narrow self-interest led them occasionally to imaginative thought and action—led them to seek out legal, institutional, political, and cultural forms which would better serve the realities of town life, and the illusions of bourgeois *amour propre*.

Regardless, then, of the temporary stagnation in the economic growth of western Europe, it is from the documents that reveal the workings of the business communities that one first senses the familiar, the characteristically modern. The twentieth-century student who struggles to penetrate the mysteries of Dantean symbolism, of Thomistic logic, of chivalric allegory, or the arcane realities of feudal institutions and law, comes upon the letters, business instruments, and partnership agreements of the early capitalists with the shock of recognition. More appealing to the imagination, and as impressively modern, is the rationality and cupidity of the bourgeois orientation looking to exploit the late medieval technology of maps and ships which finally opened the seas to even more adventures than Ser Marco Polo had bragged of. We Americans learn early the name Christopher Columbus; in the following letter which he wrote to one Gabriel Sanchez,* the treasurer of Aragon, note the clear-headed emphasis on economic goals, the spiritual delight in the excitement of acquisition. The Crusades may have been imperialist adventures too, but in the Age of Exploration that opens in the sixteenth century, the ideological trappings of religious zeal are wearing pretty thin. The expansion of European power from Christopher Columbus to Joseph Chamberlain is justified in much the same terms of "white man's burden"; the difference is that Columbus and the early European imperialists were less hypocritical about their greed:

As I know that it will please you that I have carried to completion the duty which I assumed, I decided to write you this letter to advise you of every single event and discovery of this voyage of ours. On the thirty-third day after I left Cadiz, I reached the Indian Sea; there I found very many

---

* A scholarly controversy exists over the authenticity of various accounts of his first voyage, but the Sanchez letter is essentially the same as the other extant versions.

Islands, inhabited by numberless people, of all of which I took possession
without opposition in the name of our most fortunate king by making
formal proclamation and raising standards; and to the first of them I gave
the name of San Salvador, the blessed Savior, through dependence on
whose aid we reached both this and the others. The Indians however call
it Guanahani. I gave each one of the others too a new name; to wit, one
Santa Maria de la Concepción, another Fernandina, another Isabella,
another Juana, and I ordered similar names to be used for the rest.

When we first put in at the island which I have just said was named
Juana, I proceeded along its shore westward a little way, and found it so
large (for no end to it appeared) that I believed it to be no island but the
continental province of Cathay; without seeing, however, any towns or
cities situated in its coastal parts except a few villages and rustic farms,
with whose inhabitants I could not talk because they took to flight as soon
as they saw us.

I went on further, thinking that I would find a city or some farmhouses.
Finally, seeing that nothing new turned up, though we had gone far
enough, and that this course was carrying us off to the north (a thing
which I myself wanted to avoid, for winter prevailed on those lands, and it
was my hope to hasten to the south) and since the winds too were
favorable to our desires, I concluded that no other means of accomplishment offered, and thus reversing my course I returned to a certain harbor
which I had marked and from that point sent ashore two men of our
number to find out whether there was a king in that province, or any cities.
These men proceeded afoot for three days and found countless people
and inhabited places, but all small and without any government; and
therefore they returned.

In the meantime I had already learned from some Indians whom I had
taken aboard at this same place that this province was in fact an island;
and so I went on toward the east, always skirting close to its shores, for
322 miles, where is the extremity of the island. From this point I observed
another island to eastward, 54 miles from this island Juana, which I
immediately called Hispana. I withdrew to it, and set my course along its
northern coast, as I had at Juana, to the east for 564 miles.

The before-mentioned island Juana and the other islands of the region,
too, are as fertile as they can be. This one is surrounded by harbors,
numerous, very safe and broad, and not to be compared with any others
that I have seen anywhere; many large, wholesome rivers flow through
this land; and there are also many very lofty mountains in it. All these
islands are most beautiful and distinguished by various forms; one can
travel through them, and they are full of trees of the greatest variety,
which brush at the stars; and I believe they never lose their foliage. At any
rate, I found them as green and beautiful as they usually are in the month
of May in Spain; some of them were in bloom, some loaded with fruit,
some flourished in one state, others in the other, each according to its
kind; the nightingale was singing and there were countless other birds of
many kinds in the month of November when I myself was making my way
through them. There are furthermore, in the before-mentioned island
Juana, seven or eight kinds of palm trees, which easily surpass ours in

height and beauty, as do all the other trees, grasses, and fruits. There are also remarkable pines, vast fields and meadows, many kinds of birds, many kinds of honey, and many kinds of metals, except iron.

There are moreover in that island which I said above was called Hispaniola fine, high mountains, broad stretches of country, forests, and extremely fruitful fields excellently adapted for sowing, grazing, and building dwelling houses. The convenience and superiority of the harbors in this island and its wealth in rivers, joined with wholesomeness for man, is such as to surpass belief unless one has seen them. The trees, coverage, and fruits of this island are very different from those of Juana. Besides, this Hispaniola is rich in various kinds of spice and in gold and in mines, and its inhabitants (and those of all the others which I saw, and of which I have knowledge) of either sex always go as naked as when they were born, except some women who cover their private parts with a leaf or a branch of some sort, or with a skirt of cotton which they themselves prepare for the purpose.

They all of them lack, as I said above, iron of whatever kind, as well as arms, for these are unknown to them; nor are they fitted for weapons, not because of any bodily deformity, for they are well built, but in that they are timid and fearful. However, instead of arms they carry reeds baked in the sun, in the roots of which they fasten a sort of spearhead made of dry wood and sharpened to a point. And they do not dare to use these at close quarters; for it often happened that when I had sent two or three of my men to certain farmhouses to talk with their inhabitants a closely packed body of Indians would come out and when they saw our men approach they would quickly take flight, children deserted by father and vice versa; and that too not that any hurt or injury had been brought upon a single one of them; on the contrary, whenever I approached any of them and whenever I could talk with any of them I was generous in giving them whatever I had, cloth and very many other things, without any return being made to me; but they are naturally fearful and timid.

However when they see that they are safe and all fear has been dispelled they are exceedingly straightforward and trustworthy and most liberal with all that they have; none of them denies to the asker anything that he possesses; on the contrary they themselves invite us to ask for it. They exhibit great affection to all and always give much for little, content with very little or nothing in return. However I forbade such insignificant and valueless things to be given to them, as pieces of platters, dishes, and glass, or again nails and lace points; though if they could acquire such it seemed to them that they possessed the most beautiful trinkets in the world. For it happened that one sailor got in return for one lace point a weight of gold equivalent to three golden solidi, and similarly others in exchange for other things of slighter value; especially in exchange for brand-new blancas, certain gold coins, to secure which they would give whatever the seller asks, for example, an ounce and a half or two ounces of gold, or thirty or forty [pounds] of cotton by weight, which they themselves had spun; likewise they bought pieces of hoops, pots, pitchers, and jars for cotton and gold, like dumb beasts. I forbade this, because it was clearly unjust, and gave them free many pretty and acceptable

objects that I had brought with me, in order more easily to win them over to me. . . .

Finally, to compress into a few words the advantage and profit of our journey hence and our speedy return, I make this promise, that supported by only small aid from them I will give our invincible sovereigns as much gold as they need, as much spices, cotton, and the mastic, which is found only in Chios, as much of the wood of the aloe, as many slaves to serve as sailors as their Majesties wish to demand; furthermore, rhubarb and other kinds of spices which I suppose those whom I left in the before-mentioned fort have already discovered and will discover, since indeed I lingered nowhere longer than the winds compelled, except at the village of Navidad while I took care to establish the fort and to make all safe. Though these things are great and unheard of, nevertheless they would have been much greater if the ships had served me as they reasonably should. . . . □

In such ways, then, and in others I have not the space to discuss, the western European capitalist entrepreneur of the Middle Ages was shaping forms of life that were destined to prevail over those which constituted the "medieval synthesis," i.e., the power and ideological structure of the country aristocracy. They were creating or reinforcing long-range, often slow-working patterns of desire, modes of perception, and mechanisms of power which tended increasingly to confuse and weaken the barons.

The Genesis of Nationalism

As well as, and in conjunction with, the town-centered, basically economic innovations of the bourgeoisie proper, the late medieval generations experimented with political organization and thought which bear a profound relevancy to the modern state. In England particularly—and we shall later see the importance of England's political precocity in preparing that country for the first modern political revolution within a large nation—it is fascinating to trace the institutional, juristic, and cultist developments out of Norman feudalism which are the foundation of nationhood as we have come to know it in the modern world. However, for the purposes of this survey, the appropriate documents are mostly too recondite to demonstrate the emergence from feudal and Catholic concepts of the idea of a "state" and require training in the special mysteries of medieval symbolism: one must learn to interpret the novelties couched in the rites of the new coronation ceremonies designed to celebrate the monarchs as God-instituted power transcending feudal limits, and the newly devised funerary rites for kings which emphasized the immortality of the king's other body—the body politic, the fictive "state." Similarly, the expert can cull, from the inquests and statutes and royal commissions and charters and the generality of the innovating common-law procedures, a great deal of evidence indicating a tendency for the English state to become centralized, laicized, professionalized, and ultimately nationalized.

It is the nationalization of political feeling and organization in medieval Europe that is hardest of all to indicate; the sources are inconclusive and demand a great deal of experienced ingenuity from the interested student. Obviously, there are important elements of nationalism in the new monarchies referred to above. Then one must assess the relationship to the development of modern nationalism of the great disputes between the Roman church hierarchy and the lay authority systems in England, France, the Empire, and Italy. One might argue, indeed, that the political future of Europe is already adumbrated by the end of the thirteenth century in the dramatic struggle for power and prestige between Pope Boniface VIII and the kings of France and England. For the course of the dispute (the chief explicit issue was whether the Pope had a legal right to restrict certain financial demands made by the French and English kings upon their respective clerical subjects) made both the ascendancy of royalism over feudalism and the emotional supremacy of national patriotism to Catholic loyalty shockingly clear. The amazing revelation was that not only ambitious bureaucrats looking for power within the new monarchist institutions, but also the hierarchy of churchmen themselves, were conspiring to defeat and humiliate the pontiff. National church politics were becoming a reality long before the sixteenth-century reformations.

The nationalization of the outlook of the French and English ruling classes in the course of the thirteenth century is a major (I would judge the primary cultural) cause of the crisis in the feudal and clerical civilization which first became apparent in the reign of Pope Boniface. From the triumphs of Innocent III over lay and particularistic forces, which were climaxed by the extravagantly cooperative and saintly kings Louis IX in France and Henry III in England, to the complete and irredeemable degradation of the proud and able Boniface VIII at the hands of French and English national bureaucrats—this transformation in the workings of European power is one of the coordinates by which one can graph the origins of modern Europe. Here is the deep and ultimately decisive fissure in the unity of aristocratic rule, a split in the mechanisms and psychology of authority which will widen to confound the barons in the fifteenth and sixteenth centuries, and to engulf them in the seventeenth and eighteenth centuries. The process of nationalization in the thirteenth century is a largely subterranean one, and subtle, in so far as it is a cultural concomitant of language and custom; however, in such passages as the following from the *Chronica Majora* of Matthew Paris, the historian of St. Alban's, one can recognize familiar ingredients:

During all this time, through the many-shaped cunning of Satan, the people of England in general—barons, knights, citizens, merchants and laborers, and especially religious men, were laboring under a most pestilential infliction; for the higher ranks of the foreigners imposed on the lower classes so many laborious services and harassed them by so many robberies and injuries, that of all nations existing, England appeared to be in the lowest condition. In one place the houses of merchants, in another

their carts, and their small possessions, were forcibly seized on, and nothing was left as an indemnity for them, save tallages and ridicule. On seeing these proceedings, some even of the more noble of the English, whom I am ashamed to mention by name, said in their pride, and with accompanying oaths, "There are now many kings and tyrants in England, and we ought to be kings, and tyrannize the same as others"; and so they became worse than the rest. If anyone who had been grievously injured laid his complaint before the Poitevins, whose heads were turned by their vast riches and possessions, and asked for justice to be done to him according to the law of the land, they replied, "We care nothing for the law of the land: what are the ordinances or customs to us?" Thus the natives of the country, especially the religious men, were as dirt in the sight of foreigners, in whose steps some of the English were not ashamed to follow. On one occasion, Brother Matthew Paris, the writer of this book, and Roger de Thurkeby, a knight and a man of letters, were taking their meal together at one table, when Brother Matthew mentioned the aforesaid oppressions, and the above-named knight said seriously in reply, "The time is coming, O religious men! and, indeed, now is, when everyone who oppresses you thinks he is doing God a service; indeed, I think that these injurious oppressions and troubles are not far short of utter ruin." When the said Matthew heard this speech, it brought to his mind the saying, that "in the last days of the world, there will be men, loving themselves, who have no regard to the advantage of their neighbors."   □

Or again, from the raging, open dispute between Boniface and the Christian kings of Europe's two most important states, we might look at one of the polemical items from the hand of the *légiste*, Pierre du Bois, replying to a renewal of the arguments in the bull *Clericis laicos*, in which the sophistry of the Roman legal tradition is invoked on the side of lay sovereignty:

It can be clearly proved by the following arguments that the pope, writing in this fashion, is and ought to be considered a heretic unless he should be willing to withdraw his letters and publicly correct his flagrant error and give satisfaction to the Most Christian King, the defender of the church, for such injurious statements which were published throughout his realm and almost all the world to the extreme scandal and infamy of Christian peoples, especially those of the realm of France. In addition the pope has presumed falsely to call certain friends of the king heretics, thus doing great injury as will appear below. . . .

The pope desires, steals, and bears away knowingly the supreme privilege of the king which always has been and is subject to no one, and he wishes to rule all the realm without fearing the objections of men. The pope cannot deny that ever since the establishment of private property, from a time beyond the memory of man, the invasion of things in individual possession was forbidden and was mortal sin. The king has possessed his supreme jurisdiction and temporal privileges for over 1,000 years. This same king and his ancestors from the time of Charlemagne from whom he descends possessed the collation of prebends and the fruits of the

custody of churches. And he possessed these rights not by usage without title but by the gift by Pope Adrian who with the consent of a general council granted to Charlemagne that he and his heirs forever should nominate and elect whomever they wished as Roman pontiffs, cardinals, patriarchs, primates, archbishops, and bishops.   □

The above document represents a moderate usurpation by the state of erstwhile papal powers; it was followed in France by a fantastic outpouring of verbal vilification of the Pope and the whole shocking episode was sealed by an act of atrocious daring. The author of the worst accusations against Boniface (which had been presented formally to a national assembly), a royal functionary named Nogaret, set out with a troop of soldiers and arrested the Pope in his own palace at Anagni for the purpose of bringing him to trial in France! Boniface narrowly escaped this ultimate humiliation of his person and office when he was belatedly rescued by the citizens of the town, but he died shortly after the incident, borne down by the pall of indignities and defeat. The Church was never to recover the prestige, and therefore power, lost in this conflict of elites. Boniface was succeeded by a French prelate who gave praises to Philip for his zeal, and who moved the residence of the papacy to the French-speaking city of Avignon. Formal victories of the papal monarchy over the national monarchies of France and England were sometimes won in the ensuing two centuries, but the chief power of the Church—its control of thought, the means of propaganda, and the instruments of magic—was eroded away by the rising winds and torrents of national culture.

Following upon the rift in the ruling class over the power position and function of the Roman hierarchy, the way was opened to more effective heresy at the individual and popular level. Allegedly, Nogaret's ancestors were anonymously persecuted and murdered victims of the Inquisition; yet this son of the heretic Cathari, with the mantle of nationhood and royalty upon him, could grind the Pope himself to dust. For once the issue of sovereignty began to be raised in the maturing culture of Europe, two previously concealed truths were bared: first, that religious superstitions, though the most wordy and traditional, were replaceable by other superstitions (nationalism, greed, love, etc.); second, that the real sanction for any institution or group in crisis was the unsheathed sword—and not even the Inquisition could ultimately command the brute nature of this decisive instrument of power. Thus the fourteenth and fifteenth centuries are filled with popular religious heresies, mysticism (that is, essentially, religious individualism), and anticlericalism—a swelling tide of mass disaffection and protest. And a part of this mass movement were a few significantly talented and alienated individuals—humanists, mystics, reformers—whose defection from the prevailing church culture may have been as decisive in shaping the future of Europe as the raw power principles at work in the new states. Let us consider, then, all too briefly, some of the rare moments in medieval Europe when masses of people made history—always in anger, often in despair, and never with success.

Insurrections of the Late Middle Ages

The fourteenth century was almost as gloomy and stressful an epoch for the barons and prelates of Europe as the tenth century had been. In the tenth century civilization had, in its embryonic feudal and clerical organization, barely survived the predations of invading tribes from the southern, eastern, and northern periphery of Europe. From the monastic and baronial redoubts which held up against the terrible forces of social chaos in the dark age that followed the collapse of Charlemagne's effort to impose order and literacy upon the ruling classes, there had finally emerged that astonishingly resilient pattern of life we celebrate under such epithets as "the medieval synthesis." In the fourteenth century the adaptability of those institutions and customs that had so well served the ruling classes in weathering the terrible crises of the past began to fail. But the failure of a vast and complicated civilization like that of medieval Europe is a process, not an event, and it is a very uneven and confusing process. Thus the "breakdown of feudal society" is evident in northern Italy in the thirteenth century, yet the process is incomplete in other parts of Europe five hundred years later.

The history of the communes of Italy from Rome northward is so fascinatingly special, so precocious and yet strangulated, that in many ways the history of modern Europe simply repeats the experience of the Italians of the Middle Ages. The more one knows of cities like Venice, Siena, Genoa, Milan, and, above all, Florence, the more one comes to feel they are microcosmic experiments in modernity—rather like laboratory cultures of new organisms, too select and isolated to survive the glacial realities of the outside European environment. Of course, the cultural contribution of the Italians to the revolutionizing of European taste and thought is a permanent, on-going, and integrated aspect of modern European history; what I am thinking of here are the unique social and political revolutions within the Italian cities—much like later European national revolutions, yet unlike them in their limited nurture of power. Leviathan would need stronger meat to feed on.

Nevertheless, what a brilliant fossil discovery for the historian of modern revolutions is the act of Giano della Bella, which was promulgated in 1293 by his fellow priors as the Ordinances of Justice. This remarkable document represented the political victory of the big business interests of the city (the *arti maggiori*) over the old ruling elite of nobles. Not even Cromwell's Instrument of Government is as radically a republican—nor as explicitly an antifeudal—constitutional document. There followed in Florentine history, as in the parallel history of England three hundred years later, a political struggle between the power elite of merchant-aristocrat and the lesser guildsmen, complicated briefly but sensationally by a revolt of these lesser citizens of the republic in which the disenfranchised workers in the great woolen mills were drawn in to create the sociology of the modern revolution. Just as in later European revolutions, the lower middle classes quickly turned on the working classes at the moment of success, seduced by their social superiors and frightened by their social inferiors, fumbling hopelessly

through a morass of prejudice that betrayed every ideal of democratic cooperation espoused in the passionate June days of 1378 when Salvestro de' Medici was calling for the people to assert their rights.

Certainly the history of the Italian communes is important evidence of the disintegration of feudal authority in Europe, but the leap from feudalism to the sophisticated merchant oligarchies of the fourteenth and fifteenth centuries, and their precocious use of legal stratagems and propaganda and economic coercion—all of this Renaissance state making was hardly typical of the failure of feudalism in the larger states of Europe. For in Europe generally, the power of the barons was greater and the strength of the bourgeoisie less than in Italy. (It is one of the ironies of modern history that the Italian bourgeoisie, first victors over the nobility, should have been among the last of European business elites to taste the fruits of bourgeois revolution on a world scale. The slow-working revolutions of the transalpine peoples ultimately brought —on any quantitative scale of rewards—richer prizes.) If we look over the communities of Europe in the later Middle Ages, we can find not the emergence of brilliant cadres of bourgeois political leaders as in Florence, but increasingly obvious indications of the failure of the feudal state, especially in its church organization and ideology, to command obedience from the common people of village and town. To be sure, the feudal state was weakened at the top by the endemic disinclination of the barons to work at governing, and by the financial and psychological excesses of the so-called Hundred Years' War (which turned out to be rather more than the sort of aristocratic warfare characteristic of classical feudalism). But the wars among the upper classes and the laziness and short-sightedness of the barons were weaknesses in feudalism which could only be exploited if the docility of the lower classes were ended. It is the restive thrust of popular agitation which marks out the decisive decline of feudal power in the West. The great revolutions of the sixteenth and seventeenth centuries all based their sanctions and success upon this popular, tradition-rich hostility to the old order.

The geography of popular revolt in the later Middle Ages is impressive: nearly every corner of Europe was affected, and great kingdoms as well as city-states were shaken by the new violence. There are also complexes of revolution and power politics in the fourteenth century which, superficially at least, remind one of the daily papers. For example, note the pattern of events which led up to the outbreak of the Hundred Years' War between France and England. The industrialization of the Flemish towns in the thirteenth century and the class war which resulted directly impinged on the major dynastic dispute of the century. Edward III of England was able to fish in the troubled waters of proletarian revolt in the weaving towns of Flanders to catch for himself the crown of France! The power struggle in the Flemish towns would make a case study of Marxist sociology—much purer than the later "modern" revolutions in Holland and England. Briefly, the capitalist classes in the new industrial towns were struggling to keep their workers in order. This was a problem in many of the cities of industrial capitalism: the capitalist elites were new and they had neither the

posture of military aristocracy nor the traditions of customary law that kept the barons in control of the country areas. The long-range device for controlling industrial workers most effectively was, of course, the national state with its vast reserves of military power and ideological sanction. However, the Flemish capitalists had only a weak count for a sovereign. As the material and psychological conditions of work in the wool industries grew worse in the fourteenth century, and the resentment of the workers reached the danger point, the industrial patriciate felt their control of the town governments an inadequate safeguard of their property and lives—so they turned for a safer sanction to the King of France. It was at this juncture in the social history of Flanders that the agents of Edward III proposed to the leaders of the Flemish workers that they look to the English monarch for a countervailing support against the intrusion of France on behalf of the rich oligarchs. The most notable of the leaders of a series of successful revolts of workers in the Flemish towns, one Jacques van Artevelde, threw the support of the proletariat to Edward upon the condition that the English king would renew his claim to the throne of France. The greatest of medieval wars was thus launched from the politics of industrial misery. Needless to say, the futility of the workers' uprisings was even greater than that of Edward's knightly megalomania; they had not yet learned to hate and act with the durable passion that makes a revolution.

France in the fourteenth century was spared none of the calamities of faltering feudal society in other parts of Europe—her villages were laid waste by the most brutal and stupid of medieval military adventures, her kings seemed to have lost the touch of Capetian genius in the Valois line, she was ravaged horribly by the Black Death, and hideously frustrated revolution stalked the land. So bad were things in France after the visitation of plague and the defeat at Poitiers (1356) which resulted in lodging the King of France in the Tower of London, that even the timid merchants of Paris were pushed to revolt under the leadership of Étienne Marcel who demanded middle-class councilors in the royal government, and killed the ones held responsible for national disaster. The revolt at Paris led, in what would become a classic pattern, to uprisings in the countryside. With the King happily in prison in England, the Dauphin cowering in the provinces, the council murdered or in flight, it would seem that almost any organized group with a will could have ruled France. But the conditions which lead to revolution were not present. The bourgeoisie wanted only reform in the central government, the peasants wanted only relief for their hopeless anger. The entire episode ended, predictably, with everyone turning on the peasants, and the flower of French chivalry butchering the villagers in one of the most gruesome blood-baths in history.

Not twenty-five years later there was another great peasant uprising, this time in the best governed large state in Europe—England. Although the pretext for revolt was a tax grievance against the government of Richard II's minority, and was linked therefore to the heavy and unpopular burden of the Hundred Years' War, the motives of the insurgents went deeper. Their anger, like that of the German peasants

one hundred and fifty years later, was directed against primary mechanisms within the social system: the customary manorial services to the lord, the restrictive aristocratic forest laws, the wealth of the Church. These demands for the freer sharing of the land and game of England, for greater security and opportunity for the farmer in the village through fixed rents, and the animus expressed against institutional Christianity represented more than a temporary disaffection resulting from the fortuitous bad luck with nature and disease and the stupid wars of the century. The English historian, G. M. Trevelyan, puts the case strongly, perhaps, but interestingly:

Nothing is more remarkable than the change in the temper and mental activity of the lower orders during the fourteenth century. Professor Davis has summed up the reign of Henry III with the words: "Of all the contrasts which strike us in medieval life, none is so acute as that between the intellectual ferment in the upper class and the oriental passivity of their inferiors." But in the reign of Edward III the peasants could no longer be accused of "oriental passivity," and the "intellectual ferment" in their ranks reminds us of a modern labor movement. Village unions strike for higher wages, villeins demand freedom in return for 4d. an acre rent, and men ask each other in every field that deep-probing question—

When Adam delved and Eve span
Who was then the gentleman?   □

The intellectual radicalism of the rebellion was, of course, expressed in Christian symbols—the powerful and beautiful phrases of egalitarian morality torn out of the aseptic swaddling of medieval theology by a daring band of itinerant preachers to villagers and occasional artisan gatherings. Indeed, the English poet William Langland, in his splendid *Piers the Plowman*, also warned of the subversive results of university education in the humanities upon the students of the lower classes (who might, like the inflammatory preacher John Ball, come upon a lively teacher of the caliber of John Wyclif):

Envy heard this; and bade friars go to school,
And learn Logic and Law, and also Contemplation,
And preach to men of Plato, and prove it by Seneca,
That all things under heaven ought to be in common.
He lies, as I live, who to the unlearned so preaches,
For God made to men a law, and Moses taught it:
Thou shalt not covet any thing that is thy neighbor's.   □

There is some evidence in the chronicles of Thomas Walsingham and Jean Froissart that the ancient fantasy of a Golden Age when men lived as brothers—in material as well as spiritual equality—was for the first time in European history invoked as a social prospect, as a millenarian certainty, by John Ball and his fellow preachers. The host of the Lord were the commonalty of England, and the justice of God would reign

with the destruction by the common man, the peasant villager, of the rich oppressors, the barons and prelates. Here is Froissart's account (he, of course, was completely on the side of the upper classes) of the critical events of June 1381:

While these conferences were going forward, there happened in England great commotions among the lower ranks of the people, by which England was near ruined without resource. Never was a country in such jeopardy as this was at that period, and all through the too great comfort of the commonalty. Rebellion was stirred up, as it was formerly done in France by the Jacques Bons hommes, who did much evil, and sore troubled the kingdom of France.

It is marvelous from what a trifle this pestilence raged in England. In order that it may serve as an example to mankind, I will speak of all that was done, from the information I had at the time on the subject.

It is customary in England, as well as in several other countries, for the nobility to have great privileges over the commonalty, whom they keep in bondage; that is to say, they are bound by law and custom to plow the lands of gentlemen, to harvest the grain, to carry it home to the barn, to thrash and winnow it: they are also bound to harvest the hay and carry it home. All these services they are obliged to perform for their lords, and many more in England than in other countries. The prelates and gentlemen are thus served. In the counties of Kent, Essex, Sussex and Bedford, these services are more oppressive than in all the rest of the kingdom.

The evil-disposed in these districts began to rise, saying, they were too severely oppressed; that at the beginning of the world there were no slaves, and that no one ought to be treated as such, unless he had committed treason against his lord, as Lucifer had done against God: but they had done no such thing, for they were neither angels nor spirits, but men formed after the same likeness with their lords, who treated them as beasts. This they would not longer bear, but had determined to be free, and if they labored or did any other works for their lords, they would be paid for it.

A crazy priest in the county of Kent, called John Ball, who, for his absurd preaching, had been thrice confined in the prison of the arch-bishop of Canterbury, was greatly instrumental in inflaming them with those ideas. He was accustomed every Sunday after mass, as the people were coming out of the church, to preach to them in the market-place and assemble a crowd around him; to whom he would say, "My good friends, things cannot go on well in England, nor ever will until everything shall be in common; when there shall neither be vassal nor lord, and all distinc-tions leveled; when the lords shall be no more masters than ourselves. How ill have they used us? and for what reason do they thus hold us in bondage? Are we not all descended from the same parents, Adam and Eve? and what can they show, or what reasons give, why they should be more the masters than ourselves? except, perhaps, in making us labor and work for them to spend. They are clothed in velvets and rich stuffs, ornamented with ermine and other furs, while we are forced to wear poor cloth. They have wines, spices and fine bread, when we have only rye and

the refuse of the straw; and, if we drink, it must be water. They have handsome seats and manors, when we must brave the wind and rain in our labors in the fields; but it is from our labor they have wherewith to support their pomp. We are called slaves; and, if we do not perform our services, we are beaten, and we have not any sovereign to whom we can complain, or who wishes to hear us and do us justice. Let us go to the king, who is young, and remonstrate with him on our servitude, telling him we must have it otherwise or that we shall find a remedy for it ourselves. If we wait on him in a body, all those who come under the appellation of slaves, or are held in bondage, will follow us in the hopes of being free. When the king shall see us, we shall obtain a favorable answer, or we must then seek ourselves to amend our condition."

With such words as these did John Ball harangue the people, at his village every Sunday after mass, for which he was much beloved by them. Some who wished no good declared it was very true, and murmuring to each other as they were going to the fields on the road from one village to another, or at their different houses said, "John Ball preaches such and such things, and he speaks truth."

The archbishop of Canterbury, on being informed of this, had John Ball arrested, and imprisoned for two or three months by way of punishment; but it would have been better if he had been confined during his life, or been put to death, than to have been suffered thus to act. The archbishop set him at liberty, for he could not for conscience sake have put him to death. The moment John Ball was out of prison, he returned to his former errors.

Numbers in the city of London having heard of his preaching, being envious of the rich men and nobility, began to say among themselves, that the kingdom was too badly governed, and the nobility had seized on all the gold and silver coin. These wicked Londoners, therefore, began to assemble and to rebel: they sent to tell those in the adjoining counties, they might come boldly to London, and bring their companions with them, for they would find the town open to them, and the commonalty in the same way of thinking; that they would press the king so much, there should no longer be a slave in England.

These promises stirred up those in the counties of Kent, Essex, Sussex and Bedford, and the adjoining country, so that they marched toward London; and, when they arrived near, they were upward of 60,000. They had a leader called Wat Tyler, and with him were Jack Straw and John Ball: these three were their commanders, but the principal was Wat Tyler. This Wat had been a tiler of houses, a bad man, and a great enemy to the nobility. When these wicked people first began to rise, all London, except their friends, were very much frightened. The mayor and rich citizens assembled in council, on hearing they were coming to London, and debated whether they should shut the gates and refuse to admit them; but, having well considered, they determined not to do so, as they should run a risk of having the suburbs burned.

The gates were therefore thrown open, when they entered in troops of one or two hundred, by twenties or thirties, according to the populousness of the towns they came from; and as they came into London they lodged

themselves. But it is a truth, that full two-thirds of these people knew not what they wanted, nor what they sought for: they followed one another like sheep, or like to the shepherds of old, who said they were going to conquer the holy land, and afterward accomplished nothing. In such manner did these poor fellows and vassals come to London from distances of a hundred and sixty leagues, but the greater part from those counties I have mentioned, and on their arrival they demanded to see the king.

The gentlemen of the country, the knights and squires, began to be alarmed when they saw the people thus rise; and, if they were frightened, they had sufficient reason, for less causes create fear. They began to collect together as well as they could. . . .

In order that gentlemen and others may take example, and correct wicked rebels, I will most amply detail how this business was conducted.   ◻

The rebellion was broken with astonishing ease—essentially because the leadership were willing to leave too much to God, and not, like Cromwell later, act for Him. The organization of rebellion lacked depth, the obvious stratagems of the monarchy and the upper classes were not anticipated, and the fires of resentment and hate had not been stoked to form the lava beds of ideology. The King handled the rebels in London by very simply—in person and by royal letters—lying to them; he promised them emancipation from serfdom. Their most ambitious and effective leader, Wat Tyler, was murdered while in conference with the King, and London was lost. The rest is silence—and terror.

Suggested Reading

At the end of each chapter I will give a brief annotated list of reading available in English. These lists will necessarily vary in length and quality and kinds of scholarship (source collections, monographs, surveys, etc.), but each will give the student a good start in deepening his understanding of the particulars of revolution in Europe. Those books which are available in softbound editions will be designated by an asterisk.

A good place to begin reading about late medieval Europe is in Chapters 11–14 of J. R. Strayer and Dana C. Munro, *The Middle Ages,* Fourth Edition (New York: Appleton-Century-Crofts, 1959). This is much more than a good textbook. Then probably E. P. Cheyney, *The Dawn of a New Era** (New York: Harper & Bros., 1936; Torchbook*) which remains a suggestive interpretation. A counterargument to Cheyney's can be considered in J. Huizinga, *The Waning of the Middle Ages** (London: Edward Arnold Ltd., 1924; Anchor*); Henri Pirenne, *Economic and Social History of Medieval Europe** (New York: Century Co., 1931) is a solid book. Volumes two and three of *The Cambridge Economic History of Europe* (London: Cambridge University Press, 1963) have some excellent essays. And there is a fine Marxist essay, *Feudal Order** (New York: Henry Schuman Inc., 1953; Schuman Paperbacks*) by Marion Gibbs which is an insightful excursion into the civilization which was first really illuminated by Marc Bloch in his classic, immensely influential *Feudal Society** (Chi-

cago: University of Chicago Press, 1961; Phoenix*). Finally, perhaps the most brilliant and enduring of all economic studies of England—one which I will refer to for a later period as well—is by the Marxist doyen of the English-speaking world, Maurice Dobb, whose *Studies in the Development of Capitalism** (New York: International Publishers Co., Inc., 1947) is indispensable.

On economic and social matters, in addition to the above, there is a solid history of business by N. S. B. Gras, *Business and Capitalism* (New York: F. S. Crofts Co., 1939). Peasant and lord on the land are treated in volume one of *The Cambridge Economic History of Europe* (London: Cambridge University Press, 1941). For England there is G. G. Coulton, *The Medieval Village** (London: Cambridge University Press, 1926; Torchbook*) and for France another classic study by Marc Bloch translated as *French Rural History** (Berkeley: University of California Press, 1966). For the towns see Henri Pirenne, *Medieval Cities** (Princeton: Princeton University Press, 1925; Princeton Paperbacks*); F. Schevill, *A History of Florence** in two volumes (New York: Harcourt, Brace & Co., 1936; Torchbook*) is a minor masterpiece; Gene Brucker, *Florentine Politics and Society, 1343–1376* (Princeton: Princeton University Press, 1962) is a model study; and another fine reconstruction of a medieval city is David Herlihy, *Pisa in the Early Renaissance* (New Haven: Yale University Press, 1958). For further information about the bourgeoisie and their activities, see Eleanora Carus-Wilson, *Medieval Merchant Ventures* (London: Methuen & Co., Ltd., 1954); F. C. Lane and Jelle C. Riemersma, eds., *Enterprise and Secular Change* (London: George Allen & Unwin Ltd., 1953); and the documents edited by Robert S. Lopez and Irving W. Raymond, *Medieval Trade in the Mediterranean World* (New York: Cornell University Press, 1955). Finally, the most important of all changes which created modern capitalism can be surveyed in C. E. Nowell, *The Great Discoveries and the First Colonial Empires** (Ithaca, New York: Cornell University Press, 1954; Cornell Paperback*), and one of the great adventurers into new worlds is well re-created in S. E. Morison, *Admiral of the Ocean Sea* (Boston: Little, Brown and Company, 1942).

The Church and English heresy and revolt are well introduced by Geoffrey Barraclough, *The Medieval Papacy** (New York: Harcourt, Brace & World, Inc., 1968); R. H. Bainton, ed., *The Medieval Church** (Princeton: Anvil Books, D. Van Nostrand Co., Inc., 1964); G. M. Trevelyan, *England in the Age of Wyclif* (London: Longmans, Green & Co., Ltd., 1900); and H. B. Workman, *John Wyclif,* two volumes (London: The Clarendon Press, 1926).

2　The Bohemian Fight for Freedom

Bohemia in the Fifteenth Century

The fourteenth-century ruling classes in Europe staggered successfully through the tense months when the newly articulated and organized anger of the lower classes had exploded into revolution. The peasant and artisan insurrectionists seemed never really to believe in themselves as makers of a new social order—they always hoped that they could frighten their masters by a few murders and much noise into better government, juster laws, a vaguely reformed way of life for the common man. Briefly, in the English peasant uprising described above, a more positive sense of identity and mission appeared in the chiliastic vision of the revolutionary leadership—a sense too utopian for immediate success against the inherited realities of the barons' pride of rule, but one that marked off a new era in the genesis of modern revolution. Then, at the opposite border of European civilization, in Bohemia, the fifteenth century opened with an antifeudal social convulsion that very nearly grew to the universalistic dimensions of the Lutheran revolt of a century later. To the historian of modern Europe, the Bohemian revolution as revealed in recent historiography seems a kind of "Great Rehearsal" for the first modern revolutions in Holland and England.

Bohemia was no backwater in medieval Europe: until the destruction wrought by the Hapsburgs and the Jesuits in the seventeenth century, she was one of the richest and most cultured lands in the West. The fact that Bohemian castles, monasteries, and towns were the equal in splendor of any in Europe is a surface indication of the fact that social tension in the area ruled by the Bohemian Crown was as great as that in France or England.

Most significant as an aspect of this social tension was the position of the Church. The ecclesiastical hierarchy controlled about one third of the arable land and vast wealth in buildings and gold; in the towns the churchmen were exempt from taxes, yet collected heavy interest on loans to the burghers; and in the villages the Church was not only a staunch opponent to manumission of servile labor, but also was the hated collector of fees for every moment of religious ceremony from baptism to burial. All of this clerical privilege and wealth was, of

course, typical of a feudal state. What I want to emphasize in the Bohemian situation is that for the first time in European history this most universal, pervasive, and characteristic of feudal institutions became the direct target of attack from a vast and complicated coalition of social groups—lesser nobles jealous of the Church lands and eager for spoliation, burgher patricians angry over Church privilege and restrictions in business, and artisans and peasants who deeply resented the cost of the apparatus of salvation. Congealing for crucial moments the diverse elements of disaffection and greed into common policy was the vital and growing sentiment of Czech nationalism. The Church was not only the feudal institution which impinged on the greatest number of Czech lives, but was also the one institution with a foreign head, expensive, arrogant, and remote. The psychological attrition that had beset Church leadership since the disastrous reign of Pope Boniface VIII—the Babylonian Captivity, the clerical failure of heroism before the challenge of the Black Death, the worldliness of the prelates, and finally the shocking scurrility of the endless propaganda wars of popes against popes which occupied the energies of the Roman Catholic hierarchy from the papal conclave of 1378 to the end of the Council of Constance in 1418—this cumulative and public display by the top levels of professional Christianity of all the sins of man enormously weakened that controlling power of the local clergy which had been based upon traditional reverence.

So it was that the Bohemian revolution began as heresy and lasted for eighteen years (where previous revolts had ended in weeks or months); for it was the first revolution outside of Italy to rally opposition against a major institutional component of feudal society. Why this remarkable achievement in the thrust toward fresh perspectives in religious matters, and the adventurous building of a new society should have been the special glory of the Bohemians rather than the more familiar heroes of European creativeness—the French, Italians, or English—cannot really be explained, except to say that all of the factors making for a daring and original social and cultural effort anywhere in Europe were present in Bohemia—and the genius of leadership, the most absolutely unpredictable of historical forces, was somehow there in the pulpits of Prague and the camps of Tabor.

The Martyrdom of Jan Hus and the Outbreak of Insurrection

The master spirit of the religious revolt was the Czech, Jan Hus. While a student at the university in Prague, Hus read the work of the English theologian John Wyclif whose ideas had already been an inspiration to one revolution—that of the English peasantry in 1381. From Wyclif and a long, anonymous line of heresy stretching to the Waldensians, Hus learned and developed a radical Christian primitivism. From the most influential pulpit in Prague he introduced concepts which would form the base of revolutionary millenarianism: above all, the vision of true Christianity as a *revelation,* simple, universal, overwhelming, personal—and not essentially a mystery commanded by priests. His at-

tacks on the Church as a worldly and simoniacal institution, and his general reputation as a Wyclifite radical, alarmed the prelates who banned Wyclif's works and Hus' preaching. Hus defied the ban. Then in the year 1412 the struggle between the brilliant preacher and the prelates was climaxed on exactly the issue that a hundred years later in Wittenberg would begin the Reformation—the issue of "indulgences." The Pope needed money for his war with the King of Naples and so sent agents to Prague, among other places, to sell these Church-invented instrumentalities which promised remission of the penalties for sin. Indulgences had been attacked by Wyclif; Hus launched a blistering indictment of the practice of traffic in what he regarded as the shameful usurpation by the Pope of God's absolute prerogative, and the degrading superstition of the faithful who paid their coins for a blissful release from Purgatory. Hus' sermons fired the resolve of three artisans of the city to protest openly in church against the peddlers of God's grace—and they died, the first martyrs of the Czech revolution. The execution of the three journeymen brought the people of Prague into the streets before the town hall in angry protest. Hus was excommunicated and driven into southern Bohemia where he joined forces with an already radical rural clergy in defiance of both excommunication and interdiction. The final act in this horrifying and yet somehow dignified drama was played out in the year 1415 in the imperial city of Constance where the machinations of the Emperor Sigismund had succeeded in convening a general Church Council to deal with the issues of schism, reformation, and heresy. Hus welcomed the chance for a public hearing —which he was promised—of his reforming convictions. The Emperor granted him a safe conduct as insurance against the misgivings of his friends. Almost immediately upon his arrival in the city choked with the holy men of Europe, the Czech professor was thrown into prison, tortured exquisitely, and sent up in flames when he refused to recant. He was followed in martyrdom by his learned friend and fellow heretic, Jerome of Prague. The flames of the stakes that consumed the finest Christian scholars in Europe lighted also a fuse in their native land which soon exploded with a violence that shook the medieval Church to its foundations.

It was in southern Bohemia that the incendiary pile of fourteenth-century distress reacted most dangerously to the agitation of the Hussite preachers who were more active than ever following the martyrdom of their leader. The great feudal family of Rožmberk and the monastery of Zlata Koruna were threatened by a revolt of their serfs; in Plzeň a preacher named Václav Koranda led a revolt of townspeople against the higher clergy and patriciate, while similar revolts took place in Písek, Klatovy, and Domažlice. The pattern of revolutionary strategy was uniform: in towns all over Bohemia the revolutionary cadre seized control of the urban centers as fortified and provisioned strongholds where a peasant militia could be rallied and protected. And everywhere the words of Hus were hurled at the feudal hierarchy, the chalice—Hus had demanded the cup of wine which represented the blood of Christ in the Mass be given to the lay communicant, not kept as in Catholic practice

for the priest alone as a sign of clerical supremacy in the worship of God
—became the symbol of a united defiance of Pope, Emperor, prelates,
and barons.

Since certain special features of the Bohemian social and political
situation determined much of the course of the revolution, it might be
well to consider them before describing the events themselves. Throughout the period of increasing social tension and nationalist fervor Bohemia had been ruled by the drunken German Wenceslaus and his
brother Sigismund, King of Germany, the former amazingly incompetent even for the age, and the latter having little comprehension of, or
time for Bohemian affairs, and both of them irrevocably German. The
town patriciate, who were conservative allies of the Church, and the
great barons were heavily German and could therefore be dealt with as
part of the foreign oppression of Church and Emperor. The city of
Prague is another special matter: recent Czech research seems to
indicate that the condition of the poor, who were half the population
and proportionately the largest group of poor in any town east of the
Rhine, was worsening to a point where no solution short of revolution
was even possible. In addition, within the city was the formidable
intellectual community of Charles University, which was the center of a
new national culture. Jan Hus, as Dean and Rector of the University,
had taken control out of the hands of the German Masters and given it
to the Czechs, while as lecturer, preacher, and writer he enormously
enriched the national language and quickened the hearts and imaginations not only of his students but as well the crowds of poor who flocked
to hear him in the Bethlehem Chapel. Finally, in attempting to assess
the unique character of the historical complex which generated revolution in Bohemia and Moravia, I would emphasize the solidarity of
interests which in the beginning bound town to village, and all to
Prague. The revolution of 1419 began with assemblies of gentry working in close cooperation with committees of burghers. While the friends
and disciples of Hus provided leadership, the working classes in towns
around Prague, in southern and northeastern Bohemia, joined the poor
of Prague and the peasants of all regions in an unexampled coalition of
grievance and ideology, the kind of coalition which the revolts in
France and England had never produced.

Thus in the spring of 1419 the feudal ruling classes of Bohemia and
their allies in Empire and Papacy were faced with a population in town
and country united by a terrible and compelling motivation compounded
by hatred of the rich, greed, fear, rejection of the superstition and corruption of the Church, loathing of the perfidious Emperor Sigismund,
resentment of the anti-Czech decrees of the Council of Constance, and,
most universally, anger over the humiliation, betrayal, and martyrdom of
the greatest Czech, Jan Hus. This conjunction and cooperation of revolutionary forces—economic, religious, and ethnic—was absolutely essential to the crucial task of unseating the great lords of the Church in
Bohemia and defeating the vast army of crusaders sent by Pope Martin V
at the behest of Sigismund to cut down by sword "the abominable
Czech heretics."

When the array of crusaders arrived before Prague on June 30, 1420, the inevitable factions had not yet begun to split the revolutionary movement, so that the Emperor was confronted by a city whose burghers made common cause with the masses of the poor who were led by the priest Jan Želivský (and who under his leadership had a year earlier driven the German patricians from the town hall). Even the hitherto timid Masters of the University agreed, following the lead of Jakoubek of Stříbro, that the victory of the chalice must be defended with mortal blood. One of the great revolutionary documents of European history resulted from the united Hussite opposition, the set of demands known as the "Four Articles of Prague," the key phrases of which are these:

I. The word of God shall be preached and made known in the kingdom of Bohemia freely. . . .

II. The sacrament of the most Holy Eucharist shall be freely administered in the two kinds, that is bread and wine, to all the faithful in Christ. . . .

III. The secular power over riches and worldly goods which the clergy possesses in contradiction to Christ's precept, to the prejudice of its office and to the detriment of the secular arm, shall be taken and withdrawn from it, and the clergy itself shall be brought back to the evangelical rule and apostolic life such as that which Christ and his apostles led. . . .

IV. All mortal sins, and in particular all public and other disorders, which are contrary to God's law, shall in every rank of life be duly and judiciously prohibited and destroyed by those whose office it is.   ◻

What needs stressing about this document is that it represents the early, united, and conservative phase of the revolution—a broad class alliance which set its sights on destroying the central institution of feudal society.

The siege of Prague and the resistance to it triggered all of the mechanisms of hostility and hope throughout the land: most interesting and aggressive were the Taborites, about whom we shall have more to say shortly, but other peasant and burgher groups from northwestern Bohemia, and pilgrims from the Mount Horeb region of northeastern Bohemia, all added their numbers and zeal to the united front whose ideological leader in 1420 seems to have been the priest Ambrose. The military direction of the revolutionary forces which poured from countryside and town to drive out the foreign papists who were brutally ravaging the vicinity of Prague fell principally to one Jan Žižka, the Cromwell of the Bohemian revolution. Žižka is the most attractive revolutionary general of what was to be a long and distinguished European breed: resolute, brilliant, touched with the special genius that inspires ordinary men to extraordinary deeds, and absolutely incorruptible. His personality and career reveal—in the four years of struggle which he led before the plague struck him down on his way to another great battle in October 1424—the whole complex of forces that were at once pushing on and pulling apart the revolution. Žižka had begun his rise to prominence

as a Hussite radical intransigent in July of 1419 when he headed a mob which threw the burgomaster and several town councilors from the town-hall windows to their deaths at the hands of the crowd below. There followed the death of Wenceslaus upon hearing the news, and the spreading attacks upon Romanists (mostly Germans) in the Bohemian towns. In Prague the revolutionary fervor cooled after a large part of the city had been destroyed by mercenary troops collected by Queen Sophia (widow of Wenceslaus) and the Hussite nobles had thrown in their support to the Queen. The burghers lost heart to the point of negotiating a truce that restored to the Romanists a castle that had been hard won by the revolutionaries earlier. Žižka thereupon had left the city in disgust, collected an army in southern Bohemia with which he defeated the Romanists at Sudomer, and finally joined the radical democratic community of Tabor where he was quickly elected one of the four captains of the people. It was a Taborite army which Žižka led to raise the siege of Prague. On July 14, 1420, inspired by the brilliant heroism of Žižka, it launched a great attack on Vitkov hill (which later became Mount Žižka). Sigismund's army was beaten and the siege of Prague was lifted.

The Taborites

Before relating the events which constitute the later history of the revolution, I should like to pause to look more closely at the most interesting, original, and tragic people in the movement—the hard core of imaginative and courageous radicals from whom Žižka drew early support after he left Prague, with whom he smashed the crusaders before Prague, and whom he finally had to destroy as heretics to preserve the unity of the Hussite camp. Žižka's relation to the millenarians of Tabor is very like that of Cromwell's relation to the Levellers in the English revolution; even more than Cromwell, he was forced to betray the radicals by the logic of his position as head of a revolutionary coalition. For the Taborite radicals ("Pikarts" and "Adamites") were not only democrats—they were religious free-thinkers (Martin Húska went beyond utraquism* to deny the importance of the eucharist) and communists. Cromwell, over two hundred years later, had only a handful of such people to deal with in the so-called Diggers; the millenarians numbered hundreds in southern Bohemia. Of course for those who enjoy proving the fruitlessness of radical ideology, of patronizing the visionary, and dismissing the "unsuccessful," the chiliastic wing of the Taborites is a mere episode. To me, however, the most interesting aspect of the entire Bohemian revolution is in the thought and action of the radical Taborite communities.

What we know of the Taborite revolutionaries is drawn necessarily from the hostile accounts of those who represented the old order in religion and politics that survived the challenge of the mountain preachers and the radicalized towns. But there is a great deal of

---

*   From medieval Latin, *sub utraque specie,* meaning communion in both kinds—the cup to the laity.

evidence that violent, large-scale, organized action produced a series of remarkably egalitarian communities in south Bohemia. By 1420 the walled city of Písek had been revolutionized under a regime built around common chests; in the same year an even tougher society emerged in the form of a completely new, fortified town which bore the proud name Tabor for the mountain which saw the first of the hilltop communists. In such towns and in the countryside around them the millenarians devoted intense months to realizing in social practice God's radical commands while planning the liberation of the entire sinning world.

Jan Žižka

Žižka's complicity in the murder of the utopian radicals in the Hussite movement did not open the door to a general rout of the lower classes. He remained the leader of a genuinely popular upsurge of urban poor and village peasantry who continued to trust him, as did the burghers and gentry, to lead the fight against the Romanists and the barons. Tabor, even after the destruction of its millenarians, was an amazingly radical community which drew up a new political program, giving to "the people" all power to punish mortal sins and civil misdeeds—power legally to punish Pope, Emperor, and barons! Taborites remained at the head of a town alliance in southern Bohemia which was brought by Žižka into military cooperation with the greater league of towns dominated (some through conquest) by Prague. Žižka's chief ally in Prague was at first the priest Želivský who led the poor of the city and whose loyalty to the revolutionary cause forced the burghers (sated with the loot from confiscations and fearful of lower-class needs and demands) on more than one occasion to end their negotiations with the barons and Romanists.

The revolution had by the end of 1421 reached a point of success beyond which the Prague bourgeoisie were reluctant to venture: they had enriched themselves from the property of the German patricians, the crusaders had been convincingly smashed again near Žatec, they had taken over control of the city government, and in the Diet of Cáslav which met in June of 1421 four "burgesses of Prague" and four burghers from provincial towns controlled by Prague were among the twenty-man regency designated to rule the country. (Tabor had only two representatives, Žižka one of them; the other half of the government was turned over to five barons and five gentry.) From the perspective of the new ruling class of Prague, all that remained to be won was security for their gains. So they first arranged the murder of Želivský and his lieutenants in the Old Town Hall on March 9, 1422, thereby disarming the poor of leadership, after which it was safe to open negotiations for a king to reestablish order in the country. The king whom the Prague burghers selected in consultation with the barons (and with Žižka's approval) was Sigismund Korybut, Prince of Poland. However, the scheme to impose order and unity on Bohemia was premature; the control of the lower classes in Prague was maintained well enough, but the Taborites and

Žižka were not so cheaply won over. Korybut was never to sit on the throne of Czech kings.

In all internal dynamics the Bohemian revolution began in 1422 to fragment as succeeding groups either felt satisfied or lost hope. Žižka and the Taborites almost alone fought on with a vision of national social goals and with hearts of patriotic and religious zeal. Tabor remained a vigorous bastion of radical thought and warrior determination as the loss of the millenarians was made up by an influx of peasants from the heretical countryside who joined the artisans of the town in a remarkably cohesive front against feudalism and Romanism. Indeed, the stubborn consistency of Taborite ideology created a dilemma for Žižka; for Prague was dickering with the barons and Korybut and the provincial towns around Prague were floundering in confusion—how, then, to maintain the momentum of the revolution against the selfishness and cowardice of the Praguers?

Žižka decided to leave Tabor and to reform the center of his revolutionary alliance in a new brotherhood of towns, gentry, and peasants in eastern Bohemia. From this new base brother Žižka, as he was called by his soldiers, now totally blind (his right eye was lost in the siege of Rábi in 1421—he is represented in the sculptured head from the town arms of Tabor with a patch over the left which he lost in the civil wars under Wenceslaus), was called upon to display his finest qualities. He was almost constantly on the march against a bewildering variety of enemies, a blind genius whose grim art was played out in the dust and death which followed his brilliant phalanxes of fortified wagons, the dazzling maneuvering of his marvelously disciplined infantry. Žižka's armies were, like the great revolutionary armies of the future, much more than military units—they were communities in arms, men who trained and fought for political and religious and social ideas, thoughtful and passionate men, preachers who went into battle with their congregations, a host roaring to battle against barons and crusaders with the Hussite hymn "Ye Who Are the Warriors of God" in their throats.

Shakespeare has taught us to thrill to the exploits of Žižka's dashing contemporary, King Henry V, but Agincourt is nothing more than a spectacular feudal farce compared to a dozen bloody battles fought by Žižka's legions against the mightiest forces feudal Europe could muster for their destruction. The year 1422 was spent smashing armies led by the Emperor. In 1423 the Praguers in alliance with utraquist nobles were defecting from the revolutionary course and preparing to destroy the armies that persisted in vision and courage; Žižka's troops defeated them in two big campaigns in the spring and summer of that year. The next year, the last of his life, was spent in unswerving service to the terribly demanding cause of a national and social revolution as the moderate Taborites preached it. In two brutal battles at Skalic and Malesov, Žižka decisively broke the Barons' League and their allied armies of Prague, marched to the walls of Prague, and forced the burghers to promise loyalty and cooperation in a bold and brilliant plan to invade Moravia with the objective already conceived of driving Sigismund from Hungary as well. Žižka died, October 11, 1424, probably of plague, on

his way to assume command of this hard-won national revolutionary army.

Prokop Holý

The death of Žižka immediately splintered the great design. Even the army was rent by the loss of so masterful a commander, his own troops thereafter calling themselves "Orphans" to memorialize their grief, and for almost two years no man stood forth from the ranks of the Hussites to lead as Žižka had led. Then in 1426 a vast force of Germans was assembled at Ústí to smash the disunited Hussites; at that critical hour from the ranks of the "Warriors of God" the successor to Žižka was revealed—the priest Prokop Holý.* Prokop, soon also called "Veliky" (the Great), emerged suddenly from distinguished officer service in the frontier skirmishes which followed the death of Žižka to organize and lead a reunited Czech army in a rout of the Germans. And the next year Prokop directed the same armies to what would become a legendary triumph over a tremendous crusading force assembled from all parts of Europe.

The years which followed the victory at Tachov over the crusaders were unusually exciting and are hard to explain. For the energy and successes of Hussitism reached out to every corner of Europe while insidiously at Prague the frightened and glutted and cunning were at work negotiating a surrender. But before the surrender what magnificent feats! Czech armies for almost a decade swept across frontiers in every direction on what were called "glorious raids"—partly, they were looting expeditions, but they were superbly organized to keep their great feudal enemies off balance and to spread Hussite propaganda. One such expedition led by Prokop in 1428 went through Moravia, Hungary, Slovakia, and Silesia, burning churches and manor houses while sparing the peasants and poor of the towns all but sermons and manifestoes extolling the Hussite program. In Slovakia the "armies of liberation" were welcomed by Slovak burghers as aids in their struggles against the German ruling classes, and German peasantry there and elsewhere in eastern Europe deserted their servile occupations sometimes to revolt, more often to join Hussite units in their marches. The following year Prokop took his armies westward and raided from Leipzig to Nuremberg, aiding revolts as in Bamberg where the prelates and patriciates were driven out, spreading Hussite propaganda, recruiting troops from the common people of town and village, and generally terrifying the lords of Germany. Finally, the Burgrave of Nuremberg and the Margrave of Brandenburg were able to conclude a truce which required a large immediate cash payment, a pledge of a yearly levy, and a treaty obligation to attempt to secure a hearing in Nuremberg for the political program of the Hussites! The vigor and geographical extent of the propaganda campaign waged by the Hussites has only recently been

---

* "Holý" means clean-shaven, an epithet applied to Prokop because he went against the practice of Hussite priests and shaved his beard.

discovered: pamphlets in Picardy, manifestoes in Paris, Barcelona, Venice, Rome, and Cambridge, England. In Tournai the Hussite agitation of one Gilles Mersault led to a revolt; in England, the Chancellor of the University at Cambridge felt obliged to refute the Hussite manifesto.

The high tide of this tremendous surge of Hussite armies and words can be marked in the sessions of the great Church Council of Basel which began in 1431. This had originally been summoned at the behest of a reforming party within the Church who were arguing for a parliamentary system to replace the Italian monarchy as the supreme governing power for the Church; but the Czech heresy intruded upon the fight within the hierarchy. Princes and prelates, especially in Germany, were pressing for peace with the heretics to keep them at home. The papacy made one final desperate effort to retrieve the situation by force: in August of 1431, after having already consented to invite the Hussites to negotiate at Basel, Cardinal Julian Cesarini was charged as papal legate to assemble the greatest crusading army yet seen to destroy the terrible and growing monster from Bohemia. An enormous international host of the faithful was duly recruited and led into Bohemia; at the first approach of Prokop's armies of heretics singing their blasphemous confidence in God, the Romanists fled in hysterical awe, leaving behind most of their supplies and a splendid trophy in the cardinal's hat of Cesarini. On October 15 after the crusade, the council at Basel formally invited the Hussites to share its deliberations. In the prolonged negotiations to get the Czechs to attend (a Hussite embassy did not arrive in Basel until January 1433), Cardinal Cesarini made a most interesting report to the Pope on the urgency of the problem:

Great is the tension in the souls of men, to bridle which is still the only hope of the synod; if it perishes the laymen will rise in the Hussite manner and destroy us, thinking thus to please God. In these very days the people of Magdeburg drove the Archbishop and priests out of their town, surrounded themselves with fortified wagons like the Hussites and are said to have asked for a captain from them; the matter is the more dangerous that many surrounding towns enter into alliance with them. So the town of Passau drove out their bishop and now besiege him in a castle. Both these towns are near Bohemia and if they ally with the Czechs, as must be feared, they will find many helpers and followers.   □

With such fears pressed upon them, the Council not only had to talk with heretics, it had to make concessions to them. The negotiated basis for all talks was to be that of the so-called "Judgment of Cheb" which stipulated that the hierarchy at Basel would dispute all questions with the Czech delegation as absolute equals and that the supreme arbiter of all propositions in debate was to be not the settled dogmas of the Church but simply the Bible. One cannot re-create the drama of Basel without feeling one of those rare moments of unreasoning pride in the superb vindication of the betrayed Hus, who had written from Constance ". . . in chains, awaiting on the morrow to be condemned to death, having

full hope in God, that I may not swerve from the truth of God, and that I may not disavow what the false witnesses have witnessed against me as errors." For now the exalted and terrible powers of the Roman Church had to sit helplessly while Prokop the Great, heretic priest and warrior, explained with passion and learning the program of the Hussite Four Articles.

Betrayal and Failure

But at the moment Prokop the Great was leading the Czech delegation in this new battle of scholastic disputation at Basel, the tide of the revolution had begun its inexorable ebb. At Prague, while publicly, and motivated primarily by fear, the wealthy and well-born professed support of Prokop and the Hussite program, privately he was regarded as too radical and too incorruptible, and secretly he was being betrayed. The agents of treachery were Masters of the University Hus had made immortal; they let it be known to the hierarchs at Basel that they and the conservative forces behind them at Prague wanted reconciliation with the Church even at the sacrifice of the charter of Hussite liberties, the Four Articles. They limited their demands for a return to Romanism to retention of the utraquist rite of the mass. Other signs of betrayal appeared, as in the siege of Plzeň in 1433–1434 where the Taborite forces were unsuccessful because one of the Taborite barons was providing clandestine supplies to the besieged. More serious, a coup against the only radical group left in Prague was engineered in May of 1434. Prague was essentially two cities, the New Town where small craftsmen and the poor had responded earlier to Želivský and after his murder had continued a source of agitation and vigilance for the social and religious ambitions of Hussitism, and the Old Town in which the rich burghers had exercised their rule unchallenged for a decade since the overthrow of the radicals. Although warned repeatedly of the perfidy of the men of Basel and their allies in the Old Town by a former follower of Želivský, Jacob Vlk, the people of the New Town were helpless when an army broke upon them on May 9 and seized the town hall.

The rapid sinking of revolutionary fortunes from the apparent invincibility of the Hussite united front I cannot explain, but I can offer a few background suggestions that may help one to understand it. Perhaps the most persistent cause of ultimate failure was the first clearly to manifest itself: that is, the early success of the Prague business elite and their relatively unambitious goals. They were not a revolutionary class in the Marxist sense; their economic self-interest did not demand the destruction of feudalism in Bohemia or in Europe; they were not prepared to exploit national markets or revolutionize the use of the land. In a sense, the Praguers were simply pushing for the kind of entrepreneurial opportunities won by the burghers of northern Italy and Flanders much earlier. Similarly, as we have seen, the religious enthusiasm and originality of the city elite were modest and shallow. Further, their national patriotism vis-à-vis Church and Empire was from the beginning tempered with fear of isolating themselves from outside help

in controlling the lower orders in Bohemia. Finally, so far as middle-class motivation in the revolution is concerned, one must stress the economic disadvantage to business of interminable war, the dislocation of all normal industry and merchandising, and the really serious effects on foreign trade of the papal interdiction which seems to have brought this lucrative Czech business to a standstill. In short, the Czech business classes (Prague and the client towns) had to do business with a feudal and Catholic Europe and therefore a social revolution in Bohemia would have been self-destructive. The brilliant successes of the Taborite armies in the field did nothing to enlarge the economic prospects of Bohemian merchants; each victory brought only loot for the soldiers, chaos along the trade routes, and arrogance from the masses.

The economic penalties of revolution were far greater, of course, for the lower classes. A terrible inflation of prices and lagging wages combined with drought in the 1430's to produce widespread famine, disease, and starvation. Prokop and his revolutionary councils appear to have made no effort to deal with distress among the poor in the villages and towns at home—only in the armies was there any sort of hope of enough to eat and the excitement of the booty of victory. Still, it was the poor, the lesser folk generally, who remained faithful to the boldest revolutionary visions of religious reformation and national glory. But their leaders—those not with the armies—began to soften; the radical priests grew reflective. A perfect illustration of the dimming of the idealism of the Hussite intellectuals is the following passage from the "Comments" of one of the master spirits in all Czech literature, Peter Chelčický, an early radical disciple of Hus, a man of the people, a founder of the enduring Bohemian Brethren, but as he wrote these words in 1434, a man weary of war:

This sound of the cruel sea and of the billows thereof our Czech land hath suffered much; for wellnigh all the lands round about rose up against it from dissension in faith, so that the sound of those waves could be heard almost throughout the world. Also the raging of this sea can be, and often times is wont to be, over earthly things; for them doth the one party ever wage war against the other, desiring to exalt themselves above the others and to be their betters, and therefore do they wrangle and seize upon each other's possessions, upon men and honor, and therefore do they buffet one the other, burn one another, shed blood. Likewise also other sinful folk, like the sea unquiet and unquelled in evil, who are stirred by devils to unrest, that ever evil may go against evil, as waves of the sea against other waves, quarrel against quarrel, pride against pride, hardship against hardship—in one place they have slain one another, in another place robbed one another, in another place challenged one another, as desiring to slay or rob one another. And thus is the most mournful sound of the sea to be heard.   □

Peter Chelčický, it must be emphasized, was a courageous and profoundly dissenting intellectual whose Hussitism was incomparably deeper than the utraquist issue which alone separated the generality of

the peace party from accommodation to the Romanists. But just as it was precisely the quality of imagination and courage which Chelčický possessed that had distinguished the leadership of the revolution and lifted it out of the morass of selfish factionalist unrest which threatened at every moment to preserve the status quo, so after fifteen years of struggle to achieve a new reality it was the attrition of the struggle itself—the hate and greed and betrayal and death—which finally eroded the idealist illusions into tattered banners which could no longer inspire either leader or follower. It is doubtful if the human spirit has ever sustained a longer period of dedication.

The end came quickly. Prokop the Great, whose energy never deserted him, rushed back from Basel to fight the Barons' League and their allies in the Prague confederacy. The battle which took place at Lipany on May 30, 1434, symbolized the futility of the Taborite struggle. Prokop faced a Czech army employing the tactic of the fortified wagon with which Žižka had originally made revolution possible. The Barons' League also had superior numbers. And to complete the tragic irony of the situation, a captain of the "Orphans"—the hard core of Taborite arms—betrayed his command at a crucial point in the battle. Nearly the whole leadership of the Taborite movement was killed on the field that terrible day, Prokop the Great among them. Taborite prisoners were herded into barns and burned to death during the night that followed the battle.

After Lipany the revolution retained only sporadic life; the last dangerous embers were stamped out with the murder of the radical priest Ambrose and the execution in Prague in the year 1437 of the last of the Taborite captains, John Roháč of Dubá and sixty of his revolutionary following who had been able to hold out in the castle Zion. All was not lost, however—so great and prolonged a struggle brought forth at least the mouse* of the utraquist communion for Bohemia, so that Bohemia had a kind of national church, at least in the ceremonial sense, until the Jesuits took that too in 1620. And perhaps beneath the surface of history there was more gained (not, of course, to argue that courage and imagination are ever a loss, however short-lived). We know that the Bohemian Brethren were related to the Hussite mind, and from their ranks came gentle and passively dissenting spirits for generations into the modern era.

Suggested Reading

There is not very much literature in English on the Bohemian Revolution. For a generally reliable overview see R. W. Seton-Watson, *A History of the Czechs and Slovaks* (London: Hutchinson & Co, (Publishers) Ltd, 1943). Fortunately, there is a recent study which may prove definitive and which certainly is the best thing in English: Howard Kaminsky, *A History of the Hussite Revolution* (Berkeley: University of California Press, 1967). It should be published in paperback. Also useful is Frederick Heymann,

---

* I can't resist the tragic appropriateness of Horace's metaphor about "The mountains were in labor; a ridiculous mouse was born."

John Žižka and the Hussite Revolution (Princeton: Princeton University Press, 1955).

For the study of the great Jan Hus there is Herbert Workman's old standard *The Age of Huss* (New York: Kelly Publishing Co., 1902) and the same author with R. Pope, *The Letters of John Huss* (London: Hodder & Stoughton Ltd., 1904). A good recent study is Matthew Spinka, *John Hus' Concept of the Church* (Princeton: Princeton University Press, 1966). Finally, see the collected essays of R. R. Betts, *Essays in Czech History* (London: The Athlone Press of the University of London, 1969).

3 The Christian Revolutions of the Sixteenth Century

The Revolutionary Character of Humanism

While Bohemia was exploding in religious heresy, another, subtler, far more durable heresy was developing in the very homeland of the princes of the Church. This was the heresy of humanism—the idealism of the self, the individualization of perception, the philosophy of man. Humanism has for the scholar many definitions because it has been and is many kinds of reality: in its broadest sense it simply means the study of the "humanities," or literature of the ancient world, but it can more narrowly and explicitly apply to the antischolastic learning and *belles-lettres* of the Renaissance, or to the secular, anti-Christian scholarship and writing of the eighteenth-century Enlightenment, or, as I should like to use the term here, it can mean the tendency of European thought since Petrarch to regard individual perception rather than group or traditional authority as the ultimate arbiter of truth. Humanism as a heresy—as the substitution of individual truth for group truth, of personal discovery for inherited culture—was the most deceptive foe the Church and European authority systems ever had to contend with. For the humanists themselves (some of them prelates like Aeneas Sylvius) were generally content to live double lives, granting authority over their actions and much of their thought to the traditional forces of society, and only freeing their personal perceptions in the solitude of the study or intimate communication with trusted friends. Most humanists felt then, as now, that the price of honest reflection must be peace with the tribal idols—not only outside obedience but inside reverence for accepted canons of truth.

The danger to established culture and institutions of the humanist preoccupation with independent thought was that in moments of social crisis the growing body of literature and talk, however harmless and irrelevant it may have seemed in times of greater stability, would suddenly assume revolutionary perspectives. For the insidious essence of individualism is change. That aspect of European culture which looks to the inmost, searching self for truth always has and always will discover a unique consciousness. The humanist passion to know the heart's spontaneous secret, to trust the wit and imagination of the

intellect, creates a perpetually challenging dialogue with the conventions of society. The very act of learning in the humanist way is revolt —reaching back in time and across barriers of space to read of and ponder other realities than one's own is to threaten the authority, in personal terms at least, of what is. Thus, the European humanist has always been an adventurer; he has become a revolutionist only rarely in the social sense as a result of some neurotically compelling need to find a new identity in association with other men, or because other men have found humanist insights convenient weapons with which to fight their masters.

But in our reconstruction of the cultural sources of revolution in Europe, the great masters of humanist perception—Leonardo da Vinci, Machiavelli, Montaigne, and Shakespeare—are both too large for our canvas and too complex in their relations to revolution to be included in this history. The most basic reason the humanists have not yet been looked at by historians in their roles as makers of revolutionaries is that the rhetoric of the early European revolutionaries was biblical rather than classical. In time—but not here or now!—it will become clearer that the crucial revolutionary concepts, and indeed much of the language, that changed the societies of early modern Europe were of classical and secular origin.

Meantime let us return to those men whose deep involvement in the popular culture of Christianity, combined with their sensitivity to social crisis, exploded the civilization of the past at its institutional foundations. For the dynamics of the Hussite revolution were to be repeated in western Europe in the sixteenth century on a larger stage but with less radical social theory and therefore with greater social impact.

Eckhart's Mysticism

The sources of Christian radicalism ran deep into the European consciousness by the opening of the 1500's: the legacy of heresy and dissent, especially of Hussitism, retained a stubborn relevancy amid the insecurities and futility of feudal culture in decline. Within the resources of the radical Christian imagination there were both social revolt and individual revolt, both Tabor and Eckhart. Tabor should mean something to anyone who has got this far—Meister Eckhart requires an introduction. He was a German contemporary of Dante, a Dominican monk who died accused by the Franciscan monks of heresy, and whose collected works are an excellent introduction to the kind of in-working revolt of the Catholic mind against orthodoxy which will make Luther comprehensible. The individualistic religiosity of the (especially Rhineland) mystics was a greater immediate threat to European security than was individualistic humanism, precisely because, like Luther, the mystics developed their ideas in resolutely Christian terms.

What does one do with a learned Thomist who uses sexual images to express his relation to the Godhead, and is fond of concepts which stress, in almost Hegelian fashion, the creation of God through man? The Church can—and did—force recantation from the quiet-souled heretic, but the words and ideas still remain:

What is truth? Truth is something so noble that if God could turn aside from it, I could keep to the truth and let God go.

If it is true that God became man, it is also true that man became God . . . and so . . . you haven't got to borrow from God, for he is your own and therefore, whatever you get, you get from yourself. Before God, work that does not come from your [inmost] self is dead. . . . If a man's work is to live, it must come from the depths of him—not from alien sources outside himself—but from within.

God is love . . . and out of love he gives existence and life to every creature, supporting them all with his love. The color of the wall depends on the wall, and so the existence of creatures depends on the love of God. Separate the color from the wall and it would cease to be; so all creation would cease to exist if separated from the love that God is. God is love, so loving that whatever he can love he must love, whether he will or not. There is no creature so vile that it can love what is evil; for what one loves must either be good or appear to be so.

If God should give my soul all he ever made or might make, apart from himself, and giving it, he stayed away even by as much as a hairbreadth, my soul would not be satisfied, for I would not be blessed. If I am blessed, the whole world is mine and God too, and where I am there is God, and where God is there I am.

I tell you that the soul knows the eternal Word better than any philosopher can describe it. What anyone can set forth with words is far too little —less than the soul learns in one lesson from the eternal Word. Thus the authorities say we shall do well to hurry to that school in which the Holy Spirit is the lecturer; but I tell you that when the Holy Spirit is the teacher, his students must be well prepared if they are to understand his excellent teaching—which proceeds out of the Father's heart.

When God laughs at the soul and the soul laughs back at God, the persons of the Trinity are begotten. To speak in hyperbole, when the Father laughs to the Son and the Son laughs back to the Father, that laughter gives pleasure, that pleasure gives joy, that joy gives love, and love gives the persons [of the Trinity] of which the Holy Spirit is one.

To get at the core of God at his greatest, one must first get into the core of himself at his least, for no one can know God who has not first known himself. Go to the depths of the soul, the secret place of the Most High, to the roots, to the heights; for all that God can do is focused there.

The just man lives in God and God in him, for God is born in him and he in God. With each virtue of the just person, God is born and made glad, and not only with each virtue, but with each deed, however trifling, done out of virtue and justice, and resulting in justice, God is made glad—glad through and through!—so that there is nothing in the core of the Godhead that does not dance for joy! Ordinary persons can only believe this; but the enlightened know it.   □

Erasmus and Christian Satire

Humanism, which had been safely isolated from Christian thought in Italy during the fifteenth century, became in northern Europe a source (or vehicle) of individual religious perception to rival the impact of

mysticism. The culmination and conjunction of the two traditions in the sixteenth century greatly increased the potential of explosive feeling and idea. The most famous and in fact most interesting of the men who shaped the original precepts of radical Christian humanism was a Dutchman, a reluctant monk, a university lecturer from Cambridge to Freiburg, easily the most influential and celebrated man of learning in Europe—Desiderius Erasmus of Rotterdam. Although Erasmus avoided the open break with Catholicism of the Protestant party, and broke with Luther over the issue of freedom of the will (he could not reconcile what he called Luther's "self-hatred" with his own feeling for the dignity of man), his widely popular satirical thrusts at the hypocrisy and injustice of Catholic and feudal civilization altered the sensibilities of generations of Europeans. How can one calculate the impact of the laughter of humanists at the foibles and cruelty of the sacrosanct institutions and precepts of their society? To some extent, obviously, laughter is a safety valve, letting out steam that might otherwise blow off as anger and action. But radical change—over time—can come through laughter: for the eroded prestige of the establishment (contempt is the ultimate fruit of satire) may become critically inadequate to surmount crises of protest. Contempt and hatred are the twin devils of orthodoxy, the driving psychology of revolution. France produced a greater satirist than Erasmus in François Rabelais, but I haven't space for a sufficiently long selection from *Gargantua and Pantagruel* so the more delicate—and popular—Erasmian satire will do to illustrate a genre which includes not only Rabelais but also eminent writers as different as Crotus Rubianus, Ulrich von Hutten and Sebastian Brant.

The Praise of Folly was written by Erasmus in seven days while suffering from lumbago in the home of his friend Thomas More. It had a fantastic and immediate success. Holbein sketches were added by enterprising publishers and the work went through forty editions in his lifetime and was found by Milton "in every one's hands" at Cambridge over a century later. Some characteristic passages follow:

Then what shall I say of the people who so happily fool themselves with forged pardons for sins, measuring out time to be spent in purgatory as if with an hour-glass, and figuring its centuries, years, months, days, and hours as if from a mathematical table, beyond possibility of error? Or I might speak of those who will promise themselves any and every thing, relying upon certain charms or prayers devised by some pious impostor either for his soul's sake or for money, to bring them wealth, reputation, pleasure, plenty, good health, long life, and a green old age, and at last a seat next to Christ's in heaven—but they do not wish to get it too soon. That is to say, when the pleasures of this life have finally failed them, willy-nilly, though they struggled tooth and nail to hold on to them, then it is time for the bliss of heaven to arrive.

I fancy that I see some merchant or soldier or judge laying down one small coin from his extensive booty and expecting that the whole cesspool of his life will be at once purified. He conceives that just so many perjuries, so many lustful acts, so many debauches, so many fights,

murders, frauds, lies, and so many breaches of faith, are bought off as by contract; and so bought off that with a clean slate he may start from scratch upon a new round of sins. And who are more foolish, yet who more happy, than those who promise themselves something more than the highest felicity if they daily recite those seven verses of the *Psalms*? The seven, I mean, which some devil, a playful one, but blabbing rather than crafty, is believed to have pointed out to St. Bernard after he had been duped by the saint's trick. Things like that are so foolish, you know, that I am almost ashamed of them myself; yet they stand approved not only by the common people but even by teachers of religion. . . .

Yet what do men ask of these saints except things that pertain to folly? Think a bit: among all those consecrated gifts which you see covering the walls of some churches, and even hung on the ceiling, do you ever find one given in gratitude for an escape from folly, or because the giver has been made any whit wiser? One person has come safe to land. A second survived being run through in a duel. One no less fortunately than bravely got away from a battlefield, leaving the rest to fight. Another was brought near to the gallows, but by favor of some saint who is friendly to thieves he has decided that he should go on relieving those who are burdened with too much wealth. Another escaped in a jail-break. Another came through a fever, in spite of his doctor. The poisoned drink of another, by loosening his bowels, served to cure him instead of kill him, not at all to the joy of his wife, who lost both her labor and her expenses. Another's cart was turned over, but he drove both horses home safely. Another was dug out of the debris of a fallen house. Another, caught in the act by a husband, made good his escape. No one gives thanks for a recovery from being a fool. So sweet it is not to be wise that mortal men will pray to be delivered from anything sooner than from Folly.

But why should I launch out upon this ocean of superstition? "For if I had a hundred tongues, a hundred mouths, a voice of brass, I could not set forth all the shapes of fools or run over all the names of folly." Yet the whole life of Christian folk everywhere is full of fanaticisms of this kind. Our priests allow them, without regret, and even foster them, being aware of how much money is wont to accrue from this source. In this posture of affairs, suppose that some odious wise man were to step up and sing out this, which is true: "You will not die badly if you live well. You get quit of your sins if you add to the money payment a hatred of evil-doing, add tears, watchings, prayers, fastings; and if you alter the whole basis of your life. This or that saint will be gracious to you if you emulate his goodness." If the wise man, I say, were to start howling out things like that, just see from what contentment, and into what a turmoil, he would all of a sudden drive the souls of men! . . .

Although I must hasten on, I cannot pass over in silence those who, while differing in no respect from the meanest tinker, flatter themselves beyond measure with the empty title of nobility. One will trace his family back to Aeneas, one to Brutus, and a third to King Arthur. In every room they display pictures and busts of their ancestors. They specify their grandfathers and great-grandfathers, and have by heart the ancient names, while all the time they are not so different from senseless statues

themselves and are worth, it may be, less than the ones they show off. Yet by virtue of my lovely companion Philautia, they lead a pleasant life. There will always be other fools, too, to admire specimens of this breed as if they were gods. . . .

Among men of learned professions, the lawyers may claim first place for themselves, nor is there any other class quite so self-satisfied; for while they industriously roll up the stone of Sisyphus by dint of weaving together six hundred laws in the same breath, no matter how little to the purpose, and by dint of piling glosses upon glosses and opinions upon opinions, they contrive to make their profession seem the most difficult of all. What is really tedious commends itself to them as brilliant. Let us put in with them the logicians and sophists, a breed of men more loquacious than the famed brass kettles at Dodona; any one of them can out-chat twenty picked women. They would be happier, however, if they were merely talkative, and not quarrelsome as well, to such a degree that they will stubbornly cut and thrust over a lock of goat's wool, quite losing track of the truth in question while they go on disputing. Their self-love makes them happy, and equipped with three syllogisms they will unhesitatingly dare to join battle upon any subject with any man. Mere frowardness brings them back unbeaten, though you match Stentor against them.

Near these march the scientists, reverenced for their beards and the fur on their gowns, who teach that they alone are wise while the rest of mortal men flit about as shadows. How pleasantly they dote, indeed, while they construct their numberless worlds, and measure the sun, moon, stars, and spheres as with thumb and line. They assign causes for lightning, winds, eclipses, and other inexplicable things, never hesitating a whit, as if they were privy to the secrets of nature, artificer of things, or as if they visited us fresh from the council of the gods. Yet all the while nature is laughing grandly at them and their conjectures. For to prove that they have good intelligence of nothing, this is a sufficient argument: they can never explain why they disagree with each other on every subject. Thus knowing nothing in general, they profess to know all things in particular; though they are ignorant even of themselves, and on occasion do not see the ditch or the stone lying across their path, because many of them are blear-eyed or absent-minded; yet they proclaim that they perceive ideas, universals, forms without matter, primary substances, quiddities, and ecceities—things so tenuous, I fear, that Lynceus himself could not see them. When they especially disdain the vulgar crowd is when they bring out their triangles, quadrangles, circles, and mathematical pictures of the sort, lay one upon the other, intertwine them into a maze, then deploy some letters as if in line of battle, and presently do it over in reverse order —and all to involve the uninitiated in darkness. Their fraternity does not lack those who predict future events by consulting the stars, and promise wonders even more magical; and these lucky scientists find people to believe them.

Perhaps it were better to pass over the theologians in silence, and not to move such a Lake Camarina, or to handle such an herb *Anagyris foetida,* as that marvellously supercilious and irascible race. For they may attack me with six hundred arguments, in squadrons, and drive me to

make a recantation; which if I refuse, they will straightway proclaim me an heretic. By this thunderbolt they are wont to terrify any toward whom they are ill-disposed. No other people are so loth to acknowledge my favors to them; yet the divines are bound to me by no ordinary obligations. They are happy in their self-love, and as if they already inhabited the third heaven they look down from a height on all other mortal men as on creatures that crawl on the ground, and they come near to pitying them. They are protected by a wall of scholastic definitions, arguments, corollaries, implicit and explicit propositions; they have so many hideaways that they could not be caught even by the net of Vulcan; for they slip out on their distinctions, by which also they cut through all knots as easily as with a double-bitted axe from Tenedos; and they abound with newly-invented terms and prodigious vocables. Furthermore, they explain as pleases them the most arcane matters, such as by what method the world was founded and set in order, through what conduits original sin has been passed down along the generations, by what means, in what measure, and how long the perfect Christ was in the Virgin's womb, and how accidents subsist in the Eucharist without their subject.

But those are hackneyed. Here are questions worthy of the great and (as some call them) illuminated theologians, questions to make them prick up their ears—if ever they chance upon them. Whether divine generation took place at a particular time? Whether there are several sonships in Christ? Whether this is a possible proposition: God the Father hates the Son? Whether God could have taken upon Himself the likeness of a woman? Or of a devil? Of an ass? Of a gourd? Of a piece of flint? Then how would that gourd have preached, performed miracles, or been crucified? Also, what would Peter have consecrated if he had administered the sacrament while Christ's body hung upon the Cross? Also whether at that moment Christ could be said to be a man? And whether after the resurrection it will be forbidden to eat and drink? (Now, while there is time, they are providing against hunger and thirst!) These finespun trifles are numberless, with others even more subtle, having to do with instants of time, notions, relations, accidents, quiddities, entities, which no one can perceive with his eyes unless, like Lynceus, he can see in blackest darkness things that are not there. . . .

Coming nearest to these in felicity are the men who generally call themselves "the religious" and "monks"—utterly false names both, since most of them keep as far away as they can from religion and no people are more in evidence in every sort of place. But I do not see how anything could be more dismal than these monks if I did not succor them in many ways. For though people as a whole so detest this race of men that meeting one by accident is supposed to be bad luck, yet they flatter themselves to the queen's taste. For one thing, they reckon it the highest degree of piety to have no contact with literature, and hence they see to it that they do not know how to read. For another, when with asinine voices they bray out in church those psalms they have learned, by rote rather than by heart, they are convinced that they are anointing God's ears with the blandest of oil. Some of them make a good profit from their dirtiness and mendicancy, collecting their food from door to door with importunate

bellowing; nay, there is not an inn, public conveyance, or ship where they do not intrude, to the great disadvantage of the other common beggars. Yet according to their account, by their very dirtiness, ignorance, want of manners, and insolence, these delightful fellows are representing to us the lives of the apostles.

What is funnier than to find that they do everything by rule, employing, as it were, the methods of mathematics; and to slip up is a great crime. There must be just so many knots for each shoe and the shoe-string must be of a certain color; the habit must be decked with just so much trimming; the girdle must be of a certain material and the width of so many straws; the cowl of a certain shape and a certain number of bushels in capacity; the hair so many fingers long; and one must sleep just so many hours. Who does not see that all this equality is really very unequal, in view of the great diversity of bodies and temperaments? Yet on the basis of such details they hold other people as mere nutshells. What is more, the members of one order, amid all their professions of apostolic charity, will turn and condemn the members of some other, making an admirable hubbub over the way their habit is belted or the slightly darker color of it. Among the monks you will see some so rigorously pious that they will wear no outer garment unless it be of Cilician goat's hair, while their inner garment is of Milesian wool; some others, on the contrary, are linen on the outside, but still wool underneath. Members of certain orders start back from the mere touch of a piece of money as if it were aconite. They do not, however, withdraw from the touch of a glass of wine, or of a woman. In short, all orders take remarkable care that nothing in their way of life shall be consistent; nor is it so much their concern to be like Christ as to be unlike each other. . . .

The greater number of them work so hard at their ceremonies and at maintaining the minutiae of tradition that they deem one heaven hardly a suitable reward for their labors; never recalling that the time will come when, with all these things held of no account, Christ will demand a reckoning of that which He has prescribed, namely, charity. One friar will then show a paunch which has been padded out with every kind of fish; another will spill out a hundred bushels of hymns. Another will count off so many myriads of fasts, and will lay the blame for his almost bursting belly upon his having always broken his fasts by a single dinner. Another will point to a pile of ceremonies so big that seven ships could scarcely carry it. Another will boast that for sixty years he never touched money, except when his fingers were protected by two pairs of gloves. Another will wear a cowl so dirty and greasy that no sailor would deign to put it on. Another will celebrate the fact that for more than fifty-five years he lived the life of a sponge, always fastened to one spot. Another will show a voice grown hoarse with assiduous chanting; another, a lethargy contracted by living alone; another, a tongue grown dumb under his vow of silence. But Christ, interrupting their boasts, which otherwise would go on endlessly, will say: "Whence comes this new race of Jews? I recognize one commandment which is truly mine, and of that I hear nothing. Of old in the sight of all men and using no device of parable I promised the

Inheritance of my Father, not to cowls, orisons, or fasts, but to works of charity."   □

I want to emphasize that although Erasmus and his followers share a general moral sense about values in life with humanists like Ficino or Montaigne, the important difference is that the Erasmians were agitating for humanist goals in a direct and profound Christian context which by implication at least was more of a threat to the Church than the sophisticated and alienated paganism of the great humanist minds in Italy and France. Erasmus could not leave the Church alone to go its own way; he stunned educated Christians with his Greek New Testament which in the facing Latin translation made obvious the errors of the Vulgate; his *Colloquies* were designed as school exercises in Latin style but with the objective of insinuating the "philosophy of Christ" into generations of the young (there is evidence that the youthful Shakespeare imbibed Erasmian Christianity with his Latin lessons).

Martin Luther's Attack on Ecclesiastical Authority

But humanism was, like mysticism, a very special kind of revolution. It was relatively slow in pace because it was an intellectual movement, and the humanists often seemed cowardly because they were reflective. Another very different sort of Christian revolutionary was the monk Martin Luther. Luther was not an intellectual in the humanist sense at all; he was not, like Erasmus, a lonely man believing most deeply in the beauty and dignity of human life and trying to save these fragile qualities in a Catholic religious culture. Luther was brutally religious in the way Augustine and Bernard of Clairvaux and Hus were religious. He was religious in the way most people were and are religious—out of fear and superstition. Thus it was that when Luther rebelled against the Church with all of the fury of his vulgar genius, he was understood and followed. His rebellion expressed fears and aroused hopes about the established Church at so low a level of human imagination that Europe exploded from its foundations.

Luther is the first great modern European whom the student of our culture will find baffling to the point of almost complete incomprehension; that is, once he has discarded the first inevitable impression that Luther is understandable as a "Lutheran" or "Protestant" in the contemporary sense of those words. There is a fine biography, *Here I Stand,* available in English, by Roland Bainton which will do as much as can be done to explain Luther to the beginner. For my purposes here, I want to stress what is perhaps the hardest quality of Luther's mind for us to fathom—its intense need for punishment and reassurance in terms of the popular medieval theology of sacramental magic and the arbitrary, inscrutable will of God. Luther seems to me the epitome of late medieval Christianity in his psychological immersion in the atmosphere of relics, saints' days, vesper bells, miracles at shrines, indulgence vending, pilgrimages, religious processions, theological debates, Satan wor-

ship, necromancy, and, in art and literature, the pervasive themes of horrific decay and death.

The great Dutch historian, Huizinga, in a brilliant book, *The Waning of the Middle Ages*, insists that "at the close of the Middle Ages, a somber melancholy weighs on people's souls. Whether we read a chronicle, a poem, a sermon, a legal document even, the same impression of immense sadness is produced by them all." Further, Huizinga argues that the rich and complicated image-making of Catholic Europe was at a dead-end: the "too systematic idealism" had by the fifteenth century degenerated into a conventional symbolism so oppressively familiar and authoritative that the individual could find little for himself emotionally in having everything decreed by the tribe. For most people—for the vast majority about whom we know little—the rigid hierarchical pattern of symbols which drew its authority from God must have offered some comfort. For the humanists the very certainty and prescription of the Catholic system allowed a measure of easy freedom for their aristocratic paganism which in a formal logical as well as practical sense could not be construed as a rival system of absolutes and power, but merely as the plaything of a few aberrant souls. But what of the man of the tribe raised in the supersaturated atmosphere of systematic absolutes, whose identity and security depend upon the felt reality of God's profusely revealed design of life-for-death—what of such a man if he feels fraud behind the authority, and lies in the holy terror of revelation? Doubtless there were many men who were struck down in their secret hearts by the need for the Church to do what a church must do and could no longer do—grant respite from self-hatred and justification for the ambiguity and cruelty of life. The monk Luther was the man singled out by the accident of genius to proclaim his need and his desperate resolution of the dilemma inherited from generations of failing imagination.

Martin Luther was a man of coarse and common sensibilities, of great credulity and intellectual inconsistency. But his honesty and courage made him a giant among the churchmen who have shaped the European tradition, and a revolutionary of the caliber of Newton and Marx. Born in dank Thuringia, schooled in the Latin language and Gothic humors of the University of Erfurt, suffering the usual problems of parental affection and guilt, Martin—how fateful for the future of Europe!—turned from his intended career in law to the uniquely central religious vocation of the monk. The decision which made Luther a monk was dramatically and appropriately the result of a superstitious vow made in terror at being struck down by a bolt of lightning one day in July of the year 1505. The sudden closeness and violence of death triggered the complex of guilt mechanisms inherited from an old culture and neurotic parents to produce an anguished cry, "Saint Anne help me! I will become a monk." The moment of fear passed and life went on but the vow remained spoken to the patron saint of his father, and so, in defiance of his father's wishes, and in response to the kinds of fears his culture made possible to a powerful imagination, Luther, at the age of 21, did indeed take the cowl. The order he chose in which to work out his destiny was a strict one (the newly reformed congregation

of German Augustinians), and the path he chose to salvation was an assured one if he could walk it in faith and obedience.

Fra Martin stalked the treasure of blessedness with all the dogged zeal we should expect of his driven personality: he was not only assiduous in performing his duties as priest, in keeping all the offices of ritual and prayer faithfully, but in addition he starved and froze himself with such shockingly proper rigor that his reputation for sanctity grew apace. The successful revolutionary, chatting easily of the period some twenty years later, tells us: "Certain it is, I was a pious monk and followed the rule of my order so strictly that I could say, if ever a monk got to heaven by his monkery, I should certainly have got there. All my fellow monks who knew me will bear me out. If I had kept on any longer, I should have killed myself with vigils, prayers, reading, and other work." The very tone of Luther's words in 1533—something like that of a mature man reflecting on the amusingly stupid behavior of his youth—conveys the depth of conflict which divides Protestant religiosity from the Catholic faith. For again Luther the monk was playing no game with his soul. He was searching, with a passion as desperate as that of the young Benedict or Savonarola, for a personal assurance of salvation from Hell. One must juxtapose the Luther who said "if ever a monk got to heaven by his monkery, I should certainly have got there" to the Luther who in the year 1510 had crawled painfully up the *Scala Sancta** on his hands and knees, saying over a *Pater Noster* and kissing each step for the release of one of his dead relatives from purgatory, and ending at the top with the bitter honesty of his punitive imagination forcing the words, "Who knows whether it is so?" For an Erasmus or for the ordinary Catholic, for the Christian humanist or for the run-of-mill faithful, doubts about the efficacy of the treasure of merits (the pope's storehouse of righteousness accumulated from centuries of martyrdoms and monkishness and other superfluously good works) or the authenticity of various relics or, in general, the reliability of the sanctifying "good works" basic to Catholic religious practice—any and all such doubts could be smiled upon, lost in the business of the day, or forgotten. But for Luther, an Augustinian caught in the nightmarish spiritual junkyard which had once been Augustine's church, there was only terror.

Luther returned from his journey to Rome (where he was blind to the antiquities and art which were stirring the men of the Renaissance) to resume the long and intense labor of saving his soul. Soon the gentle and fatherly Staupitz, Vicar-General of the order, who discerned that the monk Luther was both promising and difficult, decided Luther's desperation was growing as he pursued piety through asceticism and magic. As Luther's confessor and spiritual guide, the Vicar was baffled by the agonies of striving which drove Luther "to the very abyss of despair so that I wished I had never been created. Love God? I hated him!" Staupitz ordered his amazed charge to begin teaching the Bible

---

*   The twenty-eight stairs in front of the Lateran Church which were reputed to have been taken from the palace of Pontius Pilate.

at the University of Wittenberg. In the course of preparing lectures on the Bible, Luther found his salvation and a new dogma for Europe—one that with suitable accoutrements would constitute the Protestant Reformation.

The public view to which Luther's personality was now exposed consisted of a large part of Europe. The specific issue which drew attention began modestly enough: it was a familiar theological problem —that of the indulgence—raised by the outrageous interpretations of one preacher, a Dominican friar named John Tetzel. But with the stunning speed of great revolutionary events, the local and specific issue was transformed into a universal and basic struggle. The proclamation of an indulgence was a characteristic activity of the popes— such proclamations were perfect expressions of the central ambition of the Church. In the bull *Unigenitus* Clement VI had generalized the practice which began with the Crusades into a doctrine intended to reinforce the role of the Church in salvation, and the prestige of the pope in the Church: first, the claim was made that the "treasure" of Christ's redemption was "acquired" by the Church and "through blessed Peter, bearer of heaven's keys, and his successors as vicars on earth" was to be "healthfully dispensed" for "fitting and reasonable causes, now for total, now partial remission of punishment due for temporal sins, as well generally as specially." Then to add to the monopoly by the Church of this wonder-working magic, and further to exalt the power of the pope to stand between the wrath of God and the fear of man (surely to the average believer the control by the pope of the *penalties* for sin was a more significant power than that reserved to God, which was *forgiveness*—a quite theological and mystical concept), the bull continued: "And to this heap of treasure the merits of the blessed Mother of God and of all the elect, from the first just man to the last, are known to have supplied their increment" to create an inexhaustible store of goodness. Pope Sixtus IV, in another bull in 1476 had declared the efficacy of indulgences extended to the dead already in purgatory.

But more aspiring than official doctrine were the bulls of indulgence themselves and the sermons which advertised them—frequently offering plenary remission of both punishment and sins. Indulgences were available in every corner of Europe for cash purchase or as inducements to visit holy sites long before Luther was born. They had become not only a leading feature of religious life, a prime mechanism of Church magic—they were an important source of revenue for European rulers. The ecclesiastical hierarchy at Rome was heavily endowed with indulgence revenue, and Luther's own respected prince, Frederick the Wise, commanded one of the richest treasures of papal indulgence in Europe —he could sell each All Saints' Day, remissions from purgatory drawn on a capital fund totaling 1,902,202 years and 270 days (free from punishment, that is). And his Castle Church could grant plenary remission of sins. The funds collected were very large and helped support both the Castle Church and the University of Wittenberg where Luther taught.

Luther had begun to criticize the purchasing of indulgences at Wit-

tenberg in 1516 and Frederick did not like it. Then in the following year, just as his private theological speculations were maturing in a radical Nominalist sense, emphasizing increasingly the inscrutable will of God, the ineffable and majestic nature of spiritual overlordship, the logical implications of the sovereignty of a creating divinity, and the consequent inadequacy of even the sanctified traditions of "good works" and "merit" to the achievement of so miraculous a boon as salvation, Luther's parishioners began buying indulgences from an old hand at vending this kind of Church merchandise, the Dominican Tetzel. Tetzel was commissioned to undertake the largest selling campaign of his career: Pope Leo X proclaimed the sale to finance the building of the new Basilica of St. Peter's at Rome, and before all the necessary negotiations were concluded a large number of the power figures in Europe had a stake in the operation which was bedded in simony, nepotism, usury, dynastic ambitions, and general fraud—mostly unknown to Luther. What Luther did know was that he could not in conscience let Tetzel represent the Church from which he expected salvation. Here is an account by a Franciscan of a Tetzel operation five years earlier:

He gained by his preaching in Germany an immense sum of money, all of which he sent to Rome; and especially at the new mining works at St. Annaberg, where I, Frederick Mecum, heard him for two years, a large sum was collected. It is incredible what this ignorant and impudent monk gave out. He said that if a Christian had slept with his mother, and placed the sum of money in the Pope's indulgence chest, the Pope had power in Heaven and earth to forgive the sin, and if he forgave it, God must do so also. Item—if they contributed readily, and bought grace and indulgence, all the hills of St. Annaberg would become pure massive silver. Item—so soon as the coin rang in the chest, the soul for whom the money was paid would go straightway to Heaven.

The indulgence was so highly prized, that when the commissary entered a city, the Bull was borne on a satin or gold-embroidered cushion, and all the priests and monks, the town council, schoolmaster, scholars, men, women, maidens, and children, went out to meet him with banners and tapers, with songs, and procession. Then all the bells were rung, all the organs played; he was conducted into the church, a red cross was erected in the midst of the church, and the Pope's banner displayed; in short, God Himself could not have been welcomed and entertained with greater honor.

It is incredible what this ignorant monk gave out in speaking and preaching. He gave sealed letters stating that even the sins which a man might wish to do hereafter were forgiven. The Pope had more power than all the apostles, all the angels and saints, even than the Virgin Mary Herself. For these were all subject to Christ, but the Pope was equal to Christ. After His ascension into Heaven Christ had nothing more to do with the government of the Church till the last day, but had entrusted all to the Pope as His vicar and vicegerent.   □

Now this representative of the Pope was preaching on the borders of electoral Saxony. His voice was the blatant trumpet of the worldliness,

the clerical arrogance, and the fantastic dishonesty of Roman Catholicism. He ignored all of the crucial theological and psychological implications of his sermons to concentrate on the single objective of selling by lies, deliberate and repeated, and with the connivance of the hierarchy. This was the Church become an end in a sense far from that of Luther's passionate interpretation of the drama of individual salvation by unmerited and inscrutable grace. Tetzel's sermons were the abdication of the pastoral function; think how words like the following from one of his sermons must have struck the tortured sensibilities of a Luther who had gone through Hell and was trying now to communicate the experience of salvation as he had lived it and as he was laboring to relate it to a general theology:

How many mortal sins are committed in a day, how many in a week, how many in a month, how many in a year, how many in the whole course of life! They are well-nigh numberless, and those that commit them must needs suffer endless punishment in the burning pains of Purgatory. But with these confessional letters you will be able at any time of life to obtain full indulgence for all the penalties imposed upon you, in all cases except the four reserved to the Apostolic See. . . . Do you not know that when it is necessary for anyone to go to Rome, or undertake any other dangerous journey, he takes his money to a broker and gives a certain per cent—five or six or ten—in order that at Rome or elsewhere he may receive again his funds intact, by means of the letter of this same broker? Are you not willing then, for the fourth part of a florin, to obtain these letters, by virtue of which you may bring, not your money, but your divine and immortal soul safe and sound into the land of Paradise?   □

The Pope and his minions—brokers of souls, peddlers of salvation.

As soon as the coin in the coffer rings,
The soul from purgatory springs.   □

Luther struck. On October 31, 1517, he posted on the door of Castle Church a comprehensive invitation to debate all of the issues relevant to the indulgences scandal:

In the desire and with the purpose of elucidating the truth, a disputation will be held on the underwritten propositions at Wittenberg, under the presidency of the Reverend Father Martin Luther, Monk of the Order of St. Augustine, Master of Arts and of Sacred Theology, and ordinary Reader of the same in that place. He therefore asks those who cannot be present and discuss the subject with us orally, to do so by letter in their absence. In the name of our Lord Jesus Christ. Amen.   □

There followed in hard, direct language, freighted with the sarcasm and anger which distinguishes Luther's fine prose for the next five years (and which always reminds me of Marx's language), a list of 95 "Theses." To cover his rage, perhaps unconsciously to protect himself

from the consequences of the rush of hostility which would soon overwhelm him, Luther wove into his propositions a number of innocuous items stressing conservative theology which we can ignore, and very many which are repetitive, but the challenge of the document as a whole was unmistakable:

28. It is certain that, when the money rattles in the chest, avarice and gain may be increased, but the effect of the intercession of the Church depends on the will of God alone. 30. No man is sure of the reality of his own contrition, much less of the attainment of plenary remission. 37. Every true Christian, whether living or dead, has a share in all the benefits of Christ and of the Church, given by God, even without letters of pardon. 71. He who speaks against the truth of apostolical pardons, let him be anathema and accursed. 72. But he, on the other hand, who exerts himself against the wantonness and license of speech of the preachers of pardons, let him be blessed. 75. To think that the Papal pardons have such power that they could absolve a man even if—by an impossibility—he had violated the Mother of God, is madness. 76. We affirm on the contrary that Papal pardons cannot take away even the least of venial sins, as regards its guilt. 77. The saying that, even if St. Peter were now Pope, he could grant no greater graces, is blasphemy against St. Peter and the Pope. 78. We affirm on the contrary that both he and any other Pope has greater graces to grant, namely, the Gospel, powers, gifts of healing, etc. (I Cor. XII). 79. To say that the cross set up among the insignia of the Papal arms is of equal power with the cross of Christ, is blasphemy. 80. Those bishops, priests and theologians who allow such discourses to have currency among the people will have to render an account. 81. This license in the preaching of pardons makes it no easy thing, even for learned men, to protect the reverence due to the Pope against the calumnies, or at all events, the keen questioning of the laity. 82. As for instance: Why does not the Pope empty Purgatory for the sake of most holy charity and of the supreme necessity of souls—this being the most just of all reasons—if he redeems an infinite number of souls for the sake of that most fatal thing, money, to be spent on building a basilica—this being a very slight reason? 83. Again; why do funeral masses and anniversary masses for the deceased continue, and why does not the Pope return, or permit the withdrawal of, the funds bequeathed for this purpose, since it is a wrong to pray for those who are already redeemed? 84. Again; what is this new kindness of God and the Pope, in that, for money's sake, they permit an impious man and an enemy of God to redeem a pious soul which loves God, and yet do not redeem that same pious and beloved soul out of free charity on account of its own need? 85. Again; why is it that the penitential canons, long since abrogated and dead in themselves, in very fact and not only by usage, are yet still redeemed with money, through the granting of indulgences, as if they were full of life? 86. Again; why does not the Pope, whose riches are at this day more ample than those of the wealthiest of the wealthy, build the single Basilica of St. Peter with his own money rather than with that of poor believers? 87. Again; what does the Pope remit or impart to those who through perfect contrition have a right

to plenary remission and participation? 88. Again; what greater good could the Church receive than if the Pope, instead of once, as he does now, were to bestow these remissions and participations a hundred times a day on any one of the faithful? 89. Since it is the salvation of souls, rather than money, that the Pope seeks by his pardons, why does he suspend the letters and pardons granted long ago, since they are equally efficacious? 90. To repress these scruples and arguments of the laity by force alone, and not to resolve them by giving reasons, is to expose the Church and the Pope to the ridicule of their enemies, and to make Christian men unhappy. 91. If then pardons were preached according to the spirit and mind of the Pope, all these questions would be resolved with ease; nay, would not exist. 92. Away then with all those prophets who say to the people of Christ: "Peace, peace," and there is no peace. 93. Blessed be all those prophets who say to the people of Christ: "The cross, the cross," and there is no cross. 94. Christians should be exhorted to strive to follow Christ their head through pains, deaths, and hells. 95. And thus trust to enter heaven through many tribulations rather than in the security of peace.   ◻

The pace of Luther's revolt against Thomistic theology and medieval ecclesiasticism quickened as the dangers increased. The earnest, introverted monk was transformed by his God into a fiery, flamboyant warrior. Luther now needed an audience before whom his terrible struggle could be confirmed; he needed opponents against whom his victories in cloister and classroom would assume the reality of social conflict. The Theses were printed, circulated among his acquaintances in various towns, translated, and elaborated on in sermons. The sale of indulgences was virtually ended by Luther's onslaught but he was after bigger game than Tetzel. In May of 1518 he defied the efforts of a general meeting of his order (commanded by the pope) to get him to recant. In October of the same year he appeared as directed before the papal legate, Cardinal Cajetan, at Augsburg and refused to retract anything; instead he wrote to Leo an appeal "from pope badly informed and his pretended commission . . . to our holy lord Leo X, by divine providence pope, to be better informed" and followed with an appeal to "a future General Council." Then in the summer of 1519 Luther entered the lists against the most formidable disputant in the ranks of Catholic orthodoxy, a fellow German and former friend, John Eck. The resulting debate began the Reformation.

Luther's party of theologians and heavily-armed students came to Duke George's Leipzig in July. The debate was held in an auditorium of the castle before an enormous assembly of clerical and secular dignitaries. Judges for the disputation were to be theologians from the universities of Paris and Erfurt. The chief contestants were described by an eyewitness as an emaciated, silver-tongued monk set against a giant priest with the voice of a town crier.

Luther's gentle friend and theological cohort, Carlstadt, was crushed by the Church's Goliath in the first days of dispute and Eck then turned with every confidence to destroy with power of memory and length of lung the leader of the Saxon heretics. Luther, however, was at his most

brilliant. He denied by an act of extraordinary historical imagination the authenticity of the decretals which Eck used to establish the first-century authority of the Roman pontiff. Then when the masterly Eck decided upon the tactic of crowding Luther into the dread Hussite corner by suggesting the similarity of his views to those of the Bohemian heretics so feared by the Saxon hosts of the debate, Luther reacted with stunning daring. He defended Hus—condemned though he stood by pope, council, and the universal opinion of German princes—on the essential grounds of his Christian rejection of Church authority.

Eck pressed the new line of attack for what he felt was a certain kill, but Luther's genius soared in anticipated, yet uncharted, fatefulness. In German he asserted to "the people" that a mere layman armed with Scripture was to be believed in matters of faith before pope or council acting without Scripture. Eck identified again the "Bohemian virus." For eighteen days the theological battle alternately raged grandly or subsided into the incredible trivialities of that discourse which distinguishes the Queen of Sciences. All the agreed-upon rules were violated, the university judgments were never resolved, and the controversy moved from Duke George's entertainment hall to the presses of Europe. Eck was confident that Luther's heretic pyre was banked for the greatest conflagration since the Bohemian dogs died their terrible and merited deaths.

But the Saxon Hus was not for burning. The power relations of pope, emperor, and princes were such that Luther had time and opportunity never granted to Hus. In the year after Leipzig Luther became a one-man revolution. He flooded Germany and Europe with the brutal beauty of his conviction and integrity. Like the Hussite revolutionaries before him, he turned to the language and myths of his own people as he took up his final stance of defiance. Excommunicated, both in the fall of 1520 and in January of 1521, the heretic stood alone and yet not alone—a powerful, stubborn, silent people were reading his pamphlets, and danger was riding on his anger. In his *Appeal to the German Nobility,* he found the voice that has launched great revolutions, the sense of outrage, hope, and the demand for leadership. "It is not out of mere arrogance and perversity that I, an individual, poor and insignificant, have taken it upon me to address your lordships. The distress and misery which oppress all ranks of Christendom, especially in Germany, have moved not me alone, but everybody, to cry aloud for help. . . ." Then he created his great image of the "three walls" of Romanism designed to preserve their corruption from reform, and before outlining his attack on their fortress in detail, cried, "Now may God help us, and give us one of those trumpets that overthrew the walls of Jericho, so that we may blow down these walls of straw and paper. . . ." His trumpet blasts made Hus look like a boy playing with a toy horn: the whole medieval church hierarchy Luther blasted as the Antichrist, not by the accident of bad character, but by the presumption of the institution; the sacramental system was basically corrupt; the theology of the schools defiled; and the remedy could only be drastic. Further, the work of revolt and reconstruction must be the task of Germans. "Now that Italy is sucked dry, they come to Germany. They begin in a quiet way,

but we shall soon see Germany brought into the same state as Italy. We have a few cardinals already. What the Romanists really mean to do, the 'drunken Germans' are not to see until they have lost everything. . . ." And even more strikingly, frighteningly, familiar is the climax of this his greatest tract: "Poor Germans that we are—we have been deceived! We were born to be masters, and we have been compelled to bow the head beneath the yoke of our tyrants, and to become slaves. Name, title, outward signs of royalty, we possess all these; force, power, right, liberty, all these have gone over to the popes, who have robbed us of them. They get the kernel, we get the husk. . . . It is time the glorious Teutonic people should cease to be the puppet of the Roman pontiff."

In the month of April of the year 1521 Luther became wholly himself. He was superb, one of the thrilling moments for humanity. Summoned to explain himself to the Diet at Worms, before the whole antagonistic power elite of Germany and the Empire, an assembly designed to overawe, expose, and destroy the heretic monk, Luther entered Worms in a Saxon cart. The new emperor, Charles, spoke only French, ruled over the greatest inheritance of power in the history of Europe, and was a simple-minded, fanatically devout Catholic.

Luther's perception of the ensuing confrontation is instructive. He was far less impressed with the historical drama we value—the miner's son in a monk's cowl defying the mightiest of emperors—than he was with the intense and fateful religious drama about to unfold before the invisible but terrible judgment of Almighty God.

The proceeding was typically elaborate and ponderous, opening with a formal examination of Luther's alleged authorship of a stack of books displayed before the assembly. Luther's reply—avowing his authorship and refusing to repudiate the substance of any—was given in the form of a great speech during which he reviewed the entire range of his theological and evangelical assault upon the clerical hierarchy which was charged once more with corrupting the very word of Christ while reducing all Germany to slavery. Eck would not enter the debate on substantive matters but pressed brutally forward the single demand that the confessed heretic and abettor of Infidels and Jews make an immediate and complete public recantation.

Luther quietly reaffirmed his heresy as the only recourse of conscience even before the awesome and threatening power and prestige of popes, councils, and kingdoms. "I will recant nothing . . . God help me . . . Here I stand; I can do no other."

Amid a swirl of conciliatory last-ditch ecclesiastical meetings, an eloquent threat from the emperor, and a series of ambiguous social protests and declarations, Luther departed Worms branded by secular edict of the Empire a "devil in monk's habit."

Extensions of Lutheranism

From the moment he left Worms Luther became less interesting; he entered upon a career of fame and success and he worked well at the creation of a new church for his followers, and continued to dispute

with relish and skill. But as a revolutionary his imagination and personality were exhausted. Germany was astir. All sorts of distressed people
became espousers of the Gospel truths revealed by the monk Luther—
there was now a banner to carry for every manner of grievance or
greed. Luther himself was offended and frightened by the unintended
relevance of his boldness. He was even angered when his old friend and
disciple Carlstadt put the principles of their new theology into church
practice at Wittenberg; indeed, Luther was brought from hiding back to
Wittenberg to stem the tide of reforming zeal! Then there was a
"Lutheran" revolt of disgruntled German knights under an unpleasant
man named Francis von Sickingen—a fiasco. The playwright Hans
Sachs, the artist Dürer, a hundred agitators of one sort or another,
became "Lutherans." The tide of revolution swelled, authority was
challenged at many levels of German culture, and finally the dread in
the minds of the ruling classes became social reality.

The Hussite nightmare stalked the lords of Germany from the borders of Switzerland where peasants had long fought with some success
for the freedom of their cantons. Luther had written stirring words
against the "tyranny" of the nobles who "drove and hunted men like
wild beasts"; he had recognized the "distress and misery" of the common man; he had attacked the usury that sucked what little blood there
was from the poor; and, above all, he had assailed the wealthy lords of
the Church and defied the authority of the most repressive institution in
Europe. He was for the *Bundschuh* (the peasantry) a symbol of struggle against their ancient masters. Luther had projected the image of
himself as champion of the downtrodden, the dispossessed, fighters for
religious liberty and justice; but Luther was no Amos or Prokop—he
was a Paul, an Augustine. His problems were intensely personal and his
imagination was religious in the medieval sense—the words about
social tyranny and injustice to be avenged were, like those of the
medieval sermon and the flood of Protestant sermonizing after him, a
kind of conventional pulpit rhetoric, the ritual of breast-beating and
denunciation expected of the genre.

Nevertheless, to the *Bundschuh,* who were ready for not only Hus but
Žižka, the eloquent and rebellious monk seemed a leader sent by God.
They were not social radicals; at least the early agitation in southern
Germany was extremely circumspect and unbloody. Often the chief activity of the rebels was to protest the enforcement of the Edict of Worms
which deprived them of a popular Lutheran pastor, and to ask redress of
manorial grievances. A good sample of the sort of revolution which had
become generalized in the winter of 1525 is afforded by the so-called
Twelve Articles, a compilation of regional demands that was widely distributed:

The Fundamental and Righteous Articles of the Peasants and Subjects of
the Lay and Ecclesiastical Lords by whom They Consider Themselves
Oppressed.
  Peace to the Christian reader and the grace of God through Christ:
  There are many evil writings put forth of late which take occasion, on
account of the assembling of the peasants, to cast scorn upon the gospel,

saying, "Is this the fruit of the new teaching, that no one should obey but that all should everywhere rise in revolt, and rush together to reform, or perhaps destroy altogether, the authorities, both ecclesiastic and lay?" The articles below shall answer these godless and criminal fault-finders, and serve, in the first place, to remove the reproach from the Word of God and, in the second place, to give a Christian excuse for the disobedience or even the revolt of the entire peasantry.

In the first place the gospel is not the cause of revolt and disorder, since it is the message of Christ, the promised Messiah; the word of life, teaching only love, peace, patience and concord. Thus all who believe in Christ should learn to be loving, peaceful, long-suffering and harmonious. This is the foundation of all the articles of the peasants (as will be seen), who accept the gospel and live according to it. How then can the evil reports declare the gospel to be a cause of revolt and disobedience? That the authors of the evil reports and the enemies of the gospel oppose themselves to these demands is due not to the gospel, but to the devil, the worst enemy of the gospel, who causes this opposition by raising doubts in the minds of his followers, and thus the Word of God, which teaches love, peace and concord, is overcome.

In the second place, it is clear that the peasants demand that this gospel be taught them as a guide in life, and they ought not to be called disobedient or disorderly. Whether or no, God grant the peasants, earnestly wishing to live according to His word, their requests, who shall find fault with the will of the Most High? Who shall meddle in His Judgments or oppose His Majesty? Did He not hear the Children of Israel when they called upon Him to save them out of the hands of Pharaoh? Can He not save His own today? Yea, He will save them and that speedily. Therefore, Christian reader, read the following articles with care and then judge. Here follow the articles:

I. First, it is our humble petition and desire, as also our will and resolution, that in the future we shall have power and authority so that each community shall choose and appoint a pastor, and that we shall have the right to depose him should he conduct himself improperly. The pastor thus chosen should teach us the gospel pure and simple, without any additional doctrine or ordinance of man. For to teach us continually the true faith will lead us to pray God that through His grace this faith may increase within us and become part of us. For if His grace work not within us we remain flesh and blood, which availeth nothing; since the Scripture clearly teaches that only through faith can we come to God. Only through His mercy can we become holy. Hence such a guide and pastor is necessary and in this fashion grounded upon the Scriptures.

II. According as the just tithe is established by the Old Testament and fulfilled in the New, we are ready and willing to pay the fair tithe of grain. The word of God plainly provides that in giving rightly to God and distributing to His people the services of a pastor are required. We desire that for the future our church provost, whomsoever the community may appoint, shall gather and distribute this tithe. From this he shall give to the pastor, elected by the whole community, a decent and sufficient maintenance for him and his, as shall seem right to the whole community.

What remains over shall be given to the poor of the place, as the circumstances and the general opinion demand. Should anything farther remain, let it be kept, lest anyone should have to leave the country on account of poverty. In case one or more villages themselves have sold the tithe on account of want, and formal testimony to this effect is given by an entire village, the claims of those to collect this tithe shall not be considered valid; but we will, as behooves us, make an agreement with such claimants to the end that we may repay the same in due time and manner. But those who have tithes which they have not purchased from a village, but which were appropriated by their ancestors, should not, and ought not to be paid any farther by the village, which shall apply its tithes to the support of the pastors elected as above indicated, or to assist the poor as is taught by the Scriptures. The small tithes, whether ecclesiastical or lay, we will not pay at all, for the Lord God created cattle for the free use of man. We will not, therefore, pay farther an unseemly tithe which is of man's invention.

III. It has been the custom hitherto for men to hold us as their own property, which is pitiable enough, considering that Christ has delivered and redeemed us all, the lowly as well as the great, without exception, by the shedding of His precious blood. Accordingly it is consistent with Scripture that we should be free and should wish to be so. Not that we would wish to be absolutely free and under no authority. God does not teach us that we should lead a disorderly life in the lusts of the flesh, but that we should love the Lord our God and our neighbor. We would gladly observe all this as God has commanded us in the celebration of the communion. He has not commanded us not to obey the authorities, but rather that we should be humble, not only toward those in authority, but toward everyone. We are thus ready to yield obedience according to God's law to our elected and regular authorities in all proper things becoming a Christian. We therefore take it for granted that you will release us from serfdom as true Christians, unless it should be shown us from the Gospel that we are serfs.

IV. In the fourth place, it has been the custom heretofore that no poor man should be allowed to touch venison or wild fowl, or fish in flowing water, which seems to us quite unseemly and unbrotherly as well as selfish and not agreeable to the Word of God. In some places the authorities preserve the game to our great annoyance and loss, recklessly permitting the unreasoning animals to destroy to no purpose our crops, which God suffers to grow for the use of man; and yet we must submit quietly. This is neither godly nor neighborly; for when God created man He gave him dominion over all the animals, over the birds of the air and over the fish in the water. Accordingly it is our desire, if a man holds possession of waters, that he should prove from satisfactory documents that his right has been unwittingly acquired by purchase. We do not wish to take it from him by force, but his rights should be exercised in a Christian and brotherly fashion. But whosoever cannot produce such evidence should surrender his claim with good grace.

V. In the fifth place, we are aggrieved in the matter of wood-cutting, for the noble folk have appropriated all the woods to themselves alone. If a

poor man requires wood, he must pay double price for it. It is our opinion in regard to a wood which has fallen into the hands of a lord, whether spiritual or temporal, that unless it was duly purchased it should revert again to the community. It should, moreover, be free to every member of the community to help himself to such firewood as he needs in his home. Also, if a man requires wood for carpenter's purposes he should have it free, but with the knowledge of a person appointed by the community for that purpose. Should, however, no such forest be at the disposal of the community let that which has been duly bought be administered in a brotherly and Christian manner. If the forest, although unfairly appropriated in the first instance, was later duly sold, let the matter be adjusted in a friendly spirit and according to the Scriptures.

VI. Our sixth complaint is in regard to the excessive services which are demanded of us and which are increased from day to day. We ask that this matter be properly looked into so that we shall not continue to be oppressed in this way, but that some gracious consideration be given us, since our forefathers were required only to serve according to the Word of God.

VII. Seventh, we will not hereafter allow ourselves to be further oppressed by our lords, but will let them demand only what is just and proper according to the word of agreement between the lord and the peasant. The lord should no longer try to force more services or other dues from the peasant without payment, but should permit the peasant to enjoy his holding in peace and quiet. The peasant should, however, help the lord when it is necessary, and at proper times, when it will not be disadvantageous to the peasant, and for a suitable payment.

VIII. In the eighth place, we are greatly burdened by holdings which cannot support the rent exacted from them. The peasants suffer loss in this way and are ruined; and we ask that the lords may appoint persons of honor to inspect these holdings, and fix a rent in accordance with justice, so that the peasant shall not work for nothing, since the laborer is worthy of his hire.

IX. In the ninth place, we are burdened with a great evil in the constant making of new laws. We are not judged according to the offense, but sometimes with great ill-will and sometimes much too leniently. In our opinion, we should be judged according to the old written law, so that the case shall be decided according to its merits, and not with partiality.

X. In the tenth place, we are aggrieved by the appropriation by individuals of meadows and fields which at one time belonged to the community. These we will take again into our own hands. It may, however, happen that the land was rightfully purchased; when, however, the land has unfortunately been purchased in this way, some brotherly arrangement should be made according to the circumstances.

XI. In the eleventh place, we will entirely abolish the due called "heriot," and will no longer endure it, nor allow widows and orphans to be thus shamefully robbed against God's will, and in violation of justice and right, as has been done in many places, and by those who should shield and protect them. These lords have disgraced and despoiled us, and although they had little authority they assumed it. God will suffer this no

more, and it shall be wholly done away with, and for the future no man shall be bound to give little or much.

XII. In the twelfth place, it is our conclusion and final resolution that if any one or more of the articles here set forth should not be in agreement with the Word of God, as we think they are, such article we will willingly retract if it is proved really to be against the Word of God by a clear explanation of the Scripture. Or if articles should now be conceded to us that are hereafter discovered to be unjust, from that hour they shall be void and null and without force. Likewise, if more complaints should be discovered which are based upon truth and the Scriptures and relate to offenses against God and our neighbor we are determined to reserve the right to present these also, and to exercise ourselves in all Christian teaching. For this we shall pray to God, since He can grant our demands, and He alone. The peace of Christ abide with us all.   ▢

Obviously, this was not a radical program—it was entirely within the conceptual limits of medieval orthodoxy, including the attack on serfdom. But Luther was worried over the presumption of inferior social classes, concerned that the lords would attribute the uprisings to their proclaimed evangelical motivation (he even denied the demand for free choice of pastor against the wishes of the prince), and hysterical over the possibility of violence.

Thomas Müntzer

As the peasant bands of southern and western Germany spent their energies on petitions and random orgies of vandalism, attempting in the tradition of the "*Jacquerie*"* to wrest a modicum of justice from the lords of Church and State, an equally futile but much more interesting uprising took place in Luther's Saxony. Saxon peasants had throughout the Middle Ages been particularly supine; now, however, they were not only subjected to Lutheran radicalism—they were suddenly visited by a thundering prophet straight out of the Old Testament. Thomas Müntzer was a learned priest and mystic who struggled for faith as Luther had—desperately—but found it not in the historic Jesus, not in the revelation of words, but in the blinding visions of immediate knowledge, and in association with an amazing group of militant prophets in the town of Zwickau. Zwickau is on the border of Bohemia, and there a weaver named Storch had made Tabor live again. Müntzer began to preach in Zwickau a prophecy of millennial revolution—in his vision, a terrible final blood-bath in which the elect of God would rise up to destroy first the Turkish Antichrist, and then the masses of the unrighteous. Before long he and Storch led their evangelized weavers in a revolt which failed, and Müntzer fled to Bohemia where he searched for the embers of Taborite chiliasm, and ended up being driven from Prague.

For two years he wandered in central Germany, his delusions now

---

* The term has generic reference to peasant insurrections.

settled into doctrine: ("The living God is sharpening his scythe in me, so that later I can cut down the red poppies and the blue cornflowers"). In 1523 he was invited to preach in Allstedt, and from there he created a revolutionary organization, the League of the Elect, made up of peasants and miners. His church became the most radical center of Christianity in Europe—for it he created the first liturgy in German, and to it came hundreds of miners from Mansfeld and peasants from the countryside as well as artisans from Allstedt.

Müntzer's revolution was not, like Luther's, a proposed reformation of men and institutions. To him Luther was a Pharisee bound to books and Wittenberg was the center of "the unspiritual soft-living flesh." He attacked the emasculated social imagination of the reformers, branded them tools of the rich and powerful, and when Luther wrote his *Letter to the Princes of Saxony* warning of the danger of this radical agitation, Müntzer reacted by openly declaring social revolution to be indispensably a part of faith in Christ: "The wretched flatterer is silent . . . about the origin of all theft. . . . Look, the seed-grounds of usury and theft and robbery are our lords and princes, they take all creatures as their property. . . . These robbers use the Law to forbid others to rob. . . . They oppress all people, and shear and shave the poor plowman and everything that lives—yet if (the plowman) commits the slightest offense, he must hang." Like the magnificent Hebrew prophets from whom he took his texts, Müntzer denounced the princes to their faces (Duke John, the Elector's brother, came to Allstedt to hear him, and he was summoned to Weimar to explain himself as a result of Luther's complaint) and left them shaken. Müntzer, with red crucifix and sword, led another frustrated revolt in Mühlhausen, wandered to Nuremberg and the Swiss border, preaching revolution and distributing his pamphlets, and finally was called back to Mühlhausen as Saxony caught the fever that was agitating the rest of Germany.

In April of 1525, under the rainbow banner of his covenanted church, Müntzer declared war on the unrighteous, and sent out this letter to the members of the League of the Elect:

Start and fight the Lord's fight. It's high time. Keep all your brethren to it, so that they don't mock the divine testimony, otherwise they must all be destroyed. All Germany, France and Italy are on the alert . . . the peasants in Klettgau and Hegau and in the Black Forest have risen, 3,000 strong, and the crowd is getting bigger all the time. My only fear is that the foolish fellows will let themselves be taken in by some treacherous agreement. . . .

If there are but three of you who, trusting in God, seek only his name and honor, you will not fear a hundred thousand.

Now go at them, and at them, and at them! It is time. The scoundrels are as dispirited as dogs. . . . It is very, very necessary, beyond measure necessary. . . . Take no notice of the lamentations of the godless! . . . Don't be moved to pity. . . . Stir up people in villages and towns, and most of all the miners and other good fellows who will be good at the job. We must sleep no more! . . . Get this letter to the miners! . . .

At them, at them, while the fire is hot! Don't let your sword get cold! Don't let it get lame! Hammer cling, clang on Nimrod's anvil! Throw their tower to the ground! So long as they are alive you will never shake off the fear of men. One can't speak to you about God so long as they are reigning over you. At them, at them, while you have daylight! God goes ahead of you, so follow, follow!　　　　　　　　　　　　　　　　□

Norman Cohn, from whose book, *The Pursuit of the Millennium*, I have taken the letter from Müntzer, regards all this as paranoid fantasy. Müntzer's contemporaries did not. Frederick the Wise wrote to his brother the following:

Perhaps the peasants have been given just occasion for their uprising through the impeding of the Word of God. In many ways the poor folk have been wronged by the rulers, and now God is visiting his wrath upon us. If it be his will, the common man will come to rule; and if it be not his will, the end will soon be otherwise.　　　　　　　　　　　　□

Duke John wrote: "As princes we are ruined." Luther was less passive before the will of God; although hooted out of countenance by the groups of peasants whom he tried to command into submission to their prince, he continued to fight the rude social rooting of the heresy he had spawned. Müntzer presented a graphic portrait of Luther's confrontation with the peasants:

He claims that the Word of God is sufficient. Doesn't he realize that men whose every moment is consumed in the making of a living have no time to learn to read the Word of God? The princes bleed the people with usury and count as their own the fish in the stream, the bird of the air, and the grass of the field, and Dr. Liar says 'Amen!' What courage has he, Dr. Pussyfoot, the new pope of Wittenberg, Dr. Easychair, the basking sycophant? He says there should be no rebellion because the sword has been committed by God to the ruler, but the power of the sword belongs to the whole community. In the good old days the people stood by when judgment was rendered lest the ruler pervert justice, and the rulers have perverted justice.　　　　　　　　　　　　　　　　　□

Luther's final stand, as the peasants rose to Müntzer's call for a radical reconstitution of the state as well as the soul, was sent to the printer after the Zurich Protestants had already decreed death to all who preached or held ideas of pacifism, communism, and the separation of church and state (the "Anabaptists"). Nevertheless, *Against the Robbing and Murdering Hordes of Peasants* is an amazing document in the tortured history of Christian ethical perception:

Against the rioting peasants, Martin Luther.
In my earlier book on this matter, I did not venture to judge the peasants, since they had offered to be corrected and to be instructed; and Christ in Matthew 7 [:1] commands us not to judge. But before I could

even inspect the situation, they forgot their promise and violently took matters into their own hands and are robbing and raging like mad dogs. All this now makes it clear that they were trying to deceive us and that the assertions they made in their *Twelve Articles* were nothing but lies presented under the name of the gospel. To put it briefly, they are doing the devil's work. This is particularly the work of that archdevil who rules at Mühlhausen, and does nothing except stir up robbery, murder, and bloodshed; as Christ describes him in John 8 [:44], "He was a murderer from the beginning." Since these peasants and wretched people have now let themselves be misled and are acting differently than they promised, I, too, must write differently of them than I have written, and begin by setting their sin before them, as God commands Isaiah [58:1] and Ezekiel [2:7], on the chance that some of them may see themselves for what they are. Then I must instruct the rulers how they are to conduct themselves in these circumstances.

The peasants have taken upon themselves the burden of three terrible sins against God and man; by this they have abundantly merited death in body and soul. In the first place, they have sworn to be true and faithful, submissive and obedient, to their rulers, as Christ commands when he says, "Render to Caesar the things that are Caesar's" [Luke 20:25]. And Romans 13 [:1] says, "Let every person be subject to the governing authorities." Since they are now deliberately and violently breaking this oath of obedience and setting themselves in opposition to their masters, they have forfeited body and soul, as faithless, perjured, lying, disobedient rascals and scoundrels usually do. St. Paul passed this judgment on them in Romans 13 [:2] when he said that those who resist the authorities will bring a judgment upon themselves. This saying will smite the peasants sooner or later, for God wants people to be loyal and to do their duty.

In the second place, they are starting a rebellion, and are violently robbing and plundering monasteries and castles which are not theirs; by this they have doubly deserved death in body and soul as highwaymen and murderers. Furthermore, anyone who can be proved to be a seditious person is an outlaw before God and the emperor; and whoever is the first to put him to death does right and well. For if a man is in open rebellion, everyone is both his judge and his executioner; just as when a fire starts, the first man who can put it out is the best man to do the job. For rebellion is not just simple murder; it is like a great fire, which attacks and devastates a whole land. Thus rebellion brings with it a land filled with murder and bloodshed; it makes widows and orphans, and turns everything upside down, like the worst disaster. Therefore let everyone who can, smite, slay, and stab, secretly or openly, remembering that nothing can be more poisonous, hurtful, or devilish than a rebel. It is just as when one must kill a mad dog; if you do not strike him, he will strike you, and a whole land with you.

In the third place, they cloak this terrible and horrible sin with the gospel, call themselves "Christian brethren," take oaths and submit to them, and compel people to go along with them in these abominations. Thus they become the worst blasphemers of God and slanderers of his holy name. Under the outward appearance of the gospel, they honor and

serve the devil, thus deserving death in body and soul ten times over. I have never heard of a more hideous sin. I suspect that the devil feels that the Last Day is coming and therefore he undertakes such an unheard-of act, as though saying to himself, "This is the end, therefore it shall be the worst; I will stir up the dregs and knock out the bottom." God will guard us against him! . . .

It does not help the peasants when they pretend that according to Genesis 1 and 2 all things were created free and common, and that all of us alike have been baptized. For under the New Testament, Moses does not count; for there stands our Master, Christ, and subjects us, along with our bodies and our property, to the emperor and the law of this world, when he says, "Render to Caesar the things that are Caesar's" [Luke 20:25]. Paul, too, speaking in Romans [13:1] to all baptized Christians, says, "Let every person be subject to the governing authorities." And Peter says, "Be subject to every ordinance of man" [I Pet. 2:13]. We are bound to live according to this teaching of Christ, as the Father commands from heaven, saying, "This is my beloved Son, listen to him" [Matt. 17:5]. . . .

Now since the peasants have brought [the wrath of] both God and man down upon themselves and are already many times guilty of death in body and soul, and since they submit to no court and wait for no verdict, but only rage on, I must instruct the temporal authorities on how they may act with a clear conscience in this matter.

First, I will not oppose a ruler who, even though he does not tolerate the gospel, will smite and punish these peasants without first offering to submit the case to judgment. He is within his rights, since the peasants are not contending any longer for the gospel, but have become faithless, perjured, disobedient, rebellious murderers, robbers, and blasphemers, whom even a heathen ruler has the right and authority to punish. Indeed, it is his duty to punish such scoundrels, for this is why he bears the sword and is "the servant of God to execute his wrath on the wrongdoer," Romans 13 [:4].

But if the ruler is a Christian and tolerates the gospel, so that the peasants have no appearance of a case against him, he should proceed with fear. First he must take the matter to God, confessing that we have deserved these things, and remembering that God may, perhaps, have thus aroused the devil as a punishment upon all Germany. Then he should humbly pray for help against the devil, for we are contending not only "against flesh and blood," but "against the spiritual hosts of wickedness in the air" [Eph. 6:12; 2:2], which must be attacked with prayer. Then, when our hearts are so turned to God that we are ready to let his divine will be done, whether he will or will not have us to be princes and lords, we must go beyond our duty, and offer the mad peasants an opportunity to come to terms, even though they are not worthy of it. Finally, if that does not help, then swiftly take to the sword.

For in this case a prince and lord must remember that according to Romans 13 [:4] he is God's minister and the servant of his wrath and that the sword has been given him to use against such people. If he does not fulfil the duties of his office by punishing some and protecting others, he

commits as great a sin before God as when someone who has not been given the sword commits murder. If he is able to punish and does not do it —even though he would have had to kill someone or shed blood—he becomes guilty of all the murder and evil that these people commit. For by deliberately disregarding God's command he permits such rascals to go about their wicked business, even though he was able to prevent it and it was his duty to do so. This is not a time to sleep. And there is no place for patience or mercy. This is the time of the sword, not the day of grace. . . .

Therefore, dear lords, here is a place where you can release, rescue, help. Have mercy on these poor people! Let whoever can stab, smite, slay. If you die in doing it, good for you! A more blessed death can never be yours, for you die while obeying the divine word and commandment in Romans 13 [:1, 2], and in loving service of your neighbor, whom you are rescuing from the bonds of hell and of the devil. And so I beg everyone who can to flee from the peasants as from the devil himself; those who do not flee, I pray that God will enlighten and convert. As for those who are not to be converted, God grant that they may have neither fortune nor success. To this let every pious Christian say, "Amen!" For this prayer is right and good, and pleases God; this I know. If anyone thinks this too harsh, let him remember that rebellion is intolerable and that the destruction of the world is to be expected every hour.   □

Luther's pamphlet was not needed to crush the peasants. The troops of the empire were returning from Italy and everywhere in May of 1525 the insurrections were in trouble. Müntzer and his peasants stood like cattle behind their wagons near Frankenhausen while by taking advantage of a truce the German lords slaughtered five thousand—including Müntzer himself. Between Prokop and Cromwell, military genius was not in the ranks of revolutionists. The events of the next weeks would sicken the most unimaginative observer of history: perhaps 100,000 peasants were butchered (and that is a fairly accurate estimate) by the armies of the ruling classes. Luther's friend, John Ruehl, wrote, "To many of those who are favorable to you it is a strange thing that you allow the tyrants to slay without mercy and say that they can become martyrs."

The German revolution failed because the peasants did not sufficiently believe in the positive goals of their boldest ambitions (they were deeply experienced in failure so that except for moments of exhilaration provided by the genius of Müntzer, moments that could be sustained only by Müntzer himself, the peasants *knew* God would fail them and their masters would rule as before). This sense of failure is, I think, much of the explanation for the lack of inspired military leadership without which a revolution is a tragic farce. Also, of course, the revolutionaries had no adequate appreciation of the need for organization in depth—for echelons of command and reserves of interlocked units coordinated in a common purpose but with specialized functions. These dimensions of morale and organization appeared for the first time in European history in the Netherlands at the end of the century,

and reappeared in still more interesting combination in England in the middle of the seventeenth century.

Impact of the Reformation

The religious revolt of Luther was thus only in oblique and subterranean ways a factor in the shaping of the modern revolutionary social movements. What, after all, *are* the implications of Christian individualism? There is no necessary logic which carries from Luther's individualistic theology of salvation into the natural world. It was not dishonest or illogical of Luther to believe that his salvation lay in Paul's revelation of the will of God, or to create a dogmatic illusion about this central precept, while denying that the freedom of the Christian man through faith meant freedom of opinion about salvation and freedom of action to reform society. Luther's freedom was absolutely his own and could be shared only on his terms. All religious systems and personalities are ultimately intolerant and closed to rigorous inquiry because they are all founded upon an absolute truth apprehended by supernatural and historical revelation. Further, the absolutist precepts of any faith force quite inevitably into the arena of social and political debate and action the hopelessly irrelevant search for answers as enduring as those which solve the riddle of death. What can the psychology of sin and beatitude do for man in the complicated turmoil of living reality?

Generally, the religious mind can either endow social reality with the qualities of acceptance appropriate to the absolute supernature of which society is but the pale reflection, or it can totally reject existing reality as either a terrible offense to God or an impossible dross in the scheme of creation—a penalty to be suffered but not questioned. Most Christians, including Luther and his spiritual progeny, fall in the first class of religiousness—they do not see much of reality, their illusions are personal and death-centered, and with perfect integrity they adjust to whatever does not threaten their illusions about salvation by miracle. The religious radicals—mystics, humanists, millenarians, and assorted madmen—fall into the second category: they want either to tear apart and rebuild the hideous reality which offends their illusions about God, or they have to retire into the isolation of the intransigent self which wills a world of spiritual reality that transcends the reality that cannot be God's but is too terrifying to change.

The anti-Catholic religiosity of the sixteenth and seventeenth centuries was consistently a revolutionary force; the problem is to understand the complex patterns of interaction by which Protestantism hurried on and in some instances made possible the political and social changes in Europe. Perhaps the universal effects were all related to the failure of Catholic culture to hold popular support and to meet the interests and needs of the "new" men in city and court who wanted power and adventure. Protestantism was pre-eminently an experimental, bookish, talkative, argumentative religion. From Luther and his school at Wittenberg, in Paris, Strasbourg, Zurich, Basel, Geneva, in the Netherlands, Scandinavia, Poland, Scotland, and England, Christianity be-

came a religion of the press and pulpit. Millions of words made public property the inner torments, flashes of inspiration, and basic humanity of the imaginative Christian. The European consciousness was flooded with ideas for churches, personal morality, art, learning, political states, holy wars, witch detection, and money making—not much of all the writing and talking was original, but the total impact was revolutionary. It was as though Europeans had taken the meaning and direction of their lives back from a discredited trusteeship—even where Catholic culture survived, it was forced by the aggression of the heretics to reconstitute itself.

The old patterns of authority, the prescriptions of custom and the sanctity of institutions, were in the era of Protestantism replaced by the modern techniques of control—power went to the leaders and groups who could organize and discipline and inspire. The ways of God to man were being looked into, the traditional illusions smashed, and the future was given over to the bold and the persuasive in a way not previously exampled in our history. The instinct for authority, the need for certainty, was not gone; only the mechanisms for stabilizing power relationships were gone. And so kings in Scandinavia and England were able with vigor and imagination to create with the iconoclasm and individualism of the Protestant heresy stronger and richer and more popular political regimes.

The Revolt of the Netherlands

Of all the remarkable works of the Protestant imagination and energy, none is more interesting than the revolution in the Netherlands. The creation of the Dutch Republic is in itself a recapitulation and an apotheosis of the best and worst of European culture. The cities of the Netherlands had always been among the most exciting and creative centers of European civilization: in the sixteenth century, with Lutheran and Calvinist theology as a catalyst, the history of the provinces of the Netherlands (there were seventeen of them under the rule of the Hapsburgs) took an extraordinary turn. Nationalism began to assert itself against the dynastic rule of the Spanish Hapsburg Philip II. In spite of provincial differences, the gallicization of the southern provinces, and foreign rule in Church and State, there was a distinct rise in consciousness of the realities of a Netherlandish civilization. The economic inventiveness and productivity of the provincial towns and great cities like Antwerp and Brussels and Amsterdam was the talk and envy of Europe. In many important respects, the combination of a rising sense of national identity with a tremendous economic expansion fettered and drained by the stupid parasitism of the Hapsburg bureaucracy, resembles the etiology of revolt in the American colonies of the eighteenth century. But in the minds of most rebellious Netherlanders, the crucial issues which made Spanish rule intolerable, and the destruction of Spain's allies among the native nobility and clergy desirable, were those between Catholicism and Protestantism.

Protestantism was at its best in the Netherlands—contentious, var-

ious, and imaginative. Lutheran scholarship was grafted on the already flourishing humanistic piety of the Brethren of the Common Life; Anabaptism from the fire-breathing chiliasm of Melchior Hoffmann to the quietism of Menno Simons survived the terrifying persecution of the Spanish Inquisition as well as the vicious acts of the Flemish bourgeoisie; and Calvinism, finally, enjoyed a rich reception in the towns—developing political and social theories and an elitist psychology of opposition. As in England later, the divisiveness of the Protestant sects in the Netherlands was not an indication of their importance in the formation of a revolutionary élan and leadership. Protestant sectarianism in the revolutionary milieu of the sixteenth and seventeenth centuries may be likened to socialist sectarianism in the twentieth century. Varieties of competing groups and theories may in fact sharpen the effectiveness of the whole movement in its drive to destroy and reform the social establishment.

It is not possible to date the onset of revolution in the Netherlands as it is in England. The guilds of Ghent had revolted against paying taxes to the Emperor Charles V in 1539; religious martyrs and heretic defiance had challenged the Inquisition and the Council of State. William, Prince of Orange, and the counts of Egmont and Horn, the richest and most powerful lords of the Netherlands, led a patriotic opposition to Spanish rule and in 1565 gave their signatures to a secret compact pledging resistance to the new tyranny. In the following year from Brabant to Zeeland the "Beggars," as the opposition nobles were called by the party of the regent (one of those chance epithets that quickly and permanently came to denote the rebels), were given militant Calvinist support in a burst of iconoclastic rioting. Civil war ensued as William's brother, Louis of Nassau, invaded Flanders with a small makeshift army which won no victories but brought the Duke of Alva from Italy with a great army of Spanish veterans to restore and maintain order. Alva ruled the Netherlands with one of the notable reigns of terror in the modern world: he executed for heresy every patriot he could find, including Egmont and Horn, drove hundreds of thousands into exile, smashed the army which Orange in desperation put in the field, and generally contrived a brilliantly repressive regime, except that he adopted the characteristically stupid Spanish policy of ruinous tax measures that alienated the wealthy and left his regime in serious fiscal difficulties. But the rebels seemed utterly dispirited and beaten by 1572.

Then on April 1, 1572, in the province of Holland there began a new insurrection which became the center of perhaps the first successful revolution of the modern world—a prototype of many revolutions to come. As it was the first, so it was the longest, cruelest and most complicated. The forces of the status quo were formidable—great generals, master politicians, endless resources of troops, and an able and fanatical king who from the 60's had insisted, "These rascals can only be made to do right through fear, and not always even by that means." The rebels fought with new and untried weapons—secret organizations, massive propaganda, a war of terrain, and a strategy rooted solidly in the social aspirations of the most aggressive groups in the population.

The classical American account of the revolution, that of John Motley, saw the opening of the movement as "purely the work of the people. . . . By the same spontaneous movement, nearly all the important cities of Holland and Zeeland raised the standard of him* in whom they recognized their deliverer. . . . With one fierce bound of enthusiasm the nation shook off its chains." Motley believed the rebels motivated by zeal for the true God of Protestant revelation. A greater historian, the Dutchman Pieter Geyl, identifies the Protestant idealism primarily as that which inspired to action "the urban lower middle class," while the town oligarchies "felt themselves . . . the guardians of the privileges and welfare of town and country, rather than the champions of a particular new religious faith. In other words, they regarded matters from a secular standpoint, and, while the new Church had in their scheme of things its indispensable place, they felt it incumbent on them carefully to circumscribe this place. From one point of view . . . the great European movement of the Reformation was a revolt of the lay community under the leadership of their rulers—a revolt, that is to say, of the State against priestly influence."

The *opstand*, as the Dutch called it, seems to have been the work of a small, socially complex elite composed of those disaffected nobles who officered the Beggars, the ranks of the guerilla Beggars, and a coalition of new men in the towns who opposed the old ruling families. All of the revolutionary elements were anti-Catholic, though not doctrinally Calvinist. The strategy devised to take Holland and Zeeland was one of "fifth-column" subversion of town security by the Protestant revolutionists in contact with Beggar forces outside the city walls. Once taken, the town itself was revolutionized: the "Spanish" (i.e., Catholic and Imperial sympathizers) were driven into exile, town administrations were increasingly staffed by Protestant militants—and the majority of townsmen soon ended as collaborators with the new regimes.

The larger political scene remained confusing for two basic reasons. First, the rebels were opposed to centralized government—to that characteristic aspect of modernity which for them bore the stamp of foreign rule and heavy taxes. The institutions of Burgundian and Hapsburg bureaucracy were rejected for what seems a reactionary medieval emphasis on local liberties and privileges. This historical oddity may explain why there is almost no political thought worth recalling in the long, tortured history of the Dutch Revolution. The second factor that accounts for much in the political vagaries of the revolution is that of religious division and hatred. For while anti-Catholic sentiment bound together the small band that revolutionized the northern provinces, religious conservatism in the villages and towns to the south proved a stronger force working to isolate the leadership of the various radical coups.

The events of the almost incredible Eighty-Years War, as Dutch historians style it (to the recognition of United Netherlands' indepen-

* William the Silent, count of Nassau and prince of Orange—the rich and able leader of the united Netherlands in the revolt against Spain.

dence at the Peace of Westphalia in 1648) are harder to classify and make sense of than those of any subsequent civil war in modern history. Only the struggle of the Vietnamese revolutionaries in our own time can be compared to that of the Netherlanders in complexity, courageous commitment, and tragedy. The patterns of radical activity vary in sociology, ideology, chronology, and geography. Successes and failures explode unexpectedly from the first appearance of "the Beggars" in Brabant to the triumphant truce negotiated by the exhausted revolutionary nation of the north forty years later.

One further analytical peculiarity of this momentous struggle makes it impossible to describe with documents—the revolt of the Netherlands produced no geniuses, nor any really exciting and illuminating documentary testaments. The written thought of the revolution is conceptually uninspired and artistically insignificant. There are no Luthers, Cromwells, or Miltons. Creativity of the imperishable sort awaited the peace and relative freedom which were the gifts of the revolutionary generation to its posterity.

The essential action of the radical revolution was concentrated in a ten-year period following the establishment of a revolutionary base north of the Meuse. The rule of the Spanish and their minions in the south was seriously and often brilliantly (although ultimately unavailingly) challenged in the years from 1576 to 1585. The savage mutiny of Philip's mercenary army, brought in to destroy the rebellion of the northerners, alienated the pro-Spanish oligarchies in the southern towns that now feared for property and order, and gave the radicals their chance.

The first results of the degeneration of Spanish military control of the south were efforts led by the richest feudal lord of the Netherlands, William of Orange, to create a national resistance to Spain. In the fall of 1576 delegates of the conservative south met at Ghent with those of the revolutionary north to work out a program of unified opposition to Spanish rule. But of course a coalition divided in basic religious and social ideology could not produce a national revolution. The Pacification of Ghent (as the alliance of Netherlanders was called) was shattered in a little over a year by the catastrophic failure of the armies raised to fight the Spanish, although the ideal of a national union survived in the Union of Utrecht and in the entourage of William. To radical groups the destruction of Netherlands' armies in 1578 proved that the aristocratic architects of the Pacification not only stood in the way of political and social progress but also were incapable of exercising their traditional function of military prowess.

There followed hard on the failure of aristocratic national leadership a remarkable usurpation of political power in Flemish towns with a view to getting rid of the whole power complex of Spanish bureaucracy and native oligarchies. In Ghent itself the Duke of Aerschot, Stadholder of Flanders and most important leader of the national baronial party after William, was arrested and the old medieval city constitution restored. The leader of the coup d'état, Jan van Hembyze, in open defiance of the national Protestant leader pressed on to create a more

democratic and very Protestant enclave on the model of the Hollanders of the *opstand*. A revolutionary committee was set up, iconoclasm was encouraged, monks and priests were driven into exile, and Roman Catholic worship was forbidden. The revolutionized city then attempted to carry its Protestant and social revolution to the whole of Flanders. Civil war raged in the richest province of the Netherlands. The radicals expanded their power for almost two exciting years before the conservative national leadership of William the Silent found effective allies among the moderates at Ghent who finally engineered the removal of Hembyze and his radical Calvinist cohorts.

Brussels, capital of Brabant, went through a similar revolutionary phase with the extraordinary difference that the medieval guilds who dominated the city in its initial revolt of 1579 were Catholic (though anticlerical). But soon the pattern of Protestant social revolution was reasserted in the person of Van den Tympel, a brilliant military leader who seized the Brussels–Antwerp canal from the Catholic foe, thereby saving the city from starvation and providing a popular base for Protestant revolutionary leadership in Brabant. The Catholic guilds were broken in political power, and Church property was seized along with that of the crown and the *émigré* nobility. Calvinist ministries and schools were established with part of the wealth confiscated from the old regime. Catholic services were then prohibited in the name of religious freedom (Catholics were accused of plotting the return of Inquisition and Spain) while generous toleration of non-Catholic worship was the rule of revolutionary Brussels.

Finally, dramatically, in 1580 the internal hierarchies of the ancient city were exploded by the appointment of a plebeian magistrate who became burgomaster and brought other plebeians into the magistracy and therefore into the power structure of the guilds themselves. For the next five years Brabant joined Flanders in radical emulation of the north. That this major social and cultural revolution failed to stabilize its success in the style of Holland and Zeeland was an accident of military power. The armies of Spain proved simply too formidable for the southern revolutionists to contain.

William the Silent died at the hand of an assassin in 1584 with the cry, "God have pity on my soul and on this poor people!" But God's poor Dutchmen needed no pity. In the decades which followed, the United Provinces under the leadership of resourceful men like Maurice of Nassau, William's son, and Oldenbarnevelt, the Advocate of Holland, held off the armies of Parma and his successors at the Meuse, and forged ahead as traders and industrialists. Brabant and Flanders were lost to Parma, ending forever the Netherlandish state constituted by the Union of Utrecht (reconquest of Brabant was actively hindered by the burghers of Amsterdam who were happy to see Antwerp, the former giant of the province, reduced by their blockade to economic ruin); but fading Spanish power and the surging energies of the Dutch combined to give the first nation created by revolution brilliant achievements and prospects in the seventeenth century. Dutch universities—Leiden espe-

cially—and Dutch artists, writers, and scientists provided magnificent justification for the revolutionary state. Seventeenth-century Dutch culture is one of the glories of all civilization—it is known by the names of Rembrandt, Huygens, and Spinoza. Less glorious but more enduring was the bourgeois power which henceforth ruled the destinies of the Netherlanders.

Suggested Reading

The Christian Revolutions of the sixteenth century have attracted good scholars with the result that there is excellent reading on the major themes. The best single volume is probably Preserved Smith, *The Age of the Reformation* (New York: The Macmillan Company, 1920); a very useful short history is R. H. Bainton, *The Reformation of the Sixteenth Century** (Boston: Beacon Press, 1952). There are two comprehensive and intelligent surveys of the most interesting varieties of religious thought: J. T. McNeil, *The History and Character of Calvinism* (Oxford: Oxford University Press, 1954), and G. H. Williams, *The Radical Reformation* (Philadelphia: The Westminster Press, 1962).

For a brilliant account of Erasmus, see J. Huizinga, *Erasmus of Rotterdam* (London: Phaidon Press Ltd, 1952). On Luther I would begin with R. H. Bainton, *Here I Stand* (Nashville: Abingdon Press, 1950). Two interesting and very different efforts to reconstruct the genesis of Luther's revolt are Heinrich Boehmer, *Martin Luther: Road to Reformation** (Muhlenberg Press, 1946), and a psychiatric reconstruction by Erik Erikson, *Young Man Luther** (New York: W. W. Norton & Company, Inc., 1958). An adequate introduction to Luther's writing is provided by T. G. Tappert, ed., *Selected Writings of Martin Luther** (Philadelphia: Fortress Press, 1967). Two impressive Marxist interpretations of the Reformation are Frederick Engels, *The Peasant War in Germany** (International Publishers Co., Inc., 1927), and Roy Pascal, *The Social Basis of the German Reformation* (New York: Franklin Watts, Inc., 1933).

Concerning the revolutionary Netherlanders, there is an old classic available in many editions by J. L. Motley, *The Rise of the Dutch Republic* (London: J. M. Dent & Sons Ltd, 1906), and Pieter Geyl, *The Revolt of the Netherlands** (New York: Barnes and Noble, Inc., 1958), is the best recent account in English. (The superior work of J. Presser remains untranslated.) J. Huizinga, *Dutch Civilization in the 17th Century** (New York: William Collins Sons & Co., Ltd, 1968) has some interesting essays, and a good economic study is Violet Barbour, *Capitalism in Amsterdam in the 17th Century** (Baltimore: The Johns Hopkins Press, 1950). Finally, there is a biography of *William the Silent* (New Haven: Yale University Press, 1945) by C. V. Wedgwood.

4 The Great Rebellion: England 1640–1660

Background to the Revolution

The pace of change in western Europe quickened in the seventeenth century, and the frequency and intensity of conflict which had characterized the sixteenth century carried into the age of Galileo and Milton. The most obvious patterns of conflict were those between oligarchies—county, court, church; old guild elites and new entrepreneurial associations; the old "orders" and "estates" and "constituted bodies"; and the new central bureaucracies. The wars of competing oligarchies in some cases involved popular movements. In fact, the universal problem of revolting oligarchies in the seventeenth and eighteenth centuries was the danger over their shoulders—the open and persistent fear that the peasants and urban poor, whose support they actively sought, would seize the opportunities of crisis in the old regimes to achieve radical social objectives. In the Catalan Revolution of 1640, which began as a revolt against Madrid and the ambitions of Olivares to destroy the provincial "liberties" of the native oligarchies, the eventual defeat of the Catalans resulted from the fact that the ruling classes in Catalonia feared their own angry poor more than Castile—the national revolution against outside tyranny became a civil war, and the traditional elites sold out the revolution to Madrid just as similar groups had done in the Netherlands. Similar revolutions—all unsuccessful combinations of defensive oligarchies and elements of popular anger and hope—occurred in Portugal and France.

In certain ways—very difficult for the historian to assess—the seventeenth century appears altogether the most revolutionary century in history. For not only is it the century of the pivotal English Revolution, the nature of which will be the subject of this chapter, it is also the century of Galileo, Descartes, and Newton. It is impossible for me in the scope of this book even to suggestively document or comment upon the qualities and impact of the "scientific revolution" which many historians feel is the cultural watershed of modernity. Simply to list the achievements in rational technique and imagination of seventeenth-century Europeans would weary the attentive reader: the subject matter painfully mastered by students in our schools regarding the descrip-

tions of the heavens, of matter in motion, of light, and the mechanics of the animal body was substantially the creation of the fabulous 1600's. The nature of our commonest perception and usual analysis was given us—by acts of genius—in the generations between Galileo's *Dialogues* and Newton's *Principia*. Along with these singularly insightful ideas, the century laid the foundations of modern technology—basic conceptual tools like the new mathematics were supplemented by basic perceptual tools like the telescope, the microscope, the pump, clock and barometer.

The relevance of this tremendous alteration in the perceptions and argument of the learned in Europe to the revolutionary thought and actions of the generality of intellectuals (still mostly clerics) and politicians and ordinary people is not at all clear and needs much more research before anything can be established. In broad cultural terms, one can note the increasing prestige of "scientific method" not only in the specific matters of question posing, experiment, and analysis, but also in the push toward new universals, secular, international, nonsectarian, and intellectually elegant. Yet not until the eighteenth-century enthusiasm for popular science, not until the *philosophes* hammered the essentials of scientific rationalism into public consciousness by means of the press (secondary schooling for the masses is, of course, a recent development) can one detect any deep psychological dimension by which the new science affected the political and moral and animal passions which are the stuff of revolutions. Indeed, I think not into our own age has there been any very profound alteration of the sensibilities engaged in revolutionary activities as a result of the continuous revolutionizing of scientific perspectives. The industrial and technological by-products of scientific thought have, of course, profoundly set the social stage in the past two hundred years of political revolt, and the humanistic and naturalistic psychology and ethics of liberals and socialists have borrowed their vocabularies and some of their insights from the treasury of European science; but I cannot explain any important revolutionary event or idea or leader by reference to a primary scientific precept or procedure (no—not even evolution!). Thus science is a part of our story only by the kind of indirection which relates revolution to the art and learning and literature of Europe—it is present and real but narratively less crucial than the rawer facts that cry out from the documents.

The most interesting and important story of the wonder-filled seventeenth century is that of the English Revolution. The story is mostly fine in itself, but it is also one which has determined a great deal of the course of world history in the past three hundred years. The bourgeois triumph in seventeenth-century England decided, I would argue, the geography and timing of the Industrial Revolution. The basis of English capitalism, industry, and empire was created—and with it how much of our lives!—by the forces and men of revolution in the England of the Stuarts and Cromwell. Further, and more exciting, the English Revolution completed the religious and humanistic rhetoric of liberty and justice begun in the tension-ridden Europe of the fourteenth century.

The ideals which have lifted the hearts and strengthened the arms of millions in revolt since Cromwell rode with the Levellers were fired in the genius of the English Renaissance by men who struggled for all the freedoms of which the European imagination has proven capable. The dynamic secular dogmas which move our world—democracy, socialism, and libertarianism—were given imperishable form and life by Cromwell's England.

In order to read with discrimination the documents of the English revolt, the first necessity for the student is to appreciate the extraordinary nature of the Renaissance in England. Seldom in history has a society performed so brilliantly at so many levels of culture. English religious thought I consider the most various and elegant in our tradition; the names Harvey, Gilbert, Boyle, Hooke, and Newton represent the most brilliant galaxy of talents in the history of science; English music was in its one period of real distinction; historians, architects, antiquarians, philosophers, classical scholars, political theorists, and jurists were equal to the best Europe has produced; and the poets and dramatists are the wonder of all ages. Further, as Professor W. K. Jordan and Lawrence Stone have shown, the seventeenth century was not only a time of numerous foundations and societies for discussion and dissemination of the new learning, but also "educational opportunities were more widespread and stronger than they had ever been before or were to be again until well into the nineteenth century." In other words, I would argue that the greatness of the Cromwellian revolution is in the realm of ideas, and that one cannot understand or explain the discursive and poetic genius of the revolution—the work of Harrington, Baxter, Hobbes, Walwyn, Lilburne, Winstanley, and Milton—except in relation to the range and quality of the English Renaissance from which the intellectuals of the revolution drew the rare and magic resources of eloquence, originality, and significance.

But great revolutions are not the result simply of richly endowed imaginations. The search for a "self" in the humanist and Protestant tradition has been a tremendously dynamic factor in furnishing agitators and leaders for European revolutions; still, the relations of classes and power groups have determined how far and in what directions revolt would go. What of the class structure in English society of the seventeenth century? To begin formulating a general answer, one may say "classes" in both the modern Marxist analysis and in current varieties of sociological analysis were realities in a way that had not been true in the Middle Ages. Power and privilege in medieval England were organized in "estates" or "orders": nobles and clergy functioned with inherited, magical power sustained by illusions of supernatural fiat and immutability. The lesser, inferior orders—those below the eternal hierarchy of God-mandated rule—were variously graded and economically rewarded, but essentially were all lumped together as a third estate (commoners who developed and controlled oligarchies in the new towns and in the counties being considered the "political" voice and social aspect of the masses of workers, craftsmen, free farmers, serfs, slaves, urban poor, etc., who were created by God to be ruled and to serve their

masters). In the sixteenth and seventeenth centuries, as we have other-wise seen, the organization of economic life in western Europe changed radically, and with that change the fixed allocation of privilege and the realities of group power in the medieval status hierarchies were chal-lenged in a revolutionary way. Increasingly, money meant power and illusions of higher status. The "rise of the middle classes" is this process of infiltrating at first the precincts of older status (the ennoblement of rich gentry and burghers, or their promotion to the church hierarchies) and then, when the limits of this process were reached, as they had very nearly been by the middle of the seventeenth century in England (France was more enterprising in selling "offices" and status to the ambitious and envious new men)—when the old status hierarchy in England could not adequately deal with the greed and numbers and aggression of the "third estate," a major crisis was inevitable. The Stuart kings and their nobles and bishops and bureaucrats failed to do what the same groups in France succeeded in doing—keeping the rich, influential, talented, and aggressive commoners from becoming an organized opposition with popular support.

It is sometimes said that revolution came to England and not to France in the seventeenth century (the countries had for hundreds of years been the twins of European civilization) because the English ruling classes were split while the French were not. Yet in the wars of the Frondes, as in many earlier civil wars, the French ruling classes seemed as divided along provincial, religious, and economic lines as any power elite in Europe. Indeed, it is one of the explanations for the success of the monarchy of Louis XIV that he could divide and rule the ruling classes. In the past, at any rate, the English upper classes had been remarkably united in interest with the monarchy, and institutions like Parliament and the common law represented as much strength for the Crown as for the estates of privilege. At this point of analysis the Marxian hypothesis proves useful in explaining the division in the nature of English rulership, as it does later for the same split in French power. For if one looks very closely into the economic self-interest of the leading oligarchies of power, their conflicts help explain the loss of the medieval sense of alliance between the wellborn, the priests, and the rich. The increasing opportunities for wealth and power in business, farming, and the State, induced an increasing competition which placed great strain on the social structure and political mechanisms of old England. The traditional ruling barons used their status to grab trading and industrial "monopolies" from the Court; they were hated by excluded entrepreneurs from the towns, and in turn were themselves divided into peers who made out at Court and those "Country" aristo-crats who did not. The lesser county aristocracy were also increasingly divided in their relations to one another and the government by the new economics of estate management and its relation to the cloth industry. Finally, the masses of the economically undistinguished in town and village found almost nothing they liked in the emerging order of things —the "drones" at Court, monopolists, enclosing landlords, rack-renters, price-riggers, usurers, and the like, meant unemployment, depopulation,

dislocation, pauperism, and a generally terrifying rise in insecurities about the most basic needs of life. Bread and shelter and dignity of person were harder to come by in Stuart England than they had been in the England of the Plantagenets.

There were also religious issues which divided the ruling classes, though they were not of great importance. This was not a "Puritan" revolution. The Church of England was generally amazingly successful in achieving a national Christian polity and institutional conformism. A marvelous vernacular Bible, a beautiful liturgy, preachers of fire, elbow room for dogmatic clashes, the sense of unity against the Catholics, and the relaxed "Englishness" of the church establishment were the dominant characteristics of the "middle way" of Protestantism in England from the days of Elizabeth down to the decade before the revolution. Of course there were instances of dissent, "separation," deprivations of ministers for political reasons, a few executions for radicalism or Catholicism, a minor amount of censorship of the pulpit and press, but there were none of the deep, bitter, widespreading religious issues which had characterized Protestant churches like Luther's in Germany, or the Calvinist churches in the Netherlands.

Cromwell and Selden, both observers of the revolution, agreed that the calling in of religion as an issue to discredit the government was a late reinforcement of the grievances of the opposition. "King" Pym, who forged the Parliamentary opposition that carried out the initial phases of the revolution, and who used the London "mob" to intimidate the Court, deliberately manipulated the anger of the poor by religious propaganda. Hostility in the seventeenth century, as well as most other passions, was expressed in religious terms. In Protestant England the war of the competing oligarchies and the anger and idealism of the masses were all represented in Scriptural symbolism by the popular images of pulpit rhetoric. Stereotypes of abusive religious epithets became party labels and slogans to motivate heroic action. But I am convinced that in basic human terms English Protestantism was more of a bond between classes, more of a "nationalism," than it was a divisive force. The civil war among Protestants was not an intrinsic struggle over religious matters; it was rather a struggle for power and "liberty" which necessitated religious justification by each group. Primarily, the course of conflict from 1640 to 1660 meant that in religious terms each faction of Protestants attempted to draw from the richly vague treasury of their national pulpit oratory ideas which would distinguish their party and seal their ambitions with the authority of God's necessity.

Parliamentary Advances on the Crown

The historian who searches for the causes of the English Revolution finds himself pleasantly lost in a society of unusual creativity and energy, with the result that conflict is found everywhere one looks. In law, business, government, and church, dispute simmers or rages. Of all the disputes around which the classes ranged their forces, that which

seems to me next in importance to economics is the constitutional struggle. Briefly, the fight was carried on by a new species of man—the politician—who served neither one of the traditional bureaucracies nor the Court, but the propertied interests of the state. The center of the politicians' stage was the House of Commons in Parliament, with the Inns of Court (where the practitioners of common law were trained and licensed) and county and city offices providing the supporting wings to this drama of the rise of the Property State. Out of all the welter of contradiction and conflict in the economic development of England from the Reformation to the Revolution, the great consistency was a concern for the rights of owners of property which transcended all the older definitions of rights in feudal and status terms. In the course of defining and providing sanctions for these rights, the "constitution" had to be revolutionized by the agents of property. The legal revolution went on relatively quietly and almost continuously until the common law had become the morality and practical sanction for the new property-centered society of the seventeenth century. The constitutional revolution in the public and self-advertising institutions was more sporadic, much noisier, and finally led to violence. The key agency for the politicians in this basic redefinition of the nature of the English state was Parliament—a familiar medieval institution designed originally to make tax collection and royal propaganda more efficient, and used with great skill and success by the Tudors to command popular support for their own revolution in the relations of the church to the state.

The changing of the English Parliament from a tool of monarchy to a weapon against it, from a sitting of feudal orders to a political institutionalization of the will of the propertied classes, is one of the most fascinating stories of Elizabethan and Stuart history, and one there is not space to do justice to here. From the reign of Mary Tudor, after the heyday of royalist Parliaments, opposition groups of propertied Protestants began to convert the King's High Court into a modern instrument of political action. The process was not unlike that by which the customary law of Anglo-Saxon and Norman England was revolutionized by procedural innovations which created a substantively new "common law." Just as the great justiciars from the reign of Henry II on had professed fidelity to traditional ways while in "finding" the law they made it, so—but much more consciously—the great Parliamentarians from the reign of Elizabeth set about defending the "ancient constitution of the realm," righting the abuses of Magna Carta, and similar "conservative" enterprises, while in fact building procedures and precedents and organizational devices intended to alter radically the relation of Parliament to the King and his non-Parliamentary councils. All the initiative came from the Commons, but the House of Lords was skillfully used by the Commoners so that the potentially radical nature of the change from power organized by hierarchy to power based on property was not perceived until too late by the peers.

Once the organizational mechanisms (committee systems, House control of the Speaker, and, above all, the informal caucuses about which we know least but which were crucially the genius of the new

English politicians) were fixed, and the interior lines of communication among the interested oligarchies established, the Commons elite increasingly ventured public argument for their revolutionary precepts. In 1604 the new King, James I, was greeted with a document drafted by the House of Commons that would have been inconceivable in the generation which hailed the accession of Elizabeth—a long, rambling, theoretical, and blatantly propagandistic statement of the constitutional position of Parliament. More significant than the actual words of the document is the fact that the Commoners could feel themselves ready for such a redefinition of their power in terms completely alien to the form and spirit of that "ancient" constitution they purported to defend. The *Apology* argued at length and with heat that the Commons (which they already are beginning to make synonymous with Parliament) alone represented "the voice of the people" and the generality of the commonwealth (and there is an interesting assumption that the vaguer terms "generality," "people," "subjects"—the nationalistic concepts—stand for a higher, more authoritative political reality than "estates" and "orders"). Based upon this claim to speak for the whole of the commonwealth, Commons asserted a very broad right to consultation and decision in matters of religion, foreign policy, and other matters of state which in the medieval constitution had been no concern of the knights and burgesses summoned to "hear and do." In the *Petition of Right* of 1610 they repeated their attack on the prerogative of the Crown (this time in financial matters) and reasserted that they "held it an ancient, general, and undoubted right of Parliament to debate freely all matters which do properly concern the subject and his right or state."

The institutional struggle—or, more properly, to correct the Whiggish cast the history of this period is usually given, the revolutionary usurpation of the Commons—continued as a public debate for forty years before the decision was left to the armies. James wrote a letter to the Commons warning of his displeasure with those "fiery and popular spirits" who were meddling in "matters far above their reach and capacity" and commanding the Speaker "to make known, in our name, unto the House that none therein shall presume henceforth to meddle with anything concerning our government or deep matters of State." Under the leadership of the great jurist Sir Edward Coke, the House stood up intractably for its revolutionary dogma:

That the liberties, franchises, privileges, and jurisdictions of Parliament are the ancient and undoubted birthright and inheritance of the subjects of England; and that the arduous and urgent affairs concerning the King, State, and defense of the Realm and of the Church of England, and the maintenance and making of laws, and redress of mischiefs and grievances which daily happen within this Realm, are proper subjects and matter of counsel and debate in Parliament; and that in the handling and proceeding of those businesses every member of the House of Parliament hath, and of right ought to have, freedom of speech . . . and that every member of the said House hath like freedom from all impeachment, imprisonment, and molestation.   □

The strategy which put teeth into the rhetoric of the Commons was the withholding of the revenue upon which the operation of the state depended. The battle joined on the issue of revenues forced the monarchy to exploit every possible legal ruse to raise monies for the increasing expenses of the state. This desperation in the Privy Council of the King thoroughly alarmed the community of the prosperous—the exigencies of the government, a government which the propertied classes felt irresponsible, began to threaten the security of property even in the courts of common law. Coke once more led the attack; he proposed a bill in 1628 "for the better securing of every freeman touching the propriety of his goods and liberty of his person," and helped send to King Charles in the same year a meticulously drawn document which summed up the revolutionary argument as a *Petition of Right*. Here are some of the key words and precepts:

The Petition exhibited to His Majesty by the Lords Spiritual and Temporal, and Commons in this present Parliament assembled, concerning divers Rights and Liberties of the Subjects, with the King's Majesty's Royal Answer thereunto in full Parliament.

TO THE KING'S MOST EXCELLENT MAJESTY

Humbly show unto our Sovereign Lord the King, the Lords Spiritual and Temporal, and Commons in Parliament assembled, that whereas it is declared and enacted by a statute made in the time of the reign of King Edward the First, commonly called *Statutum de Tallagio non concedendo,* that no tallage or aid shall be laid or levied by the King or his heirs in this realm, without the goodwill and assent of the Archbishops, Bishops, Earls, Barons, Knights, Burgesses, and other the freemen of the commonalty of this realm: and by authority of Parliament holden in the five and twentieth year of the reign of King Edward the Third, it is declared and enacted, that from thenceforth no person shall be compelled to make any loans to the King against his will, because such loans were against reason and the franchise of the land; and by other laws of this realm it is provided, that none should be charged by any charge or imposition, called a Benevolence, or by such like charge, by which the statutes before-mentioned, and other the good laws and statutes of this realm, your subjects have inherited this freedom, that they should not be compelled to contribute to any tax, tallage, aid, or other like charge, not set by common consent in Parliament:

Yet nevertheless, of late divers commissions directed to sundry Commissioners in several counties with instructions have issued, by means whereof your people have been in divers places assembled, and required to lend certain sums of money unto your Majesty, and many of them upon their refusal so to do, have had an oath administered unto them, not warrantable by the laws or statutes of this realm, and have been constrained to become bound to make appearance and give attendance before your Privy Council, and in other places, and others of them have been therefore imprisoned, confined, and sundry other ways molested and disquieted: and divers other charges have been laid and levied upon your

people in several counties, by Lords Lieutenants, Deputy Lieutenants, Commissioners for Musters, Justices of Peace and others, by command or direction from your Majesty or your Privy Council, against the laws and free customs of this realm:

And where also by the statute called, "The Great Charter of the Liberties of England," it is declared and enacted, that no freeman may be taken or imprisoned or be disseized of his freeholds or liberties, or his free customs, or be outlawed or exiled; or in any manner destroyed, but by the lawful judgment of his peers, or by the law of the land:

And in the eight and twentieth year of the reign of King Edward the Third, it was declared and enacted by authority of Parliament, that no man of what estate or condition that he be, should be put out of his lands or tenements, nor taken, nor imprisoned, nor disherited, nor put to death, without being brought to answer by due process of law:

Nevertheless, against the tenor of the said statutes, and other the good laws and statutes of your realm, to that end provided, divers of your subjects have of late been imprisoned without any cause showed, and when for their deliverance they were brought before your Justices, by your Majesty's writs of Habeas Corpus, there to undergo and receive as the Court should order, and their keepers commanded to certify the causes of their detainer; no cause was certified, but that they were detained by your Majesty's special command, signified by the Lords of your Privy Council, and yet were returned back to several prisons, without being charged with anything to which they might make answer according to the law. . . .

They do therefore humbly pray your Most Excellent Majesty, that no man hereafter be compelled to make or yield any gift, loan, benevolence, tax, or such like charge, without common consent by Act of Parliament; and that none be called to make answer, or take such oath, or to give attendance, or be confined, or otherwise molested or disquieted concerning the same, or for refusal thereof; and that no freeman, in any such manner as is before-mentioned, be imprisoned or detained; and that your Majesty will be pleased to remove the said soldiers and mariners, and that your people may not be so burdened in time to come; and that the foresaid commissions for proceeding by martial law, may be revoked and annulled; and that hereafter no commissions of like nature may issue forth to any person or persons whatsoever, to be executed as aforesaid, lest by color of them any of your Majesty's subjects be destroyed or put to death, contrary to the laws and franchise of the land. . . .   □

A genuine and deep impasse was reached in the functioning of the medieval monarchy. The increasingly expensive bureaucracy and programs of the central government (the Privy Council was moving in the direction of Big Government in the style of Henry IV and Richelieu in France) required not only quick and easy access to all of the traditional sources of revenue, but the tapping of increasing amounts of the new wealth. In the past when revenue demands from the monarchy had been considered unjust (as was often the case), resistance by the barons and burgesses had been piecemeal and defensive—the initiative

in an organizational and institutional sense had remained with the Court and its agencies. Beginning in the reign of Elizabeth I, and climaxing in the reign of Charles I, the government confronted not just the old problems of rising costs and inadequate revenue, but the revolutionary new problem of the *organized, institutionalized,* and *idealized* opposition of wealthy, ambitious, and disaffected oligarchies that centered their attack in the magnificently convenient legal and political instrument of Parliament.

The *Petition of Right* was followed in a few weeks by a general "Remonstrance" directed against the chief figure at Court—the Duke of Buckingham—and complaining of unconscionable government. The debates in Commons pushed the new theories of Parliamentary power to extreme limits; it was even demanded that the King renounce his ancient right to the desperately important revenues from Tonnage and Poundage. ". . . forced by that duty which they owe to your Majesty, and to those whom they represent, to declare, that there ought not any imposition to be laid upon the goods of merchants, exported or imported, without common consent by Act of Parliament, which is the right and inheritance of your subjects, founded not only upon the most ancient and original constitution of this kingdom, but often confirmed and declared in divers statute laws." Charles could retreat no farther without defaulting the throne he was born to; with the following words he prorogued the Parliament he could not control:

It may seem strange, that I come so suddenly to end this Session; wherefore before I give my assent to the Bills, I will tell you the cause, though I must avow, that I owe an account of my actions to none but to God alone. It is known to every one, that a while ago the House of Commons gave me a Remonstrance, how acceptable every man may judge; and for the merit of it, I will not call that in question, for I am sure no wise man can justify it.

Now since I am certainly informed, that a second Remonstrance is preparing for me to take away my profit of Tonnage and Poundage, one of the chief maintenances of my Crown, by alleging I have given away my right thereof by my answer to your Petition; this is so prejudicial unto me, that I am forced to end this Session some few hours before I meant it, being willing not to receive any more Remonstrances, to which I must give a harsh answer.

And since I see that even the House of Commons begins already to make false constructions of what I granted in your Petition, lest it might be worse interpreted in the country, I will now make a declaration concerning the true meaning therof:

The profession of both Houses, in time of hammering this Petition, was no ways to intrench upon my Prerogative, saying, they had neither intention nor power to hurt it. Therefore it must needs be conceived that I have granted no new, but only confirmed the ancient liberties of my subjects: yet to show the clearness of my intentions, that I neither repent, nor mean to recede from anything I have promised you, I do here declare, that those things which have been done, whereby men had some cause to suspect

the liberties of the subjects to be trenched upon—which indeed was the first and true ground of the Petition—shall not hereafter be drawn into example for your prejudice; and in time to come, on the word of a king, you shall not have the like cause to complain.

But as for Tonnage and Poundage, it is a thing I cannot want, and was never intended by you to ask, nor meant—I am sure—by me to grant.

To conclude, I command you all that are here to take notice of what I have spoken at this time, to be the true intent and meaning of what I granted you in your Petition; but especially, you my Lords the Judges, for to you only under me belongs the interpretation of laws; for none of the House of Commons, joint or separate, (what new doctrine soever may be raised) have any power either to make or declare a law without my consent.   □

For eleven years Charles I ruled his kingdom without Parliament. In the course of those years the hierarchy in Church and State functioned well enough, but the tensions mounted in the country. The Court became a scandal to zealous Protestants because of the Catholicizing influence of the Queen; Archbishop Laud's ceremonial preferences angered the "puritans" and his economic policy alarmed the avaricious; and, above all, the government's tax policy increased the anxieties of the propertied classes who were not only being denied the opportunity to use the withholding of revenue as a general political weapon, but felt threatened in the security of their investments. Charles resorted to medieval financial expedients of forced loans, arbitrary seizure of bullion, fraudulent sales, extortionate fees and fines, and added the later techniques of juggling the Crown's power to grant and rescind monopolies. The most notorious of the government's measures to remain solvent was that which extended the old Ship Money tax on port towns to the inland towns. The importance of Ship Money was that it worked, was repeated, and seemed to be a brilliant solution to the problem of obtaining adequate revenue without Parliamentary grants. John Hampden, one of the stalwarts of the opposition, forced the case into the courts, where the King won. The loss of the Ship Money case proved to the politically conscious propertied classes that they could not rely upon the courts either to protect their property or to bargain with it for political ends (they had failed to challenge successfully the legality of the sanctions for forced loans in 1627). The courts were the King's and no writ ran against him.

But the key to understanding the sudden failure of the monarchy in 1640 after a decade of apparent success, is that the informal organizations of the former Parliamentary opposition remained active, so that any expensive crisis which would require a Parliament would open the gates to articulate, experienced political leaders of the new property consciousness. The inevitable crisis came essentially from the dynastic inheritance of the Stuart kings—to their rulership in England they brought the right to rule the ancient kingdom of Scotland. Ruling Scotland had never been an easy task for kings working full time at it;

for James and Charles, caught in the complexities of the Scottish Reformation and the high winds of Scottish nationalism, working with a very
limited bureaucracy absorbed in the revolutionary difficulties of English
affairs and with bad communications and organization, the task was
unmanageable (although all sorts of modern historians volunteer the
advice that would have saved the day for Charles and his ministers). In
1638 the opposition of the Scotch nobles to the Crown's efforts to
recover for the Church lands which they had seized, widespread hostility to the ecclesiastical and liturgical impositions of the Church of
England, and a generalized and deep-running nationalism, resulted in
the National Covenant, and the raising of a Scotch army to defend
Scotch property, religion, and liberty.

Charles had not the money to fight a war, nor would he give up his
program for rule in his ancestral kingdom. The leaders of the opposition
spread the word that the Scotch were allies in the fight against popery
and tyranny, and Charles could not find any popular support for his
war. In April of 1640 Charles summoned a Parliament to appeal for
help but found the opposition had done their homework well ("some
few cunning and some ill-affected men" as he styled them) and the
mood of the *Petition of Right* was more stubbornly manifest than ever.
Charles dissolved the Short Parliament after three weeks and turned
frantically to makeshift financial expedients: Convocation, in defiance
of custom, was held over after the dissolution of Parliament, and
granted a "free" gift of £20,000; the City of London refused a demand
for a loan even under the threat that such refusal would bring distraint
of their property (this from the men who had once been "the King's
serfs," and whose monies had rescued the monarchy a hundred times!);
"coat and conduct" money was demanded of the militia and resulted
only in widening the resistance; borrowing from France, Spain, and
Rome was tried with no success. The peers could only be taxed in
Parliament. Thus only from the Church could the King get real help
(even Ship Money, for all its established legality, could not be collected
by royal agents without the cooperation of the local oligarchies whose
strike now diminished these revenues to the vanishing point)—and the
Church had been robbed of its wealth by the groups now defying the
monarchy.

In August a group of twelve radical peers, in conference with the
great Commoners, John Pym and John Hampden, petitioned the King to
summon a new Parliament to meet the "great distempers and dangers
now threatening the Church and State and your Royal person," and
listed not only the Scottish army, but all the grievances of the past
twenty years. Even the conservative Great Council of peers which
Charles met with in York in September recommended a Parliament. The
Scots were in England with an army that could walk to London, and
had to be paid £850 a day until a final settlement was reached—which
the Scots wanted to be with Parliament and their London friends.
Charles surrendered at last and writs went out for a new Parliament.
The elections were brilliantly managed by Pym's coterie to assure an

anti-Court majority. The Parliament which thus assembled in November sat, with significant intermissions, through thirteen years of the greatest revolutionary upheaval and achievement the world had known.

Revolutionists in Action

The events which constitute the revolutionary activity of the years 1640–1660 are too many and too interesting for me either to narrate in proper detail or to document from the extraordinarily rich sources available. From the English Revolution to the Russian, the historian must exercise the most painfully rigorous principles of selection. My own predilection is to use the space I have to illustrate quite fully the most original and exciting aspect of English revolutionary energy—its political and social thought. The emergence of secular, liberal, democratic, and socialist ideas and ideals makes the English Revolution the most radical and fertile of all European revolutions in the rhetoric of the spirit. But in concentrating on the rhetoric, I must warn the reader that I am seriously neglecting fascinating materials in the Parliamentary records, and fine human drama in the intrigues and battles of this long struggle. I urge the reader especially to become acquainted with Oliver Cromwell—as talented as Caesar or Napoleon, and infinitely more complex and attractive. (A good way to begin is with the pamphlet by Christopher Hill for the Historical Association, *Oliver Cromwell, 1658–1958,* and from there browse in W. C. Abbott's edition of *The Writings and Speeches.*) But I do not wish to seem apologetic either about concentrating on the social thought of the revolution, or about the central place this thought occupies in the book as a whole; for seldom has there been a more secure relationship between reality and perception, between action and theory, between crisis and creativity, and between the immediate and the permanent, than in the outpouring of the revolutionary press in England. The rhetoric is true, it vibrates with the specific qualities of human passion and imagination engaged, and the ordeals and triumphs of Englishmen in these twenty years have changed Europe, the world, and the insides of each of us.

Still, even in an interpretive work like this, it would be bad editing to plunge the reader into the rhetoric of the revolution without some account of the events of the long struggle which in the years 1640–1660 at once reflected and precipitated conflicts that had existed for generations and are not yet resolved. In the months which followed the sitting of the Long Parliament the revolution resembled very much that led by Marcel in the Estates-General at Paris three hundred years earlier—a political, quasi-legal attack on the councilors of the King, and constitutional demands for a major share in policy-making by the middle classes through the redefinition of the political functions of Parliament. Marcel had proceeded in the more direct medieval fashion to murder the unpopular councilors; Pym manipulated by legal forms the exile, imprisonment, or execution of the King's chief ministers. Parliament—or, rather, Pym's revolutionary cadre through Parliament—seized the political initiative and pushed through a self-creating act of perma-

nence and regular meetings, abolished the vitally important administrative courts of the monarchy as well as the ecclesiastical court of High Commission, emptied the prisons of political opponents of the Court, and, turning to the key issue of the previous decade, declared all taxes levied in the past without Parliamentary consent to be illegal.

Finally, openly, the Hobbesian issue of sovereignty, the issue of the ultimate sanction of public power, was raised by events in Ireland. The Irish had revolted again, the King urgently needed an army; but with control of such an army would go the substance of sovereignty. Parliament wanted to appoint its own representatives to command the army for Ireland. Simultaneously, a very broad general indictment of royal policies was drawn up (including talk of impeaching the Queen for conspiracy against the state) which forced Charles to display whatever power of the sword he could command. The King's response was pure *opera bouffe*. He assembled a ridiculously large body of swordsmen whom he led personally into the hall of the Commons for the purpose of arresting Pym and four of his member associates—to find them all absent. They had taken refuge in the city and the King was powerless to command their surrender. One need not adopt the absurd argument of Whiggish historians regarding the impropriety of the King's action (the actions of Parliament were far more of an offense to legal propriety) to see that the planned coup symbolized—whether it had succeeded or not—the loss of control by the monarchy of the most indispensable resource of political power—the illusion of legality, of rightness.

Following the disastrous ignominy of the Five Members episode, Charles left London hoping to rally the loyalist and conservative forces outside the city for a military decision—the only decision still in doubt. The legal and political battle had become decisively one-sided; the King no longer had even a staff of competent advisers. And the military possibilities of a monarchist triumph were also less than brilliant. For the royalist party were—in spite of their advantage in tradition and experience—weighed down with the crushing necessity of having now to demonstrate decisive superiority in power against a massive, rich, excited opposition which somehow had managed to seize the moral initiative, the rhetorical and organizational initiative, and therefore needed only to hold its own on the battlefields to win. When the armies of the revolutionaries proved they could do much more than hold their own, the whole course of the revolution was changed—as we shall see.

In the past, the monarchy had met revolts with feudal levies of loyal barons and their men. In 1642 Charles called, as his ancestors had done, upon the swords of the aristocracy to uphold the settled order of the realm. And once again the aristocracy took to the field in defense of privilege and God's immutable hierarchies. But their numbers and arms were not overwhelming (the religious issues and Pym's strategy with the peers in the House of Lords divided even the barons), and they were opposed by a vast coalition of groups similar to the Hussite forces which had brought the Holy Roman Empire to its knees in the fifteenth century. The military resourcefulness of this "national" opposition to

Court, bishops, and peers proved one of the crucial surprises of the civil wars—an equal to and sanction for the rhetoric pouring from London pulpits and the halls of Westminster. From the trained bands who stopped Charles at Turnham Green in the first year of fighting, through the levies recruited by the Eastern Association, the expedient diplomacy that added the Scottish army at the border to that of the sturdy Fairfax and won the north, to the final triumph of Cromwell's brilliant New Model Army at Naseby in June of 1645, the revolutionaries distinguished themselves in the indispensable art of violence.

Meantime, the legal, political, and organizational forms of revolution almost kept pace with the feats performed by the saints in arms. At the local level, the County Committees raised money, rallied and disciplined the opposition; at Westminster, the momentum of the first two years of radical legal action was sufficient to bring down the church hierarchy —Archbishop Laud was executed in 1645, episcopacy abolished the next year, and the estates of the bishops put up for public sale.

The decisive military defeat of the King, and the reality of success in revolutionizing the laws and institutions of the old regime, soon led the progressive elements, who had hitherto combined their forces, into conflict. What sort of constitution was the new state to settle upon? Which groups were to have their needs and ideals best served? The more radical groups (rather misleadingly but traditionally labeled "Independents") had their chief strength in the rank and file of the Army; the conservatives ("Presbyterians"), who wanted the revolution to consolidate around the achievements of the first two years of revolt, were entrenched in Parliament and the ordinary instrumentalities of the state.

Oliver Cromwell, the creator of the New Model Army, rapidly emerged at the head of the radicals. He at first gave a sympathetic ear to the agitators who had led the mutiny against Parliament, and working through a General Council of the Army which represented rank and file as well as officers, carried aggressively forward the policies of religious toleration and suspicion of the membership of the Long Parliament. But then the pace of revolution quickened, and the London radicals ("Levellers") began to talk for themselves and for a much more democratic fundamental law than Cromwell or the generals could stomach. Cromwell ended the debate arbitrarily, unavoidably from the point of view of the groups who shared leadership with him, and therewith began a familiar process of alienating the popular forces from the central drama of the revolution.

While Cromwell was isolating the London radicals, and revolutionary counsels were divided even at the top level between Army and Parliament, the conservatives made a last effort to regain power. The King compacted with the Scots in London for an army while the "Presbyterian" Parliament entered into negotiations with Charles. Cromwell smashed the Scottish army at Preston in 1648. He responded to the conspiracy in Parliament by occupying London, driving the conservative ("Presbyterian") members from Parliament, and putting the King on trial for treason. Charles was executed as a traitor to the Common-

wealth January 30, 1649—the first victim of legal and moral arguments which herald the advent in the modern world of the revolutionized nation-state, the Leviathan that would feed on the blood of royalty.

The new call to violence and sacrifice briefly renewed Cromwell's ties with the Levellers, and the months following the courageous act of regicide (the formal political murder of God's anointed required more than average strength of will) were filled with daring political acts and exciting ideas. Monarchy and the House of Lords were abolished. We shall see in the documents which follow how far-ranging and interesting the thought of London became. Yet Cromwell, like his great Bohemian prototype, Žižka, chose the middle course of power—hoping to stabilize the revolution even at the sacrifice of his own ideals of justice and dignity. He put the Leveller leaders in prison, as he had driven the conservatives from Parliament (middle courses usually involve such delicate discrimination in awarding punishment for radicals compared to that felt appropriate for their social betters).

Cromwell had no sooner dug in to defend the new order in England, than he was on the march to expand and secure the revolution beyond the national borders. Great revolutions always betray a similar zeal and necessity. Brilliantly and brutally, Cromwell became the first Englishman to really conquer the Irish, in the process settling his soldiers on the land expropriated from its former Irish owners. Meantime, Charles II and his Scottish allies were crushed (first, at Dunbar in Scotland, in one of the most miraculous victories in military history) and Scotland was brought firmly to heel.

The remainder of Cromwell's years of power were spent in the effort to give his establishment the authority of a functional national organization, to identify the new order with the "state." In economic and social matters, his relations to the merchants and lesser aristocracy—once he closed his ears to the radical groups—were complicated only by the inevitable conflicts resulting from the experimental and competitive character of early capitalism, and the complexities of the new colonialism. The expulsion of the Rump of the Long Parliament was followed by a rigged assembly of trusted Independents which, however, proved too radical in temper (the religious integrity which Cromwell admired and trusted once again was combined with an inconvenient disposition to be plain speaking in social matters) and was therefore dissolved. Next a new constitution (the "Instrument of Government") was drafted by the Army under which crucial power was vested in Cromwell as Lord Protector. But the first Parliament under this constitution revolted against the ascendancy of the Army, and had to be sent home. Then a Royalist revolt provided the pretext for an extension of Army rule under a new system headed by the Major-Generals. Again, a Parliament called in 1656 fought the policies of the government (the rule of the military and religious toleration) by refusing taxes, and ended by offering Cromwell the crown! Cromwell was tempted by this solution, but finally rejected it. In 1658, with no political formula yet worked out, Cromwell died. Had he lived ten years longer, there would probably have been no Stuart restoration.

The new Protector was Cromwell's son, and he desperately needed the authority that would have gone with the crown his father refused. The complex forces of old self-interest within the new order finally asserted themselves against the dwindling energy and imagination of the rump of revolutionary idealists. The army of the Protectorate in Scotland marched to London and drove Richard Cromwell and the Cromwellians from power. A new Parliament (with the non-Royalist peers restored in a revived House of Lords) offered Charles II the crown on conditions which protected the majority of the propertied and religious interests of the London oligarchies and the leading gentry in the counties.

Literature of the Revolutionary Period

It should be clear from the barest narrative of the events of the revolution that the idealists of the various classes and factions who struggled to command the nature and direction of England's future would not be arguing a common morality. Generally speaking, the only consistent division among the ideologues was that of the ethics of property. Most of them shared Protestant religiosity and many professed humanist ideals of individualism and liberty—so that much of the rhetoric and argument is shared. But freedom, franchise, and rights were all concepts whose meaning depended upon class loyalties.

One of the least exciting yet most intelligent and representative spokesmen for the revolution that succeeded—that which gave political sovereignty to the propertied classes—was James Harrington. It took John Locke, some years after the revolution, to make a carefully articulated myth of the morality of property which would rescind the traditional Christian suspicion of the ethics of ownership, but Harrington is the ideological father of Madison and the liberalism of clear-sighted rationalism about property relations as the necessary determinant of history. He interpreted the revolution not in terms of irrational factionalism or incompetent government, but as the political necessity of redressing the growing imbalance in the power relations of propertied groups. The old regime did not represent politically the new wealth in land and trade. Harrington was wealthy, related to the leading nobility of England, educated at Oxford and widely traveled, a friend of Charles I, and throughout the civil wars a middle-of-the-roader. After the execution of the King, he set about writing a general critique of politics in the style of Aristotle and Machiavelli as a basis for conceiving a new order of society, a utopian commonwealth constructed by reason and experience which could replace the defunct old regime. His *Oceana* is a long, discursive piece of small literary merit, and it is hard to excerpt key ideas, but it was a widely read and much argued-about book which came directly from the press of revolutionary experience. It would prove to be a book of great influence upon subsequent generations of bourgeois revolutionaries: the draft of a French constitution in 1792 and the leading American political theorists of the eighteenth century drew heavily upon Harrington's rationale of a property owner's republic.

But the most famous and important of the political theorists who wrote during the revolution was Thomas Hobbes. Like Harrington, he was on the side of the men of property, and, indeed, went into exile as a royalist for a time; but his genius was spurred by the magnitude of the revolution into insights of such daring that men of property, religion, and any sort of traditionalism were shaken. Hobbes is the voice of the kind of simple (though his rhetoric and logic are often not so) and brutal truth which emerged from the power struggle between the English oligarchies. An educated man of leisure, Hobbes was the first political writer to unite with the humanist tradition of reasoning the ambitions of the scientific imagination—he wanted to make a geometry, a deductively exact and convincing analysis of the nature of man and society. He wanted to penetrate to the fundamentals (and simple ones) that motivated social behavior, to strip aside the ephemeral trappings of cant and myth which were failing the ruling classes in England and to see where indeed lay the sources of power and order. What he saw pleased no one, for men live by illusions as surely as by bread, and Hobbes saw that all possible illusions as to the nature of a just social order are a function of the greater reality of coercive power. Order to Hobbes is the power to command, and might makes right. Sovereignty is indivisible and eternal and absolute as the principle of force. All states, all constitutions, are politically viable (whatever the varying rationales of virtue and fiat) just so long as they can force obedience. The *Leviathan* was published in 1651 and is too great a book to be read only here—I wish merely to whet the reader's curiosity and to illustrate with a chapter from the second part the revolutionary perceptions of a brilliant humanist contemplating Cromwell's England:

OF THE CAUSES, GENERATION, AND DEFINITION OF A COMMONWEALTH

The final cause, end, or design of men, who naturally love liberty, and dominion over others, in the introduction of that restraint upon themselves, in which we see them live in commonwealths, is the foresight of their own preservation, and of a more contented life thereby; that is to say, of getting themselves out from that miserable condition of war, which is necessarily consequent, as hath been shown in chapter xiii, to the natural passions of men, when there is no visible power to keep them in awe, and tie them by fear of punishment to the performance of their covenants, and observation of those laws of nature set down in the fourteenth and fifteenth chapters.

For the laws of nature, as *justice, equity, modesty, mercy,* and, in sum, *doing to others, as we would be done to,* of themselves, without the terror of some power, to cause them to be observed, are contrary to our natural passions, that carry us to partiality, pride, revenge, and the like. And covenants, without the sword, are but words, and of no strength to secure a man at all. Therefore notwithstanding the laws of nature, which every one hath then kept, when he has the will to keep them, when he can do it safely, if there be no power erected, or not great enough for our security;

every man will, and may lawfully rely on his own strength and art, for caution against all other men. And in all places, where men have lived by small families, to rob and spoil one another, has been a trade, and so far from being reputed against the law of nature, that the greater spoils they gained, the greater was their honour; and men observed no other laws therein, but the laws of honour; that is, to abstain from cruelty, leaving to men their lives, and instruments of husbandry. And as small families did then; so now do cities and kingdoms which are but greater families, for their own security, enlarge their dominions, upon all pretences of danger, and fear of invasion, or assistance that may be given to invaders, and endeavour as much as they can, to subdue, or weaken their neighbours, by open force, and secret arts, for want of other caution, justly; and are remembered for it in after ages with honour.

Nor is it the joining together of a small number of men, that gives them this security; because in small numbers, small additions on the one side or the other, make the advantage of strength so great, as is sufficient to carry the victory; and therefore gives encouragement to an invasion. The multitude sufficient to confide in for our security, is not determined by any certain number, but by comparison with the enemy we fear; and is then sufficient, when the odds of the enemy is not of so visible and conspicuous moment, to determine the event of war, as to move him to attempt.

And be there never so great a multitude; yet if their actions be directed according to their particular judgments, and particular appetites, they can expect thereby no defence, nor protection, neither against a common enemy, nor against the injuries of one another. For being distracted in opinions concerning the best use and application of their strength, they do not help but hinder one another; and reduce their strength by mutual opposition to nothing: whereby they are easily, not only subdued by a very few that agree together; but also when there is no common enemy, they make war upon each other, for their particular interests. For if we could suppose a great multitude of men to consent in the observation of justice, and other laws of nature, without a common power to keep them all in awe; we might as well suppose all mankind to do the same; and then there neither would be, nor need to be any civil government, or commonwealth at all; because there would be peace without subjection.

Nor is it enough for the security, which men desire should last all the time of their life, that they be governed, and directed by one judgment, for a limited time; as in one battle, or one war. For though they obtain a victory by their unanimous endeavour against a foreign enemy; yet afterwards, when either they have no common enemy, or he that by one part is held for an enemy, is by another part held for a friend, they must needs by the difference of their interests dissolve, and fall again into a war amongst themselves.

It is true, that certain living creatures, as bees, and ants, live sociably one with another, which are therefore by Aristotle numbered amongst political creatures; and yet have no other direction, than their particular judgments and appetites; nor speech, whereby one of them can signify to another, what he thinks expedient for the common benefit: and therefore

some man may perhaps desire to know, why mankind cannot do the same. To which I answer,

First, that men are continually in competition for honour and dignity, which these creatures are not; and consequently amongst men there ariseth on that ground, envy and hatred, and finally war; but amongst these not so.

Secondly, that amongst these creatures, the common good differeth not from the private; and being by nature inclined to their private, they procure thereby the common benefit. But man, whose joy consisteth in comparing himself with other men, can relish nothing but what is eminent.

Thirdly, that these creatures, having not, as man, the use of reason, do not see, nor think they see any fault, in the administration of their common business; whereas amongst men, there are very many, that think themselves wiser, and able to govern the public, better than the rest; and these strive to reform and innovate, one this way, another that way; and thereby bring it into distraction and civil war.

Fourthly, that these creatures, though they have some use of voice, in making known to one another their desires, and other affections; yet they want that art of words, by which some men can represent to others, that which is good, in the likeness of evil; and evil, in the likeness of good; and augment, or diminish the apparent greatness of good and evil; discontenting men, and troubling their peace at their pleasure.

Fifthly, irrational creatures cannot distinguish between *injury,* and *damage;* and therefore as long as they be at ease, they are not offended with their fellows: whereas man is then most troublesome, when he is most at ease: for then it is that he loves to shew his wisdom, and control the actions of them that govern the commonwealth.

Lastly, the agreement of these creatures is natural; that of men, is by covenant only, which is artificial: and therefore it is no wonder if there be somewhat else required, besides covenant, to make their agreement constant and lasting; which is a common power, to keep them in awe, and to direct their actions to the common benefit.

The only way to erect such a common power, as may be able to defend them from the invasion of foreigners, and the injuries of one another, and thereby to secure them in such sort, as that by their own industry, and by the fruits of the earth, they may nourish themselves and live contentedly; is, to confer all their power and strength upon one man, or upon one assembly of men, that may reduce all their wills, by plurality of voices, unto one will: which is as much as to say, to appoint one man, or assembly of men, to bear their person; and every one to own, and acknowledge himself to be author of whatsoever he that so beareth their person, shall act, or cause to be acted, in those things which concern the common peace and safety; and therein to submit their wills, every one to his will, and their judgments, to his judgment. This is more than consent, or concord; it is a real unity of them all, in one and the same person, made by covenant of every man with every man, in such manner, as if every man should say to every man, *I authorize and give up my right of governing myself, to this man, or to this assembly of men, on this*

condition, that thou give up thy right to him, and authorize all his actions in like manner. This done, the multitude so united in one person, is called a COMMONWEALTH, in Latin CIVITAS. This is the generation of that great LEVIATHAN, or rather, to speak more reverently, of that *mortal god,* to which we owe under the *immortal God,* our peace and defence. For by this authority, given him by every particular man in the commonwealth, he hath the use of so much power and strength conferred on him, that by terror thereof, he is enabled to perform the wills of them all, to peace at home, and mutual aid against their enemies abroad. And in him consisteth the essence of the commonwealth; which, to define it, is *one person, of whose acts a great multitude, by mutual covenants one with another, have made themselves every one the author, to the end he may use the strength and means of them all, as he shall think expedient, for their peace and common defence.*

And he that carrieth this person, is called SOVEREIGN, and said to have *sovereign power;* and every one besides, his SUBJECT.

The attaining to this sovereign power, is by two ways. One, by natural force; as when a man maketh his children, to submit themselves, and their children, to his government, as being able to destroy them if they refuse; or by war subdueth his enemies to his will, giving them their lives on that condition. The other, is when men agree amongst themselves, to submit to some man, or assembly of men, voluntarily, on confidence to be protected by him against all others. This latter, may be called a political commonwealth, or commonwealth by *institution;* and the former, a commonwealth by *acquisition.*   □

By no means was all of the social thought of the revolution as secular and rational as Harrington and Hobbes. Radicalism in its more familiar forms of millenarianism reappeared and flourished splendidly among the English. Abiezer Coppe left Oxford when the revolution broke out, and after experimenting with every variety of Protestant enthusiasm, ended a Ranter, spent most of his time in the prisons of the Commonwealth for his "many horrid Blasphemies, and damnable and detestable Opinions," the chief of which, condemned by Parliament to be burned by the public hangman, were published in 1649 under the title *A Fiery Flying Roll: a word from the Lord to all the great ones of the earth.* . . . Coppe's fury communicates the living tradition of Christian communism and the messianic passion which had made the rich and powerful tremble—but seldom fall. Here are some characteristic passages:

Thus saith the Lord: Be wise now therefore, O ye Rulers, &c. Be instructed, &c. Kisse the Sunne, &c. Yea, kisse Beggers, Prisoners, warme them, feed them, cloathe them, money them, relieve them, release them, take them into your houses, don't serve them as dogs without doore, &c.

Owne them, they are flesh of your flesh, your owne brethren, your owne Sisters, every whit as good (and if I should stand in competition with you) in some degrees better than your selves.

Once more, I say, own them; they are your self, make them one with

you, or else go howling into hell; howle for the miseries that are comming upon you, howle.

The very shadow of levelling, sword-levelling, man-levelling, frighted you, (and who, like your selves, can blame you, because it shook your Kingdome?) but now the substantiality of levelling is coming.

The Eternall God, the mighty Leveller is comming, yea come, even at the door; and what will you do in that day. . . .

Mine eares are filled brim full with cryes of poore prisoners, Newgate, Ludgate cryes (of late) are seldome out of mine eares. Those dolefull cryes, Bread, bread, bread for the Lords sake, pierce mine eares, and heart, I can no longer forebeare.

Werefore high you apace to all prisons in the Kingdome,

Bow before those poore, nasty, lousie, ragged wretches, say to them, your humble servants, Sirs, (without a complement) we let you go free, and serve you, &c.

Do this or (as I live saith the Lord) thine eyes (at least) shall be boared out, and thou carried captive into a strange Land. . . .

Loose the bands of wickednesse, undo the heavy burdens, let the oppressed go free, and breake every yoake. Deale thy bread to the hungry, and bring the poore that are cast out (both of houses and Synagogues) to thy house. Cover the naked: Hide not thy self from thine owne flesh, from a creeple, a rogue, a begger, he's thine owne flesh. From a Whoremonger, a thief, &c. he's flesh of thy flesh, and his theft, and whoredome is flesh of thy flesh also, thine owne flesh. Thou maist have ten times more of each within thee, then he that acts outwardly in either, Remember, turn not away thine eyes from thine OWN FLESH.

Give over, give over thy midnight mischief.

Let branding with the letter B. alone.*

Be no longer so horridly, hellishly, impudently, arrogantly wicked, as to judge what is sinne, what not, what evill, and what not, what blasphemy, and what not.

For thou and all thy reverend Divines, so called (who Divine for Tythes, hire, and money, and serve the Lord Jesus Christ for their owne bellyes) are ignorant of this one thing.

That sinne and transgression is finisht, its a meere riddle, that they, with all their humane learning can never reade. . . .

The plague of God is in your purses, barns, houses, horses, murrain will take your hogs, (O ye fat swine of the earth) who shall shortly go to the knife, and be hung up i'th roof, except . . . blasting, mill-dew, locusts, caterpillars, yea fire your houses and goods, take your corn and fruit, the moth your garments, and the rot your sheep, did you not see my hand, this last year, stretched out?

You did not see.

My hand is stretched out still.

Your gold and silver, though you can't see it, is cankered, the rust of them is a witnesse against you, and suddainly, because by the eternall

* For 'Blasphemer.'

God, my self, its the dreadful day of Judgement, saith the Lord, shall eat
your flesh as it were fire, *Jam. 5.* 1 to 7.
   The rust of your silver, I say, shall eat your flesh as it were fire. . . .
give, give, give, give up, give up your houses, horses, goods, gold,
Lands, give up, account nothing your own, have *ALL THINGS* common, or
els the plague of God will rot and consume all that you have.
   By God, by my self, saith the Lord, its true.
   Come! give all to the poore and follow me, and you shall have treasure
in heaven.   □

The Levellers

It is time now to look at the most solidly characteristic genius of the
revolution that failed—that represented by the Levellers. This was the
intellectual formulation of the feelings and hopes of the mass of Londoners and the Army rank and file. From Marston Moor to the decision
to execute the King, the revolutionary forces that had precipitated the
crisis in the old order floundered in search of illusions that would
justify a new order. And as the debate widened, and the lesser folk of
England found themselves armed and organized, the propertied elite
were suddenly challenged in their monopoly of the ideals by which the
ancient community of England was to live. "The people as sovereigns"
had Hobbesian-clear implications so long as they were armed and led.
From the heat of the struggle, from the heart of the best imagination
awakened by the opportunity to make radical change a reality, came the
first political radicals in the modern sense—the proto-democrats, the
ancestors of Jacobins and Jacksonians, and one amazing communist.
   We do not know who the Levellers were in any very documented
fact. Certainly they were mostly Londoners; they were overwhelmingly
small property owners; in religion they were "Independents" (a vague
term denoting anti-Presbyterians) and Baptists and Quakers—from the
radical sects, although when the going got rough the Baptist and Independent leaders deserted them and proclaimed themselves nonpolitical.
The leadership of the Levellers was astonishingly nonreligious. One
could, indeed, make an argument that Levellerism was the first popular
movement in European history to be organized, led, and inspired by
laymen. Certainly it is the first great popular movement whose ideology
is fundamentally humanistic. The ideals of isolated giants of the humanistic past—the emphasis on individualism, freedom, courage, eloquence, and the supreme dignity of independent thought—became in
the publications and agitation of the Levellers the heart of a vast political movement. Never before or since has a popular, agitational, and
revolutionary social movement produced ideas and ideals which so
nearly unite the qualities of humanistic literature with the necessities
of propaganda and action. John Lilburne, William Walwyn, Thomas
Prince, and Richard Overton fall short of Milton at his best, but compared to the manifesto writers in the French Revolution, or the dreary
propaganda of the 1848-and-after revolutions, they demonstrate a fresh-
ness and vigor of perception and argument that is unique.

The greatest personality of the group of Levellers was John Lilburne, who in 1638 entered the public stage being whipped from the Fleet prison to the Palace Yard in Westminster for circulating copies of the antiecclesiastical works of Prynne and Bastwick—he was kept in prison until 1640 when Oliver Cromwell supported a petition for his release. He was voted the very handsome indemnification of £3000, and entered the army where he quickly earned the rank of lieutenant-colonel. Then, feeling the steam was going out of the revolution with the ending of the "first civil war" and the dominance of covenanting Presbyterians, Lilburne resigned his commission, petitioned Parliament for his arrears in pay, and resumed his career in the prisons of England —possibly the first professional political agitator in European history. For food and lodging Lilburne relied upon the prisons of the Commonwealth while he wrote pamphlets and drafted manifestos and party programs. He spent the rest of his life (he died in 1657) attacking the coalitions of power in Parliament and the Army which were slowing the revolution in the interests of the rich and respectable. Banished from the country in 1652, he still returned to prison and a trial in which he won acquittal and the adoration of London. Lilburne was too dangerously popular to be executed, but it is also a mark of the character of Cromwell that he died in peace and freedom living quietly in Kent. He fought hard and to the complete exhaustion of himself, his ideas, and the organizational possibilities of his movement. He was beaten by Cromwell's choice of Grandees over the Leveller-infested agitators in the rank and file of the army. The army controlled London by force of arms, and the Leveller movement, vast and popular and well organized though it was, had not the guns and horses to prevail over the genius of Cromwell and the privileges he defended.

Richard Overton was a printer who, during the revolution, ran an illegal press which came to the defense of Lilburne when he was sent to prison by the Lords. His vigorous and brilliant defense of Lilburne put him in Newgate prison in 1646 where he continued to argue. William Walwyn was a well-to-do merchant who joined in the defense of Lilburne in 1646 and not only wrote copiously but was the organizational genius behind the Leveller agitation. Almost nothing is known of Thomas Prince except that he was extraordinarily courageous and energetic in defense and propagation of Leveller principles.

The Levellers (a term of opprobrium, of course, and one they always rejected) led, like all of us, a kind of double life; but because they were radicals, their contemporaries and posterity have sat in unusually stern judgment of their sincerity and consistency. What is only human and good sense and practical wisdom in the compromises and double-talk of the successful man, is damnable cowardice and futility in the radical. So let us defer to the tradition, and note immediately that the rhetoric of freedom and equality which will fill the pages to follow outruns the commitment and integrity of the authors. The Levellers did not include the lower classes of labor, servants, and women among those whom they would restore to "freeborn" rights, nor did they see that an attack on privilege could not by any moral logic exclude the complaints of the

propertyless. Indeed, recent research has shown that the Leveller concept of democracy did not even include the advocacy of manhood suffrage. In short, there is a lot of hot air in this as in most rhetoric; but only a great revolution could have thrown up as much courageous effort of the spirit to speak with selfless honesty, so much vindication of the individual ego in a class society.

Rhetoric is one of the few things man does sublimely well, and what follows is a treasury of language at its best, language rooted in reality and consecrated to enlightened defiance. This seems to me Europe's finest hour of revolutionary perception and idealism especially, and necessarily, when one adds the "True Leveller," Winstanley, and Milton. Let us begin with the introductory section from the famous *Declaration,* probably composed by Henry Ireton, Cromwell's chief political adviser at the time, and the same Grandee who in the Putney Debates of the Army warned that the Leveller program would end in communism ("And liberty cannot be provided for in a general sense if property be preserved."), but whose draft of this document demonstrates the immense impact of Leveller ideas and words upon even the top elite of the Army. Lilburne always considered this document to represent the true principles for which the Army was fighting; it does in fact represent the moment of time (from June, 1647, when the Army seized the King from Parliament and the Generals agreed to set up the Army Council with all ranks represented, and take over the political direction of the revolution, to October of the same year, when the debates in the new Army Council over the kind of constitution wanted, split the Army on class lines)—the moment of time when a democratic revolution was conceivable. The Declaration was printed June 14, 1647; note, among other contemporary-sounding ideas, the references to the international character of the struggle for "right and freedom":

A Declaration, or Representation from his Excellency, Sir Tho. Fairfax, and of the Army under his Command, Humbly tendred to the Parliament.

That we may no longer be the dis-satisfaction of our friends, the subject of our enemies malice (to worke jealousies and misrepresentations upon) and the suspition (if not astonishment) of many in the Kingdome, in our late or present transactions and conduct of businesse; we shal in all faithfulnesse and clearnesse professe, and declare unto you, those things which have of late protracted and hindred our disbanding, the present grievances which possesse our Army, and are yet unremedied, with our desires, as to the compleat settlement of the liberties, and peace of the kingdome; which is that blessing of God, then which (of all worldly things) nothing is more dear unto us, or more pretious in our thoughts, we having hitherto thought all our present enjoyments (whether of life or livelihood, or nearest relations) a price but sufficient to the purchase of so rich a blessing; that we, and all the free-born people of this Nation, may sit down in quiet under our Vines, under the glorious administration of Justice, and righteousnesse, and in the full possession of those Fundamentall Rights and Liberties, without which we can have little hopes (as to humane considerations) to enjoy either any comforts of life, or so much as life it

selfe, but at the pleasures of some men, ruling meerly according to will and power. . . .

Nor will it now (wee hope) seeme strange or unseasonable to rationall and honest men, who consider the consequence of our present case, to their own, and the Kingdoms, (as well as our) future concernments in point of right, freedome, peace and safety, if (from a deep sence of the high consequence of our present case, both to our selves (in future) and all other people) we shall, before disbanding, proceed, in our own and the Kingdoms behalf, to propound, and plead, for some provision, for our, and the Kingdoms satisfaction, and future security in relacion to those things, especially considering, that we were not a meere mercinary Army, hired to serve any Arbitrary power of a State; but called forth and conjured, by the severall Declarations of Parliament, to the defence of our owne and the peoples just rights, and liberties; And so we tooke up Armes, in judgement and conscience to those ends, and have so continued them, and are resolved according to your first just desires in your Declarations, and such principles as we have received from your frequent informations, and our own common sence concerning those our fundamentall Rights and Liberties, to assert and vindicate, the just power, and Rights of this Kingdom in Parliament for those common ends premised, against all arbitrary power, violence and oppression, and against all particular parties, or interests whatsoever. The said Declarations still directing us to the equitable sence of all Laws and constitutions as dispencing with the very Letter of the same, and being supreame to it, when the safety and preservation of all is concerned, and assuring us, that all authority is fundamentally seated, in the office, and but ministerially in the persons, neither doe or will these our proceedings (as we are fully and in conscience perswaded) amount to any thing, not warrantable before God and men, being thus far, much short of the common proceedings in other Nations, to things of an higher nature then we have yet appeared to. And we cannot but be sencible of the great complaints, that have been made generally to us of the Kingdome, from the people where we march, of arbitrarinesse and injustice, to their great and insupportable oppressions.

And truly such Kingdomes, as have according both to the law of Nature and Nations, appeared to the vindication and defence, of their just rights and liberties, have proceeded much higher; As our brethren of Scotland: who in the first beginning of these late differences, associated in Covenant, from the very same grounds and principles (having no vissible form, either of Parliament or King to countenance them) and as they were therein justified, and protected by their own, and this Kingdome also, so we justly shall expect to be.

We need not mention the States of the Netherlands, the Portugals, and others, all proceeding upon the same Principles of right and freedome; And accordingly the Parliament hath declared it no resistance of Magistracie, to side with the just Principles, and law of Nature and Nations, being that Law upon which we have assisted you. And that the Souldiery may lawfully hold the hands of that Generall, who will turne his Cannon against his Army on purpose to destroy them; the Sea-men the hands of that Pylot, who wilfully runnes the Ship upon a Rock, (as our brethren of

Scotland argued.) And such were the proceedings of our Ancestors of famous memory, to the purchasing of such Rights and Liberties as they have enjoyed through the price of their blood; and we (both by that and the later blood of our deare friends and fellow-Souldiers, with the hazard of our own) doe now lay claim unto.   □

On January 30, 1649, the King was executed as a traitor to England. Monarchy and the House of Lords were abolished. The Generals sought again in these tense and decisive days the popular support the Levellers could bring. Lilburne and his colleagues were fired with hope that all was not yet lost. Great Leveller demonstrations were organized in London to force a showdown on the democratic demands of the radicals. In March the leaders of the Levellers were back in prison. From the Tower of London, in May, the indomitable four—Lilburne, Walwyn, Prince, and Overton—sent to the press a finished version of the constitution they had been arguing for since the Putney Debates. The Council of State (understandably!) demanded the removal of the licenser, Gilbert Mabbot, who had sanctioned the publication of so persuasively radical a document. And before the month was out, Cromwell crushed the Leveller mutinies at Burford and ended forever his alliance with the radicals.

An agreement of the Free People of England. Tendered as a *Peace-Offering* to this distressed *Nation.* by Lieutenant Colonel *John Lilburne,* Master *William Walwyn,* Master *Thomas Prince,* and Master *Richard Overton,* Prisoners in the Tower of London, May the 1. 1649. Matth. 5. verse 9. Blessed are the Peacemakers for they shall be called the children of God.

A PREPARATIVE TO ALL SORTS OF PEOPLE.

If Afflictions make men wise, and wisdom direct to happiness, then certainly this Nation is not far from such a degree therof, as may compare if not far exceed, any part of the world: having for some yeares by-past, drunk deep of the Cup of misery and sorrow. We blesse God our consciences are cleer from adding affliction to affliction, having ever laboured from the beginning, of our publick distractions, to compose and reconcile them: & should esteem it the Crown of all our temporal felicity that yet we might be instrumentall in procuring the peace and prosperity of this Common-wealth the land of our Nativity.

And therefore according to our promise in our late *Manifestation* of the 14 April 1649. (being perswaded of the necessitie and justnesse thereof) as a Peace-Offering to the Free people of this Nation, we tender this ensuing Agreement, not knowing any more effectuall means to put a finall period to all our feares and troubles.

It is a way of settlement, though at first much startled at by some in high authority; yet according to the nature of truth, it hath made its own way into the understanding, and taken root in most mens hearts and affections, so that we have reall ground to hope (what ever shall become of us) that our earnest desires and indeavours for good to the people will not altogether be null and frustrate.

The life of all things is in the right use and application, which is not our worke only, but every mans conscience must look to it selfe, and not dreame out more seasons and opportunities. And this we trust will satisfie all ingenuous people that we are not such wilde, irrationall, dangerous Creatures as we have been aspersed to be; This agreement being the ultimate end and full scope of all our desires and intentions concerning the Government of this Nation, and wherein we shall absolutely rest satisfied and acquiesce; nor did we ever give just cause for any to beleeve worse of us by any thing either said or done by us, and which would not in the least be doubted, but that men consider not the interest of those that have so unchristian-like made bold with our good names; but we must bear with men of such interests as are opposite to any part of this Agreement, when neither our Saviour nor his Apostles innocency could stop such mens mouthes whose interests their doctrines and practises did extirpate; And therefore if friends at least would but consider what interest men relate to, whilst they are telling or whispering their aspersions against us, they would find the reason and save us a great deale of labour in clearing our selves, it being a remarkable signe of an ill cause when aspersions supply the place of Arguments.

We blesse God that he hath given us time and hearts to bring it to this issue, what further he hath for us to do is yet only knowne to his wisedom, to whose will and pleasure we shall willingly submit; we have if we look with the eyes of frailty, enemies like the sons of Anak, but if with the eyes of faith and confidence in a righteous God and a just cause, we see more with us then against us.

John Lilburn.	William Walwyn.
Thomas Prince.	Richard Overton.

From our causelesse captivity
in the Tower of London,
May 1. 1649.

THE AGREEMENT IT SELFE THUS FOLLOWETH.

After the long and tedious prosecution of a most unnaturall cruell, home-bred war, occasioned by divisions and distempers amongst our selves, and those distempers arising from the uncertaintie of our Government, and the exercise of an unlimited or Arbitrary power, by such as have been trusted with Supreme and subordinate Authority, whereby multitudes of grievances and intolerable oppressions have been brought upon us. And finding after eight yeares experience and expectation all indeavours hitherto used, or remedies hitherto applyed, to have encreased rather then diminished our distractions, and that if not speedily prevented our falling againe into factions and divisions, will not only deprive us of the benefit of all those wonderful Victories God hath vouchsafed against such as sought our bondage, but expose us first to poverty and misery, and then to be destroyed by forraigne enemies.

And being earnestly desirous to make a right use of that opportunity God hath given us to make this Nation Free and Happy, to reconcile our

differences, and beget a perfect amitie and friendship once more amongst us, that we may stand clear in our consciences before Almighty God, as unbyassed by any corrupt Interest or particular advantages, and manifest to all the world that our indeavours have not proceeded from malice to the persons of any, or enmity against opinions; but in reference to the peace and prosperity of the Common-wealth, and for prevention of like distractions, and removall of all grievances; We the free People of England, to whom God hath given hearts, means and opportunity to effect the same, do with submission to his wisdom, in his name, and desiring the equity thereof may be to his praise and glory; Agree to ascertain our Government, to abolish all arbitrary Power, and to set bounds and limits both to our Supreme, and all Subordinate Authority, and remove all known Grievances.

AND ACCORDINGLY DO DECLARE AND PUBLISH TO ALL THE WORLD, THAT WE ARE AGREED AS FOLLOWETH,

I. That the Supreme Authority of England and the Territories therewith incorporate, shall be and reside henceforward in a Representative of the People consisting of four hundred persons, but no more; in the choice of whom (according to naturall right) all men of the age of one and twenty yeers and upwards (not being servants, or receiving alms, or having served the late King in Arms or voluntary Contributions) shall have their voices; and be capable of being elected to that Supreme Trust, those who served the King being disabled for ten years onely. . . .

III. And to the end all publick Officers may be certainly accountable, and no Factions made to maintain corrupt Interests, no Officer of any salary, Forces in Army or Garison, nor any Treasurer or Receiver of publick monies, shall (while such) be elected a Member for any Representative; and if any Lawyer shall at any time be chosen, he shall be uncapable of practice as a Lawyer, during the whole time of that Trust. And for the same reason, and that all persons may be capable of subjection as well as rule. . . .

For security whereof, having by wofull experience found the prevalence of corrupt interests powerfully inclining most men once entrusted with authority, to pervert the same to their own domination, and to the prejudice of our Peace and Liberties, we therefore further agree and declare.

X. That we do not impower or entrust our said Representatives to continue in force, or to make any Lawes, Oaths, or Covenants, whereby to compell by penalties or otherwise any person to any thing in or about matters of faith, Religion or Gods worship or to restrain any person from the profession of his faith, or exercise of Religion according to his Conscience, nothing having caused more distractions, and heart burnings in all ages, then persecution and molestation for matters of Conscience in and about Religion:

XI. We doe not impower them to impresse or constrain any person to serve in war by Sea or Land every mans Conscience being to be satisfied in the justness of that cause wherein he hazards his own life, or may destroy an others.

And for the quieting of all differences, and abolishing of all enmity and rancour, as much as is now possible for us to effect.

XII. We agree, That after the end of this present Parliament, no person shall be questioned for any thing said or done in reference to the late Warres, or publique differences; otherwise then in pursuance of the determinations of the present Parliament, against such as have adhered to the King against the Liberties of the people: And saving that Accomptants for publick moneys received, shall remain accomptable for the same.

XIII. That all privileges or exemptions of any persons from the Lawes, or from the ordinary course of Legall proceedings, by vertue of any Tenure, Grant, Charter, Patent, Degree, or Birth, or of any place of residence, or refuge, or priviledge of Parliament, shall be henceforth void and null; and the like not to be made nor revived again.

XIIII. We doe not impower them to give judgment upon any ones person or estate, where no Law hath been before provided, nor to give power to any other Court or Jurisdiction so to do, Because where there is no Law, there is no transgression, for men or Magistrates to take Cognisance of; neither doe we impower them to intermeddle with the execution of any Law whatsoever.

XV. And that we may remove all long setled Grievances, and thereby as farre as we are able, take away all cause of complaints, and no longer depend upon the uncertain inclination of Parliaments to remove them, nor trouble our selves or them with Petitions after Petitions, as hath been accustomed, without fruit or benefit; and knowing no cause why any should repine at our removall of them, except such as make advantage of their continuance, or are related to some corrupt Interests, which we are not to regard.

WE AGREE AND DECLARE,

XVI. That it shall not be in the power of any Representative, to punish, or cause to be punished, any person or persons for refusing to answer to questions against themselves in Criminall cases.

XVII. That it shall not be in their power, after the end of the next Representative, to continue or constitute any proceedings in Law that shall be longer than Six months in the final determination of any cause past all Appeal, nor to continue the Laws or proceedings therein in any other Language then English, nor to hinder any person or persons from pleading their own Causes, or of making use of whom they please to plead for them.

The reducing of these and other the like provisions of this nature in this Agreement provided, and which could not now in all particulars be perfected by us, is intended by us to be the proper works of faithful Representatives. . . .

XXII. That it shall not be in their power to continue or make any Law, to deprive any person, in case of Tryals for Life, Limb, Liberty, or Estate, from the benefit of witnesses, on his, or their behalf; nor deprive any person of those priviledges, and liberties, contained in the Petition of Right, made in the third yeer of the late King Charls.

XXIII. That it shall not be in their power to continue the Grievance of Tithes, longer then to the end of the next Representative; in which time, they shall provide to give reasonable satisfaction to all Impropriators: neither shall they force by penalties or otherwise, any person to pay towards the maintenance of any Ministers, who out of conscience cannot submit thereunto.

XXIV. That it shall not be in their power to impose Ministers upon any the respective Parishes, but shall give free liberty to the parishioners of every particular parish, to chuse such as themselves shall approve; and upon such terms, and for such reward, as themselves shall be willing to contribute, or shall contract for. Provided, none be chusers but such as are capable of electing Representatives.

XXV. That it shal not be in their power, to continue or make a law, for any other way of Judgments, or Conviction of life, limb, liberty, or estate, but onely by twelve sworn men of the Neighbor-hood; to be chosen in some free way by the people; to be directed before the end of the next Representative, and not picked and imposed, as hitherto in many places they have been.

XXVI. They shall not disable any person from bearing any office in the Common-wealth, for any opinion or practice in Religion, excepting such as maintain the Popes (or other forraign) Supremacy.

XXVII. That it shal not be in their power to impose any publike officer upon any Counties, Hundreds, Cities, Towns, or Borroughs; but the people capable by this Agreement to chuse Representatives, shall chuse all their publike Officers that are in any kinde to administer the Law for their respective places, for one whole yeer, and no longer, and so from yeer to yeer: and this as an especial means to avoyd Factions, and Parties. . . .

And for as much as nothing threateneth greater danger to the Common-wealth, then that the Military power should by any means come to be superior to the Civil Authority.

XXIX. We declare and agree, That no Forces shal be raised, but by the Representatives, for the time being; and in raising thereof, that they exactly observe these Rules, namely, That they allot to each particular County, City, Town, and Borrugh, the raising, furnishing, agreeing, and paying of a due proportion, according to the whole number to be levyed; and shall to the Electors of Representatives in each respective place, give Free liberty, to nominate and appoint all Officers appertaining to Regiments, Troops, and Companies, and to remove them as they shall see cause, Reserving to the Representative, the nominating, and appointing onely of the General, and all General-Officers; and the ordering, regulating, and commanding of them all, upon what service shall seem to them necessary for the Safety, Peace, and Freedom of the Common-wealth.

And in as much as we have found by sad experience, That generally men make little or nothing, to innovate in Government, to exceed their time and power in places of trust, to introduce an Arbitrary, and Tyrannical power, and to overturn all things into Anarchy and Confusion, where there are no penalties imposed for such destructive crimes and offences.

XXX. We therefore agree and declare, That it shall not be in the power of any Representative, in any wise, to render up, or give, or take away any

part of this Agreement, nor level mens Estates, destroy Propriety, or make all things Common: And if any Representative shall endeavour, as a Representative, to destroy this Agreement, every Member present in the House, not entering or immediately publishing his dissent, shall incur the pain due for High Treason, and be proceeded against accordingly; and if any person or persons, shall by force endeavour to contrive, the destruction thereof, each person so doing, shall likewise be dealt withal as in cases of Treason.

And if any person shall by force of Arms disturb Elections of Representatives, he shall incurr the penalty of a Riot; and if any person not capable of being an Elector, or Elected, shall intrude themselves amongst those that are, or any persons shall behave themselves rudely and disorderly, such persons shall be liable to a presentment by a grant Inquest and to an indictment upon misdemeanor; and be fined and otherwise punish'd according to the discretion and verdict of a Jury. And all Laws made, or that shall be made contrary to any part of this Agreement, are hereby made null and void.

Thus, as becometh a free People, thankfull unto God for this blessed opportunity, and desirous to make use thereof to his glory, in taking off every yoak, and removing every burthen, in delivering the captive, and setting the oppressed free; we have in all the particular Heads forementioned, done as we would be done unto, and as we trust in God will abolish all occasion of offence and discord, and produce the lasting Peace and Prosperity of this Common-wealth: and accordingly do in the sincerity of our hearts and consciences, as in the presence of Almighty God, give cleer testimony of our absolute agreement to all and every part hereof by subscribing our hands thereunto. Dated the first day of May, in the Year of our Lord 1649.

> John Lilburn
> William Walwyn
> Thomas Prince
> Richard Overton

April 30, 1649
Imprimatur

> Gilbert Mabbot
> finis

London, Printed for Gyles Calvert at the black spread-Eagle at the West end of Pauls.   ◻

Gerrard Winstanley

Near London, in the same critical year of 1649, a man named Gerrard Winstanley led a group of some twenty poor men to the waste lands of St. George's Hill where they began to cultivate the field as communists, and invited all England to join them. The local gentry were frightened and horrified and asked the Council of State for troops to run them off. The Council of State sent troops who came, saw, and sent in a marvel-

ously sympathetic report on the Cobham "Diggers"! Winstanley and his fellow revolutionist, William Everard, a Leveller agitator from the New Model Army, were brought before General Fairfax who listened to their proposal for cultivating waste lands in common, and convincing by example all men to surrender their estates to the new freedom and justice, and dismissed them as harmlessly mad. And, of course, the Council was right. The local oligarchy roused itself to a suitable pitch of bullying and within a year the Diggers were off St. George's Hill. Winstanley continued to write and be published, however; he lived through the era of Cromwell and died somewhere, sometime after the Restoration.

But as a writer and thinker Winstanley was the most exciting and original of a generation of genius. All things considered, he may be the most gifted socialist intellectual next to Marx. He is easily the most eloquent socialist in a tradition rich in eloquence.

But he is more important than all such nonhistorical praise of his talents can indicate. The special quality of Winstanley is that his writing brings to detailed life one of the most crtical and electrifying changes in the thought processes of our civilization. For he begins as a Christian dreamer (in the radical and mystical tradition) and in his last work emerges as a sensationally secular thinker. The intellectual distance between THE MYSTERY OF GOD and THE LAW OF FREEDOM can scarcely be measured. The latter retains religious rhetoric as precious ornament and the necessary matrix of communication—but conceptually Winstanley has renounced the Christian tradition. His brief and brilliant historical life recapitulates the development of centuries.

Since, however, the abrupt and profound nature of this metamorphosis can be adequately illustrated only by the whole CORPUS of his work, I have limited myself to selections which reflect his mature experience in the revolution. I invite the reader to explore this marvelous intelligence further in the WORKS edited by George Sabine.

First, here is his preface to the embattled WATCH WORD TO THE CITY OF LONDON:

TO THE CITY OF LONDON, FREEDOME AND PEACE DESIRED

Thou City of London, I am one of thy sons by freedome, and I do truly love thy peace; while I had an estate in thee, I was free to offer my Mite into thy publike Treasury Guild-hall, for a preservation to thee, and the whole Land; but by thy cheating sons in the theeving art of buying and selling, and by the burdens of, and for the Souldiery in the beginning of the war, I was beaten out both of estate and trade, and forced to accept of the good will of friends crediting of me, to live a Countrey-life, and there likewise by the burthen of Taxes and much Free-quarter, my weak back found the burthen heavier then I could bear; yet in all the passages of these eight yeers troubles I have been willing to lay out what my Talent was, to procure Englands peace inward and outward, and yet all along I have found such as in words have professed the same cause, to be enemies to me. Not a full yeere since, being quiet at my work, my heart was filled with

sweet thoughts, and many things were revealed to me which I never read in books, nor heard from the mouth of any flesh, and when I began to speak of them, some people could not bear my words, and amongst those revelations this was one, *That the earth shall be made a common Treasury of livelihood to whole mankind, without respect of persons;* and I had a voice within me bad me declare it all abroad, which I did obey, for I declared it by word of mouth wheresoever I came, then I was made to write a little book called, *The new Law of righteousnesse,* and therein I declared it; yet my mind was not at rest, because nothing was acted, and thoughts run in me, that words and writings were all nothing, and must die, for action is the life of all, and if thou dost not act, thou dost nothing. Within a little time I was made obedient to the word in that particular likewise; for I tooke my spade and went and broke the ground upon *George-hill* in Surrey, thereby declaring freedome to the Creation, and that the earth must be set free from intanglements of Lords and Landlords, and that it shall become a common Treasury to all, as it was first made and given to the sonnes of men: For which doing the Dragon presently casts a flood of water to drown the manchild, even that freedom that now is declared, for the old Norman Prerogative Lord of that Mannour Mr. *Drake,* caused me to be arrested for a trespasse against him, in digging upon that barren Heath, and the unrighteous proceedings of Kingstone Court in this businesse I have here declared to thee, and to the whole land, that you may consider the case that England is in; all men have stood for freedom, thou hast kept fasting daies, and prayed in morning exercises for freedom; thou hast given thanks for victories, because hopes of freedome; plentie of Petitions and promises thereupon have been made for freedome, and now the common enemy is gone, you are all like men in a mist, seeking for freedom, and know not where, nor what it is: and those of the richer sort of you that see it, are ashamed and afraid to owne it, because it comes clothed in a clownish garment, and open to the best language that scoffing *Ishmael* can afford, or that railing *Rabsheka* can speak, or furious *Pharaoh* can act against him; for freedom is the man that will turn the world upside downe, therefore no wonder he hath enemies.

And assure your selves, if you pitch not right now upon the right point of freedome in action, as your Covenant hath it in words, you will wrap up your children in greater slavery then ever you were in; the Word of God is Love, and when all thy actions are done in love to the whole Creation, then thou advancest freedome, and freedome is Christ in you, and Christ among you; bondage is Satan in you, and Satan among you: no true freedom can be established for Englands peace, or prove you faithfull in Covenant, but such a one as hath respect to the poor, as well as the rich; for if thou consent to freedom to the rich in the City, and givest freedome to the Free-holders in the Countrey, and to Priests and Lawyers, and Lords of Mannours, and Impropriators, and yet allowest the poor no freedome, thou art then a declared hypocrite, and all thy prayers, fasts, and thanksgivings are, and will be proved an abomination to the Lord, and freedome himselfe will be the poors portion, when thou shalt lie groaning in bondage.

I have declared this truth to the Army and Parliament, and now I have declared it to thee likewise, that none of you that are the fleshly strength of this Land may be left without excuse, for now you have been all spoken to, and because I have obeyed the voice of the Lord in this thing, therefore doe the Free-holders and Lords of Mannours seek to oppresse me in the outward livelihood of the world, but I am in peace. And London, nay England, look to thy freedom; I'le assure thee, thou art very neere to be cheated of it, and if thou lose it now after all thy boasting, truly thy posterity will curse thee, for thy unfaithfulnesse to them: every one talks of freedome, but there are but few that act for freedome, and the actors for freedome are oppressed by the talkers and verball professors of freedome; if thou wouldst know what true freedome is, read over this and other my writings, and thou shalt see it lies in the community in spirit, and community in the earthly treasury, and this is Christ the true manchild spread abroad in the Creation, restoring all things into himselfe; and so I leave thee,
August 26. 1649.

> Being a free Denizen of thee, and a true
> lover of thy peace,
> *Jerrard Winstanly.*   □

Finally, a sample of the bold, original, and thoroughly secular perceptions and arguments of Winstanley's masterpiece, THE LAW OF FREEDOM, which saw the light of revolutionary day in 1651. I have chosen his examination of "your Divinity," some of his thoughts on education, and a bit of his prospectus for a just legal state:

Examine your self, and look likewise into the ways of all Professors, and you shall finde, That the Enjoyment of the Earth below, which you call a low and a carnal Knowledg, is that, which you and all professors (as well as the men of the world, as you call them) strive and seek after.

Wherefore are you so covetous after the World, in buying and selling? counting your self a happy man, if you be rich, and a miserable man if you be poor. And though you say, *Heaven after death is a place of glory, where you shall enjoy God face to face,* yet you are loth to leave the Earth to go thither.

Do not your Ministers preach for to enjoy the Earth? Do not professing Lawyers, as well as others, buy and sell the Conquerors Justice, that they may enjoy the Earth? Do not professing Soldiers fight for the Earth, and seat themselves in that Land, which is the Birth-Right of others, as well as theirs, shutting others out? Do not all professors strive to get Earth, that they may live in plenty by other mens labors?

Do you not make the Earth your very Rest? Doth not the enjoying of the Earth please the spirit in you? and then you say, God is pleased with your ways, and blesseth you. If you want Earth, and become poor, do you not say, God is angry with you, and crosseth you?

Why do you heap up riches? why do you eat and drink, and wear clothes? why do you take a woman, and lie with her to beget children? Are not all these carnal and low things of the Earth? and do you not live in

them, and covet them as much as any? nay more then many which you call men of the world?

And it being thus with you, what other spiritual or heavenly things do you seek after more then others? And what is in you more then in others? If you say, there is; then surely you ought to let these earthly things alone to the men of the world, as you call them, whose portions these are, and keep you within the compass of your own sphere, that others seeing you live a life above the world in peace and freedom, neither working your self, nor deceiving, nor compelling others to work for you, they may be drawn to embrace the same spiritual life by your single-hearted conversation. Well, I have done here.

Let us now examine your Divinity,

Which you call heavenly, and spiritual things, for herein speeches are made not to advance knowledge, but to destroy the true knowledge of God; for Divinity does not speak the truth, as it is hid in every body, but it leaves the motional knowledge of a thing as it is, And imagins, studies, or thinks what may be, and so runs the hazzard true or false: And this Divinity is always speaking words to deceive the simple, that he may make them work for him, and maintain him, but he never comes to action himself to do as he would be done by; for he is a monster who is all tongue and no hand.

This divining Doctrine, which you call spiritual and heavenly things, is the thief and the robber; he comes to spoile the Vinyard of a mans peace, and does not enter in at the door, but he climbes up another way: And this Doctrine is two fold.

First he takes upon him to tell you the meaning of other mens words, and writing by his studying or imagining what another mans knowledge might be, and by thus doing darkens knowledge, and wrongs the spirit of the Authors who did write and speak those things which he takes upon him to interpret.

Secondly, he takes upon him, to foretell what shall befall a man after he is dead, and what that world is beyond the Sun, and beyond the Moon, &c. And if any man tell him there is no reason for what you say, he answers you must not judge of heavenly and spiritual things by reason, but you must believe what is told you, whether it be reason or no: There is a three-fold discovery of falsehood in this Doctrine.

For first it is a Doctrine of a sickly and weak spirit, who hath lost his understanding in the knowledge of the Creation, and of the temper of his own Heart and Nature, and so runs into fancies, either of joy or sorrow.

And if the passion of joy predominate, then he fancies to himself a personal God, personal Angels, and a local place of glory which he saith, he, and all who beleives what he saith, shall go to, after they are dead.

And if sorrow predominate, then he fancies to himself a personal Devil, and a locall place of torment, that he shall go to after he is dead, and this he speaks with great confidence.

Or Secondly, this is the Doctrine of a subtle running spirit, to make an ungrounded wise man mad. That he might be called the more excellent

man in knowledge; for many times when a wise understanding heart is assaulted with this Doctrine of a God, a Devil, a Heaven, and a Hell, Salvation and Damnation after a man is dead, his spirit being not strongly grounded in the knowledge of the Creation, nor in the temper of his own heart,

He strives and stretches his brains to find out the depth of that doctrine and cannot attain to it; for indeed it is not knowledg, but imagination: and so by poring and puzling himself in it, loses that wisdom he had, and becomes distracted and mad: and if the passion of joy predominate, then he is merry, and sings, and laughs, and is ripe in the expressions of his words, and will speak strange things; but all by imagination. But if the passion of sorrow predominate, then he is heavy and sad, crying out, *He is damned, God hath forsaken him, and he must go to Hell when he dys, he cannot make his calling and election sure:* And in that distemper many times a man doth hang, kil, or drown himself: so that this divining Doctrine, which you call *spiritual and heavenly things,* torments people always when they are weak, sickly, and under any distemper; therefore it cannot be the Doctrine of Christ the Saviour.

For my own part, my spirit hath waded deep to finde the bottom of this divining spiritual Doctrine: and the more I searched, the more I was at a loss; and I never came to quiet rest, and to know God in my spirit, till I came to the knowledg of the things in this Book: And let me tell you, They who preach this divining Doctrine are the murtherers of many a poor heart, who is bashful and simple, and that cannot speak for himself, but that keeps his thoughts to himself.

Or thirdly, This Doctrine is made a cloke of policy by the subtil elder Brother, to cheat his simple younger Brother of the Freedoms of the Earth: For saith the elder Brother, *The Earth is mine, and not yours, Brother; and you must not work upon it, unless you will hire it of me: and you must not take the fruits of it, unless you will buy them of me, by that which I pay you for your Labor: for if you should do otherwise, God will not love you, and you shall not go to Heaven when you dye, but the Devil will have you, and you must be damned in Hell.*

If the younger reply, and say, *The Earth is my Birth-Right, as well as yours, and God who made us both, is no Respecter of persons: Therefore there is no Reason but I should enjoy the Freedoms of the Earth for my comfortable Livelyhood, as well as you, Brother.*

I, but saith the elder Brother, *You must not trust to your own Reason and Understanding, but you must beleeve what is written and what is told you; and if you will not beleeve, your Damnation will be the greater.*

I cannot beleeve, saith the younger Brother, *that our righteous Creator should be so partial in his Dispensations of the Earth, seeing our bodies cannot live upon Earth without the use of the Earth.*

The elder brother replies, What, will you be an Atheist, and a factious man, will you not believe God?

Yes, saith the younger brother, If I knew God said so I should believe, for I desire to serve him.

Why, saith the elder brother, this is his Word, and if you will not believe it, you must be damned; but if you will believe it, you must go to Heaven.

Well, the younger brother being weak in spirit, and having not a grounded knowledg of the Creation, nor of himself, is terrified, and lets go his hold in the Earth, and submits himself to be a slave to his brother, for fear of damnation in Hell after death, and in hopes to get Heaven thereby after he is dead; and so his eyes are put out, and his Reason is blinded.

So that this divining spiritual Doctrine is a cheat; for while men are gazing up to Heaven, imagining after a happiness, or fearing a Hell after they are dead, their eyes are put out, that they see not what is their birthrights, and what is to be done by them here on Earth while they are living: This is the filthy Dreamer, and the Cloud without rain.

And indeed the subtle Clergy do know, that if they can but charm the people by this their divining Doctrine, to look after riches, Heaven and Glory when they are dead, that then they shall easily be the Inheritors of the Earth, and have the deceived people to be their servants.

This divining Doctrine, which you call spiritual and heavenly, was not the Doctrine of Christ, for his words were pure knowledg, they were words of life; for he said, *He spoke what he had seen with his Father,* for he had the knowledg of the Creation, and spake as every thing was.

And this Divinity came in after Christ to darken his Knowledg; and it is the language of the Mystery of Iniquity and Antichrist, whereby the covetous, ambitious and serpentine spirit cozens the plain-hearted of his portions in the Earth.

And Divinity cozens a plain heart two ways: First, If a man have an Estate, according to the Kings Laws, he is made by this charm to give it, or bazle [i.e., waste] it away to the Priests, or to religious uses, in hopes to get Heaven when he is dead.

Or secondly, A man by running to hear Divinity Sermons, and dancing after his charming pipe, neglects his labour, and so runs into debt, and then his fellow professors will cast him into prison, and starve him there, and there Divinity will call him a hypocrite and wicked man, and become a Devil to torment him in that Hell. . . .

CHAP. V. EDUCATION OF MANKINDE, IN SCHOOLS AND TRADES.

Mankinde in the days of his youth, is like a young Colt, wanton and foolish, till he be broke by Education and correction, and the neglect of this care, or the want of wisdom in the performance of it hath been, and is, the cause of much division and trouble in the world.

Therefore the Law of a *Common-wealth* does require, that not onely a father, but that all Overseers, and Officers should make it their work to educate children in good manners, and to see them brought up in some trade or other, and to suffer no children in any Parish to live in idleness, and youthful pleasure, all their days, as many have been; but that they be brought up like men, and not like beasts: That so the *Common-wealth* may be planted with laborious and wise experienced men, and not with idle fools.

Mankinde may be considered in a fourfold degree, his childhood, youth, manhood and old age; his childhood and his youth, may be considered from his birth till forty yeers of age; and within this compass of time, after

he is weaned from his mother, who shall be the nurse her self, if there be no defect in Nature, his parents shall teach him a civil and humble behavior toward all men. Then send him to School, to learn to read the Laws of the *Common-wealth,* to ripen his wits from his childhood, and so to proceed in his learning, till he be acquainted with all Arts and Languages: and the reason is threefold.

First, By being acquainted with the knowledge of the affairs of the world; by this traditional knowledge they may be the better able to govern themselves like rational men.

Secondly, they may become thereby good *Common-wealths men,* in supporting the government thereof, by being acquainted with the nature of government.

Thirdly, If *England* have occasion to send Embassadors to any other Land, we may have such as are acquainted with their Language; or if any Embassador come from other Lands, we may have such as can understand their speech.

But one sort of Children shall not be trained up onely to book learning, and no other imployment, called Schollars, as they are in the Government of Monarchy, for then through idleness, and exercised wit therein, they spend their time to finde out pollicies to advance themselves, to be Lords and Masters above their laboring brethren, as *Simeon* and *Levi* do, which occasions all the trouble in the world.

Therefore, to prevent the dangerous events of idleness in Scholars, it is reason, and safe for common peace, that after Children have been brought up at Schools, to ripen their wits, they shall then be set to such Trades, Arts and Sciences, as their bodies and wits are capable of; and therein continue till they come to fourty years of age.

For all the work of the Earth, or in Trades, is to be managed by youth, and by such as have lost their Freedoms.

Then from fourty years of age till fourscore, if he live so long, which is the degree of manhood and old age; they shall be freed from all labor and work, unless they will themselves.

And from among this degree of Mankind shal be chosen all Officers and Overseers, to see the Laws of the Commonwealth observed.

For as all men shall be Workers or Waiters in Storehouses till they be fourty years of age, so none shall be chosen a publique Officer till he be full fourty years of age: for by this time Man hath learned experience to govern himself and others: for when young wits are set to govern, they wax wanton, &c.

What Trades should Mankinde be brought up in?

In every Trade, Art, and Science, whereby they may finde out the Secrets of the Creation, and that they may know how to govern the Earth in right order.

There are five Fountains from whence all Arts and Sciences have their influences: he that is an actor in any or in all the five parts, is a profitable son of mankinde: he that onely contemplates and talks of what he reads and hears, and doth not employ his Talent in some bodily action, for the

encrease of fruitfulness, freedom, and peace in the Earth, is an unprofitable son.

The first Fountain is the right planting of the Earth to make it fruitful, and this is called Husbandry: And there are two branches of it;

As first, planting, digging, dunging, liming, burning, grubbing, and right ordering of Land, to make it fit to receive seed, that it may bring forth a plentiful crop: And under this Head all Millers, Maltsters, Bakers, Harness-makers for Plows and Carts, Rope-makers, Spinners, and Weavers of linnen, and such like, are all but good Husbandry.

The second Branch of Husbandry is Gardening, how to plant, graft, and set all sort of fruit-trees, and how to order the ground for flowers, Herbs and Roots for pleasure, food, or medicinal. And here all Physicians, Chyrurgeons, Distillers of all sorts of Waters, Gatherers of Drugs, Makers of Wines, and Oyl, and Preservers of fruits, and such like, may learn by Observation, what is good for all bodies, both man and beasts.

The second Fountain is Mineral employment, and that is to search into the Earth to finde out Mynes of Gold and Silver, Brass, Iron, Tin, Lead, Cannel, Coal, and Stone of all sorts, Salt-peter, Salt, and Allomsprings,— and such like: And here all Chymists, Gunpowdermakers, Masons, Smiths, and such like, as would finde out the strength and power of the Earth, may learn how to order these for the use and profit of Mankinde.

The third Fountain is the right ordering of Cattel, whether by Shepherds or Herds-men; and such may learn here how to breed and train up Cows for the Daries, Bulls and Horses for the saddle or yoke. And here all Tanners, Hatters, Shoomakers, Glovers, Spinners of Wool, Clothiers, Taylors, Dyers, and such like, may learn how to order and look to these.

The fourth Fountain is the right ordering of Woods and Timber trees, for planting, dressing, felling, framing of Timber for all uses, for building houses or ships. And here all Carpenters, Joyners, Throsters, Plow-makers, Instrument-makers for musick, and all who work in wood and timber, may finde out the Secret of Nature, to make Trees more plentiful and thriving in their growth, and profitable for use.

The fifth Fountain, from whence Reason is exercised to finde out the Secrets of Nature, is [to] observe the rising and setting of the Sun, Moon, and the Powers of the Heavens above; and the motion of the Tydes, and Seas, and their several effects, powers, and operations upon the bodies of Man and Beast. And here may be learned Astrology, Astronomy, and Navigation, and the motions of the Winds, and the causes of several Appearances of the Face of Heaven, either in Storms, or in Fareness.

And in all these five Fountains here is Knowledg in the practice, and it is good.

But there is Traditional Knowledg, which is attained by reading, or by the instruction of others, and not practical, but leads to an idle life; and this is not good.

The first is a laborious Knowledg, and a Preserver of common Peace, which we finde God himself acting; for he put forth his own wisdom in practise, when he set his strength to work to make the Creation: for God is an active Power, not an imaginary Fancy.

The latter is an idle, lazy contemplation the Scholars would call Knowl-

edg, but it is no knowledg, but a shew of Knowledg, like a *Parrat* who speaks words, but he knows not what he saith: This same shew of knowledg rests in reading or contemplating, or hearing others speak, and speaks so too, but will not set his hand to work: And from this Traditional Knowledg and Learning rise up both Clergy and Lawyer, who by their cunning insinuations live meerly upon the labor of other men, and teach Laws which they themselves will not do, and layes burdens upon others which they themselves will not touch with the least of their fingers; and from hence arises all oppressions, wars, and troubles in the world, the one is the son of contention, the other the son of darkness, but both the supporters of bondage, which the Creation groans under.

Therefore to prevent idleness and the danger of Machivilian cheats, it is profitable for the Common-wealth, that children be trained up in Trades and some bodily imployment, as well as in learning Languages, or the Histories of former ages.

And as boyes are trained up in Learning and in Trades, so all Maides shall be trained up in reading, sewing, kniting, spining of Lynnen and Woollen, Musique, and all other easie neat works, either for to furnish Storehouses with Lynnen and Woollen cloth, or for the ornament of particular houses with needle work.

And if this course were taken, there would be no Idle person nor Beggers in the Land, and much work would be done by that now lazie generation for the enlarging of the common Treasuries.

And in the manageing of any Trade, let no young wit be crushed in his Invention, for if any man desire to make a new tryall of his skil in any Trade or Science, the Overseers shall not hinder him, but incourage him therein; that so the Spirit of knowledge may have his full growth in man, to finde out the secret in every Art.

And let every one who finds out a new Invention have a deserved honour given him, and certainly when men are sure of food and raiment, their reason will be ripe, and ready to dive into the secrets of the Creation, that they may learn to see and know God (the Spirit of the whole Creation) in all his works; for fear of want, and care to pay Rent to Task-masters, hath hindred many rare Inventions.

So that Kingly Power hath crushed the Spirit of Knowledg, and would not suffer it to rise up in its beauty and fulness, but by his Club Law hath preferred the spirit of Imagination, which is a Deceiver, before it.

There shal be no buying and selling of the Earth, nor of the fruits thereof.

For by the Government under Kings, the cheaters hereby have cozened the plain hearted of their creation birth-rights, and have possessed themselves in the earth and cals it theirs and not the others, and so have brought in that poverty and misery which lies upon many men.

And whereas the wise should help the foolish, and the strong help the weak; the wise and the strong destroys the weak and the simple.

And are not all children generally simple and weak and know not the things that belong to their peace till they come to ripe age, but before they come to that understanding, the cunning ones who have more strength

and policy, have by this hypocriticall, lying, unrighteous and cheating Art of buying and selling, wrung the freedoms of the earth out of their hands, and cozened them of their birth-rights.

So that when they come to understanding, they see themselves beggers in the middest of a fruitfull Land, and so the Proverb is true, *Plain dealing is a jewel, but he who uses it shal dye a begger.* And why?

Because this buying and selling is the nursery of cheaters, It is the Law of the Conqueror, and the Righteousness of the Scribes and Pharisees, which both killed Christ and hindred his Resurrection, as much as darkness can to put out light.

And these cunning cheaters commonly become the Rulers of the earth, and then the City Man-kind mourns, for not the wise poor man, but the cunning rich man, was always made an Officer and Ruler, such a one as by his stolen interest in the earth would be sure to hold others in bondage of poverty and servitude to him and his party.

And hence arise oppression and tyranny in the earth upon the backs of the weak younger brethren, who are made younger brothers indeed, as the Proverb is, by their cunning elder brother; and as *Daniel* said, *The basest of men under Kingly government were set to Rule, who can command but not obey, who can take other mens labors to live at ease, but not work themselvs.*

Therefore there shal be no buying and selling in a Free Commonwealth, neither shall any one hire his brother to work for him.

If the Common-wealth might be governed without buying and selling here is a Platform of Government for it, which is the ancientest Law of Righteousness to Mankind in the use of the Earth, and which is the very height of earthly Freedoms. But if the minds of the people, through Covetousness and proud Ignorance, wil have the Earth governed by buying and selling still, this same Platform, with a few things subtracted, declares an easie way of Government of the Earth for the quiet of peoples minds, and preserving of Peace in the Land.

For, as like a Tradesman, I ask the highest price,
Yet I may fall (if you will rise) upon a good advice. . . .

Laws to choose Officers.

34. All Overseers and State-Officers shall be chosen new every year, to prevent the rise of Ambition and Covetousness; for the Nations have smarted sufficiently by suffering Officers to continue long in an Office, or to remain in an Office by hereditary succession.

35. A man that is of a turbulent spirit, given to quarreling, and provoking words to his neighbor, shall not be chosen any Officer while he so continues.

36. All men from twenty years of age upwards shall have freedom of voyce to choose Officers, unless they be such as lie under the sentence of the Law.

37. Such shall be chosen Officers, as are rational men of moderate conversation, and who have experience in the Laws of the Commonwealth.

38. All men from forty years of age upwards shal be capable to be chosen State Officers, and none younger, unless any one by his industry and moderate conversation doth move the people to choose him.

39. If any man make suit to move the people to choose him an Officer, that man shall not be chose at all that time: If another man perswade the people to choose him who makes suit for himself, they shall both lose their freedom at that time, *viz.* they shall neither have a voyce to choose another, nor be chosen themselves.

Laws against Treachery.

40. He who professes the service of a righteous God by preaching and prayer, and makes a Trade to get the possessions of the Earth, shall be put to death for a Witch and a Cheater.

41. He who pretends one thing in words, and his actions declare his intent was another thing, shall never bear Office in the Common-wealth.

What is Freedom?

Every Freeman shall have a Freedom in the Earth, to plant or build, to fetch from the Store-houses any thing he wants, and shall enjoy the fruits of his labours without restraint from any; he shall not pay Rent to any Landlord, and he shall be capable to be chosen any Officer, so he be above forty years of age, and he shall have a voyce to choose Officers though he be under forty years of age.   ◻

John Milton

The last piece I have selected is more available and better known than the other literature from the revolution. It is John Milton's *Areopagitica*. This tract seems to me the supreme vindication of humanist morality, and one of the greatest monuments of the English Revolution. No other revolution has been able to draw such dignity and beauty from the tensions and terrors of conflict. It is an amusing sidelight on the perversity of human drama that Milton was moved to pour forth his greatest rhetoric on the greatest of humanist themes because of the action of the Presbyterians in censoring his pamphlets on the less than exalted theme of divorce (". . . he did set on foot and maintained very odd and novel positions concerning divorce." His biographer, Anthony Wood, agreed). Here, then, is the voice of Milton, idealist of a republic of virtue and quality, admirer of Cromwell, servant of the Commonwealth, ultimately the disillusioned but intransigent blind poet in search of a new inward vision. But in this moment he is the poet of revolution before the illusions faded—his voice has the strength and beauty of the best in his time:

AREOPAGITICA;

"This is true liberty, when free-born men,
Having to advise the public, may speak free,

Which he who can, and will, deserves high praise;
Who neither can, nor will, may hold his peace:
What can be juster in a state than this?"

—Euripid. Hicetid.

I deny not, but that it is of greatest concernment in the Church and Commonwealth, to have a vigilant eye how Bookes demeane themselves as well as men; and thereafter to confine, imprison, and do sharpest justice on them as malefactors: For Books are not absolutely dead things, but doe contain a potencie of life in them to be as active as that soule was whose progeny they are; nay they do preserve as in a violl the purest efficacie and extraction of that living intellect that bred them. I know they are as lively, and as vigorously productive, as those fabulous Dragons teeth; and being sown up and down, may chance to spring up armed men. And yet on the other hand unlesse warinesse be us'd, as good almost kill a Man as kill a good Book; who kills a Man kills a reasonable creature, Gods Image; but hee who destroyes a good Booke, kills reason it selfe, kills the Image of God, as it were in the eye. Many a man lives a burden to the Earth; but a good Booke is the pretious life-blood of a master spirit, imbalm'd and treasur'd up on purpose to a life beyond life. 'Tis true, no age can restore a life, whereof perhaps there is no great losse; and revolutions of ages doe not oft recover the losse of a rejected truth, for the want of which whole Nations fare the worse. . . .

I conceive therefore, that when God did enlarge the universall diet of mans body, saving ever the rules of temperance, he then also, as before, left arbitrary the dyeting and repasting of our minds; as wherein every mature man might have to exercise his owne leading capacity. How great a vertue is temperance, how much of moment through the whole life of man? yet God committs the managing so great a trust, without particular Law or prescription, wholly to the demeanour of every grown man. And therefore when he himself tabl'd the Jews from heaven, that Omer which was every mans daily portion of Manna, is computed to have bin more then might have well suffic'd the heartiest feeder thrice as many meals. For those actions which enter into a man, rather then issue out of him, and therefore defile not, God uses not to captivat under a perpetuall childhood of prescription, but trusts him with the gift of reason to be his own chooser; there were but little work left for preaching, if law and compulsion should grow so fast upon those things which hertofore were govern'd only by exhortation. *Salomon* informs us that much reading is a wearines to the flesh; but neither he, nor other inspir'd author tells us that such, or such reading is unlawfull: yet certainly had God thought good to limit us herein, it had bin much more expedient to have told us what was unlawfull, then what was wearisome. . . .

As therefore the state of man now is; what wisdome can there be to choose, what continence to forbeare without the knowledge of evill? He that can apprehend and consider vice with all her baits and seeming pleasures, and yet abstain, and yet distinguish, and yet prefer that which is truly better, he is the true warfaring Christian. I cannot praise a fugitive and cloister'd vertue, unexercis'd and unbreath'd, that never sallies out

and sees her adversary, but slinks out of the race, where that immortall garland is to be run for, not without dust and heat. Assuredly we bring not innocence into the world, we bring impurity much rather: that which purifies us is triall, and triall is by what is contrary. That vertue therefore which is but a youngling in the contemplation of evill, and knows not the utmost that vice promises to her followers, and rejects it, is but a blank vertue, not a pure; her whitenesse is but an excrementall whitenesse; Which was the reason why our sage and serious Poet *Spencer,* whom I dare be known to think a better teacher then *Scotus* or *Aquinas,* describing true temperance under the person of *Guion,* brings him in with his palmer through the cave of Mammon, and the bowr of earthly blisse that he might see and know, and yet abstain. Since therefore the knowledge and survay of vice is in this world so necessary to the constituting of human vertue, and the scanning of error to the confirmation of truth, how can we more safely, and with lesse danger scout into the regions of sin and falsity then by reading all manner of tractats, and hearing all manner of reason? . . .

Let us therefore be more considerat builders, more wise in spirituall architecture, when great reformation is expected. For now the time seems come, wherein *Moses* the great Prophet may sit in heav'n rejoycing to see that memorable and glorious wish of his fulfill'd, when not only our sev'nty Elders, but all the Lords people are become Prophets. No marvell then though some men, and some good men too perhaps, but young in goodnesse, as *Joshua* then was, envy them. They fret, and out of their own weaknes are in agony, lest those divisions and subdivisions will undoe us. The adversarie again applauds, and waits the hour, when they have brancht themselves out, saith he, small anough into parties and partitions, then will be our time. Fool! he sees not the firm root, out of which we all grow, though into branches: nor will beware untill hee see our small divided maniples cutting through at every angle of his ill united and unweildy brigade. And that we are to hope better of all these supposed sects and schisms, and that we shall not need that solicitude honest perhaps though over timorous of them that vex in his behalf, but shall laugh in the end, at those malicious applauders of our differences, I have these reasons to perswade me.

First, when a City shall be as it were besieg'd and blockt about, her navigable river infested, inrodes and incursions round, defiance and battell oft rumor'd to be marching up ev'n to her walls, and suburb trenches, that then the people, or the greater part, more then at other times, wholly tak'n up with the study of highest and most important matters to be reform'd, should be disputing, reasoning, reading, inventing, discoursing, ev'n to a rarity, and admiration, things not before discourst or writt'n of, argues first a singular good will, contentednesse and confidence in your prudent foresight, and safe government, Lords and Commons; and from thence derives it self to a gallant bravery and well grounded contempt of their enemies, as if there were no small number of as great spirits among us, as his was, who when Rome was nigh besieg'd by *Hanibal,* being in the City, bought that peece of ground at no cheap rate, whereon *Hanibal* himself encampt his own regiment. Next it is a lively and cherfull presage of our

happy successe and victory. For as In a body, when the blood is fresh, the spirits pure and vigorous, not only to vital, but to rationall faculties, and those in the acutest, and the pertest operations of wit and suttlety, it argues in what good plight and constitution the body is, so when the cheerfulnesse of the people is so sprightly up, as that it has, not only wherewith to guard well its own freedom and safety, but to spare, and to bestow upon the solidest and sublimest points of controversie, and new invention, it betok'n us not degenerated, nor drooping to a fatall decay, but casting off the old and wrincl'd skin of corruption to outlive these pangs and wax young again, entring the glorious waies of Truth and prosperous vertue destin'd to become great and honourable in these latter ages. Methinks I see in my mind a noble and puissant Nation rousing herself like a strong man after sleep, and shaking her invincible locks: Methinks I see her as an Eagle muing her mighty youth, and kindling her undazl'd eyes at the full midday beam; purging and unscaling her long abused sight at the fountain it self of heav'nly radiance, while the whole noise of timorous and flocking birds, with those also that love the twilight, flutter about, amaz'd at what she means, and in their envious gabble would prognosticat a year of sects and schisms.

What should ye doe then, should ye suppresse all this flowry crop of knowledge and new light sprung up and yet springing daily in this City, should ye set an *Oligarchy* of twenty ingrossers over it, to bring a famin upon our minds again, when we shall know nothing but what is measur'd to us by their bushel? Beleeve it, Lords and Commons, they who counsell ye to such a suppressing, doe as good as bid ye suppresse yourselves; and I will soon shew how. If it be desir'd to know the immediat cause of all this free writing and free speaking, there cannot be assign'd a truer then your own mild, and free, and human government; it is the liberty, Lords and Commons, which your own valorous and happy counsels have purchast us, liberty which is the nurse of all great wits; this is that which hath rarify'd and enlightn'd our spirits like the influence of heav'n; this is that which hath enfranchis'd, enlarg'd and lifted up our apprehensions degrees above themselves. Ye cannot make us now lesse capable, lesse knowing, lesse eagarly pursuing of the truth, unlesse ye first make your selves, that made us so, lesse the lovers, lesse the founders of our true liberty. We can grow ignorant again, brutish, formall, and slavish, as ye found us; but you then must first become that which ye cannot be, oppressive, arbitrary, and tyrannous, as they were from whom ye have free'd us. That our hearts are now more capacious, our thoughts more erected to the search and expectation of greatest and exactest things, is the issue of your owne vertu propagated in us; ye cannot suppresse that unlesse ye reinforce an abrogated and mercilesse law, that fathers may dispatch at will their own children. And who shall then sticke closest to ye, and excite others? not he who takes up armes for cote and conduct, and his four nobles of Danegelt. Although I dispraise not the defence of just immunities, yet love my peace better, if that were all. Give me the liberty to know, to utter, and to argue freely according to conscience, above all liberties. . . .

And now the time in speciall is, by priviledge to write and speak what

may help to the further discussing of matters in agitation. The Temple of *Janus* with his two *controversal* faces might now not unsignificantly be set open. And though all the windes of doctrin were let loose to play upon the earth, so Truth be in the field we do injuriously by licencing and prohibiting to misdoubt her strength. Let her and Falshood grapple; who ever knew Truth put to the wors, in a free and open encounter. Her confuting is the best and surest suppressing. He who hears what praying there is for light and clearer knowledge to be sent down among us, would think of other matters to be constituted beyond the discipline of *Geneva*, fram'd and fabric't already to our hands. Yet when the new light which we beg for shines in upon us, there be who envy, and oppose, if it come not first in at their casements. What a collusion is this, whenas we are exhorted by the wise man to use diligence, *to seek for wisdom as for hidd'n treasures* early and late, that another order shall enjoyn us to know nothing but by statute. When a man hath bin labouring the hardest labour in the deep mines of knowledge, hath furnisht out his findings in all their equipage, drawn forth his reasons as it were a battell raung'd, scatter'd and defeated all objections in his way, calls out his adversary into the plain, offers him the advantage of wind and sun, if he please; only that he may try the matter by dint of argument, for his opponents then to sculk, to lay ambushments, to keep a narrow bridge of licencing where the challenger should passe, though it be valour anough in shouldiership, is but weaknes and cowardise in the wars of Truth. For who knows not that Truth is strong next to the Almighty; she needs no policies, no strategems, no licencings to make her victorious, those are the shifts and the defences that error uses against her power: give her but room, and do not bind her when she sleeps, for then she speaks not true, as the old *Proteus* did, who spake oracles only when he was caught and bound, but then rather she turns herself into all shapes, except her own, and perhaps tunes her voice according to the time, as *Micaiah* did before Ahab, untill she be adjur'd into her own likenes. Yet is it not impossible that she may have more shapes then one. What else is all that rank of things indifferent, wherein Truth may be on this side, or on the other, without being unlike her self. What but a vain shadow else is the abolition of *those ordinances, that hand writing nayl'd to the crosse,* what great purchase is this Christian liberty which *Paul* so often boasts of. His doctrine is, that he who eats or eats not, regards a day, or regards it not, may doe either to the Lord. How many other things might be tolerated in peace, and left to conscience, had we but charity, and were it not the chief strong hold of our hypocrisie to be ever judging one another. I fear yet this iron yoke of outward conformity hath left a slavish print upon our necks; the ghost of a linnen decency yet haunts us.   □

For most people, the triumphs of the English Revolution in the humanism of Hobbes, the Levellers, and Milton, were unreal, and in this important sense the revolution was a failure even in its finest work. But there were other solid accomplishments. The business classes won greater security for their investments and operations through the destruction of the prerogative courts and the establishment of Parliamen-

tary control over taxation. The deprived egos of generations of rising men were nourished by the defeat of the old ruling classes. The bitter and fruitless quarrels over religion abated after the decades of intensity and struggle in the revolution—the pulpit and the Protestant imagination at last were played out, and creative energies were thereby released for other and more interesting enterprises of the mind. The gentry in the counties were happier; no longer worried about losing their control of the country to decadent courtiers or papists, they could become Squire Allworthies and Squire Westerns and consolidate their ties with new money and old families to give England the most durable aristocracy in Europe. The revolution made England a good country for capitalist initiative, and for the informal, experienced, and relaxed controls of the interlocking oligarchies of landed families. Somehow this England has never lost the fire of the miraculous conjunction of Renaissance and Revolution which destroyed the feudal church and state—the embers seem never quite extinguished. And even embers of that fire are a legacy of wonder—and hope. For is it not really a bit silly to speak of the "failure" of men who fought and wrote and committed themselves as the great English revolutionaries did? What more is possible in life than defiance of known evil and the courage to create and fight for new illusions? Cromwell's generation was no failure.

Suggested Reading

Strangely enough, the best general history of the English Revolution may be a book written by a group of Soviet historians whose work remains untranslated fifteen years after its publication. By far the best short account is Christopher Hill, *Century of Revolution, 1603–1714* (Camden, N.J.: Thomas Nelson & Sons, 1961; Norton*). The same author with Edmund Dell edited a fine collection of sources, *The Good Old Cause*, second edition (London: Frank Cass & Co, Ltd, 1969).

For an introduction to the many problems of describing early capitalism, one must consult the *Studies* by Maurice Dobb cited for Chapter 1. See also Dobb and others in a discussion of *The Transition from Feudalism to Capitalism** (*Our History*, Pamphlet No. 29, 1954). The economic destruction of the feudal church is marvelously described by Christopher Hill, *Economic Problems of the Church* (London: Oxford University Press, 1956). An impressive effort to tell the complicated economic story of the barons in this period of revolution is that by Lawrence Stone, *The Crisis of the Aristocracy** (London: Oxford University Press, 1965; severely abridged for the Oxford softbound edition). Farming has found an able historian in Eric Kerridge, *The Agricultural Revolution* (New York: Augustus M. Kelley, 1969). For the social results of all this see E. P. Thompson, "The Peculiarities of the English" in *The Socialist Register* (New York: Monthly Review Press, 1965).

On the relations of Protestantism to the new society and its revolution —an almost insanely controversial subject—perhaps one should begin with M. J. Kitch's edition of *Capitalism and the Reformation** (London: Longmans, Green & Co, Ltd, 1967), and then read the essays (some on

political thought and esthetics) by Christopher Hill, *Puritanism and Revolution** (London: Martin Secker & Warburg, Ltd, 1958; Schocken Paperback*). My own efforts (with Katherine George) to explain the relevance of Protestant thought to revolution can be examined in *The Protestant Mind of the English Reformation* (Princeton: Princeton University Press, 1961).

The political thought of England in her revolutionary days is well documented and described. By far the most important book of analysis is C. B. Macpherson, *The Political Theory of Possessive Individualism: Hobbes to Locke** (London: Oxford University Press, 1962; Oxford Paperback*). An excellent account of the thought of the Revolution is Perez Zagorin, *A History of Political Thought in the English Revolution* (New York: Humanities Press, Inc., 1969). On the Levellers, probably the best single book is H. N. Brailsford, *The Levellers and the English Revolution,* C. Hill, ed. (Stanford: Stanford University Press, 1961). The major writings are published in *Leveller Manifestoes of the Puritan Revolution,* edited by Don M. Wolfe (London: Frank Case & Co, Ltd, 1967). The best introduction to Winstanley is that of George Sabine in his edition of *The Works of Gerrard Winstanley* (New York: Russell & Russell Publishers, 1965). There is a recent paperback edition of *The Leviathan* by Macpherson for Pelican. For Milton see the paperback edition for Viking by Douglas Bush, *Portable Milton:* William Empson's brilliant *Milton's God,* revised edition; (London: Chatto & Windus Ltd, 1965); and Don Wolfe, *John Milton in the Puritan Revolution* (New York: Humanities Press, Inc., 1963).

5 Revolution in France: the Creative Years, 1789–1794

Economic & Social Conditions in Eighteenth-Century France

Europe in the eighteenth century was filled with agitation for change in the structure and functioning of the old orders of society—it was a century of "political science," of endless schemes for new constitutions, statements of the rights of competing groups, all sorts of meetings of consultative and planning bodies. The victories of seventeenth-century science and rationalism were acknowledged by the ruling classes as well as by the general reading public. Above all, this new climate of opinion meant that society was something to plan and argue about—there was a "right" way, a reasonably superior way, to run things. The authority of the state was being questioned as it had not been since the Catholic Church put the seal of God on the varieties of rulership which imposed public order on the feudal lords. All Europe seemed unable to resist the kind of arguments which had grown out of the revolutionary experience in England. Absolutism was still the characteristic form and spirit of governing, and in size and technique the absolutist state made progress everywhere on the continent; but absolutism was conceived neither in the old terms of a religious fiat nor in the later terms of nationalist sovereignty. Kings and princes increasingly looked on themselves as servants of the "state" and its power groups; theories about the nature of sovereignty and the science of governing tended to make the exercise of authority a problem.

This continuing revolution in the consciousness of elites and of masses was no isolated psychological phenomenon. The commercial and industrial dynamism of England, Holland and France pushed men and events to postures and conclusions that made any economic or social status quo in Europe, or, indeed, the world, a thing of the moment. Economic change affects the whole man—and the whole of society. Europe entered the age of the machine and factory production of goods for mass consumption in the eighteenth century. The consequent impact on the lives and tempers of Europeans was quantitatively and qualitatively gross. The new resources for wealth-getting, the manipulative excitement of the accumulating technology, the organizational opportunities for ego gratification—all such attributes of the

industrial age reinforced the thrust of the previous era of intellectual and emotional daring and political adventuring. In the realms of the spirit, the eighteenth century is very largely a further working out of the novelties of the seventeenth century; but the economics of the 1700's (as of all subsequent time) very radically and rapidly altered the sociology and therefore the qualities of European culture. Science, political theories, literature, education, were all profoundly a function of the devastating milieux of capitalist enterprises. Threatening the fate of the new imagination—scarcely granting it time for self-consciousness—were the forces grinding powerfully to produce the ugliness and insecurities that came to dominate European civilization in the nineteenth century. Never in history has an economic system so tragically betrayed the culture of a creative society as capitalism has done the arts and letters of Europe. The greatness of mind that would survive the triumphs of capitalism is a tribute to the vigor and genius of the Renaissance—to the revolutionary impulse of humanism—which has fought a brilliantly futile battle for humanistic ideals against the persuasive and inexorable cannibalism of the economics of acquisition. But this is a digression which we cannot afford to follow in argument and illustration—the major fact about capitalism as a background force in preparing revolution in France was its accelerating dynamism. The old regime was incapable (for very respectable reasons) of dealing with the financial problems newly hatched by the conjunction of capitalism and imperialism. Success in terms of "statism" in the modern world of the eighteenth century required taxing powers that could be expanded to meet the rising costs of rule and to take advantage of the new wealth. Furthermore, power politics was increasingly a game played best by men wise in the way of economics. The French monarchy was lacking the personnel and stratagems to operate a modern capitalist state.

The first great revolution of the eighteenth century took place outside Europe—in the colonial possessions of England on the North American continent. The American Revolution is an interesting one—the first revolution precipitated by the economic and social configurations and resulting tensions in the expanding capitalism of Europe. It was also a patriotic and popular revolt on behalf of principles inherited from the radicals of the English seventeenth century. But it is not an integral part of our story. The French monarchy gave crucially important help to the American revolutionaries in order to embarrass their English rivals —and ended with a budgetary crisis which in turn led to the political crisis that triggered revolution in France. And in France as elsewhere in Europe the brilliant successes of the American revolutionaries created a legend of the popular revolution unlike any of the earlier myths of the irrational horrors of revolution—a kind of massive reinforcement of the image of the "Glorious Revolution" in England. The rationality of the American Revolution (which included its emotional congruity with the temper of the *philosophes* and gentlemen of good will) drew into the international party of radical ideologues even nobles of the French court like the Marquis de Lafayette, or conservative gentry like Edmund Burke in England. The American experience had about it just enough

blood, abuse, corruption, and the smell of the masses to titillate the imaginations of the more sensitive Europeans; it was a revolution that seemed both ideal and real. The rhetoric of the English radicals was there in the Declaration of Independence and the Bill of Rights, and the Constitution drafted at Philadelphia stood as a proud monument to the defeat of the wrong sort of radicalism—that of the propertyless.

It is of course immensely difficult to describe the sociology of the opposition that was moving in the direction of revolution in France. Certainly contemporaries did not understand it. The agitators were not given to social analysis, but to universalistic interpretation (based on Newtonian geometric and dynamic assumptions) and schemes for improvement which depended upon the altruistic enlightenment of rulers rather than upon the illusions of self-interest among the varieties of power groups that made up the nation. Until the elections to the Estates-General were held, and the bills of grievance were drawn, the social character of disaffection in France is remarkably unclear—especially from the testimony of the intellectuals. Therefore the genesis of revolution is unclear. We know that rural France, the France of villages and farms, the France of a centuries-old tradition of blind revolt, was in the eighteenth century a chaos of conflicting interests and status. On the whole, for most sections of the country, the peasants were well off by the standards of other European states. But they were very heavily taxed in a staggeringly complex and vexing pattern of Crown, Church, and feudal dues. Furthermore, there is evidence of an increasingly bitter perception among the peasants (though they were themselves endlessly divided in wealth and legal status) of the *concept* of traditional privilege—the peasant was developing an ego in the social sense, and with it a sense of rational and articulate right to shape the deeper sense of irrational anger.

The French middle classes are more baffling to identify in accurate analytical terms than are the peasants. Perhaps four millions of France's twenty-six millions in 1789 lived in towns, and at least twenty of these towns (with populations over 30,000) were growing rapidly and changing dramatically in social composition as trade and industry and government boomed and the nobility of church and state moved into the great cities from the country. Most of the townsmen were clearly not "middle class" by any conceivable definition—journeymen in the trades, apprentices, laborers from the landless peasantry of the surrounding countryside, artisans, masses of domestic servants, and the permanent aggregations of the unemployed and poor. The bourgeoisie controlled the urban communities (and often large areas of hinterland in mining and factory districts) but were by no means a homogeneous class. The majority were small entrepreneurs and guildsmen of conservative inclinations. A minority were extremely wealthy, powerful and socially mobile: the brilliant careerists known as financiers, the tax farmers and other office holders with connections at Court, lawyers, and, of course, the older elite of merchants and industrialists. These upper reaches of the bourgeoisie could buy *lettres de noblesse* or sometimes marry into nobility, and a large amount of capital was invested in

this way. But the politically significant development of the century was the sensitivity of the middle class to the political ineptitude of the monarchy and the arrogance of the privileged orders—a sensitivity given voice by the lawyers and intellectuals who have been the creators of bourgeois consciousness. In the crisis of 1789 the petty social ambitions and manipulations of the town oligarchs were transformed into the myth of the great historic definition of the "Third Estate."

The clergy and nobility in the Old Regime are much easier to give an account of—they are fewer in number, predominant in the sources, and legally and socially better defined. The First Estate, which theoretically included the whole of the clergy, was misleading fiction. Clerical orders were "first" only in the traditional sense of a Catholic society; in terms of modern analysis the clergy were institutionally and functionally a branch of the aristocratic state. The hierarchy of the Church was dominated by noble families whose younger sons were given the lucrative and powerful offices. The mass of parish clergy, on the other hand, were peasants who had almost no voice in the policy affairs of the Church—who, indeed, were mostly salaried *vicaires* under the thumb of an absentee tithe-holder. The monasteries were in a characteristic decline in the eighteenth century after the vigorous reforms of the previous century. Intellectually, the Church was generally in bad shape; the French nobility showed their unfitness to rule first and most dramatically in the Church. Bishops and abbots treated their posts as sinecures (note the very derivation of the word, "without a care of souls") and were utterly incapable of defending the Church against the charges of parasitism and corruption with which the press of the *philosophes* pilloried them. For the most part, the challenges of the culture of the Enlightenment (science, rationalism, individualism, secularism, humanitarianism, libertarianism) which were undermining the entire spiritual foundation of the Old Regime, met with not even fanatical stubbornness—the Church simply withered away in acquiescence or boredom. The proud and zealous prelates confined their aggression to Jansenists and Protestants or to rivals in the hierarchy, while the intellectual lower clergy became leaders of free-thinking humanism and in 1789 a fount of revolutionary ideology. For the privilege of this powerful and enormously wealthy order of the clergy was quite entirely structured to exclude both the poor and the merely talented.

The Second Order of the estates of the realm was the one which held the real monopoly of privilege by secure legal and social right. The French nobility were the largest and wealthiest and most powerful class in the European world of the 1700's. Within the class there were of course many divisions and much hostility. The rise of the elaborate and absorbing mechanisms of the modern absolutist state was a particularly significant source of dilemma for the nobles. The Age of Louis XIV had turned most of even the great families into courtiers—Versailles had become at once the center of the State and the social center of aristocracy. The result was that the operation of the State and its policy decisions were intimately related to the social intrigues of aristocratic families. Further complicating the relations of monarchy and nobility

were the varieties of corporate bodies with which feudal society abounded but which were especially an obstruction to rational government when vigorously used by the educated and sophisticated *noblesse de robe* (the service nobility who had once been much looked down upon by the blood nobility of the sword but who in the 1700's became the articulate leaders of the "aristocracy" of France). Above all, the defense of aristocratic privilege in the eighteenth century came to find its political center in the Parlements, or regional courts, which used their right of remonstrance against edicts of the government to make a public case of the rights of nobility against the usurpations of absolutist "tyranny." It is a remarkable fact that the most continuous and open and virulent attacks upon the Crown came from the noble judges of the "sovereign courts" of the regions—with the Parlement of Paris assuming the lead. In defending their privileges in the new age of the press and with the new arguments of the *philosophes*, they dramatized the arbitrary character of the government at Versailles and greatly weakened the effectiveness of the royal ministries to deal with crises. The nobility brought on the revolution of 1789, as we shall see, but even before the events of the 1780's, they had created a basis for public criticism of the government which was fatal to the success of an absolutist state.

One of the useful contemporary observers of the French social and economic scene before the Revolution was the English agricultural expert, Arthur Young, whose comments on his travels during the years 1787 and 1788 provide some interesting insights:

[Paris, Oct. 17, 1787] Dined to-day with a party, whose conversation was entirely political. Mons. de Calonne's *Requéte au Roi* is come over, and all the world are reading and disputing on it. It seems, however, generally agreed that, without exonerating himself from the charge of the agiotage, he has thrown no inconsiderable load on the shoulders of the archbishop of Toulouze, the present premier, who will be puzzled to get rid of the attack. But both these ministers were condemned on all hands in the lump; as being absolutely unequal to the difficulties of so arduous a period. One opinion pervaded the whole company, that they are on the eve of some great revolution in the government: that every thing points to it: the confusion in the finances great; with a *deficit* impossible to provide for without the states-general of the kingdom, yet no ideas formed of what would be the consequence of their meeting: no minister existing, or to be looked to in or out of power, with such decisive talents as to promise any other remedy than palliative ones: a prince on the throne, with excellent dispositions, but without the resources of a mind that could govern in such a moment without ministers: a court buried in pleasure and dissipation; and adding to the distress, instead of endeavouring to be placed in a more independent situation: a great ferment amongst all ranks of men, who are eager for some change, without knowing what to look to, or to hope for: and a strong leaven of liberty, increasing every hour since the American revolution; altogether form a combination of circumstances that promise ere long to ferment into motion, if some master hand, of very

superior talents, and inflexible courage, be not found at the helm to guide events, instead of being driven by them. It is very remarkable, that such conversation never occurs, but a bankruptcy is a topic: the curious question on which is, *would a bankruptcy occasion a civil war, and a total overthrow of the government?* The answers that I have received to this question appear to be just: such a measure, conducted by a man of abilities, vigour, and firmness, would certainly not occasion either one or the other. But the same measure, attempted by a man of a different character, might possibly do both. All agree, that the states of the kingdom cannot assemble without more liberty being the consequence; but I meet with so few men who have any just ideas of freedom, that I question much the species of this new liberty that is to arise. They know not how to value the privileges of THE PEOPLE: as to the nobility and the clergy, if a revolution added any thing to their scale, I think it would do more mischief than good.

September 1st, 1788. To Combourg, the country has a savage aspect; husbandry not much further advanced, at least in skill, than among the Hurons, which appears incredible amidst inclosures; the people almost as wild as their country, and their town of Combourg one of the most brutal filthy places that can be seen; mud houses, no windows, and a pavement so broken, as to impede all passengers, but ease none—yet here is a chateau, and inhabited; who is this Mons. de Chateaubriant, the owner, that has nerves strung for a residence amidst such filth and poverty? Below this hideous heap of wretchedness is a fine lake, surrounded by well wooded inclosures. Coming out of Hedé, there is a beautiful lake belonging to Mons. de Blassac, intendant of Poictiers, with a fine accompanyment of wood. A very little cleaning would make here a delicious scenery. There is a chateau, with four rows of trees, and nothing else to be seen from the windows in the true French style. Forbid it, taste, that this should be the house of the owner of that beautiful water; and yet this Mons. de Blassac has made at Poictiers the finest promenade in France! But that taste which draws a strait line, and that which traces a waving one, are founded on feelings and ideas as separate and distinct as painting and music—as poetry or sculpture. The lake abounds with fish, pike to 36lb. carp to 24lb. perch 14lb. and tench 5lb. To Rennes the same strange wild mixture of desert and cultivation, half savage, half human.— 31 miles.

The 2d. Rennes is well built, and has two good squares; that particularly of Louis XV. where is his statue. The parliament being in exile, the house is not to be seen. The Benedictines garden, called the *Tabour,* is worth viewing. But the object at Rennes most remarkable at present is a camp, with a marshal of France (de Stainville,) and four regiments of infantry, and two of dragoons, close to the gates. The discontents of the people have been doubled, first on account of the high price of bread, and secondly for the banishment of the parliament. The former cause is natural enough; but why the people should love their parliament was what I could not understand, since the members, as well as of the states, are all noble, and the distinction between the *noblesse* and *roturiers* no where stronger, more offensive, or more abominable than in Bretagne. They

assured me, however, that the populace have been blown up to violence by every art of deception, and even by money distributed for that purpose. The commotions rose to such a height before the camp was established, that the troops here were utterly unable to keep the peace. Mons. Argentaise, to whom I had brought letters, had the goodness, during the four days I was here, to shew and explain every thing to be seen. I find Rennes very cheap; and it appears the more so to me just come from Normandy, where every thing is extravagantly dear. The *table d'hôte,* at the *grand maison,* is well served; they give two courses, containing plenty of good things, and a very ample regular dessert: the supper one good course, with a large joint of mutton, and another good dessert; each meal, with the common wine, 40s. and for 20 more you have very good wine, instead of the ordinary sort; 30s. for the horse: thus, with good wine, it is no more than 6 liv. 10s. a day, or 5s. 1od. Yet a camp of which they complain has raised prices enormously.

The 5th. To Montauban. The poor people seem poor indeed; the children terribly ragged, if possible worse clad than if with no cloaths at all; as to shoes and stockings they are luxuries. A beautiful girl of six or seven years playing with a stick, and smiling under such a bundle of rags as made my heart ache to see her: they did not beg, and when I gave them any thing, seemed more surprized than obliged. One third of what I have seen of this province seems uncultivated, and nearly all of it in misery. What have kings, and ministers, and parliaments, and states, to answer for, seeing millions of hands that would be industrious, yet idle and starving, through the execrable maxims of despotism, or the equally detestable prejudices of a feudal nobility? Sleep at the *lion d'or,* at Montauban, an abominable hole.—20 miles.

The 6th. The same inclosed country to Brooms; but near that town improves to the eye, from being more hilly. At the little town of Lamballe, there are above fifty families of noblesse that live in winter, who reside on their estates in the summer. There is probably as much foppery and nonsense in their circles, and for what I know as much happiness, as in those of Paris. Both would be better employed in cultivating their lands, and rendering the poor industrious.—30 miles.

[Nantes, September 21, 1788] Come to an improvement in the midst of these deserts, four good houses of stone and slate, and a few acres run to wretched grass, which have been tilled, but all savage, and become almost as rough as the rest. I was afterwards informed that this improvement, as it is called, was wrought by Englishmen, at the expence of a gentleman they ruined as well as themselves.—I demanded how it had been done? Pare and burn, and sow wheat, then rye, and then oats. Thus it is for ever and ever! the same follies, the same blundering, the same ignorance; and then all the fools in the country said, as they do now, that these wastes are good for nothing. To my amazement find the incredible circumstance, that they reach within three miles of the great commercial city of Nantes! This is a problem and a lesson to work at, but not at present. Arrive—go to the theatre, new built of fine white stone, having a magnificent portico of eight elegant Corinthian pillars in front, and four others, to separate the portico from a grand vestibule. Within all is gold

and painting, and a *coup d'oeil* at entering, that struck me forcibly. It is, I believe, twice as large as Drury-Lane, and five times as magnificent. It was Sunday, and therefore full. *Mon Dieu!* cried I to myself, do all the wastes, the deserts, the heath, ling, furz, broom, and bog, that I have passed for 300 miles, lead to this spectacle? What a miracle, that all this splendour and wealth of the cities in France should be so unconnected with the country! There are no gentle transitions from ease to comfort, from comfort to wealth: you pass at once from beggary to profusion,—from misery in mud cabins to Mademoiselle St. Huberti in splendid spectacles at 500 liv. a night (21l. 17s. 6d.). The country deserted, or if a gentleman in it, you find him in some wretched hole, to save that money which is lavished with profusion in the luxuries of a capital.—20 miles.

The 22d. Deliver my letters. As much as agriculture is the chief object of my journey, it is necessary to acquire such intelligence of the state of commerce, as can be best done from merchants, for abundance of useful information is to be gained, without putting any questions that a man would be cautious of answering, and even without putting any questions at all. Mons. Riédy was very polite, and satisfied many of my enquiries; I dined once with him, and was pleased to find the conversation take an important turn on the relative situations of France and England in trade, particularly in the West-Indies. I had a letter also to Mons. Epivent, *consilier* in the parliament of Rennes, whose brother, Mons. Epivent de la Villesboisnet, is a very considerable merchant here. It was not possible for any person to be more obliging than these two gentlemen; their attentions to me were marked and friendly, and rendered a few days residence here equally instructive and agreeable. The town has that sign of prosperity of new buildings, which never deceives. The quarter of the *comedie* is magnificent, all the streets at right angles and of white stone. I am in doubt whether the *hotel de Henri IV.* is not the finest inn in Europe: Dessein's at Calais is larger, but neither built, fitted up, nor furnished like this, which is new. It cost 400,000 liv. (17,500l. furnished,) and is let at 14,000 liv. per ann. (612l. 10s.) with no rent for the first year. It contains 60 beds for masters, and 25 stalls for horses. Some of the apartments of two rooms, very neat, are 6 liv. a day; one good 3 liv. but for merchants 5 liv. per diem for dinner, supper, wine, and chamber, and 35s. for his horse. It is, without comparison, the first inn I have seen in France, and very cheap. It is in a small square close to the theatre, as convenient for pleasure or trade as the votaries of either can wish. The theatre cost 450,000 liv. and lets to the comedians at 17,000 liv. a year; it holds, when full, to the value of 120 *louis d'or.* The land the inn stands on was bought at 9 liv. a foot: in some parts of the city it sells as high as 15 liv. This value of the ground induces them to build so high as to be destructive of beauty. The quay has nothing remarkable; the river is choaked with islands, but at the furthest part next to the sea is a large range of houses regularly fronted. . . . □

As important as the crisis in economic affairs in the old order, was the psychological crisis. A thousand times in history the material factors disposed to revolution; very seldom has a revolutionary psychology developed to realize in action the possibilities latent in the social contin-

gency. Great revolutionary upheavals usually are the work not only of vast complexes of social disorientation, but also of the anger and imagination of powerful, alienated personalities. Luther is the perfect illustration of the indispensable revolutionary personality. In the eighteenth century there were a hundred important radical intellectuals—look at the articles in the magnificent *Encyclopédie* for the corrosive brilliance of these aggressively disaffected citizens of aristocratic France. And we shall see in the *cahiers de doléance* which poured out of the elections of the Estates-General a massive indication of the articulate grievances of lesser minds almost equally radical in feeling. But to comprehend the depth and magnitude and staying power of the revolutionary temper of France it is necessary to know the work of Jean Jacques Rousseau. Everyone should try to understand the inner dynamics of this most revealing and seminal personality of modern times. The restless, engaged alienation of this man can most intimately be discovered in his *Confessions,* but perhaps within the limits of this book it will be best to read the more general and abstract thought of the "father of the Revolution"—selections from his writings on political theory in 1762. First, I would encourage the reader to surrender to the rhetoric and peculiar logic of a few characteristic passages from *The Social Contract,* and then to reinforce what is learned there by consulting the actual constitution that Rousseau devised for Corsica:

BOOK 1

It is my purpose to inquire whether it is possible for there to be any legitimate and certain rule of administration in civil society, taking men as they are and laws as they may be. In this inquiry I shall endeavour at all times to ally the obligations of law and right with the requirements of interest, in order that justice and utility may never be disjoined.

I shall enter upon my subject without demonstrating its importance. It may be asked whether I am a prince or legislator to be writing on politics. I answer that I am not, and that that is the very reason why I am writing on them. If I were a prince or legislator, I should not waste my time saying what ought to be done; I should do it, or be silent.

Since I am by birth the citizen of a free state, and a member of the sovereign, my right to vote in that state, no matter how little influence my voice may have in public affairs, is enough to make it my duty to study them. And whenever I reflect on governments, how happy I am to find that my investigations always give me new reasons for loving that of my own country!

Chapter I
The subject of the first book

Man is born free, and everywhere he is in chains. One thinks himself master of others, but is himself the greater slave. How did this change take place? I do not know. What can render it legitimate? I believe I can answer this question.

If I were to consider nothing but force and its effects, I should say: 'As long as a people is compelled to obey, and does so, it does well; as soon as it can shake off the yoke, and does so, it does even better; for in recovering its liberty on the same grounds on which it was stolen away, it either is right in resuming it, or was wrongly deprived in the first place.' But the social order is a sacred right which serves as the basis for all others. And yet this right does not come from nature; thus it is founded on conventions. The problem is to know what these conventions are. Before considering this question, I must prove the points I have just been making.

Chapter II
The first societies

The most ancient of all societies, and the only natural one, is that of the family. But children remain bound to their father only so long as they need him for their own self-preservation. The moment this need ceases, the natural bond is dissolved. The children are exempted from the obedience they owed their father, the father from the cares he owed his children, and all alike return to a state of independence. If they continue together, their connexion is no longer natural, but voluntary; and the family itself is maintained by convention only.

This common liberty is a consequence of the nature of man. Self-preservation is the first law of human nature, our first cares are those we owe ourselves; and as soon as a man has reached the age of reason, he becomes the sole judge of the means appropriate to his own self-preservation, and thus his own master.

The family may be taken, therefore, as the prototype of political societies; the ruler represents the father, the people the children; and since all are free and equal by birth, they will not alienate their liberty except in their own interest. The only difference is that, in the family, the love the father bears his children repays him for the care he gives them; while, in the state, the pleasure of ruling takes the place of the love that the ruler does not have for his peoples.

Grotius denies that all human power is established for the benefit of the governed, and cites slavery as an example. His regular method of reasoning is to keep arguing from fact to right. A more logical method might be used, but none more favourable to tyrants.

According to Grotius, therefore, it is doubtful whether the human race belongs to a hundred-odd men, or those men to the human race; all through his book he seems to incline to the former opinion. This is also the sentiment of Hobbes. And so we see the human species divided into herds of cattle, each with its own ruler, who watches over it in order to devour it.

As the nature of the shepherd is superior to that of his flock, so also is the nature of the rulers or shepherds of men superior to that of their peoples. Such was the reasoning, according to Philo, of the Emperor Caligula, who from this analogy concluded, logically enough, that kings were gods, or else that their peoples were beasts.

Caligula's reasoning comes to the same thing as that of Hobbes and

Grotius. Aristotle, before them all, had also said that men are not naturally equal, but that some are born for slavery, and others for dominion.

Aristotle was right, but he mistook the effect for the cause. Nothing is more certain than that every man born in slavery is born for slavery. Slaves in their chains lose everything, even the desire to leave them; they love their servitude as the companions of Ulysses loved their brutishness. If there are slaves by nature, therefore, it is because there have been slaves against nature. Force made the first slaves, and their cowardice has perpetuated them.

I have said nothing of King Adam or of the Emperor Noah, father of three great monarchs, who, like the children of Saturn, with whom some have tried to identify them, divided the universe between them. I hope that my moderation will be properly appreciated; for as the direct descendant of one of these princes, and perhaps in the senior line, how do I know that, if titles were verified, I would not find myself the legitimate king of the human race? Be that as it may, there can be no doubt that Adam was sovereign of the world, just as Robinson Crusoe was sovereign of his island, so long as he was its sole inhabitant; and the great advantage of this empire was that the monarch, secure on his throne, had neither rebellions, nor wars, nor conspirators to fear.

Chapter III
The right of the strongest

The strongest is never strong enough to be always the master, unless he transforms his might into right, and obedience into duty. Hence the right of the strongest, a 'right' which looks like an ironical pleasantry, but in fact is a well-established principle. But will no one ever tell us what this word means? Force is a form of physical power; I am at a loss to see how it can produce any moral consequences. To yield to force is an act of necessity, not of will; at the very most it is an act of prudence. In what sense can it be a duty?

Let us for a moment take this alleged right for granted. I say that it leads to nothing but a meaningless farrago of nonsense. For if it is might that makes right, the effect changes with the cause and any might which exceeds the first inherits its right. As soon as you are able to disobey with impunity, you can do so legitimately; and since the strongest is always right, to become the strongest is all that matters. But what kind of a right is it that expires when might ceases? If we must obey by force, we have no need to obey by duty; and if we are no longer forced to obey, we are no longer obliged to do so. Thus we see that the word *right* adds nothing to might; in this context it is absolutely meaningless.

"Obey the powers that be." If this means "Yield to force," the precept is good but superfluous; I warrant that it will never be violated. All power comes from God, I admit, but so does all illness; does that mean we are forbidden to call a doctor? If a brigand surprises me in a dark forest, am I not only forced to give my purse, but also obliged in conscience to let him have it, though able to withhold it? For the pistol in his hand is, after all, a form of power.

Let us agree, then, that might does not make right, and that we are obliged to obey none but legitimate powers. Thus we keep coming back to my original question.

Chapter IV
Slavery

Since no man has natural authority over his fellow men, and since might in no sense makes right, conventions remain as the basis of all legitimate authority among men.

If an individual, says Grotius, can alienate his liberty and enslave himself to a master, why should not a whole people be able to alienate its liberty and subject itself to a king? There are many ambiguous words here that call for explanation; but let us confine our attention to the word *alienate.* To alienate is to give or sell. Now a man who enslaves himself to another does not give himself away; he sells himself, at the very least, for his subsistence. But why does a people sell itself? Far from providing his subjects with their subsistence, a king derives his own wholly from them; and as Rabelais says, a king does not live on a pittance. Do the subjects, then, give their persons on condition that their goods be taken too? I cannot see what they have left to preserve.

You will say that the despot guarantees civil tranquillity to his subjects. So be it; but what does it profit them if the wars his ambition brings upon them, if his insatiable greed, if the oppressions of his ministers, make them more desolate than their own dissensions would have done? What does it profit them, if this very tranquillity is one of their misfortunes? Men also live tranquilly in dungeons; is that enough to make prisoners content? The Greeks pent up in the cave of the Cyclops lived tranquilly, while awaiting their turn to be devoured.

To say that a man gives himself gratuitously is to say something absurd and inconceivable; an act of this sort is illegal and void, for the simple reason that the man who performs it is not in his right mind. To say the same thing of a whole people is to postulate a people of madmen, and madness does not make right.

Even if it were possible for each man to alienate himself, he would not be able to alienate his children; by birth they are men, and free; their liberty belongs to them, and they alone have the right to dispose of it. Before they have reached the age of reason, their father may, in their name, lay down conditions for their preservation and well-being, but he cannot give them irrevocably and unconditionally; for such a gift is contrary to the purposes of nature, and exceeds the rights of paternity. For an arbitrary government to be legitimate, therefore, it would be necessary for the people of each generation to be able to accept or reject it; but then the government would no longer be arbitrary.

To renounce your liberty is to renounce your very quality of manhood; it is to renounce not only the rights, but even the duties of humanity. There can be no possible compensation for anyone who renounces everything. Such a renunciation is incompatible with the nature of man; and to deprive your will of all freedom is to deprive your actions of all morality.

Finally, a convention which stipulates absolute authority on the one hand, and unlimited obedience on the other, is vain and contradictory. Is it not clear that you are under no obligation whatsoever to a person of whom you have the right to demand everything? And does not this unilateral and unequal stipulation in itself render the act null and void? For what claim could my slave have against me, when he himself, and all that belongs to him, is mine? His rights belong to me, and to say that they can be asserted against me is nonsense.

Grotius and the rest use war as yet another basis for the alleged right of slavery. Since the conqueror, according to them, has the right to kill the vanquished, the latter may buy back his life at the cost of his liberty; and this convention is all the more legitimate in that it is advantageous to both parties.

But it is clear that this alleged right to kill the vanquished is in no sense a result of the state of war. Men are not natural enemies, for the simple reason that, while living in their original independence, they have no mutual relations sufficiently stable to constitute either a state of peace or a state of war. It is the relationship between things, not men, that constitutes war; and since the state of war cannot arise from relations purely between persons, but only from relations involving things, private warfare, or the war of man against man, can exist neither in the state of nature, where there is no settled property, nor in the social state, where everything is subject to law.

Individual combats, duels and encounters are insufficient to constitute a state of any kind; and as for the private wars authorised by the Establishments of King Louis IX of France, and suspended by the Peace of God, they were abuses of feudalism, an absurd system if ever there was one, contrary to the principles of natural law and to all good polity.

Thus war is a relationship not between man and man but between state and state, a relationship in which individuals are enemies only incidentally, not as men, or even as citizens, but as soldiers; not as members of their native country, but as its defenders. Finally, the only enemies a state can have are other states, not men; for as between things of diverse nature, no true relationship can be established. . . .

Chapter VI
The social compact

Let us assume that men have reached the point where the obstacles to their self-preservation in the state of nature are too great to be overcome by the forces each individual is capable of exerting to maintain himself in that state. This original state can then no longer continue; and the human race would perish if it did not change its mode of existence.

Now, since men cannot engender new forces, but can only combine and direct those already in existence, their only means of self-preservation is to form by aggregation a sum of forces capable of overcoming all obstacles, to place these forces under common direction, and to make them act in concert.

This sum of forces can only arise from the concurrence of many; but the

force and liberty of each man being the primary instruments of his own self-preservation, how can he pledge them without harming himself and neglecting the cares he owes his own person? This problem, in relation to my subject, may be expressed in the following terms: "To find a form of association which defends and protects the person and property of each member with the whole force of the community, and where each, while joining with all the rest, still obeys no one but himself, and remains as free as before." This is the fundamental problem to which the social contract provides the answer.

The clauses of this contract are so completely determined by the nature of the act that the slightest modification would render them null and void; so that, though they may never have been formally declared, they are everywhere the same, everywhere tacitly admitted and recognised, until the moment when the violation of the social compact causes each individual to recover his original rights, and to resume his natural liberty as he loses the conventional liberty for which he renounced it.

These clauses, rightly understood, can be reduced to the following only: the total alienation of each member, with all his rights, to the community as a whole. For, in the first place, since each gives himself entirely, the condition is equal for all; and since the condition is equal for all, it is in the interest of no one to make it burdensome to the rest.

Furthermore, since the alienation is made without reservations, the union is as perfect as possible, and no member has anything more to ask. For if the individuals retained certain rights, each, in the absence of any common superior capable of judging between him and the public, would be his own judge in certain matters, and would soon claim to be so in all; the state of nature would continue, and the association would necessarily become tyrannical or meaningless.

Finally, each individual, by giving himself to all, gives himself to no one; and since there is no member over whom you do not acquire the same rights that you give him over yourself, you gain the equivalent of all you lose, and greater force to preserve what you have.

If the social compact is stripped to its essentials, therefore, you will find that it can be reduced to the following terms: "Each of us puts in common his person and all his powers under the supreme direction of the general will; and in our corporate capacity we receive each member as an indivisible part of the whole."

In place of the private and particular person of each of the contracting parties, this act of association immediately produces an artificial and collective body, made up of as many members as there are voices in the assembly, and receiving from this same act its unity, its collective personality, its life and its will. The public person thus formed by the union of all the rest was formerly known as a *city,* and is now called a *republic* or *body politic;* when passive it is known to its members as the *state,* when active as the *sovereign,* and as a *power* when it is being compared with its fellows. The members are known collectively as the *people;* and individually they are called, as participants in the sovereign authority, *citizens,* and, as men owing obedience to the laws of the state, *subjects.* But these terms are often confused and mistaken for one another; it is enough to be

able to distinguish between them when they are used with absolute accuracy.   ◻

The *Constitutional Project for Corsica* was written at the request of Corsican revolutionaries of the 1750's. Rousseau wrote while in flight from the problems resulting from the publication of *The Social Contract;* only fragments exist of this effort to construct his ideal constitution. The following passages will give a good idea of the whole:

You ask for a plan of government suitable for Corsica. It is asking for more than you think. There are peoples who, do what you may, are incapable of being well governed, for the law has no hold over them, and a government without laws cannot be a good government. I do not say that the Corsican people is in that condition; on the contrary, no people impresses me as being so fortunately disposed by nature to receive a good administration. But even this is not enough, for all things lead to abuses, which are often inevitable; and the abuse of political institutions follows so closely upon their establishment that it is hardly worthwhile to set them up, only to see them degenerate so rapidly.

Attempts are made to overcome this difficulty by mechanical devices designed to keep the government in its original condition; it is bound with a thousand chains and fetters to prevent it from declining, and is hampered to such an extent that, dragged down by the weight of its irons, it remains inactive and motionless and, if it does not go downhill, neither does it advance toward its goal.

All this is the consequence of an undue separation of two inseparable things, the body which governs and the body which is governed. In the original constitution of government, these two bodies are but one; they become separate only through the abuse of that constitution.

Really shrewd men, in such cases, follow the line of expediency, and shape the government to fit the nation. There is, however, something far better to be done, namely to shape the nation to fit the government. In the first case, to the extent that the government declines while the nation remains unchanged, expediency vanishes. But in the second case, everything changes simultaneously; the nation, carrying the government with it, supports it while it itself remains stable, and causes it to decline when it itself declines. Both remain at all times suited to each other.

The Corsican people are in that fortunate condition which makes possible the establishment of a good constitution; they can begin at the beginning, and take steps to prevent degeneration. Full of health and vigour, they can give themselves a government which will keep them healthy and vigorous. But even now the establishment of such a government will have certain obstacles to overcome. The Corsicans have not yet adopted the vices of other nations, but they have already adopted their prejudices; these prejudices are what will have to be combated and destroyed in order to create good institutions.

The advantageous location of the island of Corsica, and the fortunate natural qualities of its inhabitants, seem to offer them a reasonable hope

of being able to become a flourishing people and to make their mark in Europe if, in the constitution they are thinking of adopting, they turn their sights in that direction. But the extreme exhaustion into which they have been plunged by forty years of uninterrupted warfare, the existing poverty of the island, and the state of depopulation and devastation in which it finds itself, will not allow them immediately to provide for an expensive form of administration, such as would be needed if they were to organise with such an end in view. Furthermore, a thousand insuperable obstacles would stand in the way of the execution of such a plan. Genoa, still mistress of a part of the seacoast and almost all the seaports, would repeatedly crush their rising merchant marine, constantly exposed as it is to the double danger of the Genoese and of the Barbary pirates. The Corsicans would be able to control the seas only with the aid of warships, which would cost them ten times more than they could earn by trade. Exposed on land and sea, forced to defend themselves on all sides, what would become of them? At the mercy of everyone, unable in their weakness to make a single advantageous trade treaty, they would be dictated to by one and all; surrounded by so many risks, they would earn only such profits as others would not deign to take, profits which would always shrink to nothing. And if, by incredible good fortune, they were to overcome all these difficulties, their very prosperity, by attracting the attention of their neighbours, would be a new source of danger to their ill-established freedom. A constant object of covetousness to the great powers and of jealousy to the small, their island would never for a moment cease to be threatened with a new enslavement from which it could never again be extricated.

No matter what object the Corsican nation may have in view in forming a constitution, the first thing it has to do is to give itself, by its own efforts, all the stability of which it is capable. No one who depends on others, and lacks resources of his own, can ever be free. Alliances, treaties, gentlemen's agreements, such things may bind the weak to the strong, but never the strong to the weak.

Leave negotiations, then, to the powers, and depend on yourselves only. Worthy Corsicans, who knows better than you how much can be done alone? Without friends, without support, without money, without armies, enslaved by formidable masters, single-handed you have thrown off the yoke. You have seen them ally against you, one by one, the most redoubtable potentates of Europe, and flood your island with foreign armies; all this you have surmounted. Your fortitude alone has accomplished what money could never have done; if you had sought to preserve your wealth, you would have lost your liberty. Do not draw conclusions about your own nation from the experience of others; rules drawn from your own experience are the best by which to govern yourselves.

It is not so much a question of becoming different as of knowing how to stay as you are. The Corsicans have improved greatly since becoming free; they have added prudence to courage, they have learned to obey their equals, they have acquired virtue and morality, and all this without the use of laws; if they could continue thus, I would see little need to do more. But when the danger that has united them grows distant, the

factions which are now repressed will revive among them; and instead of joining forces for the maintenance of their independence, they will wear out those forces against one another, and will have none left for self-defence if the attack upon them is renewed. That even now is what you must forestall. The divisions of the Corsicans have ever been a trick of their masters to make them weak and dependent; but this trick, incessantly used, has finally resulted in a propensity to dissension, and has made them naturally restless, turbulent and hard to govern, even by their own leaders. Good laws and a new constitution are needed to reestablish that concord the very desire for which has hitherto been destroyed by tyranny. Corsica, when subject to foreign masters whose hard yoke was never patiently borne, was in constant turmoil. Her people must now reconsider its position, and look in freedom for peace.

The following, then, are the principles which ought, in my opinion, to serve as the basis for their laws: to make use of their own people and their own country as far as possible; to cultivate and regroup their own forces; to depend on those forces only; and to pay no more attention to foreign powers than as if they did not exist.

Let us proceed on this basis to establish the fundamental rules of our new constitution.

The island of Corsica, being incapable of growing rich in money, should try to grow rich in men. The power derived from population is more real than that derived from finance, and is more certain in its effects. Since the use of manpower cannot be concealed from view, it always reaches its public objective. It is not thus with the use of money, which flows off and is lost in private destinations; it is collected for one purpose and spent for another; the people pay for protection, and their payments are used to oppress them. That is why a state rich in money is always weak, and a state rich in men is always strong.

To multiply men it is necessary to multiply their means of subsistence; hence agriculture. By this I do not mean the art of theorising on agriculture, of setting up academies to talk about it, or of writing books on the subject. I mean a constitution which will lead a people to spread out over the whole extent of its territory, to settle there, and to cultivate it throughout; this will make it love country life and labour, finding them so replete with the necessaries and pleasures of life that it will have no wish to leave them.

A taste for agriculture promotes population not only by multiplying the means of human subsistence, but also by giving the body of the nation a temperament and a way of life conducive to an increased birth-rate. In all countries, the inhabitants of the countryside have more children than city-dwellers, partly as a result of the simplicity of rural life, which creates healthier bodies, and partly as a result of its severe working-conditions, which prevent disorder and vice. For, other things being equal, those women who are most chaste, and whose senses have been least inflamed by habits of pleasure, produce more children than others; and it is no less certain that men enervated by debauchery, the inevitable fruit of idleness, are less fit for generation than those who have been made more temperate by an industrious way of life.

Peasants are much more attached to their soil than are townsmen to their cities. The equality and simplicity of rural life have, for those acquainted with no other mode of existence, an attraction which leaves them with no desire to change it. Hence that satisfaction with his own way of life which makes a man peaceful; hence that love of country which attaches him to its constitution.

Tilling the soil makes men patient and robust, which is what is needed to make good soldiers. Those recruited from the cities are flabby and mutinous; they cannot bear the fatigues of war; they break down under the strain of marching; they are consumed by illnesses; they fight among themselves and fly before the enemy. Trained militias are the best and most reliable troops; the true education of a soldier is to work on a farm.

Agriculture is the only means of maintaining the external independence of a state. With all the wealth in the world, if you lack food you will be dependent on others; your neighbours can set any value they like on your money, since they can afford to wait. But the bread we need has an indisputable value for us; and in every kind of commerce, it is always the less eager party who dictates to the other. I admit that in a system based on financial power, it would be necessary to operate on different principles; it all depends on the final goal you have in view. Commerce produces wealth, but agriculture ensures freedom.

You may say that it would be better to have both; but they are incompatible, as we shall show presently. In all countries, it will be added, the land is cultivated. True, just as there is more or less trade and commerce in all countries; but that is not to say that agriculture and commerce flourish everywhere. I am not concerned here with the consequences which flow from natural necessities, but with those which result from the nature of the government and general spirit of the nation.

Although the form of government adopted by a people is more often the work of chance and fortune than of its own choice, there are nevertheless certain qualities in the nature and soil of each country which make one government more appropriate to it than another; and each form of government has a particular force which leads people toward a particular occupation.

The form of government we choose must be, on the one hand, the least expensive, since Corsica is poor; and it must be, on the other hand, the most favourable to agriculture, since agriculture is, at the present time, the only occupation which can preserve to the Corsican people the freedom it has won, and give it the firmness it requires.

The least costly administration is that which has the shortest chain of command, and requires the smallest number of official categories. It is in general the republican, and in particular the democratic state.

The administration most favourable to agriculture is the one where power, not being entirely concentrated at any one point, does not carry with it an unequal distribution of population, but leaves people dispersed equally throughout the territory: such is democracy.

Switzerland illustrates these principles in a most striking fashion. Switzerland is, for the most part, a poor and sterile country. Her government is everywhere republican. But in those cantons, like Berne, Solothurn, and

Freiburg, which are more fertile than the rest, the government is aristocratic. In the poorest, where agriculture is less productive and requires more effort, the government is democratic. Even under the simplest administration, the state has no more than it needs to subsist. Under any other it would exhaust itself and die.

You may say that Corsica, being more fertile and having a milder climate, can support a more onerous form of government. In other times that would be true; but now, crushed by long years of slavery, and devastated by long wars, the nation first of all must recover its health. When it has put its fertile soil into production, it can dream of becoming rich and of adopting a more brilliant administration. Indeed, if the constitution we are about to establish is successful, further constitutional change will become necessary. Cultivation of the land cultivates the spirit; all agricultural peoples multiply; they multiply in proportion to the product of their soil; and when that soil is fertile, they finally multiply to such an extent that it no longer suffices to support them; then they are forced either to found colonies or to change their form of government.

When the country is saturated with inhabitants, the surplus can no longer be employed in agriculture, but must be used in industry, commerce, or the arts; and this new system demands a different type of administration. Let us hope that the institutions Corsica is about to establish will soon require her to make such changes! But as long as she has no more men than she can use in agriculture, as long as an inch of fallow land remains on the island, she should cleave to the rural system, and change it only when the island no longer suffices.

The rural system, as I have said, involves a democratic state; we have therefore no choice as to the form of government to be adopted. It is true that this form must be somewhat modified in practice by reason of the size of the island, for a purely democratic government is suitable rather to a small town than to a nation. It would be impossible to bring together the whole people of an island like those of a city; and when the supreme authority is entrusted to delegates, the government changes and becomes aristocratic. What Corsica needs is a mixed government, where the people assemble by sections rather than as a whole, and where the repositories of its power are changed at frequent intervals. This was well understood by the author of the Vescovado Report of 1764, an excellent report, to be consulted with confidence on all matters which have been omitted from the present discussion.

The firm establishment of this form of government will produce two great advantages. First, by confining the work of administration to a small number only, it will permit the choice of enlightened men. Secondly, by requiring the concurrence of all members of the state in the exercise of the supreme authority, it will place all on a plane of perfect equality, thus permitting them to spread throughout the whole extent of the island and to populate it uniformly. This is the fundamental principle of our new constitution. If we make it such that it will keep the population everywhere in equilibrium, we shall by that fact alone have made it as perfect as possible. If this principle is correct, our regulations become clear, and our work is simplified to an astonishing degree. □

Aristocratic Crisis

The actual political steps taken by the monarchy to resolve the fiscal crisis were not unintelligent and on reasonable calculation should no more have led to revolution than the summoning of Parliament in 1640 by Charles I. In both cases kings of ordinary competence advised by ministers and courtiers of at least normal insight were brought down by men and events impossible to predict—or at any rate, impossible to manage with the usual resources of rule.

In fact, King Louis XVI and his ministers showed rather extraordinary daring and political imagination once Calonne had made the shocking discovery of the size and character of the national debt. Professor R. R. Palmer points out that the monarchy consistently did a bad job of public relations, always revealing its failures; and certainly the publicizing of the annual deficit (budgets were not much more than accounting in the eighteenth century anywhere) when no one knew what could be done about it seems not a very good idea. But Calonne, backed strongly by the King, proposed a radical and reasonable reform of the financial structure of the state in order to solve both the immediate and future need of the government for increased revenue. Calonne's plan involved features of advanced physiocratic precepts (ending of internal tariffs, restrictions on grain trade, the royal *corvée*), but its boldness was in attacking the whole maze of privilege which protected the wealthy and the well-born from paying a reasonable (and now necessary) share of the cost of government. He proposed a new tax (the nobles were exempt from the chief tax of the realm, the *taille*, and the other principal tax, the *vingtième*, was evaded by most of those whose incomes would have brought the needed revenue) which was intended to raise revenue from all landowners by a levy on landed income that cut through all legal and regional and social distinctions to define a taxpayer as simply a propertied citizen of France.

The aristocracy of France rebelled in 1787. Their rebellion was less violent and bloody than that of the noble Frondes in the previous century; the barons and prelates were now led by lawyers and judges from their ranks, men who fought the monarchy not with swords but with words, not with conspiracy and treason but with the legal mechanisms of the establishment. But this time the stakes were higher than anyone knew. For the opposition proved to be not a handful of court politicians and state builders, but a nation of upthrusting egos led by men of revolutionary genius.

The monarchy searched in vain for a legal, institutionally conservative instrumentality with which to put Calonne's plan into operation. The parlements and provincial estates were obviously impossible after a century of experience in fighting royal government on behalf of local privilege. What was needed was a method of using "popular" appeals and pressure to help coerce the aristocracy; but the Estates-General, which had not met since 1615, was at first rejected as too cumbersome and organizationally dominated by the privileged. So, in desperation, a similar "emergency" and "national" device of medieval politics was tried

—an "Assembly of Notables" designated by the King—which it was hoped would salve aristocratic egos and at the same time permit the government to insist that a solvent Versailles was the responsibility of the privileged orders which that government chiefly served. But the Notables were angry, frightened, and unsympathetic. The old issues of privilege against "despotism" which the parlements had popularized dominated the rhetoric once again. As a tactic made inevitable by the reality of the financial crisis, the Assembly in principle agreed to equality in taxation; but they were unwilling to implement the principle and began plans to return to the proven techniques of obstructionism "under the banners of libertarian principles" in the parlements. Calonne's ministry fell and the Parlement of Paris very successfully and with wide popular approval fought the tax demands of the monarchy until the King felt obliged to strike at the political pretensions of the courts and in May of 1788 (the "May Edicts") Louis virtually destroyed the legal base of the usurping parliamentarian "constitutionalism." From all over France the response was hostile, a barrage of antiroyalist pamphlets proved how well the privileged orders had prepared all classes to accept the medieval courts as defenders of the liberties of everyone.

Stimulated by success, the aristocracy rushed to destruction in the exciting months of 1788. The despots at Versailles were brought to their knees by the rallying of the hundreds of medieval corporative bodies which stood up for "liberty" in its ancient sense of custom. The parlements were reinvested with their former powers. Caught up in their own rhetoric, the aristocracy—or a decisively active party among them—made common cause with bourgeois intellectuals in demanding for France the freedoms won in England a century earlier (press and assembly and freedom from arbitrary arrest) as well as English-like constitutionalism and equality of taxation. The King had already summoned for the following May, 1789, an Estates-General. The leaders of all classes welcomed the opportunity to reshape the political structure of France. But before the year 1788 was out, the national union for liberty against despotic Versailles was split wide open by the deep fissures of class. The leadership of the nobles in reconstructing France was rejected by the almost magically politicized Third Estate who quickly saw in such things as the proposed voting procedures of the Estates-General (by Orders—allowing the first two orders of nobility always to outvote the third of commoners) that the rhetoric of opposition to Versailles on behalf of "liberty" concealed the realities of a social order in which they had a decidedly and gallingly minor status.

Revolt of the Third Estate

Looking back on the decades since Louis XIV seemed finally to have completed the work of Richelieu, and France was the universally admired model of the stable aristocratic society, one can only feel amazement at the political and social weakness of the Old Regime revealed by the elections to the Estates-General. The King had begun an extraordi-

nary procedure for arousing excitement over the elections with an Order in Council in July 1788 which solicited information from all his subjects on how best to convoke and manage the deliberations of an Estates-General which would reflect the national will, protect individual and corporate rights, and generally prove "useful to his people." The response had been enthusiastic and basic political thinking was thus deliberately stirred up in a way few regimes could easily afford. The Third Estate was being courted by both monarchy and aristocracy, and the process discredited both. The elections were not only a rare event in themselves, they were also intended to be discussion groups, local centers of debate and information. Neither monarchy nor aristocracy had the resources to control the thousands of open electoral meetings which took place in France during the spring of 1789. An unexampled opportunity was given all dissidents to become politically effective: in all the months that preceded the meeting of the Estates General, France was deluged with pamphlets and the famous *cahiers de doléances* drawn up to instruct the delegates selected for the national meeting. The position of the clergy and the nobility was already fairly clear—the Parlement of Paris and the second Assembly of Notables insisted that voting in the Estates-General must be by Order and that no radical political solutions were contemplated. The conservatism of the clergy was weakened by allowing the parish priests discussion and delegates, and there were liberal nobles like Lafayette, but the real surprise was the Third Estate.

Most of the Third or common Estate were, of course, peasants. By occupation and tradition they were nonpolitical and inclined to either cynical or reverent passivity toward their social superiors. So that although there were radical peasant leaders who later in the year frightened and astonished everyone by another, final, and completely successful *Jacquerie,* there were almost no peasant deputies sent to Versailles. Nor were there any working-class deputies one can identify for certain. The electoral meetings were almost entirely taken over by the most activist, ego-starved members of the middle class. Over half of all the 648 deputies of the Third Estate were lawyers. The inevitable result was that the commoners of France were represented by literate and articulate men brought up on the literature of the Enlightenment, experienced in debate and shrewd dealing, and hungry for prestige. Fired up by the idea of a great reconstruction of the nation and the sense that the ruling classes were soft and uncertain, feeling that the risks of boldness were not great, the deputies of the Third assembled for the opening of the Estates-General on May 4 in what may be called a revolutionary frame of mind. The change in psychology from even the early months of 1788 is striking—so clearly defiant and lucidly revolutionary are the spokesmen for the commonalty that one can only feel astonishment that so much hate and frustration were so long suppressed by this very class of office-seeking toadies to the nobility of the Old Regime.

Let me illustrate now the lively and imaginative propaganda which characterized the Third Estate in the months of revolutionary prepara-

tion for the sessions of the Estates-General. Here first is a fine example of political imagination and eloquence from the pen of the "Abbé" Sieyès, a rather unpleasant opportunist once caught in the tides of later revolutionary events; but in 1789 he was perhaps the leading voice of bourgeois nationalism, rationalism, and social self-consciousness. The whole pamphlet is too long to print; however, a few selections from it will indicate the line and tone of argument:

WHAT IS THE THIRD ESTATE?

The plan of this work is quite simple. We have three questions to consider:
   (1) What is the third estate? Everything.
   (2) What has it been in the political order up to the present? Nothing.
   (3) What does it demand? To become something. . . .

The Third Estate is a Complete Nation

What is necessary for the subsistence and prosperity of a nation? *Particular* labors and *public* functions.

Particular labors can be divided into four classes: 1) the soil and water furnish the primary materials for the satisfaction of human needs, and the first class in this order will be that of all the families attached to the work of the field. 2) From the first sale of materials until their consumption or use, a new handiwork, more or less multifarious, adds to these materials a secondary value more or less compound. Human industry succeeds in perfecting the goods of nature and multiplies their value as raw materials twofold, tenfold, a hundredfold. Such are the works of the second class. 3) Between production and consumption, and also between the various stages of production, there is a multitude of intermediary agents, useful as much to the producers as to the consumers: these are the merchants. . . . This useful group makes up the third class. 4) In addition to these three classes of productive citizens who are busy with the *objects* of consumption and use, society requires a group of special works and services *directly* useful or pleasing to the *person*. This fourth class embraces everything from the most liberal and distinguished scientific professions to the least esteemed domestic services. Such are the works which maintain society. Who supports them? The third estate.

Public functions may similarly, in the existing state, be arranged under the four recognized denominations, the Sword, the Robe, the Church and the Administration. It would be superfluous to run through them in detail, in order to show how the third estate is nineteen-twentieths of these, with this difference, that it is responsible for all that is truly laborious, all the services that the privileged order refuses to perform. The lucrative and titulary positions are occupied by members of the privileged order. Should we give them credit for that? It would be justifiable if the third estate either refused to fill these positions or if it were not so capable of performing their functions. The truth of the matter is known; yet they have

dared to place the third estate under interdiction. They have said to it: "Whatever your services, whatever your talents, you shall go just so far; you shall not pass beyond. It is not a good thing for you to be honored." . . . If this exclusion is a social crime against the third estate, might one at least be able to say that it serves the public interest? Well, are not the effects of monopoly known? If it discourages those whom it excludes, does it not also render unskilled those whom it favors? Isn't it known that every work removed from free competition will be at once more expensive and less well done?

What Has the Third Estate Been up to the Present?
Nothing.

We shall not examine the state of servitude in which the people has groaned for so long, no more than the state of constraint and humiliation in which it is still held. Its civil condition has changed; it ought to change more: it is quite impossible that the body of the nation or even that any particular order should become free if the third estate is not free. Privileges do not make one free, but rather the rights that belong to everyone.

If the aristocrats should attempt, even at the cost of this liberty of which they have shown themselves unworthy, to keep the people oppressed, it is fair to ask by what right. If the answer is by the right of conquest, then, it must be agreed, the matter must be pushed a bit farther. The third estate need not fear going back to the past in this way. For it will go back to the year preceding the conquest; and since it is today strong enough not to allow itself to be conquered, its opposition will be more effective. Why should not all these families that maintain the foolish pretension that they are descended from the conquerors and are the inheritors of their rights return to the forests of Franconie?

The nation, thus purged, will be able to console itself, I think, with being reduced to regard itself as made up of only the descendants of the Gauls and the Romans. In truth, if one insists upon making distinctions based on birth, might it not be revealed to our poor compatriots that those that are descended from the Gauls and the Romans are at least worthy as those that come from the Sicambres, the Welches and other savages come out of the woods and swamps of ancient Germany? Yes, it will be said; but the conquest has upset all relationships, and nobility of birth has passed to the side of the conquerors. Well! then it must change sides again, and the third estate will get back its nobility by becoming the conqueror in its turn. . . .

Let us continue. By the third estate must be understood the mass of citizens who belong to the common order. Everyone who is privileged by law, in whatever manner, departs from the common order, is an exception to the common law, and, consequently, does not belong to the third estate. We have said that a common law and a common representation are what make *one* nation. It is only too true that one is *nothing* in France, when one is only under the protection of the common law; if one does not hold some privilege he must make up his mind to endure scorn, insult and vexations of all kinds. In order to prevent his being completely crushed

the only resource of the unfortunate unprivileged person is to attach himself by all sorts of sordid tricks to some dignitary; only at this price does he buy the power, on occasions, to call himself *somebody.*

But it is less in its civil estate than in its relations to the constitution that we have to consider the third estate here. Let us study it with respect to the Estates General.

Who have been its pretended representatives? Either the newly ennobled or the temporarily privileged. These false deputies have not even always been freely chosen in a popular election. Sometimes in the Estates General, and almost always in the provincial estates, the representation of the people is looked upon as the peculiar right of certain positions or offices.

The old nobility cannot stand the new nobles; it only permits them to sit with it when they can claim, as is said, four generations and a hundred years. So it thrusts them back into the third estate to which they obviously no longer belong. However, in the eyes of the law all nobles are equal, those of yesterday and those who succeed greatly or very little in hiding their origin or their usurpation. All have the same privileges. Only opinion distinguishes between them. But if the third estate is compelled to support a prejudice sanctioned by the law there is hardly any reason for its submitting to a prejudice which is against the text of the law.

No matter who is made a noble, it is certain that from the moment that a citizen acquires privileges contrary to the common right he is no longer a member of the common order. His new interest is opposed to the general interest; he is incapacitated from voting for the people. . . .

Is separating from the third estate not only the hereditarily privileged, but also those who are enjoying privileges only temporarily, . . . is this an attempt to weaken this order by depriving it of its most enlightened, most courageous and most respected members?

. . . The third estate is always identified in my mind with the idea of a nation. Whatever our motive may be, can we make the truth not the truth? Because an army has had the misfortune of seeing its best troops desert it, does it follow that it must depend upon them to defend it? All privilege, it cannot be repeated too much, is opposed to the common right; therefore all the privileged, without distinction, form a class that is different from and opposed to the third estate. At the same time, this truth ought to contain nothing that will alarm the friends of the people. On the contrary, it serves the national interest, by making forcefully apparent the necessity of immediately suppressing all temporary privileges, which divide the third estate and would appear to condemn this order to placing its destinies in the hands of its enemies. Besides, this observation must not be separated from the one that follows: the abolition of privileges in the third estate is not the loss of exemptions which a few of its members enjoy. These exemptions are nothing but the common right. It has been supremely unjust to deprive the generality of people of them. So I demand not the loss of a right but its restitution; and if it is objected that by making some of these privileges common, like that of not being drafted for the militia, the means of filling a social need is prevented, I answer that every public need ought to be the responsibility of everybody, and not of a

particular class of citizens, and that one must be as much a stranger to all reflection as to all justice not to find a more national means of completing and maintaining such military establishment as one wishes to have. . . .

Let one read history with the intention of examining whether the facts are in conformity with or contrary to this assertion, and he will be assured, I have had the experience, that it is a great error to believe that France is subject to a monarchical regime.

It is enough at this point to have made it apparent that the pretended utility of a privilege order for the public service is only a chimera; that without it, everything that is laborious in this service is discharged by the third estate; that without it the superior places would be infinitely better filled; that they ought to be the natural portion and reward of recognized talents and services; and that if the privileged have succeeded in usurping every lucrative and titulary post, it is at once an odious crime against the generality of citizens and a betrayal of the public interest.

Who would dare to say, therefore, that the third estate does not contain in itself all that is necessary to constitute a complete nation? It is like a strong and robust man whose arms are still in chains. If the privileged order were removed the nation would not be something less but something more. So, what is the third estate? Everything, but an "everything" shackled and oppressed. What would it be without the privileged order? Everything, but an "everything" free and flourishing. Nothing can get along without it, everything will get along infinitely better without the others. Nor is the whole case stated when it is shown that the privileged, far from being useful to the nation, can only weaken it and harm it; further, it must be proved that the nobility does not enter into the social order; that it can well be a *burden* on the nation, but that it is not capable of being a part of it.

First, it is impossible to know where to place the nobles among the various elements in the nation. I know that there are many individuals, indeed too many, in whom infirmity, incompetence, incurable laziness, or the force of bad habits, operate to make them strangers to the work of society. Everywhere the exception and the abuse is side by side with the rule, especially in a vast empire. But at least it will be agreed that the fewer these abuses the better the State is regulated. The worst regulated of all will be that State in which not only are there particular persons isolated, but an entire class of citizens finds its glory in remaining inactive in the midst of general activity and is able to consume the best part of the produce without having helped in any way to bring it into existence. Such a class is surely foreign to the nation in its *sloth.*

The noble order is foreign among us not less because of its civil and public prerogatives.

What is a nation? A body of associates living under a *common law* and represented by the same *legislature.*

Is it not all too certain that the noble order has privileges, exemptions, and even rights separated from the rights of the great body of citizens? It departs in this respect from the common order, from the common law. Its civil rights make it already a people apart in the nation at large. It is truly *imperium in imperio.*

With regard to its *political* rights, it also exists apart. It has representa-

tives of its own, who are not responsible in any way for acting on behalf of the people. The body of its deputies sits apart; and when it assembles in the same room with the deputies of simple citizens it is no less true that its representation is essentially distinct and separate: it is foreign to the nation in its principle, since its commission does not come from the people, and in its object, since it consists in defending not the general interest, but a particular one.

The third estate therefore includes everything that belongs to the nation; and everything that is not the third estate cannot be regarded as being of the nation. What is the third estate? Everything.

Remove from our annals a few years of Louis XI, of Richelieu, and a few moments of Louis XIV, where one sees only pure despotism, and you would believe that you were reading the history of an *aulic* aristocracy. It is the court which has reigned and not the monarch. It is the court which makes and unmakes, which calls and recalls the ministers, which creates and distributes positions, etc. And what is the court, if not the head of that immense aristocracy which covers every part of France, which, through its members, attains to everything and exercises everywhere what is essential to every part of the public interest? Thus the people has accustomed itself to separate in its grumblings the monarch from the powers behind the throne. It has always regarded the king as a man so surely deceived and so without protection in the middle of an active and all-powerful court, that it has never thought to blame him for all the evil that is done in his name.

To sum up: the third estate has not had up to the present true representatives in the Estates General. Therefore its political rights are nought.

What Does the Third Estate Demand?
To Become Something.

It is not necessary to judge its demands on the basis of the isolated observations of a few authors more or less informed about the rights of man. The third estate is still very backward in this respect, not only with regard to the insights of those who have studied the social order, but also with regard to that mass of common ideas which constitutes public opinion. The true petitions of this estate cannot be appreciated except in terms of the authentic protests which the great municipalities of the kingdom have addressed to the government. What do these show? That the people want to be *something,* and in truth the least possible. It wants to have genuine representatives in the Estates General, that is to say, deputies *drawn from its own ranks,* who are capable of being the interpreters of its desire and the protectors of its interests. But of what use is it to this estate to be present in the Estates General if the interest contrary to its own predominates there! It would only serve to give sanction by its presence to the oppression of which it is the eternal victim. Therefore it is quite certain that it cannot come to vote at the Estates General if it ought not to have there *an influence which is at least equal to that of the privileged classes,* and it demands a number of representatives equal to the number of the two other orders together. Finally, this equality of representation would become completely illusory if every

chamber had its separate voice. The third estate demands therefore that the votes be taken *by heads and not by order.* These protests which have created such alarm in the circles of the privileged amount to this, because it is only from this that the reform of abuses would follow. The true intention of the third estate is to have in the Estates General an influence *equal* to that of the privileged. I repeat, can it ask less? And is it not clear that if its influence there is not equal, one cannot hope that it will leave its state of political nullity and become *something?*   □

No revolution has ever produced such a remarkable record of itself as the French, and the most overwhelming part of that record is made up of the bills of grievance drafted in the course of instructing the delegates who were in good medieval fashion to petition the King for redress when the Estates General met. In substance this was an old device, but it took on new meaning in the crisis of 1789. Each of the three estates met separately to frame their respective petitions and to choose their delegates. The *cahiers* of the privileged orders vary interestingly from region to region and reflect tensions between the clergy and nobility as well as within the respective orders (particularly noticeable is the animosity between parish and cathedral and monastic clergy). More appropriate for our story, however, are the twenty thousand or so *cahiers* drawn up in local and district assemblies by the commoners of the realm. Obviously it is not possible to excerpt from such a large body of literature model *cahiers* which will represent all the shades of opinion expressed in these assemblies of villagers and townsmen and their electors. But the district or "general" *cahiers* drawn up by the district electors sent from the constituent assemblies at the local level were supposed to synthesize the "particular" documents of their constituents, and furthermore, the total fund of ideas and criticism was not great so that one tends to get largely repetition of familiar dogmas of the Enlightenment and the clichés of sound, statist, legalistic opinion common to Europe since the seventeenth century. Finally, and importantly, the over-arching uniformity in these documents—as in most which we shall subsequently see—is their bourgeois orientation. The commoners of France, one would think from the *cahiers,* were primarily businessmen and lawyers. The "Third Estate" is not only equated with the nation (a reasonable dogma) but also (not a reasonable dogma) with the needs and aspirations of the capitalist world. From the district of Versailles, here is a fairly typical "general" *cahier* of the Third Estate:

CAHIER OF THE GRIEVANCES, COMPLAINTS AND REMONSTRANCES OF THE MEMBERS OF THE THIRD ESTATE OF THE BAILLIAGE OF VERSAILLES

Constitution

Art. 1. The power of making laws resides in the king and the nation.

Art. 2. The nation being too numerous for a personal exercise of this right, has confided its trust to representatives freely chosen from all

classes of citizens. These representatives constitute the national assembly.

Art. 3. Frenchmen should regard as laws of the kingdom those alone which have been prepared by the national assembly and sanctioned by the king.

Art. 4. Succession in the male line and primogeniture are usages as ancient as the monarchy, and ought to be maintained and consecrated by solemn and irrevocable enactment.

Art. 5. The laws prepared by the States General and sanctioned by the king shall be binding upon all classes of citizens and upon all provinces of the kingdom. They shall be registered literally and accurately in all courts of law. They shall be open for consultation at all seats of municipal and communal government; and shall be read at sermon time in all parishes.

Art. 6. That the nation may not be deprived of that portion of legislation which is its due, and that the affairs of the kingdom may not suffer neglect and delay, the States General shall be convoked at least every two or three years.

Art. 7. No intermediate commission of the States General may ever be established, since deputies of the nation have no right to delegate the powers confirmed to them.

Art. 8. Powers shall be conferred upon delegates for one year only; but they may be continued or confirmed by a single reelection.

Art. 9. The persons of deputies shall be inviolable. They may not be prosecuted in civil cases during their term of office; nor held responsible to the executive authorities for any speech made in the assembly; but they shall be responsible to the States General alone.

Art. 10. Deputies of the Third Estate, or their president or speaker, shall preserve the same attitude and demeanor as the representatives of the two upper orders, when they address the sovereign. As regards the three orders there shall be no difference observed in the ceremonial made use of at the convocation of the estates.

Art. 11. Personal liberty, proprietary rights and the security of citizens shall be established in a clear, precise and irrevocable manner. All *lettres de cachet* shall be abolished for ever, subject to certain modifications which the States General may see fit to impose.

Art. 12. And to remove forever the possibility of injury to the personal and proprietary rights of Frenchmen, the jury system shall be introduced in all criminal cases, and in civil cases for the determination of fact, in all the courts of the realm.

Art. 13. All persons accused of crimes not involving the death penalty shall be released on bail within twenty-four hours. This release shall be pronounced by the judge upon the decision of the jury.

Art. 14. All persons who shall have been imprisoned upon suspicion, and afterward proved innocent, shall be entitled to satisfaction and damages from the state, if they are able to show that their honor or property has suffered injury.

Art. 15. A wider liberty of the press shall be accorded, with this provision alone: that all manuscripts sent to the printer shall be signed by

the author, who shall be obliged to disclose his identity and bear the responsibility of his work; and to prevent judges and other persons in power from taking advantage of their authority, no writing shall be held a libel until it is so determined by twelve jurors, chosen according to the forms of a law which shall be enacted upon this subject.

Art. 16. Letters shall never be opened in transit; and effectual measures shall be taken to the end that this trust shall remain inviolable.

Art. 17. All distinctions in penalties shall be abolished; and crimes committed by citizens of the different orders shall be punished irrespectively, according to the same forms of law and in the same manner. The States General shall seek to bring it about that the effects of transgression shall be confined to the individual, and shall not be reflected upon the relatives of the transgressor, themselves innocent of all participation.

Art. 18. Penalties shall in all cases be moderate and proportionate to the crime. All kinds of torture, the rack and the stake, shall be abolished. Sentences of death shall be pronounced only for atrocious crimes in rare instances, determined by the law.

Art. 19. Civil and criminal laws shall be reformed.

Art. 20. The military throughout the kingdom shall be subject to the general law and to the civil authorities, in the same manner as other citizens.

Art. 21. No tax shall be legal unless accepted by the representatives of the people and sanctioned by the king.

Art. 22. Since all Frenchmen receive the same advantage from the government, and are equally interested in its maintenance they ought to be placed upon the same footing in the matter of taxation.

Art. 23. All taxes now in operation are contrary to these principles and for the most part vexatious, oppressive and humiliating to the people. They ought to be abolished as soon as possible, and replaced by others common to the three orders and to all classes of citizens, without exception.

Art. 24. In case the present taxes are provisionally retained, it should be for a short time, not longer than the session of the States General, and it shall be ordered that the proportional contribution of the two upper orders shall be due from them on the day of the promulgation of the law of the constitution.

Art. 25. After the establishment of the new taxes, which shall be paid by the three orders, the present exceptional method of collecting from the clergy shall be done away with, and their future assemblies shall deal exclusively with matters of discipline and dogma.

Art. 26. All new taxes, real and personal, shall be established only for a limited time, never to exceed two or three years. At the expiration of this term, they shall be no longer collected, and collectors or other officials soliciting the same shall be proceeded against as guilty of extortion.

Art. 27. The anticipation of future revenues, loans in whatsoever disguise, and all other financial expedients of the kind, of which so great abuse has been made, shall be forbidden.

Art. 28. In case of war, or other exceptional necessity, no loan shall be made without the consent of the States General, and it shall be enacted

that no loan shall be effected, without provision being made by taxation for the payment of interest, and of the principal at a specified time.

Art. 29. The amount which each citizen shall be obliged to pay, in case of war, by reason of an increase in the existing taxes, at a certain rate per livre, shall be determined beforehand by the States General in conjunction with the king. The certainty of increase ought to have a marked effect in preventing useless and unjust wars, since it clearly indicates to Frenchmen the new burden they will have to bear, and to foreign nations the resources which the nation has in reserve and at hand to repulse unjust attacks.

Art. 30. The exact debt of the government shall be established by the States General, and after verification it shall be declared the national debt.

Art. 31. Perpetual and time annuities shall be funded at their present value.

Art. 32. The expenses of the departments shall be determined by their actual needs, and so established by a committee of the States General, in such a manner that the expenditures may never exceed the sums appropriated.

Art. 33. There shall be no increase in taxation, until the receipts and expenditures have been compared with the utmost care, and a real deficit discovered; in fact, not until all possible reductions have been made in the expenses of each department.

Art. 34. The expenses of the war department call for the special attention of the States General. These expenses mount annually to the appalling sums of 110 and 120 millions. In order to effect their reduction, the States General shall demand the accounts of this department under the recent ministries, particularly under the ministry of the Duc de Choiseul.

Art. 35. The present militia system, which is burdensome, oppressive and humiliating to the people, shall be abolished; and the States General shall devise means for its reformation.

Art. 36. A statement of Pensions shall be presented to the States General; they shall be granted only in moderate amounts, and then only for services rendered. The total annual expenditure for this purpose should not exceed a fixed sum. A list of pensions should be printed and made public each year.

Art. 37. Since the nation undertakes to provide for the personal expenses of the sovereign, as well as for the crown and state, the law providing for the inalienability of the domain shall be repealed. As a result, all the domanial possessions immediately in the king's possession, as well as those already pledged, and the forests of his majesty as well, shall be sold, and transferred in small lots, in so far as possible, and always at public auction to the highest bidder; and the proceeds applied to the reduction of the public debt. In the meanwhile all woods and forests shall continue to be controlled and administered, whoever may be the actual proprietors, according to the provisions of the law of 1669.

Art. 38. The execution of this law shall be confided to the provincial estates, which shall prosecute violations of the law before judges in ordinary.

Art. 39. Apanages shall be abolished and replaced, in the case of princes who possess them, with cash salaries, which shall be included in the expenses of the crown.

Art. 40. The States General shall take under advisement these transfers which have not yet been verified and completed.

Art. 40. b. Ministers and all government officials shall be responsible to the States General for their conduct of affairs. They may be impeached according to fixed forms of law and punished according to the statute.

Art. 41. All general and particular statements and accounts relative to the administration shall be printed and made public each year.

Art. 42. The coinage may not be altered without the consent of the Estates; and no bank established without their approval.

Art. 43. A new subdivision shall be made of the provinces of the realm; provincial estates shall be established, members of which, not excepting their presidents, shall be elected.

Art. 44. The constitution of the provincial estates shall be uniform throughout the kingdom, and fixed by the States General. Their powers shall be limited to the interior administration of the provinces, under the supervision of his majesty, who shall communicate to them the national laws which have received the consent of the States General and the royal sanction: to which laws all the provincial estates shall be obliged to submit without reservation.

Art. 45. All members of the municipal assemblies of towns, and villages shall be elected. They may be chosen from all classes of citizens. All municipal offices, now existing, shall be abolished; and their redemption shall be provided for by the States General.

Art. 46. All offices and positions, civil, ecclesiastical and military, shall be open to all orders; and no humiliating and unjust exception (in the case of the third estate), destructive to emulation and injurious to the interests of the state, shall be perpetuated.

Art. 47. The right of *aubaine* shall be abolished with regard to all nationalities. All foreigners, after three years residence in the kingdom, shall enjoy the rights of citizenship.

Art. 48. Deputies of French colonies in America and in the Indies, which form an important part of our possessions, shall be admitted to the States General, if not at the next meeting, at least at the one following.

Art. 49. All relics of serfdom, agrarian or personal, still remaining in certain provinces, shall be abolished.

Art. 50. New laws shall be made in favor of the Negroes in our colonies; and the States General shall take measures toward the abolition of slavery. Meanwhile let a law be passed, that Negroes in the colonies who desire to purchase their freedom, as well as those whom their masters are willing to set free, shall no longer be compelled to pay a tax to the domain.

Art. 51. The three functions, legislative, executive and judicial, shall be separated and carefully distinguished.

The communes of the bailliage of Versailles have already expressed themselves in respect to the necessity of adopting the form of deliberation *per capita* in the coming States General. The reform of the constitution

will be one of their principal duties. This magnificent monument of liberty and public felicity should be the work of the three orders in common session; if they are separated, certain pretensions, anxieties and jealousies are bound to arise; the two upper orders are likely to oppose obstacles, perhaps invincible, to the reform of abuses and the enactment of laws destined to suppress such abuses. It seems indispensable that in this first assembly votes should be taken *per capita* and not by order. After the renunciation by the two upper orders of their pecuniary privileges; after all distinctions before the law have been abolished; when the exclusion of the third estate from certain offices and positions has been done away with—then the reasons which today necessitate deliberation *per capita* will no longer exist.

The communes of Versailles therefore refrain from expressing a positive opinion upon the future composition of the national assemblies and upon the method of their deliberation. They defer, with all confidence, the decision of this important question to the wisdom of the States General.

Our prayer is that the methods determined upon shall be such as will assure forever, to the king and to the nation those portions of the legislative power which respectively belong to them; that they shall maintain between them a perfect equilibrium in the employment of this power; that they shall conserve, forever, to the nation its rights and liberties; to the king his prerogatives and the executive power in all its fullness. Finally that these methods should be so combined as to produce that circumspectness and lack of haste so necessary to the enactment of laws, and that they will effectually prevent all hasty counsels, dissensions amongst deputies and immature conclusions.

May all deputies to this august assembly, impressed with the sanctity and extent of their obligations, forget that they are the mandatories of some special order, and remember only that they are representatives of the people. May they never be forgetful of the fact, that they are about to fix the destinies of the foremost nation of the world!

The Executive

Art. 52. It shall be ordained by the constitution that the executive power be vested in the king alone.

Art. 53. The king shall dispose of all offices, places and positions, ecclesiastical, civil and military, to which he has at present the right of appointment.

Art. 54. All the provincial estates, or commissions representing them, shall receive his immediate orders which it shall be their duty to obey provisionally.

Art. 55. His consent shall be necessary to all bills approved by the States General in order that they may acquire the force of law throughout the realm. He may reject all bills presented to him, without being obliged to state the reasons of his disapproval.

Art. 56. He shall have the sole right of convening, proroguing and dissolving the States General.

The Judiciary

Art. 57. The sale of the judicial office shall be suppressed as soon as circumstances will permit, and provision made for the indemnification of holders.

Art. 58. There shall be established in the provinces as many superior courts as there are provincial estates. They shall be courts of final jurisdiction.

Art. 59. All exceptional and privileged seignorial courts shall be abolished, as well as other courts rendered useless by the abolition of certain taxes which caused their erection, and by the adoption of a new system of accounts under the exclusive control of the States General. . . .

Art. 64. Judges of all courts shall be obliged to adhere to the letter of the law and may never be permitted to change, modify or interpret it at their pleasure.

Art. 65. The fees received by all officers of justice shall be fixed at a moderate rate and clearly understood; and judges who extort fees in excess of the fixed rates shall be condemned to pay a fine of four times the amount they have received.

Such are the bases of a constitution founded upon the eternal principles of justice and reason, which alone ought to regulate henceforward the government of the realm. Once they are adopted, all false pretensions, all burdensome privileges, all abuses of all kinds will be seen to disappear. . . .

General Demands

Art. 66. The deputies of the *prévôté* and *vicomté* of Paris shall be instructed to unite themselves with the deputies of other provinces, in order to join with them in securing, as soon as possible, the following abolitions:

Of the *taille;*
Of the *gabelle;*
Of the *aides;*
Of the *corvée;*
Of the *ferme* of tobacco;
Of the registry-duties;
Of the free-hold tax;
Of the taxes on leather;
Of the government stamp upon iron;
Of the stamps upon gold and silver;
Of the interprovincial customs duties;
Of the taxes upon fairs and markets;

Finally, of all taxes that are burdensome and oppressive, whether on account of their nature or of the expense of collection, or because they have been paid almost wholly by agriculturists and by the poorer classes. They shall be replaced with other taxes, less complicated and easier of collection, which shall fall alike upon all classes and orders of the state without exception.

Art. 67. We demand also the abolition of the royal preserves *(capitaineries);*

Of the game laws;

Of jurisdictions of *prévôtés;*

Of *banalités;*

Of tolls;

Of useless authorities and governments in cities and provinces.

Art. 68. We solicit the establishment of public granaries in the provinces, under the control of the provincial estates, in order that by accumulating reserves during years of plenty, famine and excessive dearness of grain, such as we have experienced in the past may be prevented.

Art. 69. We solicit also the establishment of free schools in all country parishes.

Art. 70. We demand, for the benefit of commerce, the abolition of all exclusive privileges:

The removal of customs barriers to the frontiers;

The most complete freedom in trade;

The revision and reform of all laws relative to commerce;

Encouragement for all kinds of manufacture: *viz.* premiums, bounties and advances:

Rewards to artisans and laborers for useful inventions.

The communes desire that prizes and rewards shall always be preferred to exclusive privileges, which extinguish emulation and lessen competition.

Art. 71. We demand the suppression of various hindrances, such as stamps, special taxes, inspections; and the annoyances and visitations, to which many manufacturing establishments, particularly tanneries, are subjected.

Art. 72. The States General are entreated to devise means for abolishing guild organizations, indemnifying the holders of masterships; and to fix by law the conditions, under which the arts, trades and professions may be followed, without the payment of an admission tax, and at the same time to provide that public security and confidence be undisturbed. . . .

Art. 81. That civil and military offices may not be held simultaneously by the same person, and that each citizen may hold only one office.

Art. 82. That all the honorary rights of nobles shall be maintained; but that they shall be allowed to hunt only upon their own lands, and not upon the lands of their vassals or tenants.

Art. 83. That nobility may be acquired neither through office nor by purchase.

Art. 84. That inheritances shall be divided equally among coheiritors of the same degree, without regard to sex or right of primogeniture, nor to the status of the coparticipants, and without distinction between nobles and non-nobles.

Art. 85. That all entails shall be limited to one generation.

Art. 86. That day laborers may not be taxed to exceed the amount of one day's labor. . . .

Art. 93. Since clergymen in general ought not to occupy themselves

with worldly affairs, there ought to be provided for bishops, archbishops and all holders of benefices a decent income and one suitable to their dignity: accordingly the property of the church in each province ought to be sold under the supervision of the provincial estates, which shall assume the duty of paying to holders of benefices the sums accorded to them by the States General.

Art. 94. That in case the above change should not be made, then it shall be ordained that no clergymen may hold two benefices at the same time, and that all persons now possessing two or more benefices shall be obliged to choose and to declare, within a prescribed time, which one of them they desire to retain.

Art. 95. That all commendatory abbacies, benefices without functions and useless convents shall be suppressed, their possessions sold for the benefit of the state, and the funds thus realized made to constitute an endowment, the income of which shall be used for the benefit of country parish priests for the establishment of free schools, hospitals and other charitable institutions.

Art. 96. That continuous residence of archbishops and bishops in their dioceses and of beneficiaries in their benefices shall be required; and that resignations be not permitted. . . .

Art. 98. That girls may not enter religious orders until after they are twenty-five years of age, nor men until after thirty.

Art. 99. That it be forbidden to go to the Roman Curia for provisions, nominations, bulls and dispensations of all kinds; and each bishop in his diocese shall have full powers in these matters.

Art. 100. That the right of the pope to grant livings in France be suppressed.

Art. 101. That the Concordat be revoked, and all intervention on the part of the Roman Curia be made to cease. . . .

Various Matters

Art. 2. That inhabitants of towns and rural places be paid and indemnified for troops of war quartered upon them, for the transportation of troops and of military baggage.

Art. 3. That the ordinances concerning the king's guard be revised, particularly those clauses which abolish the wise provision of Louis XIV for the safety of his person, and the regulations made by him relative to his bodyguard.

Art. 4. That barbarous punishments, taken from the codes of foreign nations and introduced into the new military regulations, be abolished, and replaced with regulations more in conformity with the genius of the nation. . . .

Art. 10. That canals be constructed in all provinces of the kingdom where they will be useful.

Art. 11. That the working of mines be encouraged.

Art. 12. That a new schedule be made of the expenses of funerals, marriages and other church functions.

Art. 13. That cemeteries be located outside of cities, towns and villages; that the same be done with places of deposit for refuse.

Art. 14. That the funds for the support of the lazarettos, formerly located in rural parishes, having been united with the endowments of hospitals, country people shall be permitted to send their sick to the city hospitals.

Art. 15. That the laws of the kingdom shall be equally the laws of the French colonies.

Art. 16. That all kinds of employment suitable for women shall be reserved for them by special enactment.   □

The Politics of Bourgeois Revolution

The first and final meeting on May 5th of the plenary session of the Estates General was an emotional anticlimax to the months of preparation and excited imagination. Archaic and anachronistic ceremonial forms dramatized the conservative frame of reference within which reformist agitation was circumscribed, and the speeches of Louis and his ministers were singularly uninspired. With no strong lead coming from the throne, and the announcement that on the following day the estates would meet separately to verify credentials, the delegates of the commons were both disappointed and encouraged to look to their own leadership. Evidently none of the power figures had made any real decisions: there were no threats. The political deadlock was produced far more by the softness and reasonableness of the government (which had also lost them the political decision against the nobility) than by any revolutionary daring or zeal in the ranks of the commoners. Out of the impasse over voting procedure, which dragged on for weeks—the commons refused to carry out the royal instructions for separate sessions of the three orders—the psychological and organizational features of a genuine revolutionary crisis emerged. The King's constitutional ideas were now seen in practice to be irreformably at odds with those of the intellectuals of the Third Estate whose pamphlets made them leaders in a time of fear and hope—men like Sieyès or the renegade Comte de Mirabeau. Now at last the commons recognized what Mirabeau and the American radicals had been proclaiming for a decade: that aristocratic privilege was inimical to "constitutionalism," to the free exercise of property rights and the protection of individual liberties. The "constitutionalism" which they had supported against the King a year earlier—that of the medieval corporations led by the parlements and provincial estates—they were now, when the King seemed to have capitulated to the demands of the aristocracy, rejecting. Under the leadership of Sieyès and Mirabeau, the Third Estate chose a President and a Secretary, declared themselves the representatives of the nation, and invited the other two estates to join them in their deliberations. Here are Arthur Young's impressions of these exciting June days:

[Paris, June 9–10, 1789] Those who are warm for the interest of the people declare that it will be impossible to reform some of the grossest abuses in the state, if the nobility, by sitting in a separate chamber, shall have a negative on the wishes of the people: and that to give such a *veto* to the clergy would be still more preposterous; if therefore, by the verification of

their powers in one chamber, they shall once come together, the popular party hope that there will remain no power afterwards to separate. The nobility and clergy foresee the same result, and will not therefore agree to it. In this dilemma it is curious to remark the *feelings* of the moment. It is not my business to write memoirs of what passes, but I am intent to catch, as well as I can, the opinions of the day most prevalent. While I remain at Paris, I shall see people of all descriptions, from the coffee-house politicians to the leaders in the states; and the chief object of such rapid notes as I throw on paper, will be to catch the ideas of the moment; to compare them afterwards with the actual events that shall happen, will afford amusement at least. The most prominent feature that appears at present is, that an idea of common interest and common danger does not seem to unite those, who, if not united, may find themselves too weak to oppose the danger that must arise from the people being sensible of a strength the result of *their* weakness. The king, court, nobility, clergy, army, and parliament, are nearly in the same situation. All these consider, with equal dread, the ideas of liberty, now afloat; except the first, who, for reasons obvious to those who know his character, troubles himself little, even with circumstances that concern his power the most intimately. Among the rest, the feeling of danger is common, and they would unite, were there a head to render it easy, in order to do without the states at all. That the commons themselves look for some such hostile union as more than probable, appears from an idea which gains ground, that they will find it necessary, should the other two orders continue to unite with them in one chamber, to declare themselves boldly the representatives of the kingdom at large, calling on the nobility and clergy to take their places— and to enter upon deliberations of business without them, should they refuse it. All conversation at present is on this topic, but opinions are more divided than I should have expected. There seem to be many who hate the clergy so cordially, that rather than permit them to form a distinct chamber, they would venture on a new system, dangerous as it might prove.

The 9th. The business going forward at present in the pamphlet shops of Paris is incredible. I went to the Palais Royal to see what new things were published, and to procure a catalogue of all. Every hour produces something new. Thirteen came out to-day, sixteen yesterday, and ninety-two last week. We think sometimes that Debrett's or Stockdale's shops at London are crouded, but they are mere deserts, compared to Desein's, and some others here, in which one can scarcely squeeze from the door to the counter. The price of printing two years ago was from 27 liv. to 30 liv. per sheet, but now it is from 60 liv. to 80 liv. This spirit of reading political tracts, they say, spreads into the provinces, so that all the presses of France are equally employed. Nineteen-twentieths of these productions are in favour of liberty, and commonly violent against the clergy and nobility; I have to-day bespoken many of this description, that have reputation; but enquiring for such as had appeared on the other side of the question, to my astonishment I find there are but two or three that have merit enough to be known. Is it not wonderful, that while the press teems with the most levelling and even seditious principles, which put in

execution would overturn the monarchy, nothing in reply appears, and not the least step is taken by the court to restrain this extreme licentiousness of publication? It is easy to conceive the spirit that must thus be raised among the people. But the coffee-houses in the Palais Royal present yet more singular and astonishing spectacles; they are not only crouded within, but other expectant crouds are at the doors and windows, listening *à gorge deployeé* to certain orators, who from chairs or tables harangue each his little audience: the eagerness with which they are heard, and the thunder of applause they receive for every sentiment of more than common hardiness or violence against the present government, cannot easily be imagined. I am all amazement at the ministry permitting such nests and hotbeds of sedition and revolt, which disseminate amongst the people, every hour, principles that by and by must be opposed with vigour, and therefore it seems little short of madness to allow the propagation at present.

The 10th. Every thing conspires to render the present period in France critical: the want of bread is terrible: accounts arrive every moment from the provinces of riots and disturbances, and calling in the military, to preserve the peace of the markets. The prices reported are the same as I found at Abbeville and Amiens 5s. (2½ d.) a pound for white bread, and 3½ s. to 4s. for the common sort, eaten by the poor: these rates are beyond their faculties, and occasion great misery. At Meudon, the police, that is to say the intendant, ordered that no wheat should be sold in the market without the person taking at the same time an equal quantity of barley. What a stupid and ridiculous regulation, to lay obstacles on the supply, in order to be better supplied; and to shew the people the fears and apprehensions of government, creating thereby an alarm, and raising the price at the very moment they wish to sink it!   □

On June 17th a formal declaration of revolution was promulgated by the commoners, the calm audacity of which has seldom been equaled:

The Assembly, deliberating after the verification of powers, recognizes that this assembly is already composed of deputies sent directly by at least ninety-six per cent of the nation.

Such a deputation could not remain inactive because of the absence of the deputies of some *baillages,* or of some classes of citizens; for the absentees who have been summoned cannot prevent those present from exercising their full rights. . . .

Furthermore, since only verified representatives may concur in the formation of the national will, and since all verified representatives must be in this assembly, it is further necessary to conclude that it and it alone, may interpret and present the general will of the nation; no veto, no negative power may exist between the throne and this assembly.

Accordingly, the Assembly declares that the common work of national restoration can and must be begun immediately by the deputies present, and that they must pursue it without interruption or hindrance.

. . . The Assembly will never lose hope of uniting within its midst all the deputies who are absent today; it will not cease to summon them to

fulfill the obligation imposed upon them to cooperate in the session of the Estates General. At whatever moment the absent deputies present themselves during the course of the session which is about to open, it declares in advance that it will hasten to receive them, and after verification of their powers, to share with them the continuation of the noble efforts which are to effect the regeneration of France. . . .

□

The Court was baffled, and, absurd as the word seems in the context of the next ten years of revolution, piqued. Louis and Necker hesitated to use force (partly because they were uncertain of the French Guard —a fact in itself an amazing demonstration of the reliance of the older "absolutisms" on customary psychology rather than guns to do their will) when it was obvious that force should be used if revolution were to be forestalled. The hard-nosed nobles had been right all along in warning of the usurping menace of the Third Estate; but they no longer were feudal lords—the monarchy had stripped the barons of their armed retainers. Thus the essentially timid, excited, talkative men who now called themselves the National Assembly found they could defy the authority of the mightiest monarchy on earth without facing the "whiff of grapeshot" that would have ended their bluff. What Louis desperately needed was not Necker, but Bonaparte. The verbal intrepidity of the commoners began to win support not only among the masses in Paris but impressively with the lower clergy and even certain liberal nobles. The Court maneuvered for time. A special "Royal Session" was planned for June 23rd, to settle all questions of procedure and, to prevent further meetings of the "National Assembly" until then, their hall was locked and surrounded with soldiers—the first use of force by the government! Like poor Charles trying to arrest the five members of Parliament in the English Revolution, the gesture of force (with even the trappings of an excuse that the hall needed preparation for the Royal Session) merely stimulated the delegates of the Third Estate to a bolder step. They adjourned to a nearby tennis court and there took a solemn oath—individually and subscribed both orally and by signature before all the delegates—"not to separate and to reassemble wherever circumstances require until the constitution of the kingdom is established and consolidated upon firm foundations. . . ." The Royal Session was an inevitable and total failure: the King's program was very reasonable and even conciliatory, but the commoners had tasted blood. And they now clearly saw the social realities of power, so that when with all moderation and rationality the King talked of liberty and equality in a nation whose "essential" constitution was one which would preserve the "ancient distinction of the three orders," he lost the good faith of the politicized and sophisticated Third. Louis ended the special session with the humiliating and infuriating phrases of lost glory and power: "It is I who, hitherto, have accomplished everything for the happiness of my people. . . . I order you, Gentlemen, to separate immediately, and to go tomorrow morning to the chambers allotted to your respective orders to resume your sessions. Accordingly, I order the Grand Master of Ceremonies to have the halls prepared."

From this confrontation of forces and classes until the fall of Robespierre and the stabilization of the state under the Directory, events
crowd so quickly and bewilderingly that we can do no more than try to
give a kind of impressionistic account of the drift of affairs with some
modest analytical ordering of the chaotic reality that distinguishes this
complicated revolution. The key to understanding the motion and direction of these events is one we have used before: for the struggle
among oligarchic groups which had been centered in legal and ideological terms at Versailles became in July of 1789 a popular and violent
struggle throughout the nation. Early in July, soldiers—mercenaries
from the provinces—began to arrive in Paris ostensibly to maintain
"order," actually and obviously to intimidate the Assembly. At this
critical juncture, when neither the King nor the delegates of the Third
Estate at Versailles were prepared resolutely to use or resist force, the
commonalty of Paris acted decisively. The electors who had been chosen
to select the delegates from Paris to the Estates General had remained
together, and they now invested themselves with the authoriy of an
emergency government.

A citizen army was called into being, street orators and mob action
replaced the polite defiance at Versailles. And on July 14th, three days
after the Parisian radicals were further incited by news that the King
had dismissed Necker (which might have meant the final decision to
dismiss the Assembly), the Bastille fell. The Court failed even then to
use the army assembled (again, the delay seems crucial and is hard to
understand) and instead the King appeared to capitulate to the new
force of popular anger. He recalled Necker, then went in person to Paris
to sanction the new communal government there, and to legalize the
"National Guard" formed by the revolutionary Parisians! Of course, the
capitulation was intended to be a long-range strategy—basically the
Court counted on subduing the revolutionary lesser classes as had been
done a hundred times before in European crises, by waiting for the
thieves to fall out amongst themselves and for the inertia of traditional
obedience to superiors to overcome the temporary imbalance of emotional rebellion. But the King's failure to strike with full violence and all
his armed strength immediately made all his later schemes for secret
subversion of the political programs of the bourgeoisie simply the
frustrated flailing of counterrevolutionary agitation. Eventually, only
the vast levies of *émigrés* and foreign princes could hope to restore the
old order by the massing of violence and terror.

While successful dissent raged in Paris, the peasants in the provinces
undertook an even more radical attack on the social base of the Old
Regime. Spurred on by a mysterious and pervasive fear—rooted in
generations of hate and guilt and failure—that the nobles were plotting
a terrible vengeance in blood, they assaulted the citadels of the most
ancient economic privilege by burning manorial documents and refusing any obligation under the systems of feudal tenure. The men in the
Assembly were somewhat aghast at the unexpected and universal movement of the peasants against legal tenures which hurt many bourgeois
investors and gentlemen as well as aristocrats—and which was an

affront to the sanctity of property—but the peasants were destroying the very base of the authority of the barons, so the political value of the *Jacqueries* was recognized by the more astute members of the Assembly. The counsels of revolution prevailed and in the course of one amazing night of August 4th the economic institutions of France were altered more radically in law than had ever been the case in the history of any country. Here are the decrees:

1. The National Assembly completely abolishes the feudal régime. It decrees that, among the rights and dues, both fedual and *censuel,* all those originating in real or personal serfdom, personal servitude, and those which represent them, are abolished without indemnification; all others are declared redeemable, and that the price and mode of the redemption shall be fixed by the National Assembly. Those of the said dues which are not extinguished by this decree shall, nevertheless, continue to be collected until indemnification takes place.

2. The exclusive right to maintain pigeon-houses and dove-cotes is abolished; the pigeons shall be confined during the seasons fixed by the communities; and during that time, they shall be regarded as game, and every one shall have the right to kill them upon his own land.

3. The exclusive right to hunt and to maintain unenclosed warrens is likewise abolished; and every land-owner shall have the right to kill or to have destroyed upon his own land only, all kinds of game, observing, however, such police regulations as may be established with a view to the safety of the public.

All *capitaineries,* royal included, and all hunting reserves, under whatever denominations, are likewise abolished, and provision shall be made, in a manner compatible with the respect due to property and liberty, for maintaining the personal pleasures of the king.

The president of the assembly shall be commissioned to ask of the king the recall of those sent to the galleys or exiled simply for violations of the hunting regulations, as well as for the release of those at present imprisoned for offences of this kind, and the dismissal of such cases as are now pending.

4. All manorial courts are suppressed without indemnification; nevertheless the magistrates of these courts shall continue to perform their functions until such time as the National Assembly shall provide for the establishment of a new judicial system.

5. Tithes of every description and the dues which have been substituted for them, under whatever denomination they are known or collected, even when compounded for, possessed by secular or regular congregations, by holders of benefices, members of corporations, including the Order of Malta and other religious and military orders, as well as those impropriated to lay persons and those substituted for the *portion congrue,* are abolished, on condition, however, that some other method be devised to provide for the expenses of divine worship, the support of the officiating clergy, the relief of the poor, repairs and rebuilding of churches and parsonages, and for all establishments, seminaries, schools, academies, asylums, communities and other institutions, for the maintenance of which

they are actually devoted. And moreover, until such provision shall be made and the former possessors shall enter upon the enjoyment of an income on the new system, the National Assembly decrees that the said tithes shall continue to be collected according to law and in the customary manner. Other tithes of whatever nature they may be, shall be redeemable in such manner as the Assembly shall determine. Until such regulation shall be issued, the National Assembly decrees that these, too, shall continue to be collected.

6. All perpetual ground rents, payable either in money or in kind, of whatever nature they may be, whatever their origin, and to whomsoever they may be due, as to members of corporations, domanial apanagists, or to the Order of Malta, shall be redeemable; *champarts,* of every kind and under every denomination, shall likewise be redeemable at a rate fixed by the assembly. No due shall in the future be created which is not redeemable.

7. The sale of judicial and municipal offices shall be suppressed forthwith. Justice shall be dispensed gratis; nevertheless, the magistrates at present holding such offices shall continue to exercise their functions and to receive their emoluments until the assembly shall have made provision for indemnifying them.

8. The fees of the country *curés* are abolished, and shall be discontinued as soon as provision shall be made for increasing the minimum salary (*portion congrue*) for priests and for the payment to the curates; and there shall be a regulation drawn up to determine the status of the priests in the towns.

9. Pecuniary privileges, personal or real, in the payment of taxes are abolished forever. The assessment shall be made upon all the citizens and upon all property, in the same manner and in the same form; and plans shall be considered by which the taxes shall be paid proportionally by all, even for the last six months of the current year.

10. Inasmuch as a national constitution and public liberty are of more advantage to the provinces than the privileges which some of these enjoy, and inasmuch as the surrender of such privileges is essential to the intimate union of all parts of the realm, it is declared that all the peculiar privileges, pecuniary or otherwise, of the provinces, principalities, districts, cantons, cities and communes, are once for all abolished and are absorbed into the law common to all Frenchmen.

11. All citizens, without distinction of birth, are eligible to any office or dignity, whether ecclesiastical, civil or military; and no profession shall imply any derogation.

12. Hereafter no remittances shall be made for annates or for any other purpose to the court of Rome, the vice-legation at Avignon, or to the nunciature at Lucerne; but the clergy of the diocese shall apply to their bishops for all provisions in regard to benefices and dispensations, which shall be granted gratis, without regard to reservations, expectancies, and monthly divisions, all the churches of France enjoying the same freedom.

13. The rights of *déport,* of *côte-morte, dépouilles, vacat, censaux,* Peter's pence, and other dues of the same kind, under whatever denomination, established in favor of bishops, archdeacons, archpresbyters,

chapters, *curés primitifs* and all others, are abolished, but appropriate provision shall be made for those benefices of archdeacons and archpresbyters which are not sufficiently endowed.

14. Pluralities shall not be permitted hereafter in cases where the revenue from the benefice or benefices held shall exceed the sum of three thousand livres. Nor shall any individual be allowed to enjoy several pensions from benefices, or a pension and a benefice, if the revenue which he already enjoys from such sources exceeds the same sum of three thousand livres.

15. The National Assembly shall consider, in conjunction with the king, the report which is to be submitted to it relating to pensions, favors and salaries, with a view to suppressing all such as are not deserved and reducing those which shall prove excessive; and the amount shall be fixed which the king may in the future disburse for this purpose.

16. The National Assembly decrees that a medal shall be struck in memory of the recent grave and important deliberations for the welfare of France, and that a *Te Deum* shall be chanted in gratitude in all the parishes and the churches of France.

17. The National Assembly solemnly proclaims the king, Lous XVI, the *Restorer of French Liberty.*

18. The National Assembly shall present itself in a body before the king, in order to submit to His Majesty the decree which has just been passed, to tender to him the tokens of its most respectful gratitude, and to pray him to permit the *Te Deum* to be chanted in his chapel, and to be present himself at this service.

19. The National Assembly shall consider, immediately after the constitution, the drawing up of the laws necessary for the development of the principles which it has laid down in the present decree which shall be transmitted without delay by the deputies to all the provinces, together with the decree of the tenth of this month, in order that both may be printed, published, announced from the parish pulpits, and posted up wherever it shall be deemed necessary.   □

Following the legalizing of social revolution in the August decrees, the Assembly turned to constitutional deliberations—a passion of the eighteenth century—the most remarkable result of which was the document issued in late August as a general statement of revolutionary ideals and intentions, "The Declaration of the Rights of Man and Citizen." This is a perfect specimen of the species of bourgeois libertarianism born in the English Revolution and flourishing in the American state constitutions and the publications of the presses of the Enlightenment:

The representatives of the French people, organized in National Assembly, considering that ignorance, forgetfulness, or contempt of the rights of man are the sole causes of public misfortunes and of the corruption of governments, have resolved to set forth in a solemn declaration the natural, inalienable, and sacred rights of man, in order that such declaration, continually before all members of the social body, may be a perpet-

ual reminder of their rights and duties; in order that the acts of the legislative power and those of the executive power may constantly be compared with the aim of every political institution and may accordingly be more respected; in order that the demands of the citizens, founded henceforth upon simple and incontestable principles, may always be directed toward the maintenance of the Constitution and the welfare of all.

Accordingly, the National Assembly recognizes and proclaims, in the presence and under the auspices of the Supreme Being, the following rights of man and citizen.

1. Men are born and remain free and equal in rights; social distinctions may be based only upon general usefulness.

2. The aim of every political association is the preservation of the natural and inalienable rights of man; these rights are liberty, property, security, and resistance to oppression.

3. The source of all sovereignty resides essentially in the nation; no group, no individual may exercise authority not emanating expressly therefrom.

4. Liberty consists of the power to do whatever is not injurious to others; thus the enjoyment of the natural rights of every man has for its limits only those that assure other members of society the enjoyment of those same rights; such limits may be determined only by law.

5. The law has the right to forbid only actions which are injurious to society. Whatever is not forbidden by law may not be prevented, and no one may be constrained to do what it does not prescribe.

6. Law is the expression of the general will; all citizens have the right to concur personally, or through their representatives, in its formation; it must be the same for all whether it protects or punishes. All citizens, being equal before it, are equally admissible to all public offices, positions, and employments, according to their capacity, and without other distinction than that of virtues and talents.

7. No man may be accused, arrested, or detained except in the cases determined by law, and according to the forms prescribed thereby. Whoever solicit, expedite, or execute arbitrary orders, or have them executed, must be punished; but every citizen summoned or apprehended in pursuance of the law must obey immediately; he renders himself culpable by resistance.

8. The law is to establish only penalties that are absolutely and obviously necessary; and no one may be punished except by virtue of a law established and promulgated prior to the offense and legally applied.

9. Since every man is presumed innocent until declared guilty, if arrest be deemed indispensable, all unnecessary severity for securing the person of the accused must be severely repressed by law.

10. No one is to be disquieted because of his opinions, even religious, provided their manifestation does not disturb the public order established by law.

11. Free communication of ideas and opinions is one of the most precious of the rights of man. Consequently, every citizen may speak, write, and print freely, subject to responsibility for the abuse of such liberty in the cases determined by law.

12. The guarantee of the rights of man and citizen necessitates a public

force; such a force, therefore, is instituted for the advantage of all and not for the particular benefit of those to whom it is entrusted.

13. For the maintenance of the public force and for the expenses of administration a common tax is indispensable; it must be assessed equally on all citizens in proportion to their means.

14. Citizens have the right to ascertain, by themselves or through their representatives, the necessity of the public tax, to consent to it freely, to supervise its use, and to determine its quota, assessment, payment, and duration.

15. Society has the right to require of every public agent an accounting of his administration.

16. Every society in which the guarantee of rights is not assured or the separation of powers not determined has no constitution at all.

17. Since property is a sacred and inviolable right, no one may be deprived thereof unless a legally established public necessity obviously requires it, and upon condition of a just and previous indemnity.　　　□

Thus the rhetoric flowed on, and the King temporized but delayed promulgating the revolutionary legislation until the pressure of the Assembly forced him again to try his troops. And once again the masses of Paris rose to defend the revolution in the October Days which so shook the Court that they moved to Paris as hostages against further antirevolutionary efforts. The Assembly also came to Paris, decreed martial law, and resumed their sessions. For the next two years this revolutionary body, proclaiming itself the voice and arm of the "people" of France, recreated the state in its own image—bourgeois, secular, national. From Rousseau and the *philosophes* the men of the old Third Estate drew the idealism which they now attempted to legislate in terms of their own experience and needs; the great ideals were those of equality of rights, freedom of expression, the sovereignty of the general will, and the secular base of truth and value. The new constitution ended the arbitrary powers of the monarch more completely than was true in England by very careful definitions of his functions (the power so to define being a major legal revolution in itself) and allegiance to the revolution. ("There is no authority in France superior to that of the law; the King reigns only thereby, and only in the name of the law may he exact obedience. On his accession to the throne, or as soon as he has attained his majority, the King, in the presence of the legislative body, shall take oath to the nation *to be faithful to the nation and to the law, to employ all the power delegated to him to maintain the Constitution decreed by the National Constituent Assembly in the years 1789, 1790, and 1791, and to have the laws executed.*") The preamble and Title I of the constitution of 1791 contain a good statement of bourgeois radicalism:

PREAMBLE

The National Assembly, wishing to establish the French constitution upon the principles which it has just recognized and declared, abolishes irrevocably the institutions that have injured liberty and the equality of rights.

There is no longer nobility, nor peerage, nor hereditary distinctions, nor distinctions of orders, nor feudal régime, nor patrimonial jurisdictions, nor any titles, denominations, or prerogatives derived therefrom, nor any order of chivalry, nor any corporations or decorations which demanded proofs of nobility or that were grounded upon distinctions of birth, nor any superiority other than that of public officials in the exercise of their functions.

There is no longer either sale or inheritance of any public office.

There is no longer for any part of the nation nor for any individual any privilege or exception to the law that is common to all Frenchmen.

There are no longer *jurandes,* nor corporations of professions, arts, and crafts.

The law no longer recognizes religious vows, nor any other obligation which may be contrary to natural rights or to the constitution.

Title I. Fundamental Provisions Recognized by the Constitution.

The constitution guarantees as natural and civil rights:

1. That all the citizens are eligible to offices and employments, without any other distinction than that of virtue and talent;

2. That all the taxes shall be equally apportioned among all the citizens in proportion to their means;

3. That like offences shall be punished by like penalties, without any distinction of persons.

The constitution likewise guarantees as natural and civil rights:

Liberty to every man to move about, to remain, and to depart without liability to arrest or detention, except according to the forms determined by the constitution;

Liberty to every man to speak, to write, to print and publish his ideas without having his writings subjected to any censorship or inspection before their publication, and to follow the religous worship to which he is attached;

Liberty to the citizens to meet peaceably and without arms, in obedience to the police laws;

Liberty to address individually signed petitions to the constituted authorities.

The legislative power cannot make any law that attacks and impedes the exercise of the natural and civil rights contained in the present title and guaranteed by the constitution; but as liberty consists only in the power to do anything that is not injurious to the rights of others or to the public security, the law can establish penalties against acts which, in attacking the public security or the rights of others, may be injurious to society.

The constitution guarantees the inviolability of property or a just and prior indemnity for that of which a legally established public necessity may demand the sacrifice.

Property intended for the expenses of worship and for all services of public utility belongs to the nation and is at all times at its disposal.

The constitution guarantees the alienations that have been or that shall be made under the forms established by law.

The citizens have the right to elect or choose the ministers of their religious sects.

There shall be created and organized a general establishment of *public relief* in order to bring up abandoned children, relieve infirm paupers, and provide work for the able-bodied poor who may not have been able to obtain it for themselves.

There shall be created and organized a *system of public instruction*, common to all citizens, gratuitous as regards the parts of education indispensable for all men, and whose establishments shall be gradually distributed in accordance with the division of the kingdom.

There shall be established national *fêtes* to preserve the memory of the French revolution, to maintain fraternity among the citizens, and to attach them to the constitution, the fatherland, and the laws.

A code of civil laws common to all the kingdom shall be made.   □

Of course the rhetoric was much better than the performance of the politicians, but the practical and legal achievements of the Assembly were not unimpressive. To begin with, the political power in the French nation was by the constitution of 1791 not only centered in the legislative body—elections to that body were remarkably democratic in structure. There was a real effort to give the government a popular base which would exclude only the poor (and therefore irresponsible). Lay and secular principles were validated by the reorganization of the church as an elective organization responsible to the citizens of France, and the removal of civil disabilities for Protestants and Jews. Church property was confiscated and the old clerical responsibilities for public worship and general education were assumed financially and morally by the revolutionized state. The provincial and central administrations were radically altered; legal institutions, the army, and varieties of learned and cultural societies all came under the rationalized programs of the increasingly politicized bourgeoisie and their allies.

The Defense of the Republic

The future leader of democratic radicalism, Maximilien Robespierre, whose very name has become a symbol of the kind of revolution anathematized by the conservatives and liberals of the world, was satisfied that in the constitution of 1791 the revolution in France had found its full realization in law—but the great question still unanswered was whether the revolutionary dispensation could be maintained against its enemies: the dispossessed privileged classes, their hangers-on, and the armed regimes of the old order beyond the borders of the revolutionary state. Even before the first legislature elected under the new constitution could meet, the attempted flight of the King in June made dramatically apparent the intransigence of the forces of counterrevolution. The political leadership in the Assembly which met in October of 1791 was necessarily inexperienced (the deputies of the

Constituent Assembly had decreed themselves ineligible for election to the new body), and there was as yet no organizational discipline or party orientation from which leaders might be recruited and through which the programs indicated by the constitution could be implemented. The result was that making the crucial and frightening decisions of the powerful revolutionary legislature (working with an "executive" monarch who while proclaiming "The Revolution is over" prepared treason) left the deputies divided in counsel and often ineffectual in action. There were over seven hundred of them, and the dynamics of their interaction in policy-making is very hard to chart. They were not bound by their constituents even as much as had been the deputies to the Estates General through the *cahiers*. Socially they were a less distinguished group than their predecessors—most were in the lower ranks of the capitalist hierarchy. The organizational nuclei which took the place of party affiliation were a variety of "clubs" where the like-minded gathered to drink and talk and plan action. Conservative, monarchist members belonged to the Feuillant Club; the radicals were in the Jacobin and Cordelier Clubs. And some three hundred of the members shifted, clubless and leaderless, between "Right" and "Left." To further complicate things, the Left split into two major groups—the moderate republicans (Girondins) and the radical democrats (*Enragés* or "Jacobins," as the term came to be applied only to radicals).

The first year of efforts to rule the most complicated and powerful society in the world under a revolutionary fundamental law, was, not surprisingly, more than a subversive King and a leaderless Assembly could manage with success. The issues were basic, life-and-death matters—war, economic and financial chaos, and, above all, the forces of counterrevolution. For the advantage in the struggle between the old order and the new had now passed to the unseated but undefeated aristocrats. They had unity, the support of all the power elements in Europe, a popular base in masses of Catholic peasants, the continuing economic recession, and the confusion and inexperience of the revolutionary politicians—all working toward what seemed a very probable restoration of Church and privilege. Decrees were issued by the Legislative Assembly for the return of the *émigrés* under a general amnesty, and for the disciplining of the counterrevolutionary clergy of the Vendée and elsewhere; but the King vetoed them, and the machinery for enforcement was in any case inadequate. War was declared on Austria, "considering that the Court of Vienna, in contempt of treaties, has continued to grant open protection to the French rebels; that it has instigated and formed a concert with several European powers against the independence and security of the French nation. . . ." But of course the new government was in no position to fight a war; the King was feeding military information to the Austrian Court, and there was no revolutionary army to support the aggressiveness of the Assembly. By the end of July, 1792, the monarchy had succeeded in subverting effective action under the constitution while awaiting the armies from the East to destroy the new France entirely, and the Assembly was too divided and moderate to cope with the mounting crisis.

The crisis of the summer of 1792 revealed once again the social depth and emotional fire of the revolution. In the ranks of the Assembly's emergency army of *Fédérés* (the symbol of whose spirit is superbly evoked by the marching song of the troops from Marseilles—*La Marseillaise*), in the resolutions of the Left Clubs, in petitions from the provinces and the working-class districts of the sections of Paris, anger and defiance confronted the schemes of the Court and the blundering of the monarchist politicians in the Assembly. The troops summoned to Paris by the Assembly petitioned that body on July 23rd in words that rang with the metal of a great revolution:

Representatives, elected by the people to defend and preserve their rights, hearken again today to the cry of grief!

Some weeks have passed since you declared that the *Patrie* was in danger, and you show us no means of saving it. Can it be that you are still ignorant of the cause of our ills, or can it be that you are ignorant of the remedies for them? Well, legislators, we citizens of the eighty-three departments, we, whom love of liberty alone has assembled here, we who are strong in the well-considered and vigorously expressed opinion of all Frenchmen, we show you that remedy, we tell you that the source of our ills lies in the abuse which the head of the executive power has made of his authority; we tell you that it exists, moreover, in the general staffs of the army, in a large proportion of the departmental and district directories, and in the courts. We tell you further, with the candor of a free people, a people standing together to defend its rights, that it is present, in part, in your own midst.

Legislators, the danger is imminent! It can no longer be dissembled! The reign of truth must begin! We are courageous enough to come to tell you about it; be courageous enough to listen.

Deliberate, forthwith and without intermission, upon the only means of remedying our ills. Suspend the executive power as was done last year. Thereby you will cut the root of all our ills. We know that the Constitution does not mention dethronement; but in order to declare that the King has forfeited the throne, he must be judged; and in order to judge him, he must be provisionally suspended. Convoke the primary assemblies in order to place yourselves in a position to learn, in a mediate manner, the will of the majority of the people concerning a national convocation with regard to the so-called constitutional articles relative to the executive power.

Legislators, there is not an hour, not a second to lose! The evil is at its height! Spare your *Patrie* a universal shock! Make use of all the power it has entrusted to you, and save it yourselves! Would you fear to call down upon your heads a terrible responsibility, or else (which we do not believe) would you give the nation a proof of impotence? Only one recourse would remain to it, namely, that of deploying all its force and crushing its tyrants. All of us, you as well as ourselves, have sworn a hundred times to live free and to die defending our rights. Well, we have just renewed that oath, which makes despots tremble when it is pro-

nounced by men of determination. Either we shall emerge from this
struggle free, or the tomb of liberty will encompass us.   □

The demands for the deposition of the King were pressed by the Paris
sections; the famous "Brunswick Manifesto" advertised the counterrevolutionary plans of the *émigrés;* the moderates in the Assembly hesitated, fearing the lower-class rage in Paris more than the Court's
treason; and so the radical masses of Paris proved once again that they
had the imagination and courage to gamble life for an ideal of life. On
the night of August 9, a revolutionary commune declared itself in
existence in Paris, took over the National Guard in key positions, and
the following morning ordered the storming of the palace by a rabble in
arms. The monarchy was in fact ended, and the Assembly, which still
would not depose Louis, became a hollow shell of debate and fruitless
edicts. The governing power in France had become the communards of
Paris. The following day, August 11, the Assembly decreed a new
election for a National Convention to draw up a new constitution, an
election significantly more democratic in franchise; for "The division of
Frenchmen into active and passive citizens shall be suppressed, and in
order to be admitted to citizenship, it shall suffice to be a Frenchman,
aged twenty-one years, domiciled for a year, living from his income or
the product of his labor, and not in a position of domesticity."
    In the six weeks which passed before the Convention met, the Com-
mune increasingly usurped the functions as well as the powers of the
Assembly. At the end of August the ultimate crisis in the revolution was
reached: the long-feared armies from the East, led by the Prussians,
were on the march to destroy the work of 1789. On September 2 the
Prussians were before Verdun. If Verdun fell, the revolution was lost. It
was this tremendous historical moment which created the Terror—
though as an organized regime it awaited Robespierre. The communards felt that the military crisis demanded national unity behind the
revolution, and they were fearful not only of defeat on the field of
battle, but of the bloody repression being plotted by the growing forces
of counterrevolution in Paris and the provinces as well. The era of
edicts seemed over to them, a paper wall against the traitors planning to
massacre patriots and return France to darkness. And so began the
terrible hunting out of "suspects," and the trials before the newly
created "Special Court" which began to feed the newly "humanized"
instrument of execution, the guillotine (the Academy of Surgery had
recommended the instrument because "humanity requires that the
death penalty be as painless as possible"; all previous methods were
barbaric, so the need was for a "machine, the performance of which
would be unfailing . . . according to the spirit and aim of the new
law"). So also the horrible massacre of suspected prisoners in Paris was
effected before the volunteers left their homes unguarded for the battle
at Verdun.
    In one of the strangest and most crucial battles in history, the citizen
armies of the revolution under the command of the unpredictable

Dumouriez forced the legions from Prussia to retreat from the field at Valmy. The daring *esprit* of the radicals seemed triumphantly vindicated. Paris was saved, there was time to rally support and prepare for the final trial of strength with all the enemies of the new France. The Convention met on the day of victory at Valmy, September 20th. All of the members were republicans, but they divided along class lines in trying to direct the course of the churning energies released by the general crisis. Sieyès was now in the Center, the Girondins represented provincial landowners and bourgeoisie and were the Right, and the Left was now practically the spokesmen for the lower classes of Paris, Jacobins, or Montagnards (for their high seats in the hall). In spite of the factionalism in the Convention, there was agreement on pushing the war to an international crusade "in the name of the French nation, the sovereignty of the people, the suppression of all established authorities . . . the abolition of the tithe, of feudalism, of seigneurial rights . . . of real and personal servitude . . . of nobility, and generally of all privileges.

"They shall announce to the people that they bring it peace, aid, fraternity, liberty, and equality, and they shall convoke it thereafter in primary or communal assemblies, in order to create and organize a provisional administration and justice; they shall supervise the security of persons and property; they shall have the present decree and the proclamation annexed thereto printed in the language or idiom of the territory and posted and executed without delay in every commune."

The revolutionary republic, having barely survived annihilation, now proclaimed the boldest political program in European history: "The French nation declares that it will treat as an enemy of the people anyone who, refusing liberty and equality, or renouncing them, might wish to preserve, recall, or treat with the prince and the privileged castes; it promises and engages itself not to subscribe to any treaty, and not to lay down its arms until after the establishment of the sovereignty and independence of the people upon whose territory the troops of the Republic have entered [in this case, Belgium] who shall have adopted the principles of equality and established a free and popular government."

The Convention also proceeded with dramatic decisiveness to put the King on trial for treason. Louis was voted a traitor almost unanimously, and the death penalty (by the humane science of the revolutionary blade) was voted by a majority. The King died by the guillotine on January 21st, 1793, and the Convention proclaimed, "Citizens, the tyrant is no more. . . . We have had to combat inveterate prejudices, and the superstition of centuries concerning monarchy. Involuntary uncertainties and inevitable disturbances always accompany great changes and revolutions as profound as ours. This political crisis has suddenly surrounded us with contradictions and tumults . . . but the cause has ceased, and the motives disappeared. . . . Now, above all, we need peace in the interior of the Republic, and the most active surveillance of the domestic enemies of liberty. . . ."

But peace and revolution the new republic could not have so cheaply.

Great Britain now forged a giant chain of powers to bring down the dangerous upstart—Austria, Prussia, Sardinia, and Holland, joined in the First Coalition of many which would throw the military might of Europe against the Revolution. The armies of the Convention were defeated in the Netherlands. There was no time now for debate or mistakes. All constitutional and social issues must be settled in the midst of war and counterrevolution. The men and measures had to be special, or all was lost. The year of Terror was at hand. It was a year made by a vastly complex historical process. It may not have been inevitable, but it is hard to imagine how otherwise the Revolution could have maintained itself. And it is impossible to imagine the revolutionaries of the Left acting with moderation and kindness when they felt their ideals and their lives threatened and betrayed.

The complicated and bitter struggle in the Convention between the Girondins and the Jacobins for control of the extraordinary mechanisms of power created by emergency decrees to meet the military and domestic crisis is a story we cannot tell properly within the limits of our book. In a general way, it is true to say that the democratic radicals were given their moment in history by the awesome nature of the problems confronting the government. The qualities of fanatical idealism and psychological daring (as well, perhaps, as the displaced aggression of the intellectual personality) are always rare, and seldom valued or useful, but the revolutionary movement in 1793 fed on its fanatics with the greed of a life-force. The hard decisions to kill or be killed, to feel challenged by defeat and stimulated by opposition, were for a critical year the prime stuff of leadership as the Revolution faced civil war in the Vendée, economic chaos in Paris and the provincial towns, fear and disillusionment and fatigue throughout the land, and the armies of the great powers closing for the kill. In the spring of 1793 the emergency Special Criminal Court began feeding the guillotine by thousands. In May the Parisian radicals were in the streets again—this time demanding the Convention purge itself of the untrustworthy (and provincial) deputies of moderation, the Girondins. The radicals within the Convention reacted with decision, and the moderates were driven out to deepen the forces opposing the government and thus make the work of war and crisis rule that much more tense and brutal.

The newly created Committee of Public Safety, a kind of ad hoc cabinet of the Convention, now began to govern under the banners of the most democratic and resolute ideals of the whole amazing generation. Their beloved *Patrie* stood beleaguered and battered by war, civil war, food riots, inflation, mob hysteria, and every sort of treason and treachery. Their answer was essentially twofold: a soaring restatement of the ideals of the Revolution, and the Terror. Here on May 8th is the voice of Robespierre addressing Paris on the issue of the counterrevolution in the provinces:

The armies of the Vendée, the armies of Brittany and of Coblenz are marching against Paris.

Parisians! The feudal masters are arming themselves because you are

the vanguard of humanity. All the great powers of Europe are equipping themselves against you and all the base and depraved persons in France support them.

We now know the entire plan of our enemies, and have means for our defense in our hands. I am not stating secrets to you, I am merely repeating the speech I delivered this morning in the Convention. I declared this morning in the Convention that the Parisians will march to La Vendée, and that on all the roads and in all the cities on our journey we shall gather friends and brothers, and that we must extinguish in a single blow all of them, all the rebels. All the friends of the Republic must rise in order to annihilate all the aristocrats in La Vendée.

This morning in the Convention I said that the rascals in La Vendée have allies in the very heart of Paris, and I demanded emphatically that the Parisian fighters who have borne the terrible burden of the Revolution for five years, a portion of whom will now take the field—that these republicans must not lose their wives and children during their absence, at the murderous hands of the counterrevolution. And no one today dared in the Convention to dispute the necessity of these measures.

Parisians! Let us hasten to meet the bandits of La Vendée!

Do you know why La Vendée is becoming a danger to us? La Vendée is a danger because great precautions have been taken to disarm a section of the population. But we shall create new republican legions and we shall not hand over our wives and children to the daggers of the counterrevolution.

This morning, in the Convention, I demanded the destruction of the rebels from La Vendée, and I also demanded that all aristocrats and moderates should at once be excluded from the Paris sections, and I also demanded that these suspected persons should be jailed.

We do not regard a person as a suspect merely because he was once a nobleman, a farmer general or a trader. Those persons are suspects who have not proved their quality as citizens, and they shall remain in our prisons until such time as the war may be terminated victoriously.

I asked money this morning in the Convention for the *sans-culottes,* for we must deliberate in the sections, and the workingman cannot deliberate and work at home at the same time. But he must receive pay for his task of guarding the city. I have asked millions for the *sans-culottes* of Paris. . . . I have asked that people cease calumniating in the Convention the people of Paris and that the newspaper writers who desire to contaminate public opinion have their mouths stopped for them.

I demanded this morning in the Convention, and I demand it here again —and neither in the Convention nor here do I hear any contrary voices— that an army be held in readiness in Paris, an army not like that of Dumouriez, but an army consisting of *sans-culottes* and workingmen. And this army must investigate Paris, must keep the moderates in check, must occupy all posts and inspire all enemies with terror.

I asked in the Convention that the forges in all public squares be set to work in order to forge weapons, weapons, and again weapons, and I asked that the Council of Ministers should supervise this production of arms.

The tyrants of this earth have made their plans. The defenders of the Republic are to be their sacrifices. Very well—in this most grave of all moments, we shall save freedom by the severest measures, we shall not consent to be murdered one by one.

Citizens! Certain representatives of the people have attempted to play off the Parisians against the Departments, the Departments against Paris, the Convention against the provinces, and the people in the galleries against the masses of the Parisians. They will not succeed. I have informed these gentlemen to this effect, and if the entire people of France could hear me, the entire people of France would be on my side.

Citizens! Do not be dismayed. We are told of immeasurably large foreign armies, of their connections with La Vendée, of their connections with Paris. Very well! What will all their efforts avail them against millions of *sans-culottes*?

We have an immense people of strong *sans-culottes* at our disposal, who cannot be permitted to drop their work. Let the rich pay! We have a Convention; perhaps not all its members are poor and resolute, but the corrupt section will for all that not be able to prevent us from fighting. Do you believe that the Mountain has not enough forces to defeat the adherents of Dumouriez, Orléans and Coburg combined? Parisians, the fate of all France, of all Europe, and all humanity is in your hands. The Mountain needs the People. The People needs the Mountain. And I brand the reports that the provinces are turning their arms against the Jacobins as fabrications on the part of our enemies.

In conclusion, I demand what I demanded in the Convention this morning, namely, that the Parisians shall be the revolutionary nucleus of the army, strong enough to drag the *sans-culottes* with them, that an army should remain in Paris in order to keep our enemies in check, that all enemies who are caught shall be placed under arrest, and that money must be confiscated from the rich in order to enable the poor to continue the struggle.   □

Here is the same voice, the voice of the man soon to become the master Terrorist, proposing a new Declaration of Rights as part of the reaffirmed and strengthened constitutionalism of the Revolution:

The representatives of the French people, met in National Convention recognizing that human laws which do not flow from the eternal laws of justice and reason are only the outrages of ignorance and despotism upon humanity; convinced that neglect and contempt of the natural rights of man are the sole causes of the crimes and misfortunes of the world; have resolved to set forth in a solemn declaration these sacred and inalienable rights, in order that all citizens, being enabled to compare constantly the acts of the government with the purpose of every social institution, may never permit themselves to be oppressed and disgraced by tyranny; and in order that the people may always have before their eyes the foundations of their liberty and their welfare; the magistrate, the rule of his duties; the legislator, the purpose of his mission.

In consequence, the National Convention proclaims in the face of the

world and under the eyes of the Immortal Legislator the following declaration of the rights of man and citizen.

1. The purposes of every political association is the maintenance of the natural and imprescriptible rights of man and the development of all his faculties.

2. The principal rights of man are those of providing for the preservation of his existence and his liberty.

3. These rights belong equally to all men, whatever may be the difference of their physical and mental powers.

4. Equality of rights is established by nature: society, far from impairing it, exists only to guarantee it against the abuse of power which renders it illusory.

5. Liberty is the power which belongs to man to exercise at his will all his faculties; it has justice for rule, the rights of others for limits, nature for principle, and the law for safeguard.

6. The right to assemble peaceably, the right to express one's opinions, either by means of the press or in any other manner, are such necessary consequences of the principle of the liberty of man, that the necessity to enunciate them supposes either the presence or the fresh recollection of despotism.

7. The law can forbid only that which is injurious to society; it can order only that which is useful.

8. Every law which violates the imprescriptible rights of man is essentially unjust and tyrannical; it is not a law.

9. Property is the right which each citizen has, to enjoy and dispose of the portion of goods which the law guarantees to him.

10. The right of property is restricted, as are all the others, by the obligation to respect the possessions of others.

11. It cannot prejudice the security, nor the liberty, nor the existence, nor the property of our fellow creatures.

12. All traffic which violates this principle is essentially illicit and immoral.

13. Society is under obligation to provide for the support of all its members either by procuring work for them or by assuring the means of existence to those who are not in condition to work.

14. The relief indispensable for those who lack the necessities of life is a debt of those who possess a superfluity; it belongs to the law to determine the manner in which this debt must be discharged.

15. The citizens whose incomes do not exceed what is necessary for their subsistence are exempted from contributing to the public expenses; the others shall support them progressively, according to the extent of their fortunes.

16. Society ought to favor with all its power the progress of public reason and to put instruction at the door of all the citizens.

17. Law is the free and solemn expression of the will of the people.

18. The people are the sovereign, the government is their creation, the public functionaries are their agents; the people can, when they please, change their government and recall their mandatories.

19. No portion of the people can exercise the power of the entire

people; but the opinion which it expresses shall be respected as the opinion of a portion of the people who ought to participate in the formation of the general will. Each section of the assembled sovereign ought to enjoy the right to express its will with entire liberty; it is essentially independent of all the constituted authorities and is capable of regulating its police and its deliberations.

20. The law ought to be equal for all.

21. All citizens are admissible to all public offices, without any other distinctions than those of their virtues and talents and without any other title than the confidence of the people.

22. All citizens have an equal right to participate in the selection of the mandatories of the people and in the formation of the law.

23. In order that these rights may not be illusory and equality chimerical, society ought to give salaries to the public functionaries and to provide so that all the citizens who live by their labor can be present in the public assemblies to which the law calls them, without compromising their existence or that of their families.

24. Every citizen ought to obey religiously the magistrates and the agents of the government, when they are the organs or the executors of the law.

25. But every act against the liberty, security, or property of a man, committed by anyone whomsoever, even in the name of the law outside of the cases determined by it and the forms which it prescribes, is arbitrary and void; respect for the law even forbids submission to it; and if an attempt is made to execute it by violence, it is permissible to repel it by force.

26. The right to present petitions to the depositories of the public authority belongs to every person. Those to whom they are addressed ought to pass upon the points which are the object thereof; but they can never interdict, nor restrain, nor condemn their use.

27. Resistance to oppression is a consequence of the other rights of man and citizen.

28. There is opposition against the social body when one of its members is oppressed. There is opposition against each member of the social body when the social body shall be oppressed.

29. When the government violates the rights of the people, insurrection is for the people and for each portion of the people the most sacred of rights and the most indispensable of duties.

30. When the social guarantee is lacking to a citizen he re-enters into the natural right to defend all his rights himself.

31. In either case, to tie down to legal forms resistance to oppression is the last refinement of tyranny. In every free State the law ought especially to defend public and personal liberty against the abuse of the authority of those who govern: every institution which is not based upon the assumption that the people are good and the magistrate is corruptible is vicious.

32. The public offices cannot be considered as distinctions, nor as rewards, but only as duties.

33. The offenses of the mandatories of the people ought to be severely and quickly punished. No one has the right to claim for himself more

inviolability than other citizens. The people have the right to know all the transactions of their mandatories: these ought to render to them a faithful account of their own administration and to submit to their judgment with respect.

34. Men of all countries are brothers and the different peoples ought to aid one another, according to their power, as if citizens of the same State.

35. The one who oppresses a single nation declares himself the enemy of all.

36. Those who make war on a people in order to arrest the progress of liberty and to destroy the rights of man ought to be pursued by all, not as ordinary enemies, but as assassins and rebellious brigands.

37. Kings, aristocrats, and tyrants, whoever they may be, are slaves in rebellion against the sovereign of the earth, which is mankind, and against the legislator of the universe, which is nature.   □

The Terror

The Terror I shall not be able to illustrate very well. The Twelve, led by Robespierre, were so busy, frightened, and brilliant in action that their work and its cost must be examined in the leisure of a monograph. They began by getting from the purged Convention the first democratic constitution in history—one that would have satisfied Andrew Jackson. The constitution of 1793 was ratified by an overwhelming vote of acclamation, but it was suspended as the fundamental law until the emergency should end—and when the emergency ended the democrats were driven from power, and France waited a hundred years for their return. I resist printing the constitution here because it is a long document and much like the earlier constitutions except for its rigorous provision for political egalitarianism.

The leaders of the Jacobin Convention and its Committee of Public Safety were, for both technical and ideological reasons, least able to cope successfully with the economic distress of the common people. They fulminated in the liberal and physiocratic stereotypes, issued decrees against all the economic villainies pilloried since the English Revolution (e.g., "Monopoly is a capital crime"), strengthened existing legislation for price-fixing, tried to stabilize the value of money, and established regulatory agencies to keep the basic needs of the citizens of the Republic from being sacrificed to corruption and profiteering. But the radicals were too unorganized and inexperienced to administer their laws, and too sensitive to the feelings of the propertied citizenry to resort to some form of "war communism," which alone could have relieved the pain of hunger and economic insecurity for the city masses. The radicals showed more imagination and resourcefulness in dealing with public finance, although again their reluctance to offend the bourgeois community left them tax-poor. They also attempted some very contemporary-sounding measures for creating and running by government initiative essential "war industries."

Politically, the Terror was more interesting. The provincial revolts were the immediate reason for the centralization of governing power in

the Committee, but even after they had collapsed in the late summer of 1793, the foreign wars required extraordinary rule by extraordinary men. The most brilliant and decisive achievement in the defense of *la Patrie* was the August decree for universal conscription and the total mobilization of the nation—for the first time in history the masses were armed by their ruling classes. Such was the power of radical eloquence, the sweep of radical imagination, the integrity of radical ideology, and the insidious assurance of nationalistic propaganda. "Henceforth, until the enemies have been driven from the territory of the Republic, the French people are in permanent requisition for army service.

"The young men shall go to battle; the married men shall forge arms and transport provisions; the women shall make tents and clothes, and shall serve in the hospitals; the children shall turn old linen into lint; the old men shall repair to the public places, to stimulate the courage of the warriors and preach the unity of the Republic and hatred of kings.

"National buildings shall be converted into barracks; public places into armament workshops; the soil of cellars shall be washed in lye to extract saltpeter therefrom. . . .

"The Committee of Public Safety is charged with taking all measures necessary for establishing, without delay, a special manufacture of arms of all kinds, in harmony with the élan and the energy of the French people. . . ."

The results of this mobilization stand as a monument to Jacobin genius and the contagious human reality of a great revolution. The "élan and the energy" released by radical agitation and organization would now for a generation roll back the mighty of the old world, and shake the foundations of the old world until no repair could restore the ancient tyranny of priest and caste.

Conservative Reaction and Radical Protest

The principles of 1789, Jacobin organization, and the *esprit* of the *levée en masse* mark out, for me, the essential outlines of the revolutionary story. As the vast armies of the Republic smashed the forces of the coalition on all frontiers and went on the offensive in the winter of 1793 (Napoleon Bonaparte drove the British from the Mediterranean port of Toulon in December), my interest flags. The real historical tension in the situation slackens; the remaining years (which run to yesterday) are those of adjustment of class interests, the settling in of the inevitable. The Terror continues to be interesting from a socio-psychiatric point of view for some months (the plodding Culture, the propaganda of Virtue, the legislation of the fine educational philosophy of the Enlightenment, the amusing Calendar—all bound up with the brutal butchery of "suspects" and the frenzied betrayals of comrades) until it is ended with the ghastly fall of Robespierre in July of 1794. But the story of the Terror most particularly demands detailed and subtle telling which it cannot have here. Robert Palmer's *Twelve Who Ruled* is a superb account that all should read.

After the fall of the radicals from control of the revolutionary govern-

ment, rule passed to the best organized, most ambitious, and wealthiest sections of the French middle classes. This is what seems "inevitable" to me. The radicals based their strength on popularity and emergency fears—transient passions. With the counterrevolutionaries destroyed, the armies of the Powers on the run, a fowl in most peasant pots, and bread in the mouths of most of the poor, the radical program had served its purpose. Nor should one forget the certainty of emotional exhaustion which had to overtake the radical leaders and their activist support. Radicalism is probably essentially an intellectual way of being, and social action has seldom proved a healthy milieu for the intellectual. So in 1795 the men of solid social self-interest, the "responsible" men, the opportunists, the men whose ideals were a function of their economic situation, became the inheritors of the power created by the great anger spurred and led by the radicals, which had brought down the empire of privilege. The dinosaurs were driven from the land; now the tigers could hunt. Here is a sample of the new code of the new predators, the Constitution of the Year III, a law drawn by the "best Elements" to replace the irresponsible instrument of the radicals of 1793. It is a thoroughly bourgeois, legalistic, lengthy, and uninspired piece of work which not even Sieyès could approve; but the bourgeois Republic has never been given to elegance. The interest of the document is in the revelation of the specific gravity of the forces which had made and would now stabilize the social revolution; something, at least, of the tone and intention of the whole endless formulation can be gathered from the preamble:

DECLARATION OF THE RIGHTS AND DUTIES OF MAN AND CITIZEN.

The French people proclaim in the presence of the Supreme Being the following declaration of the rights of man and citizen:

Rights.

1. The rights of man in society are liberty, equality, security, property.
2. Liberty consists in the power to do that which does not injure the rights of others.
3. Equality consists in this, that the law is the same for all, whether it protects or punishes.

Equality does not admit of any distinction of birth, nor of any inheritance of authority.
4. Security results from the co-operation of all in order to assure the rights of each.
5. Property is the right to enjoy and to dispose of one's goods, income, and the fruit of one's labor and industry.
6. The law is the general will expressed by the majority of the citizens or their representatives.
7. That which is not forbidden by the law cannot be prevented.

No one can be constrained to do that which it does not ordain.
8. No one can be summoned into court, accused, arrested, or detained

except in the cases determined by the law and according to the forms which it has prescribed.

9. Those who incite, promote, sign, execute, or cause to be executed arbitrary acts are guilty and ought to be punished.

10. Every severity which may not be necessary to secure the person of a prisoner ought to be severely repressed by the law.

11. No one can be tried until after he has been heard or legally summoned.

12. The law ought to decree only such penalties as are strictly necessary and proportionate to the offence.

13. All treatment which increases the penalty fixed by the law is a crime.

14. No law, either civil or criminal, can have retroactive effect.

15. Every man can contract his time and his services, but he cannot sell himself nor be sold; his person is not an alienable property.

16. Every tax is established for the public utility; it ought to be apportioned among those liable for taxes, according to their means.

17. Sovereignty resides essentially in the totality of the citizens.

18. No individual nor assembly of part of the citizens can assume the sovereignty.

19. No one can without legal delegation exercise any authority or fill any public function.

20. Each citizen has a legal right to participate directly or indirectly in the formation of the law and in the selection of the representatives of the people and of the public functionaries.

21. The public offices cannot become the property of those who hold them.

22. The social guarantee cannot exist if the division of powers is not established, if their limits are not fixed, and if the responsibility of the public functionaries is not assured.   □

A final voice from the party of radicals is worth attending to—that of the first socialist of the revolution, François ("Gracchus") Babeuf. He had been an activist in the revolutionary movement since 1789 in minor posts of power; when the radicals faltered and failed in 1794 he began to publish a newspaper (*Le Tribun du Peuple*) which was an analysis of the rightward drift of the Revolution and which ended with the suppression of the paper and prison for Babeuf. His argument was that of Winstanley against the same drift in the English Revolution: political reforms were unstable—above all the ideal of equality—so long as the economic institutions of the state favored the strong, and clever, and rich. The movement gathered its strength from the disaffected radicals in the dying days of French radicalism, and from the poor in Paris. The "Conspiracy of the Equals" commanded just enough power in the France of 1795–1796 to be worth destroying. The Directory infiltrated their meetings with spies, learned every detail of their intended revolt for a socialist France, and let Bonaparte dissolve them with even less effort than the "whiff of grapeshot" used to disperse the conservative insurrection a few months earlier. But the words remained to serve

the revolutions of the next century. Here is the famous manifesto from the hand of Babeuf's friend, Maréchal, written after all was lost:

MANIFESTO OF THE EQUALS

People of France! During fifteen centuries you have lived as slaves, and in consequence unhappily. It is scarcely six years that you have begun to breathe, in the expectation of independence, happiness, equality! The first demand of nature, the first need of man, and the chief knot binding together all legitimate association! People of France! you have not been more favored than other nations who vegetate on this unfortunate growth! Always and everywhere the poor human race, delivered over to more or less adroit cannibals, has served as a plaything for all ambitions, as a pasture for all tyrannies. Always and everywhere men have been lulled by fine words; never and nowhere have they obtained the thing with the word. From time immemorial it has been repeated, with hypocrisy, that *men are equal;* and from time immemorial the most degrading and the most monstrous inequality ceaselessly weighs on the human race. Since the dawn of civil society this noblest appanage of man has been recognized without contradiction, but has on no single occasion been realized; equality has never been anything but a beautiful and sterile fiction of the law. Today, when it is demanded with a stronger voice, they reply to us "Be silent, wretches! Equality of fact is nought but a chimera; be contented with conditional equality; you are all equal before the law. Canaille, what do you want more?" What do we want more? Legislators, governors, rich proprietors, listen, in your turn! We are all equal, are we not? This principle remains uncontested. For, unless attacked by madness, no one could seriously say that it was night when it was day.

Well! we demand henceforth to live and to die equal, as we have been born equal. We demand real equality or death; that is what we want.

And we shall have it, this real equality, it matters not at what price! Woe betide those who place themselves between us and it! Woe betide him who offers resistance to a vow thus pronounced!

The French Revolution is but the precursor of another, and a greater and more solemn revolution, and which will be the last!

The People has marched over the bodies of kings and priests who coalesced against it: it will be the same with the new tyrants, with the new political hypocrites, seated in the place of the old ones! What do we want more than equality of rights? We want not only the equality transcribed in the declaration of the Rights of Man and the citizens; we will have it in the midst of us, under the roof of our houses. We consent to everything for its sake; to make a clear board, that we may hold to it alone. Perish, if it must be, all the arts, provided real equality be left us! Legislators and governors, who have neither genius nor good faith; rich proprietors without bowels of compassion, you will try in vain to neutralize our holy enterprise by saying that it does no more than reproduce that agrarian law already demanded more than once before! Calumniators! be silent in your turn, and, in the silence of confusion, listen to our demands, dictated by nature and based upon justice!

The agrarian law, or the partition of lands, was the immediate aim of certain soldiers without principles, of certain peoples moved by their instinct rather than by reason. We aim at something more sublime and more equitable—the common good, or the community of goods. No more individual property in land; the land belongs to no one. We demand we would have, the communal enjoyment of the fruits of the earth, fruits which are for everyone!

We declare that we can no longer suffer, with the enormous majority of men, labor and sweat in the service and for the good pleasure of a small minority! Enough and too long have less than a million of individuals disposed of that which belongs to more than twenty millions of their kind!

Let this great scandal, that our grandchildren will hardly be willing to believe in, cease!

Let disappear, once for all, the revolting distinction of rich and poor, of great and small, of masters and valets, of governors and governed!

Let there be no other difference between human beings than those of age and sex. Since all have the same needs and the same faculties, let there be one education for all, one food for all. We are contented with one sun and one air for all. Why should the same portion and the same quality of nourishment not suffice for each of us? But already the enemies of an order of things the most natural that can be imagined, declaim against us. Disorganizers and factious persons, say they, you only seek massacre and plunder. People of France! we shall not waste our time in replying to them, but we shall tell you: the holy enterprise which we organize has no other aim than to put an end to civil dissensions and to the public misery.

Never has a vaster design been conceived or put into execution. From time to time some men of genius, some sages, have spoken of it in a low and trembling voice. Not one of them has had the courage to tell the whole truth.

The moment for great measures has come. The evil is at its height. It covers the face of the earth. Chaos, under the name of politics, reigns there throughout too many centuries. Let everything return once more to order, and reassume its just place!

At the voice of equality, let the elements of justice and well-being organize themselves. The moment has arrived for founding the Republic of the Equals, that grand refuge open for all men. The days of general restitution have come. Families groaning in misery, come and seat yourselves at the common table prepared by nature for all her children! People of France! the purest form of all glory has been reserved for thee! Yes, it is you who may first offer to the world this touching spectacle!

Ancient customs, antiquated conventions, would anew raise an obstacle to the establishment of the Republic of the Equals. The organization of real equality, the only kind that answers all needs without making victims, without costing sacrifices, will not perhaps please everybody at first. The egoist, the ambitious man, will tremble with rage. Those who possess unjustly will cry aloud against its injustice. Exclusive enjoyments, solitary pleasures, personal ease, will cause sharp regrets on the part of individuals who have fattened on the labor of others. The lovers of absolute power, the vile supporters of arbitrary authority, will scarcely bend their

arrogant chiefs to the level of real equality. Their narrow view will penetrate with difficulty, it may be, the near future of common well-being. But what can a few thousand malcontents do against a mass of men, all of them happy, and surprised to have sought so long for a happiness which they had beneath their hand?

The day after this veritable revolution they will say, with astonishment, What? the common well-being was to be had for so little? We had only to will it. Ah! why did we not will it sooner? Why had we to be told about it so many times? Yes, doubtless, with one man on earth richer, more powerful than his neighbors, than his equals, the equilibrium is broken, crime and misery are already in the world. People of France! by what sign ought you henceforward to recognize the excellence of a constitution? That which rests entirely on an equality of fact is the only one that can benefit you and satisfy all your wants.

The aristocratic charters of 1791 to 1795 have only riveted your bonds instead of rending them. That of 1793 was a great step indeed toward real equality, and never before had it been approached so closely; but yet, it did not achieve the aim and did not touch the common well-being, of which, nevertheless, it solemnly consecrated the great principle.

People of France! open your eyes and your heart to the fullness of happiness. Recognize and proclaim with us the "Republic of the Equals"! ▫

The Lost Generation

The bourgeois revolution in Europe was nearing completion. The greatest of European nations, the most powerful society on earth, had the contagion in its body. No one was henceforth safe. But for some years after the forces of conservatism had defeated Napoleon, the revolutionaries floundered, unable to reform their secret battalions or rekindle the great language of defiance and hope. There was a "lost generation" of radicals. The intellectual and emotional hiatus in the culture of the Europeans, the fear and reproach of the esthete, the man of letters, in contemplating the burdens of the *philosophes*, are beautifully expressed by Alfred de Musset in his *Confessions of a Child of the Century:*

During the wars of the Empire, while the husbands and brothers were in Germany, the anxious mothers brought forth an ardent, pale, nervous generation. Conceived between two battles, educated amidst the noises of war, thousands of children looked about them with a somber eye while testing their puny muscles. From time to time their blood-stained fathers would appear, raise them on their gold-laced bosoms, then place them on the ground and remount their horses.

The life of Europe was centered in one man; all were trying to fill their lungs with the air which he had breathed. Every year France presented that man with three hundred thousand of her youth; it was the tax paid to Caesar, and, without that troop behind him, he could not follow his fortune. It was the escort he needed that he might traverse the world, and then perish in a little valley in a deserted island, under the weeping willow. . . . Nevertheless, the immortal emperor stood one day on a hill

watching seven nations engaged in mutual slaughter; as he did not know whether he would be master of all the world or only half, Azrael passed along, touched him with the tip of his wing, and pushed him into the Ocean. At the noise of his fall, the dying powers sat up in their beds of pain; and stealthily advancing with furtive tread, all the royal spiders made the partition of Europe, and the purple of Caesar became the frock of Harlequin.

Then there seated itself on a world in ruins an anxious youth. All the children were drops of burning blood which had inundated the earth; they were born in the bosom of war, for war. For fifteen years they had dreamed of the snows of Moscow and of the sun of the pyramids. They had not gone beyond their native towns; but they were told that through each gate of these towns lay the road to a capital of Europe. They had in their heads all the world; they beheld the earth, the sky, the streets and the highways; all these were empty, and the bells of parish churches resounded faintly in the distance.

Pale phantoms, shrouded in black robes, slowly traversed the country; others knocked at the doors of houses, and when admitted, drew from their pockets large well-worn documents with which they drove out the tenants. From every direction came men still trembling with the fear which had seized them when they fled twenty years before. All began to urge their claims, disputing loudly and crying for help; it was strange that a single death should attract so many crows.

Three elements entered into the life which offered itself to these children: behind them a past forever destroyed, moving uneasily on its ruins with all the fossils of centuries of absolutism; before them the aurora of an immense horizon, the first gleams of the future; and between these two worlds—something like the Ocean which separates the old world from Young America, something vague and floating, a troubled sea filled with wreckage, traversed from time to time by some distant sail or some ship breathing out a heavy vapor; the present, in a word, which separates the past from the future, which is neither the one nor the other, which resembles both, and where one cannot know whether, at each step, one is treading on a seed or a piece of refuse.

It was in this chaos that choice must be made; this was the aspect presented to children full of spirit and of audacity, sons of the Empire and grandsons of the Revolution.

A feeling of extreme uneasiness began to ferment in all young hearts. Condemned to inaction by the powers which governed the world, delivered to vulgar pedants of every kind, to idleness and to ennui, the youth saw the foaming billows which they had prepared to meet, subside. All these gladiators, glistening with oil, felt in the bottom of their souls an insupportable wretchedness. The richest became libertines; those of moderate fortune followed some profession and resigned themselves to the sword or to the robe. The poorest gave themselves up with cold enthusiasm to great thoughts, plunged into the frightful sea of aimless effort. As human weakness seeks association and as men are herds by nature, politics became mingled with it. There were struggles with the *garde du corps* on the steps of the legislative assembly; at the theater, Talma wore

a peruke which made him resemble Caesar; everyone flocked to the burial of a liberal deputy.

The customs of students and artists, those customs so free, so beautiful, so full of youth, began to experience the universal change. Men in taking leave of women whispered the word which wounds to the death: contempt. They plunged into the dissipation of wine and courtesans. Students and artists did the same; love was treated as glory and religion: it was an old illusion. The *grisette,* that class so dreamy, so romantic, so tender, and so sweet in love, abandoned herself to the counting-house and to the shop.

Then they formed into two camps; on the one side the exalted spirits, sufferers, all the expansive souls who had need of the infinite, bowed their heads and wept; they wrapped themselves in unhealthy dreams and there could be seen nothing but broken reeds on an ocean of bitterness. On the other side the men of the flesh remained standing, inflexible in the midst of positive joys, and cared for nothing except to count the money they had acquired. It was only a sob and a burst of laughter, the one coming from the soul, the other from the body.

This is what the soul said:

"Alas! Alas! religion has departed; the clouds of heaven fall in rain; we have no longer either hope or expectation, not even two little pieces of black wood in the shape of a cross before which to clasp our hands. The star of the future is loath to rise; it cannot get above the horizon; it is enveloped in clouds, and like the sun in winter its disk is the color of blood, as in '93. There is no more love, no more glory. What heavy darkness over all the earth! And we shall be dead when the day breaks."

This is what the body said:

"Man is here below to satisfy his senses, he has more or less of white or yellow metal to which he owes more or less esteem. To eat, to drink, and to sleep, that is life. As for the bonds which exist between men, friendship consists in loaning money; but one rarely has a friend whom he loves enough for that. Kinship determines inheritance; love is an exercise of the body; the only intellectual joy is vanity."

Like the Asiatic plague exhaled from the vapors of the Ganges, frightful despair stalked over the earth. Already Chateaubriand, prince of poesy, wrapping the horrible idol in his pilgrim's mantle, had placed it on a marble altar in the midst of perfumes and holy incense. Already the children were tightening their idle hands and drinking in their bitter cup the poisoned brewage of doubt. Already things were drifting toward the abyss, when the jackals suddenly emerged from the earth. A cadaverous and infected literature which had no form but that of ugliness, began to sprinkle with fetid blood all the monsters of nature.

Who will dare to recount what was passing in the colleges? Men doubted everything: the young men denied everything. The poets sang of despair; the youth came from the schools with serene brow, their faces glowing with health and blasphemy in their mouths. Moreover, the French character, being by nature gay and open, readily assimilated English and German ideas; but hearts too light to struggle and to suffer withered like crushed flowers. Thus the principle of death descended slowly and with-

out shock from the head to the bowels. Instead of having the enthusiasm of evil we had only the negation of the good; instead of despair, insensibility. Children of fifteen, seated listlessly under flowering shrubs, conversed for pastime on subjects which would have caused the motionless groves of Versailles to shudder with terror. The Communion of Christ, the host, those wafers that stand as the eternal symbol of divine love, were used to seal letters; the children spat upon the bread of God.

Happy they who escaped those times! Happy they who passed over the abyss while looking up to Heaven. There are such, doubtless, and they will pity us.

It is unfortunately true that there is in blasphemy a certain discharge of power which solaces the burdened heart. When an atheist, drawing his watch, gave God a quarter of an hour in which to strike him dead, it is certain that it was a quarter of an hour of wrath and of atrocious joy. It was the paroxysm of despair, a nameless appeal to all celestial powers; it was a poor wretched creature squirming under the foot that was crushing him; it was a loud cry of pain. And who knows? In the eyes of Him who sees all things, it was perhaps a prayer.

Thus these youth found employment for their idle powers in a fondness of despair. To scoff at glory, at religion, at love, at all the world, is a great consolation for those who do not know what to do; they mock at themselves and in doing so prove the correctness of their view. And then it is pleasant to believe oneself unhappy when one is only idle and tired. Debauchery, moreover, the first conclusion of the principle of death, is a terrible millstone for grinding the energies.

The rich said: "There is nothing real but riches, all else is a dream; let us enjoy and then let us die." Those of moderate fortune said: "There is nothing real but oblivion, all else is a dream; let us forget and let us die." And the poor said: "There is nothing real but unhappiness, all else is a dream; let us blaspheme and die."

All the evils of the present come from two causes: the people who have passed through 1793 and 1814 nurse wounds in their hearts. That which was is no more; what will be is not yet. Do not seek elsewhere the cause of our malady.   ◻

Suggested Reading

The French Revolution is without question the best studied of all such phenomena in the modern world. I can only suggest from a huge literature (mostly French and often bitterly controversial) those books which embody the essentials of traditional scholarship and a few of the more brilliant new ventures into untrod paths of historical inquiry. The first book to read is Henri Sée, *Economic and Social Conditions in France During the Eighteenth Century* (New York: F. S. Crofts Co., 1927); then perhaps a general sample of the debate over *The Economic Origins of the French Revolution** edited by Ralph Greenlaw (Boston: D. C. Heath & Company, 1958*). Elinor Barber has attempted to define *The Bourgeoisie in Eighteenth Century France,** (Princeton: Princeton University Press, 1955; Princeton Paperback*). A brilliant book by a man close to the events is

Alexis de Tocqueville, *The Old Regime and the French Revolution** (Garden City, N. Y.: Doubleday & Company, Inc., 1955; Anchor*) and most valuable of all is the contemporary account of *Arthur Young's Travel in France During the Years 1781, 1788, 1789,* C. Maxwell, ed., (London: Cambridge University Press, 1929).

On the culture of the Age of Reason, see Volume II of Preserved Smith, *A History of Modern Culture** (New York: Henry Holt & Co., 1934; Crowell Collier*) and Ernst Cassirer, *The Philosophy of the Enlightenment** (Princeton: Princeton University Press, 1951; Beacon*). Of newer interpretations the most important is probably Peter Gay, *The Enlightenment,** two volumes, (New York: Alfred A. Knopf, Inc., 1966; Vintage*) and by the same author *Party of Humanity* (New York: Alfred A. Knopf, Inc., 1963). Very readable is Alfred Cobban, *In Search of Humanity* (New York: George Braziller, Inc., 1960). Crane Brinton edited the useful *Portable Age of Reason Reader** for Viking.

For the revolution itself, the indispensable beginning is with Georges Lefebvre, *The Coming of the French Revolution** (Princeton: Princeton University Press, 1947; Princeton Paperback*), and the same author's *The French Revolution from Its Origins to 1793* (New York: Columbia University Press, 1962). Then probably the best short account of events remains Albert Mathiez, *The French Revolution** (New York: Alfred A. Knopf, Inc., 1928; Universal Library*). The Terror is sensitively and dramatically portrayed by R. R. Palmer, *Twelve Who Ruled** (Princeton: Princeton University Press, 1941; Atheneum*). Albert Mathiez, *After Robespierre** (Alfred A. Knopf, Inc., 1931; Universal Library*) is a classic. Finally, in addition to the Marxist classics of Mathiez and Lefebvre, two brilliant new departures in Marxist scholarship which have profoundly affected all recent historical writing are George Rudé, *The Crowd in the French Revolution** (London: Oxford University Press, 1959; Oxford Paperback*) and Albert Soboul, *Parisian Sans-Culottes and the French Revolution, 1793–1794* (London: Oxford University Press, 1964).

6 Revolution in the Nineteenth Century

1848—Annus Mirabilis

In late February of 1848 a quarrel within the French upper bourgeoisie —a reform movement against the ministry of Guizot—once again put the torch to the revolutionary tinderbox of Paris. Parisian crowds poured out to insurrectionary demonstrations, and, in rapid sequence, the initial rallying cry of *à bas Guizot* was replaced by the demand for *la république.* Louis Philippe, once hailed as the most progressive of constitutional monarchs, abdicated in a panic, a provisional government was hastily formed, and the Republic proclaimed to the nation and to an intensely watchful European public. The continental response was not long in coming: news of the Parisian events reverberated in Berlin, Vienna, Budapest and Milan; from Prussia and the lesser German states, through the multi-national sections of the Austrian Empire, from North Italy to Rome, middle-class liberals rose to the latest French example; in Central and Southern Europe exhilarated bourgeois revolutionists, stiffened by the muscle support of the working classes, presented to frightened rulers programs for written constitutions, representative government, freedom of speech and of the press. Everywhere the pattern was the same—indeed, by the spring of 1848 bourgeois liberalism seemed on the way to a clean sweep of the crowned heads of Europe, to the obliteration of the age and the aims of Metternich.

It was a glorious, an intoxicating victory in that "peoples' spring" of '48: "The strongholds of reaction had fallen, rubble had to be carted away, new structures were to arise; there was a great void, filled by sun and air; and over it brooded a singularly enlightened *Zeitgeist.* Men dreamed dreams and saw visions, and anything the spirit could conceive seemed attainable in that year of unlimited possibilities." The cooperation of all classes in the ordered freedom of the Republic, universal suffrage, women's rights, mitigation of the social frightfulness of the factory system, an end to aristocratic privilege, exploitation and class inequality—such soaring hopes as these enthused the revolutionists of the West; in Germany, in Austria, Hungary or Italy the ideologues planned beyond the disappearance of foreign and despotic princes, to the dream-construction of modern nation-states, stripped of feudal vestiges, pacific, forward-looking states, responsive to the needs and desires of all their citizens. Truly, this was, as Namier called it, the

revolution of the intellectuals, with its poets in Paris and professors in Frankfurt, its passionate nationalists, flamboyant orators and political theorists. And theoretically perfect it seemed, with the magnificent successes of the early months, an almost bloodless insurrection in which the progressive majority of Europeans had simply brushed aside the anachronism of an autocratic political order.

But—for reasons mysterious to most bourgeois contemporaries—both the idea and the practical construct of the liberal state proved to be merely a stage, rather than a final solution, in the course of revolution. Once again Parisians led the way to a second point of revolutionary development: on June 23 workers in Paris rose in rebellion against middle-class leadership, and for three days the French capital rocked with the violence of the proletarian attempt to push beyond the political revolution, beyond the achievement of bourgeois republicanism. Inevitably, the French example was contagious; in even the barely industrialized center of Europe the working classes, aroused and fully engaged, pressed on toward the goal—however vaguely defined—of social revolution, an inchoate, swelling demand for social justice and reconstruction.

Here was the critical hour: the horrified bourgeoisie, and attendant intellectuals, hesitated, debated, divided, and finally ran from revolution, scuttling for protection to the traditional wardens of peace and order in their respective lands. Middle-class liberals, who had gone so proudly to battle against aristocratic monopoly and arbitrary rule, who had fought in the name of mystically united national citizenries, were brought perforce to reality in the face of radical revolution—civil war —from below. After the June uprisings ruler and bourgeois joined, in familiar partnership, in defense of property, privilege, and social peace. After the rapprochement the liberal bourgeoisie seceded from revolution, and, predictably enough, lost not only momentum but the constitutional gains already won: by 1851 Europe was restored its monarchical cast, rigidly controlled by the old ruling houses of Austria, Prussia and Russia, and by an interesting new adventure-in-dictatorship with the second Bonaparte in France.

As an attempt to change the political and social facts of European life, the revolutions of 1848 accomplished nothing, except to expose insurrectionary groups to more efficient methods of police repression, and to provide a springboard for the quasi-modern rule of Louis Napoleon. Yet as a chapter in the revolutionary history of Europe—and especially of France—the events of 1848 have a large measure of meaning and fascination. It is the obvious things that are important: the ignominious failure of liberal nationalism and the shattering disillusionment of bourgeois intellectuals; and the worker rebellions that are less and less the actions of desperate mobs, more and more those of disciplined, self-conscious minority movements.

The heart of the action in 1848 was in France; France, the most advanced of continental nations with her cultural brilliance, her revolutionary traditions, her writers, poets, and historians who embodied all the enlightened ideals of this confident age. Into the '48 revolution

French intellectuals poured a fund of hopes—and convictions—that had been building for a quarter century. This was the uprising that would not only complete the task of the Great Revolution and consummate the political transformation of ancient monarchical France. In the revolutionized liberal state all things modern would flourish, and its body of citizens, held together by the common bond of celebration of the *gloire* of the nation, freed for invention and experimentation, for pursuit of social and scientific knowledge, would explore the countless new paths that had opened for the benefit of man. The liberals' dream—how hollow it seemed in the June Days in Paris, during the savage action that checked the working-class rebellion, and how empty and hopeless it was after 1851, measured against the tawdry reality of the Second Empire.

The point is that bourgeois intellectuals of the mid-nineteenth century lived in a dream-image of their society. Like so much in the French scene, their concern for the unreal can be traced to the Revolution of 1789: heirs of the Revolution they most certainly were, trained to the expectation of progress and social change; but reaction to the course and the outcome of the eighteenth-century movement had marked the post-revolutionary generation. Somehow, sometime, as the later intellectuals saw it, the Revolution would be redone, but without violence, without class hatred and "Jacobin excesses"; they convinced themselves that in the enlightenment of the new century, a reproduction of the class struggles of 1793–1795 was impossible, and that the French Revolution would proceed through voluntary and harmonious social action, a monument of hope to the entire world. Nor was it only liberals and republicans who were essentially antirevolutionary; utopian socialists like Saint Simon and Fourier, and practical men of the Left like Louis Blanc—such voices, too, contributed to an intellectual climate of belief in persuasion, in peaceful transition to reform of society misshapen by capitalist exploitation, bourgeois hypocrisy and industrial abuses. Men of the nineteenth century refused to see the inevitable divisiveness of class interests—that the age of Voltaire had recognized clearly—and it was this social myopia that exposed them to swift and bitter disillusionment after June of 1848.

The strange phenomenon of nonrevolutionary revolutionists is documented in much of the social literature of the first half of the nineteenth century. To the Romantic historian Jules Michelet the Revolution *was* France, or rather France was revolutionary Idea, and thus true to herself only in movement toward the revolutionary future. The Great Revolution is with Michelet a glorious moment of history but it is a truncated memory that he treasures, a national regeneration proceeding without internal and external strife. The passage that follows is from Michelet's *Historical View of the Revolution:*

Every year, when I descend from my chair, at the close of my academic labors, when I see the crowd disperse—another generation that I shall behold no more—my mind is lost in inward contemplation. . . .

I commune with my own mind. I interrogate myself as to my teaching,

my history, and its all-powerful interpreter—the spirit of the Revolution.

It possesses a knowledge of which others are ignorant. It contains the secret of all bygone times. In it alone France was conscious of herself. When, in a moment of weakness, we may appear forgetful of our own worth, it is to this point we should recur in order to seek and recover ourselves again. Here, the inextinguishable spark, the profound mystery of life, is ever glowing within us.

The Revolution lives in ourselves—in our souls; it has no outward monument. Living spirit of France, where shall I seize thee, but within myself?—The governments that have succeeded each other, hostile in all other respects, appear at least agreed in this, to resuscitate, to awaken remote and departed ages. But thee they would have wished to bury. Yet why? Thou, thou alone dost live.

Thou livest! I feel this truth perpetually impressed upon me at the present period of the year, when my teaching is suspended—when labor grows fatiguing, and the season becomes oppressive. Then I wander to the Champ de Mars, I sit me down on the parched grass, and inhale the strong breeze that is wafted across the arid plain.

The Champ de Mars! This is the only monument that the Revolution has left. . . . Her monument is this sandy plain, flat as Arabia. . . .

And though the plain be arid, and the grass be withered, it will, one day, renew its verdure.

For in that soil is profoundly mingled the fruitful sweat of their brows who, on a sacred day, piled up those hills—that day when, aroused by the cannon of the Bastille, France from the North and France from the South came forward and embraced; that day when three millions of heroes in arms rose with the unanimity of one man, and decreed eternal peace.

Alas! poor Revolution. How confidingly on thy first day didst thou invite the world to love and peace. "O my enemies," didst thou exclaim, "there are no longer any enemies!" Thou didst stretch forth thy hand to all, and offer them thy cup to drink to the peace of nations—but they would not.

And even when they advanced to inflict a treacherous wound, the sword drawn by France was the sword of peace. It was to deliver the nations, and give them true peace—liberty—that she struck the tyrants. Dante asserts Eternal Love to be the founder of the gates of hell. And thus the Revolution wrote *Peace* upon her flag of war. . . .

France had so completely identified herself with this thought, that she did her utmost to restrain herself from achieving conquests. Every nation needing the same blessing—liberty—and pursuing the same right, whence could war possibly arise? Could the Revolution, which, in its principle, was but the triumph of right, the resurrection of justice, the tardy reaction of thought against brute force—could it, without provocation, have recourse to violence?

This utterly pacific, benevolent, loving character of the Revolution seems today a paradox:—so unknown is its origin, so misunderstood its nature, and so obscured its tradition, in so short a time!

The violent, terrible efforts which it was obliged to make, in order not to perish in a struggle with the conspiring world, has been mistaken for the Revolution itself by a blind, forgetful generation. . . .

Thus, two evils, the greatest that can afflict a people, fell upon France at once. Her own tradition slipped away from her, she forgot herself. And, every day more uncertain, paler, and more fleeting, the doubtful image of Right flitted before her eyes. . . .

Weak and unarmed, and ready for temptation, it [the nation] had lost sight of the idea by which alone it had been sustained; like a wretched man deprived of sight, it groped its way in a miry road: it no longer saw its star. What! the star of victory? No, the sun of Justice and of the Revolution. . . .   □

By 1848 idealization of the revolutionary nation-state was the common currency of expression, whether the speaker was liberal, democrat, democratic-socialist. The selection following is by Alphonse de Lamartine, liberal-republican leader, and minister in the Provisional Government:

France is a Republic. The French Republic does not need to be recognized in order to exist; it *is* by natural right and by national might. It is the will of a great nation authorized by itself alone. However, since the French Republic wishes to enter into the family of established nations as a regular power and not as a force disruptive of European order, it is fitting that you should promptly make known to the governments to which you are accredited the principles and policies which hereafter will govern the foreign policies of the French government.

The proclamation of the French Republic is not an act of aggression against any form of government anywhere in the world. The diversity of forms of government is just as legitimate as is the diversity of character, geographical situation, and intellectual, moral and material development among peoples. Nations, like individuals, are not all the same age; the principles which govern them pass through successive phases. Monarchic, aristocratic, constitutional and republican forms of government express the varying degrees of maturity of the mind of the people. They demand more liberty in proportion to their readiness for it; they demand more equality and democracy as they become more animated by justice and love toward fellow man. It is a question of time. A people is as much lost by setting ahead the clock of this maturity as it would be dishonored by failing to profit by it. Monarchies and the republics do not, in the eyes of true statesmen, represent absolute principles locked in a death struggle; rather they are contrasting facts which can coexist providing they have mutual respect and understanding.

War, then, is not now one of the principles of the French Republic as it was its fatal and glorious necessity in 1792. Between 1792 and 1848 lies half a century. To go back, after this half century, to the principles of 1792, to the period of Empire and conquest, would not be advancing but regressing. Yesterday's revolution [February, 1848] was a step forward, not backward. We and the world alike wish to go forward in brotherhood and peace. . . .

In 1792, the nation was not united, two peoples existed on the same soil. . . . Today there are no longer any distinct and unequal classes, all are

enfranchised by liberty, all are leveled by equality before the law. . . . There is not a single French citizen, whatever his political belief, who does not put his fatherland first and who, by this very unity, makes her impregnable in the face of attempted invasion. . . .

In 1792 neither France nor Europe was ready to understand and accept a harmonious interrelation of nations with its resultant of benefits to mankind. . . . Fifty years freedom of thought, freedom of speech, freedom of the press have had their effect; books, newspapers and speeches have propagated European enlightenment. Reason, shining over all, passing over national boundaries, has given men's minds a fatherland of the spirit which will be the crowning achievement of the French Revolution and the establishment of international brotherhood throughout the world.

In 1792, liberty was a novelty, equality a scandal, the Republic a problem. . . . [Thrones and peoples] will realize that there is such a thing as conservative liberty; that there may exist in a Republic not only a better system but also that there is more true order in government by all for all than in government by and for a few.

Make no mistake, however. These ideas which the Government charges you to present to the European powers as a pledge of European security are not to be taken as suing for forgiveness by the Republic for daring to be born, still less as a humble petition for the right to exist as a great state. . . .

The French people will declare war on no one; needless to say, she would accept the challenge were she to be attacked. The thoughts of those now governing France run as follows: France would be fortunate, in case war should be imposed upon her, thus forcing her to grow in strength and glory despite her moderation. France would be guilty were she to declare war without being forced to do so. . . .

Although the French Republic proclaims that the treaties of 1815 no longer exist except as facts to be modified by mutual consent, and that it is her right and her duty to bring about this modification, legally and peacefully, nevertheless, the good sense, moderation, conscientiousness, and prudence of the Republic exist and these are, for Europe, a better and more honorable guarantee than the letter of those treaties which have been frequently violated or modified.

Endeavor, Sir, to achieve comprehension and acceptance of the Republic's emancipation from the treaties of 1815 and, at the same time, show that this freedom is not irreconcilable with the peace of Europe. Thus, we proclaim it aloud, were Providence to decree that the hour of reconstruction of certain oppressed European nations had struck—were Switzerland, our faithful ally since the days of Francis I, either hindered or threatened in her political progress . . . , were Italy's independent states to be invaded, their internal transformation to be limited or thwarted, or were these states to be forcibly prevented from joining in the formation of an Italian nation, then the French Republic would believe she had the right to take arms herself in order to protect these legitimate movements of state growth and nationality.

The Republic, you see, in one bound has passed by the age of proscription and dictatorships. She is equally resolved never to let liberty be

veiled at home nor her democratic principles be obscured abroad. Let no man place his hand between the peaceful radiance of her liberty and the eyes of mankind. She declares herself to be allied by heart and mind to all rights, progress and legitimate development of the institutions of all nations who wish to live by the same principles as her own. Never will she carry on hidden and inflammatory propaganda among her neighbors. Well she knows that the only liberties which endure are those which spring from their native soil. Nonetheless, she will strive, by the example of order and peace she sets to the world, to indulge in the only real and honest propagandizing, that of winning admiration and sympathy. This is no war, it is nature; this is no agitation of Europe, it is life; this is no torch to set the world aflame, it is a beacon light to summon and guide the peoples of the world! . . .

These three words [Liberty, Equality and Fraternity] in their application to our foreign affairs mean this: setting France free from the chains which outrage her principles and her dignity; restoration of the position she should hold among the great European powers; finally, the proclamation of her alliance and amity with all peoples. If France is aware of her role in the liberal, civilizing mission of this century, no one of these words means war. If Europe is wise and just, there is not one which does not say peace.   ◻

But if the revolution of '48 possessed a surplus of participants bred to and immersed in a process of self-delusion, there was one observer who cut through the maze of rhetoric to the core-meaning of the revolution and its aftermath. For coincidental with the '48 revolutions were the first published works of Karl Marx—of a mind which combined the analytic brilliance of the *philosophes* with the idealistic humanism of the Romantics. The mystic vagaries of bourgeois intellectualism fade beside the incisiveness of Marx's interpretation and the clarity of his narration. Marx's writings had no effect on the revolutionary events at mid-century—their impact would be felt later—but the essays that appeared between 1848 and 1852 described and summarized the period with an insight into French political behavior wholly lacking in other contemporary products. *The Eighteenth Brumaire of Louis Bonaparte,* excerpts of which are reproduced below, was the last of these essays, the monograph in which Marx, explaining the final stages of the bourgeois class struggles, rounded off his analysis of the revolution in France:

Hegel remarks somewhere that all facts and personages of great importance in world history occur, as it were, twice. He forgot to add: the first time as tragedy, the second as farce. Caussidière for Danton, Louis Blanc for Robespierre, the *Montagne* of 1848 to 1851 for the *Montagne* of 1793 to 1795, the Nephew for the Uncle. And the same caricature occurs in the circumstances attending the second edition of the eighteenth Brumaire!

Men make their own history, but they do not make it just as they please; they do not make it under circumstances chosen by themselves, but under circumstances directly encountered, given and transmitted from the past.

The tradition of all the dead generations weighs like a nightmare on the brain of the living. And just when they seem engaged in revolutionising themselves and things, in creating something that has never yet existed, precisely in such periods of revolutionary crisis they anxiously conjure up the spirits of the past to their service and borrow from them names, battle cries and costumes in order to present the new scene of world history in this time-honoured disguise and this borrowed language. Thus Luther donned the mask of the Apostle Paul, the Revolution of 1789 to 1814 draped itself alternately as the Roman republic and the Roman empire, and the Revolution of 1848 knew nothing better to do than to parody, now 1789, now the revolutionary tradition of 1793 to 1795. In like manner a beginner who has learnt a new language always translates it back into his mother tongue, but he has assimilated the spirit of the new language and can freely express himself in it only when he finds his way in it without recalling the old and forgets his native tongue in the use of the new.

Consideration of this conjuring up of the dead of world history reveals at once a salient difference. Camille Desmoulins, Danton, Robespierre, Saint-Just, Napoleon, the heroes as well as the parties and the masses of the old French Revolution, performed the task of their time in Roman costume and with Roman phrases, the task of unchaining and setting up modern *bourgeois* society. The first ones knocked the feudal basis to pieces and mowed off the feudal heads which had grown on it. The other created inside France the conditions under which alone free competition could be developed, parcelled landed property exploited and the unchained industrial productive power of the nation employed; and beyond the French borders he everywhere swept the feudal institutions away, so far as was necessary to furnish bourgeois society in France with a suitable up-to-date environment on the European Continent. The new social formation once established, the antediluvian Colossi disappeared and with them resurrected Romanity—the Brutuses, Gracchi, Publicolas, the tribunes, the senators, and Caesar himself. Bourgeois society in its sober reality had begotten its true interpreters and mouthpieces in the Says, Cousins, Royer-Collards, Benjamin Constants and Guizots; its real military leaders sat behind the office desks, and the hogheaded Louis XVIII was its political chief. Wholly absorbed in the production of wealth and in peaceful competitive struggle, it no longer comprehended that ghosts from the days of Rome had watched over its cradle. But unheroic as bourgeois society is, it nevertheless took heroism, sacrifice, terror, civil war and battles of peoples to bring it into being. And in the classically austere traditions of the Roman republic its gladiators found the ideals and the art forms, the self-deceptions that they needed in order to conceal from themselves the bourgeois limitations of the content of their struggles and to keep their enthusiasm on the high plane of the great historical tragedy. Similarly, at another stage of development, a century earlier, Cromwell and the English people had borrowed speech, passions and illusions from the Old Testament for their bourgeois revolution. When the real aim had been achieved, when the bourgeois transformation of English society had been accomplished, Locke supplanted Habakkuk.

Thus the awakening of the dead in those revolutions served the purpose

of glorifying the new struggles, not of parodying the old; of magnifying the given task in imagination, not of fleeing from its solution in reality; of finding once more the spirit of revolution, not of making its ghost walk about again.

From 1848 to 1851 only the ghost of the old revolution walked about, from Marrast, the *républicain en gants jaunes,* who disguised himself as the old Bailly, down to the adventurer, who hides his commonplace repulsive features under the iron death mask of Napoleon. An entire people, which had imagined that by means of a revolution it had imparted to itself an accelerated power of motion, suddenly finds itself set back into a defunct epoch and, in order that no doubt as to the relapse may be possible, the old dates arise again, the old chronology, the old names, the old edicts, which had long become a subject of antiquarian erudition, and the old minions of the law, who had seemed long decayed. The nation feels like that mad Englishman in Bedlam who fancies that he lives in the times of the ancient Pharaohs and daily bemoans the hard labour that he must perform in the Ethiopian mines as a gold digger, immured in this subterranean prison, a dimly burning lamp fastened to his head, the overseer of the slaves behind him with a long whip, and at the exits a confused welter of barbarian mercenaries, who understand neither the forced labourers in the mines nor one another, since they speak no common language. "And all this is expected of me," sighs the mad Englishman, "of me, a freeborn Briton, in order to make gold for the old Pharaohs." "In order to pay the debts of the Bonaparte family," sighs the French nation. The Englishman, so long as he was in his right mind, could not get rid of the fixed idea of making gold. The French, so long as they were engaged in revolution, could not get rid of the memory of Napoleon, as the election of December 10 proved. They hankered to return from the perils of revolution to the flesh-pots of Egypt, and December 2, 1851 was the answer. They have not only a caricature of the old Napoleon, they have the old Napoleon himself, caricatured as he must appear in the middle of the nineteenth century.

The social revolution of the nineteenth century cannot draw its poetry from the past, but only from the future. It cannot begin with itself before it has stripped off all superstition in regard to the past. Earlier revolutions required recollections of past world history in order to drug themselves concerning their own content. In order to arrive at its own content, the revolution of the nineteenth century must let the dead bury their dead. There the phrase went beyond the content; here the content goes beyond the phrase.

The February Revolution was a surprise attack, a *taking* of the old society *unawares,* and the people proclaimed this unexpected *stroke* as a deed of world importance, ushering in a new epoch. On December 2 the February Revolution is conjured away by a cardsharper's trick, and what seems overthrown is no longer the monarchy but the liberal concessions that were wrung from it by centuries of struggle. Instead of *society* having conquered a new content for itself, it seems that the *state* only returned to its oldest form, to the shamelessly simple domination of the sabre and the cowl. This is the answer to the *coup de main* of February 1848, given by

the *coup de tête* of December 1851. Easy come, easy go. Meanwhile the interval of time has not passed by unused. During the years 1848 to 1851 French society has made up, and that by an abbreviated because revolutionary method, for the studies and experiences which, in a regular, so to speak, textbook course of development would have had to precede the February Revolution, if it was to be more than a ruffling of the surface. Society now seems to have fallen back behind its point of departure; it has in truth first to create for itself the revolutionary point of departure, the situation, the relations, the conditions under which alone modern revolution becomes serious.

Bourgeois revolutions, like those of the eighteenth century, storm swiftly from success to success; their dramatic effects outdo each other; men and things seem set in sparkling brilliants; ecstasy is the everyday spirit; but they are short-lived; soon they have attained their zenith, and a long crapulent depression lays hold of society before it learns soberly to assimilate the results of its storm-and-stress period. On the other hand, proletarian revolutions, like those of the nineteenth century, criticise themselves constantly, interrupt themselves continually in their own course, come back to the apparently accomplished in order to begin it afresh, deride with unmerciful thoroughness the inadequacies, weaknesses and paltrinesses of their first attempts, seem to throw down their adversary only in order that he may draw new strength from the earth and rise again, more gigantic, before them, recoil ever and anon from the indefinite prodigiousness of their own aims, until a situation has been created which makes all turning back impossible, and the conditions themselves cry out:
Hic Rhodus, hic salta! . . . .

The *first period,* from February 24, or the overthrow of Louis Philippe, to May 4, 1848, the meeting of the Constituent Assembly, the *February period* proper, may be described as the *prologue* to the revolution. Its character was officially expressed in the fact that the government improvised by it itself declared that it was *provisional* and, like the government, everything that was mooted, attempted or enunciated during this period proclaimed itself to be only *provisional.* Nothing and nobody ventured to lay claim to the right of existence and of real action. All the elements that had prepared or determined the revolution, the dynastic opposition, the republican bourgeoisie, the democratic-republican petty bourgeoisie and the social-democratic workers, provisionally found their place in the February *government.*

It could not be otherwise. The February days originally intended an electoral reform, by which the circle of the politically privileged among the possessing class itself was to be widened and the exclusive domination of the aristocracy of finance overthrown. When it came to the actual conflict, however, when the people mounted the barricades, the National Guard maintained a passive attitude, the army offered no serious resistance and the monarchy ran away, the republic appeared to be a matter of course. Every party construed it in its own way. Having secured it arms in hand, the proletariat impressed its stamp upon it and proclaimed it to be a *social republic.* There was thus indicated the general content of the modern revolution, a content which was in most singular contradiction to

everything that, with the material available, with the degree of education attained by the masses, under the given circumstances and relations, could be immediately realised in practice. On the other hand, the claims of all the remaining elements that had collaborated in the February Revolution were recognised by the lion's share that they obtained in the government. In no period do we, therefore, find a more confused mixture of high-flown phrases and actual uncertainty and clumsiness, of more enthusiastic striving for innovation and more deeply-rooted domination of the old routine, of more apparent harmony of the whole of society and more profound estrangement of its elements. While the Paris proletariat still revelled in the vision of the wide prospects that had opened before it and indulged in seriously-meant discussions on social problems, the old powers of society had grouped themselves, assembled, reflected and found unexpected support in the mass of the nation, the peasants and petty bourgeois, who all at once stormed on to the political stage, after the barriers of the July monarchy had fallen.

The *second period,* from May 4, 1848, to the end of May 1849, is the period of the *constitution,* the *foundation, of the bourgeois republic.* Directly after the February days not only had the dynastic opposition been surprised by the republicans and the republicans by the Socialists, but all France by Paris. The National Assembly, which met on May 4, 1848, had emerged from the national elections and represented the nation. It was a living protest against the pretensions of the February days and was to reduce the results of the revolution to the bourgeois scale. In vain the Paris proletariat, which immediately grasped the character of this National Assembly, attempted on May 15, a few days after it met, forcibly to negate its existence, to dissolve it, to disintegrate again into its constituent parts the organic form in which the proletariat was threatened by the reacting spirit of the nation. As is known, May 15 had no other result save that of removing Blanqui and his comrades, that is, the real leaders of the proletarian party, from the public stage for the entire duration of the cycle we are considering.

The *bourgeois monarchy* of Louis Philippe can be followed only by a *bourgeois republic,* that is to say, whereas a limited section of the bourgeoisie ruled in the name of the king, the whole of the bourgeoisie will now rule on behalf of the people. The demands of the Paris proletariat are utopian nonsense, to which an end must be put. To this declaration of the Constituent National Assembly the Paris proletariat replied with the *June Insurrection,* the most colossal event in the history of European civil wars. The bourgeois republic triumphed. On its side stood the aristocracy of finance, the industrial bourgeoisie, the middle class, the petty bourgeois, the army, the *lumpenproletariat* organised as the Mobile Guard, the intellectual lights, the clergy and the rural population. On the side of the Paris proletariat stood none but itself. More than three thousand insurgents were butchered after the victory, and fifteen thousand were transported without trial. With this defeat the proletariat passes into the *background* of the revolutionary stage. It attempts to press forward again on every occasion, as soon as the movement appears to make a fresh start, but with ever decreased expenditure of strength and always slighter

results. As soon as one of the social strata situated above it gets into revolutionary ferment, the proletariat enters into an alliance with it and so shares all the defeats that the different parties suffer, one after another. But these subsequent blows become the weaker, the greater the surface of society over which they are distributed. The more important leaders of the proletariat in the Assembly and in the press successively fall victims to the courts, and ever more equivocal figures come to head it. In part it throws itself into *doctrinaire experiments, exchange banks and workers' associations, hence into a movement in which it renounces the revolutionising of the old world by means of the latter's own great, combined resources, and seeks, rather, to achieve its salvation behind society's back, in private fashion, within its limited conditions of existence, and hence necessarily suffers shipwreck.* It seems to be unable either to rediscover revolutionary greatness in itself or to win new energy from the connections newly entered into, until *all classes* with which it contended in June themselves lie prostrate beside it. But at least it succumbs with the honours of the great, world-historic struggle; not only France, but all Europe trembles at the June earthquake, while the ensuing defeats of the upper classes are so cheaply bought that they require bare-faced exaggeration by the victorious party to be able to pass for events at all, and become the more ignominious the further the defeated party is removed from the proletarian party.

The defeat of the June insurgents, to be sure, had now prepared, had levelled the ground on which the bourgeois republic could be founded and built up, but it had shown at the same time that in Europe the questions at issue are other than that of "republic or monarchy." It had revealed that here *bourgeois republic* signifies the unlimited despotism of one class over other classes. It had proved that in countries with an old civilisation, with a developed formation of classes, with modern conditions of production and with an intellectual consciousness in which all traditional ideas have been dissolved by the work of centuries, *the republic* signifies *in general only the political form of revolution of bourgeois society* and not its *conservative form of life,* as, for example, in the United States of North America, where, though classes already exist, they have not yet become fixed, but continually change and interchange their elements in constant flux, where the modern means of production, instead of coinciding with a stagnant surplus population, rather compensate for the relative deficiency of heads and hands, and where, finally, the feverish, youthful movement of material production, which has to make a new world its own, has left neither time nor opportunity for abolishing the old spirit world.

During the June days all classes and parties had united in the *party of Order* against the proletarian class as the *party of Anarchy,* of socialism, of communism. They had "saved" society from *"the enemies of society."* They had given out the watchwords of the old society, *"property, family, religion, order,"* to their army as passwords and had proclaimed to the counter-revolutionary crusaders: "In this sign thou shalt conquer!" From that moment, as soon as one of the numerous parties which had gathered under this sign against the June insurgents seeks to hold the revolutionary battlefield in its own class interest, it goes down before the cry: "Property,

family, religion, order." Society is saved just as often as the circle of its rulers contracts, as a more exclusive interest is maintained against a wider one. Every demand of the simplest bourgeois financial reform, of the most ordinary liberalism, of the most formal republicanism, of the most shallow democracy, is simultaneously castigated as an "attempt on society" and stigmatised as "socialism." And, finally, the high priests of "the religion of order" themselves are driven with kicks from their Pythian tripods, hauled out of their beds in the darkness of night, put in prison-vans, thrown into dungeons or sent into exile; their temple is razed to the ground, their mouths are sealed, their pens broken, their law torn to pieces in the name of religion, of property, of the family, of order. Bourgeois fanatics for order are shot down on their balconies by mobs of drunken soldiers, their domestic sanctuaries profaned, their houses bombarded for amusement—in the name of property, of the family, of religion and of order. Finally, the scum of bourgeois society forms the *holy phalanx of order* and the hero Crapulinski installs himself in the Tuileries as the *saviour of society*. . . .

Legitimists and Orleanists, as we have said, formed the two great factions of the party of Order. Was that which held these factions fast to their pretenders and kept them apart from one another nothing but lily and tricolour, House of Bourbon and House of Orleans, different shades of royalism, was it at all the confession of faith of royalism? Under the Bourbons, *big landed property* had governed, with its priests and lackeys; under the Orleans, high finance, large-scale industry, large-scale trade, that is, *capital,* with its retinue of lawyers, professors and smooth-tongued orators. The Legitimate Monarchy was merely the political expression of the hereditary rule of the lords of the soil, as the July Monarchy was only the political expression of the usurped rule of the bourgeois *parvenus.* What kept the two factions apart, therefore, was not any so-called principles, it was their material conditions of existence, two different kinds of property, it was the old contrast between town and country, the rivalry between capital and landed property. That at the same time old memories, personal enmities, fears and hopes, prejudices and illusions, sympathies and antipathies, convictions, articles of faith and principles bound them to one or the other royal house, who is there that denies this? Upon the different forms of property, upon the social conditions of existence, rises an entire superstructure of distinct and peculiarly formed sentiments, illusions, modes of thought and views of life. The entire class creates and forms them out of its material foundations and out of the corresponding social relations. The single individual, who derives them through tradition and upbringing, may imagine that they form the real motives and the starting-point of his activity. While Orleanists and Legitimists, while each faction sought to make itself and the other believe that it was loyalty to their two royal houses which separated them, facts later proved that it was rather their divided interests which forbade the uniting of the two royal houses. And as in private life one differentiates between what a man thinks and says of himself and what he really is and does, so in historical struggles one must distinguish still more the phrases and fancies of parties from their real organism and their real interests, their conception of

themselves, from their reality. Orleanists and Legitimists found themselves side by side in the republic, with equal claims. If each side wished to effect the *restoration* of its *own* royal house against the other, that merely signified that each of the *two great interests* into which the *bourgeoisie* is split—landed property and capital—sought to restore its own supremacy and the subordination of the other. We speak of two interests of the bourgeoisie, for large landed property, despite its feudal coquetry and pride of race, has been rendered thoroughly bourgeois by the development of modern society. Thus the Tories in England long imagined that they were enthusiastic about monarchy, the church and the beauties of the old English Constitution, until the day of danger wrung from them the confession that they are enthusiastic only about *ground rent.* . . .

As against the coalesced bourgeoisie, a coalition between petty bourgeois and workers had been formed, the so-called *social-democratic* party. The petty bourgeois saw that they were badly rewarded after the June days of 1848, that their material interests were imperilled and that the democratic guarantees which were to ensure the effectuation of these interests were called in question by the counter-revolution. Accordingly, they came closer to the workers. On the other hand, their parliamentary representation, the *Montagne,* thrust aside during the dictatorship of the bourgeois republicans, had in the last half of the life of the Constituent Assembly reconquered its lost popularity through the struggle with Bonaparte and the royalist ministers. It had concluded an alliance with the socialist leaders. In February 1849, banquets celebrated the reconciliation. A joint programme was drafted, joint election committees were set up and joint candidates put forward. From the social demands of the proletariat the revolutionary point was broken off and a democratic turn given to them; from the democratic claims of the petty bourgeoisie the purely political form was stripped off and their socialist point thrust forward. Thus arose the Social-Democracy. The new *Montagne,* the result of this combination, contained, apart from some supernumeraries from the working class and some socialist sectarians, the same elements as the old *Montagne,* only numerically stronger. However, in the course of development, it had changed with the class that it represented. The peculiar character of the Social-Democracy is epitomised in the fact that democratic-republican institutions are demanded as a means, not of doing away with two extremes, capital and wage labour, but of weakening their antagonism and transforming it into harmony. However different the means proposed for the attainment of this end may be, however much it may be trimmed with more or less revolutionary notions, the content remains the same. This content is the transformation of society in a democratic way, but a transformation within the bounds of the petty bourgeoisie. Only one must not form the narrow-minded notion that the petty bourgeoisie, on principle, wishes to enforce an egoistic class interest. Rather, it believes that the *special* conditions of its emancipation are the *general* conditions within the frame of which alone modern society can be saved and the class struggle avoided. Just as little must one imagine that the democratic representatives are indeed all shopkeepers or enthusiastic champions of shopkeepers. According to their education

and their individual position they may be as far apart as heaven from earth. What makes them representatives of the petty bourgeoisie is the fact that in their minds they do not get beyond the limits which the latter do not get beyond in life, that they are consequently driven, theoretically, to the same problems and solutions to which material interest and social position drive the latter practically. This is, in general, the relationship between the *political* and *literary representatives* of a class and the class they represent. . . .

But the revolutionary threats of the petty bourgeois and their democratic representatives are mere attempts to intimidate the antagonist. And when they have run into a blind alley, when they have sufficiently compromised themselves to make it necessary to give effect to their threats, then this is done in an ambiguous fashion that avoids nothing so much as the means to the end and tries to find excuses for succumbing. The blaring overture that announced the contest dies away in a pusillanimous snarl as soon as the struggle has to begin, the actors cease to take themselves *au sérieux,* and the action collapses completely, like a pricked bubble.

No party exaggerates its means more than the democratic, none deludes itself more light-mindedly over the situation. Since a section of the army had voted for it, the *Montagne* was now convinced that the army would revolt for it. And on what occasion? On an occasion which, from the standpoint of the troops, had no other meaning than that the revolutionists took the side of the Roman soldiers against the French soldiers. On the other hand, the recollections of June 1848 were still too fresh to allow of anything but a profound aversion on the part of the proletariat towards the National Guard and a thoroughgoing mistrust of the democratic chiefs on the part of the chiefs of the secret societies. To iron out these differences, it was necessary for great, common interests to be at stake. The violation of an abstract paragraph of the Constitution could not provide these interests. Had not the Constitution been repeatedly violated, according to the assurance of the democrats themselves? Had not the most popular journals branded it as counter-revolutionary botch-work? But the democrat, because he represents the petty bourgeoisie, that is, a *transition class,* in which the interests of two classes are simultaneously mutually blunted, imagines himself elevated above class antagonism generally. The democrats concede that a privileged class confronts them, but they, along with all the rest of the nation, form the *people.* What they represent is the *people's rights;* what interests them is the *people's interest.* Accordingly, when a struggle is impending, they do not need to examine the interests and positions of the different classes. They do not need to weigh their own resources too critically. They have merely to give the signal and the *people,* with all its inexhaustible resources, will fall upon the *oppressors.* Now, if in the performance their interests prove to be uninteresting and their potency impotence, then either the fault lies with pernicious sophists, who split the *indivisible people* into different hostile camps, or the army was too brutalised and blinded to comprehend that the pure aims of democracy are the best thing for it itself, or the whole thing has been wrecked by a detail in its execution, or else an unforeseen accident has this time spoilt the game. In any case, the democrat comes

out of the most disgraceful defeat just as immaculate as he was innocent when he went into it, with the newly-won conviction that he is bound to win, not that he himself and his party have to give up the old standpoint, but, on the contrary, that conditions have to ripen to suit him. . . .

But the revolution is thoroughgoing. It is still journeying through purgatory. It does its work methodically. By December 2, 1851, it had completed one half of its preparatory work; it is now completing the other half. First it perfected the parliamentary power, in order to be able to overthrow it. Now that it has attained this, it perfects the *executive power*, reduces it to its purest expression, isolates it, sets it up against itself as the sole target, in order to concentrate all its forces of destruction against it. And when it has done this second half of its preliminary work, Europe will leap from its seat and exultantly exclaim: Well grubbed, old mole!

This executive power with its enormous bureaucratic and military organisation, with its ingenious state machinery, embracing wide strata, with a host of officials numbering half a million, besides an army of another half million, this appalling parasitic body, which enmeshes the body of French society like a net and chokes all its pores, sprang up in the days of the absolute monarchy, with the decay of the feudal system, which it helped to hasten. The seignorial privileges of the landowners and towns became transformed into so many attributes of the state power, the feudal dignitaries into paid officials and the motley pattern of conflicting mediaeval plenary powers into the regulated plan of a state authority whose work is divided and centralised as in a factory. The first French Revolution, with its task of breaking all separate local, territorial, urban and provincial powers in order to create the civil unity of the nation, was bound to develop what the absolute monarchy had begun: centralisation, but at the same time the extent, the attributes and the agents of governmental power. Napoleon perfected this state machinery. The Legitimist monarchy and the July monarchy added nothing but a greater division of labour, growing in the same measure as the division of labour within bourgeois society created new groups of interests, and, therefore, new material for state administration. Every *common* interest was straightway severed from society, counterposed to it as a higher, *general* interest, snatched from the activity of society's members themselves and made an object of government activity, from a bridge, a schoolhouse and the communal property of a village community to the railways, the national wealth and the national university of France. Finally, in its struggle against the revolution, the parliamentary republic found itself compelled to strengthen, along with the repressive measures, the resources and centralisation of governmental power. All revolutions perfected this machine instead of smashing it. The parties that contended in turn for domination regarded the possession of this huge state edifice as the principal spoils of the victor.

But under the absolute monarchy, during the first Revolution, under Napoleon, bureaucracy was only the means of preparing the class rule of the bourgeoisie. Under the Restoration, under Louis Philippe, under the parliamentary republic, it was the instrument of the ruling class, however much it strove for power of its own. . . .   □

The Paris Commune

For twenty years the second Bonaparte emperor, Louis Napoleon, ruled France as front man for the upper bourgeoisie. The Second Empire imposed a kind of unity on the fractious classes of France, and tried hard to achieve the *gloire* of the ideal nation—though the results were a sordid version of the liberal dream of 1848. Yet, significantly, when the imperial grip loosened only a little, revolution exploded again: not, this time, the work of Romantic nationalists and liberals, but the independent drive of Parisian workers. The actors were familiar—the same *sans-culottes* who had so many times before taken advantage of the quarrels of the bourgeoisie—yet the revolutionary situation was terribly unique; this was Social Revolution, the working classes with unquestioned political power, sweeping away the sacred forms of the state machine, and shaking the property foundations of society.

The Paris Commune survived only two months, before it was savagely, bloodily, crushed by the troops of Adolphe Thiers' Versailles government. One cannot, however, measure its impact on a miniscule scale. Well into the twentieth century the ghost-memory of the Commune persisted, among the French, indeed the European, ruling classes the portent of an ominous future—and ironically enough making Marxists of them all: to succeeding generations of European bourgeoisie the Armageddon of the coming proletarian revolution was as much the article of faith that it was to convinced disciples of the Marxist prophet. And on the other side of the class chasm, French workingmen, as well as the international socialist movement, enshrined the Commune as a glorious monument of revolt and hope and martyrdom. How could it have been otherwise? At the end, during *la semaine sanglante* of vengeance upon the defeated Commune, the troops of the bourgeoisie massacred thousands of Communards, the figures ranging between twenty and thirty thousand, and in the following weeks arrested perhaps forty-five thousand more, masses of whom were deported to a living death in New Caledonia.

Yet an objective examination reveals that during its brief existence the Paris Commune created neither a Red Terror nor a Marxist paradise. Nor was it a product preconceived and preplanned by Jacobin and socialist theorists deliberately exploiting a national crisis to effect the proletarian revolution. The Commune was an ad hoc affair, a desperate response to a desperate situation; it was the Parisian solution to the collapse of legally constituted authority in the vacuum of defeat that followed the 1870 Franco-Prussian War.

In 1870 the armies of the second Bonaparte had broken before the Prussian invasion. Louis Napoleon—and his imperial structure of mud and straw—had slipped into oblivion, leaving the details of formal surrender and national management to a hastily elected, conservative dominated Assembly, its chief minister the ubiquitous spokesman of the Liberal interest, Adolphe Thiers. The new government yielded—it had no alternative—to the harsh terms imposed by Bismarck, including the demand that Paris be subject to Prussian occupation. But, after the

Prussians had made only a token entrance into the capital, it was Thiers' deliberate decision to withdraw governmental authority, as it were to exclude Paris—unruly, radical, patriotic Paris—from the reforming national polity. Dutifully, government troops and government officials evacuated the city, followed by a stream of upper- and middle-class Parisians; the "decapitalization" was complete when the Assembly itself chose Versailles as the new national headquarters. Thus Paris was left to itself, and to whatever kind of authority the remaining citizens could muster. The Central Committee of the Paris National Guard provided—reluctantly—a temporary directing force, but as a guide to a more representative government Parisians turned quite naturally to the idea of the Commune, the ancient form, the traditional unit, of French local administration. The "Commune of Paris," its leaders—Radicals, Jacobins, Blanquists, National Guard members, trade-union officials—elected by manhood suffrage, became fact on March 28, 1871. Its immediate purposes—far from creating a revolutionary state—were centered on the administrative essentials of Parisian life.

To the leaders of the international socialist movement watching from abroad, the Communards, whatever their lack of explicit goals, had begun the long-awaited revolution. From London, Karl Marx poured out a steady stream of comment to his European correspondents, his letters revealing his own pounding excitement, interpreting, applauding, exulting—and criticizing—the activities of the Commune:

[London, April 12, 1871] If you look at the last chapter of my *Eighteenth Brumaire,* you will find that I say that the next attempt of the French Revolution will be no longer, as before, to transfer the bureaucratic-military machine from one hand to another, but to *smash* it, and this is the preliminary condition for every real people's revolution on the continent. And this is what our heroic Party comrades in Paris are attempting. What elasticity, what historical initiative, what a capacity for sacrifice in these Parisians! After six months of hunger and ruin, caused by internal treachery more even than by the external enemy, they rise, beneath Prussian bayonets, as if there had never been a war between France and Germany and the enemy were not still at the gates of Paris! History has no like example of like greatness! If they are defeated only their "good nature" will be to blame. They should have marched at once on Versailles, after first Vinoy and then the reactionary section of the Paris National Guard had themselves retreated. They missed their opportunity because of conscientious scruples. They did not want to *start a civil war,* as if that mischievous abortion Thiers had not already started the civil war with his attempt to disarm Paris! Second mistake: The Central Committee surrendered its power too soon, to make way for the Commune. Again from a too "honourable" scrupulosity! However that may be, the present rising in Paris—even if it be crushed by the wolves, swine and vile curs of the old society—is the most glorious deed of our Party since the June insurrection in Paris. Compare these Parisians, storming heaven, with the slaves to heaven of the German-Prussian Holy Roman Empire, with its posthu-

mous masquerades reeking of the barracks, the Church, cabbage-junkerdom and above all, of the philistine. . . .   □

On May 30, 1871, two days after the fall of the Paris Commune, Karl Marx addressed the General Council of the First International. His speech was both a tribute to the Parisians who had "stormed heaven" to achieve a society of equals and an analysis of the Commune explicitly formed as a lesson for Marxist socialists. The Commune, drowned in blood though it had been, had provided its successors, Marx said, with the concrete method of revolution; hereafter, the proletariat rising to revolt had to *smash* rather than use the organs of the bourgeois state. This address—printed in part below—became what Marx, no doubt, intended it, a guide to action for a new generation of revolutionists.

On the dawn of the 18th of March, Paris arose to the thunderburst of "Vive la Commune!" What is the Commune, that sphinx so tantalising to the bourgeois mind?

"The proletarians of Paris," said the Central Committee in its manifesto of the 18th March, "amidst the failures and treasons of the ruling classes, have understood that the hour has struck for them to save the situation by taking into their own hands the direction of public affairs. . . . They have understood that it is their imperious duty and their absolute right to render themselves masters of their own destinies, by seizing upon the governmental power." But the working class cannot simply lay hold of the ready-made state machinery, and wield it for its own purposes.

The centralised State power, with its ubiquitous organs of standing army, police, bureaucracy, clergy, and judicature—organs wrought after the plan of a systematic and hierarchic division of labour—originates from the days of absolute monarchy, serving nascent middle-class society as a mighty weapon in its struggles against feudalism. Still, its development remained clogged by all manner of mediaeval rubbish, seignorial rights, local privileges, municipal and guild monopolies and provincial constitutions. The gigantic broom of the French Revolution of the eighteenth century swept away all these relics of bygone times, thus clearing simultaneously the social soil of its last hindrances to the superstructure of the modern State edifice raised under the First Empire, itself the offspring of the coalition wars of old semi-feudal Europe against modern France. During the subsequent *régimes* the Government, placed under parliamentary control—that is, under the direct control of the propertied classes—became not only a hotbed of huge national debts and crushing taxes; with its irresistible allurements of place, pelf, and patronage, it became not only the bone of contention between the rival factions and adventurers of the ruling classes, but its political character changed simultaneously with the economic changes of society. At the same pace at which the progress of modern industry developed, widened, intensified the class antagonism between capital and labour, the State power assumed more and more the character of the national power of capital over labour, of a public force organised for social enslavement, of an engine of class despotism. After

every revolution marking a progressive phase in the class struggle, the purely repressive character of the State power stands out in bolder and bolder relief. The Revolution of 1830, resulting in the transfer of Government from the landlords to the capitalists, transferred it from the more remote to the more direct antagonists of the working men. The bourgeois Republicans, who, in the name of the Revolution of February, took the State power, used it for the June massacres, in order to convince the working class that "social" republic meant the Republic ensuring their social subjection, and in order to convince the royalist bulk of the bourgeois and landlord class that they might safely leave the cares and emoluments of Government to the bourgeois "Republicans." However, after their one heroic exploit of June, the bourgeois Republicans had, from the front, to fall back to the rear of the "Party of Order"—a combination formed by all the rival fractions and factions of the appropriating class in their now openly declared antagonism to the producing classes. The proper form of their joint-stock Government was the *Parliamentary Republic,* with Louis Bonaparte for its President. Theirs was a *régime* of avowed class terrorism and deliberate insult toward the "vile multitude." If the Parliamentary Republic, as M. Thiers said, "divided them (the different fractions of the ruling class) least," it opened an abyss between that class and the whole body of society outside their spare ranks. The restraints by which their own divisions had under former *régimes* still checked the State power, were removed by their union; and in view of the threatening upheaval of the proletariat, they now used that State power mercilessly and ostentatiously as the national war-engine of capital against labour. In their uninterrupted crusade against the producing masses they were, however, bound not only to invest the executive with continually increased powers of repression, but at the same time to divest their own parliamentary stronghold—the National Assembly—one by one, of all its own means of defence against the Executive. The Executive, in the person of Louis Bonaparte, turned them out. The natural offspring of the "Party-of-Order" Republic was the Second Empire.

The empire, with the *coup d'état* for its certificate of birth, universal suffrage for its sanction, and the sword for its sceptre, professed to rest upon the peasantry, the large mass of producers not directly involved in the struggle of capital and labour. It professed to save the working class by breaking down Parliamentarism, and, with it, the undisguised subserviency of Government to the propertied classes. It professed to save the propertied classes by upholding their economic supremacy over the working class; and, finally, it professed to unite all classes by reviving for all the chimera of national glory. In reality, it was the only form of government possible at a time when the bourgeoisie had already lost, and the working class had not yet acquired, the faculty of ruling the nation. It was acclaimed throughout the world as the saviour of society. Under its sway, bourgeois society, freed from political cares, attained a development unexpected even by itself. Its industry and commerce expanded to colossal dimensions; financial swindling celebrated cosmopolitan orgies; the misery of the masses was set off by a shameless display of gorgeous, meretricious and debased luxury. The State power, apparently soaring

high above society, was at the same time itself the greatest scandal of that society and the very hotbed of all its corruptions. Its own rottenness, and the rottenness of the society it had saved, were laid bare by the bayonet of Prussia, herself eagerly bent upon transferring the supreme seat of that *régime* from Paris to Berlin. Imperialism is, at the same time, the most prostitute and the ultimate form of the State power which nascent middle-class society had commenced to elaborate as a means of its own emancipation from feudalism, and which full-grown bourgeois society had finally transformed into a means for the enslavement of labour by capital.

The direct antithesis to the empire was the Commune. The cry of "social republic," with which the revolution of February was ushered in by the Paris proletariat, did but express a vague aspiration after a Republic that was not only to supersede the monarchical form of class-rule, but class rule itself. The Commune was the positive form of that Republic.

Paris, the central seat of the old governmental power, and, at the same time, the social stronghold of the French working class, had risen in arms against the attempt of Thiers, and the Rurals to restore and perpetuate that old governmental power bequeathed to them by the empire. Paris could resist only because, in consequence of the siege, it had got rid of the army, and replaced it by a National Guard, the bulk of which consisted of working men. This fact was now to be transformed into an institution. The first decree of the Commune, therefore, was the suppression of the standing army, and the substitution for it of the armed people.

The Commune was formed of the municipal councillors, chosen by universal suffrage in the various wards of the town, responsible and revocable at short terms. The majority of its members were naturally working men, or acknowledged representatives of the working class. The Commune was to be a working, not a parliamentary, body, executive and legislative at the same time. Instead of continuing to be the agent of the Central Government, the police was at once stripped of its political attributes, and turned into the responsible and at all times revocable agent of the Commune. So were the officials of all other branches of the Administration. From the members of the Commune downwards, the public service had to be done at *workmen's wages.* The vested interests and the representation allowances of the high dignitaries of State disappeared along with the high dignitaries themselves. Public functions ceased to be the private property of the tools of the Central Government. Not only municipal administration, but the whole initiative hitherto exercised by the State was laid into the hands of the Commune.

Having once got rid of the standing army and the police, the physical force elements of the old Government, the Commune was anxious to break the spiritual force of repression, the "parson-power," by the disestablishment and disendowment of all churches as proprietary bodies. The priests were sent back to the recesses of private life, there to feed upon the alms of the faithful in imitation of their predecessors, the Apostles. The whole of the educational institutions were opened to the people gratuitously, and at the same time cleared of all interference of Church and State. Thus, not only was education made accessible to all, but

science itself freed from the fetters which class prejudice and governmental force had imposed upon it.

The judicial functionaries were to be divested of that sham independence which had but served to mask their abject subserviency to all succeeding governments to which, in turn, they had taken, and broken, the oaths of allegiance. Like the rest of public servants, magistrates and judges were to be elective, responsible, and revocable.

The Paris Commune was, of course, to serve as a model to all the great industrial centres of France. The communal *régime* once established in Paris and the secondary centres, the old centralised Government would in the provinces, too, have to give way to the self-government of the producers. In a rough sketch of national organisation which the Commune had no time to develop, it states clearly that the Commune was to be the political form of even the smallest country hamlet, and that in the rural districts the standing army was to be replaced by a national militia, with an extremely short term of service. The rural communes of every district were to administer their common affairs by an assembly of delegates in the central town, and these district assemblies were again to send deputies to the National Delegation in Paris, each delegate to be at any time revocable and bound by the *mandat impératif* (formal instructions) of his constituents. The few but important functions which still would remain for a central government were not to be suppressed, as has been intentionally mis-stated, but were to be discharged by Communal, and therefore strictly responsible agents. The unity of the nation was not to be broken, but, on the contrary, to be organised by the Communal Constitution and to become a reality by the destruction of the State power which claimed to be the embodiment of that unity independent of, and superior to, the nation itself, from which it was but a parasitic excrescence. While the merely repressive organs of the old governmental power were to be amputated, its legitimate functions were to be wrested from an authority usurping pre-eminence over society itself, and restored to the responsible agents of society. Instead of deciding once in three or six years which member of the ruling class was to misrepresent the people in Parliament, universal suffrage was to serve the people, constituted in Communes, as individual suffrage serves every other employer in the search for the workmen and managers in his business. And it is well known that companies, like individuals, in matters of real business generally know how to put the right man in the right place, and, if they for once make a mistake, to redress it promptly. On the other hand, nothing could be more foreign to the spirit of the Commune than to supersede universal suffrage by hierarchic investiture.

It is generally the fate of completely new historical creations to be mistaken for the counterpart of older and even defunct forms of social life, to which they may bear a certain likeness. Thus, this new Commune, which breaks the modern State power, has been mistaken for a reproduction of the mediaeval Communes, which first preceded, and afterwards became the substratum of, that very State power. The Communal Constitution has been mistaken for an attempt to break up into a federation of small States, as dreamt of by Montesquieu and the Girondins, that unity of

great nations which, if originally brought about by political force, has now become a powerful coefficient of social production. The antagonism of the Commune against the State power has been mistaken for an exaggerated form of the ancient struggle against over-centralisation. Peculiar historical circumstances may have prevented the classical development, as in France, of the bourgeois form of government, and may have allowed, as in England, to complete the great central State organs by corrupt vestries, jobbing councillors, and ferocious poor-law guardians in the towns, and virtually hereditary magistrates in the counties. The Communal Constitution would have restored to the social body all the forces hitherto absorbed by the State parasite feeding upon, and clogging the free movement of, society. By this one act it would have initiated the regeneration of France. The provincial French middle class saw in the Commune an attempt to restore the sway their order had held over the country under Louis Philippe, and which, under Louis Napoleon, was supplanted by the pretended rule of the country over the towns. In reality, the Communal Constitution brought the rural producers under the intellectual lead of the central towns of their districts, and these secured to them, in the working men, the natural trustees of their interests. The very existence of the Commune involved, as a matter of course, local municipal liberty, but no longer as a check upon the, now superseded, State power. It could only enter into the head of a Bismarck, who, when not engaged on his intrigues of blood and iron, always likes to resume his old trade, so befitting his mental calibre, of contributor to *Kladderadatsch* (the Berlin *Punch*), it could only enter into such a head, to ascribe to the Paris Commune aspirations after that caricature of the old French municipal organisation of 1791, the Prussian municipal constitution which degrades the town governments to mere secondary wheels in the police-machinery of the Prussian State. The Commune made that catchword of bourgeois revolutions, cheap government, a reality, by destroying the two greatest sources of expenditure—the standing army and State functionarism. Its very existence presupposed the non-existence of monarchy, which, in Europe at least, is the normal incumbrance and indispensable cloak of class-rule. It supplied the Republic with the basis of really democratic institutions. But neither cheap Government nor the "true Republic" was its utlimate aim; they were its mere concomitants.

The multiplicity of interpretations to which the Commune has been subjected, and the multiplicity of interests which construed it in their favour, show that it was a thoroughly expansive political form, while all previous forms of government had been emphatically repressive. Its true secret was this. It was essentially a working-class government, the product of the struggle of the producing against the appropriating class, the political form at last discovered under which to work out the economic emancipation of labour.

Except on this last condition, the Communal Constitution would have been an impossibility and a delusion. The political rule of the producer cannot coexist with the perpetuation of his social slavery. The Commune was therefore to serve as a lever for uprooting the economical foundations upon which rests the existence of classes, and therefore of class-

rule. With labour emancipated, every man becomes a working man, and productive labour ceases to be a class attribute.

It is a strange fact. In spite of all the tall talk and all the immense literature, for the last sixty years, about Emancipation of Labour, no sooner do the working men anywhere take the subject into their own hands with a will, than uprises at once all the apologetic phraseology of the mouthpieces of present society with its two poles of Capital and Wages Slavery (the landlord now is but the sleeping partner of the capitalist), as if capitalist society was still in its purest state of virgin innocence, with its antagonisms still undeveloped, with its delusions still unexploded, with its prostitute realities not yet laid bare. The Commune, they exclaim, intends to abolish property, the basis of all civilisation! Yes, gentlemen, the Commune intended to abolish that class-property which makes the labour of the many the wealth of the few. It aimed at the expropriation of the expropriators. It wanted to make individual property a truth by transforming the means of production, land and capital, now chiefly the means of enslaving and exploiting labour, into mere instruments of free and associated labour. But this is Communism, "impossible" Communism! Why, those members of the ruling classes who are intelligent enough to perceive the impossibility of continuing the present system —and they are many—have become the obtrusive and full-mouthed apostles of co-operative production. If co-operative production is not to remain a sham and a snare; if it is to supersede the Capitalist system; if united co-operative societies are to regulate national production upon a common plan, thus taking it under their own control, and putting an end to the constant anarchy and periodical convulsions which are the fatality of Capitalist production—what else, gentlemen, would it be but Communism, "possible" Communism?

The working class did not expect miracles from the Commune. They have no ready-made utopias to introduce *par décret du peuple.* They know that in order to work out their own emancipation, and along with it that higher form to which present society is irresistibly tending by its own economical agencies, they will have to pass through long struggles, through a series of historic processes, transforming circumstances and men. They have no ideals to realise, but to set free the elements of the new society with which old collapsing bourgeois society itself is pregnant. In the full consciousness of their historic mission, and with the heroic resolve to act up to it, the working class can afford to smile at the coarse invective of the gentlemen's gentlemen with the pen and inkhorn, and at the didactic patronage of well-wishing bourgeois-doctrinaires, pouring forth their ignorant platitudes and sectarian crotchets in the oracular tone of scientific infallibility.

When the Paris Commune took the management of the revolution in its own hands; when plain working men for the first time dared to infringe upon the Governmental privilege of their "natural superiors," and, under circumstances of unexampled difficulty, performed their work modestly, conscientiously, and efficiently—performed it at salaries the highest of which barely amounted to one-fifth of what, according to high scientific authority, is the minimum required for a secretary to a certain metropoli-

tan school board—the old world writhed in convulsions of rage at the sight of the Red Flag, the symbol of the Republic of Labour, floating over the Hôtel de Ville.   □

But the Commune was wiped out—inevitably so, in a revolution which ranged Paris against the rest of France. This was the last of the long-drawn-out steps of the French Revolution. We would not imply that eighteenth-century problems had been solved, nor that revolutionary ideals had become reality; well into the twentieth century workers were a sullen minority, the second of Disraeli's "Two Nations," within France. But from this point the radical revolution moves beyond France, becomes explicitly, formidably, the socialist revolution. The Commune, for all its imaginative answers to the organization of a democratic polity, was a part of a specifically French tradition. The revolutions of the new century will carry a different label, the indelible imprint of Marxist ideology.

Suggested Reading

Except for the work of Marx himself, the nineteenth century is not very satisfactorily studied. However, there are some promising recent efforts which may lead to a more creative historiography in the future. A place to begin is with the sixth volume of *The Cambridge Economic History of Europe* (London: Cambridge University Press, 1965) which has articles on the Industrial Revolution. The articles in volumes IX and X of *The New Cambridge Modern History* (London: Cambridge University Press, 1960, 1965) survey much of the story pertinent to this chapter. A standard work to be consulted is J. H. Clapham, *Economic Development of France and Germany, 1815–1914** (London: Cambridge University Press, 1935; Cambridge Paperback*). For France see A. L. Dunham, *The Industrial Revolution in France, 1815–48* (Jericho, N.Y.: The Exposition Press, Inc., 1955). On the development of a European proletariat see Jürgen Kuczynski, *The Rise of the Working Class** (New York: McGraw-Hill Book Company,* 1967).

The two useful surveys of the epoch to 1848 are Eric Hobshawn, *The Age of Revolution: 1789–1848** (New York: Mentor Books,* The New American Library, Inc., 1962) and R. W. Postgate, *Revolution from 1789 to 1906** (Boston: Houghton Mifflin Company, 1921; Torchbook*). For the intellectual changes of the period there is an interesting account in J. L. Talmon, *Romanticism and Revolt** (Harcourt, Brace & World, Inc.,* 1967). The 1848 revolutions are very puzzling; except for Marx and Friedrich Engels, *Germany: Revolution and Counter Revolution** (Lawrence Publishing Co., 1933; New World Paperback*), perhaps the best analysis is that of Theodore S. Hamerow, *Restoration, Revolution, Reaction: Economics and Politics in Germany 1815–1871** (Princeton: Princeton University Press, 1958; Princeton Paperback*) and that of L. B. Namier, *Eighteen Forty-Eight: Revolution of the Intellectuals** (London: Oxford University Press, 1946; Anchor*).

For the background necessary to understand Marx, one can do worse

than Edmund Wilson, *To The Finland Station** (New York: Harcourt, Brace & Co., 1940; Anchor*); to be followed by George Lichtheim, *Origins of Socialism** (New York: Frederick A. Praeger Inc., 1969; Praeger Paperback*). Next I think it best to read Mehring, *Karl Marx** (London: George Allen & Unwin Ltd, 1951; Ann Arbor Paperbacks*). I would then go to Vernon Venable, *Human Nature: The Marxian View** (New York: Alfred A. Knopf Inc., 1945; Meridian*). For Marx himself there is no easy way. A complete English edition in some 47 volumes is now underway but until it has progressed I would suggest the edition of *Writings of the Young Marx on Philosophy and Society** edited by L. D. Easton and K. H. Guddat (Garden City, N.Y.: Anchor Books, Doubleday & Co., Inc., 1967) as a place to begin. Then *Marx and Engels: Selected Works** (New York: International Publishers Co., Inc., 1968; New World*) followed by volume I of *Capital** (New York: International Publishers Co., Inc., 1967; New World*). Finally, I would suggest the edition of a piece of Marx' most important and least known work (the so-called *Grundrisse*) by E. J. Hobsbawm who has written a brilliant introduction to the section called *Pre-Capitalist Economic Formations** (New York: International Publishers Co., Inc., 1965; New World*).

Again, the best thing to date on the Commune is by Marx, but he can be supplemented by the standard account of P. O. Lissagaray, *History of the Commune of 1871* in a new edition by Monthly Review Press, 1967.

7 The Russian Revolution

Pre-Revolutionary Russia

Although the revolutionary tradition has become increasingly Marxist in the twentieth century, it has continued to be no less rich in conflict and confusion. The difference has been in the scale and duration of political success. A truly epigonous generation of socialists has emerged —one that falls short of Marx in intellectual quality, but one that has conquered many a Thebes. Putting all the trivial pamphleteering aside, the organizational and therefore political triumphs of Marx' epigones are without precedent in the long history of revolutionary struggle.

The first major effort to put together the elements of an international revolutionary alliance had not been very encouraging in its results. Although dominated by Marx himself, the International Workingmen's Association (1864–1874) proved a factious exercise in political futility. But after the death of the master, the so-called Second International was created in 1889 from a federation of socialist parties in Europe, and it had enough importance to last until torn apart by the wars that began in 1914. The ideologues of the Second International were an interesting and competent assortment of socialists, but the intricacies of their post-Marxian theorizing have only marginal value in explaining the great events of twentieth-century revolutions. It seems more useful to me to center my effort on illustrating the nature of latter-day Marxism through the writing and organizational work of the most eclectic and influential of modern socialists, Vladimir Ilich Ulyanov, the Bolshevik's Lenin.

To introduce Lenin one must introduce for the first time in our narrative the most perplexing and challenging society of the modern world. The Russia of Tsar Nicholas II—Lenin's Russia—was a historical monstrosity. American students have the impression that Russian Marxists and other radicals emerged from a nation of backward peasants and degenerate nobles. In fact, nineteenth-century Russia was an even more complex empire than that made graphic for us in the pages of Tolstoy's WAR AND PEACE. Post-Napoleonic Russia, though still a vast ocean of impoverished villages, threw up islands of industrialized towns which were in turn dynamically transformed by the emergence of classic Western sociological structures. In addition to the basic class divisions along the lines of bourgeois property, professional groups

appeared by the score, and from the time of the "great reforms" of Tsar Alexander II, they spearheaded a very advanced, ambitious movement of politicized liberalism in the Western style.

The cultural aspect of this rapid social transformation was even more impressive. Nineteenth-century Russia kept intellectual pace with the most advanced European societies. Brilliant mathematical and scientific traditions developed in the universities where Nikolai Lobachevski's revolutionary invention of non-Euclidian geometry at the University of Kazan and Dmitri Mendeleev's formulation of the periodic law for chemical analysis at the University of St. Petersburg were merely the most dazzling successes from the ranks of numbers of exceptionally creative academic intellectuals. Historians, classical humanists, and scholars of all varieties flourished in the land of the tsars. For most of us, of course, the music, theatre, and literature of prerevolutionary Russia constitute the great legacy. The music for stage and concert hall composed by Tchaikovsky, Borodin, Rimski-Korsakov, Glazunov, and Stravinsky; the revolutionary Ballet Russe of Diaghilev; and the superb theatre of Chekhov have become commonplace delights of the Western world. And perhaps no literature of the West can match the range and quality of Pushkin, Lermontov, Gogol, Turgenev, Dostoevski, Tolstoi, Chekhov, and Gorki.

The cultural riches of Russia were not as decisive a factor in shaping revolutionary events as that of the social transformation resulting from industrialization and the incursion of world capitalism. But Western style radicalism drew heavily—perhaps crucially—on the new culture in producing the seminal work of Belinski, Herzen, Bakunin, Kropotkin, and Chernyshevski. They were joined by populist theorists (Narodniks) and the constitutional monarchists and republicans who eventually constituted themselves the Cadet party (which won over the Russian parliament in 1905). Finally, in the decade of the 1890's, there appeared a Marxist party (the Social Democrats) which completed the spectrum of nineteenth-century dissent.

The intellectual leader of the Marxist party in Russia was George Plekhanov among whose distinguished pupils were Bukharin, Trotsky, and Lenin. The first party convention (1898) ended in a police raid and mass arrests. Just five years after this convention the new party split into two major factions which continued down to 1917 as Bolsheviks and Mensheviks. Lenin's prominence among the Social Democrats was based entirely on his personal magnetism and intellectual power—from beginning to end. Even after the revolution Vladimir Ulyanov relied far less on high positions in Party and State than on his personal power for the exercise of control over his political colleagues. Let us look now at some examples of his quality as a revolutionary thinker.

First here is a section from the extraordinary assessment ("What Is To Be Done?") he made in 1902 of the revolutionary potential of *fin-de-siècle* Russia; it marks the beginning of a long theoretical struggle with not only Eduard Bernstein and the "Revisionists," but with Marxists like Plekhanov and Kautsky as well. His theory of a "van-

guard" party as the prime instrument of revolution is perhaps Lenin's major contribution to revolutionary thought; the last part of this pamphlet (which I do not reprint, but hope the student will read) details the argument that the special conditions faced by Russian Social Democrats make impossible the sort of open, democratic struggle mounted by the German Social Democrats and force instead a secret party of dedicated socialist revolutionaries who will in both theory and practice spur all groups to revolutionary perceptions and action in opposition to the governing powers. But I think the most interesting and valuable pages of "What Is To Be Done?" for American students are those in which Lenin explains his concept of the general European phenomenon of revolutionary consciousness:

The case of the Russian Social-Democrats strikingly illustrates the fact observed in the whole of Europe (and long ago observed in German Marxism) that the notorious freedom of criticism implies, not the substitution of one theory by another, but freedom from every complete and thought-out theory; it implies eclecticism and absence of principle. Those who are in the least acquainted with the actual state of our movement cannot but see that the spread of Marxism was accompanied by a certain deterioration of theoretical standards. Quite a number of people, with very little, and even totally lacking in, theoretical training, joined the movement for the sake of its practical significance and its practical successes. We can judge, therefore, how tactless *Rabocheye Dyelo* is when, with an air of invincibility, it quotes the statement of Marx that: "A single step of the real movement is worth a dozen programmes." To repeat these words in the epoch of theoretical chaos is sheer mockery. Moreover, these words of Marx are taken from his letter on the Gotha Programme, in which he *sharply condemns* eclecticism in the formulation of principles: "If you must combine," Marx wrote to the party leaders, "then enter into agreements to satisfy the practical aims of the movement, but do not haggle over principles, do not make 'concessions' in theory." This was Marx's idea, and yet there are people among us who strive—in his name!—to belittle the significance of theory.

Without a revolutionary theory there can be no revolutionary movement. This cannot be insisted upon too strongly at a time when the fashionable preaching of opportunism is combined with absorption in the narrowest forms of practical activity. The importance of theory for Russian Social-Democrats is still greater for three reasons, which are often forgotten:

The first is that our party is only in the process of formation, its features are only just becoming outlined, and it has not yet completely settled its reckoning with other tendencies in revolutionary thought which threaten to divert the movement from the proper path. Indeed, in very recent times we have observed (as Axelrod long ago warned the Economists would happen) a revival of non-Social-Democratic revolutionary tendencies. Under such circumstances, what at first sight appears to be an "unimportant" mistake, may give rise to most deplorable consequences, and only the shortsighted would consider factional disputes and strict distinction

of shades to be inopportune and superfluous. The fate of Russian Social-Democracy for many, many years to come may be determined by the strengthening of one or the other "shade."

The second reason is that the Social-Democratic movement is essentially an international movement. This does not mean merely that we must combat national chauvinism. It means also that a movement that is starting in a young country can be successful only on the condition that it assimilates the experience of other countries. In order to assimilate this experience, it is not sufficient merely to be acquainted with it, or simply to transcribe the latest resolutions. A critical attitude is required towards this experience, and ability to subject it to independent tests. Only those who realise how much the modern labour movement has grown in strength will understand what a reserve of theoretical forces and political (as well as revolutionary) experience is required to fulfil this task.

The third reason is that the national tasks of Russian Social-Democracy are such as have never confronted any other Socialist party in the world. Farther on we shall deal with the political and organisational duties which the task of emancipating the whole people from the yoke of autocracy imposes upon us. At the moment, we wish merely to state that the *rôle of vanguard can be fulfilled only by a party that is guided by an advanced theory.* . . .

Every one knows that the spread and consolidation of the economic* struggle of the Russian workers proceeded simultaneously with the creation of a "literature" exposing economic conditions, *i.e.,* factory and industrial conditions. These "leaflets" were devoted mainly to the exposure of factory conditions, and very soon a passion for exposures was roused among the workers. As soon as the workers realised that the Social-Democratic circles desired to and could supply them with a new kind of leaflet that told the whole truth about their poverty-stricken lives, about their excessive toil and their lack of rights, correspondence began to pour in from the factories and workshops. This "exposure literature" created a sensation not only in the particular factory dealt with and the conditions of which were exposed in a given leaflet, but in all the factories to which news had spread about the facts exposed. And as the poverty and want among the workers in the various enterprises and in the various trades are pretty much the same, the "Truth about the life of the workers" roused the admiration *of all.* Even among the most backward workers, a veritable passion was roused to "go into print"—a noble passion to adopt this rudimentary form of war against the whole of the modern social system which is based upon robbery and oppression. And in the overwhelming majority of cases these "leaflets" were in truth a declaration of war, because the exposures had a terrifically rousing effect upon the workers; it stimulated them to put forward demands for the removal of the most glaring evils, and roused in them a readiness to support these

---

* In order to avoid misunderstanding we would state, that here, and throughout this pamphlet, by economic struggle, we mean (in accordance with the meaning of the term as it has become accepted amongst us) the "practical economic struggle" which Engels . . . described as "resistance to capitalism," and which in free countries is known as the trade-union struggle.

demands with strikes. Finally, the employers themselves were compelled to recognise the significance of these leaflets as a declaration of war, so much so that in a large number of cases they did not even wait for the outbreak of hostilities. As is always the case, the mere publication of these exposures made them effective, and they acquired the significance of a strong moral force. On more than one occasion, the mere appearance of a leaflet proved sufficient to compel an employer to concede all or part of the demands put forward. In a word, economic (factory) exposures have been an important lever in the economic struggle and they will continue to be so as long as capitalism, which creates the need for the workers to defend themselves, exists. Even in the more progressive countries of Europe to-day, the exposure of the evils in some backward trade, or in some forgotten branch of domestic industry, serves as a starting point for the awakening of class-consciousness, for the beginning of a trade-union struggle, and for the spread of Socialism.

Recently, the overwhelming majority of Russian Social-Democrats were almost wholly engaged in this work of exposing factory conditions. It is sufficient to refer to the columns of *Rabochaya Mysl* to judge to what an extent they were engaged in it. So much so indeed, that they lost sight of the fact that this, *taken by itself,* was not substantially Social-Democratic work, but merely trade-union work. As a matter of fact, these exposures merely dealt with the relations between the workers *in a given trade,* with their immediate employers, and all that it achieved was that the vendors of labour power learned to sell their "commodity" on better terms, and to fight the purchasers of labour power over a purely commercial deal. These exposures might have served (if properly utilized by revolutionaries) as a beginning and a constituent part of Social-Democratic activity, but they might also (and with subservience to spontaneity inevitably had to) have led to a "pure and simple" trade-union struggle and to a non-Social-Democratic labour movement. Social-Democrats lead the struggle of the working class not only for better terms for the sale of labour power, but also for the abolition of the social system which compels the propertyless class to sell itself to the rich. Social-Democracy represents the working class, not in its relation to a given group of employers, but in its relation to all classes in modern society, to the state as an organised political force. Hence, it not only follows that Social-Democrats must not confine themselves entirely to the economic struggle; they must not even allow the organisation of economic exposures to become the predominant part of their activities. We must actively take up the political education of the working class, and the development of its political consciousness. *Now,* after *Zarya* and *Iskra** have made the first attack upon Economism "all are agreed" with this (although some agree only nominally, as we shall soon prove).

The question now arises: What does political education mean? Is it sufficient to confine oneself to the propaganda of working-class hostility to autocracy? Of course not. It is not enough to *explain* to the workers that

---

*   These are Social-Democratic newspapers; the latter (*Iskra*) was Lenin's principal instrument in projecting a vanguard party.

they are politically oppressed (any more than it was to *explain* to them that their interests were antagonistic to the interests of the employers). Advantage must be taken of every concrete example of this oppression for the purpose of agitation (in the same way as we began to use concrete examples of economic oppression for the purpose of agitation). And inasmuch as *political* oppression affects all sorts of classes in society, inasmuch as it manifests itself in various spheres of life and activity, in industrial life, civic life, in personal and family life, in religious life, scientific life, etc., etc., is it not evident that *we shall not be fulfilling our task* of developing the political consciousness of the workers if *we do not undertake* the organisation of the *political exposure of autocracy in all its aspects?* In order to agitate over concrete examples of oppression, these examples must be exposed (in the same way as it was necessary to expose factory evils in order to carry on economic agitation).

One would think that this was clear enough. It turns out, however, that "all" are agreed that it is necessary to develop political consciousness *in all its aspects,* only in words. It turns out that *Rabocheye Dyelo,* for example, has not only failed to take up the task of organising (or to make a start in organising) in all-sided political exposure, but is even trying to *drag Iskra,* which has undertaken this task, *away from it.* . . .

In *no other way* can the masses be trained in political consciousness and revolutionary activity except by means of such exposures. Hence, to conduct such activity is one of the most important functions of international Social-Democracy as a whole, for even in countries where political liberty exists, there is still a field for work of exposure, although in such countries the work is conducted in a different sphere. For example, the German party is strengthening its position and spreading its influence, thanks particularly to the untiring energy with which it is conducting a campaign of political exposure. Working-class consciousness cannot be genuinely political consciousness unless the workers are trained to respond to all cases of tyranny, oppression, violence and abuse, no matter *what class* is affected. Moreover, that response must be a Social-Democratic response, and not one from any other point-of-view. The consciousness of the masses of the workers cannot be genuine class consciousness, unless the workers learn to observe from concrete, and above all from topical, political facts and events, *every* other social class and *all* the manifestations of the intellectual, ethical and political life of these classes; unless they learn to apply practically the materialist analysis and the materialist estimate of *all* aspects of the life and activity of *all* classes, strata and groups of the population. Those who concentrate the attention, observation and the consciousness of the working class exclusively, or even mainly, upon itself alone, are not Social-Democrats; because, for its self-realisation the working class must not only have a theoretical . . . rather it would be more true to say: Not so much theoretical as a practical understanding acquired through experience of political life of the relationships between *all* classes of modern society. That is why the idea preached by our Economists, that the economic struggle is the most widely applicable means of drawing the masses into the political movement is so extremely harmful and extremely reactionary in practice. In

order to become a Social-Democrat, a working man must have a clear picture in his mind of the economic nature and the social and political features of the landlord, of the priest, of the high state official and of the peasant, of the student and of the tramp; he must know their strong and weak sides; he must understand all the catchwords and sophisms by which each class and each stratum *camouflages* its egotistical strivings and its real "nature"; he must understand what interests certain institutions and certain laws reflect and how they are reflected. The working man cannot obtain this "clear picture" from books. He can obtain it only from living examples and from exposures, following hot after their occurrence, of what goes on around us at a given moment, of what is being discussed, in whispers perhaps, by each one in his own way, of the meaning of such and such events, of such and such statistics, in such and such court sentences, etc., etc., etc. These universal political exposures are an essential and *fundamental* condition for training the masses in revolutionary activity.

Why is it that the Russian workers as yet display so little revolutionary activity in connection with the brutal way in which the police maltreat the people, in connection with the persecution of the religious sects, with the flogging of the peasantry, with the outrageous censorship, with the torture of soldiers, with the persecution of the most innocent cultural enterprises, etc.? Is it because the "economic struggle" does not "stimulate" them to this, because such political activity does not "promise palpable results," because it produces little that is "positive"? To advance this argument, we repeat, is merely to shift the blame to the shoulders of others, to blame the masses of the workers for our own philistinism (also Bernsteinism). We must blame ourselves, our remoteness from the mass movement; we must blame ourselves for being unable as yet to organise a sufficiently wide, striking and rapid exposure of these despicable outrages. When we do that (and we must and can do it), the most backward worker will understand, *or will feel,* that the students and religious sects, the muzhiks and the authors are being abused and outraged by the very same dark forces that are oppressing and crushing him at every step of his life, and, feeling that, he himself will be filled with an irresistible desire to respond to these things and then he will organise cat-calls against the censors one day, another day he will demonstrate outside the house of the provincial governor who has brutally suppressed peasant uprisings, another day he will teach a lesson to the gendarmes in surplices who are doing the work of the Holy Inquisition, etc. As yet we have done very little, almost nothing, to *hurl* universal and fresh exposures among the masses of the workers. Many of us as yet do not appreciate the *bounden duty* that rests upon us, but spontaneously follow in the wake of the "drab every-day struggle," in the narrow confines of factory life. . . .

As for calling the masses to action, that will come of itself immediately that energetic political agitation, live and striking exposures are set going. To catch some criminal red-handed and immediately to brand him publicly will have far more effect than any number of "appeals to action"; the effect very often will be such, that it will be impossible to tell who exactly it was that "appealed" to the crowd, and who exactly suggested this or

that plan of demonstration, etc. Calls for action, not in the general, but in the concrete sense of the term, can be made only at the place of action; only those who themselves go into action now can make appeals for action. And our business as Social-Democratic publicists is to deepen, expand and intensify political exposures and political agitation. A word in passing about "calls to action." *The only paper* that *prior to* the spring events, *called upon* the workers actively to intervene in a matter that certainly did *not promise* any *palpable results* for the workers, *i.e.,* the drafting of the students into the army, *was Iskra.* Immediately after the publication of the order of January 11 "Drafting the 183 Students into the Army," *Iskra* published an article about it (in its February issue, No. 2), and *before* any demonstration was started openly *called upon* "the workers to go to the aid of the students," called upon the "people" boldly to take up the government's open challenge. . . .

The "economic struggle between the workers and the employers and the government,"* about which you make as much fuss as if you had made a new discovery, is being carried on in all parts of Russia, even the most remote, by the workers themselves who have heard about strikes, but who have heard almost nothing about Socialism. The "activity" you want to stimulate among us workers by advancing concrete demands promising palpable results, we are already displaying and in our every-day, petty trade-union work, we put forward concrete demands, very often without any assistance from the intellectuals whatever. But *such* activity is not enough for us; we are not children to be fed on the sops of "economic" politics alone; we want to know everything that everybody else knows, we want to learn the details of *all* aspects of political life and to take part *actively* in every political event. In order that we may do this, the intellectuals must talk to us less on what we already know, and tell us more about what we do not know and what we can never learn from our factory and "economic" experience, that is, you must give us political knowledge. You intellectuals can acquire this knowledge, and it is your *duty* to bring us that knowledge in a hundred and a thousand times greater measure than you have done up till now; and you must bring us this knowledge, not only in the form of arguments, pamphlets and articles which sometimes—excuse my frankness!—are very dull, but in the form of live *exposures* of what our government and our governing classes are doing at this very moment in all spheres of life. Fulfill this duty with

---

* The demand "to give the economic struggle itself a political character" most strikingly expresses *subservience to spontaneity* in the sphere of political activity. Very often the economic struggle *spontaneously* assumes a political character, that is to say without the injection of the "revolutionary bacilli of the intelligentsia," without the intervention of the class-conscious Social-Democrats. For example, the economic struggle of the British workers assumed a political character without the intervention of the Socialists. The tasks of the Social-Democrats, however, are not exhausted by political agitation on the economic field; their task is to *convert* trade-union politics into the Social-Democratic political struggle, to *utilise* the flashes of political consciousness which gleam in the minds of the workers during their economic struggles for the purpose of *raising* them to the level of *Social-Democratic* political consciousness. . . .

greater zeal, and *talk less about "increasing the activity of the masses of the workers"!* We are far more active than you think, and we are quite able to support by open street fighting demands that do not even promise any "palpable results" whatever! You cannot "increase" our activity, because *you yourselves are not sufficiently active.* Be less subservient to spontaneity, and think more about increasing *your own* activity, gentlemen! . . .

THE WORKING CLASS AS CHAMPION OF DEMOCRACY

We have seen that the organisation of wide political agitation, and consequently, of all-sided political exposures are an absolutely necessary *and paramount* task of activity, that is, if that activity is to be truly Social-Democratic. We arrived at this conclusion *solely* on the grounds of the pressing needs of the working class for political knowledge and political training. But this ground by itself is too narrow for the presentation of the question, for it ignores the general democratic tasks of Social-Democracy as a whole, and of modern, Russian Social-Democracy in particular. In order to explain the situation more concretely we shall approach the subject from an aspect that is "nearer" to the Economist, namely, from the practical aspect. "Every one agrees" that it is necessary to develop the political consciousness of the working class. But the question arises, How is that to be done? What must be done to bring this about? The economic struggle merely brings the workers "up against" questions concerning the attitude of the government towards the working class. Consequently, *however much we may try* to "give to the economic struggle itself a political character" *we shall never be able* to develop the political consciousness of the workers (to the degree of Social-Democratic consciousness) by confining ourselves to the economic struggle, *for the limits of this task are too narrow.* . . .

The workers can acquire class political consciousness *only from without,* that is, only outside of the economic struggle, outside of the sphere of relations between workers and employers. The sphere from which alone it is possible to obtain this knowledge is the sphere of relationships between *all* classes and the state and the government—the sphere of the inter-relations between *all* classes. For that reason, the reply to the question: What must be done in order that the workers may acquire political knowledge? cannot be merely the one which, in the majority of cases, the practical workers, especially those who are inclined towards Economism, usually content themselves with, *i.e.,* "go among the workers." To bring political knowledge to the workers the Social-Democrats must *go among all classes of the population,* must despatch units of their army *in all directions.*

We deliberately select this awkward formula, we deliberately express ourselves in a simple, forcible way, not because we desire to indulge in paradoxes, but in order to "stimulate" the Economists to take up their tasks which they unpardonably ignore, to make them understand the difference between trade-union and Social-Democratic politics, which they refuse to understand. Therefore, we beg the reader not to get excited, but to hear us patiently to the end.

Take the type of Social-Democratic circle that has been most widespread during the past few years, and examine its work. It has "contact with the workers," it issues leaflets—in which, abuses in the factories, the government's partiality towards the capitalists, and the tyranny of the police are strongly condemned—and rests content with this. At meetings of workers, there are either no discussions or they do not extend beyond such subjects. Lectures and discussions on the history of the revolutionary movement, on questions of the home and foreign policy of our government, on questions of the economic evolution of Russia and of Europe, and the position of the various classes in modern society, etc., are extremely rare. Of systematically acquiring and extending contact with other classes of society, no one even dreams. The ideal leader, as the majority of the members of such circles picture him, is something more in the nature of a trade-union secretary than a Socialist political leader. Any trade-union secretary, an English one, for instance, helps the workers to conduct the economic struggle, helps to expose factory abuses, explains the injustice of the laws and of measures which hamper the freedom of strikes and the freedom to picket, to warn all and sundry that a strike is proceeding at a certain factory, explains the partiality of arbitration courts which are in the hands of the bourgeois classes, etc., etc. In a word, every trade-union secretary conducts and helps to conduct "the economic struggle against the employers and the government." It cannot be too strongly insisted that *this is not* enough to constitute Social-Democracy. The Social-Democrat's ideal should not be a trade-union secretary, but *a tribune of the people,* able to react to every manifestation of tyranny and oppression, no matter where it takes place, no matter what stratum or class of the people it affects; he must be able to group all these manifestations into a single picture of police violence and capitalist exploitation; he must be able to take advantage of every petty event in order to explain his Socialistic convictions and his Social-Democratic demands *to all,* in order to explain to *all* and every one the world historical significance of the struggle for the emancipation of the proletariat. . . .

Let us return, however, to the elucidation of our thesis. We said that a Social-Democrat, if he really believes it is necessary to develop the political consciousness of the proletariat, must "go among all classes of the people." This gives rise to the questions: How is this to be done? Have we enough forces to do this? Is there a base for such work among all the other classes? Will this not mean a retreat, or lead to a retreat from the class point-of-view? We shall deal with these questions.

We must "go among all classes of the people" as theoreticians, as propagandists, as agitators, and as organisers. No one doubts that the theoretical work of Social-Democrats should be directed towards studying all the features of the social and political position of the various classes. But extremely little is done in this direction compared with the work that is done in studying the features of factory life. In the committees and circles, you will meet men who are immersed say in the study of some special branch of the metal industry, but you will hardly ever find members of organisations (obliged, as often happens, for some reason or other to give up practical work) especially engaged in the collection of material con-

cerning some pressing question of social and political life which could serve as a means for conducting Social-Democratic work among other strata of the population. In speaking of the lack of training of the majority of present-day leaders of the labour movement, we cannot refrain from mentioning the point about training in this connection also, for it is also bound up with the "economic" conception of "close organic contact with the proletarian struggle." The principal thing, of course, is *propaganda and agitation* among all strata of the people. The Western-European Social-Democrats find their work in this field facilitated by the calling of public meetings, to which *all* are free to go, and by the parliament, in which they speak to the representatives of *all* classes. We have neither a parliament, nor the freedom to call meetings, nevertheless we are able to arrange meetings of workers who desire to listen to a *Social-Democrat.* We must also find ways and means of calling meetings of representatives of all and every other class of the population that desire to listen to a *Democrat;* for he who forgets that "the Communists support every revolutionary movement," that we are obliged for that reason to emphasize *general democratic tasks before the whole people,* without for a moment concealing our Socialistic convictions, is not a Social-Democrat. He who forgets his obligation to *be in advance of everybody* in bringing up, sharpening and solving *every* general democratic question, is not a Social-Democrat. . . .

To proceed. Have we sufficient forces to be able to direct our propaganda and agitation among *all* classes of the population? Of course we have. Our Economists are frequently inclined to deny this. They lose sight of the gigantic progress our movement has made from (approximately) 1894 to 1901. Like real Khvostists, they frequently live in the distant past, in the period of the beginning of the movement. At that time, indeed, we had astonishingly few forces, and it was perfectly natural and legitimate then to resolve to go exclusively among the workers, and severely condemn any deviation from this. The whole task then was to consolidate our position in the working class. At the present time, however, gigantic forces have been attracted to the movement; the best representatives of the young generation of the educated classes are coming over to us; everywhere, and in all provinces, there are people who have taken part in the movement in the past, who desire to do so now, who are striving towards Social-Democracy, but who are obliged to sit idle because we cannot employ them (in 1894 you could count the Social-Democrats on your fingers). One of the principal political and organisational shortcomings of our movement is that we are *unable* to utilise all these forces, and give them appropriate work (we shall deal with this in detail in the next chapter). The overwhelming majority of these forces entirely lacks the opportunity for "going to the workers," so there are no grounds for fearing that we shall deflect forces from our main cause. And in order to be able to provide the workers with real, universal, and live political knowledge, we must have "our own men," Social-Democrats, everywhere, among all social strata, and in all positions from which we can learn the inner springs of our state mechanism. Such men are required for propaganda and agitation, but in a still larger measure for organisation.

Is there scope for activity among all classes of the population? Those who fail to see this also lag intellectually behind the spontaneous awakening of the masses. The labour movement has aroused and is continuing to arouse discontent in some, hopes for support for the opposition in others, and the consciousness of the intolerableness and inevitable downfall of autocracy in still others. We would be "politicians" and Social-Democrats only in name (as very often happens), if we failed to realise that our task is to utilise every manifestation of discontent, and to collect and utilise every grain of even rudimentary protest. This is quite apart from the fact that many millions of the peasantry, handicraftsmen, petty artisans, etc., always listen eagerly to the preachings of any Social-Democrat who is at all intelligent. Is there a single class of the population in which no individuals, groups or circles are to be found who are discontented with the state of tyranny, and therefore accessible to the propaganda of Social-Democrats as the spokesmen of the most pressing general democratic needs? To those who desire to have a clear idea of what the political agitation of a Social-Democrat *among all* classes and strata of the population should be like, we would point to *political exposures* in the broad sense of the word as the principal (but of course not the sole) form of this agitation.

We must "arouse in every section of the population that is at all enlightened a passion for *political* exposure," I wrote in my article "Where to Begin" (*Iskra,* No. 4, May, 1901), with which I shall deal in greater detail later.

"We must not allow ourselves to be discouraged by the fact that the voice of political exposure is still feeble, rare and timid. This is not because of a general submission to political despotism, but because those who are able and ready to expose have no tribune from which to speak, because there is no audience to listen eagerly to and approve of what the orators say, and because the latter can nowhere perceive among the people forces to whom it would be worth while directing their complaint against the 'omnipotent' Russian government. . . . We are now in a position to set up a tribune for the national exposure of the tsarist government, and it is our duty to do so. That tribune must be a Social-Democratic paper. . . ."

The ideal audience for these political exposures is the working class, which is first and foremost in need of universal and live political knowledge, which is most capable of converting this knowledge into active struggle, even if it did not promise "palpable results." The only platform from which *public* exposures can be made is an All-Russian newspaper. "Unless we have a political organ, a movement deserving the name of political is inconceivable in modern Europe." In this connection Russia must undoubtedly be included in modern Europe. The press has long ago become a power in our country, otherwise the government would not spend tens of thousands of rubles to bribe it, and to subsidise the Katkovs, and Meshcherskys. And it is no novelty in autocratic Russia for the underground press to break through the wall of censorship and *compel* the legal and conservative press to speak openly of it. This was the case in

the seventies and even in the fifties. How much broader and deeper are now the strata of the people willing to read the illegal underground press, and to learn from it "how to live and how to die," to use the expression of the worker who sent a letter to *Iskra* [No. 7]. Political exposures are as much a declaration of war against the *government* as economic exposures are a declaration of war against the employers. And the wider and more powerful this campaign of exposure will be, the more numerous and determined the social *class* which has *declared war in order to commence the war* will be, the greater will be the moral significance of this declaration of war. Hence, political exposures in themselves serve as a powerful instrument for *disintegrating* the system we oppose, the means for diverting from the enemy his casual or temporary allies, the means for spreading enmity and distrust among those who permanently share power with the autocracy.

Only a party that will *organise* real all-national exposures can become the vanguard of the revolutionary forces in our time. The word all-national has a very profound meaning. The overwhelming majority of the non-working class exposers (and in order to become the vanguard, we must attract other classes) are sober politicians and cool business men. They know perfectly well how dangerous it is to "complain" even against a minor official, let alone against the "omnipotent" Russian government. And they will come *to us* with their complaints only when they see that these complaints really have effect, and when they see that we represent a *political* force. In order to become this political force in the eyes of outsiders, much persistent and stubborn work is required to *increase* our own consciousness, initiative and energy. For this, it is not sufficient to stick the label "vanguard" on "rearguard" theory and practice.

But if we have to undertake the organisation of the real all-national exposure of the government, then in what way will the class character of our movement be expressed?—the over-zealous advocates of "close organic contact with the proletarian struggle" will ask us. The reply is: In that we *Social-Democrats* will organise these public exposures; in that all the questions that are brought up by the agitation will be explained in the spirit of Social-Democracy, without any deliberate or unconscious distortions of Marxism; in the fact that *the party* will carry on this universal political agitation, uniting into one inseparable whole the pressure upon the government in the name of the whole people, the revolutionary training of the proletariat—while preserving its political independence—the guidance of the economic struggle of the working class, the utilisation of all its spontaneous conflicts with its exploiters, which rouse and bring into our camp increasing numbers of the proletariat! . . .   □

The Insurrections of 1905

The generation of agitation for liberal reforms, of strikes, of organization among industrial workers by the Social Democrats and among the peasants by the Social Revolutionaries (Narodniks) led finally, in a typically absurd historical moment, to a major revolutionary effort by the Russian dissidents. January 22, 1905 is "Bloody Sunday" in the

historiography of the events Lenin later termed "the beginning of the Russian Revolution." The tragic absurdity of the moment was that the blood which flowed in that Sunday massacre was from the veins of irrational workers demonstrating under the leadership of a tsarist police spy!

But shortly thereafter the opposition was multiplied to revolutionary proportions and the greatest strike in the history of the world paralyzed the empire for some ten days in October—in the course of which the historically momentous St. Petersburg Soviet (council) was organized to direct the agitation of factory workers in that area. In the same month there appeared from the hand of the tsar a manifesto of guarantees for civil liberties and a grant of genuine legislative power to the *Duma* (parliament). The government was suddenly proclaimed a constitutional monarchy.

In spite of the dizzying moments of October's revolutionary days, however, the coalition of opposition forces was soon split on class lines, and the organization of the workers proved inadequate to the task of socialist reconstruction. The liberals and moderates were satisfied with the October decrees so that when the government proceeded to arrest the members of the St. Petersburg Soviet, only the Moscow workers responded with a valiant struggle against police and soldiers. Soon the country was filled with vigilante and proto-fascist groups of the Right that based their programs on racist and ethnic hatred. There followed a period of greater moderation behind the new liberal facade directed by the minister Stolypin (under the slogan "pacification and reform") which continued until his assassination in 1911, after which there was no one in the government with even the ability to rule by repression and police spies.

Meantime, from his exile in Geneva, Lenin continued his extraordinary exercise of criticizing the Liberals and Marxists who constituted the majority of revolutionary potential in Russia as in the West. By 1917 he had written and talked himself into the position of a minority voice even within his self-created party! Yet by that same process of tough-minded, stubborn theorizing from his own unique sense of a functional Marxist critique of events, Lenin ended the master of the most awesome revolution in history. What a fateful episode in the struggle for revolutionary leadership was this triumph of Lenin over the great polemicists sprung up to answer Marx' call for vanguard intellectuals! Was he the best Marxist of the lot? Perhaps not. But he was the best political analyst and the strongest personality among the Marxists.

By the time the incompetent government of the tsar had been swallowed up in the great war of 1914, Lenin had found his audience among workers and intellectuals throughout Russia's major centers of power. It is interesting, especially in light of events in the 1960's, to note Lenin's particular rapport with teachers and students. Russia's schools were an amazingly progressive anachronism in the blighted land of the Romanovs. Education had spread very rapidly and widely; Russian teachers at all levels were unusually humanitarian and liberal; the universities were centers of freedom and press censorship was

easily circumvented. Chekhov had been worried about rebellious students in the 1880's. As early as 1908 Lenin was writing in support of the striking students of St. Petersburg University—against not only the Minister of Education, but also against their own Social Democratic leadership:

A students' strike has been called at St. Petersburg University. A number of other higher educational establishments have joined in. The movement has already spread to Moscow and Kharkov. Judging from all the reports in the foreign and Russian newspapers and in private letters from Russia, we are faced with a fairly broad *academic* movement.

Back to the old days! Back to pre-revolutionary Russia! That is what these events signify above all. As before, official reaction is tightening the screw in the universities. The eternal struggle in autocratic Russia against the student organizations has taken the form of a crusade by the Black-Hundred Minister Schwartz—acting in full agreement with 'Premier' Stolypin—against the autonomy which was promised the students in the autumn of 1905 (what did not the autocracy, faced with the onset of the revolutionary working class, 'promise' Russian citizens at that time!); against an autonomy which the students enjoyed so long as the autocracy had 'other things to think of than students,' and which the autocracy, if it was to remain such, could not but begin to take away.

As before, the liberal press laments and groans, this time together with some Octobrists—the professors lament and snivel too, imploring the government not to take the road of reaction and to make use of an excellent opportunity 'to ensure peace and order with the help of reforms' in 'a country exhausted by convulsions'—imploring the students not to resort to unlawful courses which can only play into the hands of reaction, etc. How ancient and antiquated, how hackneyed are all these tunes, and how vividly they resurrect before our eyes what took place twenty years ago or so, at the end of the eighties of last century! The similarity between that time and this is all the more striking when we take the present moment by itself, apart from the three years of revolution we have gone through. For the Duma (at first sight) with only the tiniest difference expresses that same pre-revolutionary relation of forces—the supremacy of the wild landlord, who prefers using Court connections and the influence of his friend the official to any kind of representation; the support of that same official by the merchants (the Octobrists) who do not dare to differ from their benevolent patrons; the 'opposition' of the bourgeois intellectuals who are concerned most of all to prove their loyalty, and who describe appeals to those in power as the political activity of liberalism. And the workers' deputies in the Duma recall feebly, far too feebly, the part which the proletariat was recently playing by its open mass struggle.

It may be asked, can we in such conditions attribute any importance to the old forms of primitive academic struggle of the students? If the liberals have sunk to the level of the 'politics' of the eighties (one can of course only in irony speak of politics in this connection), will it not be a debasement of the aims of Social-Democracy if it decides that it is necessary to support the academic struggle in some way or other?

Here and there, apparently, Social-Democratic students are putting this question. At any rate, our editorial board has received a letter from a group of Social-Democratic students which says, among other things:

'On September 13 a meeting of the students of St. Petersburg University resolved to call upon students for an all-Russian student strike, the reason given for this appeal being the aggressive tactics pursued by Schwartz. The platform of the strike is an academic one, and the meeting even welcomes the "first steps" of the Moscow and St. Petersburg Professional Councils in the struggle for autonomy. We are puzzled by the academic platform put forward at the St. Petersburg meeting, and consider it objectionable in present conditions, because it cannot unite the students for an active struggle on a broad front. We envisage student action only as one co-ordinated with general political action, and in no case apart from it. The elements capable of uniting the students are lacking. In view of this we are against academic action.'

The mistake which the authors of the letter are making is of much greater political importance than may appear at first sight, because their argument, strictly speaking, touches upon a theme which is incomparably more broad and important than the question of taking part in this particular strike.

'We envisage student action only as one co-ordinated with general political action. In view of this we are against academic action.'

Such an argument is radically wrong. The revolutionary slogan—to work towards co-ordinated political action of the students and the proletariat, etc.—here ceases to be a live guidance for many-sided militant agitation on a broadening basis and becomes a lifeless dogma, mechanically applied to different stages of different forms of the movement. It is not sufficient merely to proclaim political co-ordinated action, repeating the 'last word' in lessons of the revolution. One must be able to agitate for political action, making use of all possibilities, all conditions and, first and foremost, all mass conflicts between advanced elements, whatever they are, and the autocracy. It is not of course a question of us dividing every student movement beforehand into compulsory 'stages,' and making sure that each stage is properly gone through, out of fear of switching over to 'untimely' political actions, etc. Such a view would be the most harmful pedantry, and would lead only to an opportunist policy. But just as harmful is the opposite mistake, when people refuse to reckon with the actual situation that has arisen and the actual conditions of the particular mass movement, because of a slogan mis-interpreted as unchangeable. Such an application of a slogan inevitably degenerates into revolutionary phrase-mongering.

Conditions are possible when an academic movement lowers the level of a political movement, or divides it, or distracts from it—and in that case Social-Democratic students' groups would of course be bound to concentrate their agitation against such a movement. But anyone can see that the objective political conditions at the present time are different. The academic movement is expressing the beginning of a movement among the new 'generation' of students, who have more or less become accustomed

to a narrow measure of autonomy; and this movement is beginning when other forms of mass struggle are lacking at the present time, when a lull has set in, and the broad mass of the people, still silently, concentratedly and slowly are continuing to *digest* the experience of the three years of revolution.

In such conditions Social-Democrats would make a big mistake if they declared 'against academic action.' No, the groups of students belonging to our Party must use every effort to support, utilise and extend the movement. Like every other support of primitive forms of movement by Social-Democracy, the present support, too, should consist most of all in ideological and organisational influence on wider sections who have been roused by the conflict, and to whom this form of conflict, as a general rule, is their *first* experience of political conflicts. The student youth who have entered the universities during the last two years have lived a life almost completely detached from politics, and have been educated in a spirit of narrow academic autonomism, educated not only by the professors of the Establishment and the government press but also by the liberal professors and the whole Cadet Party. For this youth a strike on a large scale (if that youth is able to organise a large-scale strike: we must do everything to help it in this undertaking, but of course it is not for us socialists to guarantee the success of any bourgeois movement) is the beginning of a political conflict, whether those engaged in the fight realize it or not. Our job is to explain to the mass of 'academic' protesters the objective meaning of the conflict, to try and make it *consciously* political, to multiply tenfold the agitation carried on by the Social-Democratic groups of students, and *to direct all* this activity in such a way that revolutionary conclusions will be drawn from the history of the last three years, that the inevitability of a new revolutionary struggle is understood, and that our old —and still quite timely—slogans calling for the overthrow of the autocracy and the convocation of a constituent assembly should once again become a subject of discussion and the touchstone of political concentration for fresh generations of democrats.

Social-Democratic students have no right to shirk such work under any conditions. And however difficult this work may be at the present time, whatever reverses particular agitators may experience in this or that university, students' association, meeting, etc., we shall say: knock, and it will be opened unto you! The work of political agitation is never wasted. Its success is measured not only by whether we have succeeded here and now in winning a majority, or obtaining consent for co-ordinated political action. It is possible that we shall not achieve this all at once. But that is why we are an organised proletarian party—not to lose heart over temporary failures, but stubbornly, unswervingly and consistently to carry on *our work,* even in the most difficult conditions.

The appeal we print below from the St. Petersburg Joint Student Council shows that even the most active elements of the students obstinately cling to pure academic aims, and still sing the Cadet-Octobrist tune. And this at a time when the Cadet-Octobrist press is behaving in the most disgusting fashion towards the strike, trying to prove at the very height of

the struggle that it is harmful, criminal, etc. We cannot but welcome the rejoinder which the St. Petersburg Committee of our Party found it necessary to give the Joint Council (see 'From the Party'*).

Evidently the whips of Schwartz are not enough as yet to change the present-day students from 'academics' into 'politicians'; they need the scorpions of more and more Black-Hundred sergeant-majors to give a full revolutionary training to new cadres. These cadres, trained by all Stolypin's policy, trained by every step of the counter-revolution, require the constant attention of ourselves, the Social-Democrats, who clearly see the objective inevitability of further bourgeois-democratic conflicts on a national scale with the autocracy, which has joined forces with the Black-Hundred Octobrist Duma.

Yes, on a national scale, for the Black-Hundred counter-revolution, which is turning Russia backward, is not only tempering new fighters in the ranks of the revolutionary proletariat, but will inevitably arouse a new movement of the non-proletarian, i.e. bourgeois democrats (thereby implying, of course, not that *all the opposition* will take part in the struggle, but that there will be a wide participation of truly democratic elements of the bourgeoisie and petite bourgeoisie, i.e. those capable of struggle). The beginning of a mass student struggle in the Russia of 1908 is a political symptom, a symptom of the whole present situation brought about by the counter-revolution. Thousands and millions of threads tie the student youth with the middle and lower bourgeoisie, the petty officials, certain groups of the peasantry, the clergy, etc. If in the spring of 1908 attempts were being made to resurrect the *'Osvobozhdeniye League,'* slightly to the left of the old Cadet semi-landlord union represented by Pyotr Struve; if in the autumn the mass of youth which is closest of all to the democratic bourgeoisie in Russia is beginning to be disturbed; if the hireling hacks, with malice tenfold, have started howling once more against revolution in the schools; if base liberal professors and Cadet leaders are groaning and wailing at the untimely, dangerous, disastrous strikes which displease those dear Octobrists, which are capable of 'repelling' the Octobrists who hold power—that means new powder has begun to accumulate in the powder-flask, it means that *not only* among students is the reaction against reaction beginning!

And however weak and embryonic this beginning may be, the party of the working class must make use of it and will do so. We were able to work years and decades before the revolution, carrying our revolutionary slogans first into the study circles, then among the masses of the workers, then on to the streets, then on to the barricades. We must be capable, *now too,* of organizing first and foremost that which constitutes the task of the hour, and without which all talk about co-ordinated political action will be empty words, namely, the task of building a strong proletarian organiza-

---

* The reference is to the decision of the St. Petersburg Committee of the R.S.D.L.P. published in 'From the Party' column of *Proletary* No. 36 on October 3 (16), 1908. The Committee called on Social-Democrat student groups publicly to dissociate themselves from the appeal of the Joint Students' Council and bring the student movement in line with the tasks of Social-Democracy in the nation-wide struggle against tsarism.

tion, everywhere carrying on *political agitation* among the masses for its revolutionary watchwords. It is this task of organization in their own student midst, this agitation based on the concrete movement, that our university groups, too, should tackle.

The proletariat will not be behindhand. It often yields the palm to the bourgeois democrats in speeches at banquets, in legal unions, within the walls of universities, from the rostrum of representative institutions. It never yields the palm, and will not do so, in the serious and great revolutionary struggle of the masses. All the conditions for bringing this struggle to a head are not ripening as quickly and easily as some of us would hope—but those conditions are ripening and gathering head unswervingly. And the little beginning of little academic conflicts is a great beginning, for after it—if not today then tomorrow, if not tomorrow then the day after—will follow big continuations.

October 1908   □

The Revolutions of 1917

The final phase of the Russian Revolution was directly and decisively related to the first of the twentieth century's catastrophic wars. The Romanov empire was an early and integral partner in this most irrational exercise of power politics since the era of the mighty Bonaparte. The War of 1914 was layered with tragedy. For Socialists there had been no blacker days than those which saw the defection of every major socialist party to the cause of nationalism. The Second International was shattered. Lenin's anger proved a turning point:

The European War, which the governments and the bourgeois parties of all countries were preparing for decades, has broken out. The growth of armaments, the sharpening of the struggle for markets in the epoch of the latest, the imperialist, stage in the development of capitalism of the foremost countries, the dynastic interests of the most backward East European monarchies, were inevitably bound to bring about, and did bring about, the present war. To seize lands and to conquer foreign nations, to ruin competing nations, to pillage their wealth, to divert the attention of the labouring masses from the domestic political crises of Russia, Germany, England, and other countries, to disunite the workers and fool them with nationalism, to annihilate their vanguards in order to weaken the revolutionary movement of the proletariat, such is the only real essence, the significance and the meaning of the present war.

Upon Social-Democracy, in the first place, devolves the duty to make clear this real meaning of the war, and mercilessly to unmask the falsehoods, the sophisms and the "patriotic" phrases which are spread by the ruling classes, the landowners and the bourgeoisie, in defence of the war.

One of the belligerent groups of nations is headed by the German bourgeoisie. It has fooled the working class and the labouring masses by asserting that it wages the war for the defence of the fatherland, liberty, and civilisation, for the liberation of the peoples that are oppressed by tsarism, for the destruction of reactionary tsarism. In reality, that same

bourgeoisie, servile in face of the Prussian Junkers with Wilhelm II at their head, has always been the most faithful ally of tsarism and the enemy of the revolutionary movement of the workers and peasants in Russia. In reality, that bourgeoisie will, together with the Junkers, direct all its efforts, no matter what the outcome of the war may be, to support the tsarist monarchy against a revolution in Russia.

In reality, the German bourgeoisie undertook a predatory campaign against Serbia with the aim of subjugating it and throttling the national revolution of the Southern Slavs, at the same time directing the bulk of its military forces against freer countries, Belgium and France, in order to pillage the richer competitor. The German bourgeoisie, spreading the fable of a defensive war on its part, in reality chose the moment which was most propitious for its warfare, utilising its latest improvements in military technique and forestalling the new armaments that had already been mapped out and approved of by Russia and France.

At the head of the other group of belligerent nations are the English and French bourgeoisie which fool the working class and the labouring masses by asserting that this group leads a war for the fatherland, freedom and civilisation against the militarism and despotism of Germany. In reality, this bourgeoisie has long been buying for its billions, and preparing for an attack on Germany, the armies of Russian tsarism, the most reactionary and barbarous monarchy of Europe. . . .

Neither of the two groups of belligerent countries is behind the other in robberies, bestialities and endless brutalities of war. But in order to fool the proletarians and detract their attention from the only war for real freedom, namely, a civil war against the bourgeoisie both of "their own" and "foreign" countries, in order to further this noble aim the bourgeoisie of each country strives, by means of patriotic phrases, to extol the significance of "its own" national war and to assert that it strives to vanquish the adversary, not for the sake of robbery and seizure of lands, but for the sake of "liberating" all the other peoples except its own.

But the greater the efforts of the governments and the bourgeoisie of all countries to disunite the workers and to pit them one against the other, the more ferociously they use for this lofty purpose a system of martial law and military censorship (which measures even now, in time of war, are more successful against the "enemy within" than against the enemy without), the more urgent is the duty of the class-conscious proletariat to defend its class solidarity, its internationalism, its Socialist convictions against the orgy of chauvinism of the "patriotic" bourgeois cliques of all countries. To repudiate this task would, on the part of the class-conscious workers, mean to renounce all their striving towards freedom and democracy, not to speak of Socialism.

With a feeling of deepest chagrin it must be stated that the Socialist parties of the leading European countries have not fulfilled this duty of theirs, while the behaviour of the leaders of those parties—particularly that of the German party—borders on direct betrayal of the cause of Socialism. At this moment, which is of the greatest importance in world history, the majority of the leaders of the present, the Second (1889–1914) Socialist International, are attempting to substitute nationalism for Social-

ism. Thanks to their behaviour, the workers' parties of those countries have not counterposed their position to the criminal behaviour of the governments; on the contrary, they are appealing to the working class to identify its position with the position of the imperialist governments. The leaders of the International committed treachery with regard to Socialism when they voted for military appropriations, when they repeated the chauvinist ("patriotic") slogans of the bourgeoisie of "their" countries, when they justified and defended the war, when they entered the bourgeois cabinets of the belligerent countries, etc., etc. The point of view of the most influential Socialist leaders, and of the most influential organs of the Socialist press of present-day Europe, is chauvinist, bourgeois, and liberal, not Socialist at all. The responsibility for thus covering Socialism with shame rests, in the first place, on the German Social-Democrats who were the strongest and most influential party of the Second International. However, one cannot justify the French Socialists either, who took ministerial posts in the government of the same bourgeoisie which betrayed its fatherland and allied itself with Bismarck to crush the Commune. . . .   □

From all of the ensuing chaos of horrors, only one creative impulse seemed to salvage something for a more hopeful future—and that hope was hidden from all except Lenin in the dialectics of Russian history which were moving that enigmatic empire toward the revolution he predicted and would soon direct. Russia was to be bloodied and broken beyond saving for the conservative or liberal masters of the old regime; her losses were much the heaviest of all belligerents. In addition to the millions of dead and mutilated, the empire was strewn with destroyed property, an unexampled dislocation of social life, and an unprecedented collapse of ruling-class prestige.

While Tsar Nicholas II spent his time ineffectually at troop headquarters, the governing power of the empire was left to his stupid wife and her fantastic and incompetent consorts. None of even the simplest tasks of government were performed adequately; the towns were without food and fuel supplies, the villages were ravaged or isolated, the civilian population everywhere was in panic. Then in March of 1917 the inevitable popular revolt broke out in the likeliest of places—Petrograd. In quick order the Duma set up a Provisional Government (with one socialist in the cabinet) and Nicholas abdicated for himself and the Romanovs. The new liberal regime was immediately recognized by the United States and the Western powers, but the Petrograd Soviet of Workers' and Soldiers' Deputies, led by moderate socialists, refused to acknowledge the government and inaugurated a radical democratization of the armies. Soviets on the 1905 model sprang up all over Russia and in June an All-Russian Congress of Soviets elected an executive to supervise a socialist revolution.

The Provisional Government replied to the challenge with all sorts of enlightened legislation and promises including the convocation of a constituent assembly which was to create a liberal Russia. But the government committed itself to remain a belligerent in the war and failed utterly to meet the problems of inflation, economic disaster,

social chaos, the nationalities agitation—in short, it failed to meet the demands of leadership imposed by social trauma.

On the sixteenth of April, at the Finland Station of Petrograd, the exile Lenin stepped from a train which had been passed by the Germans in the hope of disrupting the Russian war effort. Immediately he proved, though still a minority figure in his own party, that he was a leader of genius. The "April Theses" constitute one of the most brilliant documents ever generated from a revolutionary imagination in the heat of crisis:

ON THE TASKS OF THE PROLETARIAT IN THE PRESENT REVOLUTION

As I only arrived in Petrograd on the night of April 16, I could, of course, only on my own responsibility and admittedly without sufficient preparation render a report on April 17 on the problems of the revolutionary proletariat.

The only thing I could do to facilitate matters for myself and for honest opponents was to prepare written theses. I read them, and gave the text to Comrade Tsereteli. I read them twice, very slowly: First at the meeting of the Bolsheviks, then at the joint meeting of Bolsheviks and Mensheviks.

I am publishing these personal theses, provided with very short explanatory notes, which were developed in more detail in the report:

Theses

1. In our attitude toward the war not the smallest concession must be made to "revolutionary defencism," for under the new government of Lvov and Co., owing to the capitalist nature of this government, the war on Russia's part remains a predatory imperialist war.

The class-conscious proletariat may give its consent to a revolutionary war, actually justifying revolutionary defencism, only on condition (a) that all power be transferred to the proletariat and its ally, the poorest section of the peasantry; (b) that all annexations be renounced in deeds, not merely in words; (c) that there be a complete break, in practice, with all interests of capital.

In view of the undoubted honesty of the mass of rank and file representatives of revolutionary defencism who accept the war only as a necessity and not as a means of conquest, in view of their being deceived by the bourgeoisie, it is necessary most thoroughly, persistently, patiently to explain to them their error, to explain the inseparable connection between capital and the imperialist war, to prove that without the overthrow of capital, it is *impossible* to conclude the war with a really democratic, non-oppressive peace.

This view is to be widely propagated among the army units in the field. Fraternisation.

2. The peculiarity of the present situation in Russia is that it represents a *transition* from the first stage of the revolution, which, because of the inadequate organisation and insufficient class-consciousness of the proletariat, led to the assumption of power by the bourgeoisie—to its second

stage which is to place power in the hands of the proletariat and the poorest strata of the peasantry.

This transition is characterised, on the one hand, by a maximum of legality (Russia is now the freest of all the belligerent countries of the world); on the other, by the absence of oppression of the masses, and, finally, by the trustingly ignorant attitude of the masses toward the capitalist government, the worst enemy of peace and Socialism.

This peculiar situation demands of us an ability to adapt ourselves to specific conditions of party work amidst vast masses of the proletariat just awakened to political life.

3. No support to the Provisional Government; exposure of the utter falsity of all its promises, particularly those relating to the renunciation of annexations. Unmasking, instead of admitting, the illusion-breeding "demand" that *this* government, a government of capitalists, cease being imperialistic.

4. Recognition of the fact that in most of the Soviets of Workers' Deputies our party constitutes a minority, and a small one at that, in the face of the *bloc* of all the petty-bourgeois opportunist elements from the People's Socialists, the Socialists-Revolutionists down to the Organisation Committee (Chkheidze, Tsereteli, etc., Steklov, etc., etc.) who have yielded to the influence of the bourgeoisie and have been extending this influence to the proletariat as well.

It must be explained to the masses that the Soviet of Workers' Deputies is the only possible form of revolutionary government and, therefore, our task is, while this government is submitting to the influence of the bourgeoisie, to present a patient, systematic, and persistent analysis of its errors and tactics, an analysis especially adapted to the practical needs of the masses.

While we are in the minority, we carry on the work of criticism and of exposing errors, advocating all along the necessity of transferring the entire power of state to the Soviets of Workers' Deputies, so that the masses might learn from experience how to rid themselves of errors.

5. Not a parliamentary republic—a return to it from the Soviet of Workers' Deputies would be a step backward—but a republic of Soviets of Workers', Agricultural Labourers' and Peasants' Deputies, throughout the land, from top to bottom.

Abolition of the police, the army, the bureaucracy.*

All officers to be elected and to be subject to recall at any time, their salaries not to exceed the average wage of a competent worker.

6. In the agrarian programme, the emphasis must be shifted to the Soviets of Agricultural Labourers' Deputies.

Confiscation of all private lands.

Nationalisation of all lands in the country, and management of such lands by local Soviets of Agricultural Labourers' and Peasants' Deputies. A separate organisation of Soviets of Deputies of the poorest peasants. Creation of model agricultural establishments out of large estates (from 100 to 300 desiatinas, in accordance with local and other conditions and

---

* Substituting for the standing army the universal arming of the people.

with the estimates of local institutions) under the control of the Soviet of Agricultural Labourers' Deputies, and at public expense.

7. Immediate merger of all the banks in the country into one general national bank, over which the Soviet of Workers' Deputies should have control.

8. Not the "introduction" of Socialism as an immediate task, but the immediate placing of the Soviet of Workers' Deputies in control of social production and distribution of goods.

9. Party tasks:

A. Immediate calling of a party convention.

B. Changing the party programme, mainly:

(1) Concerning imperialism and the imperialist war.

(2) Concerning our attitude toward the state and our demand for a "commune state."*

(3) Amending our antiquated minimum programme.

C. Changing the name of the party.**

10. Rebuilding the International.

Taking the initiative in the creation of a revolutionary International, an International against the social-chauvinists and against the "centre."***

In order that the reader may understand why I was compelled especially to emphasise, as a rare exception, the "case" of a conscientious opponent, I would ask him to compare the above theses with the following objection of Mr. Goldenberg: Lenin, he said, "has planted the banner of civil war in the midst of revolutionary democracy" (quoted in Mr. Plekhanov's *Yedinstvo,* No. 5).

Is this not a gem?

I write, read, and ruminate:

"In view of the undoubted honesty of the mass of rank and file representatives of 'revolutionary defencism' who accept the war only as a necessity and not as a means of conquest, in view of their being deceived by the bourgeoisie, it is necessary most thoroughly, persistently, patiently to explain to them their error."

The gentlemen of the bourgeoisie, however, who call themselves Social-Democrats, who belong neither to the masses nor to the rank and file representatives of defencism, have the insolence to present my views in such words: "Has planted (!) the banner (!) of civil war (of which there is not a word in the theses nor in my speech) in the midst (!!) of revolutionary democracy. . . ."

What is it? How does this differ from pogrom propaganda? From the *Russkaia Volia?*

I write, read, and ruminate:

---

* A state the model for which was given by the Paris Commune.

** Instead of "Social-Democracy," whose official leaders throughout the world have betrayed Socialism by going over to the bourgeoisie (defencists and vacillating Kautskians), we must call ourselves the *Communist Party.*

*** The "centre" in the international Social-Democracy is the tendency vacillating between chauvinists ("defencists") and internationalists, i.e., Kautsky and Co. in Germany, Longuet and Co. in France, Chkheidze and Co. in Russia, Turati and Co. in Italy, MacDonald and Co. in England, etc.

"The Soviet of Workers' Deputies is the only possible form of revolutionary government, and therefore, our task is . . . to present a patient, systematic, and persistent analysis of its errors and tactics, an analysis especially adapted to the practical needs of the masses."

But opponents of a certain calibre present my views as a call to "civil war in the midst of revolutionary democracy"!!

I attacked the Provisional Government because it has not fixed a date for convoking the Constituent Assembly either in the near future or at any time at all, confining itself to vague promises. I proved that without the Soviets of Workers' and Soldiers' Deputies, the convocation of the Constituent Assembly is not guaranteed and its success impossible.

A view is attributed to me that I am opposed to the speediest convocation of the Constituent Assembly!!!

I would call these expressions "delirious," had not dozens of years of political fighting taught me to regard honesty in opponents as a rare exception.

In his paper Mr. Plekhanov called my speech "delirious." Very good, Mr. Plekhanov! But how awkward, uncouth, and slow-witted you are in your polemics! If I talked delirious stuff for two whole hours, why did an audience of hundreds tolerate this "delirium"? Further, why does your paper devote a whole column to reproducing this "delirium"? You have indeed made a bad shot in this matter!

It is, of course, much easier to shout, to scold, to rave than to make an attempt to relate, to explain, to recall how Marx and Engels in 1871, 1872, and 1875 viewed the experience of the Paris Commune and the kind of state the proletariat needs.

The former Marxist, Mr. Plekhanov, probably does not wish to think about Marxism.

I quoted the words of Rosa Luxemburg who, on August 4, 1914, called the *German* Social-Democracy a "stinking corpse." Messrs. Plekhanov, Goldenberg and Co., however, feel "offended" . . . for whom?—for the German chauvinists who have been called chauvinists!

They have lost their way, these poor Russian social-chauvinists, Socialists in words and chauvinists in deeds.

N. Lenin.

Pravda, No. 26, April 20, 1917.   □

Russia was suddenly alive with cries and placards proclaiming "War to palaces, peace to the huts!" and "Expropriate the expropriators!" In July rebellion in Petrograd forced the Provisional Government to make the socialist Kerensky Prime Minister. He and his socialist colleagues then allied themselves with General Kornilov to "save the revolution" by destroying the Petrograd Soviet. Their failure gave the Bolsheviks their chance. By September they had won majorities of the Petrograd and Moscow Soviets. Lenin, now in alliance with Trotsky, was urging seizure of power before the constituent assembly met. Then on November 7 (October 25, Old Style, thus the "Great October Revolution") Red troops took over the capital, and the following day the Winter Palace fell to the workers' Red Guards after the Kronstadt sailors had seized

the power stations upon which the security of the Provisional Government rested.

Leninism and Its Consequences

The years from the *coup d'état* of 1917 to the tragic stroke of May, 1922 which incapacitated him, were Lenin's years. His theoretical position was consolidated and elaborated in the same period that he filled with the most formidable political activity the world has ever seen. Plekhanov, Bernstein, Kautsky, Luxemburg, Osinsky and a variety of "infantile" Communists—in fact, most of the Marxist intellectuals of Europe—fell before his and Trotsky's protean redefinitions of radical politics in the twentieth century. Perhaps the key issue in debate was that of Lenin's "State"—the "dictatorship of the proletariat." Kautsky, the long time friend of both Marx and Engels, chief literary executor of their work, editor of the organ of the Second International, *Die Neue Zeit,* revered by socialists down to 1914, wrote in August of 1918:

The present Russian Revolution has, for the first time in the history of the world, made a Socialist Party the rulers of a great Empire. A far more powerful event than the seizing of control of the town of Paris by the proletariat in 1871. Yet, in one important aspect, the Paris Commune was superior to the Soviet Republic. The former was the work of the entire proletariat. All shades of the Socialist movement took part in it, none drew back from it, none was excluded.

On the other hand, the Socialist Party which governs Russia today gained power in fighting against other Socialist Parties, and exercises its authority while excluding other Socialist Parties from the executive.

The antagonism of the two Socialist movements is not based on small personal jealousies: it is the clashing of two fundamentally distinct methods, that of democracy and that of dictatorship. Both movements have the same end in view: to free the proletariat, and with it humanity, through Socialism. But the view taken by the one is held by the other to be erroneous and likely to lead to destruction.

It is impossible to regard so gigantic an event as the proletarian struggle in Russia without taking sides. Each of us feels impelled to violent partisanship. And the more so because the problem which today occupies our Russian comrades will tomorrow assume practical significance for Western Europe, and does already decisively influence the character of our propaganda and tactics.

It is, however, our party duty not to decide for one or the other side in the Russian internal quarrel before we have thoroughly tested the arguments of both. In this many comrades would hinder us. They declare it to be our duty blindly to pronounce in favour of the section now at the helm. Any other attitude would endanger the Revolution, and Socialism itself. This is nothing less than to ask us to accept as already proved that which is still to be examined, viz., that one of the sections has struck out in the right path, and we must encourage it by following.

We place ourselves, of course, by asking for the fullest discussion,

already on the ground of democracy. Dictatorship does not ask for the refutation of contrary views, but the forcible suppression of their utterance. Thus, the two methods of democracy and dictatorship are already irreconcilably opposed before the discussion has started. The one demands, the other forbids it.

In the meantime, dictatorship does not yet reign in our Party; discussion amongst us is still free. And we consider it not only as our right, but as our duty to express our opinions freely, because an appropriate and fruitful decision is only possible after hearing all the arguments. One man's speech is notoriously no man's speech. Both sides must be listened to. . . .   □

Meanwhile, in the same crucial year, the most brilliant Marxist in the Western world, Rosa Luxemburg, wrote from a German prison to condemn Kautsky and to celebrate the leaders of the Bolshevik revolution for that "iron consistency" which alone had saved the Russian experience from the futility of the Second International and the Mensheviks. Trotsky and Lenin had the vision and courage to forge the principle that "all power exclusively to worker and peasant masses" through the soviets was the only engine which could at once create "democracy and drive the revolution ahead." But in the final section of her estimate of the Russian Revolution, Rosa Luxemburg, although condemning the incompetent efforts of Kautsky and his allies, returned to the theme of dictatorship and struck hard and true at the basis of Lenin's theory:

Lenin says: the bourgeois state is an instrument of oppression of the working class; the socialist state, of the bourgeoisie. To a certain extent, he says, it is only the capitalist state stood on its head. This simplified view misses the most essential thing: bourgeois class rule has no need for the political training and education of the entire mass of the people, at least not beyond certain narrow limits. But for the proletarian dictatorship that is the life element, the very air without which it is not able to exist.

"Thanks to the open and direct struggle for governmental power," writes Trotsky, "the laboring masses accumulate in the shortest time a considerable amount of political experience and advance quickly from one stage to another of their development."

Here Trotsky refutes himself and his own friends. Just because this is so, they have blocked up the fountain of political experience and the source of this rising development by their suppression of public life! Or else we would have to assume that experience and development were necessary up to the seizure of power by the Bolsheviks, and then, having reached their highest peak, became superfluous thereafter. (Lenin's speech: Russia is won for socialism!!!)

In reality, the opposite is true! It is the very giant tasks which the Bolsheviks have undertaken with courage and determination that demand the most intensive political training of the masses and the accumulation of experience.

Freedom only for the supporters of the government, only for the members of one party—however numerous they may be—is no freedom at all.

Freedom is always and exclusively freedom for the one who thinks differently. Not because of any fanatical concept of "justice" but because all that is instructive, wholesome and purifying in political freedom depends on this essential characteristic, and its effectiveness vanishes when "freedom" becomes a special privilege.

The Bolsheviks themselves will not want, with hand on heart, to deny that, step by step, they have to feel out the ground, try out, experiment, test now one way now another, and that a good many of their measures do not represent priceless pearls of wisdom. Thus it must and will be with all of us when we get to the same point—even if the same difficult circumstances may not prevail everywhere.

The tacit assumption underlying the Lenin-Trotsky theory of the dictatorship is this: that the socialist transformation is something for which a ready-made formula lies completed in the pocket of the revolutionary party, which needs only to be carried out energetically in practise. This is, unfortunately—or perhaps fortunately—not the case. Far from being a sum of ready-made prescriptions which have only to be applied, the practical realization of socialism as an economic, social and juridical system is something which lies completely hidden in the mists of the future. What we possess in our program is nothing but a few main signposts which indicate the general direction in which to look for the necessary measures, and the indications are mainly negative in character at that. Thus we know more or less what we must eliminate at the outset in order to free the road for a socialist economy. But when it comes to the nature of the thousand concrete, practical measures, large and small, necessary to introduce socialist principles into economy, law and all social relationships, there is no key in any socialist party program or textbook. That is not a shortcoming but rather the very thing that makes scientific socialism superior to the utopian varieties. The socialist system of society should only be, and can only be, an historical product, born out of the school of its own experiences, born in the course of its realization, as a result of the developments of living history, which—just like organic nature of which, in the last analysis, it forms a part—has the fine habit of always producing along with any real social need the means to its satisfaction, along with the task simultaneously the solution. However, if such is the case, then it is clear that socialism by its very nature cannot be decreed or introduced by *ukase*. It has as its prerequisite a number of measures of force—against property, etc. The negative, the tearing down, can be decreed; the building up, the positive, cannot. New territory. A thousand problems. Only experience is capable of correcting and opening new ways. Only unobstructed, effervescing life falls into a thousand new forms and improvisations, brings to light creative force, itself corrects all mistaken attempts. The public life of countries with limited freedom is so poverty-stricken, so miserable, so rigid, so unfruitful, precisely because, through the exclusion of democracy, it cuts off the living sources of all spiritual riches and progress. (Proof: the year 1905 and the months from February to October 1917.) There it was political in character; the same thing applies to economic and social life also. The whole mass of the people

must take part in it. Otherwise, socialism will be decreed from behind a few official desks by a dozen intellectuals.

Public control is indispensably necessary. Otherwise the exchange of experiences remains only with the closed circle of the officials of the new regime. Corruption becomes inevitable. (Lenin's words, Bulletin No. 29) Socialism in life demands a complete spiritual transformation in the masses degraded by centuries of bourgeois class rule. Social instincts in place of egotistical ones, mass initiative in place of inertia, idealism which conquers all suffering, etc., etc. No one knows this better, describes it more penetratingly; repeats it more stubbornly than Lenin. But he is completely mistaken in the means he employs. Decree, dictatorial force of the factory overseer, draconic penalties, rule by terror—all these things are but palliatives. The only way to a rebirth is the school of public life itself, the most unlimited, the broadest democracy and public opinion. It is rule by terror which demoralizes.

When all this is eliminated, what really remains? In place of the representative bodies created by general, popular elections, Lenin and Trotsky have laid down the soviets as the only true representation of the laboring masses. But with the repression of political life in the land as a whole, life in the soviets must also become more and more crippled. Without general elections, without unrestricted freedom of press and assembly, without a free struggle of opinion, life dies out in every public institution, becomes a mere semblance of life, in which only the bureaucracy remains as the active element. Public life gradually falls asleep, a few dozen party leaders of inexhaustible energy and boundless experience direct and rule. Among them, in reality only a dozen outstanding heads do the leading and an elite of the working class is invited from time to time to meetings where they are to applaud the speeches of the leaders, and to approve proposed resolutions unanimously—at bottom, then, a clique affair—a dictatorship, to be sure, not the dictatorship of the proletariat, however, but only the dictatorship of a handful of politicians, that is a dictatorship in the bourgeois sense, in the sense of the rule of the Jacobins (the postponement of the Soviet Congress from three-month periods to six-month periods)! Yes, we can go even further: such conditions must inevitably cause a brutalization of public life: attempted assassinations, shooting of hostages, etc. (Lenin's speech on discipline and corruption.)   □

A brutal and brutalizing period, indeed. But what fantastic creativity! Nothing was more impressive than the handling of the issue of war. The treaty of Brest-Litovsk was an unexampled practical display of Marxist morality, a vindication of that class-oriented and anti-nationalist world view which the treachery of the Second International had almost destroyed. Lenin gave up to the German Empire a good share of the Russian Empire—land, people, and industrial resources—in order to stop the dying and the other futile horrors of the Great War.

His program continued with almost equally inspired daring on a variety of social fronts. The old, decrepit empire became a land seething

with energy directed to radical—though often expedient—solutions to an incredible variety of ancient and very recent problems. The chaos and tragedy of the war was met with requisitioning, repression, militancy, expropriation and rationing. The people were fed, housed, and given useful work. Civil War raged on—counterrevolutionary terror and assassins from the Left challenged Bolshevik control. Trotsky somehow created the Red Army before the Whites (the counterrevolutionary Russians) and Allied troops from fourteen interventionist powers could take Petrograd or Moscow. There was even a war with Poland to lose! Finally, to complete what looked like the disintegration of the Empire, an imposing number of independence movements based on ethnic passions sprang up along the borders. The Bolshevik answer to the "nationalities" problem was the creation of the Union of Soviet Socialist Republics, eventually some fifteen republics whose federation replaced the old empire.

The disorder and tension of these years of "war communism" were climaxed in 1921 by a revolt of sailors in Kronstadt, heroes of the Revolution, which led the Political Bureau of the Central Committee of the Communist Party to boldly jettison previous theory and institute a New Economic Policy. The idea was to relax pressure on various sociological entities grown in the old order until the ambitious educational program for socialism could change minds as well as the Soviets could change laws. Private enterprise was permitted in small industry and retail business. Peasants (kulaks, the Russian yeomanry) were allowed to sell in the market what remained to them after taxes.

All of this backsliding was opposed by Trotsky and the Party began again to be plagued with severe factionalism. The chief issues were the New Economic Policy and the attempt to build "socialism in one country." The failure of the Communist effort in Germany after the war created another crisis for the Bolshevik theoreticians just at the tragic moment when a stroke rendered Lenin almost powerless; for the two years before his death he watched in agony the inevitably corrupt struggle for succession to that power which it seemed no one but this strange man could wield as a responsible socialist.

The Stalinist Epoch

The years which followed Lenin's death were dominated politically by Joseph Stalin. Having maneuvered an alliance with Trotsky's former "left" allies, Zinoviev and Kamenev, to destroy Trotsky and form a "triumvirate," Stalin proceeded to use the principal architect of the New Economic Policy, Bukharin, to destroy the triumvirate and help him create a Stalinist party. For his help, Bukharin was rewarded in the 1930's with a public trial for treason. By 1927, at the Fifteenth All-Union Congress of the Communist Party, Stalin's consolidation of power within Party and State was complete. Trotsky was expelled from Russia and there began the new era of collectivized agriculture, Five Year Plans, repression, and purges.

The class war which Stalin launched against the kulaks was a

success in its own brutal terms: within a decade some 95 percent of Soviet farming was being done on some form of collective. The Five-Year Plans were more amazing both sociologically and economically. The socialist achievements of the New Economic Policy had been in the *kulak* villages—the primitive industrial beginnings in the towns could not be rapidly expanded amid the chaos of postwar reconstruction and civil strife. Under Stalin's (Trotskyite!) economic policy of the 1930's, Russia became in the unbelievable period of ten years an almost totally socialized industrial society of enormously improved skills and wealth and power. Unquestionably these years represented the most ruthlessly creative economic accomplishment in the history of the world.

Tragically, however, the same decade—Stalin's decade—that bore witness to the promulgation in Russian public law of a very advanced socialist constitution (1936), also produced what the great historian Isaac Deutscher has called the "Witches' Sabbath" of 1936–1938. The Party purges and general level of paranoia related to the advances of Fascism in the West resulted in a socialist police state. There follows, first, the case for the State presented in all its ugly reasonableness by the brilliant Vyshinsky:

MORNING SESSION, MARCH 11, 1938

COMMANDANT OF THE COURT: The Court is coming. Please rise.

THE PRESIDENT: Please be seated. The session is resumed. Comrade Vyshinsky, Procurator of the U.S.S.R., will speak for the Prosecution.

VYSHINSKY: Comrades Judges, members of the Military Collegium of the Supreme Court of the U.S.S.R.

In proceeding to make my speech for the Prosecution in the present case, which constitutes an exceptional phenomenon of extraordinary public and political significance, I would like in the first place to direct your attention to certain distinguishing features of this case, to certain of its outstanding peculiarities.

It is not for the first time that the Supreme Court of our country is examining a case involving gravest crimes directed against the well-being of our country, against our Socialist fatherland, the fatherland of the working people of the whole world. But I will hardly be mistaken if I say that this is the first time that our Court has had to examine a case like this, to examine a case of such crimes and such foul deeds as those that have passed at this trial before your eyes, before the eyes of the whole world, a case of such criminals as those you now see in the prisoners' dock.

With every day and every hour that passed, as the Court investigation on the present case proceeded, it brought to light ever more of the horrors of the chain of shameful, unparalleled, monstrous crimes committed by the accused, the entire abominable chain of heinous deeds before which the base deeds of the most inveterate, vile, unbridled and despicable criminals fade and grow dim.

And indeed, what trial of all those that have taken place here—and there have been not a few of them lately due to the conditions of the class struggle and of the furious resistance of our enemies to the cause of

Socialism—can compare with the present trial in the monstrosity, brazenness and cynicism of the crimes committed by these gentlemen?

In what other trial was it possible to uncover and expose the real nature of these crimes with such force and depth, with such force to tear the mask of perfidy from the faces of scoundrels, and to show to the whole of our people and all honest people throughout the world the bestial countenance of the international brigands who cunningly and cleverly direct the hand of miscreants against our peaceful Socialist labour that has set up the new, happy, joyously flourishing Socialist society of workers and peasants?

This circumstance alone provides sufficiently clear proof of the tremendous social and political significance of this trial, of the fact that the present trial constitutes an outstanding phenomenon, that the present trial is of historic significance.

What constitutes the historic significance of the present trial? What are some of its distinguishing features?

The historic significance of this trial consists before all in the fact that at this trial it has been shown, proved and established with exceptional scrupulousness and exactitude that the Rights, Trotskyites, Mensheviks, Socialist-Revolutionaries, bourgeois nationalists, and so on and so forth, are nothing other than a gang of murderers, spies, diversionists and wreckers, without any principles or ideals.

Exactly a year ago, when analysing the shortcomings in our work and indicating the measures whereby to liquidate the Trotskyite and other double-dealers, Comrade Stalin said:

"Two words about wreckers, diversionists, spies, etc. I think it is clear to everybody now that the present-day wreckers and diversionists, no matter what disguise they may adopt, either Trotskyite or Bukharinite, have long ceased to be a political trend in the labour movement, that they have become transformed into a gang of professional wreckers, diversionists, spies and assassins, without principles and without ideals. Of course, these gentlemen must be ruthlessly smashed and uprooted as the enemies of the working class, as betrayers of our country. This is clear and requires no further explanation."

A year has gone by. The example of the present trial shows us how profoundly right was Comrade Stalin in his estimation of the Trotskyites and Bukharinites.

The Trotskyites and Bukharinites, that is to say, the "bloc of Rights and Trotskyites," the leading lights of which are now in the prisoners' dock, is not a political party, a political tendency, but a band of felonious criminals, and not simply felonious criminals, but of criminals who have sold themselves to enemy intelligence services, criminals whom even ordinary felons treat as the basest, the lowest, the most contemptible, the most depraved of the depraved.

The so-called "bloc of Rights and Trotskyites" is an organization engaged in espionage, acts of diversion and wrecking, political murder and in selling their country to the enemy.

The bloc has no ideals; there is nothing "spiritual," so to speak, nothing

ideological about it. That which some of the participants of this bloc once possessed, in some measure or other, has long ago been squandered and lost, has long ago vanished and gone rotten in the foul-smelling, abominable underworld of spies.

True, some of the accused, particularly the accused Bukharin, made attempts on more than one occasion at this trial, as the French say, to keep a straight face while the going's bad, to assume the appearance of people with "ideals," to cover up their bandit criminal activity with all kinds of "philosophical," "ideological" and other chatter.

Bukharin attempted here to reduce the whole nightmare of his heinous crimes to some sort of "ideological lines" about which he attempted to deliver lengthy and pompous speeches. Bukharin spoke here of the division of labour in this spying and wrecking organization, of some sort of "programmatic items," of some sort of "ideological orientation," albeit, he added, an ideological orientation on the kulaks.

Bukharin tried to represent his own role in this gang as that of a "theoretician." On the fourth day of the trial, when the crimes of felonious espionage committed by this so-called bloc had been fully exposed, Bukharin had the effrontery to say literally the following:

"I mainly occupied myself with the problematics of general leadership and with the ideological side; this, of course, did not exclude either my being aware of the practical side of the matter, or the adoption of a number of practical steps on my part."

Pray appraise the role of this little gentleman who alleges that he was occupied not with the direction of all kinds of crimes, and the most monstrous at that, but with the "problematics" of these crimes, not with the organization of these crimes, but with the "ideological side" of these black deeds. Appraise the role of this little gentleman who does the most rabid work of wrecking and destruction, taking advantage, on his own admission, of all the difficulties of the Soviet power, who prepares and engineers black treason, prepares the defeat of his country in war with fascist enemies and hopes to hide his treason with jaunty, cynical chatter about taking advantage of the war which "prognostically stood in perspective." Appraise the role of this garrulous little gentleman who says that the arch-bandit and Anglo-German spy Trotsky in 1932 already threw off his "Leftist uniform"—to employ Bukharin's words used here—and that he, Bukharin, together with Rykov and Tomsky armed this gang of criminals with their "ideology."

Caught red-handed in the act, Bukharin calls Hegel himself as witness, hurls himself into the jungle of linguistics, philosophy and rhetorics, mumbles some sort of learned words, so as to cover up the traces in one way or another. But he does not stand the test, and ends his scientific raving babble with the following admission:

"We all became rabid counter-revolutionaries, traitors to the Socialist fatherland, we turned into spies, terrorists, and restorers of capitalism. We embarked on treachery, crime, and treason. We turned into an insurrectionary band, we organized terrorist groups, engaged in wrecking activities, wanted to overthrow the Soviet government of the proletariat."

To this Bukharin should have added: "We became a police department of the Japanese and German intelligence services, we became shameless barterers of our country."

The bloc is an agency of foreign intelligence services. The members of the bloc and its leaders, such as Trotsky, who is not in the dock here, Bukharin, Rykov, Yagoda, Krestinsky, Rosengoltz, and its rank-and-file members, such as Zubarev, Maximov-Dikovsky and others, are slaves of these intelligence services, they are bondmen of their masters.

What room, then, is there here for ideology, "problematics" or "prognostics," for theory or philosophy?

Philosophy, behind the smoke-screen of which Bukharin tried to hide here, is only a mask wherewith to cover up espionage and treason.

Bukharin's literary-philosophical exercises are a screen behind which he tries to hide from his final exposure.

Philosophy and espionage, philosophy and wrecking, philosophy and acts of diversion, philosophy and murder, like genius and villainy, are two things that do not go together!

I know of no other instances—this is the first instance in history of a spy and murderer using philosophy, like powdered glass, to hurl it into his victim's eyes before dashing his brains out with a footpad's bludgeon.

The historical significance of this trial lies first and foremost in the fact that it has completely exposed the bandit character of the "bloc of Rights and Trotskyites," its ideological sterility, exposed the fact that the bloc—all these Rights, Trotskyites, Mensheviks, Socialist-Revolutionaries, bourgeois nationalists, etc., etc.,—are all hired agents of the fascist intelligence services.

The "bloc of Rights and Trotskyites" is no political grouping; it is a gang of spies, of agents of foreign intelligence services.

This has been proved fully and incontestably. Herein lies the enormous social, political and historical significance of the present trial.

The "bloc of Rights and Trotskyites" now in the dock—as the trial has shown with the utmost clarity—is only an advance detachment of international fascism, is a pack of hangmen and surreptitious murderers, with whose aid fascism is operating in various countries, primarily in Spain and China.

That is why the exposure of the "bloc of Rights and Trotskyites" as a gang of spies is of enormous importance not only for our Socialist revolution, but also for the whole international proletariat. It is of enormous importance for the cause of peace throughout the world. It is of enormous importance for the whole of human culture, for the fight for real democracy and the freedom of nations, for the struggle against all and sundry warmongers, against all international provocations and provocateurs.

That is why this trial is being followed with bated breath by the working people throughout the world, and particularly in those countries where the people are engaged in a heroic struggle for their freedom, against fascist tyranny.

Under the leadership of Trotsky, under the leadership of the German, Japanese, Polish and other intelligence services, the Bukharins and Ry-

kovs, Yagodas and Bulanovs, Krestinskys and Rosengoltzes, Ikramovs, Khodjayevs and Sharangoviches do their dark deeds by order of their masters not only in our country, but in Spain, in China, and wherever the class struggle of the working people is going on, wherever honest people are fighting for genuine freedom, for genuine democracy, for genuine human culture.

The Bukharins and Rykovs, Yagodas and Bulanovs, Krestinskys and Rosengoltzes, Ikramovs, Sharangoviches, Khodjayevs and others are the very same as the Fifth Column, the POUM, the Ku Klux Klan. They are one of the detachments of the fascist provocateurs and incendiaries of war operating on the international arena.

The smashing of this detachment is a great service to the cause of peace, the cause of democracy, the cause of genuine human culture.

The exceptional importance of the present trial is, however, not limited to what I have said.

Here in the dock is not some one anti-Soviet group, the agents of some one foreign intelligence service. Here in the dock is a number of anti-Soviet groups, the agents of the intelligence services of a number of foreign powers hostile to the U.S.S.R. . . .   □

The next day one of the accused, the mighty Bukharin, broken on the Stalinist rack, confessed these revolting sentiments:

EVENING SESSION, MARCH 12, 1938

THE COMMANDANT OF THE COURT: The Court is coming, please rise.

THE PRESIDENT: Please be seated. The session is resumed. Accused Bukharin, you may make your last plea.

BUKHARIN: Citizen President and Citizens Judges, I fully agree with Citizen the Procurator regarding the significance of the trial, at which were exposed our dastardly crimes, the crimes committed by the "bloc of Rights and Trotskyites," one of whose leaders I was, and for all the activities of which I bear responsibility.

This trial, which is the concluding one of a series of trials, has exposed all the crimes and the treasonable activities, it has exposed the historical significance and the roots of our struggle against the Party and the Soviet government.

I have been in prison for over a year, and I therefore do not know what is going on in the world. But, judging from those fragments of real life that sometimes reached me by chance, I see, feel, and understand that the interests which we so criminally betrayed are entering a new phase of gigantic development, are now appearing in the international arena as a great and mighty factor of the international proletarian phase.

We, the accused, are sitting on the other side of the barrier, and this barrier separates us from you, Citizens Judges. We found ourselves in the accursed ranks of the counter-revolution, became traitors to the Socialist fatherland.

At the very beginning of the trial, in answer to the question of Citizen the President, whether I pleaded guilty, I replied by a confession.

In answer to the question of Citizen the President whether I confirmed the testimony I had given, I replied that I confirmed it fully and entirely.

When, at the end of the preliminary investigation, I was summoned for interrogation to the State Prosecutor, who controlled the sum total of the materials of the investigation, he summarized them as follows (Vol. V, p. 114, December 1, 1937):

Question: Were you a member of the centre of the counter-revolutionary organization of the Rights? I answered: Yes, I admit it.

Second question: Do you admit that the centre of the anti-Soviet organization, of which you are a member, engaged in counter-revolutionary activities and set itself the aim of violently overthrowing the leadership of the Party and the government? I answered: Yes, I admit it.

Third question: Do you admit that this centre engaged in terrorist activities, organized *kulak* uprisings and prepared for White-guard *kulak* uprisings against members of the Political Bureau, against the leadership of the Party and the Soviet power? I answered: It is true.

Fourth question: Do you admit that you are guilty of treasonable activities, as expressed in preparations for a conspiracy aiming at a *coup d'état?* I answered: Yes, that is also true.

In Court I admitted and still admit my guilt in respect to the crimes which I committed and of which I was accused by Citizen the State Prosecutor at the end of the Court investigation and on the basis of the materials of the investigation in the possession of the Procurator. I declared also in Court, and I stress and repeat it now, that I regard myself politically responsible for the sum total of the crimes committed by the "bloc of Rights and Trotskyites."

I have merited the most severe punishment, and I agree with Citizen the Procurator, who several times repeated that I stand on the threshold of my hour of death.

Nevertheless, I consider that I have the right to refute certain charges which were brought: a) in the printed Indictment, b) during the Court investigation, and c) in the speech of the Prosecution made by Citizen the Procurator of the U.S.S.R.

I consider it necessary to mention that during my interrogation by Citizen the State Prosecutor, the latter declared in a very categorical form that I, as one of the accused, must not admit more than I had admitted and that I must not invent facts that have never happened, and he demanded that this statement of his should be placed on the records.

I once more repeat that I admit that I am guilty of treason to the Socialist fatherland, the most heinous of possible crimes, of the organization of *kulak* uprisings, of preparations for terrorist acts and of belonging to an underground, anti-Soviet organization. I further admit that I am guilty of organizing a conspiracy for a "palace coup." And this, incidentally, proves the incorrectness of all those passages in the speech for the prosecution made by Citizen the State Prosecutor, where he makes out that I adopted the pose of a pure theoretician, the pose of a philosopher, and so on. These are profoundly practical matters. I said, and I now repeat, that I was a leader and not a cog in the counter-revolutionary affairs. It follows from this, as will be clear to everybody, that there were

many specific things which I could not have known, and which I actually
did not know, but that this does not relieve me of responsibility.

I admit that I am responsible both politically and legally for the defeatist
orientation, for it did dominate in the "bloc of Rights and Trotskyites,"
although I affirm:

a) that personally I did not hold this position;

b) that the phrase about opening the front was not uttered by me, but
was an echo of my conversation with Tomsky;

c) that if Rykov heard this phrase for the first time from me, then, I
repeat, it was an echo of my conversation with Tomsky.

But I consider myself responsible for a grave and monstrous crime
against the Socialist fatherland and the whole international proletariat. I
further consider myself responsible both politically and legally for wrecking activities, although I personally do not remember having given directions about wrecking activities. I did not talk about this. I once spoke
positively on this subject to Grinko. Even in my testimony I mentioned that
I had once told Radek that I considered this method of struggle as not
very expedient. Yet Citizen the State Prosecutor makes me out to be a
leader of the wrecking activities.

Citizen the Procurator explained in the speech for the prosecution that
the members of a gang of brigands might commit robberies in different
places, but that they would nevertheless be responsible for each other.
That is true, but in order to be a gang the members of the gang of
brigands must know each other and be in more or less close contact with
each other. Yet I first learnt the name of Sharangovich from the Indictment, and I first saw him here in Court. It was here that I first learnt about
the existence of Maximov, I have never been acquainted with Pletnev, I
have never been acquainted with Kazakov, I have never spoken about
counter-revolutionary matters with Rakovsky, I have never spoken on this
subject with Rosengoltz, I have never spoken about it to Zelensky, I have
never in my life spoken to Bulanov, and so on. Incidentally, even the
Procurator did not ask me a single question about these people.

The "bloc of Rights and Trotskyites" is first and foremost a bloc of
Rights and Trotskyites. How then, generally, could it include Levin, for
example, who stated here in court that to this day he does not know what
a Menshevik is? How could it include Pletnev, Kazakov and others?

Consequently, the accused in this dock are not a group. They are
confederates in a conspiracy along various lines, but they are not a group
in the strict and legal sense of the word. All the accused were connected
in one way or another with the "bloc of Rights and Trotskyites," . . .

I want to say that there was one brief period of criminal conspiracy
between the "Left Communists" and the "Left" Socialist-Revolutionaries
which quickly collapsed after their action, in the suppression of which a
number of "Left Communists" took an active part.

To support his speech, the State Prosecutor advanced a number of
other points which were to provide a base for a period, a black period, in
my life.

There are a number of mistakes here. First of all, I was never an
Otzovist, although the State Prosecutor says I was.

The State Prosecutor accuses me of the fact that I worked with Trotsky as an editor of the magazine "Novy Mir," and that I had a bloc with Trotsky. I object to this.

The State Prosecutor accuses me of having opposed Comrade Stalin in 1924. I do not remember any such case. I now conclude my objections to certain charges which the State Prosecutor brought against me in the course of the trial, and I will return to the crimes I actually did commit. I have already enumerated them twice. The gravity of these crimes is immense. I think it is unnecessary to repeat how grave these crimes are; it is clear enough as it is.

I only want to say that the Trotskyite section on more than one occasion acted separately, and it is possible that individual members of the bloc, like Yagoda, may also have acted separately, because Yagoda, as Bulanov testifies, regarded Rykov and myself as his secretaries, and he himself in this Court has called me a chatterbox who organized idiotic mass uprisings when it was a question of a *coup d'état*. But I am connected with the "bloc of Rights and Trotskyites," and it is quite natural that I politically answer absolutely for everything.

The extreme gravity of the crime is obvious, the political responsibility immense, the legal responsibility such that it will justify the severest sentence. The severest sentence would be justified, because a man deserves to be shot ten times over for such crimes. This I admit quite categorically and without any hesitation at all.

I want briefly to explain the facts regarding my criminal activities and my repentance of my misdeeds.

I already said when giving my main testimony during the trial, that it was not the naked logic of the struggle that drove us, the counter-revolutionary conspirators, into this stinking underground life, which has been exposed at this trial in all its starkness. This naked logic of the struggle was accompanied by a degeneration of ideas, a degeneration of psychology, a degeneration of ourselves, a degeneration of people. There are well-known historical examples of such degeneration. One need only mention Briand, Mussolini and others. And we too degenerated, and this brought us into a camp which in its views and features was very much akin to a *kulak* praetorian fascism. As this process advanced all the time very rapidly under the conditions of a developing class struggle, this struggle, its speed, its existence, acted as the accelerator, as the catalytic agent of the process which was expressed in the acceleration of the process of degeneration.

But this process of degeneration of people, including myself, took place in absolutely different conditions from those in which the process of degeneration of the international labour leaders in Western Europe took place. It took place amidst colossal socialist construction, with its immense scope, tasks, victories, difficulties, heroism. . . .

And on this basis, it seems to me probable that every one of us sitting here in the dock suffered from a peculiar duality of mind, an incomplete faith in his counter-revolutionary cause. I will not say that the consciousness of this was absent, but it was incomplete. Hence a certain semi-paralysis of the will, a retardation of reflexes. It seems to me that we are to a

certain extent people with retarded reflexes. And this was due not to the absence of consistent thought, but to the objective grandeur of socialist construction. The contradiction that arose between the acceleration of our degeneration and these retarded reflexes expressed the position of a counter-revolutionary, or a developing counter-revolutionary, under the conditions of developing socialist construction. A dual psychology arose. Each one of us can discern this in his own soul, although I will not engage in a far-reaching psychological analysis.

Even I was sometimes carried away by the eulogies I wrote of socialist construction, although on the morrow I repudiated this by practical actions of a criminal character. There arose what in Hegel's philosophy is called a most unhappy mind. This unhappy mind differed from the ordinary unhappy mind only by the fact that it was also a criminal mind.

The might of the proletarian state found its expression not only in the fact that it smashed the counter-revolutionary bands, but also in the fact that it disintegrated its enemies from within, that it disorganized the will of its enemies. Nowhere else is this the case, nor can it be in any capitalist country.

It seems to me that when some of the West European and American intellectuals begin to entertain doubts and vacillations in connection with the trials taking place in the U.S.S.R., this is primarily due to the fact that these people do not understand the radical distinction, namely, that in our country the antagonist, the enemy, has at the same time a divided, a dual mind. And I think that this is the first thing to be understood.

I take the liberty of dwelling on these questions because I had considerable contacts with these upper intellectuals abroad, especially among scientists, and I must explain to them what every Young Pioneer in the Soviet Union knows.

Repentance is often attributed to diverse and absolutely absurd things like Thibetan powders and the like. I must say of myself that in prison, where I was confined for over a year, I worked, studied, and retained my clarity of mind. This will serve to refute by facts all fables and absurd counter-revolutionary tales.

Hypnotism is suggested. But I conducted my own defence in Court from the legal standpoint too, orientated myself on the spot, argued with the State Prosecutor; and anybody, even a man who has little experience in this branch of medicine, must admit that hypnotism of this kind is altogether impossible.

This repentance is often attributed to the Dostoyevsky mind, to the specific properties of the soul (*l'âme slave* as it is called), and this can be said of types like Alyosha Karamazov, the heroes of the *Idiot* and other Dostoyevsky characters, who are prepared to stand up in the public square and cry: "Beat me, Orthodox Christians, I am a villain!"

But that is not the case here at all. *L'âme slave* and the psychology of Dostoyevsky characters are a thing of the remote past in our country, the pluperfect tense. Such types do not exist in our country, or exist perhaps only on the outskirts of small provincial towns, if they do even there. On the contrary, such a psychology is to be found in Western Europe.

I shall now speak of myself, of the reasons for my repentance. Of

course, it must be admitted that incriminating evidence plays a very important part. For three months I refused to say anything. Then I began to testify. Why? Because while in prison I made a revaluation of my entire past. For when you ask yourself: "If you must die, what are you dying for?" an absolutely black vacuity suddenly rises before you with startling vividness. There was nothing to die for, if one wanted to die unrepented. And, on the contrary, everything positive that glistens in the Soviet Union acquires new dimensions in a man's mind. This in the end disarmed me completely and led me to bend my knees before the Party and the country. And when you ask yourself: "Very well, suppose you do not die; suppose by some miracle you remain alive, again what for? Isolated from everybody, an enemy of the people, in an inhuman position, completely isolated from everything that constitutes the essence of life . . ." And at once the same reply arises. And at such moments, Citizens Judges, everything personal, all the personal incrustation, all the rancour, pride, and a number of other things, fall away, disappear. And, in addition, when the reverberations of the broad international struggle reach your ear, all this in its entirety does its work, and the result is the complete internal moral victory of the U.S.S.R. over its kneeling opponents. I happened by chance to get Feuchtwanger's book from the prison library. There he refers to the trials of the Trotskyites. It produced a profound impression on me; but I must say that Feuchtwanger did not get at the core of the matter. He stopped half way, not everything was clear to him; when, as a matter of fact, everything is clear. World history is a world court of judgement: A number of groups of Trotskyite leaders went bankrupt and have been cast into the pit. That is true. But you cannot do what Feuchtwanger does in relation to Trotsky in particular, when he places him on the same plane as Stalin. Here his arguments are absolutely false. For in reality the whole country stands behind Stalin; he is the hope of the world; he is a creator. Napoleon once said that fate is politics. The fate of Trotsky is counter-revolutionary politics.

I am about to finish. I am perhaps speaking for the last time in my life.

I am explaining how I came to realize the necessity of capitulating to the investigating authorities and to you, Citizens Judges. We came out against the joy of the new life with the most criminal methods of struggle. I refute the accusation of having plotted against the life of Vladimir Ilyich, but my counter-revolutionary confederates, and I at their head, endeavoured to murder Lenin's cause, which is being carried on with such tremendous success by Stalin. The logic of this struggle led us step by step into the blackest quagmire. And it has once more been proved that departure from the position of Bolshevism means siding with political counter-revolutionary banditry. Counter-revolutionary banditry has now been smashed, we have been smashed, and we repent our frightful crimes.

The point, of course, is not this repentance, or my personal repentance in particular. The Court can pass its verdict without it. The confession of the accused is not essential. The confession of the accused is a medieval principle of jurisprudence. But here we also have the internal demolition

of the forces of counter-revolution. And one must be a Trotsky not to lay down one's arms.

I feel it my duty to say here that in the parallelogram of forces which went to make up the counter-revolutionary tactics, Trotsky was the principal motive force. And the most acute methods—terrorism, espionage, the dismemberment of the U.S.S.R. and wrecking—proceeded primarily from this source.

I may infer *a priori* that Trotsky and my other allies in crime, as well as the Second International, all the more since I discussed this with Nikolayevsky, will endeavour to defend us, especially and particularly myself. I reject this defence, because I am kneeling before the country, before the Party, before the whole people. The monstrousness of my crimes is immeasurable especially in the new stage of the struggle of the U.S.S.R. May this trial be the last severe lesson, and may the great might of the U.S.S.R. become clear to all. Let it be clear to all that the counter-revolutionary thesis of the national limitedness of the U.S.S.R. has remained suspended in the air like a wretched rag. Everybody perceives the wise leadership of the country that is ensured by Stalin.

It is in the consciousness of this that I await the verdict. What matters is not the personal feelings of a repentant enemy, but the flourishing progress of the U.S.S.R. and its international importance. . . .   ◻

A large part of the Old Bolshevik intellectual leadership and high Party functionaries faced similar public trials, along with eight Red Army leaders, and most were executed after their awful orgies of self-humiliation were completed.

The Unfinished Revolution

And yet amazingly and encouragingly, in spite of the horrors of the thirties, of the greater horrors and glory of the anti-Fascist war of 1939–1945, of the toll of Cold War hysteria, the stupid Cominform expulsion of Tito of Yugoslavia for communist "errors," the Red Army brutality in Eastern Europe which doomed the People's Democracies created to Stalinist specifications, Soviet intellectuals in 1961 could turn out a long treatise on the *Fundamentals of Marxism-Leninism* which concludes:

So far we have discussed primarily the immediate prospects of communism, the prospects in store for the first generations of people who will have the good fortune of living in that society. Even its general contours show that the communist system from its very first steps realises the most cherished aspirations of mankind, its dream of general sufficiency and abundance, freedom and equality, peace, brotherhood, and co-operation of people.

This is quite natural because the ideal of communism goes back deep into history, into the very depths of the life of the masses. Dreams of this ideal can already be found in folk tales about the "Golden Age" that were

composed at the dawn of civilisation. The liberation movement of the working masses in Antiquity and the Middle Ages put forward many demands which were communistic in their substance. At the boundary between the two epochs, feudal and capitalist, the outstanding thinkers of those days, the utopian socialists, made the communist ideal the cornerstone of their doctrine of the perfect society. True, those thinkers could not divine the secret of the laws of social development, could not give a scientific justification of the possibility and historic necessity of communism. Only Marxism turned communism from a utopia into a science, while the merging of scientific communism with the growing working-class movement created that irresistible force which is moving society to the next stage of social progress, from capitalism to communism.

By merging with the working-class movement, communism did not lose its great general human content. Engels was profoundly right in pointing out that "communism is a question of humanity and not of the workers alone." The victory of communism will mean the realisation of the dream of all working mankind. For the communist system signifies the triumph of humanity, the complete victory of *real humanism,* as Marx said.

What makes communist humanism practicable is not only the fact that the creation of an interesting, happy, and joyous life for all becomes a mighty, all-conquering motive of human activity. Of decisive significance is the fact that under communism society will at long last have the full opportunity of attaining such a goal. A powerful basis for production, greater power over the forces of nature, a just and rational social system, the consciousness and lofty moral qualities of people—all this makes it possible to realise the most radiant dreams of a perfect society.

It is with the victory of communism that the real history of humanity in the loftiest meaning of this term begins. Man differs fundamentally from all living creatures in that his intellect and labour save him from having to passively adjust himself to his environment, enable him to remake this environment in conformity with the interests and needs of mankind. And although mankind has existed for many thousands of years, it is only communism that ushers in the era of its full maturity and ends the prolonged prehistory when the life of each man individually and the life of society as a whole were shaped by alien forces, natural and social, which were beyond man's control. The victory of communism enables people not only to produce in abundance everything necessary for their life, but also to free society from all manifestations of inhumanity: wars, ruthless struggle within society and injustice, ignorance, crime and vice. Violence and self-interest, hypocrisy and egoism, perfidy and vainglory, will vanish for ever from the relations between people and between nations.

This is how Communists conceive the triumph of the genuine, real humanism which will prevail in the future communist society.

But even after attaining that summit, people will not stop, will not be idle, will not give themselves over to passive contemplation. On the contrary, their energies will multiply tenfold. Solved problems will be replaced by new ones; in place of the attained goals, new ones, still more entrancing, will arise. The wheels of history will continue to revolve.

Herein, if we think of it, is the greatest good fortune for mankind, a

pledge that it will never be deprived of the supreme satisfaction and happiness resulting from creative labour, active endeavour, and the bold overcoming of obstacles.

Exceptionally rapid, practically boundless development, is indeed a salient feature of communist society. Even after the victory of communism, life will confront people with ever new problems, whose solution will require the creative effort of each succeeding generation.

First of all, it is clear that the development of social production will never come to a stop. What factors will stimulate its continual progress? The constant rise in the needs of the people of communist society, moreover, a very rapid rise. Further, the growth of population, which naturally causes an expansion in the production of both the material and cultural good things of life. The social need to reduce further the working time of the people and increase their leisure is a factor acting in the same direction.

It is not difficult to foresee that the development of production itself will call for the solution of many very complex problems connected with the improvement of production organisation, the training of highly skilled personnel, the invention and application of all kinds of technical innovations.

Science, which will take an outstanding place in communist society, will be faced with ever new problems. It is already clear today that their range is truly immense. Academician V. A. Obruchev, the well-known Soviet scientist, reflecting on what people have a right to expect of science, wrote:

"It is necessary:

"to prolong man's life to 150–200 years on the average, to wipe out infectious diseases, to reduce non-infectious diseases to a minimum, to conquer old age and fatigue, to learn to restore life in case of untimely, accidental death;

"to place at the service of man all the forces of nature, the energy of the sun, the wind and subterranean heat, to apply atomic energy in industry, transport and construction, to learn how to store energy and transmit it, without wires, to any point;

"to predict and render completely harmless natural calamities: floods, hurricanes, volcanic eruptions, earthquakes;

"to produce in factories all the substances known on earth, up to most complex—protein—and also substances unknown in nature: harder than diamonds, more heat-resistant than fire-brick, more refractory than tungsten and osmium, more flexible than silk and more elastic than rubber;

"to evolve new breeds of animals and varieties of plants that grow more swiftly and yield more meat, milk, wool, grain, fruit, fibres, and wood for man's needs;

"to reduce, adapt for the needs of life and conquer unpromising areas, marshes, mountains, deserts, taiga, tundra, and perhaps even the sea bottom;

"to learn to control the weather, regulate the wind and heat, just as rivers are regulated now, to shift clouds at will, to arrange for rain or clear weather, snow or hot weather."

It goes without saying that even after coping with these magnificent and sweeping tasks, science will not have reached the limits of its potentialities. There is no limit, nor can there be any, to the inquiring human mind, to the striving of man to put the forces of nature at his service, to divine all nature's secrets.

Nor will man ever cease his efforts to improve the structure of the society in which he lives, the forms of public self-government, the way of life, the norms of human behaviour and contact in the community.

What a boundless field of activity will be open before communist society in the development of the abilities and personality of all its members, in achieving the physical and spiritual perfection of the people themselves!

The advance to the shining heights of communist civilisation will always engender in people unusual power of will and intellect, creative impulses, courage, and life-giving energy.   □

Suggested Reading

The Russian Revolution has been blessed with two historians of genius: Trotsky, perhaps more genius than historian, and Isaac Deutscher who is quite simply a historian of genius. Begin with Leon Trotsky, *The History of the Russian Revolution** (Ann Arbor: University of Michigan Press, 1932; Ann Arbor Paperback*). Isaac Deutscher's great volumes are *The Prophet Armed: Trotsky, 1879–1921** (London: Oxford University Press, 1954; Vintage*); *The Prophet Unarmed: Trotsky, 1921–1929** (London: Oxford University Press, 1959; Vintage*); *The Prophet Outcast: Trotsky, 1929–1940** (London: Oxford University Press, 1963; Vintage*); and *Stalin: A Political Biography** (London: Oxford University Press, 1949; Oxford Paperback*). A very competent general history is E. H. Carr's seven-volume *History of Soviet Russia** (New York: The Macmillan Company, 1951–1960; Pelican*). J. Bunyan and H. H. Fisher have edited documents of *The Bolshevik Revolution, 1917–1918* (Stanford: Stanford University Press, 1934).

There are two superb eyewitness accounts of the revolution by foreigners: John Reed, *Ten Days That Shook the World** (New York: International Publishers Co., Inc., 1919; New World*) and Albert Rhys Williams *Through the Russian Revolution* (New York: Boni & Liveright, 1921; New York: Monthly Review Press reissue, 1967).

A sample of Lenin's writing is available in the three-volume *Selected Works of V. I. Lenin** (New York: International Publishers Co., Inc.; New World*). Deutscher unhappily did not have time to complete a full study of Lenin and there is nothing at all adequate. There is a recent effort by Lois Fischer, *The Life of Lenin* (New York: Harper & Row, Publishers, 1964), but I like best the short life by Christopher Hill, *Lenin and the Russian Revolution* (New York: The Macmillan Company, 1950). The last terrible years are treated by Moshe Lewin, *Lenin's Last Struggle* (New York: Pantheon Books, Inc., 1968).

Literary accounts of and reactions to the revolution should be sampled in Maxim Gorky, *Untimely Thoughts* (New York: Paul S. Eriksson, Inc.,

1968) and Mikhail Sholokov's magnificent *And Quiet Flows the Don** (New York: Alfred A. Knopf, Inc., 1934; Vintage*) and *The Don Flows Home to the Sea* (New York: Alfred A. Knopf, Inc., 1940; Vintage*).

There is a superb study of the other giant of the era in two volumes by J. P. Nettl, *Rosa Luxemburg* (London: Oxford University Press, 1966).

An economic assessment of the Soviet years can be found in Maurice Dobb, *Soviet Economic Development Since Nineteen Seventeen** (London: Routledge & Kegan Paul Ltd, 1948; New World*). And the final word to our time should be read in Isaac Deutscher, *The Unfinished Revolution: Russia 1917–1967** (London: Oxford University Press, 1967; Oxford Paperback*).

8 Epilogue

There is a paradox at the heart of contemporary revolutionary history in our world. Never has radical ideology been more productive of practical social results. Not only in the West, but in every corner of the globe revolution has made over the patterns of civilization at a pace that would have kept Marx dizzy with contemplation. Although Fascism broke the revolution in Spain in the 1930's, and almost destroyed Marxist revolution in Europe, there has been an amazing recovery of radical political strength in continental Europe since World War II, and in Asia and Latin America extraordinary social revolutions are in progress at this moment.

Yet the declination in the intellectual power and emotional range of revolutionary thought since the 1920's is as unmistakable as it is mysterious. Analysis, rhetoric, and discussion have little of the quality that has in the past made radicalism one of the glories of Western intellectuality. Why so precipitant a falling off of the tradition in the epoch of its greatest success?

Here are two intelligent and articulate representatives of the discouraged minority of Marxists whose lives and thoughts may give us a clue to the failing intellectuality of our century. First, the political autobiography of an Italian Communist, Ignazio Silone:

What for us has always been much more difficult, if not impossible, has been to discern the ways and means to a political revolution, *hic et nunc,* to the creation of a free and ordered society.

I thought I had reached this discovery, when I moved to the town and made my first contact with the workers' movement. It was a kind of flight, a safety exit from unbearable solitude, the sighting of *terra firma,* the discovery of a new continent. But it was not easy to reconcile a spirit in moral mutiny against an unacceptable long-established social reality with the "scientific" demands of a minutely codified political doctrine.

For me to join the Party of Proletarian Revolution was not just a simple matter of signing up with a political organization; it meant a conversion, a complete dedication. Those were still the days when to declare oneself a Socialist or a Communist was equivalent to throwing oneself to the winds, and meant breaking with one's parents and not finding a job. If the

material consequences were harsh and hard, the difficulties of spiritual adaptation were no less painful. My own internal world, the "Middle Ages," which I had inherited and which were rooted in my soul, and from which, in the last analysis, I had derived my initial aspiration to revolt, were shaken to their foundations, as though by an earthquake. Everything was thrown into the melting-pot, everything became a problem. Life, death, love, good, evil, truth, all changed their meaning or lost it altogether. It is easy enough to court danger when one is no longer alone; but who can describe the dismay of once and for all renouncing one's faith in the individual immortality of the soul? It was too serious for me to be able to discuss it with anyone; my Party comrades would have found it a subject for mockery, and I no longer had any other friends. So, unknown to anyone, the whole world took on a different aspect. How men are to be pitied!

The conditions of life imposed on the Communists by the Fascist conquest of the State were very hard. But they also served to confirm some of the Communists' political theses, and provided an opportunity to create a type of organization which was in no way incompatible with the Communist mentality. So I too had to adapt myself, for a number of years, to living like a foreigner in my own country. One had to change one's name, abandon every former link with family and friends, and live a false life to remove any suspicion of conspiratorial activity. The Party became family, school, church, barracks; the world that lay beyond it was to be destroyed and built anew. The psychological mechanism whereby each single militant becomes progressively identified with the collective organization is the same as that used in certain religious orders and military colleges, with almost identical results. Every sacrifice was welcomed as a personal contribution to the "price of collective redemption"; and it should be emphasized that the links which bound us to the Party grew steadily firmer, not in spite of the dangers and sacrifices involved, but because of them. This explains the attraction exercised by Communism on certain categories of young men and of women, on intellectuals, and on the highly sensitive and generous people who suffer most from the wastefulness of bourgeois society. Anyone who thinks he can wean the best and most serious-minded young people away from Communism by enticing them into a well-warmed hall to play billiards, starts from an extremely limited and unintelligent conception of mankind.

It is not surprising that the first internal crises which shook the Communist International left me more or less indifferent. These crises originated from the fact that the main parties which had adhered to the new International, even after the formal acceptance of the twenty-one conditions laid down by Lenin to govern admission, were far from homogeneous. They had in common a hatred of imperialist war and of its results; they united in criticizing the reformist ideas of the Second International; but, as to the rest, for good or ill, each reflected its own country's unequal degree of historical development. That is why there were notable differences of opinion between Russian Bolshevism, formed in an atmosphere in which political liberty and a differentiated social structure were both alien

concepts, and the Left-Wing Socialist groups of the Western countries. The history of the Communist International was therefore a history of schisms, a history of intrigues and of arrogance on the part of the directing Russian group toward every independent expression of opinion by the other affiliated parties. One after another, they were forced to break with the Communist International: the currents most attached to democratic and parliamentary forms (Frossard), the groups most attached to legality and most opposed to attempts at *coups d'état* (Paul Levi), the libertarian elements who deluded themselves about Soviet Democracy (Roland-Holst), the revolutionary trade-unionists who opposed the bureaucratic submission of the trade unions to the Communist Party (Pierre Monatte, Andres Nin), the groups most reluctant to break off all collaboration with Social Democracy (Brandier, Bringolf, Tasca), and the extreme Left Wing which was intolerant of any opportunist move (Bordiga, Ruth Fischer, Boris Souvarine).

These internal crises took place in a sphere far removed from my own and so I was not involved. I do not say this boastfully; on the contrary, I am merely trying to explain the situation. The increasing degeneration of the Communist International into a tyranny and a bureaucracy filled me with repulsion and disgust, but there were some compelling reasons which made me hesitate to break with it: solidarity with comrades who were dead or in prison, the nonexistence at that time of any other organized anti-Fascist force in Italy, the rapid political, and in some cases also moral, degeneration of many who had already left Communism, and finally the illusion that the International might be made healthy again by the proletariat of the West, in the event of some crisis occurring within the Soviet regime.

Between 1921 and 1927, I had repeated occasion to go to Moscow and take part, as a member of Italian Communist delegations, in a number of congresses and meetings of the Executive. What struck me most about the Russian Communists, even in such really exceptional personalities as Lenin and Trotsky, was their utter incapacity to be fair in discussing opinions that conflicted with their own. The adversary, simply for daring to contradict, at once became a traitor, an opportunist, a hireling. *An adversary in good faith* is inconceivable to the Russian Communists. What an aberration of conscience this is, for so-called materialists and rationalists absolutely in their polemics to uphold the primacy of morals over intelligence! To find a comparable infatuation one has to go back to the Inquisition.

Just as I was leaving Moscow, in 1922, Alexandra Kollontaj said to me: "If you happen to read in the papers that Lenin has had me arrested for stealing the silver spoons in the Kremlin, that simply means that I'm not entirely in agreement with him about some little problem of agricultural or industrial policy." Kollontaj had acquired her sense of irony in the West and so only used it with people from the West. But even then, in those feverish years of building the new regime, when the new orthodoxy had not yet taken complete possession of cultural life, how difficult it was to reach an understanding with a Russian Communist on the simplest, and for us most obvious, questions; how difficult, I don't say to agree, but at

least to understand each other, when talking of what liberty means for a man of the West, even for a worker. I spent hours one day trying to explain to one of the directors of the State publishing house, why she ought at least to be ashamed of the atmosphere of discouragement and intimidation in which Soviet writers lived. She could not understand what I was trying to tell her.

"Liberty"—I had to give examples—"is the possibility of doubting, the possibility of making a mistake, the possibility of searching and experimenting, the possibility of saying 'no' to any authority—literary, artistic, philosophic, religious, social, and even political." "But that," murmured this eminent functionary of Soviet culture in horror, "that is counter-revolution." Then she added, to get a little of her own back, "We're glad we haven't got your liberty, but we've got the sanatoria in exchange." When I observed that the expression "in exchange" had no meaning, "liberty not being merchandise that could be exchanged," and that I had seen sanatoria in other countries, she laughed in my face. "You're in the mood for joking with me today," she said to me. And I was so taken aback by her candor that I no longer dared to contradict her.

The spectacle of the enthusiasm of Russian youth in those first years of the creation of a new world, which we all hoped would be more humane than the old one, was utterly convincing. And what a bitter disillusionment it was, as the years went by and the new regime strengthened itself and its economic system got into shape and the armed attacks from abroad ceased, to see the long-promised ultimate democratization failing to come, and, instead, the dictatorship accentuating its repressive character.

One of my best friends, the head of the Russian Communist Youth, Lazar Schatzky, one evening confided to me how sad he was to have been born too late, and not to have taken part either in the 1905 or the 1917 Revolutions. "But there'll still be revolutions," I said to console him, "there'll always be need of revolutions, even in Russia." We were in the Red Square, not far from the tomb of Lenin. "What kind?" he wanted to know. "And how long have we got to wait?" Then I pointed to the tomb, which was still made of wood at that time, and before which we used every day to see an interminable procession of poor ragged peasants slowly filing.

"I presume you love Lenin," I said to him. "I knew him too and have a very vivid recollection of him. You must admit with me that this superstitious cult of his mummy is an insult to his memory and a disgrace to a revolutionary city like Moscow." I suggested to him, in short, that we should get hold of a tin or two of petrol and make a "little revolution" on our own, by burning the totem-hut. I did not, to be frank, expect him to accept my proposal there and then, but at least I thought he would laugh about it; instead of which my poor friend went very pale and began to tremble violently. Then he begged me not to say dreadful things of that kind, either to him or still less to others. (Ten years later, when he was being searched for as an accomplice of Zinoviev, he committed suicide by throwing himself from the fifth floor of the house he lived in.) I have been present at the march post of immense parades of people and armies in the Red Square, but, in my mind, the recollection of that young friend's

emotion and of his frightened and affectionate voice, has remained stronger than any other image. It may be that that memory is "objectively" more important.

It is not easy to trace the history of the Communist International, and it would be undoubtedly premature. How can one separate the fatuous from the essential in the interminable discussions at its congresses and meetings? What speeches should be left to the mice in the archives to criticize, and which should be recommended to intelligent people anxious to understand? I do not know. What my memory prefers to recall may to some people seem only bizarre. They were discussing one day, in a special commission of the Executive, the ultimatum issued by the central committee of the British trade unions, ordering its local branches not to support the Communist-led minority movement, on pain of expulsion. After the representative of the English Communist Party had explained the serious disadvantages of both solutions—because one meant the liquidation of the minority movement and the other the exit of the minority from the Trades Unions—the Russian delegate Piatnisky put forward a suggestion which seemed as obvious to him as Columbus' egg. "The branches," he suggested, "should declare that they submit to the discipline demanded, and then, in practice, should do exactly the contrary." The English Communist interrupted, "But that would be a lie." Loud laughter greeted this ingenuous objection, frank, cordial, interminable laughter, the like of which the gloomy offices of the Communist International had perhaps never heard before. The joke quickly spread all over Moscow, for the Englishman's entertaining and incredible reply was telephoned at once to Stalin and to the most important offices of State, provoking new waves of mirth everywhere. The general hilarity gave the English Communist's timid, ingenuous objection its true meaning. And that is why, in my memory, the storm of laughter aroused by that short, almost childishly simple little expression—"But that would be a lie"—outweighs all the long, heavy oppressive speeches I heard during sittings of the Communist International, and has become a kind of symbol for me.

My visits to Moscow, as I have already said, were few, and limited to my functions as a member of the Italian Communist delegations. I have never been part of the organization of the Communist International, but I could follow its rapid corruption by observing a few acquaintances of mine who belonged to it. Among them, an outstanding example was the Frenchman Jacques Doriot. I had met him for the first time in Moscow in 1921; he was then a modest, willing and sentimental young working-man, and it was for his obvious docility and easy-going nature that he was chosen for the International organization in preference to other young French Communists, who were more intelligent and better educated than himself, but also less conventional. He lived up fully to expectation. Year by year, he became an increasingly important figure in the hierarchy of International Communism, and, year by year, each time I came across him, I found him changed for the worse, skeptical, cynical, unscrupulous, and rapidly becoming Fascist in his political attitude toward men and the State. If I could triumph over my natural repugnance and write a biography of Jacques Doriot, my theme would be: "Militant Communist into Fascist."

Once I met Doriot in Moscow, just after his return from a political mission in China. He gave a few friends and myself a disturbing account of the mistakes of the Communist International in the Far East. The next day, however, speaking before the Executive in full session, he affirmed the exact opposite. "It was an act of political wisdom," he confided to me after the meeting with a slight and superior smile. His case is worth mentioning because it was not isolated. Internal changes in French Communism later led Jacques Doriot to leave the Communist International, and gave him a chance to show himself openly in what had already been, for a long time, his true colors; but many others, who basically are no different from Doriot, have remained at the head of Communist Parties. Palmiro Togliatti, the Italian, referred to this phenomenon of duplicity and demoralization among the personnel of the Communist International in his speech before its Sixth Congress, and asked permission to repeat the words of the dying Goethe: "Light, more light."

In a certain sense, that speech was Togliatti's swan-song; for another year or two he kept up the effort to follow his inmost promptings and to reconcile being a Communist with speaking his mind frankly, but, in the end, even he had to capitulate and submit.

Besides internal differences resulting from its own heterogeneous composition, the Communist International felt the repercussions of every difficulty of the Soviet State. After Lenin's death, it was clear that the Soviet State could not avoid what seems to be the destiny of every dictatorship: the gradual and inexorable narrowing of its political pyramid. The Russian Communist Party, which had suppressed all rival parties and abolished any possibility of general political discussion in the Soviet assemblies, itself suffered a similar fate, and its members' political views were rapidly ousted by the policy of the Party machine. From that moment, every difference of opinion in the controlling body was destined to end in the physical extinction of the minority. The Revolution, which had extinguished its enemies, began to devour its favorite sons. The thirsty gods gave no more truce.

In May, 1927, as a representative of the Italian Communist Party, I took part with Togliatti in an extraordinary session of the enlarged Executive of the Communist International. Togliatti had come from Paris, where he was running the political secretariat of the Party, and I from Italy, where I was in charge of the underground organization. We met in Berlin and went on to Moscow together. The meeting—ostensibly summoned for an urgent discussion of what direction should be given to the Communist Parties in the struggle "against the imminent imperialist war"—was actually designed to begin the "liquidation" of Trotsky and Zinoviev, who were still members of the International Executive. As usual, to avoid surprises, the full session had been preceded and every detail prepared by the so-called Senior-convent, consisting of the heads of the most important delegations. Togliatti, on that occasion, insisted that I should accompany him to these restricted sittings. According to the rules, only he had a right to attend on behalf of the Italian delegation; but, rightly foreseeing what complications were about to arise, he preferred to have the support of the representative

of the clandestine organization. At the first sitting which we attended, I had the impression that we had arrived too late. We were in a small office in the Communist International Headquarters. The German Thälmann was presiding, and immediately began reading out a proposed resolution against Trotsky, to be presented at the full session. This resolution condemned, in the most violent terms, a document which Trotsky had addressed to the Political Office of the Russian Communist Party. The Russian delegation at that day's session of the Senior-convent was an exceptional one: Stalin, Rikov, Bukharin and Manuilsky. At the end of the reading Thälmann asked if we were in agreement with the proposed resolution. The Finn Ottomar Kuusinen found that it was not strong enough. "It should be said openly," he suggested, "that the document sent by Trotsky to the Political Office of the Russian Communist Party is of an entirely counter-revolutionary character and constitutes clear proof that the man who wrote it no longer has anything in common with the working class." As no one else asked to speak, after consulting Togliatti, I made my apologies for having arrived late and so not having been able to see the document which was to be condemned. "To tell the truth," Thälmann declared candidly, "we haven't seen the document either."

Preferring not to believe my ears, I repeated my objection in other words: "It may very well be true," I said, "that Trotsky's document should be condemned, but obviously I cannot condemn it before I've read it."

"Neither have we," repeated Thälmann, "neither have the majority of the delegates present here, except for the Russians, read the document." Thälmann spoke in German and his words were translated into Russian for Stalin, and into French for two or three of us. The reply given to me was so incredible that I rounded on the translator. "It's impossible," I said, "that Thälmann should have said that. I must ask you to repeat his answer word for word."

At this point Stalin intervened. He was standing over at one side of the room, and seemed the only person present who was calm and unruffled.

"The Political Office of the Party," said Stalin, "has considered that it would not be expedient to translate and distribute Trotsky's document to the delegates of the International Executive, because there are various allusions in it to the policy of the Soviet State." (The mysterious document was later published abroad by Trotsky himself, in a booklet entitled *Problems of the Chinese Revolution,* and as anyone can today still see for himself, it contains no mention of the policy of the Soviet State, but a closely reasoned attack on the policy practiced in China by Stalin and the Communist International.

In a speech of April 15, 1927, in the presence of the Moscow Soviets, Stalin had sung the praises of Chiang Kai-shek, and confirmed his personal confidence in the Kuomintang; this was barely a week before the famous anti-Communist *volte face* of the Chinese Nationalist leader and of his party; the Communists were expelled from the Kuomintang overnight, tens of thousands of workers were massacred in Shanghai and, a month later, in Wuhan. It was natural therefore that Stalin should have been anxious to avoid a debate on these matters, seeking to protect himself behind a screen of *raison d'état.*

Ernst Thälmann asked me if I were satisfied with Stalin's explanation. "I do not contest the right of the Political Office of the Russian Communist Party to keep any document secret," I said. "But I do not understand how others can be asked to condemn an unknown document." At this, indignation against myself and Togliatti, who appeared to agree with what I had said, knew no bounds; it was especially violent on the part of the Finn, whom I have already mentioned, a Bulgarian and one or two Hungarians.

"It's unheard-of," cried Kuusinen, very red in the face, "that we still have such petty bourgeois in the fortress of the World Revolution." He pronounced the words petty bourgeois with an extremely comical expression of contempt and disgust. The only person who remained calm and imperturbable was Stalin. He said, "If a single delegate is against the proposed resolution, it should not be presented." Then he added, "Perhaps our Italian comrades are not fully aware of our internal situation. I propose that the sitting be suspended until tomorrow and that one of those present should be assigned the task of spending the evening with our Italian comrades and explaining our internal situation to them." The Bulgarian Vasil Kolarov was given this ungrateful task.

He carried it out with tact and good humor. He invited us to have a glass of tea that evening in his room at the Hotel Lux. And he faced up to the thorny subject without much preamble. "Let's be frank," he said to us with a smile. "Do you think I've read that document? No, I haven't. To tell you the whole truth, I can add that that document doesn't even interest me. Shall I go further? Even if Trotsky sent me a copy here, secretly, I'd refuse to read it. My dear Italian friends, this isn't a question of documents. I know that Italy is the classic country of academies, but we aren't in an academy here. Here we are in the thick of a struggle for power between two rival groups of the Russian Central Directorate. Which of the two groups do we want to line up with? That's the point. Documents don't come into it. It's not a question of finding the historic truth about an unsuccessful Chinese revolution. It's a question of a struggle for power between two hostile, irreconcilable groups. One's got to choose. I, for my part, have already chosen, I'm for the majority group. Whatever the minority says or does, whatever document it draws up against the majority, I repeat to you that I'm for the majority. Documents don't interest me. We aren't in an academy here." He refilled our glasses with tea and scrutinized us with the air of a schoolmaster obliged to deal with two unruly youngsters. "Do I make myself clear?" he asked, addressing me specifically.

"Certainly," I replied, "very clear indeed." "Have I persuaded you?" he asked again. "No," I said. "And why not?" he wanted to know. "I should have to explain to you," I said, "why I'm against Fascism." Kolarov pretended to be indignant, while Togliatti expressed his opinion in more moderate, but no less succinct, terms. "One can't just declare oneself for the majority or for the minority in advance," he said. "One can't ignore the political basis of the question."

Kolarov listened to us with a benevolent smile of pity. "You're still too young," he explained, as he accompanied us to the door. "You haven't yet understood what politics are all about."

Next morning, in the Senior-convent, the scene of the day before was repeated. An unusual atmosphere of nervousness pervaded the little room into which a dozen of us were packed. "Have you explained the situation to our Italian comrades?" Stalin asked Kolarov. "Fully," the Bulgarian assured him. "If a single delegate," Stalin repeated, "is against the proposed resolution, it cannot be presented in the full session. A resolution against Trotsky can only be taken unanimously. Are our Italian comrades," he added, turning to us, "favorable to the proposed resolution?"

After consulting Togliatti, I declared: "Before taking the resolution into consideration, we must see the document concerned." The Frenchman Albert Treint and the Swiss Jules Humbert-Droz made identical declarations. (Both of them, a few years later, also ended outside the Communist International.)

"The proposed resolution is withdrawn," said Stalin. After which, we had the same hysterical scene as the day before, with the indignant, angry protests of Kuusinen, Rakosi, Pepper and the others. Thälmann argued from our "scandalous" attitude that the whole trend of our anti-Fascist activity in Italy was most probably wrong, and that if Fascism was still so firmly entrenched in Italy it must be our fault. He asked because of this that the policy of the Italian Communist Party should be subjected to a thorough sifting. This was done; and as a reprisal for our "impertinent" conduct those fanatical censors discovered that the fundamental guiding lines of our activity, traced in the course of the previous years by Antonio Gramoci, were seriously contaminated by a petty-bourgeois spirit. Togliatti decided that it would be prudent for us both to address a letter to the Political Office of the Russian Communist Party explaining the reason for our attitude at that meeting of the Executive. No Communist, the letter said in effect, would presume to question the historical pre-eminence of our Russian comrades in the leadership of the International; but this pre-eminence imposed special duties on our Russian comrades; they could not apply the rights it gave them in a mechanical and authoritarian way. The letter was received by Bukharin, who sent for us at once and advised us to withdraw it so as not to worsen our already appalling political situation.

Days of somber discouragement followed for me. I asked myself: Have we sunk to this? Those who are dead, those who are dying in prison, have sacrificed themselves for this? The vagabond, lonely, perilous lives that we ourselves are leading, strangers in our own countries—is it all for this? My depression soon reached that extreme stage when the will is paralyzed and physical resistance suddenly gives way.

Before I left Moscow an Italian working-man came to see me. He had been a refugee in Russia for some years to avoid the long term of imprisonment to which a Fascist tribunal had sentenced him. (He is still, I believe, a Communist today.) He came to complain of the humiliating conditions of the workers in the Moscow factory to which he was attached. He was ready to put up with the material shortages of every kind, since to remedy them was clearly beyond the power of individuals, but he could not understand why the workmen were entirely at the mercy of the

factory directorate and had no effective organization to protect their interests; why, in this respect also, they should be much worse off than in capitalist countries. Most of the much-vaunted rights of the working class were purely theoretical.

In Berlin, on my way back, I read in the paper that the Executive of the Communist International had severely rebuked Trotsky for a document he had prepared about recent events in China. I went to the offices of the German Communist Party and asked Thälmann for an explanation. "This is untrue," I said to him sharply.

But he explained that the statutes of the International authorized the Presidium, in case of urgency, to adopt any resolution in the name of the Executive. During the few days I had to stay in Berlin, while waiting for my false documents to be put in order, I read in the papers that the American, Hungarian and Czechoslovakian Communist Parties had energetically deplored Trotsky's letter. "Has the mysterious document finally been produced, then?" "No," he answered me. "But I hope the example set by the American, Hungarian and Czechoslovakian Communists has shown you what Communist discipline means." These things were said with no hint of irony, but indeed with dismal seriousness that befitted the nightmare reality to which they referred.

For reasons of health I had to go straight into a Swiss sanatorium, and all political decisions were suspended. One day, in a village not far from where I was taking my cure, I had a meeting with Togliatti. He explained to me at great length, clearly and frankly, the reasons for the line of conduct he had chosen. The present state of the International, he said in brief, was certainly neither satisfactory nor agreeable. But all our good intentions were powerless to change it; objective historical conditions were involved and must be taken into account. The forms of the Proletarian Revolution were not arbitrary. If they did not accord with our preferences, so much the worse for us. And besides, what alternative remained? Other Communists who had broken with the Party, how had they ended up? Consider, he said, the appalling condition of Social Democracy.

My objections to these arguments were not very coherent, mainly because Togliatti's arguments were purely political, whereas the agitation which my recent experiences had aroused in me went far beyond politics. These "inexcusable historical forms" to which we must bow down—what were they but a new version of the inhuman reality against which, in declaring ourselves Socialists, we had rebelled? I felt at that time like someone who has had a tremendous blow on the head and keeps on his feet, walking, talking and gesticulating, but without fully realizing what has happened.

Realization came, however, slowly and with difficulty during the course of the succeeding years. And to this day I go on thinking it over, trying to understand better. If I have written books, it has been to try and understand and to make others understand. I am not at all certain that I have reached the end of my efforts. The truth is this: the day I left the Communist Party was a very sad one for me, it was like a day of deep

mourning, the mourning for my lost youth. And I come from a district where mourning is worn longer than elsewhere. It is not easy to free oneself from an experience as intense as that of the underground organization of the Communist Party. Something of it remains and leaves a mark on the character which lasts all one's life. One can, in fact, notice how recognizable the ex-Communists are. They constitute a category apart, like ex-priests and ex-regular officers. The number of ex-Communists is legion today. "The final struggle," I said jokingly to Togliatti recently, "will be between the Communists and the ex-Communists."

However, I carefully avoided, after I had left the Communist Party, ending up in one of the many groups and splinter-groups of ex-Communists; and I have never regretted this in any way, as I know well the kind of fate which rules over these groups and splinter-groups, and makes little sects of them which have all the defects of official Communism—the fanaticism, the centralization, the abstraction—without the qualities and advantages which the latter derives from its vast working-class following. The logic of opposition at all costs has carried many ex-Communists far from their starting-points, in some cases as far as Fascism.

Consideration of the experience I have been through has led me to a deepening of the motives for my separation which go very much further than the circumstantial ones by which it was produced. But my faith in Socialism (to which I think I can say my entire life bears testimony) has remained more alive than ever in me. In its essence, it has gone back to what it was when I first revolted against the old social order; a refusal to admit the existence of destiny. . . . □

Finally, a Yugoslav Communist, Milovan Djilas, whose outspoken criticism of the 1950's landed him in Tito's prisons:

The roots of modern Communism reach back very far, although they were dormant before the development of modern industry in western Europe. Communism's basic ideas are the Primacy of Matter and the Reality of Change, ideas borrowed from thinkers of the period just before the inception of Communism. As Communism endures and gains strength, these basic ideas play a less and less important role. This is understandable: once in power, Communism tends to remodel the rest of the world according to its own ideas and tends less and less to change itself.

Dialectics and materialism—the changing of the world independently of human will—formed the basis of the old, classical, Marxist Communism. These basic ideas were not originated by Communist theorists, such as Marx or Engels. They borrowed them and wove them into a whole, thus forming, unintentionally, the basis for a new conception of the world.

The idea of the Primacy of Matter was borrowed from the French materialists of the eighteenth century. Earlier thinkers, including Democritus in ancient Greece, had expressed it in a different way. The idea of the reality of change, caused by the struggle of opposites, called Dialectics, was taken over from Hegel; the same idea had been expressed in a different way by Heraclitus in ancient Greece.

Without going into the details of the differences between Marxist ideas

and preceding similar theories, It is necessary to point out that Hegel, in presenting the idea of the Reality of Change, retained the concept of an unchanging supreme law, or the Idea of the Absolute. As he expressed it, in the last analysis there are unchangeable laws which, independently of human will, govern nature, society, and human beings.

Although stressing the idea of the Reality of Change, Marx, and especially Engels, stated that the laws of the objective or material world were unchangeable and independent of human beings. Marx was certain that he would discover the basic laws governing life and society, just as Darwin had discovered the laws governing living creatures. At any rate, Marx did clarify some social laws, particularly the way in which these laws operated in the period of early industrial capitalism.

This fact alone, even if accepted as accurate, cannot in itself justify the contention of modern Communists that Marx discovered all the laws of society. Still less can it justify their attempt to model society after those ideas in the same way that livestock is bred on the basis of the discoveries of Lamarck and Darwin. Human society cannot be compared to species of animals or to inanimate objects; it is composed of individuals and groups which are continuously and consciously active in it, growing and changing.

In the pretensions of contemporary Communism of being, if not the unique and absolute, but in any case the highest science, based on dialectical materialism, are hidden the seeds of its despotism. The origin of these pretensions can be found in the ideas of Marx, though Marx himself did not anticipate them.

Of course, contemporary Communism does not deny the existence of an objective or unchanging body of laws. However, when in power, it acts in an entirely different manner toward human society and the individual, and uses methods to establish its power different from those its theories would suggest.

Beginning with the premise that they alone know the laws which govern society, Communists arrive at the oversimplified and unscientific conclusion that this alleged knowledge gives them the power and the exclusive right to change society and to control its activities. This is the major error of their system.

Hegel claimed that the absolute monarchy in Prussia was the incarnation of his idea of the Absolute. The Communists, on the other hand, claim that they represent the incarnation of the objective aspirations of society. Here is more than just one difference between the Communists and Hegel; there is also a difference between the Communists and absolute monarchy. The monarchy did not think quite as highly of itself as the Communists do of themselves, nor was it as absolute as they are.

Hegel himself was probably troubled by the possible conclusions to be drawn from his own discoveries. For instance, if everything was constantly being transformed, what would happen to his own ideas and to the society which he wanted to preserve? As a professor by royal appointment he could not have dared, in any case, to make public recommendations for the improvement of society on the basis of his philosophy.

This was not the case with Marx. As a young man he took an active part

in the 1848 revolution. He went to extremes in drawing conclusions from Hegel's ideas. Was not the bloody class struggle raging all over Europe straining toward something new and higher? It appeared not only that Hegel was right—that is, Hegel as interpreted by Marx—but also that philosophical systems no longer had meaning and justification, since science was discovering objective laws so rapidly, including those applicable to society.

In science, Comte's positivism had already triumphed as a method of inquiry; the English school of political economy (Smith, Ricardo, and others) was at its height; epochal laws were being discovered from day to day in the natural sciences; modern industry was carving out its path on the basis of scientific technology; and the wounds of young capitalism revealed themselves in the suffering and the beginning struggle of the proletariat. Apparently this was the onset of the domination of science, even over society, and the elimination of the capitalistic concept of ownership as the final obstacle to human happiness and freedom.

The time was ripe for one great conclusion. Marx had both the daring and the depth to express it, but there were no social forces available on which he could rely.

Marx was a scientist and an ideologist. As a scientist, he made important discoveries, particularly in sociology. As an ideologist, he furnished the ideological basis for the greatest and most important political movements of modern history, which took place first in Europe and are now taking place in Asia.

But, just because he was a scientist, economist, and sociologist, Marx never thought of constructing an all-inclusive philosophical or ideological system. He once said: "One thing is certain; I am not a Marxist." His great scientific talent gave him the greatest advantage over all his socialist predecessors, such as Owen and Fourier. The fact that he did not insist on ideological all-inclusiveness or his own philosophical system gave him an even greater advantage over his disciples. Most of the latter were ideologists and only to a very limited degree—as the examples of Plekhanov, Labriola, Lenin, Kautsky, and Stalin will show—scientists. Their main desire was to construct a system out of Marx's ideas; this was especially true of those who knew little philosophy and had even less talent for it. As the time passed, Marx's successors revealed a tendency to present his teachings as a finite and all-inclusive concept of the world, and to regard themselves as responsible for the continuation of all of Marx's work, which they considered as being virtually complete. Science gradually yielded to propaganda, and as a result, propaganda tended more and more to represent itself as science.

Being a product of his time, Marx denied the need for any kind of philosophy. His closest friend, Engels, declared that philosophy had died with the development of science. Marx's thesis was not at all original. The so-called scientific philosophy, especially after Comte's positivism and Feuerbach's materialism, had become the general fashion.

It is easy to understand why Marx denied both the need for and the possibility of establishing any kind of philosophy. It is harder to understand why his successors tried to arrange his ideas into an all-inclusive

system, into a new, exclusive philosophy. Even though they denied the need for any kind of philosophy, in practice they created a dogma of their own which they considered to be the "most scientific" or the "only scientific" system. In a period of general scientific enthusiasm and of great changes brought about in everyday life and industry by science, they could not help but be materialists and to consider themselves the "only" representatives of the "only" scientific view and method, particularly since they represented a social stratum which was in conflict with all the accepted ideas of the time.

Marx's ideas were influenced by the scientific atmosphere of his time, by his own leanings toward science, and by his revolutionary aspiration to give to the working-class movement a more or less scientific basis. His disciples were influenced by a different environment and by different motives when they converted his views into dogma.

If the political needs of the working-class movement in Europe had not demanded a new ideology complete in itself, the philosophy that calls itself Marxist, the dialectical materialism, would have been forgotten—dismissed as something not particularly profound or even original, though Marx's economic and social studies are of the highest scientific and literary rank.

The strength of Marxist philosophy did not lie in its scientific elements, but in its connection with a mass movement, and most of all in its emphasis on the objective of changing society. It stated again and again that the existing world would change simply because it had to change, that it bore the seeds of its own opposition and destruction; that the working class wanted this change and would be able to effect it. Inevitably, the influence of this philosophy increased and created in the European working-class movement the illusion that it was omnipotent, at least as a method. In countries where similar conditions did not exist, such as Great Britain and the United States, the influence and importance of this philosophy was insignificant, despite the strength of the working class and the working-class movement.

As a science, Marxist philosophy was not important, since it was based mainly on Hegelian and materialistic ideas. As the ideology of the new, oppressed classes and especially of political movements, it marked an epoch, first in Europe, and later in Russia and Asia, providing the basis for a new political movement and a new social system.

Marx thought that the replacement of capitalist society would be brought about by a revolutionary struggle between its two basic classes, the bourgeoisie and the proletariat. The clash seemed all the more likely to him because in the capitalistic system of that time both poverty and wealth kept increasing unchecked, on the opposite poles of a society that was shaken by periodic economic crises.

In the last analysis, Marxist teaching was the product of the industrial revolution or of the struggle of the industrial proletariat for a better life. It was no accident that the frightful poverty and brutalization of the masses which accompanied industrial change had a powerful influence on Marx. His most important work, *Das Kapital,* contains a number of important and stirring pages on this topic. The recurring crises, which were characteris-

tic of the capitalism of the nineteenth century, together with the poverty and the rapid increase of the population, logically led Marx to the belief that revolution was the only solution. Marx did not consider revolution to be inevitable in all countries, particularly not in those where democratic institutions were already a tradition of social life. He cited as examples of such countries, in one of his talks, the Netherlands, Great Britain and the United States. However, one can conclude from his ideas, taken as a whole, that the inevitability of revolution was one of his basic beliefs. He believed in revolution and preached it; he was a revolutionary.

Marx's revolutionary ideas, which were conditional and not universally applicable, were changed by Lenin into absolute and universal principles. In *The Infantile Disorder of "Left-Wing" Communism,* perhaps his most dogmatic work, Lenin developed these principles still more, differing with Marx's position that revolution was avoidable in certain countries. He said that Great Britain could no longer be regarded as a country in which revolution was avoidable, because during the First World War she had become a militaristic power, and therefore the British working class had no other choice but revolution. Lenin erred, not only in his failure to understand that "British militarism" was only a temporary, wartime phase of development, but because he failed to foresee the further development of democracy and economic progress in Great Britain or other Western countries. He also did not understand the nature of the English trade-union movement. He placed too much emphasis on his own, or Marxian, deterministic, scientific ideas and paid too little attention to the objective social role and potentialities of the working class in more highly developed countries. Although he disclaimed it, he did in fact proclaim his theories and the Russian revolutionary experience to be universally applicable.

According to Marx's hypothesis and his conclusions on the subject, the revolution would occur first of all in the highly developed capitalist countries. Marx believed that the results of the revolution—that is, the new socialist society—would lead to a new and higher level of freedom than that prevalent in the existing society, in so-called liberal capitalism. This is understandable. In the very act of rejecting various types of capitalism, Marx was at the same time a product of his epoch, the liberal capitalist epoch.

In developing the Marxist stand that capitalism must be replaced not only by a higher economic and social form—that is, socialism—but by a higher form of human freedom, the Social Democrats justifiably considered themselves to be Marx's successors. They had no less right to this claim than the Communists, who cited Marx as the source of their idea that the replacement of capitalism can take place only by revolutionary means. However, both groups of Marx's followers—the Social Democrats and the Communists—were only partly right in citing him as the basis for their ideas. In citing Marx's ideas they were defending their own practices, which had originated in a different, and already changed society. And, although both cited and depended on Marxist ideas, the Social Democratic and Communist movements developed in different directions.

In countries where political and economic progress was difficult, and

where the working class played a weak role in society, the need arose slowly to make a system and a dogma out of Marxist teaching. Moreover, in countries where economic forces and social relations were not yet ripe for industrial change, as in Russia and later in China, the adoption and dogmatization of the revolutionary aspects of Marxist teachings was more rapid and complete. There was emphasis on *revolution* by the working-class movement. In such countries, Marxism grew stronger and stronger and, with the victory of the revolutionary party, it became the dominant ideology.

In countries such as Germany, where the degree of political and economic progress made revolution unnecessary, the democratic and reformist aspects of Marxist teaching, rather than the revolutionary ones, dominated. The anti-dogmatic ideological and political tendencies generated an emphasis on *reform* by the working-class movement.

In the first case, the ties with Marx were strengthened, at least in outward appearance. In the second case, they were weakened.

Social development and the development of ideas led to a severe schism in the European socialist movement. Roughly speaking, the changes in political and economic conditions coincided with changes in the ideas of the socialist theorists, because they interpreted reality in a relative manner, that is, in an incomplete and one-sided way, from their own partisan point of view.

Lenin in Russia and Bernstein in Germany are the two extremes through which the different changes, social and economic, and the different "realities" of the working-class movements found expression.

Almost nothing remained of original Marxism. In the West it had died out or was in the process of dying out; in the East, as a result of the establishment of Communist rule, only a residue of formalism and dogmatism remained of Marx's dialectics and materialism; this was used for the purpose of cementing power, justifying tyranny, and violating human conscience. Although it had in fact also been abandoned in the East, Marxism operated there as a rigid dogma with increasing power. It was more than an idea there; it was a new government, a new economy, a new social system.

Although Marx had furnished his disciples with the impetus for such development, he had very little desire for such development nor did he expect it. History betrayed this great master as it has others who have attempted to interpret its laws.

What has been the nature of the development since Marx?

In the 1870's, the formation of corporations and monopolies had begun in countries where the industrial revolution had already taken place, such as Germany, England, and the United States. This development was in full swing by the beginning of the twentieth century. Scientific analyses were made of it by Hobson, Hilferding, and others. Lenin, in *Imperialism, the Final Stage of Capitalism,* made a political analysis, based mainly on these authors, containing predictions which have proved mostly inaccurate.

Marx's theories about the increasing impoverishment of the working class were not borne out by developments in those countries from which

his theories had been derived. However, as Hugh Seton-Watson states In *From Lenin to Malenkov,* they appeared to be reasonably accurate for the most part in the case of the agrarian East European countries. Thus, while in the West his stature was reduced to that of a historian and scholar, Marx became the prophet of a new era in eastern Europe. His teachings had an intoxicating effect, similar to a new religion.

The situation in western Europe that contributed to the theories of Engels and Marx is described by André Maurois in the Yugoslav edition of *The History of England:*

> When Engels visited Manchester in 1844, he found 350,000 workers crushed and crowded into damp, dirty, broken-down houses where they breathed an atmosphere resembling a mixture of water and coal. In the mines, he saw half-naked women, who were treated like the lowest of draft animals. Children spent the day in dark tunnels, where they were employed in opening and closing the primitive openings for ventilation, and in other difficult tasks. In the lace industry, exploitation reached such a point that four-year-old children worked for virtually no pay.

Engels lived to see an entirely different picture of Great Britain, but he saw a still more horrible and—what is more important—hopeless poverty in Russia, the Balkans, Asia and Africa.

Technological improvements brought about vast and concrete changes in the West, immense from every point of view. They led to the formation of monopolies, and to the partition of the world into spheres of interest for the developed countries and for the monopolies. They also led to the First World War and the October Revolution.

In the developed countries the rapid rise in production and the acquisition of colonial sources of materials and markets materially changed the position of the working class. The struggle for reform, for better material conditions, together with the adoption of parliamentary forms of government, became more real and valuable than revolutionary ideals. In such places revolution became nonsensical and unrealistic.

The countries which were not yet industrialized, particularly Russia, were in an entirely different situation. They found themselves in a dilemma; they had either to become industrialized, or to discontinue active participation on the stage of history, turning into captives of the developed countries and their monopolies, thus doomed to degeneracy. Local capital and the class and parties representing it were too weak to solve the problems of rapid industrialization. In these countries revolution became an inescapable necessity, a vital need for the nation, and only one class could bring it about—the proletariat, or the revolutionary party representing it.

The reason for this is that there is an immutable law—that each human society and all individuals participating in it strive to increase and perfect production. In doing this they come in conflict with other societies and individuals, so that they compete with each other in order to survive. This increase and expansion of production constantly faces natural and social

barrlers, such as individual, political, legal, and international customs and relationships. Since it must overcome obstacles, society, that is, those who at a given moment represent its productive forces, must eliminate, change, or destroy the obstacles which arise either inside or outside its boundaries. Classes, parties, political systems, political ideas, are an expression of this ceaseless pattern of movement and stagnation.

No society or nation allows production to lag to such an extent that its existence is threatened. To lag means to die. People never die willingly; they are ready to undergo any sacrifice to overcome the difficulties which stand in the way of their economic production and their existence.

The environment and the material and intellectual level determine the method, forces, and means that will be used to bring about the development and expansion of production, and the social results which follow. However, the necessity for the development and expansion of production —under any ideological banner or social force—does not depend on individuals; because they wish to survive, societies and nations find the leaders and ideas which, at a given moment, are best suited to that which they must and wish to attain.

Revolutionary Marxism was transplanted during the period of monopolistic capitalism from the industrially developed West to countries of the industrially undeveloped East, such as Russia and China. This is about the time when socialist movements were developing in the East and West. This stage of the socialist movement began with its unification and centralization in the Second International, and ended with a division into the Social Democratic (reform) wing and the Communist (revolutionary) wing, leading to the revolution in Russia and the formation of the Third International.

In countries where there was no other way of bringing about industrialization, there were special national reasons for the Communist revolution. Revolutionary movements existed in semi-feudal Russia over half a century before the appearance of the Marxists in the late nineteenth century. Moreover, there were urgent and specific concrete reasons—international, economic, political—for revolution. The basic reason—the vital need for industrial change—was common to all the countries such as Russia, China, and Yugoslavia, where revolution took place.

It was historically inevitable that most of the European socialist movements after Marx were not only materialistic and Marxist, but to a considerable degree ideologically exclusive. Against them were united all the forces of the old society: church, school, private ownership, government and, more important, the vast power machinery which the European countries had developed since early times in the face of the constant continental wars.

Anyone who wants to change the world fundamentally must first of all interpret it fundamentally and "without error." Every new movement must be ideologically exclusive, especially if revolution is the only way victory can be won. And if this movement is successful, its very success must strengthen its beliefs and ideas. Though successes through "adventurous" parliamentary methods and strikes strengthened the reformist trend in the German and other Social Democratic parties, the Russian workers,

who could not improve their position by one kopeck without bloody liquidations, had no choice but to use weapons to escape despair and death by starvation.

The other countries of eastern Europe—Poland, Czechoslovakia, Hungary, Rumania, and Bulgaria—do not fall under this rule, at least not the first three countries. They did not experience a revolution, since the Communist system was imposed on them by the power of the Soviet Army. They did not even press for industrial change, at least not by the Communist method, for some of them had already attained it. In these countries, revolution was imposed from the outside and from above, by foreign bayonets and the machinery of force. The Communist movements were weak, except in the most developed of the countries, Czechoslovakia, where the Communist movement had closely resembled leftist and parliamentary socialist movements up to the time of direct Soviet intervention in the war and the *coup d'état* of February 1948. Since the Communists in these countries were weak, the substance and form of their Communism had to be identical with that of the U.S.S.R. The U.S.S.R. imposed its system on them, and the domestic Communists adopted it gladly. The weaker Communism was, the more it had to imitate even in form its "big brother"—totalitarian Russian Communism.

Countries such as France and Italy, which had relatively strong Communist movements, had a hard time keeping up with the industrially better-developed countries, and thus ran into social difficulties. Since they had already passed through democratic and industrial revolutions, their Communist movements differed greatly from those in Russia, Yugoslavia, and China. Therefore, in France and Italy revolution did not have a real chance. Since they were living and operating in an environment of political democracy, even the leaders of their Communist parties were not able to free themselves entirely of parliamentary illusions. As far as revolution was concerned, they tended to rely more on the international Communist movement and the aid of the U.S.S.R. than on their own revolutionary power. Their followers, considering their leaders to be fighters against poverty and misery, naïvely believed that the party was fighting for a broader and truer democracy.

Modern Communism began as an idea with the inception of modern industry. It is dying out or being eliminated in those countries where industrial development has achieved its basic aims. It flourishes in those countries where this has not yet happened.

The historical role of Communism in the undeveloped countries has determined the course and the character of the revolution which it has had to bring about. . . .   □

And so this account of the European revolutionary tradition ends with a paradox, not surprisingly—for it began with one: the paradox of individuals and minorities struggling for self-knowledge and freedom and animal comfort against the almost hopeless odds of civilization itself. The struggle has not won many clear victories thus far, but those it has won look permanent. Millions live in socialized economies that probably cannot revert to earlier historic forms of exploitation. Millions

are deeply committed to socialist or other kinds of radical democratic ideology, armed with the words of past genius and ambitious to create an enlarged vocabulary of freedom. Their children will carry on and may greatly expand and deepen the triumphs of twentieth-century Marxism.

Finally, the most ghastly element of paradox remains to be identified and confronted with whatever common sense remains in our ugly world. Just as hope for rational, humane societies emerging from the oppressive historic past seems an analytical certainty, the world-spanning mania for industrialization may have sold our children into the last, most terrible degradation ever visited upon humanity. For the smokestacks belching the filth that is the by-product of our new wealth are rapidly turning our beautiful and bountiful planet into a desolation that cannot support any life at all. The Atmospheric Sciences Research Center in the United States has already predicted that by 1990, at the present rate of pollution, the Northern Hemisphere will have become a graveyard. The price of technological genius and the universal craving for the American "high standard of living" would appear to be the end of the world. The USSR is also polluting its water and air at an alarming rate, and the crisis of this continent will soon be that of all industrial societies. Our only hope is that a massive, truly social morality will demand life before either profits or progress. The base of all future social advance must surely be the survival of the species! As Lord Ritchie-Calder concludes, ". . . there are no frontiers in present-day pollution and destruction of the biosphere. Mankind shares a common habitat. We have mortgaged the old homestead and nature is liable to foreclose." For the articulation of that necessity, the revolutionary ethic of the eighteenth century—that ethic which substituted for the worship of God and veneration of the dead, the love of children and dedication to their future—may yet prove the most valuable creation of the European Revolution.

Suggested Reading

The literature which reflects upon and reacts to the revolutionary traditions we have surveyed in this book is enormous and growing. Except for the Marxists, almost all of this literature responds with cynicism and despair. Much of it is disastrously incompetent. I will suggest only a few of the more intelligent and influential of the books which look back on our civilization and try to draw conclusions of a broad philosophical nature. A good place to begin is with the dark genius of Sigmund Freud's essay on *Civilization and Its Discontents** (London: The Hogarth Press Ltd, 1930; Anchor*). Then perhaps Albert Camus, *The Rebel** (New York: Alfred A. Knopf, Inc., 1954; Vintage*) and his essays published as *Resistance, Rebellion, and Death* (New York: Alfred A. Knopf, Inc., 1961) to represent the gloom of Western intellectuals faced with libertarian and existential dilemmas created by modern revolutions. Another valuable introduction to modern philosophical alarm is Karl Popper, *The Open Society and Its Enemies,** fifth edition (Princeton: Princeton University Press, 1966;

Torchbook*). For a very different, positive, and perceptive view of the revolutionary past, see Ralph E. Shikes' unique *The Indignant Eye* (Boston: Beacon Press, 1969) which traces the visual revolt of Western artists.

Finally, amazingly, it remains to be noted that little progress has been made in the general analysis of European revolution. Apart from the vast literature of ignorant or self-involved pessimism, scholarly energy has produced little of value. There is P. A. Sorokin's massive (four volumes) and rather silly *Social and Cultural Dynamics* (New York: American Book Company, 1937); Dutton has published in paper a shorter work which distills his view in *The Crisis of Our Age.* Then there is the popular effusion of Hannah Arendt on display in *On Revolution** (New York: The Viking Press, Inc., 1963; Viking*). Crane Brinton tried to see revolutions as morbid moments in otherwise healthy social environments in *The Anatomy of Revolution** (Englewood Cliffs, N.J.: Prentice-Hall, Inc., 1938, 1952; Vintage*). A more limited but useful effort at analysis was undertaken by George Pettee, *The Process of Revolution* (New York: Harper & Bros., 1938). Barrington Moore, Jr., has some interesting ideas in a study called *Social Origins of Dictatorship and Democracy** (Boston: Beacon Press, 1966; Beacon Paperbacks). A potentially encouraging methodological advance is argued (and is now being implemented by a few young scholars) by Charles Tilly and James Rule, *Measuring Political Upheaval* (Princeton: Center of International Studies, 1965).

Some beginning toward an understanding of the ecological crisis can be made with Barry Commoner, *Science and Survival* (New York: The Viking Press, Inc., 1966) and *The Environmental Handbook,** G. de Bell, ed., (New York: Ballantine Books, Inc., 1970*).

Index

DATE DUE

DEMCO 38-297

REVEALING ANTIQUITY

G. W. Bowersock, General Editor